REINDEER ENGRAVED ON BONE, FROM THE GROTTO OF TÄYNGEN (SWITZERLAND).
(TAKEN FROM "MATÉRIAUX POUR L'HISTOIRE DE L'HOMME," 1874).

(Frontispiece).

THE

RECENT ORIGIN OF MAN,

AS ILLUSTRATED BY

GEOLOGY AND THE MODERN SCIENCE OF PRE-HISTORIC ARCHÆOLOGY.

BY

JAMES C. SOUTHALL.

ILLUSTRATED.

PHILADELPHIA:
J. B. LIPPINCOTT & CO.,
LONDON: TRÜBNER & CO.
1875.

PREFACE.

I do not flatter myself that I have avoided all errors in the following pages. That, in a volume like the present, containing such a vast multitude of statements of fact, was nearly impossible.

I have been admonished by some of my friends against the retention of certain expressions which occur with regard to Science and scientific men, as well as against the theological temper of some of the early chapters. With respect to the first, I do not believe that any candid person will suspect me of an unfriendly feeling towards Science, or of any want of appreciation of its great achievements and the lofty position which it so justly occupies. A scientific fact is as much a part of the Truth as a verse of Scripture, and every rightly-constituted mind must welcome the discoveries of scientific men as the Biblical student would welcome a corrected text of the Books of Chronicles or the recovery of the original Ignatian epistles. It is not Science, but scientific theories hastily formed and inconsiderately promulged, that I venture to rebuke; *speculation*, it appears to me, is hardly within the sphere of Science, and when the theologian or the scientist undertakes to go one step beyond the Record, in the one case and in the other we have the right to call him *back*. In the past the Theologians have had it all their own way, and they uttered a cry of indignation when they were rudely checked up by Science; in the present day the Scientists appear to have it very much their way, and some of them, accordingly, fall into that overweening dogmatism and those indiscretions which characterized the reign of the Theologians.

With regard to the references to Christianity and the Bible in some of the earlier chapters, I thought them pertinent to any discussion of the origin of man, involving, as the Bible does, not only a professed revelation on the subject, but also historical statements of great antiquity.

There is a certain want of ingenuousness among many literary and scientific men with regard to the historical books of the Hebrew Scriptures which is reprehensible, and for which I have little respect. They studiously avoid all mention of these documents, when if they had been discovered in the valley of the Euphrates or the Nile they would receive great attention. I do not recollect that the "Antiquity of Man" ever recognizes that the book of Genesis is in existence; and yet every one is perfectly conscious that the author has it in mind, and is writing *at* it all the time.

It is not considered dignified, nor exactly in good taste, to make such allusions.

I venture to violate this canon of letters. I have said in a plain way whatever seemed to me to bear on my subject,—treating Moses as I would treat Herodotus.

It is impossible in this question of the antiquity of man to ignore, or be indifferent to, the statements of the Pentateuch; and Englishmen and Americans do not in fact forget them. Affectation in a scientific work is specially out of place; such a work should be characterized by the most thorough candor and by no suppressed prejudices.

If I have succeeded in establishing the very recent origin of the human race, the effect of the evidence reaches farther than the position of pre-historic archæology: it bears upon Mr. Darwin's views; for, if, as I contend, primeval man commenced his career six or eight thousand years ago in a civilized condition in the temperate regions of the East, and there are no human traces behind these, the doctrine of evolution, so far as man is concerned, is at once negatived. Even the man of Solutré, in Eastern France, the cotemporary of the mammoth, and who, as I have attempted to show, occupied that station only a few thousand years ago, had apparently domesticated the horse, and, in the words of M. Pruner-Bey, "est constitué homme dans toute la force du terme," —with regard to whom "rien dans son physique n'indique un rapprochement avec les Simiens." Behind this hunter tribe who have left their remains in the sepultures and refuse-heaps of this palæolithic village, we find—nothing; in other words, Palæolithic Man in Western Europe—though not civilized—was an intelligent savage like our Esquimaux or Red Indians; and neither Archæology nor Geology has detected any earlier human form. Such a man—civilized in Egypt—uncivilized, but employing horses, making pottery, executing such drawings as that represented in our frontispiece, in Europe—appeared abruptly on the scene a few thousand years ago,—ten, if you choose. As the facts stand, I think Mr. Darwin will find it a difficult matter to procure from the quaternary and tertiary deposits a sufficient number of earlier human types and pithecoid types, to connect the man of the Pyramids and the French River-Gravels with the brute creation.

I wish, in conclusion, to express the great obligations I have been under in the preparation of this volume to Prof. Edmund Andrews of the University of Chicago. He was kind enough in the beginning to read my manuscript, and to encourage me in its publication, and he has read the proof-sheets and corresponded with me as the work has been passing through the press. To him I am indebted for many important hints and much valuable information, which I have sometimes, but not always, recognized.

My thanks are also due to Professors Schele de Vere and Holmes of the University of Virginia, and to W. H. Ruffner, Esq., Superintendent of Public Instruction in Virginia, for their kind help in assisting me to read the proof-sheets.

JAMES C. SOUTHALL.

RICHMOND, VA., March, 1875.

CONTENTS.

CHAPTER XXVII.

CHAPTER XXVIII.

CHAPTER XXIX.

CHAPTER XXX.

CHAPTER XXXI.

CHAPTER XXXII.

CHAPTER XXXIII.

CHAPTER XXXIV.

CHAPTER XXXV.

CHAPTER XXXVI.

CHAPTER XXXVII.

THE RECENT ORIGIN OF MAN.

CHAPTER I.

THE FIRST GLIMPSES OF THE HUMAN RACE.

The Thread of History.—Results of Modern Research.—Chronology.—Probable Date of the Beginnings of Monumental History.—The Antiquity of Civilization.—Egypt, Babylon, and Nineveh in the Earliest Known Ages.—The Deluge.—Was there a Stone Age? —The Abrupt Beginnings of Civilization.—America; Early Discovery of.—The Biblical Account of the Beginning of History.—Similar to that of the Monuments.—M. Oppert on the Tower of Babel.—Account of the Confusion of Tongues by Berosus.—Egyptian Art.—Babylonian Astronomy.—What has become of the Palæolithic Races of Egypt and Mesopotamia?—The Negro Race.—Early Manifestation of Race-Marks.—Language.—The Cave-Men of Western Europe.—No Older than the Oriental Races.

If we trace back the thread of human history, we have Modern Europe; the Middle Ages; the Goths, Vandals, Huns; Rome. We can follow the Roman history back to seven hundred and fifty years before Christ. And before the Romans were the Greeks. We can trace them back through Demosthenes, Thucydides, Herodotus, Homer. Solon was about 600 B.C.; Lycurgus, a kind of mythical form, about 900 B.C. Back of that we place the Trojan war (about 1200 B.C.), the Lycians, the Lydians, the Carians, etc.; and there, excluding certain confused ideas of Egyptian, Babylonian, Assyrian, Etruscan, and Phœnician history, our thread was lost,—always excepting, of course, the earlier Hebrew chronicles, written about 1500 B.C. But modern research has laid bare the Egyptian and Mesopotamian annals, and we know now more, perhaps, of the daily life of the old Memphian and Theban monarchies than we do of that of the Romans before the Punic wars. Champollion and Young, followed by Layard, Rawlinson, Oppert, Brugsch, De Rougé, Lepsius, Mariette, have found the key to the mysterious characters that were stamped on the Babylonian bricks or traced on the walls of the Egyptian tombs. The long-sealed records of ancient India, of Phœnicia, of Palestine, Persia, Moab, have also been more or less illustrated by archæological inquiry. We find ourselves face to face with the builders of the Pyramids and the Tower of Babel, with the hoary antiquity of the Vedas, and those primeval rovers of the sea whose traces, it is supposed, have been found even in America. We can almost lay our hands upon Mizraim and Asshur and Nimrod, as they stand between the Ark and the opening drama of human history.

Egyptian and Babylonian chronology.

Authorities differ as to the precise chronology; but 2700 B.C. for Egypt, and the same date for Babylon, is, perhaps, not far from the mark. A few hundred years earlier or later will not affect the main fact: *that human history commences about four thousand five hundred or five thousand years ago.* The Chinese and the Hindoos (like the Egyptians and the Babylonians) *claim* a much greater antiquity; but by general consent it is now allowed that the Egyptian annals go back as far as any others, if not farther. There is, however, no very great difference between the antiquity of the Egyptians, the Babylonians, the Arabians, the Assyrians, the Persians, the Scythians (Turyas), the Phœnicians, the Chinese, and the Indians. They all go back some two thousand or three thousand years before the Christian era.* Zoroaster is placed by Pliny in the year 2500 B.C., which corresponds with the tradition of Berosus and the calculation of M. Oppert.

Primeval man civilized.

We find all of these primeval people suddenly appearing on the scene together, *and with a full-fledged civilization.* That was *about* four thousand six hundred years ago. The Egyptians of Manetho's Fourth Dynasty, the builders of the oldest Pyramids, assigned by Mr. Stuart Poole to about B.C. 2400–2200, are acquainted with all the arts of civilized life; they not only write, but the characters have assumed the cursive form; agriculture is in a state of considerable

* Even Lepsius places Menes at 3892 B.C.

With regard to China, in the seventh century before the Christian era it embraced only five out of the present eighteen districts; and there are no historical documents earlier than the sixth century B.C. No writings of any description, prior to those ascribed to Confucius, exist in China. This philosopher compiled a history of China in a book called the *Shoo-king.* Subsequent to this, one of the Chinese emperors, Che-wang-tse by name, under the idea of commencing a new set of annals with his own reign, caused all the records of the empire to be destroyed. Sixty years afterwards, his successor attempted to repair the mischief which had been perpetrated, and offered large rewards for the recovery of any of the lost annals. The Shoo-king is said to have been recovered from an old man who had committed it to memory. Such is Chinese history prior to this date. But, such as it is, it does not claim to go back farther than 2637 B.C.

With regard to India, the annals of this country do not go back farther than the epoch of Alexander the Great. The Rig-veda, for which an antiquity of three thousand years before our era is claimed, belongs probably to the twelfth century B.C., while the Laws of Menu are five hundred years later. The rock-cut temples of India have also been deemed of immense antiquity; but it is now ascertained, from inscriptions and other data, that none of them are older than the second century B.C. The natives will tell you that they were erected by the Pandus 3101 B.C., while others tell us that they belong to "an ante-Sanskrit race."

advancement; they have their science and their literature; the women are dressed in "brilliant scarlet," and adorned with "necklaces, bracelets, and anklets of blue and white glass beads;" the "government" is engaged in mining for copper and turquoise in the Sinaitic peninsula; "in short, the civilization represented is in every respect as high as that of any later period of the Egyptian monarchy, and the art is even higher." Well may M. Renan exclaim, "When we think of this civilization that it had known no infancy; that this art, of which there remain innumerable monuments, had no archaic epoch; that the Egypt of Cheops and Cephren is superior, in a sense, to all that followed, *on est pris de vertige.*"

It was pretty much the same at Babylon and Nineveh. In two rooms of the palace of Asshur-bani-pal at Nineveh, Mr. Layard discovered a mass of Assyrian grammatical literature. One of these documents proves to be a vast *Cyclopedia of Assyrio-Babylonian Grammar.* In the same "Chamber of Records" he found an exceedingly rich collection of mathematical and astronomical works. The Phœnicians, it is at least probable, crossed the Atlantic, and left their colonies in North and South America.*

---

* Since this was written, we have met with the following in the columns of the New York *Evening Post:*

"PHŒNICIAN INSCRIPTIONS IN BRAZIL.

"Readers of the *Evening Post* will recall a recent allusion in these columns to the discovery of inscriptions in Brazil, which upon examination proved to be Phœnician, and to record the presence there, five centuries B.C., of a Phœnician colony. The circumstances of the discovery are given as follows:

"'Visconde de Sapercahy, a member of the Emperor's Council of State, received, three months ago, a letter from Parahyba, inclosing a drawing of the inscription upon a stone which the writer's slaves had come upon during their agricultural labors on his farm, and which drawing had been taken by the writer's son, a young man who could draw a little. This copy was turned over to the Historical Society of Rio, and by it to Señor [*sic*] Ladislão Netto, Director of the Rio Museum, for an examination. On examining it he found the letters to be pure Phœnician.

"'The inscription is of a commemorate stone,—a rough monument erected by some Phœnicians of Sidonia, apparently exiles or refugees from their native land, between the ninth and tenth years of the reign of a king named Hiram. These rash or unfortunate Canaanites—the patronymic which they have used to denominate themselves—left the port of Aziongaber (now Akaba), a port upon the Red Sea, and sailed for twelve novilunes (lunar months) along the land of Egypt—that is, Africa. The number of vessels they had and the number of males and females composing the adventurous expedition are all set forth in a concise and seemingly elegant style, these particulars being placed intermediate between the invocation, some at the beginning and the others at the end of the inscription of the Alonim Valonuth,—that is, gods and goddesses, or *superos superasque*, as is the Latin translation of those well-known Phœnician words. The inscription is in eight lines of most beautiful Phœnician letters, but without separation of the words, without the vowel-points, and without quiescent letters,—three great obstacles to the interpretation, to overcome which a mere knowledge of Biblical Hebrew is insufficient.

"'Writing to the finder on the subject, Señor Netto expresses the opinion that the voyage

The records of all these nations go back, we say, to B.C. 2000 or 2700,—we there come to a dead halt,—we cannot go any farther. If we examine their religion, their language, their architecture, we find that they are related. If we question them of their origin, most of them tell us of a DELUGE, some of them of an *Ark and Eight Persons*.

Such being the facts, we may ask such a one as Sir John Lubbock what he means by his Stone Age, and his Bronze Age, and his Iron Age. The Egyptians certainly had no Stone Age; they were born civilized. Stone implements occur in Egypt, but there is no evidence that they are older than the metal implements which we know were employed to construct the Pyramids. And so in Babylonia we find traces of iron and bronze from the very first, and, associated with them, implements of stone. There is not a particle of evidence that man in his earliest seats in the East was a *savage*.

No Stone Age in Egypt.

It is certain that the Egyptians, the Arabians, the Babylonians, the Aryans of India, set out as civilized races. The remark is, perhaps, true of the Chinese, and of the Scythians. In the beginning, among some of them, certain tribes may have followed a pastoral life; in the main the arts and the building of cities appear at once.

There is nothing back of this civilization, no graduated process from the savage state. Did they pass from the lacustrine or the cave state in a day? Did the Pyramids and the Chaldæan Astronomy emerge from the Danish kjökken-möddings abruptly and instantaneously? If not,—and of course not,—where did the Pyramid-builders and the Phœnician navigators come from? We can go back to the Circus Maximus and the Aqueducts; but we can go *behind them*. Rome had her infancy, —the guilds of Numa Pompilius and the she-wolf. We can go back to Pericles and Phidias and Plato, but we have the gradual development of the Grecian drama before these figures fill the scenes.

The Parthenon did not emerge from the primeval night. Giorgione did not commence painting in Venice without some preliminary stages of art. We go back to Ghirlandajo, Angelico da Fiesole, Andrea Orcagna, Giotto, Cimabue, and the Byzantine School. But if we turn to the history of the primitive races, as preserved in their monuments, and in the pages of Manetho and Berosus, we are at the very

was made during the reign of the second Hiram, who succeeded Solomon's ally on the throne of Phœnicia. He explains their crossing, of which they themselves appeared to be unaware, by resort to Maury's observations on oceanic currents. Like Cabral, in fleeing from the storms reigning from the Cape of Good Hope up to near Senegambia, they steered in to the high sea, and, seized by the famous equatorial current, which sometimes flows with extraordinary swiftness, they unexpectedly came upon the Brazilian shores. Señor Netto writes to Ernest Renan and to Father Barges, giving them some words of his version, and asking their advice how to make his efforts of the most service to science.'" We know nothing of this, and merely give it for what it is worth.

threshold confronted by the colossal Sphinx, the Pyramids, and the Lake of Mœris; or by the *Birs-Nimrûd* and the ruins of Calah, Asshur, and Resen.

American civilization.

If we come to North and South America, there is nothing to indicate an older civilization than that of Asia and Africa and Italy. The islands of the Pacific Ocean, and the American continents, there is little doubt, were settled by the Malays, the Tatar or Scythian (Turanian) race, and perhaps the Hamitic (?) Phœnicians. Even the Negroes from south of Ethiopia and Madagascar are found in the Fiji Islands and in "Central America." It is fashionable now to claim long dates;* but the Phœnician annals do not go up higher than 1500 or 2000 B.C., and yet (as it would seem) the ships of Tyre visited America. Sir John Lubbock says, "We are quite justified in concluding that between B.C. 1500 and B.C. 1200 the Phœnicians were already acquainted with the mineral fields of Spain and Britain," and he thinks it quite probable "they pushed their explorations still farther." M. Morlot thinks he "found traces of the Phœnicians even in America." Pharaoh Necho, B.C. 600, had two great fleets of triremes manned by Phœnician sailors, one upon the Mediterranean and the other upon the Indian Ocean, a detachment of the latter having circumnavigated Africa during his reign. Diodorus Siculus speaks of "a country over against Africa, many days' sail from Libya westward," discovered by the Phœnicians. Humboldt quotes from Plutarch a passage about "a great continent beyond the ocean, called 'the Saturnian continent.'" Claudius Ælianus speaks of a similar continent beyond the Atlantic, "larger than Asia, Europe, and Libya together." Bernard de Sahagun, the leading Spanish authority at the time of the conquest of America, mentions a universal tradition among the natives of New Spain "of a foreign Atlantic colony arriving before the Christian era on the shores of Florida;" all of which is rendered the more probable by the evidence that, prior to the voyage of Columbus, America had been visited by the Chinese, the Japanese, the Irish, the Welsh, and the Northmen, if not by the Basques. We still ask, *Where did these races come from?* Did they have their Iron Age, and their Bronze Age, and their Neolithic, and their Palæolithic

---

* M. Bunsen, for example, treats us to the following delicious nonsense:

"After five thousand years from B.C. 19,752, the earliest polarization of religious consciousness issued in that formation of pure agglutinative speech which was the Eastern polarization of Sinism." Again, he tells us that man was frozen out of his Paradise by a convulsion of nature in the eleven-thousandth year of his existence. This was the Flood,—which did not extend to Egypt, which had been peopled a thousand years before directly from Eden,—yet with Osirian idolaters. From 9086 B.C. to 7231 B.C. it enjoyed a dynasty of sacerdotal kings, followed by elective, and then hereditary princes, down to 3643 B.C., when Menes ascended the throne. The Exodus took place in the year 1322 B.C., after a sojourn of one thousand four hundred and thirty-four years in Egypt."

Age? Did they live in caves, and "bee-hives," and on sea-beaches, feeding on fish, and mussels, and marrow, and human flesh?

Scientific men call us to the record, and refuse to speculate, holding us exclusively to *facts*. Historical criticism and archæology take us back to the Fourth Dynasty of Manetho and the Third of Berosus, and the East is in a blaze of light; these are the *facts*, and the date is certainly not more than 4000 B.C.,—in our opinion, not more than 2700 B.C. Neither science nor secular history has any account of what preceded this state of things.

The picture of primeval man in the Book of Genesis.

It is remarkable that the Book of Genesis, which alone undertakes to speak, gives just this representation of the beginning of human history. We find nothing there about a stone age, or a bone age, or gaunt prehistoric savages cracking the long bones and vertebræ to get at the marrow. We find, *before the flood*, Cain *building a city*; in the eighth generation, Jubal, the "father of all such as handle the harp and organ," and his brother, Tubal-Cain, "an instructor of every artificer in brass and iron;" while, after the flood, we find Nimrod, the great-grandson of Noah, "the beginning of whose kingdom was Babel, and Erech, and Accad, and Calneh;" and Abraham, four hundred years after the flood, going down to Egypt, where he finds an established government and a great kingdom, with all the paraphernalia of a busy and vigorous civilization. We read, on the other hand, of the Tower of Babel, and of Cherdorlaomer, King of Elam, and his allied kings, making war (in the days of Abraham) with the King of Sodom and the King of Gomorrah. The ruins of Erech and Calneh, two of the cities of Nimrod, are found at the modern *Warka* and *Niffar*, the *Huruk* and *Nipur* of the Babylonian inscriptions; while the *Tower of Babel* itself seems to have been identified at Birs-Nimrûd, by the great French archæologist M. Oppert, who has found an inscription which he describes as Nebuchadnezzar's own account of the building of the temple of Bel-Merodach, which was founded on the ruins of the citadel of Nimrod. Nebuchadnezzar gives a particular description of his great temple, "of the Seven Lights of the Earth," and says, "We say for the other, that is, this edifice, the House of the Seven Lights of the Earth, the most ancient monument of Borsippa; *a former king built it* (*they reckon forty-two ages*), *but he did not complete its head.* SINCE A REMOTE TIME PEOPLE HAD ABANDONED IT, WITHOUT ORDER EXPRESSING THEIR WORDS."* Abydenus, who is said to have drawn his narrative directly from Berosus, the Babylonian historian, notices the same event: "At that time the men of antiquity are said to have been so puffed up with strength and haughtiness, that they despised even the gods, and undertook to build that lofty obelisk, which

* See Smith's Dictionary of the Bible, art. Confusion of Tongues.

is now called Babylon. And when they had already built it up into the heavens, almost as high as the gods, the gods, by the help of the wind, smote the well-contrived but futile work, and prostrated it to the ground. And that rubbish took the name of Babel. For up to that time men relied upon the use of one language; but then a various and discordant confusion of tongues was sent by the gods upon those who had heretofore used but one language." See Müller's Fragm. Hist. Gr., vol. iv. p. 282, F. 26.

The Book of Genesis, we remark, gives precisely this representation of the beginnings of human history, which is thus so remarkably corroborated even in the details. It represents Egypt, and Babylon, and Assyria, and Ethiopia (Southern Arabia and Abyssinia) as established kingdoms from the very first; it affirms a knowledge of the arts of civilized life; it quietly draws a most improbable picture. The trouble with the Biblical account is to understand how the human race could have multiplied so rapidly and made such progress in a few centuries. But even so it seems to have been.

The only explanation of this wonderful knowledge on the part of these primeval races is the suggestion that Noah and his sons *inherited* the same from the antediluvian world, and that the patriarchs were also, by natural endowment and by virtue of the experience acquired in a life of from four to six hundred years, very remarkable men. However this may be (and it is no doubt the fact), the Mosaic history and the Egyptian and Babylonian records tell precisely the same story. Speaking of Egypt, an intelligent historian remarks, "In the formative arts she has had no superior except her pupil, Greece, and in majestic grandeur no rival; there is even a delicate beauty in her best colossi, partly concealed by their vast size and their attitudes of repose; and it has been said by no mean judge, 'Give motion to these rocks, and Greek art would be surpassed.'" This art was at its highest point of excellence about 2250 B.C. In one respect it was a Stone Age: architecture and sculpture afforded among the grandest forms the world has ever seen.

Of the Babylonian astronomy we are told that "it reached the highest perfection attainable without the aid of optical instruments." The Chaldæans were acquainted with the synodic period of the moon, the equinoctial and solstitial points, the true length of the year, as dependent on the annual course of the sun, and even the precession of the equinoxes. They calculated eclipses (which implies a knowledge of the "golden cycle" of two hundred and twenty-three lunations); their observations of the apparent motions of the sun, moon, and planets imply a careful identification of the fixed stars; and there is little doubt that they invented the system of constellations, of which mention is made in the Book of Job.

It is true that there is no positive evidence that the astronomy of the Babylonians reaches back to the earliest ages. But it is also true that we find among the ruins at *Abu-Shahrein* on the Euphrates the remains of a "temple-tower," apparently belonging to the earliest period, the platform of which is cased with a stone wall, in some places twenty feet thick, while the stairs leading up to the first story are made of blocks of polished marble, fastened by copper bolts above the steps of sun-dried bricks. This is merely a single example. The most ancient tombs contain vessels and lamps of pottery, chains, nails, fish-hooks of bronze, leaden pipes and jars, armlets, bracelets, and finger-rings of iron, along with knives, arrow-heads, hatchets, and other implements of *flint*. The clay tablets contain bas-reliefs, and there are curious cylindrical seals or signets made of serpentine, chalcedony, jasper, etc. The art of *writing*, as in Egypt, goes back also to the most ancient period. On the bricks of the oldest cities we find letters in use, and that not in their first stage; that is, not hieroglyphic.

Modern Archæology cannot explain the absence of records and monuments prior to the Pyramids and the Babylonian Temple-towers.

If, then, man existed a million or a quarter of a million of years ago, as Sir John Lubbock and Sir Charles Lyell affirm, where are their monuments and their records? Is it probable that different tribes, in different parts of the earth, lived on from the Pliocene and the Miocene ages, through the Glacial period, and for several hundred thousand years after the Glacial period, and left no footprints except a few uncouth flint implements, and then suddenly blazed up into the Pyramids and the abounding remains of the Mesopotamian Valley? The statement is that they lived here many hundred thousand years. When were they destroyed? Some say they are the negroes; but Dr. Livingstone tells us that he has observed the most striking coincidences between the customs of ancient Egypt and Central Africa, and declares that all the tongues now spoken south of the equator (with the exception of the Hottentot) are homogeneous, and in particular that the Sichuana tongue, as elevated by the powerful Bechuana chieftains, bears in structure a very close resemblance to the language of Egyptian monuments; while

The Negro race.

Rawlinson observes that "the original unity between the languages of Africa and Asia is confirmed by these linguistic resemblances as well as by the manifold traditions concerning the two Ethiopias." As to the American Indians, Bunsen remarks, "The linguistic data, combined with the traditions and customs, and particularly with the system of mnemonic or pictorial writing, enable me to say that the Asiatic origin of these tribes is as fully proved as the unity of a family amongst themselves."

The "Ethiopians," whom the Egyptians denominated "the vile race of Cush," and who occupied Southern Arabia and the region in Africa now known as Nubia, were nearly related to the Egyptians, and resembled them in manners, customs, institutions, and religion. They were a straight-haired race, nearly black, with regular features, and were highly civilized. The Egyptians themselves were a link between the Hamitic and Semitic races; the Ethiopians Hamitic, and nearly allied to the negroes. In fixing the ethnological place of any particular race, too little attention is paid to the fact that the races of mankind have constantly *intermingled;* which often accounts for many things that cannot be explained on the hypothesis that they belong exclusively to one particular family. This remark applies in a greater or less degree to the Babylonians, Scythians, Egyptians, and Phœnicians. We do not pretend to say positively who the negroes are; from which of the descendants of Noah they have proceeded. We find them geographically, and in the main point of *complexion*, closely connected with the Ethiopians, and, as we have seen, linguistically associated with the Egyptians. As to how they came to differ so much from the Japhetic race, is unexplained. At the present day we find a German physiognomy, a Jewish physiognomy, an Italian physiognomy, an American physiognomy (already very different from the English), and a Hindoo physiognomy. The features of the Egyptian and the Assyrian are as distinctly marked from the first as were those of the negro. If it be argued that the negro is of a different species from the Caucasian, or that it must have required the lapse of many centuries to establish the diversities between them, we desire to ask, How did the Egyptian come to differ at once from the Assyrian, and the Phœnician, and the Persian, and the Ethiopian? These people are all unquestionably related, and, as we have shown, there is no trace of any of them back of 2700 B.C., or at the utmost 4000. We will venture to remark that the diversities of complexion and physiognomy may have originated as the diversities of language originated. It may have been done *suddenly*, just as the line of Cain diverged from that of Seth; it may have been in the divine purpose to have diversities both of language and of race. There *are* the most marked diversities of language, diversities observable from the very earliest times, as far back as we can see. And yet there are, at least, indications of *one* original language. "One of the grandest results," says Meyer, "of modern comparative philology has been to show that all languages belonging to one common stock, and we may say, enlarging this view, all languages of the earth, are but scattered indications of that primitive state of human intellect, and more particularly of the imitative faculty, under the highest excitement of poetical inspiration, in which the language originated, and with which every language remains connected, as well through the physiological unity of

The diversity of type among the races of mankind.

the human race as through the historical unity of the family to which it more especially belongs." Prof. Max Müller says, "Nothing necessitates the admission of different independent beginnings for the material elements of the Turanian, Semitic, Aryan branches of speech; nay, it is possible even now to point out radicals which, under various changes and disguises, have been current in these three branches ever since their first separation." It is quite certain that the divergence of languages was *violent;* and the confusion of tongues at Babel is an adequate explanation, It is probable that the diversity of race was equally sudden and equally violent. We see negroes on the Egyptian monuments in the Sixth Dynasty.

We may quote on this subject (to show that the negro is related to the other races) the remarks of Mr. Winwood Reade, F.R.G.S., an acknowledged authority. "I have always," he says, "been anxious to impress upon men of science this *fact,* that the woolly-headed, black-skinned, fetid, prognathous negro is by no means to be regarded as the typical African. The real African is *copper-colored,* and superior in every respect to the negro, mentally and physically. I went further than this, and ascribed it as my belief that the negro inhabits only maritime districts, or the marshy regions of the interior; that he originally belonged to the copper-colored race, and that his degeneration of type is due entirely to the influence of climate and food." *

Dr. Carpenter, we may add further, observes that there is strong evidence to show that even the Syro-Arabian or Semitic nations may be referred to the African stock; at any rate, that there are numerous tribes in the interior of Africa whose affinity with the true negroes cannot be disputed, and which yet present a far superior cranial organization.

It would be according to the analogies of the early Biblical history, we think, to find marked diversities among the sons and immediate descendants of Adam and Noah. There is, we think, a plain intimation that the founders of certain races stamped a certain character and individuality on their offspring. This seems to be indicated in the account of the sons of Noah. They were to be the progenitors of different races, to whom were assigned different rôles and divergent histories. We see something similar in the descendants of Isaac and Ishmael. The Jews and the Joktan Arabians are each a peculiar people, the latter, at least, having the germ of all their national peculiarities lodged in their great progenitor.

If, then, after tracing up all the languages of the earth to some three parent stocks, it may prove impossible to trace these any farther to one

---

* Anthropological Review, November, 1864, p. 341.

original tongue; and if it is necessary to call in the Biblical narrative of the confusion of tongues to account for the remaining diversities, so there is to our mind no difficulty in accounting for the divergence of physiological types in the first generations of the human race.

But we are by no means without evidence that such divergencies are rapidly developed, under favorable conditions, even in the ordinary course of things. We find an example in the Turks of Europe and Western Asia, as compared with those of Central Asia. The former have assumed in a few centuries the European type, insomuch that many physiologists refer them to the Caucasian stock; and yet we know that they belong to the Central Asiatic stock. And Dr. Carpenter remarks that no hypothesis of the intermixture of these Turks with other races is adequate to explain the modifications which have taken place. The same great authority adduces as another similar example the Magyars of Hungary. This race, as we know from history and philology, is a branch of the great Northern Asiatic family, expelled some ten centuries ago from their homes on the borders of the Ural Mountains. Having thus changed the vigorous climate of the hunting-grounds of the Ostiaks and Samoiedes for the genial and fertile plains of Southern Europe, they changed also their modes of life, and in the course of a thousand years their cranial formation, which was originally pyramidal, has become elliptical, and nearly every trace has been lost of their primitive Tartar features. This too, it might be said, was attributable to the mixture of the conquering with the conquered race; but, as a matter of fact, the existing Magyars pride themselves particularly on the purity of their descent. We find a similar modification, though less in degree, in the case of the Finnish tribes of Scandinavia. These are believed to be of the same origin with the Lapps; but, having adopted a much more settled mode of life than the Lapps (who retain the nomadic habits of their Mongol ancestors), they have experienced a modification of their cranial conformation and of their general bodily form. The contrast between the Lapps and the Magyars is very marked,—the latter being a handsome, tall, well-formed race, the former uncouth and short of stature. Further, it is believed that the Georgian and Caucasian nations are of Mongolian origin, but, separated at an early period from the common stock, the cranium here has also changed from the pyramidal or Mongolian to the elliptical or Indo-European form. Even the Negro type, so constantly appealed to, has been modified in the course of a few centuries in America, and this, although the climate of the West Indies and the Southern States of the United States is not very different from that of the Guinea coast. Dr. Carpenter also justly calls attention to the divergence in type of the Anglo-Saxon

Historical examples of a modification of the original race-type.

population of America from that of the original and existing English stock.*

Archdeacon Pratt has a very striking observation in this connection: the population of the world, he remarks, after the Deluge, did not proceed *from a single centre:* there were *four pairs;* and *the wives of Shem, Ham, and Japhet may have belonged to different tribes.* The diversity of type may have been *antediluvian.* This is abundantly sufficient to account for the whole matter, even presuming that there was no extraordinary or miraculous feature in the transaction.

The Law of the Growth of Languages has of course been used in the same way as the above to impugn the correctness of the Biblical record. M. Bunsen attempts to show that a far longer interval than the Scripture chronology allows is necessary to explain the development and diversity of languages. To the same purport speaks the Duke of Argyll. We have no idea of entering into this discussion. We shall only state in a few words a few facts.

The Rapid Divergence and Development of Languages.

Iceland was colonized by the Northmen in the ninth century. The Scandinavian tongue has there no doubt been preserved in comparative purity. Let it be compared with the languages since that time developed in the colonies, provinces, and kingdoms of the Scandinavians of Northern Europe.

In the same ninth century the Northmen acquired and colonized Normandy, in France. These settlers adopted the Romance dialect of the district. There were then no less than *seven* Romance dialects in existence, namely, the Italian, Wallachian, Rhetian, Provençal, Spanish, Portuguese, and French,—all descended from the Latin, and all formed and developed since the downfall of the Roman Empire.

In an address before the British Association at Brighton, in 1872, Colonel A. Lane Fox made the following statement: "Amongst the one hundred islands occupied by the Melanesian race, the Bishop of Wellington informs us there are no less than two hundred languages differing from each other as much as Dutch and German, and this diversity of languages and dialects is confirmed by Mr. Turner in his account of his nineteen years' residence in Polynesia. Amongst the Penons, or savage tribes of Cambodia, Mr. Muhot speaks of dialects spoken by different tribes whose manners and customs are the same. Amongst the Musgu of Central Africa, Barth tells us that, owing to the absence of friendly intercourse between the several tribes and families, such a number of dialects had sprung up as to render communication between them

* See Archdeacon Pratt's admirable book, entitled "Scripture and Science not at Variance," p. 99.

difficult. Upon the river Amazon Mr. Bates mentions that in a single canoe he found several individuals speaking languages so different as to be unintelligible to each other."*

And yet great stress is laid on the great lapse of time that is required for the development of a language.

It is said, we may add, that there are from four thousand to six thousand languages spoken at the present time, and not a half-dozen of them, we will venture to say, are a thousand years old. We thus have some five thousand languages formed in ten centuries. In Germany the poem of the Nibelungen Lied—seven centuries old—is now unintelligible except to scholars. The modern Italian cannot be traced back much beyond the time of Dante. Polybius informs us that the language of the treaty between Rome and Carthage, concluded in the first year of the commonwealth, was so unlike the Latin of his own time (about B.C. 160) that even those who understood it best found some things in it which, with their best attention, they could scarcely explain. So the Hymns of the Salii, and of the Brotherhood of Husbandry, Fratres Arvales, required to be interpreted to the Romans of Cicero's time, like a foreign language. The hymn of the Fratres Arvales has descended to our own times, and the meaning of half of it is only to be guessed at.

But the language of Rome continued to change—even in the capital itself, where there was no intrusion of the barbarians of the North. The population of Rome in the year 1000 spoke a language quite different from that spoken in the time of Constantine, and equally different from that of their descendants, as is shown by the well-known chronicle of Benedict, of the convent of St. Andrea, on Mount Soracte, —unintelligible to any one but a profound linguist.

This was *at the centre*—in the metropolis of the world. It was at the principal seat of learning which existed for most of this time in Europe.

What would occur among unlettered savages with no written forms to fix their language?

There are nearly one hundred languages spoken at present in the Caucasus. In South America and Mexico Alexander Humboldt reckoned the languages by hundreds. There are eighteen provincial dialects even in China; and in the Himalayan Mountains the number of languages is so great as to prove a serious barrier to the advance of civilization.

The rapidity with which a language changes is governed by the existence or the absence of a *literature*. The English Bible and Shakspeare have fixed the English language, and so long as they are read the language will remain substantially what it is now. But the English

---

* See Nature, Aug. 22, 1872.

and the Dutch were originally the same; one took one direction; the other, another; *before they became fixed.* Professor Max Müller has some remarks which are pertinent to this subject. "Tribes," he says, "who have no literature, and no sort of intellectual occupation, seem occasionally to take a delight in working their language to the highest pitch of grammatical expansion. The American dialects are a well-known instance; and the greater the seclusion of a tribe, the more amazing the rank vegetation of their grammar. We can, at present, hardly form a correct idea with what feeling a savage nation looks upon its language; whether, it may be, as a plaything, a kind of intellectual amusement,—a maze in which the mind likes to lose and find itself. But the result is the same everywhere. If the work of agglutination has once commenced, and there is nothing like literature or society to keep it within limits, two villages, separated for only a few generations, will become mutually unintelligible. This takes place in America as well as on the borders of China and India; and in the north of Asia, Messerschmidt relates, that 'the Ostiakes, though really speaking the same language everywhere, have produced so many words and forms peculiar to each tribe, that even within the limits of ten or twelve German miles, conversation between them becomes extremely difficult.'"

We have been led into this digression in order to clear our subject of the idea that such races as the Negroes and the American Indians occupy different ground in this discussion from the Babylonians and Egyptians and Hindoos. We shall have farther occasion to show that they are all linked together.

The primitive races of Western Europe, and the Stone Age.

At this point the question will be asked, But did not the Cave-men of England and France—those Palæolithic savages of the archæologists—have their Stone Age? and do we not in this quarter carry back the existence of man to a far more remote antiquity than that of Egypt and Babylon? There was, undoubtedly, a Stone Age in Western Europe; but these *Iberians*, or whoever they were, *came from the East.* They are the kinsmen, at least, of the Turanians of the East.

It seems that there were wild and savage races as well as civilized races. After the dispersion, some of the descendants of (as we believe) Cush were doubtless cannibals. The descendants of Mizraim built the Pyramids. And, of course, the wild, roving races used rude weapons, just as the North American Indians did a century ago, and in that sense they had their Stone Age. And there are stone weapons delineated on the Egyptian monuments, and they are found in the Babylonian tombs; and they have been found in India, China, Japan, and were in use among the Aztecs and Peruvians; but this does not prove an indefinite antiquity. Metals were rare, if not unknown, at first; but they appear almost immediately.

Our argument is that the races which migrated to Western Europe from Central Asia were no older than their fathers; that Egypt is as old as the oldest; and that in Egypt, in Mesopotamia, in Arabia, in India,* in China, we find a high state of civilization *from the first*, and that as these races were civilized they would have left traces of the ages before the Pyramids and other similar monuments, if they had existed prior to the period when they are revealed to us. If they had been savages, we could not expect to find such traces; but organized states like Egypt and Babylon, at a high point of civilization, must show some of the tracks that led up to this state of things, if the races had existed for ages before.

Few traces of a Stone Age in Africa.

It is a very noticeable and a very remarkable fact that there are hardly any traces of the Stone Age in any part of Africa. A few stone implements have been recently discovered in the western and southern parts of the continent, and a few have been discovered in Egypt. On the contrary, as remarked by Colonel Fox (we believe it was at the International Congress of Anthropologists in London, in 1868), iron has been known in South Africa for a much longer time and at a much earlier development than elsewhere, the date of its introduction being anterior to the earliest records of its inhabitants by modern writers.

The inference from these facts is that Africa received its knowledge of iron from Egypt. It had no Stone Age back of Egypt, and if, as the anthropologists affirm, it is the oldest of the continents, and the region where Miocene man is to be discovered, it is precisely the country where we should look for a Stone Age.

A few flint implements have been found in Egypt, and Sir Gardiner Wilkinson mentions that flint arrow-heads were used as late as the period of the Eighteenth Dynasty, *but no palæolithic implements at all have been found.* Dr. Pickering, in a paper on the Gliddon mummy case in the museum of the Smithsonian Institution, says the Stone Adze is figured in the Third Dynasty, of which the hieroglyphic character continues perhaps until the Fifth (two or three hundred years). These, he says, "are all the traces I have been able to discover of a Stone Age in Egypt."†

* Certain rude Turanian tribes had penetrated into India before the Aryan migration into that region. We cannot go into this: Egypt, Babylonia, and Assyria support the argument which we have made. Our information in these cases is complete. The indications point to the same state of things on the table-land of Iran and in Arabia. All of the tribes of China and India, it is believed, migrated from Central Asia. Palæolithic implements are also found in India,—the handiwork, no doubt, of the Turanian tribes, who were not older, but ruder, than their Iranian conquerors.

† Smith. Contrib. to Knowl., vol. xvi. p. 2.

We may conclude these remarks by the following quotation from George Syncellus, in the eighth century of our era, cited by Sir G. C. Lewis in his "Astronomy of the Ancients." George Syncellus, speaking of the chronology of the Egyptians and Babylonians, observes:

"The writers on Chaldæan antiquity consider the accounts of Egyptian antiquity to be fabulous, and the writers on Egyptian antiquity hold a similar opinion with respect to the accounts of Chaldæan antiquity. Neither regards the other; but each weaves spiders' webs in glorification of its own nation and fatherland."

CHAPTER II.

THE UNITY OF THE HUMAN RACE.

The Kinship of the Different Races of Mankind, proved by the General Prevalence of Certain Traditions and Customs.—The Symbol of the Crux Ansata.—The Tradition of the Deluge.—Tradition of a Terrestrial Paradise.—The Occurrence of Dolmens, Stone Circles, and Tumuli in various Countries.—The Prevalence in Asia Minor, America, and some Parts of Europe of the Remarkable Custom of moulding the Human Head.—The Custom of Scalping common to Asia, Africa, and America.—Identity of the Sacred Edifices of Central America and the Buddhist Temples of Southern India.—The Aztecs and the Etruscans.—The Worship of the Sun and the Phallus.—Pyramidal Architecture.—The Prevalence of the Custom of placing Flint Implements in the Tombs of the Dead.—The Remarkable Resemblance between these Implements in all Parts of the World, and the Superstitions connected therewith.—The Origination of nearly all of the Domesticated Animals in Central Asia or Northern Africa.—The Recent Origin of the Cereals, and their Uniform Association with the Remains of Man.—Inferences from these Facts.—The Traditions of Mankind carry us back, not to a Brazen or Stone Age, but to a Golden Age.—The Traditions have reference to a Mythical, not to a Historical, Era.—No Trustworthy Evidences of Man beyond some 2700 or 3000 years B.C.

If we prove that the Egyptians, Babylonians, Assyrians, Hindoos, are of recent origin, and that the European and other races are nearly allied to them, we show that all are of recent origin; at least the presumption is so strong that it suffices, especially if the migrations of men originated in Central Asia.

Instances of common traditions and customs among the races of mankind.

It would be beyond the discussion which we propose to ourselves to go into the general question of the unity of the human race. We leave that to Prichard, Dr. Latham, Dr. Carpenter, and M. de Quatrefages. We would refer, however, to a few facts, which, apart from the physiological and linguistic argument, seem irresistibly to suggest the common origin of mankind.

Symbol of the Crux Ansata.

Let us begin with the symbol of the *Crux Ansata*, "the key of the Nile," the mystical *Tau*, the "hidden wisdom" at once of the Egyptians, the Chaldæans, the Phœnicians, the Mexicans, the Peruvians, and "of every other ancient people." We find this mystic sign, says a writer in the *Edinburgh Review*, alike in the ruined cities of Central America and on the breast of the Egyptian mummies; alike on the Babylonian cylinders and in the hands of Brahma, Vishnu, and Siva; on the battle-axe of Thor and on the

Pagodas of China; among the sect of Xaca Japonicus in Japan and the Knights of St. John in Malta; on the sceptre of the Bompa deities of Thibet and on the sculptured stones of Scotland; on the ancient coins of Gaul and the cinerary urns of Northern Italy; in Persia, in Britain, and in Kamschatka. It was emblematical of creative energy; of immortality; of rejuvenescence; of the "resurrection"; of the Divine Unity. It is frequently found in association with streams of water and exuberant vegetation. We see it thus on the cross-cakes of Egypt, which symbolized the supreme content of the "better land."

Tradition of the Deluge.

Take (what we have already referred to) the universal tradition of the Deluge. We can understand that there might be such a legend as that of the deluge; but how shall we explain that all nations have *the same legend?* How does it happen that the Greek and the Fiji Islander lit upon the same imagination of the destruction of the earth by water? How is it that Ovid and Berosus both carry us up to the Deluge as the beginning of human history? how is it that the Phrygians and the Cherokee Indians have the same recollection of the past? that the inhabitants of Mexico, and the Persians, and the Hindoos, and the Chinese all repeat the same story? We hear on all hands of a "Deluge." Did many races, thousands of miles apart, in different ages, dream the same dream? They all make this the beginning. Ovid, Apollodorus, Lucian, ascribe it to the *wickedness* of the antediluvian world. So also does the Persian tradition: "The world having been corrupted by Ahriman, it was necessary to bring over it a universal flood of water, that all impurity might be washed away. The rain came down in drops as big as the head of a bull," etc. The account of the flood of Deucalion, as given by Lucian, corresponds closely with the Biblical account. The Chinese account represents that Fuh-he, the founder of Chinese civilization, escaped, with his wife, his three daughters, and his three sons, from the waters of the deluge. The Jesuit M. Martinius says the Chinese compute this to have taken place four thousand years before the Christian era: The Phrygian account represents that King Annakos (Enoch), who reigned in Iconium, and who reached the age of three hundred years, foretold the flood. This tradition was commemorated by a medal struck at Apamæa in the reign of Septimius Severus. This city was formerly called "Kibotos," or "The Ark," and it is known that the coins of the cities in that age frequently exhibited some leading point in their mythological history. On the medal referred to is depicted an ark or chest floating on the waters. Two persons are seen within it and two issuing from it. There is a bird perched on the top of the ark, while another is seen flying towards it bearing a branch in its feet. On some specimens of this medal or coin are found the letters *ΝΩ*, or *ΝΩΕ*. Humboldt informs us that the Aztecs, the Zapotecs, the Tlascaltecs, and the Mechoacans, in Mexico, had paintings of the deluge. The Noah, Xisuthrus, or Manu of these nations is termed Coxcox, Teo-Cipactli, and Tezpi. He saved himself with his wife, Xochiquetzatl, on a raft. The mountain of Colhuacan in this tradition represents Ararat. The "dove" is also seen. The Mechoacan tradition speaks of Coxcox or Tezpi, and his wife, *and his children*, and several *animals*. When the Great Spirit ordered the waters to withdraw, Tezpi sent out from his bark a vulture, and subsequently a humming-bird, which returned holding in its beak a branch. Humboldt also found the tradition of the deluge among the wild Indians on the Orinoco in South America. It was found also in Brazil, in Peru, and in Cuba. The Fiji tradition speaks of *eight* persons. The Hindoo tradition lands the ark on the summit of Mount Himarat (Himalaya). The most ancient version of this story (that contained in the Catapat'ha-Bráhmána) places the locality north of the Himalaya range. Besides these, we have the Syrian, the Phœnician, and the Armenian traditions. The Babylonian account, as given by Berosus, now regarded as a very trustworthy chronicler, is as follows:

"Xisuthrus was warned by Saturn, in a dream, that all mankind would be destroyed shortly by a deluge of rain. He was bidden to bury in the city of Sippara (Sepharvaim) such written documents as existed, and then to build a huge vessel or ark, in length five furlongs, and two furlongs in width, wherein was to be placed good store of provisions, together with winged fowl and four-footed beasts of the earth; and in which he himself was to embark with his wife and children and close friends. Xisuthrus did accordingly, and the flood came at the time appointed. The ark drifted towards Armenia; and Xisuthrus, on the third day after the rain abated, sent out from the ark a bird, which, after flying for awhile over the illimitable sea of waters, and finding neither food nor a spot on which it could settle, returned to him. Some days later, Xisuthrus sent out other birds, which likewise returned, but with feet covered with mud. Sent out a third time, the birds returned no more; and Xisuthrus knew that the earth had reappeared. So he removed some of the covering of the ark, and looked, and behold the vessel had grounded upon a high mountain, and remained fixed. Then he went forth from the ark, with his wife, his daughter, and his pilot, and built an altar, and offered sacrifice; after which he suddenly disappeared from sight, together with those who had accompanied him. They who had remained in the ark, surprised that he did not return, sought him; when they heard his voice in the sky, exhorting them to continue religious, and bidding them go back to Babylonia from the land of Armenia, where they were, and recover the buried documents, and make them once more known among men. So they obeyed, and went back to the land of Babylon, and built many cities and temples, and raised up Babylon from its ruins." A similar account is given by Abydenus. Eupolemus, quoted by Eusebius, refers to the same event: "The city of Babylon," he says, "owes its foundation to those who were saved from the Deluge; they were giants, and they built the tower celebrated in history." (Euseb., Frag. Evang., x. 9.) We may add to these the account of the Deluge given in the Sibylline oracles. After that catastrophe Kronos, Titan, and Japetus ruled the world, each taking a separate portion to himself. This evidently refers to the three sons of Noah; Shem, Ham (Titan), and Japhet. It has been said that these memories are confined to the Semitic and Aryan races, but are not found in the Turanian family. This is contradicted by the legends of the Chinese, of the natives of Polynesia, of the American Indians, and, we may add, of the Tartars; for we are told by M. Malte-Brun that "the tradition of the deluge is found very distinctly among the Calmucs."*

And now we have the Chaldæan account of the deluge which Mr. George Smith has recently deciphered from the Assyrian monuments. He wrote of it to the London *Daily Telegraph* as follows:

"The cuneiform inscription which I have recently found and translated gives a long and full account of the deluge. It contains the version or tradition of this event which existed in the early Chaldean period of the city of Erech (one of the cities of Nimrod), now represented by the ruins of Warka. In this newly-discovered inscription the account of the deluge is put as a narrative into the mouth of Xisuthrus, or Noah. He relates the wickedness of the world, the command to build the ark, its building, the filling of it, the deluge, the resting of the ark on a mountain, the sending out of the birds, and other matters. The narrative has a closer resemblance to the account transmitted by the Greeks from Berosus, the Chaldean historian, than to the Biblical history, but it does not differ materially from either. The principal differences are as to the duration of the deluge, the name of the mountain on which the ark rested, the sending out of the birds, etc. The cuneiform account is much longer and fuller than that of Berosus, and has several details omitted both by the Bible and the Chaldean historian. This inscription opens up many questions of which we knew nothing previously, and it is connected with a number of other details of Chaldean history which will be both interesting and important. This is the first time any inscription has been found with an account of an event mentioned in Genesis."

These traditions prove conclusively the *fact* of the deluge; it cannot be questioned: they prove also the existence of some *bond of union*

* Précis de Géographie, vol. lx.

between the races of mankind. They prove almost certainly *community of origin.*

The tradition among nearly all nations of a Terrestrial Paradise affords a similar argument to the above. Arab legends tell of a garden in the East, on the summit of a mountain of jacinth, abounding with trees and flowers of rare colors and fragrance. The Zendavesta mentions a region which it calls *Heden,* and Zoroaster, who lived some 2000 or 2500 years B.C., is stated in the same ancient books to have been at a place called *Hedenèsh.* The Vishnu Purana tells us that in the centre of Jambudwipa is the golden mountain *Meru,* which stands like the seed-cup of the lotos of the earth. On its summit is the vast city of Brahma, encircled by the Ganges, which, issuing from the foot of Vishnu, *is divided into four streams* that flow to the four quarters of the earth. Here is the grove of Indra, and here too is the *Jamba tree,* from whose fruit are fed the Jamba waters, which bestow immortal life on all who drink of them. The Chinese, too, have their "enchanted gardens," in the midst of the summits of the Honanlun, where is the fountain of immortality dividing off into *four streams.* We read of the gardens of Laertes and Alcinoüs; of the Omphalium of the Cretans; of the sacred Asgard of the Scandinavians, springing from the centre of a fruitful land, which was watered by the four primeval rivers of milk; of the Harâmberezaitîm of the Parsi; of the Ilá of the Singalese and the Thibetans; of the Sineru of the Buddhist, with its four-limbed D'amba tree, with its never-fading blossoms, from between whose roots issue the four sacred streams that water the garden of the supreme god, Sekrá.

Tradition of a Terrestrial Paradise.

How, again, shall we account for the Tumuli, the Dolmens, the Menhirs, the Stone Circles,—almost identically the same, in so many parts of the world? We find at Carnac in Brittany immense rows of stones that seem to have been copied from the Menhirs on the Khassia Hills. In India and Algiers and Ireland we see the same dolmens. In Peru, in France, among the aborigines of North America, in Spain, in Denmark, in the Orkney Islands, on the shores of the Black Sea, in the Mediterranean islands, in Palestine, in Malabar, in the Sinaitic peninsula, we find the traces of the mound or the dolmen builders. Let any one compare the tumuli with the open dolmen on their top in Algiers with those of Sauclières and Bousquet in Aveyron, or those described by Olaus Wormius near Roeskilde. Or the dolmen at Halskov in Denmark with the similar one at Northern Moytura in Ireland. Or the dolmen sketched by Sjöborg at Oroust, in Bohuslan, with the Kits Cotty House at Aylesford, represented in this work. Or the circle near Peshawur, in

The same Megalithic Monuments in many parts of the world.

Affghanistan, with the Standing Stones of Stennis in the Orkneys. Or the tombs on the Nilgiri Hills in India with the *chouchas* of Northern Africa. Or the four cairns from Algiers figured on p. 402 of Mr. Fergusson's "Rude Stone Monuments" with the circles at Aschenrade in Livonia. Or the Trilithons at Stonehenge with those at Ksaca and Elkeb in Tripoli, and both of these with those described by Mr. Giffard Palgrave in Central Arabia; and all with the tomb of Isidorus at Khatoura, in Syria, and the Buddhist monument at Bangkok, in India. Or the cairns at Lough Crew, in Ireland, and their cells and inscribed stones, with Locmariaker in Brittany, and the chambers at Mnaidra in Malta. Or the circles at Northern Moytura with that at Pullicondah, Madras; or with that delineated by Bonstetten, near Lüneberg, Hanover; or those mentioned by Von Estorff near Uelzen. Or the great serpent-mound of Loch Nell, in Argyleshire, with the serpent-mounds of Wisconsin and Ohio.

Is all of this accident?

There are minute points of agreement that we have not time to go into,—as, for example, not only the simulated cist on the top of the real tomb, but the circles of stones at the same time on and around the mound; while one of the sides of the exterior and simulated dolmen is pierced with a circular hole six or eight inches in diameter.†

The Practice of Distorting the Skull.

Let us mention another curious custom that may be traced from the Black Sea and Lake Baikal to Switzerland on the one hand—perhaps Britain—and to the valley of the Columbia River and Peru on the other. We refer to the custom which has prevailed among certain races of *artificially moulding the human head.*

The *Macrocephali* are first mentioned by Hippocrates in the fifth century before the Christian era. He represents that these people inhabited the shores of the Euxine Sea, and that they admired those the most who had the longest heads, and states that it was a custom among them to compress the skull during infancy.

Strabo, Pliny, and Pomponius Mela repeat this statement, but do not agree about the locality or region inhabited by this race. Strabo, in his Geography, speaks of such a tribe in Western Asia, who had thus

* For example, the great serpent-mound in Adams County, Ohio, described by Messrs. Squier and Lapham. In this mound, as in that of Loch Nell, the "altar" is in the head of the snake.

† An example of a holed stone is that at Stennis, referred to in "The Pirate," by Sir Walter Scott. The oath to Woden, says Mr. Fergusson, was sworn by persons joining their hands through this hole. The person breaking this oath was regarded as infamous. The dolmen with one of the sides pierced in this way is common in France, as at Grandmont, Languedoc, and that of Trie, Oise. They are also common in Circassia and India.

elongated their heads, and who had foreheads projecting over their beards. He also mentions them as found in the valley of the Danube in Europe. He points to it as a custom common among the migratory tribes of Asia.

Stephanus Byzantinus, nearly a thousand years after Hippocrates, speaks of macrocephalic Scythians, in Colchis, on the eastern shore of the Euxine Sea. Pliny locates them in the neighborhood of Cerasus in Natolia.

These statements have been corroborated by the discoveries of William Burckhardt Barker, who in 1845 obtained a large number of terracotta images from a mound on the site of the ancient city of Tarsus, which exhibited the precise contour of head observed on some of the monuments of Central America.

Prof. Retzius gave an account in 1844 before the Royal Academy of Sciences of Stockholm of a skull found in the year 1820 near Grafenegg, in Austria. It was assigned to the Avarian Huns, who occupied this region during the seventh century. It was a brachycephalic skull, greatly elongated by artificial compression. Similar skulls have since been found near Vienna; others at St. Romain, in Savoy, and in the valley of the Doubs, near Mandeuse. Dr. Fitzinger has investigated the whole subject, and shows in a memoir in the Imperial Academy of Vienna that the skulls are unquestionably macrocephalic, mentioning in addition the interesting fact of the discovery of an ancient medal, struck to commemorate the destruction of Aquileia by Attila, the Hun, in 452. On one side of this is an effigy of this famous chieftain, presenting the same macrocephalic form of the skull.

M. Troyon has discovered a similar skull near Lausanne, in Switzerland.

When M. Tschudi, the Peruvian traveler, had his attention called to the Grafenegg skull, he wrote a memoir in Müller's *Archiv für Anatomie*, in which he insisted that it was a *Peruvian cranium*, and, by way of explanation, reminded the *savans* that although Austria and Peru were widely separated, the Emperor Charles V. embraced them both in his dominions!

The prevalence of the custom in Peru is attested by the crania found in the ancient Peruvian tombs, as well as by Garcilasso de la Vega and Torquemada. The latter, referring to the Peruvians, remarks, "As to the custom of appearing fierce in war, it was in some provinces ordered that the mothers, or their attendants, should make the faces of their children long and rough, and the foreheads broad, *as Hippocrates and Galen relate of the macrocephali, who had them moulded by art into the elevated and conical form.*"

The same custom prevailed among the Flathead Indians along the

Columbia River and on the Pacific coast, who represent some twenty different tribes, the Chinooks, the Klatsaps, the Cowlitz, the Songas, the Newatees, the Chastays, etc.

This distortion of the skull among the Flathead Indians is regarded as a mark of aristocracy. They do not allow their slaves to improve their appearance in the same way. It prevailed also among the Natchez Indians. It was practised also in Central America. We find it in the Sandwich Islands (Malay). And it is stated that the ancient inhabitants of Caledonia and Scandinavia had the same practice.

Scalping.

In this connection we may mention that the custom of *scalping* is not peculiar to the American Indians. Herodotus mentions that it was one of the most characteristic practices of the ancient Scythians. But this is not all: it is stated that the practice prevails at this day among the wild tribes of the frontier in the north-eastern district of Bengal. The "Friend of India," commenting on this statement, adds, "The Naga tribes use the scalping-knife with a ferocity that is only equaled by the American Indians, and the scalps are carefully preserved as evidences of their prowess and vengeance over their enemies. On the death of a chief, all the scalps taken by him during his warlike career are burned with his remains."

The Boomerang.

The *boomerang* is so remarkable a weapon that we should not expect to find it except among kindred tribes. It had never, until recently, been met with except in Australia. But it has now turned up among the Moqui Indians of Northern Arizona and New Mexico, the Esquimaux, the Indians of California, the Furus Furus Indians of South America, and the Dravidian races of India, and has been traced, as we learn from an address by Col. Fox before the Anthropological sub-section of the British Association, among the ancient Egyptians.*

Architecture.

Humboldt was the first to remark that many of the teocallis or sacred edifices of Central America "are identical with the Buddhist temples of Southern India, and in the islands of the Indian archipelago." The great temple of Palenque so closely corresponds in its details with that of Boro-Bodo in the province of Kedu, in Java, as "to place beyond all reasonable doubt the common purpose and origin of both." We find both of them elevated on a series of graduated platforms or terraces, and reached by successive flights of steps facing the cardinal points. The chambers of both are disproportionately small, with no apertures, excepting the doorways, for air or light; the curved ceilings, formed of stones overlapping each other "triangularwise," and constituting a Cyclopean arch, are precisely alike. The walls of both

---

* Nature, August 22, 1872.

are adorned with hieroglyphical tablets, on which the head of the Asiatic elephant* is conspicuous (the head of the elephant occurs also at Copan, and on a helmet or cap of a warrior or a priest in Plate 13 of M. de Waldeck's "Monuments anciens du Mexique et du Yucatan"); while in the sanctuaries of both Buddha is represented in colossal form, seated cross-legged upon a throne, benignly receiving an offering of fruit and flowers from a priestess kneeling before him.†

The close resemblance between the Aztecs and the Etruscans in religious practices has been remarked on, as also the facts that both nations offered human sacrifices at the graves of the chiefs; that both used *the olive branch* as the symbol of peace; and that their calendars were nearly the same,—the one fixing the length of the year at 365 days 5 h. 50 m.; the other at 365 days 5 h. 40 m.

Associated with the Sabæan worship of the sun among the Egyptians, the Assyrians, the Scythians, the Greeks, and the ancient inhabitants of Nicaragua and New England, was that of the lingham or phallus. The worship of the lingham flourished in the cities of Panuco and Tlascala in Mexico at the period of the conquest, and Mr. Stephens observed at Uxmal, in Yucatan, certain ornaments on the cornices of some of the buildings, the meaning of which was too plain to be misunderstood. This revolting worship has been traced in the southern part of the United States, and as far north as Tennessee, where many characteristic images have been ploughed up.

Worship of the Lingham or Phallus.

The worship of Priapus in Rome, of the phallus in Greece, of the lingham in India, of Peor-Apis in Egypt, of Baal-Peor among the Ammonites, seems obviously connected with these images in America.

The pyramidal architecture of Egypt, Ethiopia, and Babylon is of course recalled by the pyramids of Mexico and Central America; and this Dr. Wilson‡ dismisses as of no significance; but it is more difficult to dispose of the fact that the sides of the American pyramids are all orientated, as in Egypt and Mesopotamia. The great pyramid of Cuernavaca, known as Xochicalco, "the house of flowers," is said to be scarcely distinguishable from the ordinary type of those in Lower Egypt. Upon its stones are many sculptured figures, and among them "crocodiles spouting water."

The custom of depositing Flint Implements in the grave seems to have been wellnigh *universal.* We encounter it in all parts of Europe, in Africa, in Asia, and in America.

The *use* of these implements among all races is not very remarkable,

---

* This may be the mammoth or the mastodon.

† Edinburgh Review, cxxv. p. 342.

‡ Prehistoric Man, p. 334.

but the universality of the custom just referred to suggests kinship, and this probability is strengthened by the *identity* or resemblance of the implements all over the world. "So far as the general form is concerned," says Mr. Evans, the implements from the River-Gravels of Western Europe "are identical" with those from the lateritic beds of Southern India. Speaking of the modern Esquimaux flint scrapers, Sir John Lubbock says, they "are in form *identical* with the old ones [of the drift]." The author of the article entitled "The Present Phase of Prehistoric Archæology," in the *British Quarterly Review* for October, 1872, remarks that if the harpoons and arrow-heads of the Auvergne caves be compared with those of the Esquimaux, "the only difference is that those from Auvergne generally bear a groove on their barbs. The mode in which the head is fastened to the shaft is identical in both; the fishing-spears, bone needles, and flint scrapers are also identical in form."

The identity of form of the stone implements of different parts of the world.

Prof. Nilsson observes, "The great resemblance which exists among the stone implements of nations of different tribes, during very different periods and in most different countries, . . . is remarkable." He mentions the similarity between the implements from Scania and those from Pennsylvania, and remarks particularly on the small heart-shaped arrow-heads of flint from Scania and from Tierra del Fuego, "both of which are, with regard to shape and mode of construction, even in the most minute details and when closely viewed with the microscope, surprisingly similar, as if they had been made by the same hand on the same day." *

At the meeting of the British Association in 1871, Sir John Lubbock called attention "to the extreme similarity of these primitive implements," speaking of some specimens which had been presented from Western Africa. One of these was put in contrast with a tray of other axes. "There were examples," he said, "from New Zealand, North America, Chili,—English, Irish, German specimens,—from Spain, British Guiana, South America, the river Amazon, and Australia. That common type, therefore, may truly be said to be found all over the world." †

There is an attempt to explain all this by the suggestion that the similar wants of mankind lead to similar results. But while it is true that all mankind want, in the primitive state, knives, spear-heads, scrapers, axes, etc., it is not true that they want knives, spear-heads, scrapers, axes, etc., of precisely the same pattern. It is no more true than that such similar needs would lead to the discovery of the boom-

* Nilsson on the Stone Age, p. 103.

† Year-book of Facts, 1871, p. 174.

erang or to the practice of scalping or the adoption of the symbol of the Red Hand.

We shall see hereafter that the belief has been almost universal that the stone celts are *thunderbolts*. This wide-spread sentiment, prevailing in Cornwall, Ireland, Scotland, Norway, Denmark, Brittany, Germany, Portugal, Italy, China, Japan, Burmah, Assam, Western Africa, implies a necessary connection between these various races, separated by continents and seas.

Such, hurriedly thrown together, are some of the evidences of kinship among the races of mankind. We have mentioned only a few; they might be greatly multiplied. One such testimony suggests community of origin; many such, brought together, amount to a demonstration.

The origination of nearly all of the domesticated animals in Central Asia or Northern Africa.

Another interesting fact bearing on the origin of man is, that, as we are told by M. Geoffroy St. Hilaire, there are some forty species of domesticated animals; that of these, thirty-five, such as the horse, goat, sheep, ox, dog, pig, etc., may be called cosmopolitan; and that out of this number of thirty-five possessed by Europe, thirty-one appear to have originated in Central Asia or in Northern Africa. Nearly all of the forty are from a warm climate, which indicates that civilization pertained to primeval Asiatic man, and that he brought these animals to Europe with him. It may also be mentioned here, though not specially connected with the subject under discussion, that it was stated by Mr. Vicien, at the meeting of the British Association in Birmingham in 1865, that no trace of the existence of the *cereals* can be discovered in geological formations that can be imagined more than six thousand years old. Wheat is only found where man is found. The inference has, therefore, been drawn that man was originally *instructed* in regard to its cultivation. So strong has been the conviction, says Dr. George Moore, in his work entitled "The First Man, and his Place in Creation," that the cereals are not spontaneously produced, that the mythologies of Egypt, India, and Greece ascribe their cultivation to direct Divine interference.*

Recent date of the Cereals.

We have thus proved (as we believe) that the present races of mankind do not date back farther than several thousand years ago; secondly, that they are related to each other; and, thirdly, that they "began life" in a highly civilized state. We see no traces of a Stone Age, and encounter no Troglodytes, until we recede from the original centres. It is very true that all of the nations to whose history we have referred *claim* a vast antiquity; but it is a notable fact that, so far from their "pre-historic"

* It is proper to add to this, that it is asserted that some of our cereals grow wild in Affghanistan and India. We are not prepared to say whether this is correct or not.

age being represented as one of gross savagery and barbarism, as soon as they leave the firm ground of their monumental records they take us not to a "stone," but to a "golden" age. The lists of Manetho prefix to the human period, commencing with Menes, a "pre-historic" period of twenty-five thousand years, during which Egypt enjoyed the beneficent rule of gods, demi-gods, and heroes. The series of the seven divine rulers "looks like an allegory of the creative energy and conflicts of nature, by which the land was prepared for human habitation." The first is the creative PHTHA, the genius of *Fire*. The next is RA, the *Sun*. The third is [in Greek] AGATHODÆMON, representing the energy of *Water*. Then we have SEB or CRONOS, representing *Time*, etc. The demi-gods were eight: Mars, Anubis, Hercules, Ammon, Tithoës, etc. So Berosus gives us a mythical period of thirty-four thousand years, filled up by eighty-six demi-gods. But the history of Babylon, as developed from the *monuments*, does not go back farther than from 2400 to 2600 B.C. If there was any "pre-historic" æon, there is no trace of it. Now (as we said of the Romans), we can trace the Gauls down to Louis XIV. and Napoleon Bonaparte through the intermediate stages from the time when they were barbarians; we can look behind the era of Peter the Great in Russia; we can go behind the age of Pericles in Greece; but suppose Sir John Lubbock should tell us that for five hundred thousand years before the year in which the Parthenon was finished (no monuments or records existing before) the Athenians had been living in caves, and acquainted with no implements but those made out of flint, —should we not tell him he was out of his head? It might be true that they had been in existence as a race five hundred thousand years, but it could not be true that they should have passed in one day from the bone-caves to the Acropolis and the Stoa Pœcile. There are no monuments behind the Pyramids of any sort. There is no history, and no traces of any kind leading up to that splendid civilization. If the cave-men gradually worked their way up to the Pharaohs and a thoroughly organized state, there must necessarily have been some monuments by the way-side. The obliteration could not have been *complete*. There must have been *some* shading off—some straggling cairn or cromlech or "round tower"—some tradition—some rude Pelasgic wall—some archæolithic grotto or gravel-bed—to show that men lived before Menes and Cheops. The very religion of Egypt is the purer the farther we go back—fresh in the beginning from the patriarchs themselves.

CHAPTER III.

THE ANTIQUITY OF MAN.

The Opinion with regard to the Antiquity of Man now widely disseminated.—The Extreme Views now held among Men of Science.—Sir Charles Lyell finally converted.—The Sources from which the Evidence on the Subject is derived.—The River-Gravels.—The Views of Sir John Lubbock.—M. Boucher de Perthes on the Peat of the Somme Valley.—The Bone-Caves.—The Megalithic Monuments of Western Europe.—The Lake-Dwellings of Switzerland.—The Danish Kjökken-möddings.—The Mounds and Ruined Cities of America.—Rev. Dunbar Heath on the Shell-Mounds.—Prof. Agassiz on the Lake-Dwellings.—The Peat Bogs of Denmark and Ireland.—Dr. Dowler's Red Indian.—Mr. Horner and the Mud of the Nile.—Prof. Agassiz on the Coral Reefs of Florida.

The Antiquity of Man indorsed by scientific men.

THE wave has not fairly reached the masses yet, but it will soon be very generally believed that SCIENCE has proved the immense antiquity of man. Nearly all of the scientific men of Europe and of this country have embraced this opinion, while perhaps a decided majority have reached the conclusion of Mr. Darwin and Mr. Huxley that we are descended from apes. These convictions are observable in the works of the leading scientific minds of England, France, Belgium, Denmark, Sweden, Germany, Switzerland, and Italy. We need only mention (some of them very recently dead) Sir C. Lyell, Sir J. Lubbock, Mr. Darwin, Mr. Huxley, Dr. Falconer, Mr. Prestwich, Mr. Geikie, Mr. John Evans, Mr. Owen, Mr. Busk, Mr. Flower, M. Lartet, M. de Mortillet, M. Cartailhac, M. de Quatrefages, M. Broca, M. Pruner-Bey, M. Bourgeois, M. Boucher de Perthes, M. Dupont, M. Morlot, Nilsson, Worsaae, Steenstrup, Desor, Vogt, Gastaldi, Ponzi, Ceselli, Wilson, Agassiz,* Cope, Foster, Whitney, etc.

Most of these learned gentlemen believe in "natural selection" or "evolution," and all of them laugh to scorn the idea that Man is not more than seven or eight thousand years old. Most of them cautiously avoid specific figures, but all of them use terms which imply a great antiquity for the human race. Chevalier Bunsen ventured from his Egyptological studies to fix the date of the human period at 20,000 B.C. Mr. Jukes, one of the first English geologists, fixes it at one hundred thousand years ago. Professor Fuhlrott of Germany, who writes a work on the famous Neanderthal skull, suggests that that piece of palæontology

* Agassiz, it is well known, ridicules Darwinism.

must be some two hundred thousand or three hundred thousand years old. Dr. Hunt, formerly president of the British Anthropological Society, holds the opinion that the proper date is nine million years ago. Prof. Huxley believes that man "existed when a tropical fauna and flora flourished in our northern clime," which was in the carboniferous era,—and that is supposed to have been hundreds of millions of years ago. Sir Charles Lyell, who seems to be the Nestor of British Geology, held out for a long time against the existence of pre-Adamic man, but, after visiting the gravel-pits at St. Acheul, in the Somme Valley, in 1855, according to M. Figuier, "was able to say, *Veni, vidi, victus fui;* and at the meeting of the British Association of that year at Aberdeen, declared himself to be in favor of the existence of quaternary man." Indeed, he believes now that the remains of man will be found in the Pliocene strata; while Sir John Lubbock concurs with M. Bourgeois and M. Delaunay, and hopes to discover traces of our race in the deposits of the Miocene Age.

These views are not confined to these great teachers and expounders of science, but are current in the newspaper and magazine literature of the day,—and, in fact, so dogmatic are the assertions in favor of them, and so great is the authority of the names by which they are guaranteed, that opposition and dissent have been almost entirely *silenced,* and men like the Duke of Argyll and Prof. Tayler Lewis attempt to protect the Mosaic record by suggestions about gaps in the tables of genealogy, or the possible existence of "other" anthropoidal forms. Mr. J. P. Lesley, Secretary of the American Philosophical Society, in some lectures delivered in Boston,* regards the whole question as so completely closed by the "recent discoveries," that he considers it merely necessary to *kick* the old Theology. "All these questions have been settled for us," he says sneeringly, "as you are probably but too well aware, many centuries ago, by that science falsely so called, Theology. . . . Are we not *assured* that the world is only six thousand years old? . . . Does it not stand so within the books of Moses? Do we not also *know* that man was created upright before he fell? All this is too distinctly written by holy men of old, who wrote as they were moved by the Holy Ghost, to be called in question for a moment." After reciting the statements of the first chapter of Genesis, he proceeds:

"It is surprising how indifferent men of science seem to be to these great statements. Thousands of preachers proclaim them from the pulpit every Sunday in the year, and millions of communicants respond Amen. And yet our men of science continue skeptical,† and call them,

* Man's Origin and Destiny, p. 43.

† So Mr. Herbert Spencer declares: "The current cosmogony is not only without a single fact to stand on, but is at variance with our knowledge of nature." Essays, p. 55.

as the Apostles did, old wives' fables. They believe them indeed to be old Jew-legends so palpably heathenish and contrary to all we know, that it is not worth while to try to show their absurdity."

Mr. Lesley then gives us his scheme of the Antiquity of Man—or rather that of M. Renevier of Lausanne. The different human epochs are classified as follows:

1. Pre-glacial Epoch, in which man was cotemporary with the *Elephas antiquus*, *Rhinoceros hemitœchus*, *Ursus spelœus*.

2. Glacial Epoch, when he lived with the *Elephas primigenius* and the *Rhinoceros tichorinus*.

3. Post-glacial Epoch, when he lived with the *Elephas primigenius* and the Reindeer.

4. Present Epoch, when man lived with the *Cervus elephas* and the urus, and began to construct plank villages, on piles, in lakes.*

Finally, we learn in a note to this volume that "while putting these pages to press the news from Paris was received that at the meeting of the International Anthropological Society in that city, in August of this year (1869), 'two memoirs due to the Abbé Bourgeois and the Abbé Delaunay have established beyond doubt that man was already in existence at the epoch of the Lower Pliocene.' "

In an address made, we believe, in 1872, Mr. James Geikie, the eminent geologist, takes the ground also that man is *pre-glacial*, and inter-glacial. Mr. Croll, he says, estimates the beginning of the glacial period at two hundred and forty thousand years ago, and the period itself as having a duration of one thousand six hundred centuries.†

Mr. Evan Hopkins, F.G.S., quoted in Figuier's "The World before the Deluge," states that some geologists estimate the glacial period to have been one billion two hundred and eighty million years ago.‡ If this be the fact, and if Mr. Geikie is correct in judging man to be *pre*-glacial, his antiquity is great indeed!

The human implements found in the River-Gravel.

Anthropologists derive the evidence for the antiquity of man from various sources. One of the principal of these is the remains of human workmanship found in the river-gravels of the valleys of the Somme, the Seine, the Oise, the Thames, the Wey, the Darent, the Ouse, etc. In the valley of the Somme, rude flint hatchets have been found in association with the bones of the mammoth, the rhinoceros, the hippopotamus, the cave-bear, cave-lion, reindeer, etc., and this in the river-gravel a hundred feet above the

* Man's Origin and Destiny, p. 66.

† See Harper's Magazine for June, 1873, p. 152. Also Mr. Geikie's book, "The Great Ice Age," recently published, p. 135, Amer. edit.

‡ See p. 22, Amer. edit.

present bed of the river, and in gravel at lower levels frequently under peat from twenty-five to thirty feet thick. Sir Charles Lyell estimates that the deposition or formation of this peat occupied "thousands of years," and yet, he remarks, this deposit contains only the remains of existing animals and implements of polished flint, bronze, or iron, and is separated from the gravel "by an interval far greater than that which divides the earliest strata of the peat from the latest." He adds, "The contrast of the fauna of the ancient alluvium, whether at high or low levels, with the fauna of the oldest peat is almost as great as its contrast with the existing fauna, the memorials of man being common to the whole series: hence we may infer that the interval of time which separated the era of the large extinct mammalia from that of the earliest peat was of far longer duration than that of the entire growth of the peat. Yet we by no means need the evidence of the ancient fossil fauna to establish the antiquity of man in this part of France. The mere volume of the drift at various heights would alone suffice to demonstrate a vast lapse of time during which such heaps of shingle, derived both from the eocene and the cretaceous rocks, were thrown down in a succession of river-channels." * To all this he adds the enormous ages required to *excavate the valley*.

Sir C. Lyell on the antiquity of these remains.

On the same subject we have the following from Sir John Lubbock: "When finally the excavation of the valley [of the Somme] was completed, the climate had gradually become more like our own, and either from this change, or rather perhaps yielding to the irresistible power of man, the great Pachydermata became extinct. Under the altered conditions of level, the river, unable to carry out to sea the finer particles brought down from the higher levels, deposited them in the valley, and thus raised somewhat its general level, checking the velocity of the stream, and producing extensive marshes, in which a thick deposit of peat was gradually formed. We have, unfortunately, no trustworthy means of estimating the rate of formation of this substance, which indeed varies considerably, according to the conditions of the case; but on any supposition the production of a mass in some places more than thirty feet in thickness must have required a very considerable period. Yet it is in these beds that we find the remains of the Neolithic or later Stone period. From the tombs at St. Acheul, from the Roman remains found in the superficial layers of the peat, at about the present level of the river, we know that fifteen hundred years have produced scarcely any change in the configuration of the valley. In the peat, and at a depth of about fifteen feet in the alluvium at Abbeville, are the remains of the Neolithic period, which we have ample reason

Sir J. Lubbock on the same subject.

* Antiquity of Man, Amer. edit., p. 144.

for believing, from the researches in Denmark, Switzerland, and other countries, to be of no slight antiquity. Yet all these are subsequent to the excavation of the valley. What date, then, are we to ascribe to the men who lived when the Somme was but beginning its great task? No one can properly appreciate the lapse of time indicated, who has not stood on the heights of Liercourt, Picquigny, or on one of the other points overlooking the valley; nor, I am sure, could any geologist return from such a visit without an overpowering sense of the changes which must have elapsed since the first appearance of man in Western Europe." *

M. Boucher de Perthes, who first called attention to these phenomena in the valley of the Somme in his now famous "Antiquités Celtiques et Anté-diluviennes," estimates that the peat grows at about the rate of three centimetres, or one and one-fifth inches, per century. Taking a depth of thirty feet, this would require thirty thousand years for the deposit of the peat alone.

The remains of man—his bones as well as flint and bone implements—have also been found in many parts of Europe in association with the remains of the mammoth, rhinoceros, cave-bear, etc., in the numerous bone-caverns which have been explored during the past thirty-five or forty years. They have often been found under floors of stalagmite of considerable thickness, which, it is alleged, required ages to be deposited.

But the mere fact of the constantly recurring juxtaposition far down below the surface of these caves of the remains of men and the great extinct mammals, is sufficient evidence of a remote antiquity, according to all of our preconceived notions with regard to the existence of these animals.

Megalithic Monuments.

Other evidences of the antiquity of man are found in the Megalithic Monuments of Western Europe,—the stone circles, the dolmens, the cromlechs, the menhirs, the tumuli, the barrows, which are so abundant in England, France, Denmark, Spain, etc. These are supposed to be older than the Pyramids, and to have been erected by races which formerly lived in a state of considerable civilization in these countries. Sir John Lubbock refers the great circle at Abury, in Wiltshire, to the Stone Age.

The reader is, moreover, doubtless familiar with the Lake Villages, the remains of which, since 1854, have been found so numerously in Switzerland and elsewhere; and with the Danish Kjökken-möddings or shell-mounds. Volumes have also been written on these, to illustrate the remote appearance of man in Western and Central Europe.

Danish Shell-mounds.

The Rev. Dunbar Heath is of the opinion that the shell-mounds were occupied before man had acquired the faculty of speech. In a paper *On the Acquirement of Language by Mutes*,

* Prehistoric Times, Amer. edit., pp. 383–4.

he says, "I am about to bring before the reader a conception of certain *kitchen-middens* occupied by what I call mutes, and subjected to the rationalizing influences of a further advanced set of men whom I call speakers. . . . This view is that during and after the tertiary geological epoch, the highest mammals then on earth were becoming more erect in their way of walking, less hairy in their bodies, and more like in general to what the lowest men are now. . . . If we can by this time conceive to ourselves the clever chief of two or three hundred of such merely emotional inhabitants of a kitchen-midden, struggling into the semi-emotional, *semi-rational* state of expressing," etc.*

With regard to the antiquity of the Lake Dwellings we may quote the opinion of Prof. Agassiz. At a meeting of the Boston Society of Natural History, a few years since, he remarked that "The historians struck the first blow at the assumption [that we had a trustworthy chronology] by their Egyptological researches. Their lead was followed in other departments of science,—and now we are forced to construct our chronology on a new and independent basis. Twelve years ago, Ferdinand Keller, of Zurich, by an examination of the Swiss Lake deposits, brought to light proofs of the existence of races of men with new characters of civilization. These discoveries astonished the world, and have since given rise to a new science, new societies, and new museums. *Humanity is now connected with geological phenomena.*"

Agassiz on the antiquity of the Lake Dwellings.

The mound-builders and ruins of Central America.

The mounds and ancient earthworks of North America, as well as the ruined cities of Central America, have also been cited in this connection; while archæologists were never so busy with the monumental history of Egypt, Assyria, Babylonia, India, and Arabia.

Egypt, Assyria, etc.

Another prolific source of evidence has been the Danish and Irish peat-bogs, in which a great many remains of the Bronze and the Stone Age have been discovered.

The Danish and Irish peat.

Sir Charles Lyell and Sir John Lubbock have also referred to the skeleton of the Red Indian found some fifteen feet below the surface while digging the foundation for the gas-works in New Orleans some years ago. Dr. Dowler, who investigated the matter on the spot, calculated from the rate of formation of the delta of the Mississippi that this fossil was about fifty-seven thousand years old.

Dr. Dowler's Red Indian.

Both of the distinguished British savans referred to also give impor-

* Read before The Anthropological Society in 1867. See Anthropological Review for April, 1867.

tance to the investigations of Mr. Horner in the mud of the Nile, which seemed to carry back the civilization of Egypt at least thirteen thousand years.

The mud of the Nile.

Sir Charles Lyell refers also to the fossil human remains found by Count Pourtalis, and cited by Prof. Agassiz, in the coral reefs of Florida, and estimated by Agassiz, in Nott and Gliddon's "Types of Mankind," to be ten thousand years old "by a moderate computation."

Coral Reefs of Florida.

CHAPTER IV.

THE ANTIQUITY OF MAN—CONTINUED.

Mr. Crawfurd's Opinion that Primeval Man was without Speech.—Rev. Dunbar Heath of the Same Opinion.—Sir C. Lyell's Expectation of finding Human Remains in the Pliocene Strata.—Views of Carl Vogt.

Primeval man represented as a savage.

SCIENTIFIC men, as we have mentioned, have not contented themselves with proving the antiquity of man; but they represent, further, that primeval man was a most debased savage, and that thousands and thousands of years passed before he elevated himself to the civilization of the Neolithic Age, or the era of Polished Stone Implements. An immense period—mayhap several hundred thousand years—is supposed to have elapsed during the First Stone Age,—the age of the rude and questionable-looking flints of the "river-drift" and the older bone-caverns. Mr. Crawfurd, formerly President of the (British) Ethnological Society, like the Rev. Dunbar Heath, is of opinion that "man when he appeared on earth was destitute of language," and that "each tribe framed a separate language of its own," and "in every case had to achieve the arduous and tedious task of *constructing speech.*" * He believes that man, although the latest creation of the class of beings to which he belongs, is yet "of vast antiquity, . . . although that portion of his history which has transpired since he acquired the art of making a durable and authentic record of his own existence *forms but a very small fraction of it.*" When we find him in the Drift, "he was considerably advanced." †

Primeval man a mute.

These views have been presented in greater detail by our friend Mr. Heath, M.A., F.R.S.L., F.A.S.L., who was formerly a clergyman of the Church of England. In the paper, already referred to, read by him a few years since before the Anthropological Society, he expressed the opinion that the original inhabitants of Europe were *mutes,* and that such was the condition of man in the days of the "woolly elephants,

* Address at Manchester meeting of Brit. Assoc. for 1861.

† At the meeting of the Brit. Assoc. in 1867. See An. Sci. Discov. for 1868, p. 308.

rhinoceroses, and kitchen-middens." In the *Anthropological Review*, No. XIII. p. 36, Mr. Heath refers to the fact that at one time apes abounded in Europe, and suggests that these apes were the progenitors of European men, who were at first dumb. He says,—

"I confine myself to the accepting and explaining known and knowable phenomena. It is *known* that anthropoids existed throughout Europe. It is *knowable* that they became mute men. It is knowable that these mutes *gasped after articulation*, and in a few spots attained to it. Those who did so at one particular spot I call *Aryans*, whether that one spot was in Asia or in the submerged continent of Atlantis!"

Human remains will probably be found in the Tertiary strata.

Sir Charles Lyell also hopes to find the missing links between Man and the Apes in the pliocene and post-pliocene strata of the tropical regions of Africa, and the islands of Borneo and Sumatra, which he says have not yet been explored. He admits that so far the intermediate links have not been met with, but, as Man is an Old-World type, he is not disappointed that Dr. Lund found only a few fossil monkeys of the American type in the ossiferous caverns of Brazil.*

The learned and distinguished professor Carl Vogt entertains a similar expectation of bridging over by future discoveries the great chasm between man and the pithecoid types. He remarks in his *Lectures on Man*, "Twenty years ago, fossil monkeys were unknown; now we have nearly a dozen. Who can tell but that in fifty years we may have fifty? A year ago, no intermediate form between *Semnopithecus* and *Macacus* was known; now we possess a whole skeleton. Who can assert that in ten, twenty, or fifty years we may not possess *intermediate forms between man and ape?* . . . in short, we cannot see why American races of men cannot be derived from American apes, Negroes from African apes, or Nigritos, perhaps, from Asiatic apes."

* See Antiquity of Man, Amer. edit. p. 498.

CHAPTER V.

THE FICKLENESS OF SCIENCE.

The Object of this Work.—The Vacillations of Science.—Its Vacillation on the Question of the Unity of the Human Race.—On the Theory of Lamarck.—The Fluctuating Opinions of Sir C. Lyell.—The New Theory of Light.—The Nebular Hypothesis.—On Geological Breaks.—Sir C. Lyell and M. d'Orbigny.—On the Question of the Central Heat of the Earth.—On Spontaneous Generation.—Deep-Sea Dredgings.

The object proposed in this volume.

WE have attempted briefly in the foregoing chapters to set forth the prevailing doctrines among men of science with regard to the antiquity and origin of Man. It is not our purpose in the present volume to discuss Mr. Darwin's theory, or any similar theory of evolution: the subject which we have in hand is the antiquity of the present human race, and we propose to consider in detail the evidence which has been brought forward in favor of man's remote existence on the earth, and to *prove* that he is of *recent origin.* We are aware of the magnitude of the undertaking, and of the weight of authority that is against us; but in these days a great name has not the potent influence which it possessed in the age of a less enlightened public, and even a concurrence of opinion among scientific men, while it should undoubtedly raise a very strong presumption, cannot be regarded as conclusively *settling* any scientific question, in view of the notorious vacillation of science on a great number of leading subjects during the whole of this century. Let us glance at some of these frequent "changes of base" on the part of science.

The vacillation of science.

Former theory of the Azoic rocks.

A very few years ago, geologists divided the strata of the earth into the *Azoic*, the *Palæozoic*, the *Mesozoic*, and the *Cainozoic* or more recent. The Azoic rocks commenced with the origin of the earth's crust, and included "the oldest rocks of the globe." They were supposed to be the rocks which underlie the Silurian and the subsequent geological beds. But it appears now that the *Eozoon Canadense* has been found in the Laurentian rocks, the deepest and oldest which constitute the geological strata.

The unity of the human race.

If we interrogate science, we hardly know what opinion to form at present with regard to the Unity of the Human Race. A few years ago the preponderating opinion appeared to be in favor of multiple centres of creation and a number of species. The elaborate and learned work of Messrs. Nott and Gliddon, bearing the imprimatur of Professor Agassiz, was written to demonstrate this doctrine. Now the preponderating opinion is in favor of a single origin, although scientific men still differ very much on the subject. Mr. Crawfurd regards the idea of the earth's having been peopled from a single tribe or family as "a wild and incoherent dream." Sir John Lubbock and Sir Charles Lyell seem to countenance the unity of the race. Mr. Carter Blake and Prof. Lesley think differently, the latter affirming that the races of mankind are "as distinct as the American bison and the European cow." M. Quatrefages, Dr. Carpenter, Prof. Owen, Mr. Winwood Reade, M. Figuier, argue for a common origin. Mr. Stuart Poole and Mr. McCausland believe that the Adamic race is different from the Negro race and the Mongolian race. While Prof. Wagner believes in "one original existing," but only an "ideal" type, to which the Indo-European type approaches nearest.

The Lamarckian theory. Sir C. Lyell.

So of the Darwinian or Lamarckian theory. Sir Charles Lyell, some years ago, in his *Principles of Geology*, wrote a refutation of it. In his recent edition of that work he writes in favor of it. He has changed his opinion, and, as he has frequently done before, he avows it. But this only shows that those who read the earlier edition, and died before the appearance of the recent editions, were led grievously astray by a conscientious physicist. Sir Charles was formerly a devout follower of Hutton,—an ardent Plutonian,—and believed in the igneous origin of granite: his present opinion is that it owes its formation to the action of water. Sir Charles has also greatly modified his views with reference to the phenomena and date of the glacial period, and within a few years he has been compelled to recast his nomenclature of the pliocene and post-pliocene ages. Indeed, the scientific life of this eminent man is a history of retracted geological opinions, and serves to admonish us that the gravest and most cautious interpreters of nature are by no means exempt from false constructions of that difficult text.

Lyell formerly a follower of Hutton.

Change of views with regard to the Glacial Period.

Motion of the Solar System.

New theory of Light.

The Nebular Hypothesis.

Sir William Herschel used to teach us that the whole Solar System was moving steadily towards a certain point in space. This opinion is pronounced now to be in doubt and abeyance. So in reference to the theory of *Light*. Twenty years ago the emission theory of Newton was the prevailing theory. Now the undulatory theory of Huygens is revived, and generally accepted. So of the Nebular Hypothesis. It was thought to be exploded by Lord Rosse's great telescope, which resolved certain supposed nebulæ into stars. But the spectroscope has since shown that other supposed nebulous matter is really of that character.

Sir William Thomson affirms that the gradual cooling of the earth's crust from a state of fusion must have required about ninety-eight millions of years; while Mr. Darwin represents that it must have taken three hundred and six millions six hundred and sixty-two thousand four hundred years.

Cooling of the earth's crust.

Sir Charles Lyell insists that the fossils of the tertiary beds are in many cases identical with existing flora and fauna; that, in other words, there has been no *break* in animal and vegetable life in passing from the pliocene to the post-pliocene and quaternary strata. Hugh Miller was driven to the same conclusion, and urged that the discovery of this fact necessitated an abandonment of Dr. Chalmers's attempted reconciliation of the Mosaic record with the facts of geology. But the late eminent geologist M. Alcide d'Orbigny, who is of great authority on this subject, affirms and proceeds by powerful arguments to prove that there is not one species in common between the tertiary and present plants and animals; and he asserts, moreover, that beginning with the Silurian beds there have been, down to the present time, *twenty-seven* distinct and original creations of plants and animals, following each time some geological disturbance *which had totally destroyed living nature;* which opinion is concurred in by Prof. C. H. Hitchcock.

Geological breaks.

Geologists formerly taught that the earth was originally in a condition of igneous fluidity,—the theory of *a central heat.* But Sir Charles Lyell tells us now that the increase of heat as we descend into the earth may be explained "without the necessity of our appealing to an original central heat, or the igneous fluidity of the earth's nucleus." And yet Prof. Dana assures us (Text-book of Geology, p. 320) that "the facts of geology leave little room for doubt that the earth was once in fusion, and has been through all time a *cooling* globe;" while Prof. C. H. Hitchcock (Elementary Geology, p. 104) affirms that "previous to the formation of the lowest solid rocks the whole globe was in a state of igneous fusion."

Igneous fluidity.

So on the subject of *Spontaneous Generation.* Dr. Bastian tells us that "he has found organisms in fluids, either acid or alkaline, which, whilst inclosed within hermetically-sealed and airless flasks, had been submitted to a temperature varying from 146° C. and 153° C. for four hours." And on this Prof. Huxley remarks, "I believe that the organisms which he has got out of his tubes are exactly those which he has put into them."

Spontaneous generation.

It is evident, therefore, that Science is considerably unsettled and often in error; that the opinions of to-day are in a great many cases not the opinions of to-morrow; and that pre-eminent for instability among all the sciences is *Geology,* the latest revelation of which is the declaration of Prof. Wyville Thomson, that "we are still living in the cretaceous age" !

The deep-sea explorations of this learned investigator and of Dr. Carpenter have made the astounding revelation that if the sea-bottom at certain points of observation in the North Atlantic should become dry land, "we should find two very different-looking deposits, containing two series of remains, really cotemporaneous, but indicating such difference of conditions that our present geological theories would lead us to class them as belonging to *successive* periods, sufficiently separated to allow of climatic changes." This is due to the fact that at such points (north of Scotland and the Faroe Islands), at the depth of six hundred fathoms, Dr. Carpenter found *contiguous currents* with varying temperatures, the one ranging from 32° to 33° F., and the other being not less than 47° F. These neighboring currents presented naturally a difference of fauna, the living things in the cold area being of a different type from, and less abundant than, those of the warm area.

Deep-sea explorations.

How far this discovery will unsettle a fundamental principle of Modern Geology does not yet appear: it seems to us that it ought at least to beget a spirit of extreme caution and diffidence among geologists; for it is really like the explosion of a bomb in the laboratory of a chemist.

It had been the current opinion among geologists that the temperature of the deepest portion of the sea was everywhere about 39° F. This opinion also was overturned. Nor is this all: if the theory of oceanic currents which Dr. Carpenter has engrafted on his discoveries should prove to be true, "it will considerably modify the received doctrine of the dependence of our own climate, and of the amelioration of the temperature of the polar basin, on an extension of the Gulf Stream; it will also considerably modify the glacial doctrine of geologists, limiting its range in one direction, whilst vastly extending it in others."

Nor is this all: it has been heretofore taught that three hundred fathoms was the limit of marine life. Naturalists taught that in consequence of the enormous pressure of the water, and the diminution of light, animals and plants could not exist in "the abysmal zone." It is now demonstrated that animals exist in the ocean not only at the depth of three hundred fathoms, but at the depth of *three miles,* under a pressure of *three tons* to the square inch.

It *may,* therefore, turn out that man is *not* descended from an ape, and that the received Mosaic chronology is nearer the mark than that of Dr. Dowler or Sir Charles Lyell; and who can affirm that in the twelfth edition of the "Principles" Sir Charles may not introduce an entire recantation of his present impressions? and that his readers of to-day may not be as poorly instructed as those who were told by him only several years since that the Glacial Age was eight hundred thousand years ago,—which he now fixes at two hundred thousand?

CHAPTER VI.

THE CONFLICTS OF CHRISTIANITY.

Christianity.—The Attacks on it.—The First Three Centuries.—Modern Philosophy and Science.—The Prevailing Views not New.—The "Vestiges of Creation."—Lamarck and St. Hilaire.—Hartley.—Bonnet.—Atomic Theory of Democritus.—The Protoplasm of Anaxagoras.—Buddhism.—The Vedas.—The Unwarranted Boldness of Science.—Science and Literature necessarily Infidel.—The Difficulties presented by the Bible.—The Temper of Modern Science; its Exclusion of the Supernatural; its Disposition to Speculate and Theorize.—The Subject of the Conflicts of Christianity resumed.—Its Triumphs in the Past a Guarantee of its Triumph in the Future.—The Last Struggle with Paganism.—Doubt in the Middle Ages.—The Literary *Renaissance* of the Fifteenth Century.—The Courts of Lorenzo de Medici and Leo X.—The University of Padua.—The Seventeenth Century.—Lord Herbert, Hobbes, Spinoza, Bayle, Condillac.—Beginning of the Eighteenth Century.—Collins, Woolston, Tyndal, Morgan, Chubb, Bolingbroke.—The Latter Part of the Eighteenth Century.—Hume, Voltaire, Diderot, Helvetius, etc.—Rousseau.—Succeeded by Gibbon and Paine.—The French Revolution.—Sensational Philosophy of Cabanis.—Destutt de Tracy.—Volney.—Infidelity in Germany.—Semler, Paulus, Eichhorn.—The Philosophy of Kant.—The Nineteenth Century.—Byron and Shelley in England.—Fichte, Schelling, and Hegel in Germany.—Strauss's Leben Jesu, and the Mythical Theory.—The German Schools of Biblical Criticism.—Recent Period.—Carlyle, Theodore Parker, Emerson, James Martineau, Morell, Cousin, Feuerbach, the Bauers.—The Failure of all their Attacks.—The Present Attack by Science.

Assaults on Christianity.

CHRISTIANITY is naturally sensitive,—it has to receive the fire of every new discovery, every new system, every new opinion in philosophy and science. It has to give battle to all comers. Any knight who may please to wind his horn at her castle gates can summon her out to maintain her cause; and it is necessary for her to win in every contest. It has been thus for eighteen hundred years. It first had to encounter whatever of learning there was in the ancient Roman world. It had to deal with the wonderful traditions and memories of Egypt,—with a civilization whose art, two thousand years before, was as grand as that of Phidias or Michael Angelo, and whose priests for twenty-odd centuries had worshiped the mysterious "I AM THAT THAT I AM." It had to deal with those whose fathers, at least, had been taught the sublime precepts of Zoroaster, and whose national religion, as ancient as that of Egypt, in its purer form, went back almost to the gates of Paradise. It had to deal with the acute and polished Greek,—with the pure and almost inspired thought of Socrates and Plato and Aristotle. It had to meet the hard, practical genius of the Latin race, illuminated by the best knowledge and culture which the age of Augustus afforded. It had to encounter the flippant skepticism and ribald mockery of Lucian; the philosophy and logic of Celsus; the learning and critical acumen of Porphyry. It was branded by Tacitus and the younger Pliny as a "*prava et immodica superstitio.*" Marcus Aurelius, Mr. Lecky's ideal of what can be accomplished by a pure philosophy, instituted against it fierce and repeated persecutions; among whose victims were the venerable Polycarp, Pothinus, Bishop of Lyons, and the heroic virgin, Blandina. Under Diocletian, Eusebius relates, "the swords became at last dull and shattered; the executioners became weary, and had to relieve each other; even the wild beasts at last refused to attack the Christians, as if they had assumed the part of men in place of the heathen Romans." Eighty years later, Christianity was the State religion of the Roman Empire. Paganism, in all its gates, fell before it; and no one—as we have suggested—need deride the cultivated thought of the ancient world. If we remember that it produced the Pyramids and the palaces and temples of Thebes,—the "Ritual of the Dead,"—the "Vendidad,"—the Vedas,—the Parthenon,—the Apollo Belvedere,—the astronomy and the arts of Egypt and Babylon,—the works of Herodotus, Thucydides, Plato, Aristotle, Tacitus, Virgil, Seneca, Pliny, Strabo, Josephus, Epictetus,—we realize at once that we do not stand in modern times on any higher plane, and that our Huxleys and Tyndalls and Lubbocks and Lyells, our Grotes, our Mills, our Spencers, our Tennysons, our Bastians, our Comtes, our Emersons, our Figuiers, our Vogts, our Büchners, are not a whit abler or more cultivated men, or more advanced thinkers. The Greeks had propounded the doctrine of evolution six hundred years before the Christian era; and the Brahmins and the Buddhists had anticipated modern Pantheism and the whole German Metaphysics two thousand three hundred years ago. They were behind us in scientific *facts*, but not in generalizations; in art they were immeasurably ahead of us; in letters and philosophy they were certainly our equals; in religion we cannot see that the advantage lies on the side of our French and German and British *savans.* If we take the *Westminster Review* as a fair exponent of the materialistic school of England, these gentlemen do not compare, in the elevation and reverence of their sentiments, with Plato or Cicero.

Lucian. Celsus. Porphyry. Tacitus.

Persecutions.

Our modern skeptics not abler men than the ancient assailants.

Modern Philosophy assumes all the airs of novelty, and—a sure symptom of shallowness—seems honestly unconscious of the past. We are assaulted as if something new had been developed. The discovery of new Illuminators, and Washing-machines, and bone and flint implements—and Prof. Huxley and Mr. Herbert Spencer—have occasioned the belief that this is a very remarkable age; and the literature of the day—from the New York *Herald* to the Quarterlies—is violently excited.

The present positions of science are not new. Even we can remember the sensation made some twenty-odd years ago by the "Vestiges of Creation." At the beginning of the century MM. Lamarck and Geoffroy St. Hilaire set forth the doctrine that there had been an uninterrupted succession in the animal kingdom, effected by means of generation, from the earliest ages of the world up to the present day, and that the ancient animals whose remains have been preserved in the strata, however different, may nevertheless have been the ancestors of those now in being.

The present objections not new.

And before that day the "vibrations" of Dr. Hartley and the "fibres" of Bonnet sound very much like a page from our modern scientists. We are taught nowadays, as if it were taught for the first time, that "thought stands in the same relation to the brain as bile to the liver," and that "all vital action is the result of the molecular forces of the protoplasm which displays it;" but Monsieur Cabanis wrote a century ago (during the French Revolution), "Les nerfs, voilà tout l'homme," and more tersely than Vogt, "The brain secretes thought as the liver the bile." And as for Prof. Huxley's protoplasm, and the whole theory of Evolution, Force, Vital Atoms, etc., precisely the same theory was advocated nearly six hundred years before our era by Anaximander, who first gave to the original material substance of things the name of *principle* (ἀρχή), and who evolved the animal creation by the action of "the sunlight on the miry clay." We have very nearly the identical article of protoplasm itself in this philosopher. The sun's heat, he said, acting on the primal miry earth, produced "filmy bladders or bubbles, and these, becoming surrounded with a prickly rind, at length burst open, and, as from an egg, animals came forth. At first they were ill formed and imperfect, but subsequently they elaborated and developed." MAN he represented as "developed" from a *fish*. This reads precisely like "Half-Hours with the Modern Scientists." Where is the difference? And yet they claim to possess all the Profundity of this age, and to have made a great advance on past ages.

Hartley.
Bonnet.

Cabanis.

Anaximander.

But our "modern scientists" were anticipated not only by the Ionic philosophers. About the time of Anaximander, Buddhism propounded in India that matter was "eternal" and possessed "the property of *inherent organization*." Nor is it in the doctrine of Evolution alone that our "modern scientists" have been anticipated by the Hindoos. Mr. Mill's philosophy of Nescience or Materialistic

Buddhism.

Idealism is completely described in the following account of Vedaism:

Vedaism.

"That matter has no essence independent of mental perception; that existence and perceptibility are convertible terms; that external appearances and sensations are illusory." This, if we understand them, is the precise position of Mill and Huxley, the latter of whom avows himself a "Humist."

If the Vedas give us an anticipation of the blank Nihilism of Mr. Huxley, the following account of Buddhism gives us a perfect picture of "Positivism" in general: "The fundamental principle of Buddhism is that there is a supreme power, but no Supreme Being. From this it might be inferred that they who adopt such a creed cannot be pantheists, but must be atheists. It is a rejection of the idea of Being, an acknowledgment of that of Force. If it admits the existence of God, it declines him as Creator. It asserts an impelling power in the universe, a self-existent and plastic principle, but not a self-existent, an eternal, a personal God. *It rejects inquiry into first causes as unphilosophical, and considers that phenomena alone can be dealt with by our finite minds.* . . . Since he has no God, the Buddhist cannot expect absorption; the pantheistic Brahman looks forward to the return of his soul to the Supreme Being as a drop of rain returns to the sea. The Buddhist has no religion, but only a ceremonial."

What is there, then, to warrant so much boldness on the part of scientific men? Science has, unquestionably, made great progress in our age; but we do not see how the recognition of law throughout the universe strengthens the atheistic or the pantheistic argument. Let us resolve the material universe into FORCE, and what does that prove? Some logician still survives to put the inquiry: And WHENCE that force? No matter

The ignorance of Science.

how far Science may go, she can never call the universe from nothing, nor account for the primordial elements with which she has erected her structure. We presume the career of discovery is just entered on; the portals of the temple of science are just fairly opened; two centuries hence we shall be as far in advance of Mr. Huxley's protoplasm and Mr. Darwin's hypotheses as we now are in advance of the meagre knowledge of the Ionic and Brahminical cosmogonists. Every twenty-five or thirty years there is a new attack on Christianity. It is the sensation of the passing age. In the beginning of this century it looked as if Kant had upset everything with his metaphysics. About

Strauss.

forty years afterwards, Strauss convulsed all Germany, and from thence the advanced thought of all Europe, with what appears now a very ridiculous theory. Within our own day, also, Mr.

Carlyle.

Carlyle attracted a great deal of attention. He sat upon a hill apart, and insinuated that he could tell a great deal if he chose. The Delphic utterances of Mr. Emerson have also in his lifetime passed away. It is natural that science and literature should be infidel; for the thought of a people is reflected in its science and literature. If Germany or England is irreligious, as both are, culture will give expression to these feelings in unfriendly theories. There is no denying the fact that the New and Old Testaments offer many difficulties; every candid man will allow this. A dozen verses in the first chapter of Genesis commit the Bible on the questions of the creation of Light and the Atmosphere, and the primeval vegetation of the earth. The next dozen commit it with regard to the appearance of the Sun and the celestial luminaries; the creation of Fishes, Reptiles, Birds; the creation of Mammals and of Man; and presently the very date of man's creation is (apparently) fixed. In a few chapters the writer takes ground on the question of a Deluge destroying the entire race, excepting eight persons; then with regard to the Divergence of Languages and the Dispersion of Mankind. In a few centuries the narrative represents the existence of civilized states and a considerable population.

Science and Literature naturally infidel.

The Bible boldly takes position on a multitude of questions;

The most astounding miracles are related; men are represented as continuing to live for centuries; and even as late as the time of Joseph (not to say Moses) we are told of men living one hundred and twenty years. In geography and history we have the most minute and detailed statements; some of them of an extraordinary character. The Israelites are brought out of Egypt with signs and wonders from heaven, and preserved in the "wilderness"—a multitude of two millions—for forty years. The Canaanitish nations are *exterminated* by the command of God; the dispensation of miracles continues down to the age of Pericles,—to be resumed and revived in the first century of the Christian era. Ten thousand marks are offered to Geology, Astronomy, Archæology, Philology, Ethnology, Historical Criticism, Physiology, Geography, Psychology, Moral Science; and it is only necessary to pierce *one* of them to discredit the whole system.

The Philosophical Thought of the world is quick to discover these marks. It seems to give many scientific men particular pleasure to strike a covert blow at Christianity in decorous and fair-spoken words. It is believed by many of them that a demonstration of the "antiquity of man" will overturn the whole Biblical structure. The spirit of the prevailing science of the present time is remarkable in one particular: its proclivity to theorize on a limited number of facts. Avowedly inadequate unless future discoveries shall supply what has never yet been procured, Mr. Darwin erects his immense edifice of "natural selection;" and the surprising part of the matter is that the scientific world seems to cry out, That is exactly the thing! The explanation of such a loose and wild

And so challenges contradiction.

The speculative habits of modern Science;

speculation receiving so much favor is due to the fact, we think, that a large proportion of our scientists are determined to ignore the supernatural altogether, and to escape a creative act they are compelled to require Matter to manipulate itself. We thus have "spontaneous generation" by Mr. Bastian; protoplasm by Mr. Huxley; evolution by Mr. Spencer; and natural selection by Mr. Darwin. The question still remains, even in a case of spontaneous generation, Where did the original dead matter which generates come from? But this is disposed of by saying, We deal only with facts; we never speculate. Does not Mr. Darwin "speculate"? It is the most extensive speculation of any age—not excepting the Hindoo cosmogonists. Does not Mr. Huxley speculate when he contends that a living, intelligent being is nothing but a chemical mixture of so many parts of three or four gases? "It rejects inquiries into first causes as unphilosophical, and deals only with phenomena;" so speaks the votary of Buddha. And so speaks the modern man of "science" when you press him with the main question in this inquiry. "He rejects inquiries into *first* causes." As many secondary causes as you choose; that is all "philosophical;" that is "science;" beyond that we get out of the pale of science, and are classed with the old women and the priests. We look up into the blue vault of heaven, and see it filled with systems and worlds, moving in intricate and harmonious orbits; we see the glory of the sun by day, the peerless rule of the moon by night; we see the earth with its waving forests and verdant meadows; we see highly-organized animals, like the lion, and tiger, and leopard; beautiful and musical birds; we see human society, and its cities and towns, its laws, its government, its schools, its affections, its religion; and we are told by scientific men that it is "unscientific" to ask whether all these are more than self-perpetuating and self-originated phenomena. We must ask no questions back of what we *see*. That would be theological or metaphysical.

While professing to deal only with facts.

It is perfectly legitimate to reason that by a process of "natural selection" Napoleon Bonaparte was evolved from a Corsican crab; but we travel beyond the range of observed phenomena if we refer his organization to an intelligent and self-conscious creator. How the scientific mind, as represented by Mr. Huxley, Sir Charles Lyell, and Mr. Spencer, is constituted, we cannot say: it is able to observe, to record, and to classify physical phenomena, but it seems to be deficient in the logical faculty; and it is really difficult to deal with it. To say that it is perfectly legitimate to observe a man strike a ball with a billiard-cue; and that it is perfectly legitimate to observe that ball strike against another; and that it is perfectly legitimate to refer the motion of the second ball to the blow administered by the first; and that it is perfectly legitimate to refer the activity of the first to its being struck by the cue; and that it is perfectly legitimate to ascribe the motion of the cue to the arm of the billiard-player; but that it is *illegitimate* to ask, where did the arm of the billiard-player come from?—this we simply do not understand; a comparison of views under such circumstances is impossible.

We have dwelt on this merely to show the *unreasonableness* of this sort of science; there is nothing manly, or direct, or square, or thorough, about it. Professing to grapple with the highest questions, it contents itself with tracing everything back to *Force.*

Our present object is to estimate the evidence which Science has adduced in behalf of the current belief amongst geologists and archæologists in the great Antiquity of Man.

Further consideration of the past conflicts of Christianity.

It is exceedingly important to remember the conflicts in which Christianity has been engaged, in order to appreciate the controversies that are waged with it in the present age. We have briefly traced these conflicts during the first few centuries of the Christian era. We proceed to notice them still further during the succeeding centuries; for the war upon it has never ceased, and the philosophers of each succeeding age continue to bring up their guns, regardless of the disasters which have been visited on all previous attacks. The system has been so vehemently assailed, and has been involved in so many contentions, that it is, in fact, an act of complaisance on its part to consider any new challenge: for why should it be probable that after fighting through the first, the second, the third, the fourth, the fifth, the sixth, the seventh—and down to the nineteenth century—number nineteen should have anything new to say? Is Herbert Spencer greater than Kant? or Mr. Mill greater than Spinoza? Is there any critical genius greater than Strauss? or any theologico-metaphysical philosopher greater than Schleiermacher and Coleridge? Is there any one greater than Hume, or Voltaire? or is Darwin more ingenious than Lamarck, or St. Hilaire, or the author of the "Vestiges of Creation"? And if he is, how great is the difference?

It is undoubtedly true that we are in the possession of a greater number of scientific facts than in any preceding age, and that we have a more exact historical knowledge than our ancestors enjoyed. We have discovered new metals, new stars, new fossils, new scientific processes, and we know more about Egypt, Assyria, Babylon, India, China, than Voltaire or Gibbon or Thomas Paine knew; and it is certainly *possible* (we may say to our opponents) that some of the new facts may prove irreconcilable with Christianity. Our point is that new facts and new knowledge were constantly acquired during the first eighteen centuries of the Christian era, and that Christianity was tested during all that period. It is barely possible, we may allow, that it may be reserved for

Mr. Darwin or Sir John Lubbock or Sir Charles Lyell or Mr. Huxley to strike at last the fatal blow.

Darwinism.

We do not think they have done it. Mr. Darwin, as we have said, we leave to others, with the single remark that his whole scheme seems to us to be merely a *speculation:* it is not *science*, if science may be defined as generalizations arising out of *facts*. There is not a particle of *evidence* that man is descended from the monkey, or that any fly has ever been converted into an elephant: Mr. Darwin merely *thinks* that it *might be so*, provided the earth is a great deal older than Sir William Thomson and other eminent men of science believe it possible for it to be; and provided a great many facts are ascertained which have not yet been ascertained. Nor shall we enter into the discussion about *protoplasm*. This too is *not proven*, and if it were, it professedly declines to say where the protoplasm which possesses such rare powers itself came from.

The antiquity of man.

The statements about the antiquity of man rest on *facts* which challenge consideration: it is not so much a *theory*, as an inference from many appearances; and while some think that it might not contradict the Biblical narrative to admit all that is claimed (and that the Mosaic "days" of creation were *æons* there is little doubt), yet such is not our opinion. The man Adam is not the primeval man described by the anthropologists.* To take one single particular, he is represented to have lived nearly a thousand years. Every rule of interpretation is violated if we repudiate the longevity of the patriarchs.

Close of the third century of our era.

About the close of the third century, Christianity was everywhere triumphant; and paganism has never since, within the limits of the then Roman world, attempted to offer any resistance to it, save in one notable instance, when (to use the

---

* Their primeval man is the lowest of savages—a mute—a transitional form from the brute creation. The patriarchs of Genesis are the builders of cities. Such also is the primeval man of the Mesopotamian Valley and of Egypt. We have already referred to this. We may add to what has been stated that Comparative Philology unites with the Monumental Records of the East to point out the early civilization of our race. Before the separation of the Aryan family, before the existence of the Greek and Sanskrit languages, one supreme deity, says Max Müller, "had been invoked by the ancestors of our race, and had been invoked by a name which has never been excelled by any other name—Dyaus, Zeus, Jupiter, Tyr—all meaning light and brightness, sky and day." So in the Chinese, Mongolian, and Turkish languages there seems to be an original identity of name for the Deity—a word signifying *sky*, as among the Aryans. So in the mythology of Finland the primary conception of the Deity is associated with the same word.

Prof. Max Müller has shown that we find the same name for *town* in Sanskrit and in Greek, which proves that towns existed among the Aryans before Greek and Sanskrit were spoken,—before the Aryans were scattered from their primeval seats. From an examination of the Latin, Celtic, Teutonic and Sanskrit, we perceive, similarly, that kingly government had been established among the Aryans at an equally early period.

words of another) the power of the State, as well as the resources of a brilliant and highly-cultivated mind, were exerted in an elaborate and expiring effort to revive and re-establish the supremacy of pagan thought. After this, in the West it merely pleaded for toleration, while in the East it disappeared altogether.

Julian.

The names of John Scotus Erigena, Lanfranc, Thomas Aquinas, Anselm, Abelard, Bonaventura, Marco Polo, Roger Bacon, Duns Scotus, Wickliffe, Dante, Cimabue, Innocent III., Frederick II., are a sufficient evidence that there were able thinkers and active minds even in the middle ages. The works of Erigena, the attention bestowed on the materialistic philosophy of Averroës, the saying of Frederick II. that "Moses, Christ, and Mahomet were the three great impostors who had deceived the Jews, the Christians, and the Arabs" (as well as the celebrated book "De Tribus Impostoribus"), reveal to us that Doubt prevailed even when Alfred was at Æthelingay and in the days of the Crusaders.

The middle ages.

Wide-spread unbelief developed itself throughout Europe about the close of the fifteenth century, as evidenced by the literature of the day, as well as by the anti-Christian sympathies of men like Politian, Ficinus, Poggio, Cardinal Bembo, etc. It is called the *Renaissance*,—when at the brilliant courts of Lorenzo de Medici and Leo X. paganism was nourished at the heart of the Church, and the fifth Lateran Council found it necessary to promulgate anew the doctrine of the immortality of the soul.

The fifteenth century.

During the sixteenth century the University of Padua became a centre of scepticism, which manifested itself in a form of pantheism derived from the philosophy of Averroës, and in a gross materialism derived from the works of Alexander of Aphrodisias.

The sixteenth century.

The latter half of the seventeenth century inaugurated the assaults on Christianity in modern times. Lord Herbert and Hobbes in England, Spinoza in Holland, and Bayle in France, are familiar names. Lord Herbert may be called the father of English Deism. His principal work is the *De Veritate*. Hobbes was a materialist and a sensationalist. His chief work was his *Leviathan*, which was primarily a political treatise. As Herbert was answered by Locke, Baxter, and Leland, so Hobbes was answered by Cudworth in his *Intellectual System*, by Cumberland, by Lord Clarendon, and others.

The seventeenth century.

Lord Herbert, Hobbes, Spinoza.

And now with the dawn of the eighteenth century the conflict becomes still sharper, and the attack still bolder. Toland and Shaftesbury belonged to the transitional period.

The eighteenth century.

Toland and Shaftesbury.

It was about this time that Mills drew attention to the variety of readings in the sacred text, a subject which disturbed so much the mind of the pious Bengel. Toland opened up also the question of *the validity of the canon*.

Collins.

In 1713 Anthony Collins published "A discourse of Free-thinking, occasioned by the rise and growth of a sect called the Free-thinkers." One of the points in this book was the uncertainty of the text of Scripture, in which he was completely refuted by Bentley in his *Phileleutheros Lipsiensis*.

In 1724 Collins published his "Discourse of the Grounds and Reasons of the Christian Religion." In this work he assails the variety of readings, and indirectly the authenticity of the books. He attempts to show that the prophecies cited in the New Testament from the Old, to prove the Messiahship of Jesus, are really inapplicable in any except a fanciful or allegorical sense.

Woolston.

Woolston in 1727 published his celebrated "Discourses on the Miracles," in which he interpreted the accounts of the miracles in the Bible figuratively, and rationalized them away as was subsequently done by Paulus and the Germans. These pamphlets created a most intense excitement in England, Voltaire, who was in England at the time, stating that their sale reached thirty thousand copies.

Tindal.

In 1730 Dr. Tindal published his famous dialogue, "Christianity as old as the Creation," which is noteworthy from the fact that it was mainly in reply to this work that Butler wrote his "Analogy of Natural and Revealed Religion."

The object of the book is to show that natural religion is sufficient, and that revelation is superfluous; and, further, to show the impossibility of a revelation, on the ground that the inculcation of positive as distinct from moral duties is equivalent to establishing a new and independent rule of action. He also suggests many objections to the credibility of the Bible, such as the non-fulfilment of prophecies, the mistakes of the inspired writers, the destruction of the Canaanites, etc.

Morgan.

Morgan's "Moral Philosopher" was published in 1737. He also urges the sufficiency of the moral law without any additional revelation; and argues, as Tindal did, that neither prophecies nor miracles can avail to prove any doctrine which is contrary to the moral sense. Therefore he rejects the Old Testament on account of such passages as the sacrifice of Isaac, the oracle of Urim and Thummim, etc. Warburton's "Divine Legation of Moses" was written in reply to this work.

Chubb.

Thomas Chubb was a working-man. He wrote "A Discourse concerning Reason," and various other tracts and treatises. He denied a particular providence, the utility of prayer (like Mr.

Tyndall), and attacked the Old and New Testaments very much in the line marked out by Morgan.

Bolingbroke pronounced the Jewish history to be repugnant to the idea of a benevolent and just God, while he assails the narrative of the fall, the destruction of the Canaanites, the figures in the historical books, the absence of future rewards after death, etc. He finds the theology of Paul to differ from that of Christ, and attempts to show that the miracles of the New Testament never really occurred; but admits that if they did occur, they attest the revelation. He gives prominence to the separation by an interval of time of the miracles from the composition of the gospels.

Bolingbroke.

Spinoza had argued for the philosophical impossibility of miracles: Woolston argued that the witnesses to them contradicted one another: Bolingbroke urged that they were not attested by eye-witnesses: Hume contended that no amount of human testimony could prove what was contrary to the universal experience of mankind. His metaphysical Nihilism is well known. Since Spinoza no stronger antagonist had assailed Christianity or human beliefs.

Hume.

Voltaire lived from 1694 to 1778. While Woolston and Morgan and Tindal and Bolingbroke and Hume were writing in England, he was busy in France.

Voltaire.

Next to Voltaire in France was Diderot. Voltaire was a Deist: Diderot was an Atheist. Diderot was the projector, and the ruling spirit in the preparation, of the celebrated *Encyclopédie*.

Diderot.

Another of this band of infidels was Helvetius, the author of *De l'Esprit* and *De l'Homme*. That pleasure is the only good, and self-interest the true ground of morals, was the pith of his system.

Helvetius.

D'Holbach was the principal author of the *Système de la Nature*, published in 1774. Diderot, Helvetius, and others are supposed to have had a hand in it. Even Voltaire is said to have denounced it. The aim of the work is to show that there is no God, and no such thing as mind as distinguished from matter; no such thing as free-will, and no such thing as immortality.

Holbach.

Rousseau was cotemporary with the foregoing philosophers, but not of them. In his *Emile* he assails Christianity very much in the manner of the English Deists, attacking the external evidence of prophecy and the miracles, and insisting on the improbability of portions of the historical books. His course did not please the Encyclopedists or the clergy, and he was prosecuted and driven out of France.

Rousseau.

To these we must add Condillac, the founder of the French materialistic philosophy.

Such were the conflicts of Christianity during the second and third quarters of the eighteenth century,—George II. and Louis XV.,—unquestionably one of the most corrupt, one of the hardest, and one of the most selfish, as well as the most sensual, eras in modern history,—the age of Swift, St. John, Sterne, Le Sage, Smollett, Walpole, Alexander Pope, Lord Chesterfield. Grovelling in temper, it was materialistic in philosophy.

Christianity was passed through the furnace by some of the subtlest and finest intellects the world has ever seen—with the spirit of the age against it.

Gibbon and Paine.

Nor did these attacks cease. Bolingbroke and Hume were succeeded by Gibbon and Paine.

The French Revolution.

In France, during the storm of the Revolution, the churches were stripped, and Christianity declared to be effete. The images of the Saviour were trampled under foot; a prostitute, impersonating the Goddess of Reason, was introduced into the National Convention, and then followed by a procession to the magnificent church of Notre Dame, in the Ile de la Cité, where she was elevated on the high altar, and *adored by the audience*. This was the net result of the Encyclopedists in France. On all the public cemeteries an inscription was written declaring that "*Death is an Eternal Sleep.*"

Cabanis.

The century closed with the sensational philosophy of Cabanis and Destutt de Tracy, and Volney's "Ruins" of Empires. Cabanis was the friend and pupil of Condillac, and also the intimate personal friend of Mirabeau. The maxim of his philosophy was: "Les nerfs, voilà tout l'homme." The moral feeling, the intellect, the will, he reduced to sensation; sensation, he said, was an affection of the nerves; and "voilà," he exclaimed, "*the entire man!*" Destutt de Tracy lived till 1835. He carried out and amplified the views of M. Cabanis.

Volney.

Another notable work published by Volney was his "catechism,"—*La Loi Naturelle, ou Catéchisme du Citoyen Français*,—in which he taught that the chief end of man was "la conservation de soi-même," and that there was no evil except death: even murder he defended whenever it conduced to our security or defence.

Infidelity in Germany.

So far we have said nothing of Germany, which was not fairly aroused until the latter part of the eighteenth century. The infidelity of England and France was that of Common Sense: the objections were those of clear, strong intellects that spun no cobwebs. A more subtle and refined criticism developed itself in Germany, in connection with a more searching, if a less substantial, metaphysics. A fresh storm was about to burst on the head of Christianity, which has hardly spent itself yet.

Semler at Halle, Paulus at Jena, and Eichhorn at Göttingen, were the founders of modern *Rationalism*. Semler is the author of the "historical" method in the interpretation of Scripture. He taught that the doctrines of the New Testament were an "accommodation" on the part of our Lord to Jewish prejudices or opinions: that, for example, there was really no such thing as demoniacal possession, but that the instances mentioned were cases of lunacy or epilepsy, and that the narrative merely humored the erroneous notions of those to whom our Lord's discourses were addressed. Paulus advanced these doctrines yet further. He did not believe the apostles to be impostors, but regarded them as addicted to "oriental" modes of speech. The miracles narrated by them were merely figurative. The transfiguration was "the confused recollection of sleeping men, who saw Jesus with two friends in the beautiful light of the morning;" the resurrection was only apparent; the exorcism of the demons was the power of wisdom over a disturbed imagination. So Eichhorn affirmed the smoke of Sinai to be a *thunder-storm*.

Semler, Paulus, Eichhorn.

The close of the eighteenth century in Germany was signalized by the appearance of the *Critique of Pure Reason*, a work which is the foundation of modern metaphysics, and which practically expelled all *realities* from the world.

Kant.

We have now reached the nineteenth century. In England the battle seemed over,—for the rhapsodies of Byron and Shelley were merely the murmurs of the retiring wave.

Nineteenth century.

In France, too, there was a lull, or even an improved temper,—as seen in the anti-materialistic tone of the works of Chateaubriand.

In Germany there was a perfect carnival of doubt. Kant was followed by Fichte; Fichte by Schelling and Hegel; Semler by De Wette.

Fichte, Schelling, Hegel, De Wette.

In 1835 Strauss's work appeared, which attracted such unprecedented attention. The English Deists and Voltaire had attacked the character of the Evangelists; Eichhorn and Paulus had assailed the literal accuracy of their statements; the "legendary" theory attacked the character of the writings, and accounted for them on the principle of the Homeric myths.

Strauss.

"A legend is a group of ideas around a nucleus of fact: a myth is an idea translated by mental realism into fact." Strauss undertook to show that if a small basis of fact expanded into a legend be allowed in the gospel history, the influence of myth is sufficient to explain the remainder. There was a man named Jesus; his career was exaggerated: so far the legend; the need of a deliverer, and the Jewish expectation of a Messiah, created the Christ of the Evangelists.

Foolish as this seems in the full glare of the unequivocal historical evidences for the facts of the New Testament, it not only convulsed all Germany, but all Europe. The German mind is like that of a man of fine powers who *just feels his wine;* he is conscious that he has not the full use of his judgment, but has brilliant imaginings. They live in a sort of state of ecstasy, and dream while they are awake.

Doubt in Germany.

We have had all forms of doubt in Germany. Every book of the Old and New Testaments has been tested in the furnace "heated seven times." Every chapter, every verse, every word, has been under the microscope of modern criticism. Every historical statement has been delicately weighed. Every geographical allusion has been scrutinized by modern learning. Every reference to Egyptian, Babylonian, Ethiopian, Assyrian, Phœnician, Moabite, Philistine, Greek, Persian, Roman concerns, has been brought up for comparison with our present knowledge of the antiquities, manners, customs, laws, literature, and monumental remains of these countries.

Recent cavillers.

We have had also in this day men like Carlyle, Theodore Parker, R. W. Emerson, R. W. Mackay, James Martineau, Dickens, Morell, Cousin, Comte, Feuerbach, Moleschott, Bruno and Christian Bauer.

Failure of all these attacks.

All these attacks on Christianity *have failed.* Failed from Celsus to R. W. Mackay and Christian Bauer. The men who conducted the attacks are in large measure forgotten,—even those among the living. Not one of their works can be regarded as seriously imperilling now the authority of the Bible. Which weapon among them has left an appreciable scar behind it?

A new Knight.

But a new Knight has entered the lists, and there must be a trial of strength between the Bible and SCIENCE.

CHAPTER VII.

THE PREMATURE ANNOUNCEMENTS OF SCIENCE WITH REGARD TO THE ANTIQUITY OF MAN.

M. Bailly, Prof. Playfair, and the Edinburgh Review on the Astronomy of the Hindoos.—The Excitement created by the Discovery of the Zodiacs of Dendera and Esne.—The Edinburgh Review on these.—The Theory exploded by Champollion's Arrival in Paris.—The Fossil Man of Guadaloupe.—Nott and Gliddon thereon.—Dr. Lund's Discoveries in Brazil.—The Tombs at Marino under the Peperino.—The Fossil Man of Denise.—The Pigmy Graves of Tennessee.—The Perforated Shark's Teeth of the English Crag.—The Fossil Man of the Coral Reefs of Florida.—Ancient Stone Lance-Head of Prof. Nilsson.—The Burghs, Bee-hive Houses, Pillar Stones, etc., of Scotland and Ireland.—Dr. Mill and Dr. Moore on the Newton Stone Inscription.—Inscription on Stonehenge, thought to be Libyan.

WE have already, in a previous chapter, pointed out the unreliability of scientific theories,—how rapidly one theory succeeds another,—and how different are the teachings of one of the editions of Sir Charles Lyell's "Principles" from those which precede it and those which follow it; and how cautious we have, therefore, to be before accepting any startling scientific announcement.

Past attempts to prove the antiquity of man.

In reference especially to the evidence for the antiquity of man, experience teaches that we must be more than ordinarily mistrustful of any alleged discoveries of this character. We have been prematurely informed so often of the discovery of "fossil men," that we are compelled to pause before we yield our assent to the antiquity now claimed for the Neanderthal skull or the skeleton of Mentone. It may prepare the reader for the following discussion to enumerate some of the *misses* already made by science on this subject.

The Hindoo Astronomy.

M. Bailly.

Prof. Playfair.

1. At the close of the last century it was heralded, with all the assurance which Science assumes, that an examination of the astronomical tables of the Hindoos proved conclusively that the Hindoo astronomers had made observations of the heavenly bodies three thousand one hundred and two years before the Christian era. M. Bailly first announced this discovery in France, and Professor Playfair, of Edinburgh, one of the most distinguished mathematicians of Europe, read a paper on the subject, in 1788, before

the Royal Society of Edinburgh, in which he not only explained that the places of the sun and moon, in the beginning of the Cal-yougham, or age of misfortune, were determined by actual observation 3102 years B.C., but he added that "the equation of the sun's centre, and the obliquity of the ecliptic, when compared with those of the present time, seem to point to a period of this astronomy *one thousand or twelve hundred years earlier* (that is, four thousand three hundred years before the Christian era), and the time necessary to have brought the arts of calculation, and observing, to such perfection as they must have been, at the period spoken of, comes in support of the same conclusion."

This distinguished scientist also published a paper on the Indian Astronomy in the Philosophical Transactions for 1790, in which he makes the following fling at the Biblical chronology: "It is through the medium of astronomy *alone* that a few rays from those distant objects (*the primitive inhabitants of the earth*) can be conveyed in safety to the eye of the modern observer, so as to afford him a light which, though scanty, is pure and unbroken, and free from the false coloring of *vanity and superstition.*"

This was the first announcement of the "Antiquity of Man,"—and it came from Astronomy, not Geology.

The whole subject was re-discussed in the *Edinburgh Review* for 1807, and the conclusion was reached that M. Bailly was right, and that the arguments advanced by him "give a great probability to the opinion that the art of astronomical observation is of *the highest antiquity in India*, and goes back not less than three thousand years before the Christian era."

The Edinburgh Review.

These views made a profound impression at that time. M. Bailly was the rival of Lagrange and Laplace, the author of the valuable memoir on *The Light of the Satellites* (1771), which was marked with a degree of precision and accuracy till that time unknown in the observations of their eclipses. He was also the author of the *History of Astronomy*, published at Paris in 1775, and of (which was considered his greatest work) the *History of Indian and Oriental Astronomy*, besides various other elaborate and learned treatises. He was a member at once of the Academy of Sciences, the French Academy, and the Academy of Inscriptions and Belles-Lettres,—the only instance of the same person having been so honored since the days of Fontenelle.

Professor Playfair occupied a position in the scientific world as distinguished as M. Bailly. He succeeded Dugald Stewart in the chair of Mathematics in the University of Edinburgh, and afterwards succeeded Professor Robison in the chair of Natural Philosophy in the same institution; and he was the author of a number of scientific works: the

Origin and Investigation of Porisms, the *Elements of Geometry*, *Theorems on the Figure of the Earth*, the *Theory of the Earth*, *Illustrations of the Huttonian Theory*, *Lithological Survey of Schehallien*, *Outlines of Natural Philosophy*, the *Dissertation on the Progress of Mathematical and Physical Science* in the Encyclopædia Britannica, *Observations on the Trigonometrical Tables of the Brahmins*, etc.

The tables of Tirvalore were determined to be three thousand one hundred and two years older than the Christian era not only from the calculations with regard to the obliquity of the ecliptic and the equation of the sun's centre, but from the longitudes of the sun and moon at the commencement of the Calyougham, from the length of the tropical year as given by the tables (which varies in consequence of its being affected by the precession of the equinoxes), and also from a conjunction of the sun, moon, and planets, alleged to have occurred at that epoch.

The accurate calculations of modern astronomy have, however, shown that the conjunction in question could not have occurred at the date assigned, nor at any epoch near it; while in order to find the equation of the earth's centre given in the tables, it is necessary to go back six thousand years before our era. From which it appears that the tables of Tirvalore, which furnished such a handle to M. Bailly and Professor Playfair against the Christian chronology, were not the result of actual observation, but had been *calculated backwards* upon imperfect data.

The celebrated Delambre, in his great History of Astronomy, says that "Mr. Playfair has not calculated this table anew," and that "he has not had the discernment to perceive the error of the division, 225 being substituted, probably by an error of the copyist, for the true divisor 235.5."

"When," he also remarks, "we inquire why the Indians chose the remote and fictitious epoch of the Calyougham, or misfortune, we perceive, in the first place, that it was from national vanity, and in the next, that they might make all the planets start from one point, a conjunction which their method of calculation required. If we further ask why they adopted a complicated method which employs divisions and multiplications of enormous numbers, with so many additions, subtractions, reductions, and different precepts, the answer is that they did not wish for written tables; they wanted numbers which could be put in technical verses, even into songs, so that the calculations might be performed without writing a book. These facts, now well known, through the labors of the Asiatic Society, are alone sufficient to subvert the whole system of Bailly."

Mr. Bentley, of Calcutta, a member of the Asiatic Society, was the first to expose this theory, and to prove that the vast *yugas* of the Hindoos, which carried the creation of the world back (like the Egyptian and Babylonian dynasties of Manetho and Berosus) millions of years, was a mere myth. He not only exposed the fallacy of the "conjunction" above referred to, but he also, by a calculation of the precession of the equinoxes in the interval, showed that the very earliest of all the observations handed down in the sacred books of the Hindoos, namely, the division of the zodiac into lunar "mansions," was in the year 1421 B.C. The oldest Hindoo astronomical treatise extant, the *Surya-Siddhanta*, as indicated by the position of the Hindoo sphere, belongs to a far later period than this, namely, to the year 570 A.D.

A second set of Indian tables was sent from Chrisnabouram, in the Carnatic, about the year 1750. They are fifteen in number, and their epoch corresponds with the 10th of March, at sunrise, in the year 1491 of our era; and the probability is that all of the Indian astronomical tables (there are others which we have not referred to) are derived from these.

2. It was only a few years after the excitement created by the Indian Astronomy, that an even greater sensation was produced by the discovery of the zodiacs of Dendera and Esne in Egypt, which, it was believed, settled definitively the question of the antiquity of man.

Zodiacs of Dendera and Esne.

These zodiacs were discovered during the expedition of Napoleon to Egypt, and were found on the ceilings of two temples in the cities named. They were engraved in wood and painted. The zodiac at Dendera is headed by the sign of the Lion, followed by the Virgin, the Balance, the Scorpion, the Archer, and the Capricorn in the same line. The peculiar arrangement of these figures represented, it was said, the exact position of the constellations when the zodiac was constructed, and it was ascertained by appropriate calculations that it was much older than the beginning of the period embraced in the Christian chronology. M. Dupuis calculated that these temples must have been at least fifteen thousand years old. M. Nouet calculated that the zodiac at Esne was as old as 4600 B.C., while M. Burkard declared that it dated from about 7000 B.C.

Figures of the zodiacs were first published by M. Denon, in his work on Egypt, and excited the most intense interest in Europe, and particularly in France.

"Science," says M. Greppo (Essay on the Hieroglyphic System, 1829), "struck out into systems very bold; and the spirit of infidelity, seizing upon the discovery, flattered itself with the hope of drawing from it new support."

The *Edinburgh Review* for 1811 (article on "Hamilton's Egyptiacæ," vol. xviii.) remarked,—

"About the antiquity of these zodiacs, we find ourselves compelled to differ from Mr. Hamilton, who seems to think that they were constructed only one thousand eight hundred years ago. . . . The equinoxes recede a sign in about two thousand one hundred and fifty years; and, consequently, since the sun, at the summer solstice, is now in the first degree of *Gemini*, and was about the twenty-fourth of *Cancer* when these zodiacs of Dendera were constructed, they cannot be referred to a much later period *than three thousand eight hundred years ago.*"

The Edinburgh Review on this subject.

"The zodiac of Esne is unquestionably *much more ancient* than those of Dendera. . . . We must assign an antiquity to it of *more than five thousand three hundred years.*"

In the midst of the apparent triumph of science, a circumstance occurred which added a new excitement to the subject. This was the arrival of the planisphere of Dendera at Paris, in 1821, M. Leloraine, an enterprising young traveller, having succeeded in detaching it from the ceiling of the temple and transporting it safely to France.

M. Greppo describes the interest which it awakened: "An object of interest to educated men, and of vanity to those who thought themselves such, it could not remain unnoticed by the multitude; and classes of society, who knew not even the signification of the term Zodiac, rushed in crowds to behold it. In the journals, in the saloons, the Zodiac was the only topic of discussion. Have you seen the Zodiac? What do you think of the Zodiac? were questions to which every one was seemingly compelled to give a well-informed answer, or to be degraded from a place in polished society."

Tracts were circulated in Paris to disseminate the fact that the Christian chronology was set aside.

At this moment Champollion, the younger, arrived in Paris from a visit to Egypt. He had just previously assisted in solving the secret of the Egyptian hieroglyphics, and, having examined the Zodiac of Dendera before its removal, had there deciphered in Greek letters the word for *Emperor;* while on the walls of the temple he discovered the names, titles, and surnames of *Tiberius*, *Claudius*, *Nero*, and *Domitian.*

Upon the portico of Esne, which the *Edinburgh Review* had pronounced "much more ancient," he read the names of *Claudius* and *Antoninus Pius:* it was really *more modern.*

The truth about the Zodiacs was that they belonged to the first and second centuries of the Christian era, and that they were "*themes of nativity*," and had reference to *judicial astrology.*

3. Another scientific sensation was created by the *Fossil Man of Guadaloupe.* Nott and Gliddon suggest a high antiquity for this in their "Types of Mankind." There were two of these skeletons, which were found imbedded in the solid rock on

Fossil Man of Guadaloupe.

the northwest coast of Guadaloupe, in the West Indies. One of these skeletons is in the British Museum, the other in the Royal Cabinet in Paris.

They are the remains of Indians killed in battle two centuries ago. The rock is a limestone harder than statuary marble, which is forming daily, and which consists of minute fragments of shells and corals, incrusted with a calcareous cement, resembing travertin, by which the different grains are bound together. The skeletons still retain some of their animal matter, and all of their phosphate of lime.

Coins of Edward I., imbedded in similar shell-rock, were found at a depth of ten feet below the bed of the river Dove in England. The delta of the Rhone is a similar formation, consisting chiefly of *solid rock* deposited by the river. There is a cannon in the museum of Montpellier taken up near the mouth of this river imbedded in this rock.

New type of man in Brazil.

4. Then we had Dr. Lund's discovery in Brazil of fossil skulls having the incisive teeth with the edges parallel to the axis of the mouth—a new type of man. We learn from M. Morlot that this discovery, it is now ascertained, "was based on a *misunderstanding.*" Dr. Reinhard, of Copenhagen, had, however, to make a journey to Brazil, under the auspices of the Royal Museum of Copenhagen, to correct the mistake.*

The tombs under the peperino near Albano.

5. Then certain antique burial-places were found under an intact layer of *peperino*, at Marino, near Albano, in the then States of the Church. It was inferred that the tombs were older than this deposit. M. Morlot stated that it had been ascertained that they had been excavated in galleries by entering laterally under the peperino, and cited Prof. Ponzi and M. Pietro Rosa as his authority. But this is contradicted by Sir John Lubbock, who, in conjunction with Prof. Pigorini, made an examination of the locality, an account of which is published in the *Archæologia* for 1869. The case demonstrates, says Sir John, that the burials took place at a period when the volcanoes near Rome were in a state of full activity.

We may observe that the silence of all records with regard to the activity of these volcanoes in recent times would not by any means

* The horizontal wearing or abrasion of the teeth is regarded by the European archæologists as one of the marks of extreme antiquity. When this occurs, the man is at once remitted to the Stone Age. Last year, a human body was found in a peat-bog in Holstein, which was well preserved, and thought to be probably as old as the beginning of the Christian era. It lay in an outstretched posture, and had a wound in the forehead. It was clothed in a garment of twilled woollen material, with broad sleeves, and over it a tunic composed of pieces of sheep and wolf skins sewed together. The sewing was of the finest character, and the dress indicated (we are told) an antiquity corresponding with the beginning of our era. But the teeth were worn or abraded after the manner of those who are generally supposed to have lived in the Stone Age.

prove that no such eruptions had occurred. If Pompeii and Herculaneum had not been exhumed in modern times, we should hardly have known of their destruction, although the younger Pliny witnessed and gave an account of the catastrophe which overwhelmed them.

But the character of the contents of these tombs at once settles the fact that these volcanoes have been in a state of activity at a comparatively recent date. These articles consisted, among other objects, of pottery, a number of bronze knives, and fragments of *iron*. The presence of iron excludes the idea of any great antiquity, and, as we shall see, probably fixes the date of the sepultures during the monarchical period of Rome. Evidently it was the transitional period from the use of bronze to that of iron.

It has, furthermore, been ascertained that at various times since the human period, and even down to the historic epoch, volcanic disturbances have occurred in the neighborhood of Rome. In what is called the palæolithic age, we find the rude stone implements of the early population of Italy, associated, in volcanic deposits, with the bones of the great extinct animals. The second period of activity corresponded, as we are told by M. Ponzi, with the Age of Bronze, when the crater of Monte Cavo, near the Lake of Albano, was in eruption. The subterranean fires broke forth for the third time in the Alban mountains, and deposited the volcanic ashes (since hardened into peperino) and covered the tombs which we have been considering. This, says M. Ponzi, was the "first epoch of iron." M. de Rossi thinks hê has discovered traces of lake habitations of this epoch on the banks of the ancient lake crater of *Valle-Marciana*, which is now dried up. After a period of tranquillity, continues M. Ponzi, a new eruption took place, but less violent. It gave birth to the little crater of *Monte Pila*, which was opened by the side of that of *Monte Cavo*. M. Ponzi thinks that this period of activity was during the existence of the Roman monarchy.* This is not all: we know that there were frequent shocks of earthquakes felt at Rome A.U.C. 319, and that many houses in the city were thrown down. All this disposes of the idea of fossils from this quarter. We may add further that a number of distinguished scientific men concur in the opinion that in the progress of time the volcanic deposit in question, if originally composed of ashes, might have become hardened and solidified.

The Fossil Man of Denise.

6. The *Fossil Man of Denise*, buried under the lava of the extinct volcanoes of Auvergne, has been often adduced in proof of an "auld lang syne" in anthropological affairs; for it was alleged that these volcanoes had not been in activity in historic times, certainly not since the days of Julius Cæsar, who encamped on

* Matériaux pour l'Histoire de l'Homme, Jan. 1872, p. 25.

the spot when he was in Central Gaul. But it has been ascertained from an old Gaulish history, re-edited some years since, that from A.D. 458 to 460 this region was visited with violent convulsions of the earth, and the Rogation Days were appointed by Mamercus, Bishop of Vienne, about A.D. 460, for the purpose of chanting litanies to stay the volcanic eruptions which were then devastating his diocese.*

And M. Morlot informs us that it has been further ascertained that the burial in question "is posterior to the epoch of the activity of the volcano, and that it is explained by a land-slip." He adds, however, that it may be also true that the volcanoes of Auvergne and Vivarais might have been in action at a quite recent period, for in the diluvium of the valley of the Rhone, M. Emilien Dumas finds only peridotous basalt proceeding from the ancient veins, and no felspathic basalt, peculiar to volcanoes with craters and tap-holes.

The Pigmy Race of Tennessee.

7. It is not long since the discovery of the graves of an extinct Race of Pigmies was announced in Tennessee. Only a few years ago we read an account in *Littell's Living Age* of these wonderful graves, the skeletons of which belonged unquestionably, it was stated, to a race some two or three feet high. But at the meeting of the Academy of Natural Sciences at Philadelphia in 1866, Prof. Leidy read an extract from an article written by Col. A. W. Putnam, of Nashville, from which we learn that the story is without foundation, and originated from the small size of the graves. Dr. Leidy exhibited a skull and medallion (of shell) obtained from one of these graves, near the mouth of Stone River, in Davidson county. "The skull does not differ in general form, proportion, and size, from that of the usual North American Indian skulls." The graves are near the surface. Col. Putnam supposes that the practice was to expose the dead body, as was the custom of some recent tribes, on a high scaffold, or suspended from the trees in the open air, until the flesh decayed, after which the bones were collected and laid in the graves, which, notwithstanding their shallowness, seem never to have been disturbed by wild beasts.

Traces of Man in the English "Crag."

8. Year before last it was announced that a number of perforated Shark's Teeth had been found in the "crag" (referred to the pliocene strata) in England; and it was stated (among others, by Mr. Owen) that the borings were unquestionably the work of man. We learn, however, from a writer in the *Geological Magazine* for June, 1872, that "there is not the slightest reason for attributing the phenomena in question to the agency of man."†

* See Quarterly Review, Oct. 1844; Nature, May 16, 1872; Geolog. Mag., ii. 241.

† Mentioned in Amer. Jour. Sci., Sept. 1872, p. 241.

9. Another standard evidence of the "Antiquity of Man" has been the human bones found in the coral formation of Florida. Attention was first called to this fossil, we believe, in Nott and Gliddon's "Types of Mankind" in a letter on the subject from Prof. Agassiz,* who, by an elaborate calculation with regard to the rate of growth of coral, ascertained that these bones were, on the most moderate computation, some ten thousand years old.

Agassiz's fossil human bones from Florida.

Sir Charles Lyell lends his imprimatur to this inference,† repeating the statement in even the last edition of the "Antiquity of Man" (1873).

And now comes the contradiction. The *American Naturalist* contains the following announcement: "In regard to the alleged discovery of human bones in the coral formation of Florida (see *Naturalist*, vol. ii. p. 386), which was first published by Prof. Agassiz in Nott and Gliddon's 'Types of Mankind,' and has appeared in other works, including Lyell's 'Antiquity of Man,' we beg to give our readers the following statement, in his own words, by Count L. F. Pourtalès, the original discoverer of these bones: 'The human jaw and other bones found in Florida by myself in 1848 were not in a coral formation, but in a freshwater sandstone on the shore of Lake Monroe, associated with freshwater shells of species still living in the lake (Paludina, Ampullaria, et cet.). No date can be assigned to the formation of that deposit, at least from present observation.' "‡

10. A *Lance-head* discovered by Prof. Nilsson, and which he deposited in the Museum of Lund, was adjudged to be of great antiquity. It was of silex, and had been retouched after it was originally made. It was observed that before being re-cut it had turned white, as has happened frequently to ancient specimens. It was believed that silex required a very long time to whiten, and so this bleached lance-head was regarded as another testimony to the cycles of time which have rolled over man since the Primitive Stone Age. But Prof. Steenstrup has ascertained numerous instances of silex very much whitened in a few years, as it were under his own eyes, and by natural means. The phenomenon is dependent on the locality and position in which the silex is found.

Prof. Nilsson's ancient lance-head.

11. The "Rock-cut Temples of India" have been another example of a hoary chronology in the affairs of men. These temples excavated in the solid rock, which is extremely hard and difficult to work, occur in Central and Western India—at Ajunta, Ellora, Karli; in the islands of Elephanta and Salsette; at

The Rock-cut Temples of India.

* Types of Mankind, 8th edit., p. 352.

† See "The Antiquity of Man," Amer. edit., p. 44, and also the Eng. edit. of 1873.

‡ American Naturalist, vol. ii. p. 434.

Joonain; at Dhumnar, etc. Those of Ellora extend for about two miles along the face of the plateau. Some of them are chapels and oratories; others, large halls for worship; and all are filled with groups and images of Hindoo deities, and the walls covered with elaborate carvings. The Temple of Elephanta, in the harbor of Bombay, consists of four chambers, hewn in the basaltic rock. The face of the hill has been cut down to the depth of thirty feet and over a width of three hundred feet. The central chamber, says Mr. W. H. Seward, who visited the spot a short time before his death, "is majestic with gate-ways, abutments, porches, columns, pilasters, cornices, and vaulted ceilings, as complete and perfect as if, instead of having been carved in the rock, they had been detached from it, framed, and erected on the ground." Within is a gigantic group representing Brahma, Vishnu, and Siva,—the figures twice the size of the human form. The ceiling of the recess in which this stands is decorated with a crowd of not less than fifty or sixty figures. On either side of the principal hall or temple are chapels, the walls of which are covered with allegorical works, illustrating the transformations, incarnations, battles, triumphs, marriages, and miracles of the Hindoo trinity.

When Europeans first encountered these remarkable excavations, it was believed that they were as old as the earliest monuments of Egyptian toil.

Mr. John D. Baldwin, author of "Prehistoric Nations," regards them as the remains of a "Cushite" race,* and as "ante-Sanskrit." "That they belong to a remote antiquity is shown by the fact that there is in India no record or recollection of their origin." That some writers have denied their immense antiquity, he says, is due to "the influence of that amazing *chronological lunacy* which aims so obstinately to obscure the past, and begin the history of civilization with an age comparatively modern."† He quotes from a paper in the Journal of the Royal Asiatic Society for 1852 on "The Aboriginal Race of India," by Lieut.-Gen. Briggs. Gen. Briggs refers the rock-cut temples to these aborigines. Prof. Benfey is also quoted as referring the remains found in the Dekhan to a race which "we know preceded the Sanskrit-speaking people." Maurice in his "Indian Antiquities" assigns them, we are told, to the remotest antiquity, and believes that "a species of worship totally different from that now prevailing in India was anciently practised in these caverns."

The answer to all this is, that the oldest of these temples are Buddhist, and that they cannot be more ancient than the birth of Sakhya-Muni, which was in the year 623 B.C. Mr. James Fergusson, probably the

* Prehistoric Nations, pp. 228–238.

† Ib., p. 230.

highest authority on such a subject, assigns the group at Raja Griha, in Behar, which he believes to be the very oldest, to 200 B.C. Those of Ajunta range in his opinion from the first to the tenth or eleventh century of our era. In a review of Mr. Fergusson's work* in the *Edinburgh Review* for October, 1865, the reviewer claims a somewhat greater antiquity for most of these excavations than the dates of Mr. Fergusson. The caves of Ajunta, he thinks, were, for the most part, the works of the dynasty of Asoka (B.C. 263–178), that prince having become a convert to Buddhism and having established it as the state religion of India; though the oldest, it is remarked, may have existed before Asoka; while the latest are not much more recent than the extinction of the dynasty. This writer, however, assigns the Hindoo temples at Ellora (which succeeded, he believes, the Buddhist excavations at the same place) to a period reaching down even to the tenth century of our era; while another rock-temple at the village of Kharôsa, in the province of Nuldroog, in the Dekhan, he assigns to about 1100 A.D.

Mr. Seward, whose account of the Cave of Elephanta we have already quoted, remarks that "it is the opinion of Dr. Bhau Daji that this temple was excavated about twelve hundred years ago."

So that the antiquity of the "Rock-cut Temples of India" stands on no better foundation than the antiquity of the Indian Astronomy.

The weems and burghs of Scotland, etc.

Great antiquity was at one time claimed for the weems, bee-hive houses, burghs, and round towers of Scotland and Ireland; and for the "pillar stones" and Ogham inscriptions; but they are all of no very ancient date, and need not detain us. A bronze sword was found in a weem at Monzie, in Perthshire. A group of "bee-hive" houses on the shore of Loch Resort, in Long Island, was occupied until 1823, and even now some of them are occupied in the Island of Uig. Torfæus tells us that about the year 1150 Erling, who carried off the beautiful Margaret, mother of Harold, Earl of Orkney, was besieged in the celebrated Burgh of Moussa, in the Shetlands. The Dun of Dornadilla, another burgh, is believed to have been erected by the Scotch king of that name. The Ogham characters have been found on monuments known to be later than the subjugation of the Britons by the Romans. The Pillar Stones of Scotland range probably from the fifth to the eighth century of our era. To this class belongs the celebrated Newton Stone, which has a Latin (?) inscription. Many of them have secondary inscriptions in the Ogham characters,—a repetition of the Latin, with the names given in their more purely Celtic form. Dr. Mill, the well-known Sanskrit

The Pillar Stones of Scotland.

* "The Rock-cut Temples of India, illustrated by Seventy-four Photographs." By James Fergusson, F.R.S., M.R.A.S., London, 1864.

scholar, read the Newton Stone inscription backwards, and pronounced it *Phœnician*. According to his elaborate explanation, it commemorated "the escape from shipwreck of a high magistrate of the city of Tyre, while on a voyage to the north of Scotland." This paper was read in 1862, in section E of the British Association, at Cambridge, on which occasion a cast of the stone was exhibited. In a work written since by Dr. George Moore, M.R.C.P., entitled "The Ancient Pillar Stones of Scotland," the interpretation of Dr. Mill is rejected. Dr. Moore says the inscription is "Arian," and his theory is that "Arian" missionaries, when the whole "Arian" people were still located at one central spot in Central Asia, speaking the primal "Arian" language, made their way across Asia and Europe, to plant in North Scotland this pure monument of Buddhism! which they are supposed to have established there.

Dr. Mill.

Dr. Moore.

This is somewhat of a piece with the mysterious inscription noticed a few years since on the impost of the Great Trilithon at Stonehenge. This consisted of a figure resembling a sickle, with the two Roman letters LV within the curved blade. It was moss-grown, and had all the marks of antiquity. The discovery being noised abroad, a party from the British Association in 1864 paid Stonehenge a visit. Some declared the inscription to be Roman, and suggested that it was the work of a Roman legionary, LV standing for *legio victrix*. Others considered it yet more ancient, and compared it with the lapidary inscriptions found at Carthage, said to be Libyan, and with figures found in countries occupied by the Phœnicians. It has been ascertained, however, by Dr. Thurnam, that in 1827 or 1828 a traveller who appeared to be a mechanic, and who carried a basket of tools, stopped here, and deliberately cut the figure and letters on the stone, and then proceeded on his way to Salisbury.

The mysterious inscription at Stonehenge.

The fossil human skeleton dug out of the schist rock at Quebec, and reported to be "still preserved"* in the Museum of that city, it is hardly necessary to refer to, as it is now ascertained that no such remains have ever been found.

The Fossil Man of Quebec.

The reader will appreciate, from the examples adduced (others will be mentioned hereafter), that Science is addicted to an inconsiderate haste in the promulgation of new theories, and that in particular she has blundered repeatedly on the subject of the antiquity of man. Her anxiety to confound the theologians permits her to indulge in premature convictions of the inaccuracy of the Mosaic chronology.

"Depuis l'époque de Buffon les systèmes se sont élevés les uns à côté des autres en si grand nombre, qu'en 1806 l'Institut

Science in France.

---

* Pre-Adamite Man, Griffin Lee, p. 285.

de France comptait plus de quatre-vingts théories hostiles aux saintes Ecritures. AUCUNE n'est restée debout jusqu'à ce jour."*

This is an astonishing fact, and one feels almost impatient that these evanescent forms should assume such airs of authority and of superiority to other methods of knowledge. Think of it: eighty theories hostile to Christianity, developed in the course of forty or fifty years, brought before the Institute of France in 1806, and *not one* of them surviving to this day!

It appears that Christianity and Science have *already* measured swords, and that Science has been as unfortunate as Philosophy and Criticism.

But Science would fain have these lists fought over again, and she makes two issues: that man is descended from the ape, and that the human race (apart from that theory) has existed on the earth for many thousands, if not a million, of years.

The objection to the first is, as already suggested, that it is a mere *speculation*, adopted for the purpose of throwing the Deity into the background; the objection to the other is that the evidence breaks down on the cross-examination.

The Darwinian hypothesis is by no means necessarily atheistic: it only goes so far as to contradict the declaration of the apostle that "he is not far from every one of us."

As to the chronology of the Bible, we might enlarge somewhat the present limited scheme, if it seemed necessary to do so; but we shall proceed to show that the facts hardly appear to require it.

---

* La Bible et la Science moderne, p. 13. By M. Pauchaud.

CHAPTER VIII.

THE SOURCES OF EVIDENCE RELIED ON BY THE ANTHROPOLOGISTS TO PROVE THE ANTIQUITY OF MAN.

THE evidence for the antiquity of man is marshalled under various heads, the principal of which are: 1, the Megalithic Monuments of Europe, Africa, Asia, and America; 2, the Swiss Lake-Dwellings; 3, the Danish Shell-Mounds; 4, the Peat-Bogs of Denmark, Ireland, and France; 5, the Bone-Caverns of Europe and South America; 6, the River-Gravel or "Drift" of England and France.

To these we may add the relics found in the mud on the banks of the Nile; the fossil men alleged to have been found at Natchez and New Orleans; the human implements found in various parts of the United States in association with the remains of the mastodon, or in the so-called "drift;" and (already referred to) the long period alleged to be necessary for the formation of the different languages of mankind, for the development of the different races of man, and for the distribution of mankind over the face of the globe.

We are told that man began on this earth as a *Savage*, and that he passed through four successive ages before he became fully civilized: namely, the Palæolithic or Primitive Stone Age; the Neolithic Age or Age of Polished Stone Implements; the Bronze Age; and the Iron Age. The Dolmens and Tumuli of Europe and the Swiss Lake-Dwellings are assigned to the Neolithic, the Bronze, and the Iron Ages; the Danish Kjökken-möddings are considered still older, intermediate between the first Lake-Dwellings and the Cave-Men. The older Bone-Caves belong to the Palæolithic Age, but are regarded by some as possibly not quite so ancient as the remains found in the river-gravel of the Somme and the Thames Valleys.

What are the facts?

CHAPTER IX.

THE MEGALITHIC MONUMENTS AND TUMULI.

Found in Northern and Western Europe, in Northern Africa, in the Caucasus, the Sinaitic Peninsula, Tartary, Southern India, Arabia, Australia, Peru.—In General Sepulchral in their Character.—Assigned by the Archæologists to a Remote Antiquity.—The Large Tumuli of Brittany, the Great Circle at Avebury, and the Yorkshire Barrows, assigned by Sir J. Lubbock to the Stone Age.—Stonehenge referred to the Bronze Age.—The British Quarterly Review on Stonehenge and Avebury.—The Subject considered under the Two Heads of the Stone Circles and the Dolmens and Tumuli.—The Great Circles of England.—Penrith, Stanton Drew, Rollright, the Standing Stones of Stennis.—The Probable Age of Avebury.—Finding of Roman Coins and Iron.—Stonehenge.—Iron Armor and Roman Pottery.—Moytura in Ireland.—Assigned by Mr. Fergusson to Beginning of our Era.—The Scotch Circles.—Braavalla Heath in Östergothland.—Scene of Battle between Harald Hildetand and Sigurd Ring in A.D. 736.—The Great Barrow at Lethra, where Harald was buried.—Circles and Bauta Stones near Hwitaby, in Malmö.—Mark Battle-fields of A.D. 750 or 762.—Stiklastad in Norway also marks a Battle-Site (A.D. 1161).—The Circles at Aschenrade, near Riga.—Anglo-Saxon, Byzantine, and Kufic Coins found in the Graves (A.D. 906–1040).—The Dolmens.—The Mode of ascertaining their Age.—Flint Implements found in.—The Long-chambered Tumuli said to contain no Trace of Metal.—Review of the Tumuli noticed by Sir J. Lubbock.—Tumulus in the Island of Möen.—West Kennet.—Roman Pottery.—The Great Tumuli of Brittany.—Mont St. Michel at Carnac.—Beautiful Stone Implements.—Kerlescant.—Plouharnel.—Gold and Bronze.—Moustoir-Carnac.—Roman Tiles.—Mané er H'roëk.—Roman Medals.—Tumulus in Forest of Carnoët.—Gold and Silver Chains and Flints.—The Monuments of Locmariaker in Brittany all hewn.—The Great Monolith from the Dol ar Marchant.—Shaped of course by Metallic Tools.—The Great Tumulus of New Grange, in Ireland.—Stone Basin.—Coin of Valentinian.—Coin of Theodosius.—Gold Torques and Coin of Geta.—The Tumulus of Dowth.—Yields Iron Knives and Rings.—The Cairns at Lough Crew.—Sculptures like those at Gavr Innis.—Another Stone Basin.—Relics of Iron and Glass.—The Dolmens of France resumed.—Confolens.—Belongs to about Twelfth Century.—Crubelz.—Roman Tiles again.—Their Presence in the Dolmen considered "Accidental."—In a Neighboring Tumulus find Coin of Constantine and Two Statuettes of Latona.—The Disregard of the Evidence by the Archæologists.—The Flints found generally by the Abbé Cochet in Roman Cemeteries.—Dolmens in South of France.—The One Hundred and Forty Thousand Tumuli in Eastern France.—The Dolmens and Barrows of England.—Uley.—Roman Pottery.—The Occurrence of the Flint Implements in the Tombs under all Circumstances, and in all Parts of the World.—A Religious Sentiment associated with the Flints.—But in many Cases no Relics of any kind deposited in the Graves.—The Wiltshire and Derbyshire Barrows.—Arbor Low.—Benty Grange.—Roman Coins and Bronze Dagger.—Drinking-Cup ornamented with Silver Stars.—Numerous Examples showing the Recent Date of these Barrows.—Rev. Mr. Greenwell's Exploration of the Yorkshire Barrows.—Regarded as very Old.—Difference of Habits in Different Parts of Country.—Some more advanced than others.—Cists at Broomend,

Aberdeenshire.—Tumulus opened by Gen. Lefroy at Greenmount, in Ireland.—Bronze Plate with Runic Inscription of Ninth Century, and a Bronze Battle-axe.—Quotations from Irish Poems showing that Bronze Weapons were in Use long after Christian Era.—The Tumuli at Upsala.—Chess-man found.—Recent Date of the Tombs of Central Sweden.—The Burial-Mounds of King Gorm and his Queen at Jellinge, in Jutland (A.D. 950).—Dolmen at Heerestrup (A.D. 500–900).—Worsaae on the Bronze Age in Denmark.—In the Interments of the Early Bronze Age finds Wooden Coffins, Woollen Garments, and Bronze Swords.—Kongehoi and Treenhoi.—Worsaae fixes Beginning of Iron Age in Denmark at A.D. 200.—Burial-Mound in Lower Austria.—The Dolmens of Spain.—Antequera.—Other Examples.—Tumulus near City of Olleria in Valencia.—Bronze Coins.—No Dolmens in Italy except at Saturnia in Etruria.—The Mediterranean Islands.—Northern Africa.—Its Circles, Dolmens, Bazinas, and Couchas.—Apparently of Recent Date.—Some of them post-Christian.—Hewn Stones.—Coin of Empress Faustina.—Latin Inscription near Sidi Kacem.—Mr. Flower on the Sepulchres of Algeria.—Considers them to have been erected by the Nasamones of Herodotus.—Probably continued to be erected long after Roman Occupation.—Considers all of the Tombs later than the Romans.—The Great Burial-Mound of the Numidian Kings.—Trilithons in Tripoli.—Tumuli in Western Asia.—Were being erected in Thirteenth Century.—The Cairns, Dolmens, and Menhirs of India.—Iron in India.—The Rude Stone Monuments of the Khassia Hills, many of them erected within the past Few Years.—These Tribes surrounded by a High Civilization.—The Bhils.—The Khonds.—The Age of the Indian Monuments.—The Cross in India.

In various parts of Europe, principally in the West and North, we find certain ancient rude megalithic monuments and numerous great mounds or tumuli (often containing megalithic chambers), which have perplexed, and continue to perplex, the antiquarians. Related to these (and therefore requiring some notice), we find also humbler barrows, and certain monuments of stone which are not megalithic, and some of which are carefully and elaborately finished. In England we have Avebury and Stonehenge, and Stanton Drew, and Penrith,—great Stone Circles,—besides innumerable tumuli and barrows, and a few free-standing dolmens; in Ireland we have the circles of Moytura, the tumuli at New Grange and Dowth, the cairns at Lough Crew, the cromlechs of Glen Malin and Glen Columbkille; in Scotland we have the Clava mounds and the sculptured stones of Coilsfield and Aberlemmo; in the Orkneys, Maes-Howe and the Standing Stones of Stennis; the long barrows and circles and dolmens of Scandinavia and Germany; the one hundred and forty thousand tumuli or barrows in the east and south of France, with the dolmens of Ardèche and Poitou, and the great groups of Carnac and Locmariaker in Brittany; the Giants' Graves of Drenthe in North Holland; the dolmens of Antequera and the Tio Cagolleros in Spain; the dolmens* at Saturnia and the tumuli throughout Tuscany in Italy; the circles at Aschenrade in Livonia; the tumuli of Thrace; the Giant's Tower at Gozo in Malta; the Nurhags of Sardinia; and the Talyots of the Balearic Isles.

* The only dolmens in Italy.

Nor are these mysterious structures confined to Europe. They occur by thousands and thousands in Northern Africa,—as *bazinas*, *chouchas*, tumuli, dolmens, circles; we find them again in Palestine at Kafr en Wâl and in the Sinaitic Peninsula; we encounter them in vast numbers on the Steppes of Tartary, in Affghanistan, and on the coasts of the Black Sea; we meet them in the district of Kasim, in Arabia; in India we find them on the Khassia Hills, in the valley of the Kistnah, and thence as far south as Cape Comorin; we find the tumuli again among the mound-builders of North America, while we meet with the stone circles in Peru; and even near the Mount Elephant Plains of Australia, stone circles like those on the plain of Salisbury were found by Mr. Ormond.

Occur in Northern Africa, Western Asia, and India.

America.

Australia.

There are doubtless exceptions, but as a general rule it may be stated that all of these monuments in Europe are either places of interment or memorials of the dead.* It is true that Sir John Lubbock and other antiquaries regard Stonehenge and Avebury as *temples;* but, as Mr. Fergusson has well said, if Avebury was a temple, it was large enough to accommodate two hundred and fifty thousand people. It is more probable that they were erected to commemorate some battle. If Avebury was a temple, we may ask why not *Carnac*, which extends over several miles?

Generally Sepulchral or Cenotaphic.

These Rude Stone Monuments have been largely brought into the discussion about the Stone Age, and the Bronze Age, and the Iron Age, and nearly all the archæologists insist that a majority of them date from a remote antiquity. Sir John Lubbock assigns Avebury, for example, the barrows of Yorkshire, and the large tumuli of Brittany to the Stone Age, and remarks that "it was the examination of the tumuli which first induced Sir R. Colt Hoare, and other archæologists, to adopt for Northern Europe the division into the three great periods." Other monuments, as, for example, Stonehenge, the author of "Pre-historic Times" assigns to the Bronze Age. And others, along with all of the archæologists, he assigns to the Iron Age, and even to Saxon times.

Affirmed to be very ancient.

Some assigned to the Stone Age.

Others to the Bronze Age.

The great Swedish antiquary, Prof. Nilsson, has carefully examined Stonehenge, and, after reviewing the opinions of Stukeley, Charlton, Gibson, Brown, Thurnam, etc., decides that it was "a temple of the early fire-worshippers, and of pre-Druid origin,"—"Phœnician" in its character, and "connected with the rites of Baal, like its congeners at Tyre." M. Figuier,

Stonehenge pronounced a Temple of the Early Fire-worshippers, by Prof. Nilsson.

* It may be that the larger circles were also used as places of assembly.

who reproduces very faithfully the archæological sentiment of France, says that the tombs of the Polished Stone Age have now been "thoroughly studied," and that they "by no means belong, as has been always thought, to any historical period, that is, to the times of the Celts, for they go back to a much more remote antiquity, the prehistoric period of the Polished Stone Age."

The *British Quarterly Review*, in an article on "Pre-historic England," in 1870, spoke as follows:

The British Quarterly Review regards Stonehenge and Avebury as preceding the Pyramids.

"Stonehenge and Avebury, measured by this scale, belong to the period of megalithic, coursed, uncemented masonry. More modern than the walls of Tiryns or Mycenæ, they yet, as matter of artistic antiquity, precede the Great Pyramid." . . . . "Unless, therefore, it can be shown that the artistic knowledge of Egypt and of the Mediterranean shores was arrested in the course of travelling to England—an assumption which is at variance with the fact of the close similarity between all the circular ruins, as well as cromlechs, over the entire breadth of the Continent—*we seem to roll back the date of Stonehenge to the earliest period of the Bronze Age, and, further, to date that period before the foundation of Memphis, or, at least, before the era of that fourth Egyptian dynasty, the second king of which, it is now no longer matter of question, was the builder of the Great Pyramid.*"

Again: "Before the Julian *Gens* had its origin, or Rome herself was founded, great builders exercised their art in Britain. While wild hunters were chasing the boar on the wooded hill which is now the centre of our metropolis, and fishermen floated their coracles and leistered salmon on the sands now covered by the Palace of Westminster, a mighty race of men had overspread the swelling downs of Wiltshire with towns, and tombs, and temples. As to the origin, the duration, and the condition of that race, written history is silent. The very last link with the past, that of a corrupted and perhaps unintelligible local name, is severed."

The Passage-Graves assigned to the Stone Age.

"The Present Phase of Pre-historic Archæology" is discussed in the October number of the same Review for 1872, and we are there told that "a great many of the tumuli which lie scattered over the face of nearly every country in Europe, may also fairly be assigned to the Neolithic Age. Those which contain a stone chamber with a passage leading to it, named 'Gang-graben' by Nilsson, 'gallery-graves' by Dr. Thurnam, have been found alike in Scandinavia, France, and Britain, *and in no authenticated instance have furnished articles of bronze or iron where they have not been previously disturbed.*" (The italics are ours.)

We propose in the present chapter to discuss this question, and the general question of the age of these stone monuments, and we have made the foregoing citations in order to place the issue distinctly before the reader.

We will first consider the Stone Circles, and then take up the Dolmens and Tumuli.*

Division of the subject.

There are numbers of barrows which contain no stone chambers or dolmens. These of course are not megalithic monuments, but the gap is not a wide one between them and the chambered tumuli. They may be older, or they may be more recent, than the stone monuments; but *reasoning* on this subject is idle, and is the mistake of the archæologists; it is a matter to be decided by the *facts*, and not by *a priori* speculation. In India, as Mr. Fergusson says, within sight of the ancient city of Ougein,—the residence of Asoka 260 B.C.—famous in the days of the Greeks—the city chosen by Jey Sing for one of his observatories in the reign of Akbar,—are found tribes of Bhils with their bows and arrows, living as their fathers did some thousands of years ago,—acknowledged now as "lords of the soil," and each new-comer to the throne confirming his title by "receiving the tika at the hands of the nomad." So the Khassias of India are noted for their expertness in extracting iron from the ore and manufacturing it afterwards, and yet these people adhere at this day to the practice of erecting rude unhewn stone monuments. An archæologist, two thousand years hence, encountering the long lines of menhirs on the Khassia Hills, would scout the idea of their having been erected within sight of the temples of Kamarupa and the mosques of Sylphet. Therefore, we say, we are unwilling to speculate *a priori* that men have buried in the plain barrows first, and in the chambered tumuli afterwards. We prefer to make it all a matter of observation, and, in forming our opinions, to pursue the manner of Lord Bacon rather than that of Mr. Darwin.

---

* There is much confusion among the writers on this subject in the use of the terms dolmen, cromlech, and cairn. We define a dolmen to be a stone chamber, composed of (in general) three sides and a cap-stone. Sometimes they are covered up by a mound or tumulus; at others they are exposed or free-standing dolmens.

A cromlech (from *crom*, a circle, and *lech*, a stone) means a stone circle; but the term is only applied to sepulchres surrounded by a circle of stones, and not to the great monumental circles like Avebury and Stonehenge. A cairn is a heap of stones raised over a grave. But we find these stone-heaps sometimes surrounded (as at Moytura) by stone circles, and the term cairn still employed to designate them.

Besides the great stone circles there are groups and avenues of stones, as at Carnac, in Brittany, and near Merivale Bridge, on Dartmoor.

A menhir means literally "a long stone." They occur most frequently in clusters or rows.

THE STONE CIRCLES.

The Great Circles find their most marked development in England and the Orkneys. Less important circles occur in Scotland, Ireland, Scandinavia, Southern France, Algeria, Western Asia, Australia, Peru. There was undoubtedly a Circle-building Race. The Great Circles, deserving of special mention, are those of Avebury, Stonehenge, Penrith, Rollright, Stanton Drew, the Ring of Brogar, and Stennis. There are also circles—some of them mere rings—at Aspatria, Mule Hill (Isle of Man), Moytura (Ireland), Callernish (Isle of Lewis), Braavalla, Hwitaby, Stiklastad, Aschenrade, etc., etc. These last differ among themselves in plan, and most of them differ also essentially in type from such monuments as Stonehenge or Stennis. In many instances, of course, there is nothing to fix the date of these circles, and the remark is equally true of the dolmens and tumuli. The most reliable criterion of the age of a tomb is its contents; and it is by scrutinizing these contents that the archæologists ordinarily assign one of these structures to the Stone, the Bronze, or the Iron Age. But often the barrows and the cists and the dolmens contain nothing; very frequently they have been plundered; and so we are necessarily restricted in any discussion of the subject.

Method of determining the age of the monuments.

The manner in which the remains have been interred—as whether the skeleton has been deposited in an extended or sitting posture, or incineration practised—is also relied on by the antiquarians; but we regard this as depending also on the particular race to which the interment belongs, and on other considerations.

We can sometimes decide that a particular monument belongs to the metal age by the presence of hewn or shaped stones. Sometimes we can attach more or less importance to the *tradition* associated with the place.

Thus, among the Great Circles named—seven in number—we find at four of them no remains at all; and yet with regard to two of these we have traditions connecting them (like Stonehenge) with recent characters or events. These two are Penrith and Stanton Drew.

At Penrith, one of the circles bears the name of "King Arthur's Round Table," while the monument at Stanton Drew is linked with a tradition which represents that Keyna, a holy virgin of the fifth century, the daughter apparently of a Welsh prince, by her prayers converted the deadly serpents that infested this region into the stones now standing on this spot. At Penrith, too, attached to one of the circles is a stone, about twelve feet high, called Long Meg, which appears to be *hewn*. Of Rollright we have no information. Of the Standing Stones of Stennis (to which we shall recur

Penrith and Stanton Drew.

again) we know this, that in the neighborhood is the great monument of Maes-Howe, which probably belongs to the ninth century; and near by, some six or seven conoid barrows, in which were found silver torques and other ornaments similar to those found at Skail Bay, in the vicinity, along with coins of Athelstane (A.D. 925) and the caliphs of Bagdad (887 to 945). These graves are quite certainly Scandinavian, as is in all probability Maes-Howe.*

Stennis.

Of Avebury it has been said that "it did as much exceed Stonehenge as a cathedral does a parish church." The stones here are unhewn, while those at Stonehenge have been shaped by the axe. The diameter of the enclosing vallum is twelve hundred feet. Within this vallum of earth ran a ditch, and along the inner edge of this

Avebury.

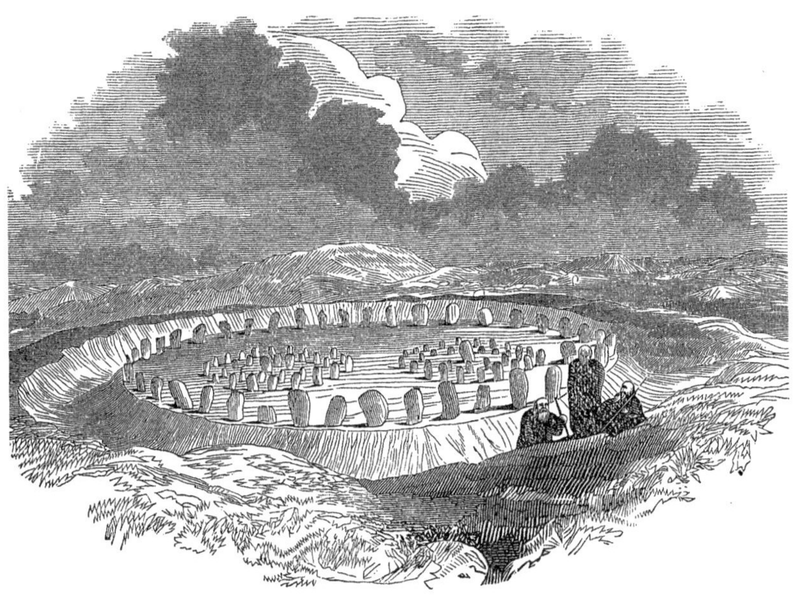

GENERAL VIEW OF AVEBURY—RESTORED.

ditch stood about one hundred vast upright stones, inside of which were two other double circles of stones. These stones measured from fifteen to seventeen feet in height, with a thickness of about thirteen feet. From the outer vallum ran a stone avenue perfectly straight for nearly a mile. There are two other members of the Avebury group,—the double

---

* We should state, however, that there are near Stennis also a few bowl-shaped barrows containing interments by cremation; and these barrows occur in great numbers in the neighboring parish. They are different from the monuments referred to, and belong doubtless to the ancient population.

circle on Hakpen Hill, and the famous Silbury Hill, about a mile south from Avebury. The antiquaries, as we have said, assign these great stones to the Neolithic Age,—about the time that Menes reigned in Egypt. We know of no warrant for this. The evidences point the other way. Nearly two centuries ago Lord Stawell levelled a portion of the vallum, and we learn from Dr. Stukeley, the well-known antiquarian of that day, that he found large quantities of buckhorns, burned bones, oyster-shells, etc.; and it is added that "some Roman coins were accidentally found in and about Abury," and that he "was informed a square bit of iron was taken up under one of the great stones upon pulling it down." It is stated that other Roman coins have been found since; but there is no authentic record of the fact. At Hakpen Hill a large number of skeletons were found in 1685, and in the great tumulus of Silbury Hill, the third member of this group, near the summit, an iron bridle-bit and traces of armor were found in Stukeley's time. We raise thus a strong presumption of the Roman or post-Roman date of this great circle. The "square bit of iron" found under one of the great stones "upon pulling it down" must be cotemporary with the monument.

Roman coins.

Iron.

Mr. Fergusson thinks Avebury commemorates the battle of Badon Hill, fought by King Arthur in the year 520.

This author urges with great force another argument for the post-Roman date of this structure. It is recognized that Silbury Hill is a member of the same group. This great mound (the largest in Europe) is a truncated straight-lined cone, while all the British tumuli known are "domical," or at least curvilinear in section. There are in England nearly one hundred examples of truncated regular cones (apart from this), every one of which is post-Roman, and there is no example of such cones which is pre-Roman. This fact of itself is almost conclusive; but we must combine with it the finding of the iron bridle-bit and the traces of armor in the mound.

Stonehenge.

Stonehenge, from some cause,—perhaps its more finished character and its better state of preservation,—is far more famous than even Avebury. It has been the subject of speculation and wonder in England among the antiquaries of the past three hundred years. It is situated in the county of Wilts (not far from Avebury), and consisted originally of two concentric circles of stones, enclosing certain interior groups, whose character and position have been matter of dispute. The diameter of the outer stone circle is *exactly* one hundred Roman feet. Surrounding these stone circles is a vallum of much larger dimensions, its diameter being about three hundred feet. The outer circle of stones consisted originally of thirty upright stones, all hewn, with an average height of fourteen feet, their sides being seven feet by three feet. Each of these uprights has tenons on its upper end, on which were laid horizontal stones or imposts, with mortises to correspond with the tenons; and these imposts being connected together formed a continuous circular architrave all around the enclosed area. Within the circles are five great *trilithons*, the great central one being nearly twenty-two feet high. Stukeley fixes the date of this monument at 400 B.C. That it belongs to the age of *iron* is clear to our mind from the character of the work which has been done on the great masses of hard rock of which it is constructed.

We have already mentioned that *tradition* assigns the circles and avenues at Stanton Drew to the fifth century, while one of the circles at Penrith comes down to us associated with the name of King Arthur.* These traditions show us at least the era to which in past ages the popular belief referred these monuments, and it is a circumstance of no inconsiderable weight that such local traditions represented them to have been erected subsequent to Roman times. With regard to Stonehenge, Geoffrey of Monmouth, in his history of Britain, in the twelfth century, followed by all the subsequent chroniclers, tells us that Ambrosius, the successor of Vortigern, with the aid of Merlin, "erected Stonehenge" as a monument to three hundred British nobles treacherously slain by Hengist, about A.D. 462. He also tells us that the stones were brought by Merlin from Ireland, to which country they had previously been brought from Africa. And this part of the story is repeated in A.D. 1187 by Giraldus Cambrensis. Geoffrey of Monmouth also informs us that Ambrosius was buried "near the convent of Ambrius within the Giant's Dance, which in his lifetime he had commanded to be made;" and again that Constantine, the successor of Arthur, was killed by Conan, "and buried close to Uther Pendragon, within the structure of stones which was set up with wonderful art, not far from Salisbury, and called in the English tongue Stonehenge." And, lastly, similar statements are found in the triads of the Welsh bards.

The tradition of Stonehenge. Geoffrey of Monmouth.

Geoffrey of Monmouth may be, as is replied to this, a great romancer, and, like his cotemporaries, he may have believed in Merlin;† but, unless there is some *evidence* that Stonehenge is several thousand years older than he represents it to be, it is fair to presume that the date of the monument is, at least, not very widely removed from the period to which he assigns it. He lived only two hundred and fifty years after Alfred the

* So at Aylesford (as we shall see)—the scene of the battle in 455 between Vortigern and Hengist and Horsa—tradition affirms one of the monuments (Kit's Cotty House) to be over the grave of Catigern, and another, Horstead, to be over the grave of Horsa,—both of whom were slain in this battle.

† He was the first to collect Merlin's prophecies.

Great, and there had been a succession of British and Saxon chroniclers before him,—Ingulphus, Ethelward, Asser, Bede, Nennius (from whom a part of this story is taken), and Gildas, who (A.D. 500) described the conquest of Britain by the Saxons.* Surely such a line of chroniclers implies intelligence and observation, and, while there may be gross inaccuracies and foolish stories, and wide mistakes with regard to the dates of distant events, it is impossible, it appears to us, for even the later writers of that age to have referred a monument as important as Stonehenge to the fifth century, if it really belonged to the age of the Pyramids. If they had sources of information, they would know; if they did not have them, according to all analogy, they would have given a *remote* rather than a *recent* date. With regard to objects of mystery, touching which men are uninformed, the imagination—and particularly in a rude age—invests them with the associations of antiquity,—never, where the object is conspicuous and of an important character, with the vivid environment of the present.†

Possibly, Stonehenge was erected long before the irruptions of the Saxons from the mouth of the Elbe; but it is incredible that it had been standing there thousands of years before the date to which tradition assigns it. Avebury and Stonehenge were as conspicuous in their day as the Pyramids were in the days of the Pharaohs, or as the Coliseum was in Imperial Rome. They were not events which had occurred and of which no record was kept: they were everlasting and ever-present monuments; and to confound them, if they were hoary with the Bronze Age and the Stone Age, with the times of Hengist and Horsa and Arthur, is an anachronism on the part of Geoffrey of Monmouth, and those who went before him, that cannot be accepted until the strongest evidence is adduced to prove it.

The statements of Geoffrey of Monmouth are too explicit and circumstantial to be lightly set aside. He not only tells us that the celebrated British hero Aurelius Ambrosius (he was of Roman descent) erected Stonehenge, but he adds that he was buried there; and then that Constantine, the nephew and successor of Arthur (who succeeded Ambrosius), was also buried there "close to Uther Pendragon." Giraldus Cambrensis, as far as he goes, corroborates Geoffrey's statement.

Both of them state that the stones were brought from Ireland. Now, among the stones within the area enclosed by the circles are certain *blue stones* (eleven of them still remain), all of which are cut from igneous rocks not found in this region, but which are found in Corn-

---

* We are aware that the age or the genuineness of the chronicles of Ingulphus, Nennius, and Gildas has been disputed.

† Tradition is wonderfully tenacious. The *Birs-Nimrûd* (the Citadel of Nimrod) commemorates in its name the site of the Tower of Babel,—a fact only recently ascertained.

wall and Ireland. The rest of the stones are a siliceous sandstone found in the vicinity. The probability is that only the Blue Stones (which are about seven feet long) were brought from Ireland; the pattern of the whole structure (as suggested by Mr. Fergusson) also coming from the same quarter.

Iron armor.

Roman pottery.

Arrow-head of iron.

Let us, however, ascertain whether we find anything in the way of relics here to correspond with the Roman coins and the objects of iron found at Avebury. We are told by Aubrey that in 1620 the Duke of Buckingham, "when King James was at Wilton, did cause the middle of Stonehenge to be digged, and this underdigging was the cause of the falling down and recumbencie of the great stone there." This was at the great central trilithon. What did they obtain here? They "found," we are told, "a great many bones of stagges and oxen, charcoal, batter dashes, *heads of arrows, and some pieces of armor eaten out with rust.*" These arrow-heads and pieces of armor, which were "eaten out with rust," must have been of *iron*. Sir R. Colt Hoare also dug here, and remarks, "We have found in digging several fragments of *Roman* as well as coarse British pottery, parts of the head and horns of deer and other animals, and *a large barbed arrow-head of iron.*" Mr. Cunnington also found "near the altar," at the depth of about three feet, some Roman pottery. Soon after the fall of the great trilithon in 1797 he dug out some of the earth that had fallen into the excavation, and "found fragments of fine black Roman pottery, and since then another piece on the same spot." This is precisely similar to the finding of "the bit of iron" under one of the great stones at Avebury. When this evidence is combined with the accounts of Geoffrey of Monmouth and Giraldus Cambrensis, and with the manner in which the stones are cut, and mortised, and fitted, it leaves an impression that cannot be removed by vague theories about the Stone or the Bronze Age. And this is greatly strengthened by the finding of exactly similar relics at Avebury.

Aylesford.

One of the most important groups of stones in England is that near Aylesford, on the Medway, in the county of Kent. This group (which we mention here for convenience, although they are not circles) includes the celebrated Kit's Cotty House; the monument known as the Countless Stones (about five hundred yards south of Kit's Cotty House); a line of great stones, in the rear of the foregoing, extending from a place called Spring Farm, three-quarters of a mile, to a place known as Hale Farm; and several collections of stones at Addington, on the opposite bank of the river, about five miles west of Aylesford. There are also some smaller monuments of a sepulchral character near Kit's Cotty House, situated on the brow of the hill above it.

It will be perceived, therefore, that these remains extend over a very considerable area. Some of the stones are nineteen feet high. We know that a battle* was fought on this spot in the year 455 between Vortigern and Hengist and Horsa, in which Catigern was slain on the side of the Britons, and the redoubted Horsa fell on that of the Saxons; and Mr. Fergusson expresses the opinion that it is, at least, extremely probable that these stones commemorate this conflict, and mark the sepulchres of the slain.

Tradition represents Kit's Cotty House to be the tomb of Catigern, while the neighboring tumulus at Horstead has been always called the grave of Horsa.

This tumulus has been examined. It yielded no relic of either stone or metal; but it was ascertained that a cremation had been performed on the natural surface of the ground, and a tumulus raised over it. Now, we learn from the Anglo-Saxon poem of "Beowulf" (written not long before this date) that after Beowulf's death, his body was burned, and a great mound raised over the spot "on the surface of the ground."

Whether the conjecture in question be true or not, no great antiquity can be assigned to such a monument as this in Britain:

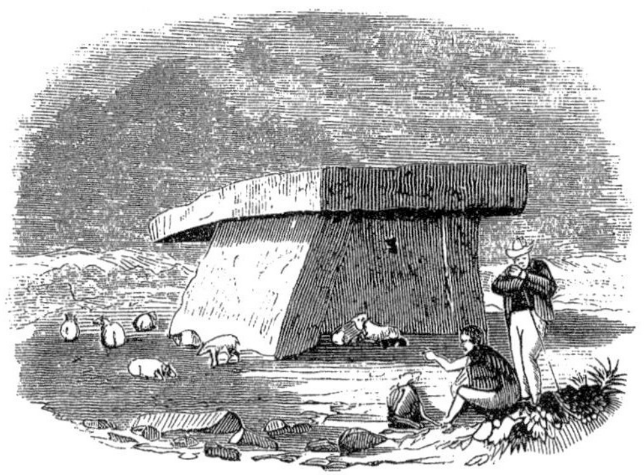

KIT'S COTTY HOUSE.

No rude tools, it is obvious to any unprejudiced eye, ever shaped these stones; or those which are represented on the following page.

The monuments at Northern and Southern Moytura, in Ireland, are not circles resembling those we have been considering. They are, for the most part, cairns or dolmens surrounded by circles of rude stones. They mark the sites of two battles in which the natives of the island were defeated by invaders from Scandinavia,

Ireland. Moytura.

* The battle of Ægeles-ford.

who no doubt erected these memorials. Mr. Fergusson assigns them to about the beginning of the Christian era. There is no evidence except the Irish annals, which are very confused; and the discovery of some flint implements, and a very elegant earthen urn. But the fact that the invaders came from the Northern Seas, and the character of the pottery, exclude the idea of a very remote date.

The circles of Scotland are very numerous, and, it is worthy of remark, occur in the North; there are none in the lowlands, or south of the Frith of Forth and Clyde. But it is not on the mainland at all, but in the Northern and Western Isles that they chiefly

Scotland.

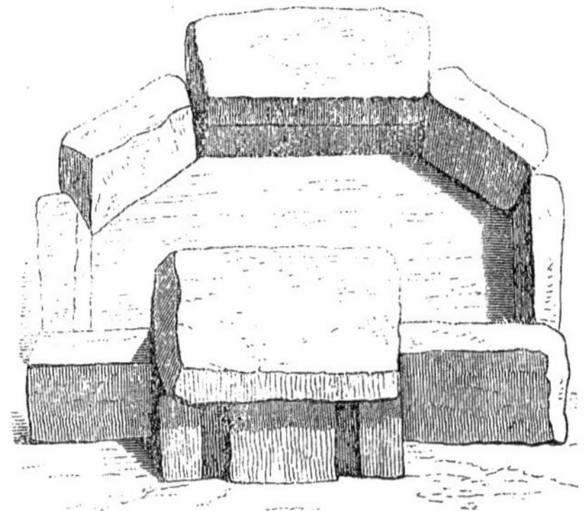

COUNTLESS STONES, AYLESFORD.

abound. This is one of the circumstances which convince us that the circle-building race came—one branch of them—from Scandinavia (whither they came originally from the East). Such evidence as we have with regard to the date of the construction of the Scotch circles, leads us to the conclusion that they possess no claim to antiquity.

The most celebrated of these monuments is that of Stennis, in the Orkneys, where also we find the Ring of Brogar (three hundred and forty feet in diameter). The Standing Stones of Stennis* are connected probably, as we have said, with the grand tumulus of Maes-Howe, and with certain conoid barrows near by. These barrows contained silver torques and other ornaments. Mr. Fergusson assigns Maes-Howe to between 800 and 1000 A.D. He goes into an extended discussion on the subject, and proves, we think, beyond all reasonable doubt, that it is a Norwegian monument of about this date. These islands were conquered by Harold Harfagar in 875. There are two other important barrows in the islands, one of which has been identified as having been

* The remains of a *dolmen* still exist within the circle.

raised by Torf Einar, a Norwegian Jarl, about A.D. 925, while we know further that another Jarl, Thorfin, "was buried on Ronaldshay under a tumulus." We know also that King Gorm and Thyra (his queen) of Denmark were buried in tumuli, resembling Maes-Howe, in 950. We know also that Havard "the happy," the son of Thorfin, was slain in battle at Stennis, and that the place afterwards went by the name of Havard-steigar. Professor Munch, of Christiania, who visited the island in 1849, arrived at the conclusion "that most of the grave-mounds [those containing the silver torques] grouped around the Brogar circle are, probably, memorials of this battle, and perhaps one of the larger [which we take to be Maes-Howe] that of Havard Earl."

The masonry of the chamber of Maes-Howe is of a character that compels us, also, to assign to it a comparatively recent date. It could never have been executed, in pre-Christian times, by the rude and barbarous natives of the Orkneys.

On a stone attached to the tumulus of King Gorm, at Jellinge, in Denmark, is sculptured, in admirable style, the figure of a dragon. A similar drawing occurs on a pillar facing the entrance of the chamber at Maes-Howe.

Among the Stennis group there is a Holed Stone, by joining hands through which the oath to Woden was taken as late as 1781, and of which Mr. Fergusson remarks that "it was certainly set up by Northmen and by them dedicated to Woden."

But the resemblance of these Orkney circles to the Great Circles of England is too striking not to suggest that they cannot be separated in point of time by many centuries. A broad ditch runs around the stones of Stennis as well as those of Brogar circle. The Ring of Brogar has a diameter of one hundred metres; the large circle at Stanton Drew has a diameter of one hundred metres. The stones of Stennis have a diameter of one hundred feet; one of the two smaller circles of Stanton Drew has a diameter of one hundred feet. The Stennis circle contains a dolmen; the corresponding circle at Stanton Drew contains a dolmen. So that the circles of Stanton Drew are the counterpart of the circles of Stennis and Brogar. There are detached stones associated with both groups. At Stanton Drew we have the fortified hill of Maes-Knoll occupying the same position with regard to it that Maes-Howe does to the circle of Stennis.

We might point out resemblances between these Orkney circles and those at Penrith, Avebury, and elsewhere in England.

Other circles in Scotland are those of Callernish, on the Isle of Lewis, of Tormore, on the Isle of Arran, those in Aberdeenshire, and elsewhere. All the information that we have about their age is the statement of Mr. John Stuart, that articles of bronze, mingled with implements of flint, have been found in many of the Scottish circles;* and the statement of Prof. Wilson, that a funicular rod or torque of gold was dug up within the great circle of Leys (near Inverness) in 1824.†

Scandinavia. Braavalla Heath.

Braavalla Heath, in Östergothland, is well known as the scene of the battle in which the blind old king Harald Hildetand was defeated and killed by his nephew Sigurd Ring. The date of this event is A.D. 736.

The numerous small circles on this field, there is no doubt, says Mr. Fergusson, are memorials of this battle. They number as many as fifty or seventy-five, and they resemble those of Moytura. According to the Saga, after the battle Sigurd Ring caused a search to be made for the body of his uncle, which he afterwards buried in a tumulus which he caused to be raised at Lethra, Harald's capital in Seeland. This was mentioned by Saxo Grammaticus in 1236, and never doubted, says Fergusson, until the Museum authorities of Copenhagen found some "wedges of flint" in the tomb, which decided them to refer it to the Stone Period.

Hwitaby, A.D. 750.

Stiklastad, A.D. 1030.

Other examples.

There are two groups of circles and Bauta stones near Hwitaby, in Malmö. These are said to mark two battle-fields in which Ragnar Lothbrok gained victories over his rebellious subjects in Scania, A.D. 750 and 762. At Stiklastad, in Norway, is a group of forty-four circles, said to mark the site of a battle in 1030 between Knut the Great and Olof the Holy. At Uppland, in Denmark, the Danish prince Magnus Henricksson was slain by Carl Sverkersson, in the year 1161, and the place is marked by twenty stone circles and ovals, most of them enclosing mounds, and two square enclosures, thirty to forty feet in diameter. Another group is said to mark the spot where, in 1150, a Swedish heroine, Blenda, overcame the Danish king Swen Grate. It is impossible that since the twelfth century these stories could have been invented. It is tradition or history fortified by monuments; and the cases are too numerous for any mistake to exist about it.

Aschenrade.

Within fifty miles of Riga, in Livonia, there is an extensive group of these circles, at Aschenrade, on the banks of the Dwina. They remind us at once of the circles in Algeria. It appears to be a cemetery, rather than a battle-field. In these graves enormous wealth of bronze and other metal was found, which consisted in part of great numbers of coins and iron implements. The coins were German coins dating from A.D. 936 to 1040; Anglo-Saxon, from 991 to 1036; Byzantine, from 911 to 1025; and Arabic or Kufic, from 906 to 999.

Coins, A.D. 906–1040.

---

* Internat. Cong. Prehist. Arch., 1868, p. 30. † Prehist. Annals Scot., vol. i. p. 163.

The circles in Algiers may be considered in connection with the discussion of the dolmens and other stone monuments of that region.

THE DOLMENS AND TUMULI.

Dolmens.

Very few dolmens, strictly so called, exist in England,—hardly half a dozen. They are numerous in Denmark and North Germany. Some very fine ones are found in Ireland. In France they abound in the west and southwest; but not one is found in the departments of the Côte-d'Or, Vosges, Haut-Rhin, Bas-Rhin, Doubs, Jura, and Ain, where, on the other hand, there are computed to be one hundred and forty thousand tumuli. They are found also in Spain, in Portugal, and elsewhere.

The Three Ages.

We have represented to the reader that archæologists speak of three ages: the Stone Age (Palæolithic and Neolithic); the Bronze Age; and the Iron Age. If a tomb contains only stone implements, they refer it to the Stone Age. If it contains only bronze, they refer it to the Bronze Age, etc. It was the custom among the ancients, and is the custom now among many savages and semi-civilized races, to place weapons, ornaments, vases, and other objects, in the grave. A warrior was buried with his arrow and spear heads, his helmet, or his horse; a female was buried with her beads and necklaces; and with both we find the funeral urns and vases. Coins occur also occasionally in the tombs.

Mode of interment.

The occurrence of the "flints," and the absence of metal, is the great point with the archæologists. The mode of interment (as we have stated) is also another criterion appealed to: thus, Sir John Lubbock states that in the Iron Age it was the custom to deposit the corpse in an extended posture, and that all cases where the skeleton is found so extended may be confidently referred to this period. In the Neolithic Age he tells us it was usual to bury the body in a sitting or contracted posture, while the prevailing mode in the Bronze Age was cremation.*

Long-chambered tumuli.

The form and construction of the tomb are also regarded as characteristic of particular epochs. Thus, the long-chambered tumuli are all referred to the Stone Age.† "No trace of metal," says Sir John Lubbock, "has yet been found in this class of tumulus." This statement is repeated, as we have seen, by the Reviewer in the *British Quarterly* for October, 1872. "Those which contain a stone chamber with a passage leading to it, named 'ganggraben' by Nilsson, 'gallery-graves' by Dr. Thurnam, have been found alike in Scandinavia, France, and Britain, *and in no authenticated*

* But see paper by Mr. Pennington, Nature, July 2, 1874, p. 177.

† Prehistoric Times, pp. 136, 152.

instance have furnished articles of bronze or iron where they have not been previously disturbed."

We shall proceed now to notice the DOLMENS and TUMULI at length, beginning with those selected by Sir John Lubbock as special representatives of the Stone Age.

Tumulus on island of Möen.

The first which he mentions is a chambered tumulus on the island of Möen in Denmark, where a great number of beautiful stone axes, spear-heads, chisels, etc., were found. Here in the mound they found cists containing burnt bones, a bent knife, a pair of pincers, and various other objects of bronze. In the main chamber below they found the stone implements, amber beads, and fragments of pottery, "ornamented with points and lines." The objects in the upper stratum, says Sir John Lubbock, "belong to the Bronze Age," and it is "evident," he says, that these interments were "secondary." Perhaps so. The original sepulchral chamber he regards as much more ancient; he selects it as a clear instance of a Stone Age interment. "Not the smallest fragment of metal was found either in the chamber or in the passage." (Prehistoric Times, Amer. ed., p. 161.) We have not access to the work from which this account is taken, and can only be guided by Sir John's own account. From that account we learn that the sepulchral chamber was quite a grand affair, eight and a half ells in length, twenty and a half in circumference, and about two and a half in height,—the walls consisting of twelve very large unhewn stones,—the roof of five great blocks. The passage leading to the chamber was five ells long and one broad, and formed by eleven side-stones and three roof-stones. Sir John has a diagram of this chamber. "About the middle," he tells us, "not far from the bottom, a skeleton was extended (at *b*), with the head towards the north." The other skeletons (with one exception) were in a sitting posture.

Indications of a recent date.

We have pointed out that Sir John Lubbock (see his work, p. 157) lays it down that "those cases in which the skeleton was extended may be referred, with little hesitation, to the Age of Iron." In the present case, in the lowest part of this chambered tumulus the *central* corpse is *extended*, and Sir John Lubbock must decide which half of his theory must be withdrawn. Nor is this all. We perceive from the cut given by Sir J. Lubbock on page 158, that the inner face of the great stones of the chamber and passage-way of this tomb was *smooth*, and it is, at least, most probable that they had been split and prepared with metal tools. This is a feature observable in all of the long-chambered tumuli of Denmark,* and of itself makes it very questionable whether they should be referred to the Stone Age.

* See Worsaae's Primeval Antiq., p. 92.

The second proof-case selected by Sir John Lubbock is the fine tumulus near West Kennet, in Wiltshire, described by Dr. Thurnam. This tumulus is three hundred and thirty-six feet in length, forty feet wide at the west end and seventy-five feet at the east, and about eight feet high. It is a long-chambered tumulus like the preceding. The find here, according to Lubbock, consisted of four skeletons, "chalk rubble, containing also bones of animals, flint implements, and fragments of pottery." There were nearly "three hundred flint flakes in different parts of the chamber, three or four flint cores, a whetstone, a scraper, part of a bone pin, a bead of Kimmeridge shale, etc.;" a veritable "flint find;" and it is only necessary to add that the "pottery" referred to was exceedingly abundant, and that a portion of it *was Roman pottery.* Besides which, the bead of "Kimmeridge shale" indicates no early date, as we may learn from Mr. Evans's recent work on "Ancient Stone Implements."

West Kennet.

Roman pottery.

The next example of Sir John Lubbock is "the large tumuli of Brittany," most of which, he says, "belong probably to the Stone Age."

The large tumuli of Brittany.

He singles out Mont St. Michel at Carnac and Mané er H'roëk (a few miles off) at Locmariaker. The former contained magnificent celts of jade and fibrolite, nine pendants in jasper, with some in turquoise, all polished and pierced so as to form a necklace. This was all. The human bones had perished. The ornaments do not seem to imply a very ancient date, but we are left in the dark. Some light, however, is thrown on the subject by a precisely similar tumulus, about a hundred paces off, at Kerlescant, where some "very fine" pottery was found; and by a double dolmen, about a mile and a half off, at Plouharnel, in which beautiful ornaments of gold and bronze were found. And to this we may add that about a half-mile off, in another direction, at Moustoir-Carnac, in a tumulus two hundred and eighty feet in length, M. René Galles, in 1865, found upon the roof of the chamber within a number of *Roman tiles.*

Mont St. Michel.

Kerlescant.

Plouharnel.

Moustoir-Carnac.

In the Mané er H'roëk, but near the surface, eleven medals of the Roman emperors from Tiberius to Trajan were found, together with fragments of bronze, glass, and pottery, but no signs of a secondary interment. We shall have occasion to notice the occurrence of Roman coins or medals near the top of these tumuli again, in England as well as in France. The archæologists dispose of them by saying that they are found above the chamber, and not in it. Perhaps we shall find them *in* it; but for the present it may suffice to remark that nearly all of these "chambers" have been rifled, and it is not to be expected that the coins should be

Mané er H'roëk.

Roman medals.

left. The "flints" are of no use, and they remain. But the Roman coins (always Roman—*never* British, or Gaulish, or Christian) occur too often in this position for it to be accidental. It is at all events unfortunate for Sir John Lubbock that in one of the four cases which he singled out from ten thousand as unquestionable examples of very ancient tumuli, we should find the corpse extended as in the Iron Age, and hewn stones; that in another we should find in the very chamber itself fragments of Roman pottery; that in juxtaposition with the third we should find Roman tiles and ornaments of gold and bronze and beautiful pottery; and that in the fourth we should find the effigies of the early Roman emperors.

We have noticed all of the examples discussed in detail by Sir John Lubbock, in order that we might not appear to avoid the precise issue presented by the archæologists.

Forest of Carnoët.

Relics of gold, silver, bronze, iron, and flint.

The Rev. W. C. Lukis, in a paper on the dolmens of Brittany, describes a round tumulus in the forest of Carnoët, Finistère, which was faced within with artificially squared walling stones, and which contained gold and silver chains, silver-plated bronze daggers, and flint arrow points.

In the *Eclectic Magazine* for January, 1844, there is an account of this same "tomb of stones," as it is called, quoted from the *Athenæum*. In this earlier account we have it mentioned that the tomb contained "a number of small arrows of sharp and transparent flint, a sword, and three lance-heads, one of silver." The material of the sword is not stated, but it was doubtless iron.

Sir John Lubbock (p. 20) informs us that "silver and lead do not occur in Bronze Age finds." This tomb, therefore, belongs to the Iron Age,—as is proved also by the sword.

We perceive also from these relics that the "bronze daggers" continued in use in the Iron Age,—a fact the importance of which will appear more clearly hereafter.

We remark, thirdly, that we find here in this recent tomb flint, bronze, and iron associated,—the three ages all co-existing at once.

We have an account of some further explorations in the dolmens or tumuli of Brittany in the "Matériaux pour l'Histoire de l'Homme" for 1873. These were made at Le Rocher, in Plougoumelen, on the Auray river, near the hamlet of Knoz, where a dolmen and a tumulus were opened. The locality is not very far from Carnac. Close together at this spot stand some seven monuments, tumuli or dolmens, among them the great *tumulus à dolmen* ordinarily called the "dolmen du Rocher." The dolmen of which we now speak is a member of this group. It is a "galleried" dolmen, and is surrounded by a circle of stones nearly forty feet in diameter. Digging into this tomb, M. Galles found, as he informs us, several dozens of bronze bracelets. Continuing his explorations, he subsequently opened one of the tumuli. At the bottom of this mound was found *a bronze vase*, twenty-six centimetres (ten inches) in diameter in its largest part. And we are told that the rim of this vase is surrounded by a thick wire of *iron*.

Before leaving Brittany (whose megalithic monuments are regarded as particularly ancient) we wish to remark that the extraordinary stone monuments of Locmariaker are all *shaped* or *hewn*, and the walls of many of them sculptured. We do not see how it is possible for the stones of such a monument as the grand Dol ar Marchant, and its great fallen obelisk, sixty-four feet long and thirteen in diameter, to have been shaped except by metallic tools.* And so of the holes in one of the stones at Gavr Innis, and the trough sunk below them; as Mr. Fergusson observes, it would appear that they could only be formed by a tool which would bear a blow on the head.†

Locmariaker Hewn Stones.

The beautiful perforated stone axes have also been found in the dolmens of Brittany, which unquestionably, it appears to us, must have been worked with iron or bronze. It may be *possible*, "with the patience and the leisure of a savage," to drill these holes with a wetted stick dipped in sand, but among all the finely-wrought implements of modern savages there are no examples of perforated stone axes (intended for service) without the aid of metal. The battle-axes of the American Indians (who were most skilful in the manufacture of their stone weapons and implements) were "fastened in a cleft piece of wood," says Father Hennepin, "with leather thongs." The stone axes of the American savages, says Lafitau, "are prepared by the process of grinding on a sandstone, and finally assume, at the sacrifice of much time and labor, nearly the shape of our axes, or of a wedge for splitting wood. The life of a savage is often insufficient for accomplishing the work. . . . When the stone is finished, the difficulty of providing it with a handle arises. They select a young tree, of which they make a handle, without cutting it. They split one end and insert the stone. The tree grows, tightens around it, and encloses it so firmly that it hardly can be torn out."

Perforated stone axes.

A few examples of perforated stone axes among the "Southern

---

* Mr. S. P. Oliver (as we have seen since this was written), in *Nature*, May 2, 1872, states that the fallen Menhir at the Dol ar Marchant, which Mr. Fergusson considers two *obelisks*, and not one, are "fragments of one huge monolith, which was, moreover, artificially fashioned, and, possibly, originally actually polished." Mr. Oliver also states that the sculptured celts at Gavr Innis are *in relief*.

Of course this work was not done with stone tools.

† The dolmen of Gavr Innis is constructed of large hewn blocks. A representation of it may be seen in Figuier's "Primitive Man," Amer. edit., Fig. 135, p. 187.

Indians" are given in his elaborate and excellent work by Mr. Jones; but he tells us that, "fashioned principally of a talcose slate, they were utterly unfit for service, and must be regarded as ornamental or ceremonial axes." Some of them, he says, were made of steatite or soapstone. Occasionally they seem to have been made of a hard stone, but the perforations seem to have been only a half-inch in diameter, and about one and one-third inches in depth. These, he says, also appear to have been intended for mere ceremony, as "so small is the perforation that no handle, other than one of metal, could prove at all lasting or serviceable." *

We know of no example from Polynesia where the stone axe was perforated to receive the handle; the custom there was to lash the axe to the handle.

Even the Mound-Builders, as we are told by Dr. Foster, attached their stone axes to the helve by "inserting the axe-head in a cleft stick, and binding it firmly with a leather thong or a deer's sinew." "It is not unusual," he adds, "to meet with perforated objects which are chiselled as axes, but when we consider the character of the material, a green-colored siliceous slate of a banded structure, ill adapted to stand repeated shocks, we are led to the conclusion that they were designed for ornament and not for use." †

Pipes made of very hard stones frequently occur in the graves of the Mound-Builders; but these pipes often represent animals or birds peculiar to South America, and we must infer, therefore, that the Mound-Builders trafficked, directly or indirectly, with that region, as we know they did with other far-distant localities.

We therefore regard the presence of perforated stone axes in the dolmens of Brittany, or elsewhere, as nearly a conclusive evidence of the employment of metal; and we are fortified in this conclusion by the following declaration of Sir John Lubbock himself. "The pierced axes," he says, "are generally found in the graves of the Bronze period, and it is most probable that this mode of attaching the handle was used very rarely, if at all, until the discovery of metal had rendered the process far more easy than could have been the case previously" (p. 95). And to the same purport Mr. John Evans, who remarks, after a full discussion of the whole subject, that "most of the perforated axes" in Britain "must be referred to the Bronze period."

We mentioned the sculptured walls of the monuments at Locmariaker. The stone which closes the end of the Dol ar Marchant is shaped into the form of two sides of an equilateral spherical

Sculptures.

* Antiq. Southern Indians, pp. 282–4.

† Prehist. Races of America, p. 212.

triangle, "and covered with sculptures," of a purely decorative character. At Gavr Innis the ornamentation consists of a number of unintelligible curved and spiral lines, very similar to those which occur at New Grange and Dowth and Lough Crew in Ireland. The pattern is in fact identical with that at Lough Crew.*

Ireland.

This leads us to speak of Ireland. The most celebrated of all these monuments in Ireland are the three great tumuli of Knowth, Dowth, and New Grange, belonging to a group of seventeen, on the banks of the Boyne. That at Knowth is in such a dilapidated condition that it has not been examined. It is a mound some fifty or sixty feet high and some two hundred feet in diameter. Less than a mile distant is New Grange. This is some seventy feet high, and more than three hundred feet in diameter. Around its base was a circle of monoliths. The number of these appears to have been thirty, the same as at Stonehenge. A stone passage leads to a central chamber within some seventy feet from the entrance, twenty feet high. The crypt extends still some twenty feet beyond, and on the east and west are two other recesses, so that the whole assumes the form of a cross. In each of the recesses thus formed stands a shallow oval *stone basin*, three feet by three feet six inches across, and from six to nine inches deep. On one stone in the passage, and on most of those in the main chamber, the decorative sculptures to which we have referred appear, while similar ones, but of more careful execution, exist on the stone at the threshold. A coin of Valentinian was found in 1699 at the top of the mound, and a coin of Theodosius has also been found, but in what part of the mound is not stated. And again in 1842 Lord Albert Cunyngham discovered near the entrance two splendid gold torques, a brooch, and a gold ring, and with them a gold coin of Geta (A.D. 205). A similar ring was found about the same time in the cell. These facts seem to determine the date

New Grange.

Stone basins.

Sculptured stones.

Roman coins.

* Since the foregoing observations were written, we have met with the following statement: The Abbé Collet has been making some excavations under the Menhirs of Carnac. The *Mané Bodegade* is a hillock situated three hundred metres to the west of the town of Ploërmel. The summit of this hillock is crowned with a small conical tumulus some thirty feet in circumference. It is in a ruined condition, but portions of a circle of rude stones, with the remains of an interior gallery, may be observed. At the entry of this gallery, at its point of junction with the dolmen, some forty pigmy vases were found, together with a great number of flint flakes. But another very significant discovery was that of an *iron axe* entirely oxidized, and near it a broken *iron ring*. We find this account in "Matériaux pour l'Histoire de l'Homme," January, 1872. The editor remarks on these facts, "This is another proof, to be added to so many others, of the existence of iron at the epoch of the Breton dolmens. Cayot-Delandre, in his annual of 1837, mentions similar hatchets of iron found at the foot of a Menhir in the Commune of Crach." See p. 63.

of the monument to about 380 or 400 A.D. The stone basins point to a date fully as recent.

Dowth.

The third of these great tumuli—that at Dowth—is supposed to have been plundered by the Danes in 862. The sculptures here are more delicate and elegant than those at New Grange, indicating a more recent date. The "find" here consisted of a number of globular stone shot, a large stone basin, and "in the chamber fragments of burned bones, many of which proved to be human, glass and amber beads of unique shape, portions of jet bracelets, a curious stone button, a fibula, bone bodkins, copper pins, and *iron knives and rings.*" And some years since in the passage were found objects of iron and a small *stone urn.*

Iron knives and rings.

The Irish chronicles affirm that the "kings of Tara" were buried at this spot from the time of Crimthann (A.D. 76) to the time of Leoghaire, son of Niall (A.D. 458).

Lough Crew.

But this is not all. Twenty-five miles west from Brugh na Boinn (the cemetery just described) are twenty-five or thirty cairns, at a place called Lough Crew. These were examined in 1867–8. The same spiral decorations occur here which we have observed on the Boyne and at Locmariaker. As we have remarked, in one of the cairns the pattern is *identical* with that at Gavr Innis, of which the writer in the *British Quarterly* for 1870 raves as follows: "The Cromlechs of Bretagne, however, have preserved a yet more startling message from the depths of their hoary antiquity. In the island of Gavr Innis, on blocks of transported granite which form one of these ancient tombs, are to be found the earliest traces of human art applied to what we must call decorative architecture. . . . Before the Romans had learned to venerate the serpent of Esculapius, or the Greeks to fear the Python destroyed by the Sun God, the Celtic tomb-builders had traced the rude outline of the mystic reptile on the granite cromlech of Morbihan." And he might have added that the artist was probably paid for his work in the coin of the Roman empire.

The spiral sculptures.

Another stone basin.

In this same cairn at Lough Crew (the chamber of which is twenty-nine feet deep and thirteen feet wide) was found another of those mysterious oval stone basins which we have described as found at New Grange. It is the largest yet discovered, being nearly six feet long by three feet broad, "the whole being tooled and picked with as much care and skill as if executed by a modern mason." All of these cairns had been rifled, excepting one. In this were found (in the passage and crypts) fragments of rude pottery, ten pieces of flint, a great number of sea-shells, numbers of pebbles and polished stones, three hundred fragments of human bones, and nearly five thousand fragments of bone implements, most of them of a knife shape (like a paper-cutter), and nearly a hundred combs engraved by compass with circles and curves of a high order of art. In addition they found also beads of amber, beads of glass, a curious molten drop of glass, one inch long, trumpet-shaped, a number of bronze rings, and seven implements of *iron* (very much corroded). One of these last appeared to be the leg of a compass, and one was an iron punch, five inches long, with a chisel-point. In another cairn they found an ornamented bronze pin.*

Glass, bronze, and iron.

We have dwelt on these examples because Sir John Lubbock attaches especial weight to the corresponding monuments in Brittany in this discussion.

To show to what a recent date the dolmens of France (to which country we now return) descend, we may instance that at Confolens, which consists of an immense rude cap-stone, twelve by fifteen feet, resting on five Gothic columns, whose style of ornamentation belongs to the twelfth century.

Confolens.

Here are some more Roman relics:

Dr. de Closmadeuc, a very distinguished French archæologist, opened a perfectly virgin tumulus at Crubelz, enclosing a dolmen. After penetrating through three distinct but undisturbed strata, he reached the roof of the chamber. In the chamber he found evidences of cremation and the usual flint arrow-heads; but, says Mr. Fergusson, he refers in triumph to the "absence de toute trace des métaux." "Aucun doute," he says, "n'est donc possible. Ce dolmen appartient bien à cette classe de monuments primitifs de l'age de pierre." He proceeds very coolly to add, "Nous tenons peu de compte des débris de tuiles antiques rencontrées à la superficie du tumulus, *et même sous les tables du dolmen.* Il est raisonnable d'admettre que ces fragments de tuiles qui dénoncent l'industrie gallo-romaine, ont *accidentellement pénétré dans l'intérieur.*"

Crubelz.

Roman tiles.

Of course there is no dealing with archæology on these terms. No amount of evidence makes any impression. If we find a beautifully perforated stone axe, they tell us it was done with a switch and a little wet sand, or that the relic belongs to a transition period; if we find a coin of the empire, they say it was found near the surface, or that it belongs to a secondary interment; if we find Roman pottery "sous les tables du dolmen," they say it is an accident; if we show them the arrow-heads and the stone axes in a Saxon tomb, they say it is an

* Dr. Conwell examined thirty-one cairns at Lough Crew in 1865. He stated before the British Association in 1870 (see *Nature*, October 20, 1870) that he found stone balls,—one beautiful specimen of syenite,—pendants of beads of different colors, bronze rings, a very perfect bronze pin with ornamented head, a fragment of iron, etc.

exceptional case; if we point them out in a great number of cases, they say the ages *lapped.*

Near this covered dolmen at Crubelz, the Baron de Bonstetten, well known for his *Essai sur les Dolmens*, opened another tumulus. At thirty centimetres (one foot) below the undisturbed surface, the flint implements were met with; and two feet below this he encountered two statuettes of Latona in terra cotta and a coin of Constantine II., but it did not shake his faith in the prehistoric character of the tomb.

Statuettes of Latona.

Even Mr. Evans,* when he finds in a tumulus on Hartshill Common, as described in Bartlett's "History and Antiquities of Manceter," a perforated stone axe, lying on a pavement of *brick* at the *bottom* of the grave, merely remarks, "There is probably some mistake as to the bricks." And when he finds a flint arrow-head in Northern Italy with ten of the degenerate imitations of the gold coin of Philip II. of Macedon, suggests that it may have been "accidental." And when he finds in Denmark fragments of iron in association with polished hatchets and other instruments of flint and stone, says, "It seems doubtful whether they were not subsequently introduced." And when in Germany (p. 131) he finds "many cases" in which iron and the stone axes have been associated, he says, "The proofs of cotemporaneity are not satisfactory."

No impression made on the antiquaries.

The utter worthlessness of the presence of the "flints" as evidence of the Stone Age, is exposed by the simple statement of Mr. Thomas Wright,† that "the Abbé Cochet found, *as the usual accompaniment* (our italics) of the urn-interments in the Roman cemeteries opened in Normandy, pieces of chipped flint, generally formed into the shape of wedges."

Roman tombs.

The Roman date of many of these monuments is further illustrated by an inscription on a menhir near Joinville, in the department of Meuse. It reads as follows: *Viromarus Istalii F.* = Viromarus, son of Istalius.

M. Lalande gives us an account of a dolmen explored by him at Peyrelevade, commune of Estivaux. He found a black bead, "like that at the dolmen of Lachassagne," *and a very small fragment* of Gallo-Roman pottery (red), "which," he says, "would seem to indicate that the dolmen of Estivaux has been *rummaged* at an epoch already very ancient"! ‡

Estivaux.

We mentioned that there were one hundred and forty thousand tumuli, or barrows, in the east of France (and no dolmens). Metal has been found in all of them which have

The tumuli of Eastern France.

---

* Ancient Stone Implements, Amer. edit., p. 166.

† Essays on Archæolog. Subjects. By Thos. Wright. Vol. i. p. 28.

‡ Congrès International d'Anthropologie, 1867, p. 174.

been examined,* and therefore no great antiquity can be claimed for the French tumuli. The dolmens of the south of France seem to be of more recent date even than those of the northwest. Here we find the external dolmen on the summit of the tumulus, a form which occurs in Scandinavia, Ireland, and Algiers, and which is certainly very modern in those countries. The tomb of Harald Hildetand at Lethra is of this character, and, as we have seen, is of the eighth century. Some of the dolmens in the north of France are peculiar; they are called "Allées couvertes," or "Grottes des Fées." One of these at Mettray, near Tours, might have come from a modern marble-yard, and the stones of most of this type of dolmens are hewn.

DOLMEN NEAR METTRAY.

In "Matériaux pour l'Histoire de l'Homme," † we have an account of a tumulus in a field near Saint-Pierre-de-Bressieux (Isère), which is from fifty to sixty-five feet high. In this tumulus were found iron keys, nails, horse-shoes, knives (resembling a modern butcher's knife), a very fine spur, etc.

In the north of France, we have an account of the tumulus of Merkeghem, one hundred metres in circumference. It contained a bronze star, pottery, etc. Near it, on the same road, is a second tumulus, four hundred metres in circumference; and, farther on, a third, about the size of the first. This contained iron nails and red tiles or bricks.‡

In the southwest of France, MM. Lacaze and Dusan describe the tumulus of Frégonville, department of Gers. It contained burials by

* The majority of the tumuli of Burgundy are more recent than the Bronze Age. See Matériaux pour l'Histoire de l'Homme, Livraisons 5e et 6e, 1873, p. 265.

† Tome i. p. 444.

‡ Matériaux, tome iii.

incineration as well as by inhumation, in graves constructed with masonry (the stones of which were cemented with mortar). On the interior walls were *fresco paintings*. Coins of the early and the lower empire occurred, with numerous débris of arms, keys, spurs, etc., all of iron. The savans who examined this tomb consider one of the more ancient pictures to be Phœnician ! *

In the west of France, the dolmens of Charente, we are told,† contain (as, for example, the Dolmen de Bernac, near Valetti) hatchets of flint and jade, worked stag-horn, and little axes of bronze.

In the south of France, M. de Malafosse has examined sixty of the dolmens of Lozère. He found in them stone implements associated with bronze ornaments, such as rings, buckles, pins, beads, etc.‡ These dolmens have also been examined by M. Prunières, who informs us that, with few exceptions, they yielded beads of bronze, amber, and glass, and objects, perhaps, even more recent than the age of bronze ; as, for example, "three small vases in red earth, witnesses of an advanced civilization." (He gives cuts of them.) In a paper on the dolmens of the neighboring department of Ardèche, M. Ollier de Marichard refers them to the same epoch, and to the same people who constructed the dolmens of Lozère, Aveyron, and Gard.§

In the south again, in Dauphiny, between Cremieu and Hières, on the site of the ancient Gaulish city of Lerins, there are several tumuli. In the only one examined were found arms of bronze.||

In the north of France, in the place called the cemetery of the English, near Pontoise, is the megalithic sepulture of Vauréal. It is constructed of great blocks of sandstone, which form a rectangle nearly fifty feet long by seven or eight broad, divided into three chambers. It contained a grand polished axe, knives, lance-heads, etc., all in flint, and a bronze ring.¶

The dolmens in southern France are noticed by M. Cartailhac. He mentions an *Allée Couverte*** (de Taurines) in the arrondissement of Saint-Affrique, Aveyron. There were many human remains, and only a few instances of cremation. He found flint arrow-heads, cut with great care, bronze rings, a bronze bead, and a pendant of bronze.

He refers in the same paper to a dolmen examined by the Abbé Cerès. On the slab covering the tomb were found fragments of bronze rings, and some "grains de collier en fer." Within the dolmen were only objects of stone.

* Mat. pour l'Hist. de l'Homme, tome ii. p. 546.

† Ib., tome iii. p. 29.

‡ Ib., tome v. p. 326.

§ Ib., 2e Série, tome iv., 1873, pp. 365, 345.

|| Ib., tome i. p. 397.

¶ Ib., tome iv. p. 189.

** Showing that Mr. Fergusson is in error in supposing that this type is peculiar to the region north of the Loire.

In another tomb M. Cartailhac found mixed up indiscriminately some flint points, four bits of unshaped iron, one of them pierced with a hole, beads of jet, bronze, and iron, and fragments of pottery.*

It is evident that these dolmens of Aveyron belong to the Bronze and Iron Ages, and it is to be remarked that we find in them the flints and the metallic objects mixed up together.

The *hache en pierre*, M. Cartailhac informs us, "is *very rare*" in these dolmens. They are abundant *outside* of them, are found in every field, but were not deposited in the tombs. Small symbolic hatchets are sometimes found in them. The weapons were too valuable to be used in this way.

The next two cuts represent "Holed Dolmens" at Trie, Oise, and at Grandmont, Bas-Languedoc:

HOLED DOLMEN, AT TRIE.

We learn from "Matériaux pour l'Histoire de l'Homme" † that some of the tumuli of the department of Creuse (Central France) belong to the epoch of stone, others to the epoch of bronze, while others enclose Roman tiles and potteries; and there are others still of the Merovingian period which contain axes of stone and instruments of iron. We have seen that the absence of metal does not prove anything. The tumuli here referred to the Stone Age may be older than the others, but it is plain that they do not possess any special antiquity.

* "Monuments Mégalithiques du Département de l'Aveyron." Internat. Cong. Prehist. Archæol., 1868, pp. 351–54.

† Ib., Août et Septembre, 1872, p. 346.

DOLMEN OF GRANDMONT.

ENGLAND.

We notice now the tumuli and dolmens of England, the exposed or free-standing dolmens, as we have stated, being very rare. Dr. Thurnam cites the large tumulus at Uley, Gloucestershire, as belonging to the long pre-historic past. It is a chambered tumulus, and in the chambers the bodies were found in great disorder, and with them a vessel resembling "a Roman lachrymatory," and pottery which was either Roman or mediæval; also flint implements; and, outside, two stone axes. Near the summit there had been another interment, and with this were found three brass coins of Constantine the Great.* Dr. Thurnam, of course, readily disposes of this, and the lachrymatory and the pottery he considers to have been "accidentally introduced."

Uley.

Roman pottery.

Coins.

The reader is prepared now to understand that the presence of the flints and the stone axes is by no means a proof of any of these interments belonging to a Stone Age. The truth is,

The universality of the flints.

* The writer in the *British Quarterly* (October, 1872), followed by the author of an article on Mr. Fergusson's book in the *Edinburgh* for July, 1873, remarks on this that a coin of Edward IV. was also found in this mound, and this (such is the idea) disposes of all the Roman coins.

There is nothing strange in finding a coin of one of the Edwards or one of the Henries in the summit of a tumulus. A child at play may have dropped it there, or it may have been hidden there. One Roman coin would prove nothing. But Roman coins and Roman pottery and Roman tiles, frequently occurring, sometimes on the chamber or in the chamber of the tomb, is of course a different matter. Some *judgment* must of course be exercised in drawing conclusions from the objects found in these graves.

they occur under all circumstances, and in association with bronze, iron, and Roman coins and pottery, as well as in Saxon and Frankish tombs. It was the custom to bury such objects with the deceased, and the custom prevailed *all over the world*, among the early Greeks as well as among the Barbarians; and it continued to prevail in England, France, Germany, and other parts of Europe, down to the Middle Ages. Modern savages—the North American Indians, for instance—have the same custom. A peculiar sentiment was cherished towards implements of stone among all races. Herodotus and Diodorus Siculus inform us that among the ancient Egyptians in the rite of embalming, while the brain was removed with a crooked iron instrument, the body was cut open with a sharp Ethiopian stone. And it is a curious and significant fact that the bodies of the chiefs of the Guanches in Teneriffe were also cut open with knives made of sharp pieces of obsidian. So the Aztecs used a knife of obsidian in their sacrifices. Among the Hebrews the rite of circumcision was performed with knives of stone. Solemn treaties were ratified among the Romans by sacrificing a pig killed with a flint stone. In Western Africa, on the occasion of the annual visit of the god Gimawong to his temple at Labode, his worshippers offer him an ox slain with a stone. We have already mentioned that there was a general belief among the ancient nations that the stone axes were thunderbolts. In Cornwall they still have medical virtues attributed to them. In the north of England, and in Scotland, the flint arrow-heads, as well as the celts, are believed to possess curative properties, especially for diseases of cattle. In Brittany the stone celt is frequently thrown into wells to purify the water. In Sweden they are believed to protect against lightning. In Germany they are called *Donnerkeile*, and are said to perspire when a storm is approaching. They are also said to increase the milk of cows, and are in requisition at the birth of children. In Holland, Portugal, Italy, Greece, the same belief prevails. In China, Japan, Burmah, Assam, they are called lightning-stones. It is the same among the Malays, and in Western Africa. We could go on, but have said enough to show that a peculiar veneration attached to these stone implements; and that they should have been laid in the tomb will not appear strange to those at all acquainted with the manners of rude and barbarous nations.

Stone axes regarded as thunderbolts.

It is not to be supposed, however, that weapons, urns, jewels, charms, etc., were in all cases deposited with the dead. "Indeed," says Sir John Lubbock, "it is quite the exception, and not the rule." Out of two hundred and sixty-seven interments described by Sir R. Colt Hoare in the first volume of his work on Ancient Wiltshire, only eighteen had any implements of

The absence of all relics of every kind very common.

stone, only thirty-one of bone, sixty-seven of bronze, and eleven of iron, —one hundred and seven containing pottery. "Sir R. C. Hoare, however," says Sir John Lubbock, "appears to have overlooked the ruder instruments and weapons of stone." He, therefore, relies principally on the evidence afforded by the researches of Mr. Bateman and Rev. Mr. Greenwell. Mr. Bateman examined two hundred and ninety-seven barrows, or tumuli, in Derbyshire which had never been opened before. In one hundred of them there were no implements at all. Of one hundred and two "primary" interments examined by Mr. Greenwell in Yorkshire, seventy-two of the graves were entirely devoid of implements. If the stone weapons and utensils are absent from so many graves, it is not strange that bronze and iron should often be absent from the interments of the bronze and iron ages. Those metals were too precious in many instances to be used in this way, and particularly in the ruder districts and among the poor.

In the Derbyshire barrows about one-third of those which yielded remains of any sort contained metal. In Wiltshire the proportion was probably even greater than this. These Wiltshire barrows, as is known, are in proximity to Stonehenge, and two of them were destroyed by the construction of the vallum, and it is pretty evident, therefore, that the antiquaries are hardly right in contending that the barrows came to Stonehenge. They are probably a little older, constructed after the introduction of iron, but when it was *precious*, and not sufficiently *venerable* for a funeral relic.*

The principal monument attached to the Derbyshire group is Arbor Low, a circular platform one hundred and sixty-seven feet in diameter, surrounded by a rampart. In a cist here were found among other things a bronze pin and a rather elegant vase. About two hundred and fifty yards distant is Gib Hill, a large tumulus seventy-five feet in diameter. The cist was found very near the summit, composed of four massive blocks of limestone, and a cap-stone four feet square. In this they found a pretty vase, a stone celt, an arrow-head of flint, and a small iron fibula, which had been enriched with precious stones.

Arbor Low.

Bronze.

Gib Hill.

Iron fibula.

Minning Low is another important monument of this group. It is a straight-lined truncated cone, three hundred feet in diameter, and eighty feet wide at the top. At the summit, the cap-stones flush with the surface, there were found in 1786 five kistvaens, each capable of containing one body. Below there was another cham-

Minning Low.

* It is important also to remark that if, as the antiquaries will have it, the barrows are more modern than Stonehenge, and if, as they allege, Stonehenge belongs to the Bronze Age, then the Wiltshire barrows also belong to the Bronze Age. And yet the majority of them which contain any works of art at all contain only stone, and no metal.

ber, or rather three chambers. The kistvaens seem to have been rifled, but *in the chambers below*, as we learn from Mr. Bateman, were found fragments of five urns, animal bones, and six brass Roman coins,* viz., one of Claudius Gothicus (270), two of Constantine the Great, two of Constantine, junior, and one of Valentinian. Some wheel-made pottery and a bronze dagger were also found, which shows this: that bronze weapons had not ceased to be used in England as late as the fourth century of our era. The wheel-made pottery implies a similar date. Iron had been long in use, but it seems that bronze and even stone weapons by no means went out with the introduction of iron. (And observe, there is no iron in this tomb.) Mr. Bateman remarks on the "striking analogy between Minning Low and the great barrow at New Grange." A strong point of connection between them, which he does not refer to, is the finding of coins of Valentinian, Theodosius, and Geta, at New Grange.

More Roman coins.

There is another notable barrow belonging to this group, about a mile from Arbor Low, at Benty Grange. In this a body was found, and with it a leather drinking-cup, ornamented in silver with stars and crosses, and with it two circular enamels adorned with an interlacing pattern found in the earliest Anglo-Saxon or Irish MSS. of the sixth or seventh centuries. A helmet was also found formed of iron bars, with bronze and silver ornaments. In Kenslow Barrow, between Minning Low and Arbor Low, were found implements of flint and bone, a bronze dagger, and a little above these an iron knife. Of course a secondary interment is alleged here, but there seems to be no ground for it.

Benty Grange. Drinking-cup. Silver.

Helmet.

Kenslow Barrow. Iron knife.

On Winster Moor Mr. Bateman found in a barrow a gold Greek cross (Christian), a gold buckle, and a number of glass and metal ornaments.

Farther examples.

At Long Roods, urns and a coin of Constantine.

In Haddon Field Barrow, eighty-two brass coins, of Constantine, Constans, Constantius, Urbs Roma, Constantinopolis, Valentinian, Valens, Gratian, etc.

On Cross Flatts with the skeleton were found an iron knife and a spear-head of flint.

In Galley Low a beautiful gold necklace, and a coin of Honorius; but towards the outer edge, and consequently, according to theory, later, a small arrow-head of gray flint, a piece of iron-stone, and pottery.

In Borther Low a flint arrow-head and a bronze celt.

---

* Mr. Jewett, in his work entitled "Grave-mounds and their Contents," states that coins have been found in the skull in Derbyshire in more than one instance.

In Rolley Low, a coin of Constantine, a brass pin, and lower down an urn, two flint arrow-heads, etc.

In a barrow on Ashford Moor, scattered, an iron arrow-head and fine implements of flint.

In Net Low, two studs of Kimmeridge coal, a large brass dagger, handle highly decorated, and fragments of flint.

In Stand Low, on digging towards the centre, stone implements and flint chippings were found, and at the centre an iron (Saxon) knife, a bronze box, bronze buckles, articles of iron, silver, glass.

In a barrow between Wetton and Ilam, flint implements, urn, and an iron pin. In a second barrow near by, urn and coin of Constantine.

At Moot Low, six rude instruments of stone, a bronze lance-head, a bronze box, iron knives, glass beads, and a silver needle.

In a barrow on Elton Moor, at eighteen inches below the surface of the natural soil, were found a skeleton, a fragment of wood encased with iron, some polished iron ore in an urn, a celt of gray flint, a beautiful cutting instrument of flint, twenty-one flints "of the circular-ended shape," and fifteen pieces of flint of various shapes, some of them arrow-heads. Even with the level of the ground, and above the foregoing, in the centre of the barrow, were found a large flint arrow or spear-head, and a neat urn.*

And so on.

In a barrow near Sarum, near Winchester Hut Enclosures, the Rev. A. B. Hutchins found at one and a half feet from the top of the barrow an urn, amber beads, a fluted lance-head of mixed metal, a metal pin, etc. In the centre he found another interment and an iron spear-head and four arrow-heads of iron. Then four feet below the surface of the soil, he found the original interment—a skeleton of immense size—the teeth all perfect, a handsome red vase, and in the vase two flint arrow-heads, one black, and one white, and a metal spear-head.†

Rev. Mr. Greenwell on the barrows of Yorkshire.

In the *Archæological Journal* for 1865 are two contributions by the Rev. Mr. Greenwell on certain "Ancient Grave Hills in the North Riding of Yorkshire." They constitute a portion of the list given by Sir J. Lubbock already referred to. It may give the reader a farther insight into the character of these barrows, if we run rapidly over the contents of this paper.

Multitude of flints.

The country, Mr. Greenwell remarks, is "covered with flints, scattered over the surface." In some places, he says, it is no exaggeration to state that they are found by "thousands," arrow-heads, knives, saws, etc. The flint used in the manufacture is

* Archæolog. Jour., vol. i. 247.

† Ibid., vol. i. 157.

foreign to the district. He examined a number of large barrows as follows:

Barrow A, two and a half miles west of Scamridge Dikes. Long barrow, one hundred and sixty-five feet in length. Within found first an extended body, which was a secondary interment. Near the centre were fourteen bodies, the bones in utter confusion. Then came upon a cairn of stones. No trace of metal, flint, or pottery.

He considers the long barrows to be "the earliest sepulchral remains in Britain." "No trace of metal in any of them," and "in many of them, as at Scamridge, no implements or weapons of any kind have occurred."

Barrows B are called—but, as Mr. Greenwell thinks, without good reason—"the Danes' Graves." They are different from and have no connection with the others. He examined fourteen of them. The bodies were doubled up. They contained hand-made urns.

C was one of these Danes' barrows, and contained a skeleton laid on the right side, and close by it a piece of oxidized *iron*. Also remains of two goats.

The other barrows of this set exhibited an almost entire absence of weapons or implements.

Two round barrows of the class first mentioned were then examined two miles west of Egton Bridge, near Whitby. One, called "William Houe," was eighty feet in diameter. It contained urns, two burnt bodies, and fifteen long perforated jet beads, evidently, as Mr. Greenwell says, "bored with a metal instrument."

Jet beads.

Barrow G, on Egton South Moor, was sixty-eight feet in diameter; it contained nothing but two burnt bodies.

Another "Houe," forty feet in diameter, contained nothing.

"Barrows next examined equally disappointing." Barrow I contained burnt earth and charcoal, and a few burnt and unburnt flint chippings among the sand. Also some shards of pottery, never entire. Barrow J, thirty feet in diameter, contained nothing. Barrow K, forty-four feet in diameter, contained an urn and some flint chippings.*

In the second paper† in the same volume of the *Archæological Journal*, on the same subject, we have:

On Wykeham Moor, in the district between Troutdale and the valley of the Derwent, the mounds called "The Three Tremblers." The largest, L, is ninety-eight feet in diameter and eleven feet high. Pottery just below the surface, but mere loose shards, occurring originally in the earth. Chippings of flint met with as they dug. At twenty-five feet from outside, and southeast of centre, a small cist, containing a

---

* Archæol. Jour., vol. xviii. pp. 107–116.

† Ib., p. 241.

small urn. About eight feet from the centre, and four feet from the natural surface, burnt earth and charcoal. At the centre, four feet from the summit, and seven feet from bottom, were found a *bronze dagger* and a beautiful flint knife side by side. Bronze dagger.

"There can be no doubt," says Mr. Greenwell, "that both the bronze dagger and the flint knife had belonged to the person buried in this houe; and we have, therefore, a valuable illustration of the cotemporaneous use of bronze and stone.

"During the highest cultivation of the bronze period, it is, I think, certain that stone implements were in common use. Poorer persons, probably, had no other articles than those of flint, or other stone; whilst the richer had some of metal and some of stone.* All who are acquainted with our early remains must have observed that no bronze arrow-heads have been found, whilst, on the contrary, flint arrow-heads are abundant; and also that spear or javelin heads of flint . . . are extremely rare."

Digging down to the surface, seven feet below the dagger and knife, they found the interment. The body apparently had not been burned. There were a thin layer of greasy dark matter and a small fragment of bronze.

A mile north of this, three houes were examined. They contained some urns, fragments of pottery, and some flints.

A mile west of "The Tremblers," examined two barrows. P was twenty-seven feet in diameter. Burnt bones near the surface, together with a small urn, a flint flake, a bronze pin, and four jet beads, two of them of an elongated oval form, and perforated like those previously mentioned. At another point, one foot from surface, found urn, bones, flints. Over centre, one foot from surface, three urns, and bones. Two feet below surface, came upon a flat stone covering an urn, containing burnt bones and a flint. Found also six feet from centre another urn and a well-made flint arrow-head. Bronze pin. Beads.

Barrows R, S, and T, near Castle Howard, contained burnt bones, calcined flints, and one of them some urns.

At Scale House, near Skipton, a barrow, thirty feet in diameter, was examined. It contained a coffin, formed out of the trunk of an oak, split and then hollowed out. The cutting was roughly done, showing marks of the tool. Ends finished off square. Contained Coffin.

* So Mr. Wright, the eminent English archæologist, remarks that "the comparison of these barrows with one another . . . would lead us to think that they may in general be placed within no very wide limits." He thinks that according to wealth and station, one man may have had weapons of bronze or iron, his neighbor having to remain content with a chisel or axe of stone, or, if a hunter, a few flint arrow-heads. He refers them in general to about the beginning of the Christian Era. *Celt, Roman, and Saxon*, pp. 81, 83.

remains of a woollen shroud, much rotted. Woven apparently by a kind of plaiting process, without the loom. Nothing else in the grave. Mr. Greenwell considers the interment of same date with the others, which he believes to be "many centuries" anterior to the appearance of the Romans. All of them he refers to the Bronze Age. He remarks that where we find one interment without bronze, and another with bronze, the other accompaniments being the same, the tomb containing the bronze and the tomb containing the flints are of the same age.* The people who constructed these barrows used, in his opinion, bronze "for certain weapons and implements, while they used for other articles the common material, namely flint."

Woollen shroud.

Mr. Greenwell also remarks that "it is possible that in many interments where no bronze is discovered, it may have existed, but have become quite destroyed." "In several instances," he says, "I have found a fragment of bronze so small, that a very little longer time, or greater exposure to the atmosphere and wet, would have destroyed all trace of it."

We have given these details about the Yorkshire barrows, because they appear to us to have more marks of antiquity than any others in England; and even these, it is admitted, belong to the age of bronze. But some of these great barrows contained jet ornaments, which Mr. Evans states belong to a quite recent date. One of them contained an oaken coffin and a woollen shroud.

Iron was doubtless rare in the north of England at the beginning of the Christian Era. Mr. Evans observes in this connection that the older inhabitants of Britain who had been driven into the north and the west, by the Belgic invaders, "were no doubt in a far more barbarous condition" than those on the southern and southeastern coasts. Of this we shall speak elsewhere. But it is important to keep in mind this distinction in considering the remains found in different regions. Cæsar in his Commentaries distinguishes between the Belgæ on the coast and the inland tribes; and, as we shall see, cannibalism prevailed in Ireland until a very recent period, and in one district, at least, of Scotland, as late as the fourth century of our era.

This region less advanced than the south of England.

It may be remarked also that in these Yorkshire barrows, the rarity of the more expensive stone weapons is as noticeable as the rarity of metal. In the one hundred and three interments given from Mr. Greenwell by Sir John Lubbock, only *two* polished stone axes were found; while in Mr. Bateman's Derbyshire tables, embracing one hundred and two interments, only *one* was found.

Few polished stone weapons in these barrows.

* Page 259.

As to arrow-heads of bronze, Mr. Evans (p. 328) tells us that with weapons so liable to be lost as arrows, flint would be preferred to metal, so long as this was scarce and costly; and he remarks in this connection "on the extreme scarcity of bronze arrowheads" in Great Britain.

Bronze arrow-heads very rare.

In the East Riding of Yorkshire Mr. Greenwell explored a great tumulus at Langton Wold, which is noticed in the *Intellectual Observer* for 1865 by a writer whom we take to be Mr. Thomas Wright. This mound contained near the top a series of Anglo-Saxon interments. Below these were other interments. Near the centre was a male skeleton, doubled up, lying on the left side. Near it was a female skeleton. By the latter were three cowrie shells, a number of red-striped snail-shells, a jet bead, three bronze bodkins, and some bone ornaments.* Mr. Wright regards these interments also as Anglo-Saxon. The cowrie shells, he observes, are peculiarly characteristic of the Anglo-Saxon graves, as are also the jet beads and the bronze pins and the objects in bone. He remarks also on the improbability of the Saxons making use of a British tumulus. Among the ancient races of Northern Europe the grave was supposed to be guarded and tenanted by spirits, and the most superstitious sentiments prevailed with regard to its sacred character. It would have been deemed a perilous thing to lay the remains of a friend in a grave occupied by hostile spirits. It was in connection with this idea of the presence of spirits, he suggests, that the grave or the tumulus was surrounded by a circle of stones. They marked the limits of the consecrated spot.

Langton Wold.

Col. A. Lane Fox mentions the cromlech of Enstone (it is in Oxfordshire, we believe). It consists of five large stones, three of which are upright, forming three sides of a cist. Mr. Jordan, the historian of Enstone, informs Col. Fox on the authority of Sir Henry Dryden, Bart., who dug beneath the monument, that all the fragments of pottery discovered there were of Roman, or Romano-British, manufacture.†

Enstone.

Dr. Daniel Wilson, in his interesting volumes, "The Prehistoric Annals of Scotland,"‡ describes a large tumulus, surrounded by an earthen vallum, near Rutherglen, Lanarkshire, which contained a gallery or long chamber of unhewn stones. The circumference of this mound was two hundred and sixty feet. It is one of those long-chambered tumuli which are said to be peculiarly characteristic of the Stone Age, and which, as we are told, "in no authenticated instance have furnished articles of bronze or

Scotland.

Tumulus near Rutherglen.

* Intel. Obs., vol. viii. p. 316.

† Jour. Ethnolog. Soc. of London, 1869, vol. i. p. 1.

‡ Vol. i. p. 80.

iron where they have not been previously disturbed." In the present case, however, as stated by Dr. Wilson, the chamber contained two brass vessels, which, from the description, were Roman patellæ, on the handle of one of which was engraved the name CONGALLUS or CONVALLUS. There were also a perforated stone and three large glass beads. Nothing is said about the mounds having been previously "disturbed," which Dr. Wilson would promptly have mentioned if there had been any reason to think that such was the fact, as he is himself a firm believer in the antiquity of these monuments. Nor do we see how any "disturbance" would occasion the presence of the Roman dishes, unless new bodies were introduced into the chamber in Roman times,—of which we have no account, and which is highly improbable. The secondary interments occur above the original one.

Dr. Wilson states that near by to the Camus Stone, in the neighborhood of Edinburgh, there formerly stood two very large conical cairns, styled the Cat-stanes (the Gaelic CATH signifying *battle*), and that beneath these cairns were found cists containing human skeletons and "various bronze and iron weapons." There were two iron spear-heads and sundry bronze celts and other weapons. We thus not only fix the date of these monuments to the Iron Age, but we find bronze and iron weapons in use at the same time.*

Broomend.

We have an account in the Proceedings of the International Congress of Pre-historic Archæology for 1868, by Mr. John Stuart, of some cists at Broomend, Aberdeenshire. In one of them there were two skeletons laid on the bottom (which was paved with pebbles) in a bent posture, and covered with a piece of ox-hide, on which the hair still remained. There were an urn and several flint flakes.

In the next cist there was a similar skeleton, and an infant skeleton in a sitting posture. Also an ox-hide, an urn much ornamented, and a lamp made of leather. Two flint flakes.

Mr. Stuart mentions that in 1864, at Bishopmill, near Elgin, a cist was discovered, which, like the above, contained an ox-hide, with the hair partly remaining. There was also a bronze dagger.†

We might cite other examples from Scotland, although, in most of the cases reported from this country which we have met with, the contents of the tombs are not specified.

Greenmount, Ireland.

There is an exceedingly interesting account in the *Archæological Journal* (No. 108) for 1870 of a tumulus in the ancient parish of Kilsaran, Barony of Ferrard, County of Louth, now united to Gernon's-town, Ireland, by Maj.-Gen. J. H. Lefroy, R.A., F.R.S., etc. This tumulus is two hundred and ten feet in circumference, and

* Prehist. Ann. Scot., vol. i. p. 137.

† See p. 27.

twelve feet high, and is situated at Greenmount, Castle Bellingham, in the parish referred to. It was opened in 1870. The depth from the top of the tumulus to the bottom was twenty-three feet. At nine or ten feet from the top, and six or seven above the level of the chamber, and incorporated with the material of the mound, and the bones of the ox, the horse, the sheep, etc., the explorers found a small *bronze plate*, containing an inscription in Runic characters. A few days later a bronze axe was found at the surface, perhaps thrown up with the earth from below.

A bronze plate with a Runic inscription.

Bronze celt.

The bronze object is a narrow plate 3.8 inches long, .6 inch wide, and nearly .5 inch thick. It is ornamented on the face, and inlaid with silver—the pattern being described as "a graceful relief of bright silver and white enamel bands." Gen. Lefroy thinks it was originally part of a sword-handle or belt-fitting. On the reverse side are the Runes.

Nothing else was found except "a bone harp-peg," very well fabricated, and a lump of iron, which was possibly the remains of an axe.

Iron.

The inscription on the bronze plate was as follows:

DOMNAL SELSHOFOTh A SOERTh ThETA

which translated reads, "Domnal Sealshead owns sword this."

Professor Stephens refers the inscription to the ninth century; Mr. Vigfusson to the eleventh. The Runes are undoubtedly Scandinavian, and belonged to the Norwegian or Danish invaders of Ireland.

Of the ninth century.

The bronze battle-axe weighed twenty ounces, and Gen. Lefroy considers it of the same date with the inscribed plate. He remarks that a Celtic tumulus opened in 1848 at Anet, near Berne, yielded, among other objects, a bronze axe, which Dr. Todd regarded as of a date long subsequent to the introduction of Christianity into that country. That is, later, and probably much later, than the end of the sixth century. See Proceedings Royal Irish Acad., vii. p. 42.

Gen. Lefroy states that there are passages in the ancient Irish books which prove that bronze weapons were used in Ireland long after the Christian era. As, for example, the following:

Bronze weapons used in Ireland long after the Christian era.

> "The stipend of the king of Drung, which is not small,
> From the king of Eira, 'tis not contemptible,
> Three curved narrow swords,
> And three ships very beautiful."
>
> *From Leabhan na g' Ceart or Book of Rights*, *O'Donovan*, 1847, p. 85.

Gen. Lefroy remarks that he "believes a *curved narrow sword* of iron is unknown in any collection," but that the description "applies exactly to the ordinary bronze weapon." "Drung" is the ancient designation for Kerry. Here are some other quotations:

"Whoever wishes for a speckled boss
And a sword of sore inflicting wounds
And a green javelin for wounding witches,
Let him go early in the morning to Ath-Cliath."

Four Masters, A.D. 917.

"This day Brinde fights a battle for the land of his grandfather,
Unless the Son of God will it otherwise, he will die in it,
To-day the son of Osery was killed in a battle with green swords."

A.D. 704. *Three Frag. translated by O'Donovan.* 1860, p. 111.

"Green" is the color assumed by bronze when not kept bright, and could not, unless, possibly, the expression had continued in use after the disappearance of bronze, be applied to iron. No one ever heard of *green iron.*

Again:

"There is Domhnall in battle.
* * * * * * *
Oh the size of the expert blue sword
Which is in his valiant right hand
And the size of his great shield beside it!
The size of his broad green spear."

A.D. 637. *The Battle of Magh Rath*, p 197.

Here the poet evidently means to employ terms which shall accurately describe the weapons mentioned. He discriminates between the "blue" iron and the "green" spear.*

We have in this example of Greenmount, evidence—1. That this great tumulus was erected by the Norwegians or the Danes in the ninth, tenth, or eleventh century. 2. That at that time they armed themselves with the bronze battle-axe. What becomes then of the Age of Bronze, and the "pre-historic" antiquity of these great sepulchral monuments?

Mr. Fergusson states that the chamber of this mound had been rifled, and raises the question whether the bronze plate may not have been dropped at this time. But it was found above the roof of the chamber. 2. It is more probable that it was *not* "dropped" than that it was. 3. Were the bone "harp peg," and the bronze axe, and the lump of iron, also "dropped"? 4. Mr. Fergusson says the chamber, from its mode of construction, is "the most modern of all the chambered sepulchral tumuli yet discovered in Ireland."

SCANDINAVIA.

We pass now to Scandinavia. The traditions of Odin do not pretend to go back of the first century B.C., and we have no doubt of their being founded on fact, and that this date is substantially correct. Frode I. lived about A.D. 35, according to these traditions. Previous to about 900 all is tradition. All this accords with the fact that Palæolithic man never entered Denmark or the regions north of it. The chief stone

---

* See Arch. Jour., No. 108, 1870, pp. 285–310.

monuments in Scandinavia are those which mark battle-fields, and the dates of many of these are approximately known. The first is that of Kongsbacka, near the coast in Halland, to which Sjöborg assigns a date about 500. Kongsbacka, A.D. 500.

The circles of Bravaalla Heath we have mentioned. We begin here to tread on sure ground—the date being, as already stated, 736 or 750.

Our present business, however, is with the dolmens and tumuli of this region.

There is a barrow at Wiskehärad, in Halland, which we are informed by Sjöborg is one of several which mark the spot where Frode V. landed in Sweden. This was about A.D. 475. A battle was fought, and the dead were interred in these mounds. There is a triple group at Upsala, known as the graves of Thor, Woden, and Freya. Marryat, in his "One Year in Sweden," states that one of these had been opened, and that in its "giant chamber" were found the bones of a woman, a fragment of a gold filigree bracelet, some dice, and a *chessman, either the king or a knight.* Mr. Fergusson informs us that Herr Hildebrand, the royal antiquary of Sweden, opened the mound known as that of Woden in 1846. He found fragments of bronze ornaments, calcined bones, and fragments of two golden bracteates, which from their workmanship he referred to the fifth or sixth century. Herr Hildebrand adds that "the tombs of Central Sweden" contain generally "nothing but an iron nail, or some such trifling object." According to him, "almost every village in Sweden, with the exception of those in some mountain-districts and the most northern provinces, has a tomb-field quite close to the side of the house."

Wiskehärad, A.D. 475. The group at Upsala. Dice and chessman. B. C. 500 or 600. Iron in Swedish tombs.

At Jellinge, on the east coast of Jutland, there are two mounds, known traditionally as those of King Gorm and his queen Thyra Danebod—the Beloved. Gorm died in A.D. 950. Saxo Grammaticus, who lived in the twelfth century, tells us Harold Blaatand, Gorm's son, buried his mother here also, and that he employed a whole army of men to remove from the Jutland shore an immense stone and bring it to the place where his mother lay. This stone still exists, and has sculptured on one side a dragon, precisely like that at Maes-Howe in the Orkneys. The tomb of Queen Thyra was opened in 1820, or thereabouts, and they found in it a silver goblet lined with gold, some tortoise-shaped fibulæ, some buckle-heads, etc. The walls and roof of the chambers were originally of oak, and hung with tapestries.

Jellinge. King Gorm. A.D. 950.

The delineations on these monuments, or the hewn stones, frequently guide us. At Herrestrup, in Zeeland, is a rude dolmen, with a very heavy cap-stone, on which are engraved some half-dozen Herrestrup.

representations of ships, such as the Vikings were in the habit of drawing, and which abound on the coast of Gottenburg. This would fix the date at between A.D. 500 and 900. The engravings must be cotemporary with the dolmen, as it was covered up under a mound until very recently. There is a very grand buried dolmen at Uby, in Zeeland, the stones of which seem to be hewn. The fine dolmen at Axevalla, in Westergothland, from the condition of the skeletons and the hewn stones, as represented by Sjöborg, must be quite recent. The correct drawings on the celebrated grave of Kivik in Southern Sweden also point to a recent date.

The Vikings.

Uby.

Axevalla.

Mr. Worsaae, in a paper on "The Antiquities of South Jutland or Sleswick," states that "the cromlechs of the Bronze Age are far more common in South Jutland than those of the Stone Age." *

Worsaae on the cromlechs of the Bronze Age.

He divides the Bronze Age into two periods: "The Early Bronze Age," and "The Late Bronze Age." Under the former head he speaks of "eight instances" in the north of Sleswick, between Aabrenraa and the frontier of North Jutland, where interments of the Bronze Age occurred without cremation. The unburnt bodies, he says, were found at the bottom of the barrows, deposited in hollow and split oak trunks, under piles of stones, covered by earth, the tops and sides sometimes containing urns with ashes, burnt bodies, and bronze objects.

Coffins.

The bodies in these oaken coffins were wrapped in "well-woven woollen cloths, with thicker mantles and caps of a peculiar kind of felt, and laid on ox- or cow-hides, sometimes with the horns on." With these were "very fine swords, sometimes with bronze hilts; a palstave, dagger, and ornaments, of bronze; a double spiral bracelet of gold; turned wooden cups, sometimes with ornamental tin nails carefully hammered in; chip-boxes; horn combs, etc."

Woollen garments.

Bronze swords.

Prof. Worsaae refers these to the *Early* Bronze Age—about 600 B.C., according to his estimate. They probably belong to about the fifth century of our era.

Date.

"Entirely corresponding barrows," he states, "have been found in the adjoining parts of North Jutland," while others "of a still later period" are scattered over parts of the same region—the coffins being made of plank.

Plank coffins.

He then describes the two barrows called "Kongehoi" and "Treenhoi," which we have referred to elsewhere as mentioned by Sir John Lubbock. The clothes in these Prof. Worsaae says "are so well preserved that they are now fit for use." We learn, he

Kongehoi and Treenhoi.

* See Archæolog. Jour. for 1866, vol. xxiii. p. 31.

also remarks, from these tombs, that a warrior's dress in those [pre-historic] days "consisted of a woollen, woven shirt tied around the waist; some pieces of finer cloth wrapped around the feet, but no trousers; a thick woven mantle, and a cap, perhaps also a kind of plaid." *

At Dragshoi, he mentions a wooden cup which "was turned on the lathe"—which fact alone proves that the interment is post-Roman.

Mr. Worsaae then speaks of the cromlechs in South Jutland of the "Late Bronze Age."

According to the scheme of this distinguished antiquary, the Iron Age in Denmark commenced about A.D. 200, which is in our opinion about the correct date. The Bronze Age, however, he ranges over some thousand years before this.

Worsaae on the Iron Age. A.D. 200.

There is a recent official report with regard to a number of tumuli, explored, on the island of Sylt, at the instance of the Schleswig-Holstein authorities. The excavations extended over the years 1870, '71, and '72, and as many as thirty mounds were opened. The bodies had been sometimes burned, and sometimes not. The relics were bronze swords, having, in some instances, wooden sheaths, richly ornamented with spiral lines, fragments of woollen stuff, and occasionally articles of gold or flint. In mound No. 24 were found a flint saw and a bronze sword and knife—showing plainly that the flint saw continued to be used in this region after the introduction of bronze swords.†

Island of Sylt.

GERMANY.

The dolmens are quite numerous in the north of Germany, along the coasts, and resemble those of Scandinavia. They abound especially in the northern districts of Hanover, in Mecklenburg, in Pomerania, and in Prussian Saxony. The whole coast of the Baltic and the North Sea, and thence up the basin of the Elbe to Prussian Saxony, seems to constitute *par excellence* the dolmen region of Germany. On the west this region includes the province of Drenthe, in North Holland. When we remember that the dolmens also abound in Jutland, and that Britain was conquered by races from these quarters—Saxons, Frisians, Angles, Jutes—in the fifth century, we might naturally suppose that some traces of such monuments would appear in England, even if none had existed there before. These Goths or Scythians may have played the same part in Kent and Wilts which their kinsmen played in the Orkneys and in Ireland. It is true there are few existing free-standing dolmens in England; but this does not necessarily overthrow such a conjecture. Britain had been civilized by the Romans when Hengist and Horsa landed there; the influence of that civilization naturally operated to arrest the

* See Archæol. Jour., vol. xxiii. p. 34.

† Academy, Apr. 15, 1873.

rude practices which the Saxon pirates brought with them from the mouth of the Elbe and the Cimbric Chersonese. The custom, after the settlement of the Saxons in Britain, while it was not discontinued altogether, was, no doubt, gradually abandoned. Lastly, it is highly probable that in such a country as England, where the population is dense, and where every foot of land has been under thorough cultivation, monuments of this sort would in most instances be destroyed, and every vestige of them obliterated.

We do not mean to suggest that all of the rude stone monuments might be as recent as the Saxons. As will appear hereafter, we believe that there was another line of migration followed by the dolmen-building race, which extended to England, and which was of earlier date than that which traversed Scandinavia and Northern Germany.

Some of the largest dolmens in Europe are found in the Grand-Duchy of Oldenburg, the very point from which the Saxons who invaded England are represented as coming. "One of these dolmens, near Wildesheim, is twenty-three feet long; another, near Engelsmanns-Becke, is surrounded by an enclosure of stones measuring thirty-seven feet by twenty-three, each stone being ten feet in height, while the cap-stone of a third is twenty feet by ten." *

While this is a very plausible method of accounting for the presence of some of the rude stone monuments of England, we do not accept it as most probably representing the facts of the case. The express affirmations of Geoffrey of Monmouth and Giraldus Cambrensis with regard to Stonehenge assign that work, not to the Saxons, but the Britons, while *tradition* associates Aylesford, Stanton Drew, and Penrith with the same race. The historical testimony, combined with the immemorial *names* of some of the monuments, we regard—taken in connection with other important facts—as almost conclusive. We shall have occasion to consider *who* were these Britons; for the present the reader may bear in mind that King Arthur was a prince of the *Silures*.

AUSTRIA.

Recently some burial-mounds have been examined in Austria. Prof. Woldich has opened one near Pulkau, Lower Austria, in which he found stone, bone, and bronze implements, together with some pottery, which is described as being "very tastefully ornamented." Animal remains were also found, including those of the dog, ox, urus, goat, sheep, fallow deer, pig, horse, and stag. This is another illustration of the cotemporaneous use of stone and metal, and of the recent existence of the *bos primigenius* in Austria.

Bronze.

Bos primigenius.

* Fergusson, p. 301.

SPAIN.

There are many dolmens in Spain, but they have not been generally explored. That at Antequera is hardly surpassed by any in any part of the world. The massive stones are hewn in such a manner as plainly to imply the use of metallic tools. The stones of the Dolmen del Tio Cogolleros, another very fine example, are also hewn. Near Dilar is another remarkable dolmen. It consists of a monolithic chamber, "hollowed out of a stone of considerable dimensions, and hewn so as to look almost like an Egyptian cell."

Dolmen of Antequera.

Tio Cogolleros.

At Cangas de Onis, in Asturias, "there is a small church built on a mound, which contains in it a dolmen of rather unusual shape." The church is built on the top of the mound, "probably in the tenth or eleventh century," to which this dolmen served as a crypt. It is plain that the dolmen was held sacred when the church was erected. There is a still more remarkable example of the same kind at Arrichinaga, near Bilbao, in Biscay. In the hermitage of St. Michael, at this place, a dolmen of considerable size "is enclosed within the walls of what seems to be a new modern church."

Cangas de Onis.

Don Juan Vilanova y Piera mentions a large tumulus near the city of Olleria, in Valencia, which was explored and almost destroyed some twenty-five years ago. Its dimensions were one hundred metres for the circumference, and ten metres in height. Seven complete skeletons were found, and with them some beautiful polished hatchets of diorite, a great quantity of coarse pottery, some teeth of a deer no longer seen in this district, and a series of bronze *coins* of several sizes. This tumulus is called "Monton de Tierra." Most of the articles found here have disappeared, "except some human bones, some fragments of pottery, and two hatchets of polished stone and bronze." *

Tumulus in Valencia.

Coins.

The coins of course bring this tomb down to a recent date, but it may have been either a few centuries before or a few centuries after the Christian era.

M. José Villamil y Castra explored the tumulus of Mondonedo, province of Galicia. He found a beautiful flint axe and fragments of iron arms and implements much oxidized.†

ITALY.

There are no dolmens in Italy except at the ancient site of Saturnia, one of the oldest cities of Etruria. And the only other uncovered

* Proc. Internat. Cong. Prehist. Archæol. for 1868, p. 398.

† Mat. pour l'Hist. de l'Homme, tome iv. p. 67.

"rude stone monument" in this country is a small stone circle at Sesto Calende, in Lombardy.

The dolmens of Saturnia (of which there are a considerable number), we think it probable, belong to a very early period—to the very oldest monuments of Europe. The early civilization of Italy probably led to the early substitution of less rude sepulchral forms, as the Etruscan cemeteries at Cære and Vulci. The dolmens at Saturnia are described by Mr. Dennis in his "Cities and Cemeteries of Etruria" as consisting of a quadrangular chamber sunk a few feet below the surface, lined with rough slabs of rock set upright, one on each side, and roofed over with two large slabs resting against each other, or else an immense single one covering the whole. There is not the slightest trace of the chisel. To most of them a passage leads, ten or twelve feet long and three feet wide. Each had a tumulus of earth piled over it, so as to cover all but the cap-stone. One tumulus was observed with a circle of small stones around it, and, in Mr. Dennis's opinion, all of them may have originally been so encircled,—the small stones having been probably removed by the peasantry.

There is, as we have said, also a small circle of thirty feet in diameter at Sesto Calende, in Lombardy, with an avenue fifty feet in length leading up to it, and with a small semicircle of stones twenty feet wide a few yards farther off.

So far as we are aware, no other "free-standing" rude stone monuments have yet been discovered in Italy.

The tumuli of Etruria, on the other hand, are exceedingly numerous and of great importance. That of Cucumella, at Vulci, is two hundred and forty feet in diameter, and must have been one hundred and twenty feet high. The tomb called the Regulini-Galeazzi tomb at Cære is supposed to have been originally surmounted by an immense mound—now destroyed. The chamber is sixty feet long, with the sides and roof vaulted like a Gothic arch with a square top. This is filled with vessels and furniture mostly of bronze, and of elaborate workmanship. Mr. Fergusson thinks it as old as the tenth century before our era. He omits to state, however, that amongst the furniture of the tomb was an *iron* altar on a tripod, and that among the articles of bronze were a bier, a four-wheeled car, a small tray on four wheels, beautifully embossed shields, etc. There were also vessels of silver, and "the most marvellous collection of gold ornaments ever found in a single tomb in modern times."

There are innumerable tombs of this sort—at Cære, Corneto (Tarquinii), Vulci, Tuscania, etc. Signor Avolta estimated that the cemetery at Tarquinii extended over sixteen square miles, and that the total number of the tombs amounted to two millions! More than six thousand tombs have been opened in a portion of the necropolis at Vulci. Many of the paintings in the chambers of these sepulchres are Greek. Some of them are as late as 500 B.C., others are supposed to be as old as 1300 B.C. The ornaments and furniture, it is important to observe, are chiefly of *bronze*, and we may, therefore, form a judgment as to the date of the Bronze Age in Etruria—where it was decidedly earlier than in the ruder parts of Italy.

MEDITERRANEAN ISLANDS.

In the islands of the Mediterranean—Malta, Sardinia, etc.—there are stone monuments akin to those we are considering, which are of considerable antiquity, but we know almost nothing about them. The Giant's Tower of the island of Gozo (one of the Maltese group) is an immense work. A still more extensive structure is found at Hagiar Khem in the south of Malta. There is a third monument at Mnaidra. Restored, these elaborate structures resemble the Kubber Roumeia near Algiers, ascertained to have been the tomb of the Mauritanian kings down to Juba II. (the Christian era), and which was two hundred feet in diameter, and one hundred and thirty feet high.

Malta.

Sardinia has a unique and peculiar class of stone monuments, called *Nurhags*. These are round towers, constructed of masonry, from twenty to sixty feet high, and from twenty to sixty feet in diameter at the base. It is difficult to conjecture what they were. Fergusson says they correspond to the "Towers of Silence" found in Persia, and that they may have been the tombs of a people who, like the Parsees of the present day, exposed their dead to be devoured by the birds of the air.

Sardinia.

In a Greek work, conjecturally ascribed to Aristotle, they are said to have been erected by Iolas, son of Iphicles. Diodorus has the same story. The stones of these monuments are generally, but not always, hewn. Bronze and stone implements are found in them.

In Minorca and Majorca we have another style of stone structures, very similar to the above—the *Talyot*—conical, truncated towers. Little or nothing is known of them.

NORTHERN AFRICA.

There are said to be ten, and, perhaps, twenty thousand stone sepulchral monuments in Northern Africa. They are circles, dolmens, menhirs, *bazinas*, *chouchas*, etc. They are found in the province of Algeria, and seem, many of them at least, to have been erected *since the Christian era*. The stones are frequently hewn. The traditions of the country ascribe them to the pagan inhabitants of this region at the time of the Mohammedan conquest. M. Féraud, who examined some of them in Algiers,

Thousands of stone monuments.

Hewn stones.

found in one (a dolmen enclosed in a circular enceinte of stones forty feet in diameter), at the foot of the skeleton, the remains of a horse and an iron bridle-bit, a ring of iron, various objects in copper, superior pottery, *worked flint implements,* and *a medal of the Empress Faustina.* We have here the Stone Age, the Bronze Age, and the Iron Age, all together.

Medal of Faustina.

On a dolmen near Sidi Kacem M. Féraud discovered a Latin inscription, too much defaced to be deciphered, but in letters of a late type. Monsieur Leternoux found stones and columnar shafts of Roman workmanship among the materials out of which the bazinas at the foot of the Aures chain had been constructed. In addition there are numerous plates given in the "Exploration scientifique de l'Algérie" where the rude stone monuments are so mixed up with those of late Roman and early Christian character that it seems impossible to doubt, says Fergusson, that they are cotemporary.* But it is more probable, we think, that some of them are older than others.

Latin inscription.

Roman columns.

Mr. J. W. Flower, who has examined a number of these monuments, states that the Chouchas are built of hewn stones, and represents the dolmen and cromlech at Tarf† as surrounded by "a pavement of flagstones perfectly well squared," and "on the road from Guelma to Constantine," he tells us, "is a dolmen . . . . . surmounting several concentrical rows of steps of hewn stone."

Mr. J. W. Flower on the prehistoric sepulchres of Algeria.

In nearly all of these interments are two or more bowls or cups, which precisely resemble those found in the bone-caves of Gibraltar, and those which are used at this day at Ceuta.

Mr. Flower describes a very extraordinary dolmen at Tiaret. The cap-stone is sixty-five feet in length by twenty-six feet broad and nine feet thick. It is placed on other rocks which raise it thirty or forty feet high. On the upper surface of this cap-stone are troughs cut in the rock, connected with each other by channels four inches in breadth. Of course all this cutting was done with iron tools. Iron, however, in this region, does not imply necessarily a later date than 600 or 700 B.C. It implies, however, that it was not much earlier.

Tiaret.

The work of iron tools.

Mr. Flower tells us that Herodotus, in the book "Melpomene," § 190, when describing various nomade tribes of Africa, says, "These Libyan nomades observe the same ceremonies with the Greeks in the interment of the dead. *We must except the Nasamones,* who bury their deceased in a sitting attitude,

Herodotus on the tombs of the Nasamones.

* Rude Stone Monuments, p. 405.

† "Prehistoric Sepulchres of Algeria." Internat. Cong. Prehist. Archæol., 1868, p. 194.

and are particularly careful, as one approaches his end, to prevent his expiring in a reclined posture. Their dwellings are easily movable, and are formed of the asphodel shrub secured with rushes." He also speaks of their tombs and sepulchral monuments. See § 172.

This people, says Mr. Flower, occupied the regency of Tripoli, seven or eight degrees east of Constantine, and were a warlike and wandering race. The plains of this region still bloom with the asphodel; and the skeletons in the tombs are in a crouching or sitting posture. He observes that long after Herodotus, and long after the Roman occupation, the natives may well have continued to practice their ancient modes of sepulture. Their weapons and implements would be probably partly of stone, and partly of metal. He believes all the existing tombs to be later than the Romans, or coeval; and this, he remarks, accords with the Arab tradition, that they were the work of pagans—*Djouhala*.

Probably post-Roman.

These views are corroborated by the character of the stupendous tomb between Constantine and Batna, which was the burial-place of Syphax and the Numidian kings, and which, as any cut of it will show, is nothing but a combination (as frequently occurs) of the choucha and the bazina.

Tomb of the Numidian kings.

M. Bertrand, who believes in the pre-historic character of the dolmens of France—who, like Mr. Flower, is a believer in the "antiquity of man"—is constrained to take the same view of the Algerian dolmen that Mr. Flower does; he remarks on the discoveries of M. Féraud:

Opinion of M. Bertrand on the date of the Algerian monuments.

"Ceux de la province de Constantine ne pouvaient, à en juger par les objets qui y ont été trouvés, être de beaucoup antérieur à l'ère chrétienne; quelques-uns même seraient postérieurs."

The Trilithons in Tripoli remind us so forcibly of the hewn trilithons at Stonehenge that, as Mr. Fergusson says, the first thing that occurs to us is Geoffrey of Monmouth's assertion that "Giants in old days brought from Africa the stones which the magic arts of Merlin brought afterwards from Kildare and set up at Stonehenge."

Trilithons in Tripoli.

Here is another link. M. Payen has noticed that in the Algerian graves there is always a quantity of earth of a much lighter and finer character than the surrounding soil; he speaks of it as *poussière legère*, and says "it was found in almost all the circular tombs (chouchas), and those which did not contain it were empty." The same fact has been observed repeatedly in England, France, and Portugal.

It is only necessary to add to what we have said, that M. Bourgignat, who has published a paper on the Symbolic Monuments of Algeria, assigns them to the Stone Age, and believes they are to be rated as dating from 8000 to 4000 B.C.

M. Bourgignat per contra.

We append representations of two of the North African monuments, for the entertainment and instruction of the reader.

CHOUCHA. FROM A DRAWING BY MR. FLOWER.

DOLMEN ON STEPS.

WESTERN AND CENTRAL ASIA.

Tumuli very numerous. Recent construction of.

Tumuli are found by thousands on the steppes of Western and Central Asia, and we learn from the monk Rubruquis, who travelled in this region in the thirteenth century, that they were still erected by the natives at that time.

The Black Sea.

Kertch.

They are found also on the peninsula of Taman and the peninsula of Kertch, on opposite sides of the straits of Yenikale, connecting the Black Sea and the Sea of Azof. A splendid one was opened at Kertch, the ancient Panticapæum, an account of which is given elsewhere. The dolmens abound in Circassia and Palestine, and the great chambered tumuli in the region which constituted ancient Lydia.

INDIA.

Innumerable cairns and dolmens are found in India. The pottery found in them everywhere is identical in form and texture with the pottery of the present day; but it would be unsafe to argue from a circumstance of this sort in India or any part of the East. Gold and silver ornaments, precisely similar to the objects seen in the bazaars in remote districts of the present day, are generally found also in these tombs. Iron spear-heads and iron utensils of the most modern shape and pattern are also among the commonest objects found. No bronze is found, though it was known to the Indians in very ancient times. Flint is found, but not in the graves. Iron was known to the Indians as early as 400 B.C., and the celebrated iron pillar of Dhava, in the court-yard of the mosque at the Kutub, near Delhi, affords a wonderful proof of their skill in the working of this metal. This pillar is a solid shaft forty feet long and five feet in circumference. It could not have been made in any country of Europe prior to the introduction of steam machinery. It was erected about A.D. 300–350.

Iron.

North of the Ganges, on the Khassia hills, there is a tribe and a state of things (referred to in the beginning of this chapter) which are full of instruction to those who are quick to speculate in ethnology and archæology. Here menhirs and dolmens exist in greater numbers, perhaps, than in any other portion of the globe. All travellers are struck with their curious resemblance to those of Europe. Many of them were erected within the last few years, and these are identical in form with those which suggest elsewhere a "hoary antiquity." If one of the Khassia tribe falls sick, he prays to one of his ancestors for assistance. If the prayer is granted, he erects a menhir in honor of the deceased. Thus one person may have a number of these stones erected to him.

The Khassia Hills.

Dolmens and menhirs erected in past few years.

Not only have these monuments been erected, some of them, within the present century and the past few years, but this custom exists in the immediate presence of two higher civilizations. At the foot of the Khassia hills, to the north, lies, as we have already remarked, the famous Hindoo kingdom of Kamarupa, where in the seventh century Hiouen Thsang found hundreds of magnificent temples. On the south lies Sylhet, adorned with mosques and palaces and all the magnificence of the Moslems. But the Khassians are not changed, nor moved. They continue to erect their rude monuments, and to cling to their primitive civilization.

Juxtaposition of different civilizations.

We spoke also of Ougein, the residence of the celebrated king Asoka, and the capital of the Visramaditya in the fifth century, in sight of which the *Bhils* are still living as their fathers did two thousand years ago—having no literature and hardly a tradition.

The Khonds afford a similar example. These people are the Druids of the East, worshipping in groves, indulging in human sacrifices, etc. They live near the beautiful caves of the Buddhists, on the Udyagiri hills, excavated before the Christian era; in sight of the great tower of the Bobaneswar temple and the numerous

The Khonds.

smaller fanes consecrated to Siva; and not far from the great tower of the temple of Juggernaut, at Puri, established in the twelfth century for the worship of Vishnu.

As to the age of the Indian monuments, Mr. Fergusson relies on this fact: there were, he says, certainly no hewn-stone buildings in India prior to the date 250 B.C. Their architecture was of wood, as is the case to-day with the palaces and monasteries of Siam and Burmah. The influence of the Bactrian Greeks first introduced the use of stone for building purposes, as the Romans introduced it into Northern and Western Europe. We are not inclined, however, to accept this reasoning. Mr. Fergusson mentions, nevertheless, a number of additional facts which seem to make the existing dolmens and other monuments comparatively modern. As for example, the greater number of the dolmens on the Nilgiri hills are sculptured; one of these drawings has been published, and it is very similar to the drawings on a class of monuments very common in the plains, called Viracull, if designed to commemorate men or heroes, and Masteecull, if erected in honor of women who sacrifice themselves on their husbands' funeral pile. There is little doubt that these drawings are of the same age as those on the Nilgiri dolmens, and most of the former are accompanied by inscriptions, and their date at least approximately known. None of them go back a thousand years, and those most like the drawing from the Nilgiri dolmen are not more than five centuries old.

Age of the Indian monuments.

On the banks of the Godavery, near Nirmul, in Central India, in 1867–8, Mr. Mulheran, attached to the Trigonometrical Survey of India, came across a great number of "cromlechs," consisting of upright stones sunk in the ground in the form of a square, and covered with one or two large slabs of sandstone. Near some of these, always on the right, a *cross* is erected. They are about seven feet high, and consist of one stone, "and are all of the latest form." The people (as usual) can give no information about them. "There can be no doubt, however," says Mr. Mulheran, "that the crosses are memorials of the faith of Christians buried in their vicinity." We know that the Nestorians had missions as far east as China about the tenth century, and that there were Christian settlements in India from Persia prior to the tenth century, and, perhaps, as early as the third. Cosmas Indicopleustes, in the sixth century, mentions Christians as residing in Ceylon and India.

All this may prove the recent date of the *existing* monuments; it does not prove that others did not precede them. Our own opinion is that the Stone Monuments originated at an early period in the East; they travelled westward, and were erected in Europe as soon as the nomad tribes to whom they belonged had become a somewhat settled and organized society.

CHAPTER X.

THE MEGALITHIC MONUMENTS, CONTINUED.

The Association of the Stone Celts with the Metals and other Recent Relics.—A Proof of the continued Use of Stone Weapons and Implements down to a Late Period.—Examples of their being found with Bronze.—Examples of their being found with Iron.—The Co-existence of the Three Ages.—The only Coins found in the Tombs, Roman; and of the Later Emperors.—No British or Gaulish Coins.—Our Indebtedness to Mr. Fergusson's Work.—Extracts therefrom, and his Opinion that the Megalithic Monuments belong to the First Ten Centuries of the Christian Era.—Not noticed by the Classical Authors.—In no Instance (excepting Etruria) where the Date has been fixed have the Monuments been Pre-Roman.—Who were the Builders of the Dolmens?—Their Distribution.—They probably belong to the Basque or Iberian Race.—The Circle-Builders of Scandinavia.—Two Lines of Migration from the Shores of the Black Sea.—The Iberians of the Caucasus.—The Saxons from the Mouth of the Elbe.—The Circles of Scotland and the Orkneys, Scandinavian.—Explanation of the Fact that there are no older Monuments.—The Saxons the same with the Scythian Tribe of the Sacæ from the Eastern Borders of the Black Sea.—The Turanian Family of Mankind.—Close Relation between the Turanian and the Japhetic Races.

We have in the preceding chapter shown pretty conclusively that the Rude Stone Monuments must be abandoned by the archæologists as an evidence for the antiquity of man. There remain, however, some few points to be noticed in this connection, before passing to the next branch of the general subject.

We have given, in describing the tombs considered in the previous chapter, various examples of the association of the flint or stone and metal implements in these graves. We desire to mention some additional examples of such association (taken chiefly from the graves) to show in particular the continued use of the stone celts after the introduction of the metals. Arrow-heads, it has been said, would naturally (as liable to be lost) continue to be made of flint. And flint "flakes," it might be said, in association with metal, in the graves, would not necessarily prove the cotemporaneous use of flint and metal weapons. But the battle-axe of stone was a more important weapon; and we propose, by farther examples, to show that even this is constantly found with the metals, or with Roman and other recent relics. These examples would be greatly more numerous but for one circumstance (already adverted to); namely, that these weapons were so valuable that in a large majority of cases they could not

The stone celts found with metal and Roman relics.

be spared by the living to deposit with the dead; and this must be borne in mind.

As we propose to recur to this subject (involving, as it does, a vital point in this discussion) in our chapter entitled "Stone, Bronze, and Iron," we shall not multiply these examples at present. It has seemed to us appropriate to add a few additional ones just here, first, because most of the instances specified fall naturally under the head of the tumuli and dolmens, in which the weapons were found, and, secondly, because we wish to illustrate still farther, just here, the point under discussion.

The examination which has been instituted into this subject is bringing out more and more clearly the fact that stone weapons continued in use in Northern, Central, and Western Europe until even post-Roman times.

We proceed to cite the following cases:

In a barrow on Upton Lovel Down, Mr. W. Cunnington, in 1802, found an extended skeleton, and above it a smaller skeleton in a contracted posture. He also found three flint celts (one rough, the others polished *at the edge*), a perforated stone axe, a number of bone instruments, some jet beads and a ring, and a small bronze awl. In the Ravenshill tumulus, near Scarborough, were an urn containing burnt bones, a broken flint celt, flint arrow-heads, and a beautiful bronze pin. Near Tynewydd, Denbighshire, a greenstone celt and a bronze socketed celt were found together. At Cantire, in the parish of Southend, three stone celts were found with a bronze socketed celt. At Campbelton, in Argyleshire, were found two polished stone axes, and with them two stone moulds for casting looped spear-heads of bronze. A double-edged axe of basalt was found with a bronze awl, and a flint spear-head, near Throwley, in Derbyshire.

So that not only the perforated axes, but the axes without holes drilled through them, and which are more ancient, are found with bronze, and must have been in use in the Bronze Age.

The cut on the next page is a superb battle-axe of fine-grained mica-schist, found in a "Druidical" circle at Crichie, near Inverary. We take it from Mr. Evans's work. It was obviously prepared with a metallic tool.

Some very beautiful cups of stone, wood, and other material, have been found in these "primeval" barrows. Stone cups with handles have been frequently found in Scotland and the adjacent islands. A beautiful cup of shale figured in "The Ancient Stone Implements," was found in a tumulus at Broad Down, near Honiton, by the Rev. Mr. Kirwan, who found another like it with a bronze spear-head in another barrow on Broad Down. These cups, we are told by Mr. Evans, have been *turned in the lathe*, a practice not known in the north of Europe until after the appearance of the Romans.

A beautiful amber cup was also found in a barrow at Hove, near Brighton. It also was turned in the lathe. With it were found a

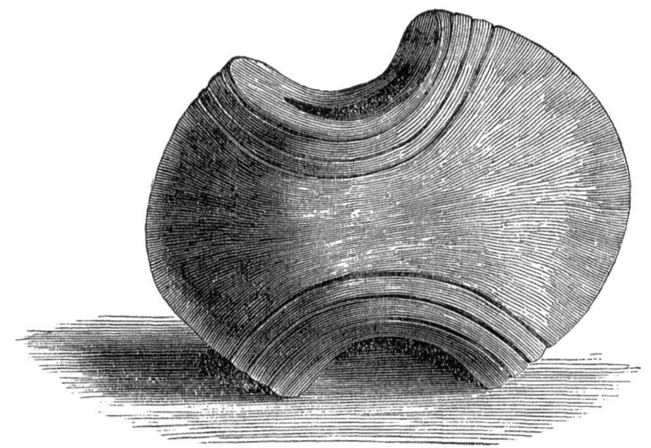

CRICHIE, ABERDEENSHIRE.

double-edged battle-axe of stone, and a bronze dagger. The corpse had been buried in a wooden coffin. Here is an obviously post-Roman interment containing a stone battle-axe and a bronze dagger.

It is usually said that the Stone Age and the Bronze Age *lapped:* of course they did; but it is our impression that the "lap" was a much broader one than the archæologists would allow.

"Lap" of the Stone Age and the Bronze Age.

The stone celts and other stone weapons are found *in association with iron implements and with Roman remains.* If the Bronze Age lasted several thousand years, as we are told, did the stone axe and the stone knife *lap* clear across this "several thousand years"? did the Stone Age "lap" the Iron Age too?

"Lap" of the Stone Age and the Iron Age.

We have already specified instances of the association of iron and stone. It will be remembered that a polished celt and iron were found together at Gib Hill. Near Claughton Hall, Lancashire, in 1822, a perforated stone axe was found in a wooden case, together with an iron axe, spear-head, sword, and hammer, in cutting through a tumulus.

"In many cases in Germany," says Mr. Evans in his "Ancient Stone Implements of Great Britain," "stone axes, for the most part perforated, are said to have been found in association with objects of iron." (Page 131.) They (not perforated) have also been found in Denmark associated with iron. Flint battle-axes were found in a Merovingian cemetery at Labruyère, in the Côte d'Or. A fibrolite hatchet was found within a building at Mont Beuvray (the ancient Bibracte), with three Gaulish coins of the time of Augustus.

Iron and stone implements occurring together.

In the Saxon burial-place at Ash, in Kent, were found a polished flint celt, a circular flint stone, and a Roman fibula. At Leicester a fragment of a flint celt was found with objects referred to a late Roman or an early Saxon period. In the Roman villa at Great Whitcombe, Gloucestershire, a "British hatchet of flint" was discovered. A greenstone celt was found in excavating a Roman building at Ickleton, Essex; and another with Roman remains at Alchester, Oxfordshire. A flint celt was also found with Roman remains at Eastbourne.

Flint arrow-heads with Roman and Saxon remains.

The flint arrow-heads are also found with objects of iron, and of the Roman and Saxon periods. A broken flint arrow-head, almost of a lozenge form, accompanied by a human skeleton, an iron sword, and an iron lance, was found in the Frankish cemetery of Samson, near Namur, and another stemmed arrow-head was found in the soil. Other cases we have already mentioned, and we shall mention others hereafter.

The tendency of all this is to show that these "ages" not only run into each other, but that all three are found together in some instances. It is by no means improbable that iron was often found on the hill, and stone in the valley; and that an army of Britons or Gauls presented oftentimes weapons of iron, and bronze, and stone in the same host—or as at Kingston, on the Thames, or at Alise in Burgundy, there may have been a conflict between the iron weapons of the Romans and the bronze or stone weapons of the Britons or Gauls. The Peruvians, as we shall see, and as has been alluded to, used knives of obsidian, and the Peruvian ladies used scissors of obsidian, when they were perfectly familiar with bronze.

Another point to which we would call attention is this:

The coins in the tombs all Roman.

We have in the course of this discussion mentioned a number of instances in England and France in which *Roman coins* occurred in the tumuli and dolmens. We have not mentioned *one* in which a British or Gaulish coin has been found. There is in fact no instance of the kind anywhere mentioned. The Gauls, according to Mr. Evans, had a coinage about 300 B.C.; the Britons were a century or two later. If these tombs are pre-Roman, why are there no British or Gaulish coins in them?

But this is not all: there is no instance on record of any Roman coin, belonging to any of the earlier emperors, having ever been found in England or Ireland—and, so far as we know, Scotland. A coin of Hadrian was found in the Bartlow Hills (A.D. 138–180); but the barrows here are known to be Roman, and do not belong to the present discussion. Nor has any coin or medal of Augustus, or of Julius Cæsar, or of the Republic, been found in any of these tombs in France. Nor, so far as we are informed, is there any trace of any of the emperors of the first two centuries of the Christian era in any of the Gaulish sepulchres, excepting at Mané er H'roëk, where, as we have stated, there was found a series of medals from Tiberius to Trajan.

Is there no inference to be drawn from these remarkable facts? That there are no traces of British or Gaulish coins, and none of the Roman Republic, or the first emperors, in these tombs, when the Roman coins after the second century frequently occur?*

It may be imagined that Roman coins of the early emperors do not occur under other circumstances. But such is not the fact. During the excavations at Carlisle, in 1857, near the ancient Roman Wall, a medal of Antoninus Pius was found, together with a large brass coin of Vespasian, struck to commemorate the capture of Jerusalem—having on one side a head aptly representative of a nation of "fierce countenance," and on the other the figure and inscription of "Judæa capta."

On the Hill of Barcombe, a half-mile south of the Wall, there were found in 1837 a number of Roman silver coins in a bronze vessel—nine of them belonging to the Consular days, and the others representing Claudius, Nero, Otho, Vespasian, Domitian, Nerva, and Trajan.

At Condercum, on Benwell Hill, two miles from Newcastle, they found brass and silver coins of Vespasian, Titus, Domitian, Nerva, Trajan, Hadrian, Antoninus Pius, Commodus, Diocletian, Constantine, Constans, Valentinian, Gratian (A.D. 364).

The late Mr. Bell, of Isthington, collected coins from the neighborhood of the Wall from the period of Julius Cæsar to that of Arcadius.

In Drake's "Eboracum" is given a catalogue of coins from Augustus to Gratian, found in York. At Bath we have them from Claudius to Honorius and Arcadius. At Cirencester from Augustus to Honorius, etc., etc.†

In 1867 excavations near Cannon Street in London brought to light a variety of Roman remains—among them coins of Agrippa, Claudius, Nero, Vespasian, Titus, Domitian, and Trajan.

We perceive, therefore, that Roman coins occur in Britain dating from the beginning of the empire, and even during the epoch of the republic. And yet in the tumuli they only occur bearing the date of the third and fourth centuries.

Mr. James Fergusson's work.

Our principal (but by no means our sole) guide in collating the facts of the previous chapter has been the learned work of Mr. James Fergusson, D.C.L., F.R.S., published in 1872, entitled "Rude Stone Monuments in all Countries: their Age and their Uses,"—a work which in our opinion cannot be answered.‡

* In a barrow near Parwich (Derbyshire) eighty coins of the later emperors were found. They have been found in other barrows in Derbyshire.

† See *The Roman Wall*, by J. Collingwood Bruce, London, 1867, pp. 418, 421, 18, 44, etc.

‡ The writer of the article in *The British Quarterly* for Oct. 1872, attempts to answer it,

The conclusions reached by him.

Mr. Fergusson, after an elaborate review of the whole field, reaches the conclusion that these tumuli, circles, dolmens, etc., are not even pre-Roman, but belong "to the first ten centuries of the Christian era." Direct literary evidence, he says, does not exist. No classical author alludes to these structures; why not, he asks, if they were in existence? When Cæsar witnessed the fight between his galleys and the fleet of the Veneti in the Morbihan, he must have stood right amongst the vast stone avenues of Carnac—if they existed. He makes no allusion to the "standing stones" of Dariorigum. So the Via Badonica in Britain passed so immediately under Silbury Hill that the Romans who occupied Old Sarum probably during their sojourn in that island, would not have been ignorant of either Stonehenge or Avebury. France too was (according to the theory) full of dolmens. And yet the voice of classical antiquity is absolutely silent as to the existence of these monuments. Cæsar goes into the minutest details about Gaul, even describing its fauna, but he makes no reference to these "pre-historic" monuments. Tacitus is equally silent. All this, of course, is merely negative evidence. "The direct written evidence," says Mr. Fergusson, "is of the most shadowy character. It amounts to little more than this: that every allusion to these monuments in mediæval authors, every local tradition, every scrap of intelligence we have regarding them, points to a post-Roman origin."

It is not possible to prove that all these monuments are later than the Christian era; possibly some of them are earlier. Our examination of the subject, however, has not afforded us the first instance where the evidence proved a pre-Roman date, except in Etruria. Whenever we have been enabled to fix the date, it has been some centuries, at least, after the Christian era. Mr. Fergusson says "few can produce such proof of their age as would stand investigation in a court of law." "But," he adds, "when all the traditions, all the analogies, all the probabilities of the case are examined, they seem to make up such an accumulation of evidence as is irresistible; and the whole appears to present an unbroken and intelligible sequence which explains everything."

Character of the evidence.

The proof of this does not rest on the evidence of two or three, or even a dozen, instances, but upon the multiplication of a great number of coincidences derived from a large number of instances, which taken together make up the strongest possible case.

---

but has by no means done so; and if he had not been conscious of impotence, he would not have fastened on a few ill-considered remarks in the book, and made them rather than the main argument the subject of his criticism.

Another important remark of Mr. Fergusson is this: that "three-fourths of the monuments have yielded sepulchral deposits to the explorer, and, including the tumuli, probably nine-tenths have proved to be burial-places." "Still, at the present stage of the enquiry, it would be at least premature to assume that the remaining tenth of the whole, or the remaining fourth of the stone section, must necessarily be sepulchral. Some may have been cenotaphic, or simply monuments, such as we erect to our great men—not necessarily where the bodies are laid. Some stones and some tumuli may have been erected to commemorate events, and some mounds certainly were erected as 'Motes' or 'Things'—places of judgment or assembly. In like manner some circles may have been originally, or may afterwards have been, used as places of assembly, or may have been what may more properly be called temples of the dead, than tombs. These, however, certainly are exceptions. The ruling idea throughout is still of a sepulchre."*

The monuments sepulchral.

We will make one other quotation from Mr. Fergusson; it is the closing paragraph of his Introduction.

"One point, I fancy, there will be very little difficulty in proving, which is that the whole [of these monuments] form one continuous group, extending in an unbroken series, from the earliest to the latest. There is no hiatus or break anywhere; and if some can be proved to belong to the tenth century, it is only a question how far you can, by attenuating the thread, extend it backwards. It can hardly be much beyond the Christian era. It seems that such a date satisfies the known conditions of the problem, in so far as the Stone Monuments at least are concerned. There is, so far as I know at present, absolutely no evidence on the other side, except what is derived from the Danish system of the three ages; if that is established as a rule of law, *cadit questio*, there is no more to be said on the subject. But this is exactly what does not appear to have been yet established on any sufficient or satisfactory basis. There need be no difficulty in granting that men used stone and bone for implements before they were acquainted with the use of the metals. [This we do not admit as regards some races.] It may also be admitted that they used bronze before they learned the art of extracting iron from its ores. But what is denied is, that they abandoned the use of those primitive implements on the introduction of the metals; and it is contended that they employed stone and bone simultaneously with bronze and iron down to a very late period. The real fact of the case seems to be, that the people on the shores of the Baltic and the North Sea were as remote from the centres of civili-

* Rude Stone Monuments, p. 26.

zation on the Mediterranean and to the eastward of it in the earlier centuries of our era, and were as little influenced by them, as the inhabitants of the islands in the Pacific and of Arctic America were by Europe in the last century. In the remote corners of the world, a stone and a bone age exists at the present day, only modified by the use of such metal implements as they can obtain by barter or exchange; and this appears to have been the state of Northern Europe, till, with their conversion to Christianity, the new civilization was domesticated among its inhabitants."*

We will simply observe on these remarks that, while, as a general rule, these monuments do seem to date either since, or not long before, the Christian era, it does not follow that they were erected then for the first time. Those which have come down to us may be, ordinarily, not more than two thousand years old; the probability, however, is, that even in Gaul and Britain such tombs were erected at least eight hundred or a thousand years before our era, while in the north of Africa and in the East they doubtless go back still farther.

Mr. Fergusson's idea that it was a "fashion" which suddenly sprang up in different parts of the world, about the beginning of the Christian era, is too improbable to be entertained. They belong to some race, and have travelled from the East to the West.

Who erected the dolmens?

The question then remains in connection with the Rude Stone Monuments which we have traced from India to the Caucasus, and thence to Northern Africa, Spain, Portugal, Western and Southern France, Britain, Ireland, North Germany, Denmark, Sweden, Russia—and finally to Peru: By whom were they erected? The fact that they exist in Western but not in Eastern France proves that they are not Celtic. It has been shown also by Mr. Fergusson that those occurring in Southwestern India were not built by the Aryan race. We miss them (saving always Etruria) in Italy, in Switzerland, in Belgium, in Central and Southern Germany, in Austria, in Greece, in Turkey.† They occur in Eastern England, but they swarm in Cornwall, in Wales, in Anglesea, and the Isle of Man. We do not find them (speaking broadly) in Western, but in Eastern and Southeastern Ireland (opposite Wales and Cornwall). They are absent from the south of Scotland, but are found in the northeast, and in the islands north and west of Scotland.

They occur on the northern coast of Spain, and in Granada, on the south coast. There are also a great many in Portugal.

They abound again in North Holland, Hanover, Mecklenburg, Pomerania, Denmark, and Southern Sweden.

---

* Rude Stone Monuments, p. 28.

† There are tumuli in Turkey.

There are thousands in North Africa; a goodly number in Southwestern India; and they are numerous in the Caucasus and on the coast of the Black Sea, and on the steppes of Tartary and Siberia. They are not Semitic. They must be Turanian. According to our observation, wherever we find the dolmens in Europe, we can detect the Basque or Iberian race.

Iberian.

We thus find them in Galicia, the Asturias, Navarre, Biscay, and Catalonia; while they abound in Portugal. They do not occur often in Central and Eastern Spain—the Iberian population having probably been driven to the North and West by the Carthaginians, the Romans, and the Christians. We find them in the Basses and the Hautes Pyrénées, in Southwestern France, and then north of the Garonne in Limousin and Auvergne and along the entire western coast to the northern limits of Brittany.

Spain and Portugal.

We learn from Tacitus that the inhabitants of Britain consisted of: 1. The red-haired Caledonians, resembling the Germans; 2. Those opposite Gaul, resembling the Gauls; and 3. The Silures, of dark complexion and curling hair; and these last he suggests were *Iberians* from Spain, inhabiting the region opposite Spain. Accordingly, it is in Wales and Cornwall that we find in full flower the dolmens of Britain. As we have stated, they are not very frequent in other parts of England, and are absent from Southern Scotland.

The Silures in Wales and Cornwall.

We find them again in Ireland, as particularly near Wexford and Donegal. And there we find traces of the Spanish immigrants "of the race of Heremon," etc., who settled in Ireland after (as is probable) the Christian era. The migrations from Spain to Ireland, even down to a late period, are a well-established fact.

Ireland.

Migrations to, from Spain.

In Northern Africa these monuments belong, we believe, to the Numidian or Berber race—and these we suspect to have been identical with the Iberians.

If we turn now to Denmark, Sweden, North Germany, we find that all the coasts of the Baltic (from the mouth of the Vistula) and, on the east, those of the North Sea, were settled by the *Goths* or the *Saxons*. Worsaae tells us that in the oldest Icelandic sagas and chronicles of the North it is stated that Denmark in the earliest time was called *Eygotland* (the island of the Goths), and, sometimes, merely *Gotland*. "In the fifth century," he proceeds, "the Goths (Jütes) went over to England from Jutland, which country was still, in the ninth century, called by the Anglo-Saxons *Gotland*." *

* Prim. Antiq., p. 144.

The Svear, or, as tradition says, Odin and his followers, came to the shores of Mäler Lake about the beginning of the Christian era, from the countries about the Black Sea, passing through Russia and Finland, and over the Aland islands. The Norwegians followed them. For some centuries after this there were great "migrations" in progress throughout Northern and Eastern Europe—and doubtless there had been similar movements before, as the arms of the Romans advanced, or in connection with the ceaseless wars of the barbarians. The southern part of Sweden was settled by the Göths, and called Götaland. These were a nearly related people to the Svear. They all came from the region of the Black Sea.

At the foot of Mount Caucasus, near the eastern shore of the Black Sea, we find the "Iberians." And, as we have stated, here again we encounter many dolmens.

Our theory is that Turanian (Scythian) tribes moved originally from this region, and from the region east of it, into India, Northern Africa, and the north of Europe. We find a thickly-studded dolmen region in Granada opposite the African coast. There were thus two great lines of migration from the original seat of the Iberians into Europe: the first, at a very early period, via Northern Africa into Spain, and thence to Aquitania, Brittany, Britain, and Ireland; the second, much later, across Russia, into North Germany, Denmark, and Sweden.*

The Goths, on their first appearance in history, are described as occupying the country about the mouth of the Vistula, north of the Tygii. They are represented as inhabiting the coast of the Baltic as early as the time of Pytheas, the Massilian navigator—about B.C. 330. They are mentioned by Tacitus, under the name of Gothones, and as still inhabiting the coast of the Baltic.†

The Saxons, along with the Frisians, the Jutes, and the Angles, came to England from the mouth of the Elbe, from Jutland, Schleswig, and the southern shores of the North Sea. They were all evidently the same family with the Goths; and all were, doubtless, Scythian tribes from the coasts of the Euxine.

It is worthy of remark, that Sharon Turner traces the Saxons to the very region in the neighborhood of the Black Sea, from which we have supposed Odin and his followers to have migrated. He regards them as

* In corroboration of this, it may be stated that Prof. Nilsson finds from an examination of the crania of present inhabitants of Sweden that they resemble the type found among the Iberians, the Lapps and Samoyedes, and the Pelasgi. See Prehist. Ann. of Scot., vol. i. p. 11.

† It is mentioned in Rawlinson's Herodotus that Dr. Donaldson regards *Scyth* as another form of *Goth*, and *Massagetæ* (a Scythian tribe of Central Asia) as equivalent to *Massa-Goths*, *Thyssegetæ* as equivalent to *Thysse-Goths*, etc. Vol. i. p. 266.

a Scythian tribe, descended from the Sakai or Sacæ. These Sacæ seized Armenia, bordering on Iberia, and Pliny calls them Sacassani, which is equivalent to Saka-Suna or Sakai-Suna, the sons of the Sakai. They gave the name of Sacasena to the part of Armenia which they occupied. Mr. Turner adds that Ptolemy mentions a Scythian people, sprung from the Sakai, by the name of Saxones. He further states that Stephanus mentions a people called Saxoi, on the shores of the Euxine.

But we shall be asked, Were the Saxons "Turanians"?

Tribes of the Caucasus.

It is very well known that the mixture of races and languages in the Caucasus is, perhaps, greater than in any other part of the world. There are Georgians, Basians, Abchasians, Tcherkessians, Oketiens, Kistiens, Lesghians, Tartars. And we may remark also that it is curious that Josephus represents Iberia (in the Caucasus) to have been first peopled by Tubal, the brother of Gomer and Magog; which opinion is sanctioned by the Septuagint, in which Meshech and Tubal are rendered *Moschi* and *Iberians*. And finally, speaking of the Scythians, Mr. Smith, in his Ancient History of the East, speaks in a note as follows: "This qualification has respect to the indications—which seem to come out more as the subject is pursued farther—of that close connection between these primitive Turanians and the Aryan type, which is sometimes expressed by calling them *Scytho-Aryans*, as if they were a mixed population, and sometimes by regarding them as an ancient type of the Japhetic race, before its decided bifurcation into the Aryan and Turanian families. There seems now to be established a close connection between the Turanian and Aryan races, on the one hand, and between the Hamitic and Semitic, on the other."*

The Scythians.

In the British Isles the two currents of the great Turanian or Scytho-Aryan migrations *meet*. The Rude Stone Monuments of these islands, therefore, are no doubt partly due to the Iberians from Spain and Brittany, and partly to the emigrants or marauders from Scandinavia and the eastern shores of the North Sea. Those in North Scotland, and in the Orkneys and the Western Isles, are probably Scandinavian. Those in Ireland are probably, in some instances, Scandinavian; in others, Iberian. Those of Wales and Cornwall are from Iberia or Brittany. Those in East England may be from either source; but there are none here to speak of, excepting Aylesford. The Circles and the Dolmens and the Barrows of England are in the West or the North. The dolmens (with a half-dozen exceptions) are all in the West—in Cornwall, in Wales, in Anglesea, in the Isle of Man—the country of the Silures. All of the

---

* Anc. Hist. of the East, p. 519.

Great Circles, so far as we remember, are in the West. Tradition connects Stonehenge with Uther Pendragon, the father of King Arthur, and with Constantine, his nephew and successor—both of whom are said to have been buried there. Now Arthur was a Prince of the Silures. One of the great circles at Penrith, in Cumberland, bears the name of "King Arthur's Round Table." Stanton Drew, in Somersetshire, as we have seen, is traditionally associated with a female saint, apparently the daughter of a Welsh prince, in the fifth century.

It will be asked how our theory that the ancient Iberian race is the race of the dolmen-builders is consistent with our representations of the recent date of these monuments? why the Iberians did not erect them from their earliest settlement in Europe? In the beginning, probably an unsettled and nomad race, they would not of course construct many monuments. They were, moreover, at that time, in a very rude and primitive condition, and the nation was hardly sufficiently organized to engage in the erection of these megalithic structures. No doubt some were erected; great numbers, and among them, most probably, the earliest, have perished. Possibly in Spain, or even in Western France, some of the existing monuments may be as old as 500 or 600 years before Christ. Many of these monuments may have been destroyed by conquering races.

Were the Etruscans "Iberians"? It is not improbable. Only in Etruria (as we have stated), excepting a single example elsewhere, are there, so far as we know, any rude stone monuments in Italy. The only dolmens are at Saturnia. But the tombs at Saturnia are supposed to be *Pelasgic*. Dionysius represents Saturnia to have been one of the four cities built by the aborigines of Italy, and no Etruscan objects have been found in these graves. All this is very vague. We know little of either the Etruscans or the Pelasgi. The latter came from the same region with the "Iberians," and their name is derived by Strabo and Myrsilus from πελαργοι, *storks*, in allusion to their wandering life, the former describing them as an unsettled and migratory race; while, as we have seen, Nilsson classes them, in respect to cranial conformation, with the Iberians, Lapps, and Samoyedes.

In any event, we probably have at Saturnia among the oldest existing dolmens in the world—survivors from the wreck of those which were pre-Christian in date.

CHAPTER XI.

THE LAKE-DWELLINGS.

First Discovery of, in 1854, by Dr. Keller.—Represent the Three Ages.—Not regarded as so Old as the Danish Shell-Mounds.—The Archæologists estimate them to be Seven Thousand Years Old.—Found on all the Swiss Lakes.—Character of the Relics.—The Lake-Dwellers Weavers.—Animal Remains found.—Agriculture amongst the Lake-Dwellers.—The Steinbergs and Pfahlbauten.—Lake-Dwelling mentioned by Herodotus.—By Hippocrates.—By Abulfeda.—Still found in Several Countries.—The Irish Crannoges.—Remains of, in Scotland, England, France, Austria, Pomerania, etc.—The "Saturday Review" on the Great Antiquity of the Lake-Habitations.—Dr. M'Causland's Estimate.—The Evidence in Detail.—Robenhausen, one of the Oldest Settlements.—Three Times destroyed by Fire.—Axes of Nephrite.—Agriculture.—Weaving.—Wangen, another Ancient Stone Age Settlement.—A Factory for Stone Implements.—The Nephrite of the East again.—Perforated Stone Axes.—Linen Garments.—Ueberlinger See, a Stone and a Bronze Station.—Nussdorf.—Destroyed by Fire.—Belongs to Stone Age.—The Horse domesticated.—Maurach.—Unter Uhldingen.—Stone and Bronze.—Roman Pottery.—Also Iron Relics.—Glass.—Sipplingen.—Some Twelve Hundred Feet from Shore.—Stone Implements.—Iron and Glass, but no Bronze.—The Lake of Zug.—The Remains here Inland, and away from Shore.—Wauwyl.—In a Peat-moss like Robenhausen, and very ancient.—Nephrite and Glass-bead.—Moosseedorf, one of the Oldest Stations.—No Metal.—A Factory.—Nephrite, Wheat, Barley, Linseed, Dog, Goat, Sheep, Cow, etc.—Lake of Bienne.—Great Bronze Station of Nidau.—Other Stations.—Roman Relics.—Möringen, another Bronze Station.—Destroyed by Fire.—Iron.—Lake of Neufchâtel.—Great Iron Station of La Tène.—Coins, Roman Tiles, etc.—Other Stations on this Lake.—Roman Remains.—Calculation with regard to Age of Station at Pont de Thièle.—Cortaillod.—Bronze.—Estavayer.—Two Stations here.—The Stone Age Settlements always near the Shore.—Remains found.—Farther Evidences of continuous Use of Stone after Introduction of Bronze.—Concise.—Belongs to Stone Age.—Bronze Relics found.—Perforated Stone Hammers.—Coral and Wheel-made Pottery.—Corcelettes, a Bronze Station.—Roman Amphora, but no Iron.—Lake of Morat.—Lake of Geneva.—Morges.—Two Stations here.—Meilen, very old, on Lake of Zurich.—The Stations in East of Switzerland generally of the Stone Age.—The Bronze and Iron Stations in the West.—Trade of Geneva with Massilia and Lugdunum.—Co-existence of the Three Ages.—Animal Remains of the Lacustrine Villages.—No Reindeer.—Similar Settlements on Land.—Ehrensberg.—Stone and Metal mixed again.—Burg.—Same Phenomenon.—Uetliberg.—Windisch.—Lacustrine Settlements in Italy, and Other Countries of Europe.—Lake of Bourgat.—Lake of Paladru.—Olmutz.—Lake-Dwellings delineated on Trajan's Column at Rome.—Those at Noville and Chavannes continued to Eighth Century.—Irish Crannoges occupied in Sixteenth Century.

In the winter of 1853–4, owing to an unusually dry season, the lakes of Switzerland fell greatly below their usual level; at Meilen, on the Lake of Zurich, the inhabitants undertook to reclaim from the water a tract of ground, which they proceeded to secure by dykes and embankments. In the execution of this work they found in the mud of the lake a number of piles, besides fragments of pottery, and implements of stone and bone. Various articles had previously been observed within the margin of other lakes, and piles had been noticed standing erect in the water. But they had not elicited any special examination. When, however, the attention of Dr. Keller, a physician of Zurich, was called to the relics observed at Meilen, he at once, we are informed, recognized them as "belonging to pre-historic times." He published five very interesting papers on the subject, and this was the signal for a general exploration. Since that time several hundred of these pile-habitations have been discovered—the remains of lacustrine villages which formerly existed over the water. Innumerable objects have been found belonging, according to the vocabulary of the archæologists, to the Stone Age, the Bronze Age, and the Iron Age—for it is assumed that they belong to different ages, and by some (as M. Troyon), even to different races. The older ones, of course, are assigned to the Stone Age, but not to the first period of the Stone Age. They belong to the Neolithic Age or The Age of Polished Stone Implements. They are not, therefore, considered as old as the Danish Kjökken-möddings, or the oldest Bone-Caverns, or the River-Gravel of the Somme Valley. Their minimum age is, according to M. Morlot and M. Figuier (Sir John Lubbock appearing to concur), about 6000 or 7000 years.

Dr. Ferdinand Keller.

The relics found.

Not older than the Neolithic Age.

The Lake-Dwellings are found in the lakes of Zurich, Constance, Geneva, Bienne, Morat, Neufchâtel, etc., and frequently in peat-moss covering the bed of former small lakes. Twenty have been found in the Lake of Bienne; twenty-five in the Lake of Geneva; thirty-two in the Lake of Constance; forty-nine in the Lake of Neufchâtel. "Some belong to the Iron Age, some few even to Roman times; but the greater number appear to be divided in almost equal proportions between the age of Stone and that of Bronze."* The antiquities found in these localities are stone axes, arrow-heads, flint flakes, stone hammers, whetstones, slingstones, instruments of bone, broken pottery, weapons and ornaments and vessels of bronze and iron, etc.

We present in the following cuts examples of the rude flint implements of the Palæolithic Age.

* Pre-historic Times, p. 179.

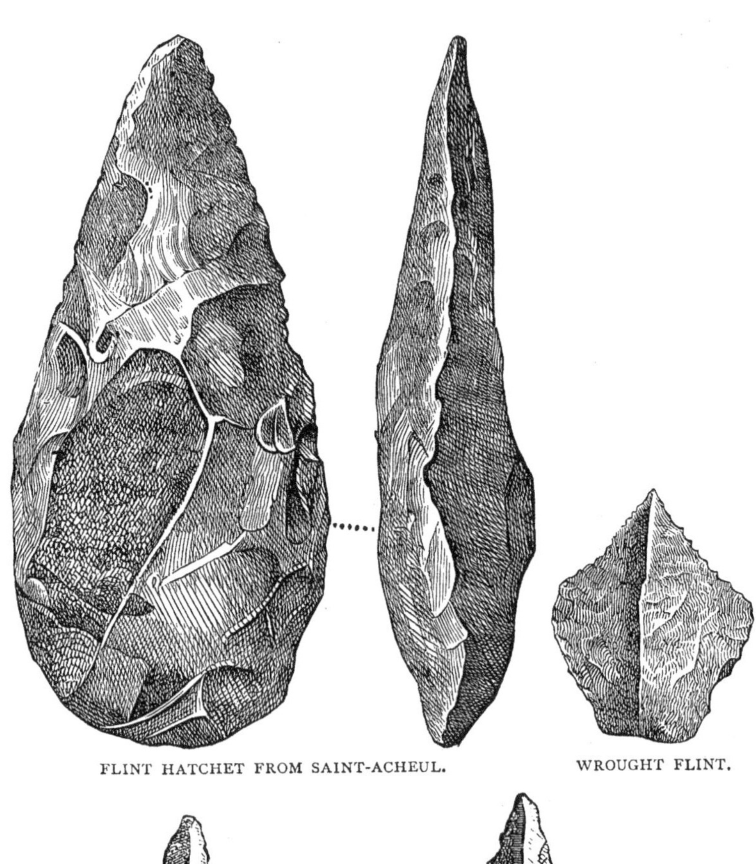

FLINT HATCHET FROM SAINT-ACHEUL.

WROUGHT FLINT.

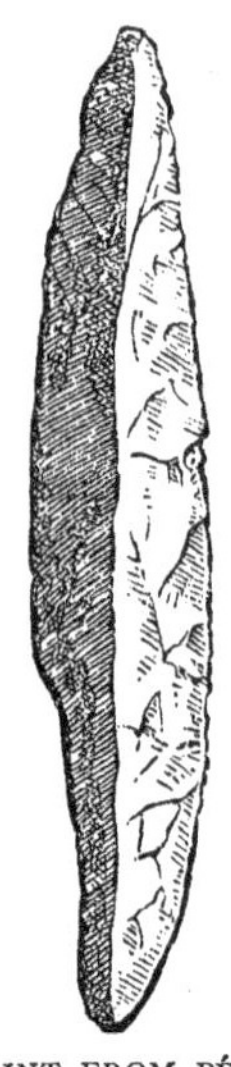

WORKED FLINT FROM PÉRIGORD (KNIFE).

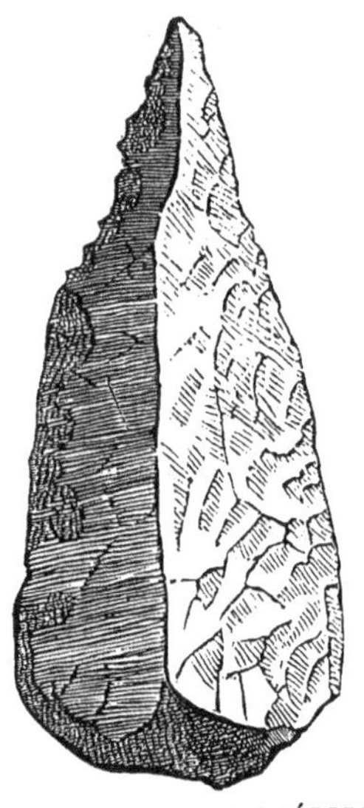

WORKED FLINT FROM PÉRIGORD (HATCHET).

The following specimens, which the reader may contrast with the foregoing, belong to the Age of the Lake-Dwellings and Polished Stone Weapons:

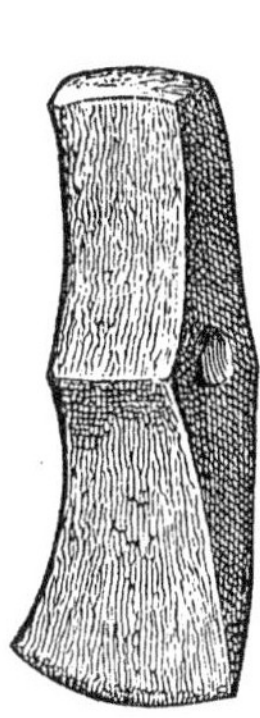

PERFORATED AXE.

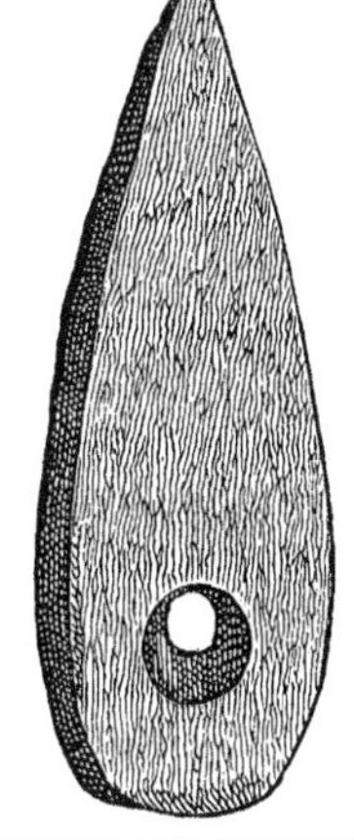

DANISH AXE-HAMMER, DRILLED FOR HANDLE.

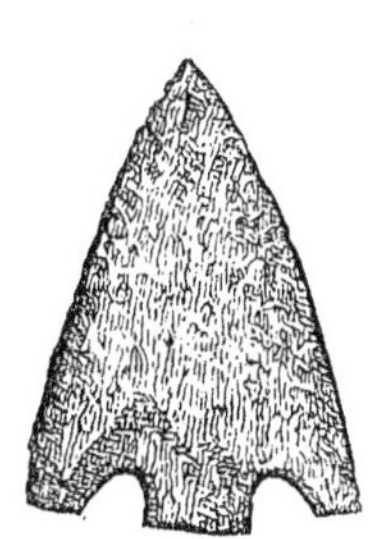

ARROW-HEAD.

FLINT PONIARD FROM DENMARK.

HARPOON MADE OF STAG'S HORN, FROM THE LACUSTRINE HABITATIONS OF SWITZERLAND.

The Lake-Dwellers weavers.

Speaking of the remains of the Stone Age, Sir John Lubbock informs us that "spindle-whorls of rude earthenware were abundant in some of the Lake villages." "This," he says, "indicates a knowledge of weaving." At Wanken and Robenhausen, both of which are assigned to the Stone Age, "pieces of rude fabric have been found in some abundance." (Pp. 190, 194.) It appears, therefore, that the Lake-Dwellers of the Stone Age understood the art of making cloth. We find, however, in the "Annual Record of Science and Industry" for 1871 (p. 181) more explicit testimony on this point. It is as follows:

"An interesting communication was presented by Dr. Weigert, before an industrial society in Prussia, upon the products of spinning and weaving discovered in the pile-dwellings of Switzerland, in which he showed that even in the stone period flax was cultivated in large quantity, and worked up in the most varied fabrics, including the making of thread, ropes, etc. Remains of spinning-wheels of stone and clay are very abundant, as also the relics of the manufactured articles themselves. Plaited fabrics, which served as mats, coverlets, and walls, showed the extended use of this branch of manufacture. The remains of spindles proved conclusively that the art of weaving was known to these people, and that they used a loom with the chain standing vertically instead of horizontally. An important conclusion was derived from this fact by the author in regard to the development of civilization on the part of these people; since of the two methods, namely, whether the chain is horizontal or vertical, the former has been peculiar to India and Egypt from the earliest period, while the latter was used among the Græco-Italian nations, a proof that the European culture was not influenced by Africa and Asia until it had itself made considerable progress.—14 c, cxcviii. 308."

Not probable that any great antiquity belongs to these relics.

It is hardly reasonable to assign a very remote antiquity to these spinners and weavers. And it will be remarked that it is not the Bronze people who spin and weave, and cultivate flax, and work up "the most varied fabrics"—thread, ropes, mats, coverlets, etc.; but the primitive "Stone Age" people—those who made the beautiful polished stone weapons of the Neolithic Age—the successors of the cotemporaries of the cave-bear, and the cave-lion, and the European mammoth, and the woolly rhinoceros.

Coral and amber from distant countries.

It appears, moreover, that these artists often procured "the flint" and the other materials of which their weapons were formed from remote countries. Fragments of Mediterranean coral also "have been found at Concise, and of Baltic amber at Meilen" (p. 191).

Pottery.

The Lake-dwellers of the Stone Age also fabricated pottery, which was rude and coarse, and made by hand (the wheel-made pottery is always associated with the industry of the Iron Age, although even then the hand-made pottery is by no means rare). The animal remains found among the pile-works of this era include, among others, the ox, the goat, the sheep, and the dog. The Lake-dwellers must, therefore, have been a pastoral people.

Domestic animals.

We are told also that "agriculture was not unknown." "This is proved in the most unexpected manner by the discovery of carbonized cereals at several points." Wheat has been discovered at Meilen, Moosseedorf, and Wangen—among the oldest of the settlements. Many bushels were found at the last-named place. Ears of the *hordeum hexastichon* L. (the six-rowed barley) have also been found. This is the species, according to M. De Candolle, which was cultivated by the Greeks and Romans. "Three varieties of wheat were cultivated;" also "two kinds of barley, and two of millet." Egyptian wheat has been discovered at Wangen and Robenhausen. Oats are found in the Bronze Age, but are absent from the Stone Age villages. (Rye was not known.) *Bread* has also been discovered—and flat round cakes. Carbonized apples have been found at Wangen, dried and put away for winter use. They have occurred also at Robenhausen and Concise. They are small, and resemble generally those which still grow wild in the Swiss forests; but at Robenhausen the specimens were larger "and were probably cultivated." (P. 212.) Seeds of the raspberry and blackberry are found.

Agriculture.

Bread.

Fruit.

It would appear, therefore, that the Lake-Dwellers of the Stone Age were an Agricultural and an Arboricultural people.

At one of the Stone Age stations—we forget which—one hundred bushels of wheat were obtained, and among them was noticed *the Cretan catch-fly*, which is found all over the Mediterranean and the south of France, but never in Switzerland or Germany. The corn-bluebottle was also found, which is from Sicily—all going to show communication, on the part of the Stone Age people of these lake settlements, with Southern Europe.

The Lacustrine dwellings are of two kinds: 1. The piles were driven in the mud of the lake-bottom, and on these platforms were laid, on which the lake-people reared their houses. 2. In the other case heavy posts were placed upright and boat-loads of stones emptied around them. This method was adopted when the bed of the lake was rocky, and the piles could not be driven readily into the bottom. The stones were merely used to hold the posts in position. This method was very common in the Stone Age. Such structures are called *tenevières* (a submerged hillock) or *steinbergs* (mountains of stone); the pile-habitations are called *pfahlbauten;* in French, *palafittes* (buildings on piles).

Steinbergs and Pfahlbauten.

At Robenhausen, we are told, there are one hundred thousand piles. The settlement of Morges, on the Lake of Geneva, covers an area of seventy thousand square yards; that of Chabrey, on the Lake of Neufchâtel, sixty thousand square yards. At Wangen there are forty thousand piles. To cut down the trees with their stone axes, to shape them into piles, to drive these piles in water from six to eight feet deep, and then prepare the platforms and rear the dwellings, implies no ordinary amount of intelligence and resolution.

These works imply great intelligence.

We do not doubt that many of these villages are very ancient—possibly as old as the time of Homer, or even older.

One of the few references we have to the subject in ancient history occurs in Herodotus. He is relating how Darius sent one of his great captains with orders to transplant the Pæonians to Asia, and proceeds:

Lake-Dwelling described by Herodotus.

"But the Pæonians about Lake Prasias were not conquered at all by Megabazus. Yet an attempt was even made to subdue those on the lake who dwell there in the following manner:

"Beams fastened together are fixed on lofty piles in the middle of the lake, having a narrow approach from the shore by a single bridge. And all the citizens in common have been wont from some very ancient time to plant the piles which support the beams. And this is the custom followed as to planting the piles. They bring them from a mountain called Obelus, and every bridegroom plants three piles for each woman that he marries; and every man marries a great many women; and they live in the following manner: each man possesses beams and a hut in which he lives, and a trap door to the beams, opening downwards to the lake. And they tie the little children by the foot with a cord, fearing lest they should tumble down into the lake. And they give to their horses and cattle fish for their food; and the multitude of fish is so great that when a man opens the trap door and lets down an empty basket into the lake, after waiting only a little while, he draws it up full of fish. And there are two sorts of these fish, which they call *paprakes* and *tilones*." Herod., v. 16.

Hippocrates, writing about the same time, describes a similar settlement. In his "De Aeribus, etc.," xxxvii., he writes:

Mentioned by Hippocrates.

"Concerning the people on the Phasis (now Rioni), that region is marshy and hot, and full of water, and woody, and at every season frequent and violent rains fall there. The inhabitants live in the marshes, and have houses of timber and of reeds, constructed in the midst of the waters; and they seldom go out to the city or to the market, but sail up and down in boats made out of a single tree-trunk; for there are numerous canals in that region."

So Abulfeda, the geographer, and a Syrian prince (A.D. 1273–1332), in his Supplementa tabulæ Syriæ, cap. ii., says:

By Abulfeda.

"The Apamæan lake consists of an innumerable number of smaller lakes and reedy places. Two of them, however, are larger than the others. . . . The water of the Orontes pours into them from the South. . . . This latter lake is reckoned amongst the land of Hesu Borgajjah, and it is commonly called the lake of the Christians, because it is inhabited by Christian fishermen who live here on the lake in wooden huts built on piles."

Lake Prasias still occupied.

Sir John Lubbock is informed by a friend living at Salonica that the fishermen of Lake Prasias *still inhabit wooden cottages over the water as in the time of Herodotus*. He mentions also a number of instances of similar villages in different parts of the world at the present day. Thus, the city of Tcherkask is built over the Don. Similar dwellings occur in the northern part of South America; Venezuela being so called because the houses resemble those of Venice in being over the water. The city of Borneo is altogether built upon piles, and similar constructions have been remarked in New Guinea, Celebes, Solo, Ceram, Mindanao, the Caroline Islands, and elsewhere. (P. 176.) Sir John Lubbock adds that Dumont d'Urville (Voyage de l'Astrolabe, vol. v. p. 635) tells us that "Jadis toute la ville de Tondano était construite sur le lac, et l'on ne communiquait d'une maison à une autre qu'en bateau." The Bishop of Labuan thus describes the dwellings of the Dyaks: "They are built along the river side, on an elevated platform, twenty or thirty feet high, in a long row, etc."

Found at present in various parts of the world.

Irish Crannoges.

Such structures were common in Ireland, where artificial islands were formed and used as strongholds by the petty chiefs. They are here called "Crannoges." As late as 1567, one Thomas Phettiplace, in his answer to an inquiry from the Government as to what castles or forts O'Neil hath, states: "For castles, I think it be not unknown to your honners, he trusteth no point thereunto for his safety, as appeareth by the raising of the strongest castles of all his countreys, and that fortification which he only dependeth upon is *in sartin ffresh-water loghes* in his countre," etc. (Quoted by Lubbock from Shirley, p. 177.) The remains of lake-dwellings have been observed also in Scotland, Ireland, England, France, Italy, Austria, Germany, and Poland. Dr. Keller has described one at Peschiera, on Lake Garda; Dr. Tisch has described similar remains in Mecklenburg; Dr. Hochstetter has traced them in the lakes of Carinthia. M. Boucher de Perthes mentions the existence of certain platforms at the bottom of the Abbeville peat, evidently belonging to the same structures. They have been found at Loch Neagh in Ireland; at Loch Etive, and in the Lochs of Wigtonshire and Dumfriesshire; on the river Nare near Norwich; and, as we believe, on the Thames, at London. They appear to have been numerous in France and Italy, as we shall have occasion presently to notice.

Such being the general evidence with regard to these Lake-Dwellings, we may well be astonished at the extravagant declarations made with regard to their antiquity. A writer in the *Saturday Review* expresses himself as follows:

Extravagant language of the archæologists.

"So, again, the people who, through a long series of ages since the time of the mammoth, dwelt in the pile-works of the Swiss lakes, passed through a succession of similar advances of civilization; but they themselves and their handiworks had sunk into oblivion before the Romans conquered Helvetia. 'Time, time, and yet more time,' is the cry of the student of antiquity, whether he work from the geological, the archæological, or the philological side; and the searcher after primeval man is as one using an inverted telescope which lengthens as he seeks, and throws the object of his investigation ever farther and farther off." Dr. McCausland in his volume entitled "Adam and the Adamite" says, "The ancient Swiss dwellings, far removed from Denmark, afford further and confirmative evidence of the succession of the stone, bronze, and iron ages" (p. 55.) And he estimates the three ages in Denmark, on "a moderate estimate," to have lasted four thousand years. This he considers, on the testimony of Sir Charles Lyell with regard to the peat-bogs of Denmark, to be "the minimum time" for the formation of the peat above the pine forests that grew there. Sir Charles thinks it might well have taken four times four thousand years for the deposition of that peat. We have seen the remarks of Agassiz. Commenting on the revelations of the Swiss lake-dwellings, he exclaims, "Humanity is now connected with geological phenomena!"

Mr. McCausland.

There was, we have no doubt, a period in Switzerland when bronze had not been introduced, and the implements during that period appear to have been of stone. At the same time, we have no doubt that after the introduction of bronze, stone was still extensively used, and in some localities perhaps exclusively. Manners and customs in such an age, in a secluded mountain-valley, are slow to change; and bronze was very expensive. We are not prepared to say when bronze was introduced, or when it was, for weapons, superseded by iron. There are no defined lines. In some places bronze was never used. The stone was followed immediately by iron. Bronze weapons never were extensively used in Switzerland.

Stone and metal often in use at the same time.

The fact that the Lake-Dwellers come down to the so-called Iron Age is a proof that they are not very ancient. The fact that these stations yield so many beautiful bronze ornaments is an evidence that there is nothing particularly "pre-historic" about them. And when we find even at Wangen and Moosseedorf and the other "Stone Age" dwellings, the remains of the horse, the ox, the goat, the sheep, the dog; wheat precisely like that now in use; two

Evidences of a recent date.

kinds of barley and two of millet; bread in the form of cakes, and roasted grains stored up in jars precisely as is now done in Germany and Switzerland; apples cut up and dried and stored away for winter use; stones of the wild plum and seeds of the raspberry and blackberry and strawberry; peas; shells of the hazel-nut and beech-nut; pottery; matting; twine; leather; ropes; cloth; spinning-wheels; corn-crushers: all this shows us that even the Stone Age people of the Swiss Lakes are very nearly related to us in their ways and customs, and not very far off in point of time.

We propose now to give the evidence on this subject more in detail, and to pass in review the principal lake-settlements in Switzerland. This is the only method of examining this question, and it is only by looking at all of the facts that we can read these disinhumed records of the past so as to arrive at a fair translation, and so as to frame an intelligible and consistent narrative out of these strange appearances. Mere general statements may be—are—made on both sides: as we have examined the tumuli and cists, so we wish now to examine the lakes and peat-moors of Switzerland, France, Italy, and Germany, and to afford the reader the full materials for weighing and judging this branch of the evidence.

ROBENHAUSEN.

Robenhausen is not only one of the oldest, but one of the most interesting, of the lake-dwellings. It is situated in a peat-moor, on the lake of Pfäffikon. There are three distinct settlements, one above the other, and all of them are referred to the Stone Age. The plan on the following page, taken from Dr. Keller's book, will illustrate the relations of these different settlements.

The first of them Dr. Keller thinks was not of long duration, and was destroyed by fire. In it have been found barley, wheat, thread, fragments of cloth, fish-nets, etc. The contents indeed seem to be identical with those of the second and third settlements, save that the axes of nephrite are found in the uppermost bed.

Above the lowest bed of charcoal the inhabitants erected new homes. This second settlement lasted during the accumulation of three feet of peat, in which are imbedded bones, pottery, the flooring, etc. The huts of this settlement were also burned, and above the peat just referred to are the remains of the conflagration. Above this layer of charred remains is another bed of peat, also three feet thick, containing the flooring and the remains of the third settlement. Among the stone implements here are some axes of nephrite.

The peat was growing all the while the second and third settlements were occupied, and seems finally to have driven the last settlers away.

	Feet deep.
½ foot of mould.	½
2 feet of peat.	2½
1 foot. No fire. Stone celts (nephrite).	3½
3 feet of peat. Broken stones. Flooring. Relics of third settlement.	6½
1 foot. Remains of conflagration. Implements, woven cloth, corn, apples.	7½
3 feet of peat. Flooring. Relics of second settlement. Excrements of cows, sheep, goats.	10½
1 foot. Conflagration. Implements, woven cloth, corn, apples, pottery.	11
4 or 5 inches. Relics of first settlement.	12
Shell marl.	

Manure-heaps.

The translator of Dr. Keller's book* in a note states that Dr. Keller has written him a letter stating that the fæces of goats occurring in regular beds lead Dr. Heer to the opinion that they do not arise from the sweepings of the stalls, but were *manure-heaps* hoarded for agricultural purposes. They were found in both the first and second settlements.

Cloth.

In Dr. Keller's work we have a picture of some Robenhausen cloth, which, and especially the "fringe," that author remarks, "betrays a certain refinement of life and a tendency to luxury."

Here we have a genuine Stone Age settlement—not an implement of metal has been found—and yet there is no occasion, we think, to feel called upon to associate any remote antiquity with the lake-dwellers of Robenhausen. But it appears that notwithstanding the apparent absence of metal, the inhabitants of Robenhausen were not ignorant of it. In concluding his remarks on this station, Dr. Keller gives us the following highly important information:

Traces of metal.

"Thirdly," he says, "the settlers, as has been supposed before, were in early times acquainted with copper and bronze, *for traces*

* "The Lake Dwellings of Switzerland and other parts of Europe. By Dr. Ferdinand Keller. Translated by John Edward Lee, F.S.A., F.G.S., etc." p. 46.

of these metals have been met with in the lower beds of the Stone Age settlements, before the appearance of nephrite." *

There is no need of any comment on such a statement; for at Robenhausen we are confessedly at one of the very oldest of all the Swiss lake villages. It is only at three stations—Moosseedorf, Wauwyl, and Robenhausen—that any remains of the aurochs have been found; and the remains of only one individual have been found at either Wauwyl or Moosseedorf, while they are very common at Robenhausen. The *Bos primigenius* (urus) has been found only at Wauwyl, Moosseedorf, Robenhausen, Wangen, Sipplingen, and Concise; and while its remains are frequent at Robenhausen, only a few individuals have been found at any of the other points. So at Moosseedorf, Wauwyl, and Robenhausen (and only here) the remains of the fox are more abundant than those of the dog. So again at Robenhausen we find no traces of the domestic hog, although we do find them at Wauwyl. All of which demonstrates the great comparative antiquity of Robenhausen. And here in the lowest beds, as we infer from Dr. Keller's remark, although we do not find any copper or bronze implements, "traces of these metals have been met with." The nephrite† at these Stone Age stations is very extraordinary. We shall have occasion to observe its presence as we proceed with our remarks.

Remains of the aurochs.

Urus.

Before leaving Robenhausen we must add that a number of articles in wood have been found here—ladles showing "astonishing skill in carving"—"very similar," says Dr. Keller, "to those now in use in the Swiss milk chalets." Also a yoke of hazel-wood, a threshing-flail, yew-wood combs, a *shoemaker's last*, a great tub cut out of maple-wood, &c. M. Messikomer also disinterred here "a remarkable canoe made out of a single trunk, *such as may now be seen* in the

Objects in wood.

---

* See p. 57. The italics are ours.

† Nephrite is not found originally in Switzerland, nor in any part of Europe. It comes (according to M. Desor) from Turkestan, China, and one or two other countries outside of Europe.

M. de Fellenberg has analyzed a nephrite hatchet from one of the lake-stations of Neufchâtel, and also a specimen which came from the palace of the Emperor of China. He found that their composition was identical.

According to M. Desor, these axes are very rare. There are only several dozens of them in Switzerland. They are found along the Alps from the Lake of Constance to the Lake of Bourget. They are also found in the south of France.

They have been obtained, however, we may mention, in Italy, in Germany, and in England. M. Desor states that for twenty years the rock has been most carefully sought for in Europe, but has never been found. He suggests that the axes in nephrite and jade may have been brought to Europe during the original migrations to that continent from Asia. See paper on the Axes of Nephrite and Jadeite, by M. Desor, in Cong. d'Anthrop. et d'Archéol., 1872, p. 351. And see also farther on some additional facts on this subject mentioned by us.

lakes of Zug and Lucerne, twelve feet long by one and a half broad, but only five inches in depth." We believe it was at Robenhausen that *leather* was found.

"Three hundred apples" were also found at Robenhausen in one place, and also "a specimen of what appeared to be a cultivated apple."

There was another station on the lake of Pfäffikon at Irgenhausen. Here they have found stone implements and the other usual remains, but also a number of pieces of *embroidered cloth.*

WANGEN,

on the Lake of Constance, is "pre-eminently" a Stone Age station. M. Löhle found here fifteen hundred stone axes, twenty-five hundred arrow-heads, one hundred and fifty corn-crushers, one hundred whetstones, three hundred and fifty bone instruments, and "not a trace of metal." But yet we find specimens of *nephrite* at Wangen; great quantities of corn; baked cakes of bread; abundance of flax; and we are told that "the inhabitants were pre-eminent as agriculturists and as handicraftsmen." Several perforated axes were also found here.

A factory of stone implements.

Nephrite again.

Speaking particularly of Niederwyl, another Stone Age station, but referring also generally to all of the Stone Age villages, Dr. Keller expresses the opinion that the inhabitants were not clothed in skins, but *in linen garments.**

Linen garments.

There is no trace of burning at Niederwyl, as at so many of the lake-villages. It was voluntarily abandoned. It probably existed some centuries.

At Allensbach and Markelfingen on the Untersee (Lake of Constance), beautiful perforated stone axes were found, "fit for the toilet table." Also beautiful saws of yellow flint. These perforated axes, as remarked in another connection, imply the use of metallic tools.

UEBERLINGER SEE (WESTERN SHORE)—LAKE OF CONSTANCE.

We find here perforated stone celts at the Stone Age station.

There is also a Bronze Age station, where were found bronze celts, an iron knife, two iron arrow-heads, the fragment of an iron fish-hook, pieces of worked stag's horn, and some flint flakes. The pottery was like that found in the Stone Age stations. No trace of the wheel.

---

* See p. 71.

UEBERLINGER SEE (EASTERN SHORE).

We have here, within a few hours' walk of each other, the Stone Age settlements of Nussdorf and Maurach, and the Bronze settlements of Unter Uhldingen and Sipplingen.

Nussdorf. This station was destroyed by fire. There were found here one hundred specimens of arrow and lance heads (flint), eighty saws, piercers, knives, etc., and one thousand axes, chisels, hammers, etc. There were fifty axes of nephrite, and fifty perforated axes,* the hole being either circular or oval, and having been drilled with a hollow tube—which must have been of metal. The core frequently left where the perforation is not completed, shows at once the use of a hollow boring instrument.

Nephrite. Perforated axes.

Many teeth of the horse (Equus caballus) were found here, showing the domestication and employment of this animal in the "stone" age. His remains are found at other Stone Age stations.

Maurach. Found here, besides the stone implements, one copper axe or celt.

Unter Uhldingen. Is one thousand feet from the shore. The stone implements found here have the same character as those found at Nussdorf and Maurach. They are arrow and lance heads, flint saws, three hundred stone axes and chisels, besides stone hammers, net-sinkers, mealing-stones, fruit-crushers, etc. The axes are mostly unperforated.

Stone.

The objects of clay show a slight improvement. There was some pottery of pretty red clay (*terra sigillata*) which was of Roman origin.

Roman pottery.

They found here also a large number of bronze tools and weapons, showing that bronze was both manufactured and used on the shores of Constance. Among the objects of bronze were a number of celts, six lance-points, twenty-five knife-blades, sickles, beautiful armlets, etc.

Bronze.

Several iron implements were also found here: one lance-head, five arrow-heads (like those of bronze), one axe or celt, two carpenter's chisels, twelve knife-blades, two pruning-knives, an iron ring, a fibula, a clothes-pin, etc. Also the remains of an iron two-edged sword, and an iron short-sword with a wooden hilt.

Iron.

Of *glass* there were found eleven bottoms of goblets, and one smooth glass slab.†

Glass.

---

* Sir John Lubbock says the perforated axe is very rare, if not altogether absent, in the Stone Age (p. 14). The fifty axes of nephrite is rather inconsistent with the statement of M. Desor, on p. 162, that there are only several dozens of them in Switzerland.

† In the volume of the "Congrès International" for 1869 (p. 267) M. Stendel mentions

The distance of this settlement from the shore, and its being classified by Dr. Keller as a "bronze age" station, warrant us in supposing that it was built in the Bronze Age, and with metallic tools.

It appears that stone and bronze were used indiscriminately together. It is to be remarked, however, that while we hear of three hundred stone axes and chisels, the bronze celts apparently were not very numerous; and there were only six bronze lance-heads. Then the Iron Age supervenes. There are a few iron weapons. It is *evident* that the stone weapons and tools continued still to be used, and *that they constituted the chief implements still used at Unter Uhldingen.*

Stone and bronze mixed together.

Sipplingen. Is a half-hour's walk from Unter Uhldingen. It is situated some twelve hundred or fifteen hundred feet from the shore. The settlement is precisely like that just described.

There are two hundred specimens of unperforated stone celts, and twenty of the perforated type. Also stone hammers, and one hundred stone implements of one form, found in a heap, whose use is not known—apparently unfinished celts.

Perforated and unperforated celts.

No bronze implements have been found so far; one celt of copper was met with. (Yet it is referred to the Bronze Age.)

Of iron, there were found one lance-head, three arrow-heads, two sickles, one single-edged sword, two pieces of a cylindrical shape, and one Roman key.

Iron.

Of glass, five pieces of a gray color.

Glass.

Also the horns of the urus, and a number of implements of horn.

Urus.

The following table exhibits the character of the finds at these two last-named stations:

	Unter Uhldingen.	Sipplingen.
Stone	400 spec.	350 spec.
Bronze	200 "	...
Copper	...	1 "
Iron	49 "	16 "
Glass	40 "	8 "

If stone continued to be used at Unter Uhldingen, it is still more evident that it constituted even to the last the chief material at Sipplingen.

But the most noticeable feature about Sipplingen is that while it had an abounding stone age, and continued down to the Iron Age, and even to Roman times, it has yielded no relics of bronze. It passed at once

---

recent discoveries in the Lake of Constance, and says the most remarkable was that of fragments of translucent and *filigreed* glass, which he had deposited in the Museum of St. Germain.

M. de Mortillet observed that the glass was moulded(*coulé*), and resembled that called *verre Gaulois.*

from the Stone Age to the Iron Age,—and even then stone continued to be chiefly used. This was certainly as late as the date of the Roman key. The glass vessels bespeak an equally recent period.

LAKE OF ZUG.

1. *Zug*. The piles sharpened by fire. Stone implements, no metal, and no pottery. A remarkable feature of this station is, that it is fifteen feet higher than the lake, and sixty feet inland from the shore.

Fall in the level of the lake.

2. *Koller*. The relic bed here is also three feet higher than the surface of the water.

3. *St. Andreas*, near Cham. Also some distance inland from lake. Stone celts found.

4. *Dusbach*. Stone implements also found here away from shore.

5 and 6. *Zweeren* and at the Bathing-place at Zug. Also inland; but in every case the relics rest on shell marl, showing the former presence of the lake.

It is evident from these facts that the level of this lake has fallen,—a fact which we shall observe elsewhere among the Swiss lakes.

Some of the clay vessels found at these last-named stations (5 and 6) are of the Bronze Age.

WAUWYL

Is situated in a peat-moss, which occupies the bed of a former lake, near Zofingen, in the Canton of Lucerne. It is one of the very oldest of all the stations. Some four or five hundred stone and flint implements have been found here, and no metal. But one of the stone celts is of *nephrite*, and a glass bead of a bluish color has been found. This last implies an occupation down to a recent period. There were two settlements here,—one above the other. The first was burned. The peat here, and the dry bed of the lake, again remind us of a higher lake-level in former times.

Very ancient.

Nephrite. Glass.

MOOSSEEDORF.

Another peat-moss station, two miles from Berne. We have here again traces of a greater body of water in the ancient lake-basins. We have also one of the very oldest lake-villages. More than three thousand three hundred instruments of stone and bone were found, but no metal. Nephrite, however, occurs, and wheat, barley, and linseed. The dog, goat, sheep, cow, and hog are also met with, and all, excepting the dog, quite frequently.

Very old.

A factory.

Nephrite.

LAKE OF BIENNE.

There are twenty-one settlements on this lake, representing all three ages.

Nidau. At this station we find stone, bronze, and iron. The piles are sharpened by fire, showing that the settlement originated in the Stone Age. There were secured thirty-three axes of stone, some of them perforated, and twenty-three bronze axes. Also perforated stones, surrounded by a band of iron, which were used as net-sinkers. The pottery is all hand-made. Iron spear-heads also were found here, and two curved pieces of iron holding a piece of wood between rivets. Dr. Keller mentions two pieces of pottery which he believes to be Roman. A *pirogue* or *einbaum* was also found, made of a single trunk, hollowed out by fire. Glass beads, strung with beads of jet, "exactly like those found in the tumuli and in Roman stations," were also found.

Called a Bronze station.

Stone.

Iron.

Roman pottery.

Graseren. These remains are two hundred feet from the shore (in the lake). A dagger ornamented with silver wire, knives, sickles, and other implements of iron were found.

Silver and iron.

Sutz. Is one hundred and twenty-five feet from the shore, in six feet of water. Destroyed by fire. Found here: a bronze celt, a bronze sword, two iron lance-points, and a Roman mill-stone. Also a stone hammer-pick, a flint flake five inches long, etc.

Stone, bronze, and iron.

Möringen. Destroyed by fire. Essentially a bronze station. A number of bronze celts, knives, sickles, bracelets, ear-rings, fish-hooks, awls, etc. Also *glass* and amber beads, a bone arrow-head, and three canoes. So far Dr. Keller.

This important station has been recently re-explored by Dr. V. Gross. He obtained great numbers of objects of bronze, among them thirty celts, twenty razors, and quite a collection of ornaments. He found also three bronze swords, and an *iron* sword with a bronze handle. Also a bronze *bridle-bit,* which seems to be a matter of great astonishment among the archæologists. A similar bit has been found at the pile-village of Vaudrenanges. At a meeting of the *Société d'Anthropologie* of Paris, May 1st, 1873, M. Bertrand called attention to these discoveries, and remarked that they "established the fact that the horse was employed as a domestic animal by the lacustrine populations of the Age of Bronze." He added that these bits indicated a horse of small size, like those mentioned by Herodotus in the valley of the Danube, unsuitable to carry a cavalier, but adapted to a cart. (This disposes of the *Equus spelæus* whose "small size" has occasioned so much remark.) M. Bertrand concluded, we are told, by saying that "we were acquainted with similar bits to that from Möringen, which would indicate that *the times* *called pre-historic must be connected very nearly with historic times.*"* M. Sanson observed that the documents presented on this subject by M. Bertrand were very interesting, and that these horses were *oriental*, in fact, of small size, such as are met with in Southern Russia and in Hungary.

Dr. Gross remarks that when this bit was brought to him, "je crus d'abord avoir affaire à un produit de l'industrie moderne, perdu fortuitement sur l'emplacement à pilotis;" but he ascertained that it had been brought up by the drag from the bottom of the bed where the other objects were found.†

Dr. Gross is equally puzzled at finding a sword of iron in association with the swords of bronze (and, he says, at the same time, "with some axes of stone") in this bed. "This sword-blade of iron," he remarks, "with its handle of bronze, associated with other objects in bronze and even with some stone axes, leads us to conclude that the station of Möringen was constructed at an epoch when concurrently with bronze stone was still in use, and that it has existed during the age of bronze and was destroyed after the appearance of iron in our countries." It seems that along with the iron sword and the objects in bronze, Dr. Gross obtained several discoidal pieces of stone, several stone hammers, a dozen stone axes, some stone anvils, stone awls, etc. We have thus the Stone Age not only running into, and lapping the Bronze Age, but actually leaping over the Bronze Age (two thousand years), and existing side by side with swords of iron!

And we not only find the bronze bridle-bit and the iron sword at this great station of the Bronze Age (Möringen, as we shall see, was a *manufactory of bronze implements*), but we are told by Dr. Keller that beads of *glass* were obtained here.

We merely add that moulds were found at Möringen in which the objects of bronze (or some of them) were cast. They are of stone or of clay. A crucible of baked earth was also found.

Little Island. Col. Schwab "found here objects of stone, bronze, and the Gallo-Roman period all mixed together."

Sutz. Dr. Gross found here (mingled together apparently) perforated stone axes, a dozen *fusaïoles* of stone, a quantity of flint chippings, a remarkable lance-head of white flint, a bronze celt, bronze pins, and an elegant fibula of the same metal.

Ile des Lapins. "The remains of all the ages here" (says Dr. Gross), "from the epoch of polished stone to the Gallo-Roman epoch, seem to testify that this station served as *a place of re-union where the merchants of different countries met together.*" In other words (the italics are ours),

---

* Matériaux, Livraisons 5e et 6e, 1873, pp. 280–81. † Ib., p. 221.

the stone, bronze, and iron are all mingled together. When a "find" of this sort is encountered, the archæologists dismiss it with some summary observation like the above. But how did the "Gallo-Roman" merchants manage to meet the merchants of the age of polished stone, who lived four or five thousand years before?

Locras. Dr. Gross describes also a very ancient station (that of Locras) on the Lake of Bienne, which yielded no metal of any kind (save at the surface two or three objects of iron). But among the stone axes found here were two of jadeite and four of nephrite. Dr. Gross remarks that the former are probably the largest jadeite axes found in the Swiss palafittes up to this time. One measured twenty-two centimetres in length by seven centimetres in breadth, and the second fifteen centimetres long by six centimetres broad. M. de Fellenberg writes to Dr. Gross (modifying slightly the statement of M. Desor) that nephrite is not native to any region except Turkestan and Siberia, in the environs of the Lake of Baikal.* The jadeite, he says, comes from China, from the province of Kiang-Si, to the south of Nanking. The presence of these axes in Switzerland, says M. de Fellenberg, can only be explained by the emigration of the people who used them, who carried with them their most precious articles of property.

There were found here also two perforated stone hammers.†

We have mentioned that at the surface of this bed there were found several objects of iron. There was no trace of bronze. Did the occupants of Locras *skip* the Bronze Age?

LAKE OF NEUFCHATEL.

The banks of this lake are studded with settlements; some of the earliest age; others continued during Helvetian times; and not a few were inhabited during the Gallo-Roman period.

Iron station.

La Tène, near Marin, and sometimes called Marin. The relics here are:

1. Flint flakes, which are scattered over the whole station. Also found a dozen stone balls.

2. A bronze hatchet, one bronze ornament, and twelve bronze "sundries."

3. A great number of iron implements, among them fifty swords, "masterpieces of the smith's art," which are very similar to, if not identical with, those from Alise, where the well-known battle occurred

---

* Jade (or nephrite) is found also in the Kouenlun range of mountains in Central Asia, on the northern frontier of India; as, for example, in the quarries of Goulbagasten, lat. 36° 9′, long. 77° 45′ E. It is called *Yaspen* by the Tourkezos. It is soft when first taken from the quarry, but soon becomes very hard. Cong. d'Anthropol., 1867, p. 123.

† Matériaux pour l'Hist. de l'Homme, 5e et 6e Livraisons, 1873, p. 209.

between Cæsar and the Gauls. M. Morlot mentions "an iron scabbard with silver inlaying."

4. Pottery. Most of this is Roman, though even this is rare. We may include under this head a great number of Roman tiles,* also found.

5. Glass.

Coins.

6. Coins. *a.* Roman and Gallic. Coins of both Claudius and Tiberius were found. Also the quarter-stater of gold, which was the current money of the Helvetii; also a bad imitation of the Macedonian coins (so widely distributed) of Philip, having on obverse head of Apollo with fillet of laurel, and on reverse a biga with the emblem of a bird under the vehicle, and the letters *ΦΙΛΙΠΠΟΥ.* *b.* Several Massilian coins (silver) from Massilia (Marseilles). *c.* Several coins, made from a mixture of copper, tin, and lead, commonly found in the districts of the Ædui, Helvetii, and Sequani. Very rude.

Date of Marin.

Marin was obviously an iron station, and continued to be occupied after the Christian era. The presence of the numerous flint flakes shows that flint was largely in requisition.

The absence of bronze ornaments here is very remarkable, for the hair-pins, rings, bracelets, etc., of bronze, were worn of course after the introduction of iron.

Hauterive. Two iron spear-heads. Subsequently Prof. Desor found only stone implements, but at a different point.

Stone implements with Roman relics.

Crêt. An implement like a cylindrical roller with an iron hook at each end, and letters I R engraved on it.

Colombier. Flint implement, celts of serpentine, and Roman tiles.

Chez Les Moines. Stag's horn, stone chisels, and Roman tiles.

Font. Articles of bronze.

Bevaix. Bronze pins and knife.

Near St. Aubin. Stone implements.

Forel. Roman tiles.

Chevroux. Bronze dagger, etc.

Above Chevroux. This station is six hundred feet from the shore. The relics consisted of stone celts, bronze swords, knives, sickles, and armlets, and a great iron fork. The distance from the shore implies deep water, and the use of bronze tools to construct the dwelling; and the association of the stone and bronze implements is again to be remarked.

Gletterens. This station is six hundred feet from shore, and yielded Roman tiles. Nothing else mentioned.

---

* The Roman tile, says Dr. Keller, was used not only for buildings, but for making the hypocaust, and for many other purposes. And both Dr. Keller and M. Desor state that the art of constructing kilns of brick was unknown to the Helvetians and the Gauls before their conquest by the Romans.

Port Alban. Is nine hundred and eighty feet from the shore, and yielded stone celts. There is probably metal behind.

No. 44. Is five hundred and ninety feet from the shore. Yielded stone celts.

A La Sauge. Is nine hundred and eighty feet from the shore. Yielded Roman tiles, and the handle of a Roman amphora.

Pont de Thièle. Is in the valley connecting the Lakes of Neufchâtel and Bienne, and a great distance away from the shore of the lake, in which it formerly stood. The relics here were stone celts and Roman pottery and tiles.

This station has been made the subject of a most extraordinary calculation, intended to ascertain the *age* of the lake-dwellings. M. Gilliéron, Professor at the College of Neuveville, has the honor of originally making this investigation; but Sir John Lubbock, in his famous chapter on the "Antiquity of Man," selects this as *one* of the illustrations of that great thesis. It will be best to let Sir John present the matter in his own language:

Sir John Lubbock's calculation.

"Not less ingenious is the attempt which has been made by M. Gilliéron, Professor at the College of Neuveville, to obtain a date for the lake-habitations at the Pont de Thièle. This stream connects the lakes of Neufchâtel and Bienne. During the first part of its course, the valley is narrow, and the bridge, close to which the lake-habitation has been discovered, is situated at the narrowest spot. A little farther down the valley suddenly expands, and from this point remains of the same width until it joins the Lake of Bienne. It is evident that the valley, as far as the bridge over the Thièle, was once occupied by the lake, which has gradually been silted up by the action of the forces still in operation, and, if we could ascertain how long it would have taken to effect this change, we should then know approximately the date of the remains found at the Pont de Thièle, which are evidently those of a lake-dwelling. The Abbey of St. Jean, which stands in the valley, about three hundred and seventy-five metres from the present shore of the lake, was founded, according to the ancient documents, between the years 1090 and 1106, and is, therefore, about seven hundred and fifty years old. It is possible that the abbey may not have been built exactly on the edge of the lake; but, even if this were the case, the gain of land will only have been three hundred and seventy-five metres in seven hundred and fifty years. Prof. Gilliéron does not compare with this the whole space between the convent and the lake-dwelling, because in the narrower part of the valley in which the latter is situated, the gain may have been more rapid; but if we only go to the point at which the basin contracts, we shall have a distance of three thousand metres, which would upon these data indicate a minimum antiquity of six thousand seven hundred and fifty years. This calculation assumes that the shape of the bottom of the valley was originally uniform. . . . These two calculations, then, appear to indicate that six thousand or seven thousand years ago Switzerland was already inhabited by men who used polished stone implements, but how long they had been there, or how many centuries elapsed before the discovery of metal, we have as yet no evidence to show." *

Now let us suppose that the Lake of Bienne, like the Lake of Geneva, and other Swiss lakes, stood in former times at a higher level than it has now,—and let us suppose that the level of the lake suddenly fell,—as seems to have been the case with the American lakes,—how long would it take *then* for the waters of the Lake of Bienne to retreat from the Pont de Thièle to the present shore-line?

Roman pottery at the Pont de Thièle.

But it seems to us we have another method of getting at the date at which the waters of Bienne stood at the Bridge of Thièle. Dr. Keller informs us that *Roman pottery and tiles* were found at this lake-station. These were deposited certainly not more than nineteen hundred years ago, and the water of the lake was probably at the Pont de Thièle then.

And, finally, M. Desor informs us (in another connection) that "landslips have been distinguished at the mouth of the Thièle." †

Cortaillod. Great numbers of bronze objects were found at this station, and also objects of stone and iron. A bronze wheel, supposed to belong to a war-chariot, and a string of amber and glass beads, were among the articles found.

Estavayer. On the east bank of the Lake of Neufchâtel is the bronze station of Estavayer. There are, indeed, two pile-dwellings found at this point; one near the shore, where only stone implements are found, and the other farther from the shore, where a large number of bronze implements have been found.

The Stone Age dwelling is forty-five paces from the shore. Among the objects gathered here was a perforated axe, the hole being of an *oval* shape.

The Bronze Age station is four hundred feet from the shore, and the water here is only six feet deep, showing that the level of the lake has fallen. Among the bronze objects found were twenty-six knives, one celt, five sickles, one arrow-head, etc. A bar of pure tin, seven and a half inches long by one-fifth of an inch thick, was also found here,—imported from abroad to be manufactured at home.

Stone and Bronze found together.

Stone celts, grinding stones, etc., were also found at this bronze station, showing again the cotemporaneous use of stone and metal. A knife has also been obtained here with a bronze handle and an iron blade.

---

* Pre-historic Times, p. 393.

† Smithsonian Report for 1865, p. 351.

The cuts below will give an idea of the bronze articles found in the Swiss lake-dwellings.

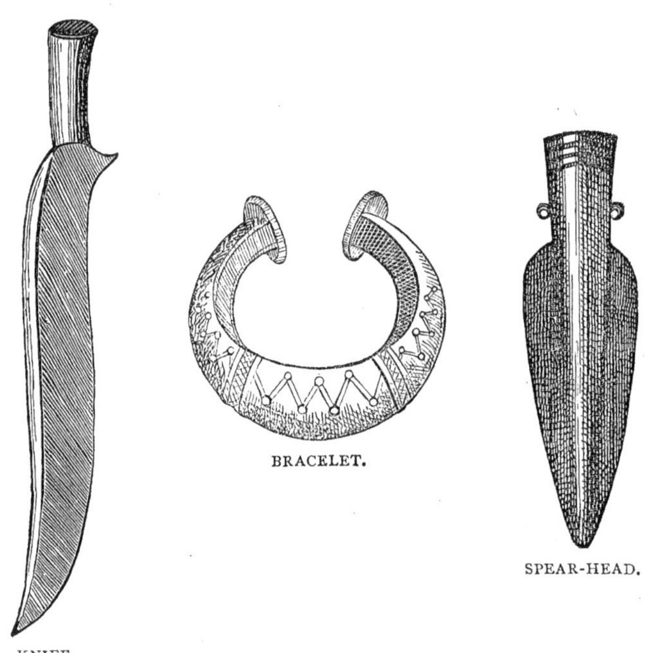

KNIFE. BRACELET. SPEAR-HEAD.

Concise, near Yverdon. This is a very old station of the Stone Age, and existed a long period. Eighty stone celts were collected here. Two beautiful bronze swords also found here in 1832. Other bronze objects also found. The bronze sword-hilts, bracelets, and hair-pins exhibit wonderful taste and skill. Beautiful flint arrow-heads also found. Amber, tin, and, we believe, nephrite, also occurred.

Stone Age station.

Amber and tin.

At Concise (as at Corcelettes) bronze objects, sawn stone celts, and perforated stone hammers were found along with sharpened pebbles and the coarsest pottery. At the station of Les Uttins, near by, a bronze bracelet was found in the same peat digging with two stone celts.

Perforated hammers.

Mediterranean coral was also found at Concise, and M. Rochat states that pottery made on the wheel was found.

Coral.

Wheel pottery.

Corcelettes, also near Yverdon. This is a bronze station, yielding more than five hundred articles of this metal, and none of iron, while the objects in stone apparently were not very numerous. The latter do not seem to have been particularly sought for.

Bronze station.

Although there is not a solitary article of iron, a Roman amphora was found, showing the fact *that after the appearance of the Romans at Corcelettes, iron was unknown to, or, at least, not used by, these lake-dwellers.* And yet at this time iron was abundant at Marin on this very lake. At one station they were using bronze, and at the other they were using iron.

Roman amphora.

LAKE OF MORAT.

Greng. Near the shore we find only implements of stone, while farther in the lake we find *a mixture of stone and bronze*, iron also appearing. When the settlers procured bronze they moved farther into the lake, but they continued to use stone.

Stone and Bronze found together.

Montellier. Col. Schwab has obtained here stone and bronze implements. Also a ring of *tin*, and an armlet or clasp of tin. Also dishes of thin bronze plate, bronze screws, etc.

Roman remains. *No. 6.* At this station found only Roman tiles.

No. 10. Here they found bronze articles of the Gallo-Roman age.

No. 14. Found here a stone celt, an iron javelin, and Roman tiles.

LAKE OF GENEVA.

There are a number of stations on this great lake, the principal of which is

Morges. There are two stations here, the larger one being opposite the town. The piles are four hundred or five hundred feet from the shore, and the water is ten feet deep. They obtained here bronze celts, swords, knives, lance-points, and many other objects in the same metal. Also one iron poignard, and "a little object in silver like a necklace-bead."

Les Roseaux is the name of the second station. Here they found stone, bronze, and iron. There was a number of iron sickles. The piles were sharpened by bronze axes. Place not inhabited long,—so says Dr. Keller; and yet here we have the *Three Ages!*

Stone, bronze, and iron.

MEILEN

Is, as already mentioned, on the Lake of Zurich. It is considered one of the oldest stations. The relics were chiefly of stone. But a bronze armilla, a bronze celt, and, at one point, a number of piles which had been sharpened by "a sharply-ground bronze celt," were also found. As was also a perforated stone hammer of very hard material like serpentine. It is beautifully bored,—evidently with a *tube.*

"The pottery resembles the specimens dug out of the tumuli."

On the *Lake of Sempach* is the station of "Mariazell," where Col. Schwab found flint flakes, a stone celt, and an iron knife.

Attention has been called to the fact that the lake-villages of the Bronze and Iron epochs are in general situated *in the west of Switzerland:* those, for example, on the Lakes of Geneva, Neufchâtel, Bienne, Morat, and Sempach. On the other hand, most of the older settlements are in the east. It is natural that the settlements next to France, and in communication, no doubt, with Northern Italy, should have been in advance of those embosomed in the solitary valleys of Pfäffikon and Zurich, and the Bavarian Alps. If there was a secluded spot in Europe in ancient times, it was on the extreme northeastern frontier of Switzerland, and it is there that we find the Stone Age settlements of the Lake of Constance. A glance at the map will show this at once. Not far off were the Lakes of Zurich and Pfäffikon, and there we find the primitive remains of Meilen and Robenhausen. Of course we find Stone Age settlements in the west, but they were superseded by the more important stations of the Bronze and the Iron ages. "One settlement of the Bronze Age," says Sir John Lubbock, "has been found on the Lake of Constance; but as the question now stands, Pileworks of the Metallic Period are almost peculiar to western and central Switzerland." Sir John Lubbock refers to Unter Uhldingen, where a number of iron implements were also found, among them a couple of iron swords, and where the fragments of glass goblets were also found. These show that the station at Unter Uhldingen was occupied after the Christian era, when the Roman arms had penetrated to that region.

The stations of the metal ages found chiefly in the West of Switzerland.

We should, as just remarked, expect the population about the lakes of Geneva, Neufchâtel, and Bienne, at the foot of the Jura Mountains, to be in advance of the population at the sources of the Rhine and the Danube. The Greek colony of Massilia was only some two hundred miles distant from Geneva. Marseilles (then Massilia) was in the days of Julius Cæsar a highly cultivated city. Strabo informs us that in his time, about A.D. 60, "this city for some little time back has become a school for the barbarians [who, he says, "now that they are under the dominion of the Romans, become daily more civilized"], and has communicated to the Galatæ such a taste for Greek literature, that they even draw contracts on the Grecian model, while at the present day it so entices the noblest of the Romans, that those desirous of studying resort thither in preference to Athens." *

Massilia.

The Massilians had cities also in Iberia "as a rampart against the Iberians;" also "around the river Rhone against the barbarians,"—such as Rhoa (probably Rhodanusia), and Agatha (Agde); also on the northwestern coast of Italy, against "the Salyes and the Ligurians who

* Strabo. Bohn's edit., vol. i. p. 270.

inhabit the Alps,"—such as Nicæa (the modern Nice), Tauroentium (Taurenti), Olbia (Eoube), Antipolis (Antibes), etc.*

Geneva had a nearer neighbor than Marseilles, from whom the Lake-Dwellers in that region probably received many hints: we refer to Lugdunum (Lyons), which, at least in the days of Strabo, had become a very important city.

Lugdunum.

The lake settlements of the Bronze and Iron ages are, then, in the West, while the Stone settlements are almost entirely in the East. The inhabitants of the West trafficked with Lugdunum, Massilia, and Nicæa, and no doubt used bronze and iron when the population of the East, separated by the barriers of the Alps, were using stone. In other words, we have here the Stone Age and the Bronze Age side by side, according to the advancement of the people and their intercourse with the outside world. And we have just seen that the Bronze Age at Möringen, Corcelettes, etc., was cotemporary with the Iron Age at Marin. But the archæologists string them out in a line. M. Figuier puts the Iron Age at B.C. 2000: the Bronze Age at B.C. 4000: an error of several thousand years.

Of course we do not mean to say that the stone or flint remains are not older ordinarily than those of metal. We only mean that the gap is not so great as is alleged,—and that we may find in the same year before Christ or after Christ men using stone celts on the eastern frontier of Switzerland and bronze celts on the western frontier; as we find them, at one and the same point, using both together.

No remains of the Reindeer.

A very remarkable fact in connection with these lacustrine settlements is the entire absence of all remains of the *Reindeer*, while those of the *Aurochs* and *Urus* are rare. We have abundant traces of the domestic animals even at Robenhausen and Moosseedorf. The reindeer and the aurochs are also absent from the Danish shell-mounds. This fact unavoidably suggests a comparatively recent date for these Swiss and Danish settlements. Gaston de Foix saw the reindeer in Norway and Sweden in the thirteenth century. They were hunted in Scotland in the twelfth. The urus existed in Europe down to the sixteenth century; the aurochs still exists in the forests of Lithuania.

Original home of the Lake-Dwellers.

In the foregoing account it may have been observed that the axes of *nephrite* are found at the Stone Age stations,—at Robenhausen, at Wangen, at Nussdorf, at Wauwyl, at Moosseedorf, at Locras. We are not informed whether they do not sometimes occur at the metal stations, but, so far as our record goes, we have only found them at those of the Stone Age.

What inference are we to draw from the presence of this material at

* Strabo, vol. i. p. 269.

the Swiss lake-villages? It is not probable that there was any *traffic*, direct or indirect, between Switzerland and the East in those days; and we are compelled to accept the suggestion of M. de Fellenberg and M. Desor, that the weapons in question were brought to Europe by immigrants from Asia. Turkestan, we are told, is one of the regions of Asia where nephrite is found. Tribes, therefore, from the shores of the Caspian—or, as is more probable, from those of the Euxine,—the population of the latter region having procured the nephrite by traffic with their more eastern kinsmen—found their way into Central Europe.* Thus everything points to the East as the starting-point of the early migrations of the human race. It is in corroboration of this conjecture, that we find this material from Central Asia at the earliest, but not at the more recent, pile settlements of Switzerland, while the small number of the axes found points to the same conclusion. It is by no means inconsistent with this opinion that Dr. Keller tells us that in these oldest Stone Âge stations traces of iron and bronze have been met with "in the lowest beds" "before the appearance of nephrite." The first comers were probably not wholly unacquainted with metal, bringing with them, perhaps, a few precious implements, obtained either in their original homes or on their journey.

SETTLEMENTS OF THE SAME PEOPLE ON LAND.

Remains resembling in all respects those of the lake-villages are found in Switzerland on land.

1. At Ehrensberg, near Berg, on the Irchel, Mr. G. von Escher, in 1851, and afterwards in 1862, examined one of these inland settlements. At the depth of five feet, in the alluvial soil, he found traces of fire, so common in the lake-villages, and a number of relics; among them three small stone celts and some cutting flint implements; a glass bead of a whitish-blue color, exactly like those found in the graves and Roman settlements; worked horns of the roebuck, and antlers which had been used for tools; a lance-point of bone; two bronze knives, several dozen bronze hair and clothes pins, several small bronze chisels, a bronze arrow-head, and a number of bronze rings.

Stone, bronze, and glass found together.

We have here again, obviously cotemporaneous, objects of stone, bone, horn, and metal, and with them the glass bead belonging to a recent period.

---

* While these sheets are passing through the press, we see the important statement made that deposits of jade have been discovered in the Caucasus and in Northern Armenia. *This* is the quarter from which the jade of the Swiss lake-villages was brought. See Harper's Magazine for September, 1874.

2. Burg (ancient castle), near Vilters, in the Canton of St. Gall. This place lies a half-hour's walk up the mountain. Upon excavating, they met with flint saws, stone celts and crushers, and bronze arrow-heads, precisely similar to those at Ehrensberg.

Stone and bronze.

3. At Uetliberg, near Zurich, on the highest point of Mount Albis, they found pottery, a stone celt, a bone piercer, bronze ornaments, and a chisel, pin, wheel, and moon-image, all of bronze.

Stone and bronze.

A "moon-image" was also found at Burg. These curious objects are constantly found in the lakes.

4. At Windisch, the Roman Vindonissa, were found celtic pottery, bronze clasps, iron implements, a flint knife, flint scraper, stone celt, etc.

5. In front of Vorbourg, in the Bernese Alps, M. Quiquerez informs us, a number of pre-historic objects were found in 1866. All three ages are represented. Wheel-made pottery was also found.

The archæologists suggest that at such places the ages have *succeeded* each other. But the remains are found all together, and, while there may have been *some* succession, it is plain that a few centuries will cover the entire occupation.

6. M. Suess gives an account of important discoveries in Lower Austria, where antiquities similar to those of the Swiss lakes are found heaped together on the summits of hills, especially in the Vitur-Berg, not far from the small village of Eggenburg. There are found here, we are told by M. Desor, "along with a prodigious quantity of flakes of silex," objects in bronze, such as brooches and poniards, some articles of iron, but chiefly utensils of stone and a vast amount of fragments of pottery.

Lake-Dwellings on Trajan's Column.

A very pregnant fact bearing on the age of these lacustrine villages is stated by Mr. Stevens in his "Flint Chips." He says that "*Pile-dwellings are delineated on Trajan's Column.*"* The date of this column is about A.D. 105; and it was erected to commemorate the conquest of Dacia. We learn, therefore, that in the region represented by modern Austria (perhaps no very great distance from the celebrated salt-works at Hallstadt,—possibly not then opened) there were lake-dwellings in the beginning of the second century. The war lasted five years, and Gibbon describes the Dacians as "the most warlike of men," and Decebalus, their king, as "proving himself a rival not unworthy of Trajan." They were, therefore, it is not improbable, fully as far advanced in civilization as the inhabitants of Central and Eastern Switzerland.

---

* Page 121.

Indeed, we know that the lake-dwellings in Switzerland continued, in some instances at least, to a much later period even than this. At Noville and Chavannes, in the Canton de Vaud, we are told that they were occupied *until the sixth century of our era.** Lake-dwellings in the sixth century.

We have mentioned that the lake-dwellings or crannoges of Ireland were occupied down to the close of the sixteenth century. All of them are of comparatively recent date. While stone and bronze are rare, iron is very commonly found in them.

Such are the facts with regard to the lake-habitations of Switzerland, which have figured so conspicuously in the recent treatises on the Antiquity of Man. We have mentioned the discovery of similar remains in other countries. It may be worth while to ascertain whether these afford better evidence of the lapse of seven or eight thousand years since their occupation.

ITALY.

After the discoveries in Switzerland, M. Desor conjectured that similar pre-historic stations, from the topographical character of the country, and certain indications in the turbaries, ought to exist in Northern Italy. His speculations have proved to have been well founded. They were first recognized by M. Stoppani in the Lake of Varese. They have since been found in all the lakes of Lombardy. Seven have been signalled in the Lake of Varese, of which four belong to the age of stone, the rest to the bronze age. Nine stations are known on the Lake of Garda. Other stations have been found in Lake Maggiore, and in those of Monate, Annone, Pusiano, Lecco, and Fimon, the last near Vicenza.

The pile-villages are found not only in the waters of existing lake-basins, but also in the turbaries, which, in ancient times, made part of these basins, and even in turbaries which are the sites of former small lakes now entirely filled up. These occur in Piedmont, Lombardy, Venetia, and the ex-Duchies, in which are found objects of ancient industry, in great part of the age of bronze. We may mention particularly the turbary of Mercurago,—those of the Parmesan—explored by MM. Strobel and Pigorini,—and those of the territory of Reggio and of Modena, explored by MM. Chierici, Pigorini, and Canestrini, and

* Antiquity of Man, p. 26, Am. edit. To the same purport Dr. V. Gross, after referring to his examination of the lake-stations on the Lake of Bienne of the stone, the bronze, and the iron epochs, remarks, "Besides the stations which I have just mentioned, and which belong to a well-defined epoch, there exist *at various places* of our lake sites covered with pile-work which have been little used, which probably remount to an epoch *much less ancient*. I have recognized two of this kind in the vicinity of Neuveville and of the Landeron." Matériaux pour l'Histoire de l'Homme, 5e et 6e Livraisons, 1873, p. 206.

which seem (with one exception) to mark the southern limit of the lacustrine stations in Italy.

Mercurago, near Arona, is a peat-moor, the site of which was formerly occupied by a lake. M. Gastaldi describes as found here: flint arrow-heads, a bronze lance, and a wooden anchor. Subsequently M. Moro found among the piles "an extraordinary quantity of objects in flint, bronze, and clay, and a canoe."

In the neighboring moor of Conturbia, a number of piles were found, driven into the peat, which are said to have had the lower ends furnished with *iron points*.

The traces of a lake-village have been found by Captain Angelucci in the province of Capitanata, on the southeastern coast of Italy. It is in the Lake of Salpi, and is assigned to the age of stone.

A coin found.

It is difficult to associate the term "pre-historic" with a coinage. We find nevertheless in "Matériaux pour l'Histoire de l'Homme" * that traces of a lake-village have been found in the marshy soil along the course of the river Chiana, in Tuscany; and that, in addition to a number of vases and utensils of copper, lances of iron, statuettes in metal, etc., there was found among these relics *a copper coin*. Thus we find the lake-dwellers right in the midst of the later Etruscan civilization. The coin, indeed, was very probably Roman.

The Terramares.

First-cousins to the Lake-Dwellings, and the most important feature offered by this country to the palæo-ethnologist, are the *Terramares* of Italy. Morlot designated them as "the kjökken-möddings of the age of bronze;" but they are, as they appear to us, more nearly related to the pile-villages of the lakes. They seem to have been constructed in the swamps and marshes. The piles were driven into the mud, and a platform laid down, on which the Terramarians erected their cabins. On this platform was gradually accumulated a quantity of rubbish and refuse matter, until finally a new platform was laid down, which may have been repeated even again. A little hillock (*tertre*, as the French call it) was thus formed. At Montale (a well-known station of this character) this eminence is some sixteen feet high and has a diameter of seventy or eighty yards.

Most of these terramares which have been recognized lie in the plain of the ancient Via Æmilia, which extends from the Arda to the Reno, between the Apennines and the Po, covering an extent of one hundred kilometres long by fifty broad. In the moiety of this area which belongs to the Parmesan, that is, in a district of two thousand five hundred square kilometres, fifty-five stations have been discovered.

These piles are found under the city of Parma, where three successive

---

* Matériaux, 10e à 12e Livraison, 1873, p. 404.

platforms have been recognized. The archæologists refer these terramares to the age of bronze. The remains in general found in them consist of pottery, objects in wood, bronze, and sometimes iron. M. Pigorini has obtained in one instance some implements in stone. A terramare near Reggio contained bronze, iron, and flints, while flints were found also everywhere on the surface of the superficial soil. This fact shows that the population continued to use stone implements after the introduction of iron.

AUSTRIA.

Lake-dwellings have been discovered in the lakes of various provinces of the Austrian Empire. Five or six stations occur on the Lake of Atter, which are assigned to the age of stone. But at several of them objects of bronze have been found; and in one case, as we are informed by Dr. Much, fragments of baked earth, partially covered with a metallic coating, were met with,—showing that these people were not only acquainted with metal, but that they knew how to melt it. At one of these stations they have found an object in *iron*.

Near Olmutz, in Moravia, on the banks of the March, the traces of a pile-village have been found. A portion of the relics belong to the age of stone. Dr. Keller recognized a stone knife and a bone hatchet, etc., precisely like those in the Swiss lakes. The greater part of the objects, however, were bronze,—bronze rings, needle, and ear-ring "of the same form," according to Dr. Keller, "with those in Switzerland and in the mounds." Also earthenware. A drinking-cup is described "as exactly similar to those which we often find in the burial-mounds of the Helvetic era (two hundred years before and until Christ), and executed in the same style with the above." The animals, according to Prof. Rutimeyer, were the wild boar, hart, horse, goat, sheep, brachyceros, dog, remains of two breeds of domestic cattle, tame hog, etc." Prof. Heer discovered some specimens of wheat, and also *rye*, "which had been previously nowhere discovered in the remains either of pile-settlements or of the Roman times." *

Stone and bronze.

Rye.

From the situation of Olmutz, this settlement must be subsequent to the Christian era.

Prof. Unger states that the great lakes of Hungary must have diminished so considerably that there is no chance of discovering any piles on their ancient banks, which, if they ever existed, have been too long exposed to the destructive agencies of the atmosphere to have been preserved.

* See Smithsonian Report for 1865.

BAVARIA.

The lake-settlements have been discovered also in six of the Bavarian lakes. At one of these stations Roman relics were found.

PRUSSIA.

The three ages together.

In Prussia, pile-villages have been met with in the marshes of Pomerania, near Lubtow. There are two distinct beds. In the lower are found fragments of pottery, vases with figures, axes in serpentine, silex, and amphibole, a chisel with a circular socket of bronze, carbonized wheat, barley, and peas. Here we have bronze and stone together. In the upper bed were found similar objects, and also utensils of iron. Here we have stone, bronze, and iron together, —and no question about the "lapping" of ages.*

M. Figuier is equally explicit with M. Desor. In the environs of Lubtow, he says, are two archæological strata, the site of an ancient pile-village. In the lower stratum are found, "all mingled together," bronze and stone instruments, pottery, wheat, etc.; the upper stratum, he tells us, belongs to the iron age.†

POLAND.

M. Przezdziecki discovered a few years since the site of a pile-village at Grobowek, on the banks of the Vistula, to the north of Warsaw. Many stone implements were found. The most eastern lacustrine station (of Europe) yet discovered is, we believe, that on Lake Czeszewo, in the grand-duchy of Posen. Objects in stone, pottery, implements formed of stag-horn, "evidently worked with instruments of metal," were found here. The ages again confounded.

FRANCE.

In the Lake of Bourget, in Savoy, various stations have been found. At one of them the piles are two hundred and twenty yards from the shore, in seven feet of water. There are traces of a conflagration at this station. M. Costa de Beauregard found here bronze relics. At the station of Grésine he found iron. Superior pottery—resembling the Greek—had been found by previous explorers. At the station of Châtillon M. Rabut found a Roman vase.

---

* Palafittes of the Lake of Neufchâtel. By E. Desor. Translated and published in Smithsonian Report for 1865, p. 402.

† Primitive Man, p. 229.

Within the past two or three years it has been ascertained that numbers of lake-villages existed also in Southwestern France,—in the Haute-Garonne, in Ariége, in Aude, and in the Pyrénées-Orientales. All of the valleys of the Pyrenees, as well as the sub-Pyrenean basin, furnish indications of these habitations. They are observed in the lakes of Saint-Pé, of Massat, of Augat, of the environs of Tarascon; in the turbaries of divers localities of the four departments mentioned; and even in the alluvions of the mountain valleys. They extend over the whole region from the Mediterranean to the ocean, from Bayonne and Dax to the eastern limits of the Pyrenees.

Lake-dwellings in the valleys of the Pyrenees.

An account is given of one of these by M. F. Garrigou, in a paper presented to the French Academy of Sciences by M. Quatrefages. The remains were found in the peat near Saint-Dos (Basses-Pyrénées), at the depth of about two and a half feet. Like most of the others in this region, it is assigned not only to the metal age, but to the age of *iron.**

We learn farther from the work of M. Chantre, entitled the "Palafittes of the Lake of Paladru," which lake is in the department of Isère, that (in the words of M. Quatrefages) "there existed in France lacustrine habitations down to the Carlovingian Epoch."† An old legend represented that there existed at the bottom of the lake the ruins of a city destroyed by the divine vengeance. At the Grands Roseaux, the most considerable of these stations, M. Chantre obtained axes, lance-points, keys, spurs, etc., all of iron, together with a Carlovingian coin. We learn, therefore, that the Lake-Dwellings must have existed in Southeastern France (some seventy-five miles from Geneva) in the ninth century.

Lake-dwellings in the ninth century in France.

We merely add here that traces of the pile-villages have been found in the peat at both Abbeville and London,—the latter associated with Roman remains. This is important as showing the former presence of larger bodies of water at these places, and in the latter case, as showing that these settlements existed in England after the Roman occupation.

JAVA.

In the International Congress at Brussels a letter was read from Col. Weitzel, giving an account of a lake-village which still exists in the island of Noëssa Kimbangan, on the southern coast of Java. The inhabitants live by fishing. When interrogated by Col. Weitzel as to their motive for establishing themselves in the midst of the water, their reply was that it was to put themselves out of the reach of the tigers.

* Comptes-Rendus, 1871, p. 476.

† Comptes-Rendus, Janvier-Juin, 1872, p. 204.

CHAPTER XII.

THE DANISH KJÖKKEN-MÖDDINGS.

The Dirt-Piles or Refuse-Heaps of Ancient Fishermen on the Coasts of Denmark.—Fauna of.—No Remains of Reindeer, Sheep, Ox, or Hog.—Pottery.—Sir J. Lubbock dates them in Beginning of Neolithic Age.—Prof. Worsaae refers them to Palæolithic Age.—Implements found generally very Rude, but some Polished and Fine Implements found.—Prof. Steenstrup thinks the Rudeness of Implements due to the Poverty of the Fishermen.—Case of American Indians.—Iron not known in Denmark before Christian Era.—Palæolithic Man never in Denmark.—Account of a Shell-Mound on Island of Herm.—Stone Implements found with Roman Pottery, Bronze, Iron, and Glass.—Shell-Mound examined by Sir J. Lubbock in Scotland.—Bronze Pin.—Date about 800 A.D.—Shell-Mounds on English Coast.—Roman Pottery.—Coin.—At St. Valéry.—On Coast of United States from Nova Scotia to Florida.—Coasts of Maine, New Jersey, Georgia, Florida.

ARCHÆOLOGISTS appeal next, in proof of the antiquity of man, to the Danish *kjökken-möddings*, or *shell-mounds*. These are the dirt-piles or refuse-heaps of a race of ancient fishermen who lived on the eastern coasts of Denmark,* the word kjökken-mödding meaning literally "kitchen-midden." These mounds were at first supposed to be raised beaches; but it was observed by Prof. Steenstrup that the shells belonged exclusively to full-grown specimens; that they consisted of four species which do not live together; and that the stratum was almost entirely devoid of gravel, and consisted almost entirely of shells.

Unpolished stone implements were found in these heaps, and in many places hearths bearing all the marks of fire. Other traces of man were also observed. The deposits are always found near the coasts, never in the interior. The four species of shells most abundant are the oyster, the cockle, the mussel, and the periwinkle. No vegetable substances have been found except burnt pieces of wood and the charred remains of a sea-plant. It does not appear that the men of that day and locality had any knowledge of agriculture.

Rude stone implements.

The remains of a few crabs have been found. Also the herring, the dorse, the dab, the eel, and other fishes. There are no traces of the domestic fowl, or the domestic swallows of Denmark, or the sparrow,

* They have been found in Zeeland, Fyen, Möen, and Samsoe, and also in Jutland, along the Liëmfjord, the Mariagerfjord, etc. The oyster does not grow in these regions now, in consequence of the amount of fresh water poured into the Baltic by its tributaries. Formerly Jutland was an archipelago, traversed by many fjords and arms of the sea, thus admitting more freely the waters of the North Sea into the Baltic.

or stork. Specimens of the capercailzie, which feeds on the buds of the pine, and several species of ducks and geese, also the wild swan, and the Great Auk, are found. Of mammalia the most frequent are the stag, the roe-deer, and the wild boar. We have also the urus, the dog, the fox, the seal, the otter, the wolf, the beaver, the bear, the mouse, a smaller species of ox, etc. The musk-ox, the domestic ox, the reindeer, the elk, the hare, the sheep, the domestic hog, are absent.

Animal remains.

The flint implements found are, ordinarily, very rude. Sir John Lubbock assigns them to the early part of the Neolithic Age; Prof. Worsaae assigns them to the Palæolithic period.

Archæological date of.

Pottery of a rude type is also found. From the fact that the flint flakes and other implements encountered in the shell-mounds are entirely unpolished, it has been argued by Prof. Worsaae that they are "the remains of a much ruder people than those who erected the large Stone Age tumuli and made the beautiful weapons found in them." He does not deny that well-worked implements have been occasionally found in the kjökken-möddings, but he regards their presence as exceptional. Prof. Steenstrup is of a different opinion. He affirms—1. That the tumuli are the tombs of the chiefs, and the kjökken-möddings the refuse-heaps of fishermen,—and that this accounts for the difference in the value and workmanship of the articles found. 2. That the long flint flakes found in those heaps are sufficient evidence of the skill which had been attained. 3. Prof. Steenstrup affirms that the ruder implements do actually occur in the tumuli, but have not heretofore been particularly observed; which last statement is corroborated by Sir John Lubbock, who remarks that the more recent researches of Mr. Bateman, Mr. Greenwell, and others, have demonstrated that the ruder implements of stone in the tumuli were overlooked by the earlier archæologists.

Pottery.

Prof. Steenstrup.

We may just add to this that all over the United States and in Canada the very rudest stone implements are constantly found lying on the surface of the ground, and are known to have been manufactured by the Indians a few centuries ago; and with them very superior and polished implements are also found. The same rude implement is also found in abundance in the Danish peat at the depth of a few feet. The people on the Danish coasts were obviously a primitive race of fishermen, who contented themselves with very primitive weapons and tools, just as we see to-day in portions of Europe agricultural implements that have been out of use in more advanced regions ever since the Reformation.

Rude and polished implements found together.

The unpolished character of these flints, and the absence of metal, constitute the whole case for the antiquity of the kjökken-möddings.

With regard to the absence of metal, the Danish antiquaries admit that iron was not known in that country before the Christian era. And we can well imagine, considering that prior to that time Denmark was unknown to the Romans, that bronze was not introduced at a very early period. Bronze had doubtless reached there in exceptional cases through Phœnician traders, but there were many tribes that did not use it, and stone implements were used all over the country.

Prof. Morlot informs us that "some rare specimens of flints of fine workmanship have been found in the kjökken-möddings." And he tells us farther that the fragments of worked bones found indicate well-made instruments. Prof. Steenstrup and Sir John Lubbock refer to similar indications of skill. The finding of a few superior implements is sufficient evidence of what the shell-mound people could do,—and in a dung-hill we do not expect often to gather jewels.

The fauna of the shell-mounds indicates by no means a very ancient period. There are no extinct animals, except the urus, or *Bos primigenius*, and this existed in Germany down to the sixteenth century, and its remains are found in the tumuli. Cæsar mentions it (as we have stated) as occurring in the Hercynian forest. It is also mentioned (as we shall see) in the Niebelungen Lied.

The fact that the reindeer and the aurochs both fail to occur in these mounds is full of significance. We alluded to the absence of the reindeer in the Swiss lake-dwellings, and the extreme rarity of the aurochs and urus.

This absence of the remains of these animals in the shell-mounds and lake-dwellings, or their extreme rarity, we do not undertake to explain; we only remark that it is wholly irreconcilable with any very ancient date; and yet Prof. Worsaae assigns the shell-mounds to the Palæolithic Age, and Sir John Lubbock is not far behind him; while, as we have seen, the Rev. Dunbar Heath thinks that man had not acquired the faculty of speech in that primal dawn of the Baltic oyster.

These views are the more extraordinary from the fact that, as is well known, Palæolithic Man never penetrated into Denmark. This country, like Scotland, was still probably in its Glacial Age when the mammoth and the rhinoceros were in Southern England, Germany, and France, and the remains of the mammoth only occur in these regions in a very few instances, while there are no traces whatever of the rhinoceros, excepting a single molar tooth from Sweden.

Palæolithic Man never in Denmark.

We are guided somewhat in determining the probable date of these Danish shell-mounds by the account which we have of one in the *Anthropological Review*, by Mr. J. W. Flower, F.G.S., on the west coast of the island of Herm, one of the Channel Islands, situated between Guernsey and Sark. He found the bones of

Shell-mound on the island of Herm.

the ox, horse, sheep, pig, goat, etc. The marrow-bones were all broken, as in Denmark; but none of the bones were gnawed by dogs; indeed, *no remains of the dog were found.* The horse belonged to a small race,—resembling the Shetland pony. This small species of horse is often referred to by the anthropologists as "pre-historic." Mr. Flower thinks the bones of the so-called ox really belonged to the *Bos longifrons.* The shells of the oyster, mussel, limpet, Mya, Haliotis, etc., were also found,—as in Denmark. These mollusks are still sold in Guernsey for food.

Bricks.

A number of small cylindrical bricks were also found—hand-made,—and were probably used in baking the pottery, the fragments of which were also found. The impression on the base of these bricks indicated that they had been "placed on the edge of a flat stone or plank." There were great numbers of these bricks, which were not adapted for building purposes.

Roman pottery.

Some of the pottery was rude and hand-made; other specimens, says Mr. Flower, "are clearly of Roman workmanship," several pieces being "undoubted Samian ware."

Stone implements.

Hand-mills, or querns, were also found,—showing that the soil was cultivated. There were no flint flakes or scrapers. The only flint implements found were "some of those rude mullers or chisels" often found in the Channel Islands, and "some rounded, and other, stones, evidently used as hammers."

Metals and glass.

A bronze pin, an instrument of iron, and a fragment of glass, were also found.

We thus have a post-Roman kjökken-mödding, and in it we find stone chisels and hammers and rude hand-made pottery, and no remains of the dog, but those of a small horse and the *Bos longifrons.*

This is not all the instruction we derive from this pile of "pre-historic" rubbish. In one of the volumes of the *Archæologia,* if we remember rightly, Rev. Mr. Lukis published his account of the cromlechs of Guernsey, in which he did not find anywhere "any trace of metal." They have, of course, been regarded as very ancient. Now, the stone implements discovered by Mr. Flower in the shell-mound are precisely like those found by Mr. Lukis in the cromlechs. We thus perceive that we may find graves without a trace of metal which may be no older, or little older, than the Christian era. The stones of these cromlechs are all rude and unshaped, and there are more than the usual appearances of antiquity. When the paper on this shell-mound was read by Mr. Flower, Col. Lane Fox remarked that he had found a kitchen-midden of the Roman age in the Isle of Thanet, in which were finger bricks like those described, and which were associated with Roman pottery.*

---

* Anthrop. Rev., 1869, p. 115.

Is it strange that on the coast of Denmark, some two thousand or two thousand five hundred years ago, a race of rude fishermen used unpolished flint implements? Is it any stranger than that the Indians of New Jersey and Canada, in the seventeenth century, used precisely similar implements? Is it any stranger than that the Japanese used stone in the eighth century of our era? that it was used in Northeastern Asia a century ago? that the bulk of the German soldiers in the days of Tacitus used sharpened stakes for spears? that the Mexican soldiers encountered by Cortez were many of them armed with spears pointed with obsidian? that the Peruvians also had arrows and spears and swords of stone?

Shell-mounds in Scotland.

Shell-mounds, similar to those of Denmark, have been found in Scotland. Some of these were examined by the Rev. Dr. Gordon and Sir John Lubbock on the shores of the Moray Firth. The largest of the Scotch kjökken-möddings is on Loch Spynie (near the sea-coast). This was visited by Sir John Lubbock. He did not find any implements or pottery, but "a laborer who had been employed in carting it away for manure had previously found some fragments of rude pottery and a bronze pin." The pin was "submitted to Mr. Franks, who gives it as his opinion that it is probably not older than 800 or 900 A.D." One is tempted to ask here why the Bronze Age in Scotland happens to be so much nearer modern times than the Bronze Age in the neighborhood of the Cattegat and the Skager Rack?

Bronze pin.

Coast of Cromarty.

Shell-mounds on the Scottish coast, in the neighborhood of Cromarty, are referred to by Hugh Miller, where, as he states, articles of bronze were found along with rude implements of bone and flint.*

A kjökken-mödding has also been discovered at Newhaven, in Sussex, containing, along with bones, shells, pottery, and flint flakes, two or three fragmentary objects of metal, including a leaden hook and a small *coin*. The pottery was apparently Roman. Two of the fragments were undoubtedly such, being Samian ware, *above* which the flint flakes occurred.†

St. Valéry.

Shell-mounds have also been found in many other parts of the world. Traces of them have been observed at St. Valéry, close to the mouth of the Somme,—that prolific theatre for the archæologists,—in whose valley they have also found remains of the lake-dwellers, and in whose "gravel" they have found those famous flints which have immortalized M. Boucher de Perthes. The shell-mounds have also been

* Jour. Anthropolog. Soc., 1865, vol. iii. p. 21.

† Intellect. Obs., vol. vii. p. 233.

found in Cornwall and Devonshire, in Australia, in Tierra del Fuego, and on the coasts of North America.

In the International Congress at Brussels, Baron Dücker stated that in a recent voyage to Greece he had found on the sea-shore, particularly in the island of Salamis, shell-heaps which he regarded as similar to the kjökken-möddings of Denmark. Recent examinations show these accumulations to be quite recent, and of an origin "entirely historic."

On the Atlantic coast of the United States.

In an address before the American Scientific Association, at Chicago, in 1867, Col. Whittlesey stated that shell-mounds were found all along the Atlantic coast from Nova Scotia to Florida.

Prof. Chadbourne, of Bowdoin College, in the "Agricultural Geology of Maine" for 1861 (second series) gives an account of the shell-mounds on that coast. They are to be found at New Castle, Damariscotta, Trenton, etc. Prof. Chadbourne states that the shells are in small piles of from ten to fifteen feet in diameter, and some two or three feet deep. He found the bones of the beaver, apparently broken by some instrument. Also bones of birds.

There are similar deposits at Sawyer's Island, covering an area of ten acres, and containing human bones, and animal and fish bones, in every stage of decomposition. The common clam or *Mya edulis* occurs frequently. The oyster, the dog, the cod, and antlers of the red deer, also occur. The oyster is the *O. Virginiana* and *O. borealis*, which are still found in Sheepscot River, not a great distance from the Indian shell-beds. The *O. Virginiana* was formerly very common here, but has been nearly exterminated by the saw-mills.

Prof. Leidy examined some of these mounds, near the town of Lewes on the Delaware Bay. They extended for a mile or so below the town to the base of a huge sand dune. He states that he found them all "quite superficial," from "a few inches to less than a foot in depth." He visited similar accumulations on the south shore of the cape. All of them examined contained "fragments of pottery, chips of jasper, and stone-arrow-heads. A few copper rings were also found, and in one heap Mr. Canby found several *English coins.*" *

Near Cape Horn, we are told, the natives of Tierra del Fuego (who still use stone tools) have their "shell-mounds" in every sheltered cove.

The coasts of Georgia and Florida.

Mr. Charles C. Jones, in his recent work on the "Antiquities of the Southern Indians," states that the coasts of Georgia and Florida are "hoary" with the shell-mounds. They range, he says, from the Bay of Fundy to Cape Sable, and also along the Gulf coast. Many of them in the southern region are *burial-mounds*,

* Proc. Phil. Acad. Nat. Sci., 1866, p. 291.

while vast numbers are little more than refuse-heaps. They contain pottery, stone axes, flint knives, etc. There is a remarkable tumulus of these shells on Stalling's Island, two hundred miles from the mouth of the Savannah River. Its diameter is three hundred feet, and its height fifteen feet. It is a huge necropolis.

CHAPTER XIII.

THE BONE-CAVES.

Fertile Source of Evidence.—The Celebrated Cave of Gailenreuth, in Bavaria.—Examined by Cuvier and Dr. Buckland.—Remains of the Cave-Bear, Elephant, Hyæna, etc.—Kirkdale Cave.—Remains of Great Numbers of Hyænas and Bears.—Flint Implements found in these Caverns in Association with the Bones of these Extinct Animals, including Mammoth, Woolly Rhinoceros, Cave-Bear, Cave-Lion, Cave-Hyæna, Reindeer, Hippopotamus, etc.—Frequently found under Floors of Stalagmite.—Bones sometimes swept into the Caves by Water.—In other Cases, Evidences of Habitation.—Bones of the great Pachyderms dragged in by Carnivores.—Bones of the Reindeer split for the Marrow, and the Horns carved into Implements.—Figures of Animals sketched on the Bones and Horns.—Review of the Caves mentioned by Sir John Lubbock in his "Pre-historic Times."—Caves examined by Dr. Schmerling near Liége.—M. Dupont.—Chaleux and Furfooz.—Kent's Hole near Torquay.—Brixham Cave.—Wokey Hole.—Aurignac.—The Caves and Grottoes of Dordogne.—Palæolithic Art.—Grotto of Maccagnone.—The Gibraltar Caves.—Pottery found in the Caves.—Other Examples of the Bone-Caves.—M. Figuier's Work on "Primitive Man."—Cave of Nabrigas.—Vergisson.—La Chaise.—Caves of Massat.—Fishing and the Use of the Needle among the Cave-Dwellers.—The Gower Caves.—Glamorganshire.—The Religious Sentiment among the Cave-Dwellers.—Traffic and Travel among the Cave-Dwellers.—Chaleux again.—M. Dupont on the Trou du Frontal at Furfooz.—Evidences here of a *Great Inundation*.—Trou Rosette.—More Pottery.—Trou des Noutons.—These Belgian Caves all show the Occurrence of a Great Flood, by which they were swept, and their Occupants, perhaps, overtaken.—Other Examples of the Art of the Cave-Dwellers. — Bruniquel. — Laugerie-Basse.—La Madelaine.—Pottery found in the Caves of Ariége by MM. Garrigou and Filhol.—Cavern at Pondres described by Messrs. Nott and Gliddon.—Cavern of Bize.—Cave of Mialet described by Sir C. Lyell and Sir H. De La Beche.—The Paviland Cave.—Flint Implement Factories at Chaleux, Laugerie-Basse, Laugerie-Haute, Grand Pressigny, Charente, Hoxne, etc. — Grime's Graves.—Capt. Brome on the Caves of Gibraltar.—Growth of Stalagmitic Floors.—Erroneous Calculations of Mr. Vivian and Mr. Evans.—Bone-Caves in the Islands of Malta and Sicily.—The newly-discovered Cave of Mentone and the Fossil Man of Baôsses-Rousses.—Burial Forms among the Cave-Men.—Cave near Luchon discovered by M. Piette.—More Drawings.—Cave near Nuremberg discovered in 1872.—Agriculture and Weaving amongst the Cave-Men.—New Discoveries in Aquitaine.—Drawing of Palæolithic Man pursuing a Bison.—Cave near Veyrier, at the Foot of Mt. Salève, in Switzerland.—Numerous Remains of the Reindeer.—Caves of South Africa.—Grottoes discovered by M. Baye in the Department of Marne, belonging to the Polished Stone Age.—Grotto of Hohlefels.—Pottery in the Palæolithic Age.—Palæolithic Music—The Use of Paint by the Palæolithic Tribes.

THE Bone-caverns constitute a fertile source of the "remains" of "Pre-historic Man." M. Figuier's work on "Primitive Man" is largely engrossed with this branch of the evidence. The caves have attracted attention now for a century, the celebrated cavern of Gailenreuth, in Bavaria, having been discovered by Esper in 1774.

Gailenreuth.

This immense cave is a series of chambers or grottoes, the first of which is eighty feet long. An orifice only two feet high leads from this into the second grotto, which is one hundred and fifty feet long, and from five to eighteen feet in height. A very tortuous passage leads to the third grotto. The loam on this floor is filled with teeth and jaw-bones, and a rift opens into a side chamber, fifteen feet long by four wide, where an immense number of hyænas' and lions' bones were found. It is to be remarked that this rift was too narrow to have allowed the animals to enter. A peculiar tunnel which terminated in this grotto afforded an incredible number of bones, and large skulls, quite entire.

Descending from grotto number three by a ladder, we come to a vault fifteen feet in diameter, and on the side is a fourth grotto bestrewed with bones. Proceeding along an arcade, we reach a fifth chamber, and a new gulf eighteen or twenty feet deep. Even below this there is another opening, filled with bones. Nor are we yet through. A passage now leads to a grotto twenty-five feet long by twelve wide; then an alley twenty feet long, leading into a cave twenty feet high; and finally, a grand grotto expands, eighty-three feet in width by twenty-four high, "more copiously furnished with bones than any of the rest."

This cavern was explored by Dr. Buckland in 1816, and it was also examined by Cuvier, who ascertained that the bones occurring in it belonged in the proportion of three-fourths to bears. There were a few bones of the elephant, and a number of the hyæna, glutton, fox, and polecat. There are other caves in this neighborhood,—all in the limestone,—and all containing animal bones, and in all of them the same species of bear occurs in the same proportion.

Kirkdale cave.

The Kirkdale cave, in England, was discovered in 1821, and here the prevailing remains were those of the hyæna,—one collector alone, according to Dr. Buckland, having obtained more than three hundred of the canine teeth of this animal, representing as many as seventy-five hyænas. But this is a small figure in comparison with the exhibit which Buckland and Cuvier give us of the cave of Külhock. Says Buckland, "there are hundreds of cart-loads of *animal dust.*" And Cuvier estimates that it contained the remains of two thousand five hundred bears.

Works of art found in the caves.

The flint implements are found in these caverns, and frequently human bones. In association with them are found the remains of the cave-bear, the cave-hyæna, the mammoth, the woolly rhinoceros, the hippopotamus, the reindeer, the aurochs, and other extinct animals. Frequently there is a floor of stalagmite in the cave, and the animal remains are often found with the flints under this floor.

In the case of the reindeer, the bones and horns of this animal are found in these caverns as far south as the Pyrenees,—a circumstance which is interpreted as proving that the climate of Southern France was at that time much colder than it is at present. It is contended that these facts demonstrate the immense antiquity of the human race.

We admit that the remains of man and the reindeer in these caves are of the same age; and we believe that those of man and the mammoth and cave-bear are also of the same age; but the latter fact is not yet universally accepted. Lubbock seems somewhat dubious about it, while Lyell, on the other hand, does not hesitate to affirm it as established; and we have no great doubt that Lyell is right in this opinion.

The mere juxtaposition of the bones alone does not prove the cotemporaneity of the remains. Man may have frequented these caves long after the bears and the hyænas, and have left his traces there. Or they may have been burial-places.

Action of water.

Or his bones and those of the animals may have been swept into the caves, at different times, by floods. We *know* that in many instances the bones were collected in this way. In speaking just now of one of the chambers of the Cavern of Gailenreuth, where there was an immense number of hyænas' and lions' bones, we pointed out that the opening was *too narrow* to have allowed the animals to enter. Their remains *must* have been borne into the fissure by water. Of course the reindeer, the aurochs, the hippopotami, and the elephants did not inhabit the caves. Their bones were swept in by floods, or dragged in by the hyænas and bears, or left there by man. Figuier also remarks that "caves often contain large heaps of bones, situated at heights which would have been absolutely inaccessible to the animals which lived in these places." "It is also," he says, "a very strange fact that no [palæolithic] cavern has ever produced an entire skeleton or even a whole limb of the skeleton of a man, and scarcely of any animal whatever."* The bones are frequently found in the utmost confusion and disorder. It is often rendered certain in these cases that they have been washed into the caves, by the fact that drift-pebbles are found in close proximity, which pebbles have come from a considerable distance. They are often accompanied by terrestrial and fluviatile shells.

Dr. Buckland informed Sir Henry De La Beche that MacEnery, at the famous cavern of Kent's Hole, discovered in 1825, found rounded portions of granite and greenstone beneath stalagmite, as also fragments of rolled sandstone and slate. The cave is of limestone. No granite

* Primitive Man, p. 59. To those familiar with the subject it is unnecessary to say that M. Dupont has found entire human limbs in the Belgian caves, that a number of entire skeletons have been found in the caves of Mentone near Nice, and that, last year, a skeleton was found at Laugerie-Basse. The remark of M. Figuier is, however, generally true.

is found nearer than Dartmoor, thirteen miles off. The same phenomena appear at Yealm Bridge.*

So in the bone breccia in the caverns of the Morea it is notorious that water has been the transporting agent; as also at Gibraltar and in the caves of Sicily and Malta.

Sir Charles Lyell concurs in these views, and in his "Principles of Geology" gives an elaborate explanation of the manner in which animal and human bones are even now swept into the caverns of the Morea.† In this connection this writer mentions another fact calculated to throw light on this subject: he states that M. Boblaye and his companions, who studied these caverns in Greece, "near the mouth of one chasm saw the carcass of a horse, in part devoured, the size of which seemed to have prevented the jackals from dragging it in; the marks of their teeth were observed on the bones, and it was evident that the floods of the ensuing winter would wash in whatsoever might remain of the skeleton." ‡

Brazilian caves.

Here is another suggestive statement, made in the "Geology and Physical Geography of Brazil by L. Agassiz and his Travelling Companions." Near Caxoeira do Campo, Dr. Lund, who has devoted so much attention to the study of the Brazilian caves, counted the bones found in a half cubic-foot of earth taken from a cave. He found in it four hundred half-underjaws of a small opossum and two thousand belonging to mice, besides those of bats, porcupines, etc. In another cave he estimated the remains of cavias, opossums, porcupines, mice, small birds, frogs, etc., as belonging to six million eight hundred and eighty-one thousand five hundred individuals! All these bones were carried into these caves, according to Dr. Lund, by *owls*.

One more illustration: During the earthquake of 1693, in Sicily, several thousand people were at once entombed in the ruins of caverns in limestone, at Sortino Vecchio.

Coprolites of the Hyæna.

That the hyænas *inhabited* many of these caves we know by their coprolites, which sometimes form a regular layer or floor.

We say this much by way of preliminary, and in order to give the reader a clear idea of all the facts.

Man and the extinct mammifers cotemporary.

How then do we know that Man and the *Cervus tarandus* of Southern France were cotemporary? and why do we believe that the mammoth and the Rhinoceros tichorinus and the great cave-bear lived at the same time? Because the bones of the reindeer are not only constantly found in association with the remains of man in the caves of Southern France and elsewhere, but these bones are *split for the marrow;* and because the bones and the horns are not only

* Geological Observer for 1850, by Sir H. De La Beche, p. 308.

† See Amer. edition of 1865, p. 734. ‡ Ib., p. 735.

carved and shaped into various implements, but there are *sketches* (and very elegant ones, sometimes) of the reindeer on bone and horn found in the caves. There seems to be some doubt entertained by Sir John Lubbock (as we have stated) with reference to the sufficiency of the evidence in regard to the cotemporaneity of man and the mammoth, the cave-tiger, the cave-bear, and the cave-hyæna. We have mentioned that we think, however, that the fact is pretty well established. Several cases of the delineation of the mammoth have—if we may rely on the reproduced figures—been discovered, and it is represented (we presume correctly) that sketches of the cave-bear, cave-lion, and rhinoceros have been found in the caves. M. Lartet also believed that he observed marks of the knife on the bones of the rhinoceros at Aurignac, as well as indications that they had been bròken by man. Farther: in one or two instances, in association with the flints, entire limbs of the cave-bear have been found, with all the bones lying in their natural order, as if they had been deposited in the caves at the time of, or soon after the death of, the animal. These cases will be noticed as we proceed, and other facts leading us to the same conclusion, that all of these animals were cotemporary with the cave-men.

We propose now to notice the caves in detail, and first in order we shall lay before the reader all the cases mentioned by Sir John Lubbock in the "Pre-historic Times."

In 1828 MM. Tournal and Christol found human bones, the bones of extinct animals, and fragments of *pottery* in certain caves in the south of France. We have not access to the original narrative of these gentlemen, and give only the meagre statement which we find in Sir J. Lubbock's work. It is important to observe that in this case the remains of the extinct animals were associated with *pottery*.

The Belgian caves. Dr. Schmerling.

A great number of these caves have been found in Belgium. In 1833 Dr. Schmerling examined as many as forty of them in the neighborhood of Liége, and found in all of them, along with the flint implements, the remains of the mammoth, woolly rhinoceros, cave-bear, cave-hyæna, cave-lion, reindeer, or some one or more of the extinct animals. In four or five of them he found also the skull or other bones of the human skeleton. In the cave of Engihoul he found the remains of at least three human individuals mingled in such a manner with the bones of the extinct animals as to leave no doubt on his mind of man having co-existed with them. None of these caves contained any *gnawed bones* or the fossil excrements of any animal species; which put an end to the hypothesis that, in these particular instances, they had been used as dens by wild beasts. The flints, as we have said, were found in all of these caves, chipped into the form of hatchets, knives, and other implements. In the cave of Chokier Dr.

Schmerling picked up a polished bone needle, having an eye pierced at the base. In the cave of Engis he found also a carved bone with the flints. It was in this last-named cave that two human skulls were found, one of them in a very perfect condition, and since made famous as *the Engis Skull* in connection with the discussions with regard to the craniology of primeval man. Huxley is of the opinion that it offers no indications of degradation; while Carl Vogt believes that it indicates an altogether rudimentary condition of the human intellect.

On the right bank of the Meuse, on the opposite side of the river to Engis, Dr. Schmerling explored the cave of Engihoul,* where he found numerous bones of the extremities of three human beings, and two small fragments of a cranium. Professor Malaise and Sir Charles Lyell explored this cave again in 1860, and "beneath a hard floor of stalagmite" they found mud full of the bones of extinct and recent animals, and two human jaw-bones retaining their teeth. "The skulls from these Belgian caverns display no marked deviation from the normal European type of the present day."†

M. Dupont.

More recently still these Belgian caves have been investigated by M. Dupont under the auspices of the Belgian Government. "They belong," says Sir John Lubbock, "to the so-called Reindeer period, and the flint implements are never ground." Out of thirty thousand worked flints found at Chaleux, and twelve hundred in the caverns of Furfooz, "not one presents a trace of polish." Some of them seem to be [are] of Pressigny flint, and must have come from a long distance. The Trou du Frontal contained the bones of thirteen individuals, who, in Sir John Lubbock's opinion, had probably been *buried* in the cave, the door of which was closed by a large block of stone.

Kent's Hole.

The celebrated cavern of Kent's Hole, near Torquay, on the coast of Devonshire, in England, was examined by Mr. MacEnery in 1825. It was again explored in 1840 by Mr. Godwin-Austen, who found flint arrow-heads and knives, and the bones of the elephant, rhinoceros, ox, deer, horse, bear, hyæna, etc.

Mr. Evans gives a very full account of this cave, which has been very thoroughly examined by a committee appointed by the British Association. The deposits are as follows:

1. Large blocks of limestone which have fallen from the roof, sometimes cemented by stalagmite.

2. A layer of black, muddy mould, three to twelve inches thick.

3. Stalagmite one foot to three feet thick, almost continuous, and in places containing large fragments of limestone.

4. Red cave-earth, varying in thickness, containing fifty per cent. of

* Not mentioned by Lubbock.

† Elements of Geology, by Lyell, Amer. edit., p. 157.

angular fragments of limestone, with bones of extinct animals, and flint and bone implements.

Above the stalagmite, and chiefly in the black mould, have been found a number of relics belonging to different periods, such as socketed celts, and a socketed knife, of bronze, smelted copper, four hundred flint flakes, cores, and chips, a polishing-stone, numerous spindle-whorls, bone instruments, pottery, marine shells, bones of existing animals, and human bones. Some of the pottery is distinctly Roman in character.

In the cave-earth below the stalagmite are flint implements, implements of bone, and the bones of extinct animals. Some of these implements, the flints as well as the utensils of bone, exhibit very considerable care and skill. Some of the wrought flakes resemble the flakes of obsidian in use as javelin-heads among the New Caledonian and other savage tribes of the present day, and may be compared, says Mr. Evans, with some of the lance-heads from the cave of Laugerie-Haute. Other forms are identical with some found at Aurignac. A very perfect harpoon-head of bone is precisely of the same character as some from La Madelaine, which we shall notice hereafter. Mr. Evans gives a list of the animals whose remains have been found below the stalagmite: it includes the cave-lion, cave-hyæna, wolf, large fox, glutton, cave-bear, grizzly bear, brown bear, mammoth, woolly rhinoceros, horse, urus, bison, Irish elk, stag, reindeer, hare, cave-pika, water-rat, field-mouse, bank-vole, beaver, and the *Machairodus latidens*. The animals above the stalagmite, where the polished stone and bronze implements occurred, were the dog, short-horn ox, roe-deer, sheep, goat, pig, and rabbit.

Brixham cave is also in the neighborhood of Torquay. It was discovered in 1858, and brought to the notice of the Royal Society by the late Dr. Hugh Falconer, F.R.S. It was explored by a committee consisting of Dr. Falconer, Sir Charles Lyell, Mr. Prestwich, Mr. Pengelly, and others. The deposits in the cave, in descending order, were— Brixham cave.

1. Irregular layer of stalagmite, one to fifteen inches thick.

2. Ochreous red cave-earth, with angular stones and some pebbles, two to thirteen feet.

3. Gravel, with pebbles.

In and on the stalagmite were found antlers of the reindeer and a humerus of a bear, and in the cave-earth numerous mammalian remains.

The organic remains, according to Sir John Lubbock, belonged chiefly to the following species:

1. Elephas primigenius.

2. Rhinoceros tichorinus—teeth in considerable numbers and an astragalus.

3. Bos spelæus—teeth, jaws, and other bones.

4. Equus spelæus.
5. Cervus tarandus—skull and horns.
6. Cervus elephas.
7. Cervus capreolus.
8. Ursus spelæus.
9. Ursus ferox.
10. Ursus arctos.
11. Hyæna spelæa.
12. Felis spelæa.
13. Lagomys.

In this Brixham cave, under the stalagmitic floor, a very perfect flint tool occurred, on the same level with, and in very close proximity to, "the entire left hind-leg of a cave-bear."

This specimen was found in what is called the reindeer-gallery. The mass of earth containing it was removed entire, and the matrix cleared away carefully by Dr. Falconer in the presence of Mr. Pengelly. Every bone was in its natural position. Even the patella or detached bone of the knee-pan was searched for, and not in vain. "Here, therefore," says Lyell, "we have evidence of an entire limb not having been washed in a fossil state out of an older alluvium, and then swept afterwards into a cave, so as to be mingled with flint implements, but having been introduced when clothed with its flesh, or at least when it had the separate bones bound together by their natural ligaments, and in that state buried in mud." *

This case, Lyell urges, and with apparent justice, proves one of two things: either the bear and the flint implement were cotemporary, or the bear *succeeded* the flint tool.

Mr. Pengelly, and after him Sir Charles Lyell, suggest that, from the nature and origin of some of the pebbles found in the cave-earth, the configuration of the land about the cave must formerly have been different,—and that the valleys adjoining the cave must have been shallower than they now are; while the currents which carried the red loam in the cavern must have run at a level seventy-eight feet above the stream now flowing in the valley. This may be so. It was that flood which swept the Belgian caves. The land, moreover, on the south coasts of England has been subject to great oscillations within the human period, and, as we shall see, the conformation of the country has been modified, not only here, but in other parts of Great Britain, as well as in France.

A number of flint flakes were found indiscriminately mixed with the animal bones, and, according to all appearances, of the same antiquity. They occurred at various depths, from ten inches to eleven feet.

---

* Antiquity of Man, p. 100, Amer. edit.

This cave was filled with *débris* up to the very roof, and it appears that the accumulation of the material was due partly to the disintegration of the dolomitic conglomerate forming the roof and walls of the cavern, and partly to the sediment washed in gradually by the rain and small streams. Here there are several layers of album græcum, that is to say, excrement of hyænas, each of which indicates (says Sir John Lubbock) an old floor, and a separate period of occupation; "so that the presence of, at least, one such floor above some of the flint implements" proves two things: first, that the hyænas which produced this album græcum occupied the cave after the savages who used the flint implements; and, secondly, that these implements have not been disturbed by water since the period of the hyæna.

Wokey Hole.

One of the most famous of all the caves is that of Aurignac, in the south of France, described by M. Lartet, and cited by Sir John Lubbock and Sir Charles Lyell. A peasant named Bonnemaison, seeing a rabbit run into a hole on a steep slope, put his hand in, and to his surprise pulled out a human bone. Prompted by curiosity, he removed a quantity of rubbish, and came to a large black stone which almost closed up the entrance to a small chamber, in which there were no less than seventeen human skeletons. Unfortunately, the mayor of Aurignac, hearing of the circumstance, collected the bones, and ordered them to be re-buried,—and some years afterwards they could not be identified.

Aurignac.

M. Lartet reached the conclusion that this had been used as a burial-place, and that "it reaches back to the highest antiquity of our race." From the remains of the bones broken for marrow, and the marks of fire immediately outside the cave, he inferred that funeral feasts had been held here. Among the animal remains found were those of the cave bear, the brown bear, the badger, the polecat, the cave-lion, the cave-hyæna, the fox, the wolf, the mammoth, the rhinoceros, the horse, the Irish elk, the reindeer, the stag, the aurochs, etc. Some of these were found in the grotto, some outside; the latter had been gnawed by some large carnivorous animal, no doubt the hyæna, coprolites of which were found among the ashes. On the other hand, the bones inside the cave were untouched, from which M. Lartet concludes that after the funeral feasts, hyænas came and gnawed the bones left outside, but could not effect an entrance into the cave.

The cotemporaneity of the reindeer with man is obvious, as all the bones are broken for the marrow, and many bear marks of the knife; besides which the greater number of the bone implements are made out of the bones or horns of this species. In one case (as at Brixham) the entire limb of a cave-bear appears to have been buried with the flesh on, as the different bones were all found together. M. Lartet conjectures that it was (as is the custom among savages) a portion of the food provided for the dead.

This cave was examined by Principal Forbes. His conclusions were as follows: "It seems very improbable that such a tomb transcends in antiquity the limits usually assigned to historic records. Clearly no considerable geologic change has happened in the valley where it occurs; for the entrance to the cave was covered over only by turf, and a little gravel through which a rabbit had worked a passage which led to the discovery of the tomb. Outside of the stone portal were lying beds of ashes, burned and gnawed bones, and other transportable relics, which a moving force of the slightest kind must at once have dislodged. As an argument of mere general probability, no one would be disposed to assign to such a place of aboriginal sepulture an antiquity of more than two or three thousand years. It appears to us to afford an argument altogether in favor of the comparatively modern date of the disappearance of the mammoth." *

Sir Charles Lyell does not seem to fancy this case himself. He remarks, "An argument, however, having an opposite bearing may, perhaps, be founded on the phenomena at Aurignac. It may—indeed it has been said that they imply that some of the extinct mammalia survived nearly to our own times. First, because of the modern style of the works of art at Aurignac; secondly, because of the absence of any sign of change in the physical geography of the country since the cave was used for a place of sepulture." †

A writer in one of the British Reviews forcibly remarks that it is "repugnant to common sense" to suppose that we have before us at Aurignac "the intact relics of *tens of thousands of years ago.*"

We omitted to state that a number of flint and bone implements were found in this cave.

THE DORDOGNE CAVES.

Caves of Dordogne.

Sir John Lubbock refers also to a number of celebrated caves or grottoes in Dordogne, which were examined by Mr. Christy in conjunction with M. Lartet. Among them are those of Laugerie, La Madelaine, Les Eyzies, Pey de l'Azé, Le Moustier, Badegoule, etc. Remains of the cave-bear have been found at Pey de l'Azé, of the cave-hyæna at Le Moustier, and separated plates of elephant molars at Le Moustier and at Laugerie, accompanied at the latter place by a piece of a pelvis. The bones of the reindeer found in these caves are all broken open for the marrow. "But," says Sir John Lub-

* Good Words, 1864, p. 436.

† In the last edition of the "Antiquity of Man," Lyell believes the interments of later date than the animal bones.

bock, "in its negative aspect the zoological evidence is very instructive. No remains have been found which, in the opinion of Messrs. Christy and Lartet, can be referred to domestic animals. It is true the bones of the ox and the horse occur, but there is no evidence that they belonged to domesticated individuals. Remains of the boar are very rare. . . . The sheep and the goat are entirely wanting, and, what is still more remarkable, even the dog appears to be absent. At the same time, the bones of the horse and the reindeer are very numerous, etc."* P. 326.

The flint implements found in these caves are "innumerable,"—scrapers, cores, awls, lance-heads, cutters, hammers, and mortar-stones. "At Laugerie and Badegoule, fragments of leaf-shaped lance-heads, *almost as well worked as some of those from Denmark*,† are far from uncommon." "If, therefore, we were to attempt any classification of the grottoes according to the periods of their occupation, we should be disposed to refer these to a somewhat later period than most of the others." P. 330.

These stations have yielded also a number of bone implements. These are square chisel-shaped implements; round, sharply-pointed, awl-like tools; harpoon-shaped lance-heads; plain or barbed arrow-heads "cut with wonderful vigor;" and, lastly, eyed needles of compact bone, finely pointed, polished, and drilled with round eyes, "so small and regular that some of the most assured and acute believers in all the other findings might well doubt whether they could indeed have been drilled with stone, until their repetition by the hand of that practical and conscientious observer, Monsieur Lartet, by the very stone implements found with them, has dispelled their honest doubts."

No representation, however rude, of any animal has yet been found in the Danish shell-mounds or the Stone Age lake-villages (excepting, perhaps, a lizard on a piece of pottery, at one of the lake-villages). It is doubtful whether they even occur on objects of the Bronze Age.

Art amongst the Cave-dwellers.

"And yet," says Sir John Lubbock, "in these archaic bone-caves, many very fair sketches have been found, scratched on bone or stone with a sharp point, probably of a flint implement. In some cases there is even an attempt at shading. Fig. 1

FIG. 1.

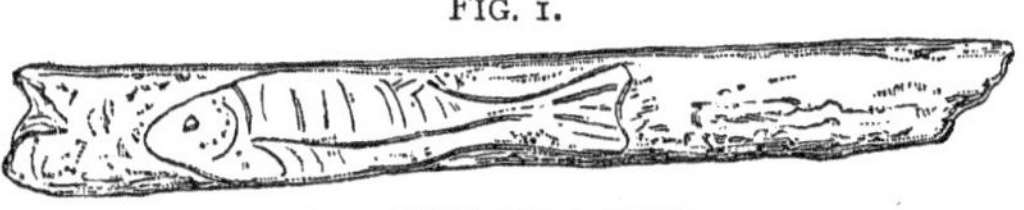

DRAWING OF A FISH.

* We learn from the *Reliquiæ Aquitanicæ* that the fauna of Moustier, the Laugeries, La Madelaine, and Les Eyzies are "near about the same." The reindeer is only numerically less frequent at Moustier. At each of them have been found the dislocated molar plates of the elephant. At Les Eyzies there is worked ivory.

† The italics are ours; but the fact is full of significance.

represents a cylindrical piece of reindeer's horn, found at La Madelaine, on which are carved two outlines of fishes, one on each side. Fig. 2

FIG. 2.

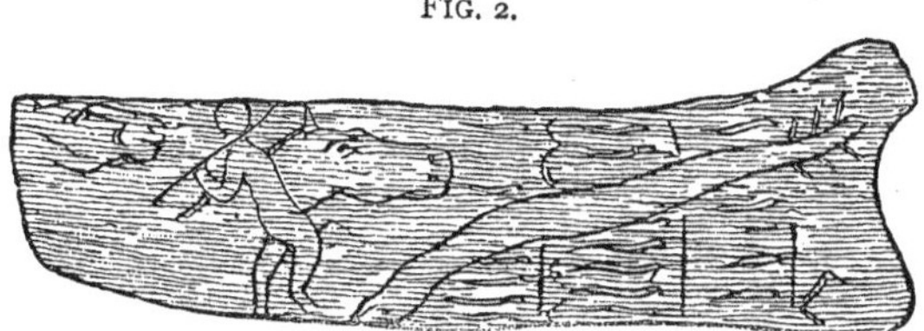

STAFF OF AUTHORITY, ON WHICH ARE GRAVEN REPRESENTATIONS OF A MAN, TWO HORSES, AND A FISH.

represents a group of a snake, or eel, a naked human figure, and two horses' heads. Fig. 3 represents a spirited group of reindeer. Fig. 4

FIG. 3.

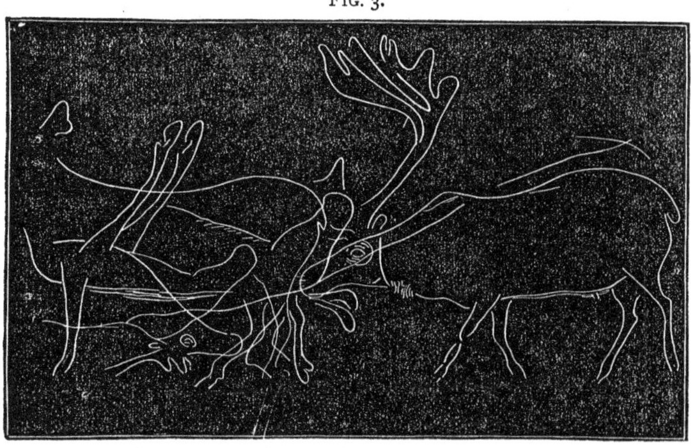

GROUP OF REINDEER.

is a representation of a hairy mammoth; it is executed on a piece

FIG. 4.

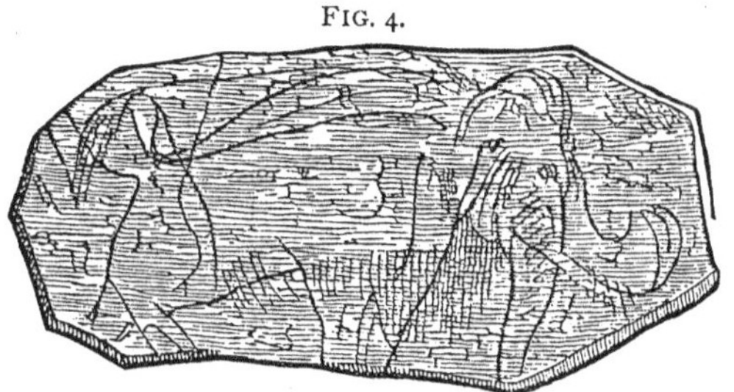

SKETCH OF A MAMMOTH, GRAVEN ON A SLAB OF IVORY.

of mammoth's tusk. Fig. 5 is a carved poniard, cut out of a reindeer's horn."

FIG. 5.

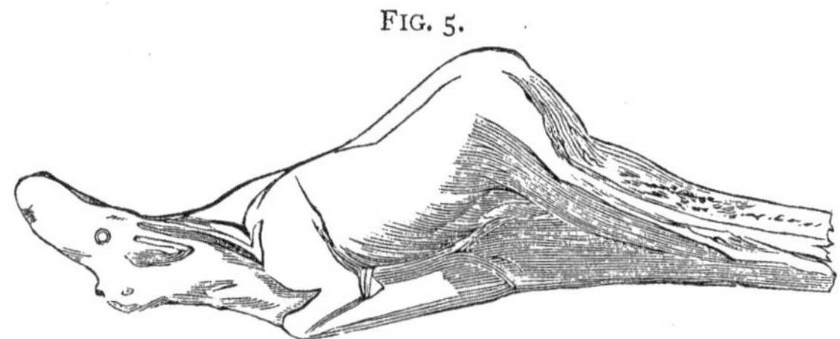

HANDLE OF A PONIARD.

Sir John Lubbock is impressed by the artistic taste of these ancient cave-men, but says there are instances among recent savages of a certain skill in drawing and sculpture being accompanied by an entire ignorance of metallurgy, as, for example, the Esquimaux.* He calls attention to the absence of metal, of polished flint implements, and even of pottery, amongst the cave-dwellers; to their ignorance of agriculture; and to the apparent absence of all domestic animals.

Sir John Lubbock mentions also the grotto of Maccagnone in Sicily. His account leaves the impression that ashes and rude flint implements were found here in association with the bones of *Elephas antiquus*, the hyæna, bear, and hippopotamus. This does not correspond with the fuller and clearer account of Sir C. Lyell, which last we shall follow. Both accounts are based on the account given of the ossiferous caves of Sicily by Dr. Falconer.

Grotto of Maccagnone.

We learn that on the northern coast of Sicily, between Termini on the east and Trapani on the west, there are many caves containing the bones of extinct animals. They are situated in the rocks of hippurite limestone, and some of them may be seen on both sides of the Bay of Palermo. Near this city, and about a mile from the shore, and at the height of about one hundred and eighty feet above it, there is a precipice of limestone, at the base of which appear the entrances of several caves. In that of San Ciro, on the east side of the bay, we find at the bottom sand with marine shells, forty species of which have been examined "and found almost all to agree specifically with Mollusca now inhabiting the Mediterranean." Higher in position, and resting on the

* Sir John Lubbock favors us in his work with some Esquimaux drawings (in another connection). We have, therefore, in his volume an opportunity to judge of the relative merits of the ancient and the modern savages (if such a term can be applied with any propriety to the Esquimaux). The drawings of the Esquimaux do not *compare* with those of the cave-dwellers.

Mr. Searles V. Wood thinks the delineation of animals on bone in so masterly a manner by the fossil man indicates a degree of culture far above that of cotemporary savages. Either these delineations throw a doubt on the antiquity of the troglodytes, argues Mr. Wood, or their evidence is in direct conflict with Lubbock's hypothesis; for the best figures that living savages can produce are too uncouth to be compared with these palæolithic relics.

sand, is a breccia composed of pieces of limestone, quartz, and schist in a matrix of brown marl, through which land-shells are dispersed, together with bones of two species of hippopotamus. These bones are so numerous that they must have belonged to several hundred individuals. With these were associated the remains of *Elephas antiquus*, and bones of the genera *Bos*, *Cervus*, *Sus*, *Ursus*, *Canis*, and a large *Felis*. Some of the bones have been rolled as if they had been subjected to the action of water, and may have been introduced by streams through rents in the hippurite limestone; "but there is now no running water in the neighborhood, no river such as the hippopotamus might frequent, not even a small brook, so that the physical geography of the district must have been altogether changed," etc.

There are no traces of man, says Lyell, at San Ciro.

But on the opposite side of the bay there is another cave, called the Grotta di Maccagnone. "In the bottom of this cave a bone deposit like that of San Ciro occurs, and above it other materials reaching to the roof, and evidently washed in from above, through crevices in the limestone. In this upper and *newer* breccia Dr. Falconer discovered flint knives, bone splinters, bits of charcoal, burnt clay, and other objects indicating human intervention, mingled with entire land-shells, teeth of horses, coprolites of hyænas, and other bones, the whole agglutinated to one another and to the roof by the infiltration of water holding lime in solution. The perfect condition of the large fragile helices (*Helix vermiculata*) afforded satisfactory evidence, says Dr. Falconer, that the various articles were carried into the cave by the tranquil agency of water, and not by any tumultuous action. At a subsequent period other geographical changes took place, so that the cave, after it had been filled, was washed out again."

All of this is very suggestive, but it does not prove the antiquity of man. We shall consider elsewhere the question about the change in the physical geography. We only remark just here that Sicily, in the first place, is the home of Mount Ætna, and there is no spot in the world where we should sooner look for a change in the physical geography. In the next place, not far off is Vesuvius. In the third place, there was a *tradition* among the ancients that Sicily was formerly joined to the main-land, and that it was detached by a violent volcanic convulsion. The coast of Sardinia, we know, has been raised three hundred feet in the human period, as will be hereafter noticed. At Puzzuoli, in the Bay of Baiæ, since the beginning of the Christian era the coast has risen and fallen twenty-five feet. On the island of Crete, one hundred and thirty-five miles long, at the western extremity there are ancient ports now twenty-five feet above the sea, while at its eastern extremity buried cities may be seen beneath the waves.

It appears from Sir C. Lyell's own statement that the sea at a very recent period covered the floor of the cave of San Ciro, as proved by the sand and shells found there.

There is no doubt of this fact. Coral as well as shell, and both intermingled with pebbles, occur within the cave, while immediately above the beach containing them *serpulæ* still adhere to the rock, and the walls of the cave are perforated by *lithodomi.*

With regard to the hippopotamus, there is no evidence from this example that he was cotemporary in Sicily with man. It is noticeable also that Dr. Falconer points out that "the perfect condition of the larger fragile helices" proves that the objects contained in "the upper and newer" breccia "were carried into the cave by the tranquil agency of water, and not by any tumultuous action." Now, this could not have been the case with the hippopotami in the lower breccia, because at San Ciro their bones "were counted in such numbers as to prove that they must have belonged to several hundred individuals." Several hundred hippopotami must have been carried into the cave by some strong current of fresh water, or by an inundation of the sea. The events are thus separated.

We do not see precisely the force of the remark that "there is now no running water in the neighborhood, no river such as the hippopotamus might frequent, . . . so that the physical geography," etc.

The hippopotamus does not confine himself to the rivers. "Indeed," says Dr. Andrew Smith, quoted by Lyell, "it is difficult to decide whether, during the daytime and when not feeding, they prefer the pools of rivers or the waters of the ocean for their abode." They are also great travellers by land, and even greater by water.

We may add to this account of the Sicilian caves the statement that Baron Anca, in 1859, found in a cave at Mondello, near Palermo, molars of *the living African elephant,* and afterwards additional remains of the same species in the neighboring grotto of Olivella.

Caves of Gibraltar.

"The rock of Gibraltar also," says Sir J. Lubbock, "abounds in caves containing human remains, with stone, bone, and bronze implements, mixed with those of domesticated animals, such as the goat and ox. In the bone breccia from the Genista cave and fissure, Mr. Busk and Dr. Falconer have found *Hyæna crocuta,* an existing African species, the leopard, lynx, serval, Barbary stag, together with Rhinoceros hemitæchus, and a species of ibex." "But," adds Sir John, "although it is more than probable, it does not appear to be proved, that man co-existed with these animals on the rock of Gibraltar." "Among some bones in another cave near Madrid, M. Lartet found molars of *the existing African elephant.*"

The remains in these Gibraltar caves or fissures, washed in chiefly by floods, are in such confusion, and the different objects are so mixed up, that it is difficult to draw clear conclusions from them. There have been "great changes in the physical geography" here too,—and probably at no very remote period.

It will be observed that we have in a cave near Madrid also the remains of the African elephant, as in Sicily; and at Gibraltar the Barbary stag, the spotted hyæna of Africa, the lynx, ibex, leopard, etc.*

We have now gone over the caves noticed by Sir John Lubbock, whose account we have supplemented in some instances by those of Sir C. Lyell and Mr. Evans. This is the strength of the anthropologist's case, as derived from the caves.

Pottery found in the caves.

We would call attention to the fact that in the first example cited by Sir John Lubbock, they discovered "pottery." Elsewhere Sir John informs us that pottery is never found in these caves.† In the present case he attempts to discredit the evidence because there was pottery. But Sir John has appealed to the caves, and we must not mutilate the record. The pottery is reported. Monsieur Figuier so states it, and adds that, along with human bones, it was "mixed up with remains of the great bear, hyæna, rhinoceros," etc. The cave-men, therefore, had pottery.

With reference to the celebrated Aurignac cave, which M. Lartet and M. Figuier consider one of the oldest yet discovered, Sir John Lubbock omits to mention that some very well-finished implements made of the horn of the reindeer were found here, as well as certain pierced discs of shell, probably intended for a necklace, and also a carved tooth of a young bear.

At Moustier, regarded as a very ancient cave, according to Figuier, "bi-convex spear-heads of very careful workmanship" were found.

In other caves of the Dordogne valley a great many ingenious implements occur made of reindeer-horn and bone,—"harpoons," "very slender and elegant" needles, "a perfect drill with a sharpened point and cutting edge" "which worked as well as our tool made of steel," a "spoon," etc. There are also needles of ivory.

The reader must bear in mind that intelligent and very able men—

* There is no occasion to fancy that it must have been at a very remote period that the African elephant, and hyæna, and stag, were to be found in Southern Europe. The *monkey* existed, it is well known, in great numbers, on the rock of Gibraltar, within a very few years past, and, perhaps, still exists there. And the existence of the monkey in Europe in the present century is fully as strange as the existence of the hyæna or the elephant on the same continent several thousand years ago.

The remains of the monkey were found in the *Grotta dei Colombi*, on the isle of Palmaria, which belongs to the Neolithic Age. They were also found in a cave, of the same period, near Cadiz. Palmaria is in Northern Italy.

† Pre-historic Times, pp. 333, 335, 550. He makes the statement several times.

the foremost thinkers of England,—Sir C. Lyell, Sir J. Lubbock, Mr. Huxley, Mr. Wallace—believe that these people lived several hundred thousand years ago: an astonishing instance of the credulity of SCIENCE.

Having considered these cases, selected no doubt as the strongest by Sir John Lubbock, we propose now to introduce new evidence, which, we think, will tend to throw additional light upon this obscure subject. We must still rely almost entirely on the materials and narratives of those who have hastily committed themselves to the conclusion of the antiquity of man; it is they who have explored these caverns and fissures, and who have given to the world their deductions from the facts which they have observed and reported. Our first examples are gathered from the lively and entertaining book of M. Louis Figuier.

Cave of Nabrigas.

Among the caves noticed by him is that of Nabrigas (Lozère), found by his teacher, Prof. Joly, of the Lyceum of Montpellier, in 1835,—one of the earliest discoveries. M. Joly found in this cavern the skull of a cave-bear, which had been struck by an arrow, and "close by a fragment of *pottery* bearing the imprint of the fingers of the man who moulded it." So that, notwithstanding Sir John Lubbock's assertion that there are "no traces of metal or pottery" in these ancient caves, we have here together the oldest of all the extinct animals, the flint, and the moulded clay. Our object is to show that these so-called links between the human and the pithecoid forms—these cotemporaries, as is alleged, of the glaciers and the drift—were by no means devoid of intelligence, and that they acted very much as our rude forefathers acted in the Celtic and Saxon forests of pre-Christian Europe.

Vergisson.

The cave of Vergisson (Saône-et-Loire) was explored by M. Ferry. Here he found the bones of the cave-bear, cave-lion, mammoth, rhinoceros, reindeer, bison, horse, wolf, and fox, mixed with wrought flints and rough *pottery*. M. Franchet found in the same cave the upper vertebral column of the human skeleton. M. Figuier naïvely remarks, "The presence of this pottery indicated that the cave of Vergisson belonged to the latter period of the great bear epoch." It is thus admitted that pottery was cotemporaneous with the great cave-bear; and he, according to M. Figuier, was older than the cave-lion and the mammoth, which in turn were older than the reindeer, which was older than the bison.

La Chaise.

The cave of La Chaise, in the department of Charente, near Vouthon, was examined by MM. Bourgeois and Delaunay. It furnished "bones of the cave-bear, rhinoceros, and reindeer, flint blades and scrapers" (these were used to clean the hair off the skins), "a bodkin and a kind of hook made of bone, an arrow-head in the shape of a willow-leaf likewise of bone, a bone perforated so as to hang on a string, and, what is more remarkable, two long rods of reindeer's horn, tapering at one end and bevelled off at the other, on which figures of animals were graven."

Massat.

In two caves in the valley of Massat (Ariége) M. Fontan found remains of the cave-bear, cave-lion, cave-hyæna, a bone arrow-head, beds of ashes and charcoal. In the upper cave he found a curious stone on which we have a rude sketch of the great cave-bear.

The caves of Chiampo and Laglio, in the north of Italy, on Lake Como, like the caves of Vergisson and Nabrigas (says M. Figuier), have yielded fragments of pottery "indicating some degree of progress in the manufacture."

Fishing.

We are informed by M. Figuier that "the men of the Reindeer Epoch" were addicted to *fishing*. They had rude pins of bone for hooks. The remains of fishes are found in the caves. In this epoch also (as likewise in the days of the great bear) they sewed skins together for garments. The sinewy fibres of the reindeer served for thread.

The Gower caves.

Mr. Evans and Sir Charles Lyell mention the Gower caves, in the peninsula of Gower, Glamorganshire. Long Hole is about a mile from the celebrated Paviland Cave, and "is about one hundred and thirty feet above ordinary high-water mark." Flint implements were found here with the remains not only of the *Elephas primigenius* and the *Rhinoceros tichorinus*, but also with those of the *Rhinoceros hemitœchus* and *Elephas antiquus*,—a very unusual circumstance. In a fissure called Bosco's Den, *no less than one thousand or twelve hundred antlers of reindeer were found*,—mostly the shed horns of young animals,—all evidently swept into the rent by a powerful current of water. With them were bones of the cave-bear, wolf, fox, ox, stag, and field-mouse.

Alterations in Line of Drainage.

In a cavernous fissure, called the Raven's Cliff, teeth of the *Hippopotamus major* were found; "and this in a district," says Sir Charles Lyell, "where there is now scarce a rill of running water, much less a river in which such quadrupeds could swim."

The Explanation.

This appears very strange; but Sir Charles tells us presently—some pages farther on—that "the Gower caves in general have their floors strewed over with sand, *containing marine shells*, all of living species; and there are raised beaches on the adjoining coast, and other geological signs of great alteration in the relative level of land and sea since the country was inhabited by the extinct mammalia."* In other words, the beach here has been raised one hundred and thirty feet. The only question is, When was this done?

* Antiquity of Man, p. 174, Amer. edit.

At one of the caves in this region (King Arthur's Cave) the evidences of antiquity are thought to be particularly strong. The flints are found under a floor of stalagmite two feet thick, and above this floor, we are told, are what appear to be the traces of an old river-bed. We simply refer to Sir Charles Lyell's statement about the raised beaches and the former presence of the sea, and to the additional fact that the flint implements found are all "*foreign to the district*, and have been imported from long distances." If Palæolithic Man lived here, we must therefore conclude that he carried on a considerable traffic. The stalagmitic floor we shall notice presently.

King Arthur's Cave.

M. Figuier believes also that there are decided indications that the Reindeer men were *religious*. We find in the tombs of this epoch "the weapons and knives which men carried during their lifetime, and sometimes even a supply of the flesh of animals used for food." M. Dupont has also remarked on the existence around the fire-hearths in the caves of large fossil elephant bones,—which custom [of placing bones around the caverns] prevails, as a religious act, among the Indians at this day. [These little incidental correspondences in the habits of different races, widely removed in time and place, are strongly suggestive of some bond of union.]

Religion among the Cave-Dwellers.

The early cave-men were also considerable *travellers* and *traffickers*. They travelled from the banks of the Lesse in Belgium to Champagne, and even to Touraine, in Western France, to find flints to their fancy, and to purchase fossil shells of which they made "fantastical necklaces." M. Dupont found in the cave of Chaleux, near Dinant, in Belgium, fifty-four of these shells, which are not found anywhere else except in Champagne.

Traffic and travel among the Cave-Dwellers.

There was a *manufactory* at Chaleux, at which in the course of three weeks twenty thousand flints were gathered,—hatchets, daggers, knives, scrapers, scratchers, etc.

The Factory at Chaleux.

Not a trace of polish, as we have stated, quoting from Sir John Lubbock, is found on any of the flints from Chaleux. It is assigned by him to the "Reindeer" period,—which, however, is a mere artificial distinction rejected by other palæontologists. The fore-arm of an elephant, we learn from M. Dupont's Report to the Belgian Government,* was found in the ashes of the hearth. We have thus at Chaleux one of the most ancient of the Bone-Caverns; and we learn from M. Dupont that all of the flint or stone here is "foreign." They found on the floor fragments of ammonite; fluvine from the Devonian limestone; shells from Champagne; slate from Fernay; flints from Pressigny; fragments

* M. Dupont's Report to the Minister of the Interior on Excavations in the Province of Namur in 1864. Printed in Mem. Anthrop. Soc. of London for 1867–8–9.

of elephants' teeth out of which they manufactured their "elegant needles;" and *nephrite* from the East.

Workshops similar to that at Chaleux were established in the settlements of Laugerie-Basse and Laugerie-Haute in Périgord. It is a singular fact that the barbed arrows found have a longitudinal groove, like those which appear on the arrows of the North American Indians,—intended to give a freer vent to the flow of the animal's blood when it may be wounded. And the same barbed darts, made out of the same material (reindeer's horn), are used by the Esquimaux in pursuing the seal.

Laugerie-Basse and Laugerie-Haute.

In a number of the caves—as at Les Eyzies, Laugerie-Basse, Chaffant —*bone whistles* (still serviceable) have been found.

The Trou du Frontal, at Furfooz, in Belgium, was also explored by M. Dupont. He here found, as we have stated, the remains of thirteen human beings, some of them infants, and among them two very perfect skulls. The bones of the reindeer and other animals were also found, and the earthen vase represented below. It is an extremely creditable piece of work, and has by no means the appearance of being two hundred thousand years old—or, as Mr. Geikie would have it, *pre-glacial.*

Trou du Frontal.

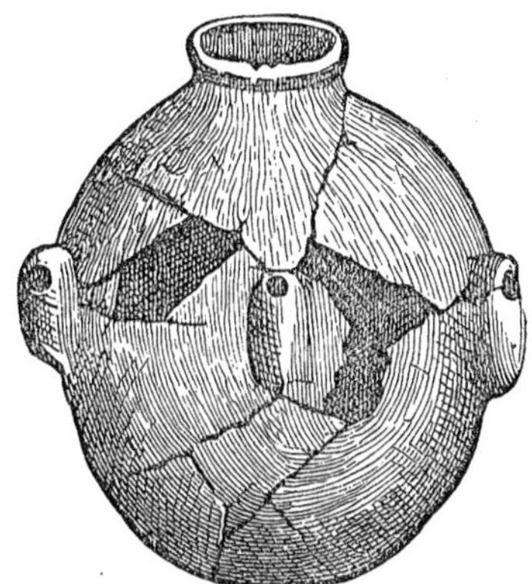

EARTHEN VASE FOUND IN A CAVE AT FURFOOZ (BELGIUM).

The human bones here, says M. Dupont, were found "in inexpressible disorder." It was, he adds, unanimously admitted that they had been mingled with stones and earth by "a great inundation." Implements of bone, arrow-tips, a whistle from the phalanx of a reindeer, and a shell (with a hole bored through it) from France, were found. The animal remains belonged to the reindeer, horse, ox, bear, and wild boar.

The Palæolithic Flood.

Very near to the Trou du Frontal is another cave, called the Trou

Rosette, in which were found human bones mingled with those of the reindeer and beaver, together with fragments of a blackish kind of pottery, roughly ornamented with grooves, and hardened in the fire. It is remarkable, with so many examples of this kind, that Sir John Lubbock should have spoken in this connection so frequently of "the absence of pottery." Referring to the human remains here, M. Dupont says that the occupants of the cave were "overwhelmed by a deluge."

Trou des Noutons.

In the same valley of the Lesse is a third cave, called the Trou des Noutons. Here M. Dupont and M. Van Beneden found in the superficial layer money and glazed pottery of the last century; fragments of vases of the middle ages; some objects of the Frankish period; vials in glass; medals of Domitian and Antoninus; fragments of Roman vases and tiles; objects in bronze; utensils in iron, etc.

In the subjacent layer—a bed two metres thick, composed of red argillaceous earth—they found one hundred and fifty horns of the reindeer, most of them broken by the violence of water; bones of the glutton, brown bear, chamois, elk, stag, fox, wolf, urus, wild goat, etc.; a large number of flints; the tibia of a goat formed into a whistle; and two *astragali* of the goat, polished, and "entirely identical with those which children still use in their play." "It is then," says M. Dupont, "to the antediluvian people that we owe the discovery of this toy." Bone needles, daggers, arrow-heads, pottery, and split bones of the horse, ox, etc., were also found.

In the Trou de la Naulette, the remains of the mammoth, rhinoceros, hyæna, etc., occurred. M. Dupont takes occasion to remark that the brown bear continued to exist in Belgium down to the tenth century.

The fact that these caves in Belgium were overwhelmed by a great inundation seems to be universally admitted. The elevation of the Trou des Noutons is thirty-three metres (about one hundred and ten feet) above the level of the Lesse, and two hundred metres above the present sea-level. The elevation of the Trou du Frontal is eighteen metres above the river,—which "puts them out of the reach of the highest floods." "Do we not see traces, then," M. Dupont asks, "of that terrible phenomenon of which all races have preserved the remembrance?" We find thus in the Belgian caves the same evidences of disturbance which we observed in the south of England, and about which we shall have more to say hereafter.

Fortifications of the Stone Age.

They do not strictly belong to the "Palæolithic" Age, but it may be well to mention here that there are remains of extensive fortifications of the Stone Age. Cissbury we shall notice elsewhere; Col. A. Lane Fox, judging from the rude and unground implements, refers this to the First Age; in our view they are all quite old, historically speaking, and all very recent, geologically speaking. But the fortifications cited by M. Figuier are assigned by him to the Polished Stone Age. In our opinion only three or four centuries separate them from the factories of Chaleux and Pressigny-le-Grand. They give us a vivid idea of the activity and intelligence of the Stone Age, and call up a humanity changed in no respect by the invention of gunpowder and our modern rifled artillery. These fortifications occur in Belgium, at Furfooz, Pont-de-Bonn, Simon, Jemelle, Hastedon, and Poilvache. They are generally established on points overhanging valleys, on a headland of rock. A wide ditch was dug across this narrow tongue of land, and the whole camp enclosed by a thick wall of stones, piled up without cement. At the camp at Hastedon this wall measured ten feet in thickness, and about the same in height. Over the whole surface of these camps we find worked flints and pottery.

Further examples of Palæolithic Art.

We have already described a number of the drawings or etchings of the Cave-men. They are not the only examples. Another figure of the *Elephas primigenius* or mammoth was found graven on a fragment of reindeer's horn from one of the rock-shelters of Bruniquel. It forms the hilt of a poniard, the blade of which springs from the front part of the animal. We recognize the trunk of the mammoth, its wide flat feet, and its tail ending in a bunch of hair. The tail is also erect. The existing elephant never erects its tail, and the tail has no tuft of hair, but only a few bristles.

Laugerie-Basse also contributes "a staff of authority" (whatever that is), the lower end of which is carved into a mammoth's head. We have, therefore, so far, three representations of the mammoth.

On another "staff of authority,"* found at Bruniquel by M. Brun, we have a carving of the cave-lion,—executed with great clearness. We have thus representations of the mammoth, the cave-bear, and the cave-lion; which demonstrates, if the parties who have seen them have not deceived themselves, the co-existence of these animals with man.

In the cave of Lavigné (Vienne), M. Joly-Leterme found a stag's bone, on which the bodies of two animals were delineated, "with hatchings to indicate shadows."

From La Madelaine we have on a staff of office a fawn with a spotted skin, accompanied by its dam, which the *Revue des Cours Scientifiques de la France et de l'Étranger* describes as a "morceau." The same Review characterizes the reindeer combat from Laugerie-Basse as "executed with remarkable sprightliness," and "with true feeling of the situation."

* One of these "commander's batons" was found by Dr. Gross at the lake-station of Locras (Bienne), showing a connection between the people of the Palæolithic and those of the second Stone Age.

We learn from M. Figuier that "during the polished stone age" (as we knew before from the Lake-Dwellings) the cave-man was acquainted with *Husbandry*. MM. Garrigoù and Filhol found in the caves of Ariége more than twenty millstones, which must have been intended for grinding corn. Stones of the same kind are in use at this day among the Mangajas, Makalolos, Landines, and other tribes of Central Africa, as well as among the American Indians.

Similar traces of agriculture are found also around the hearths in the caves of Puy-de-Dôme, where the gentlemen above-named found *carbonized wheat* intermingled with pottery and flint implements.

In that famous book published some twenty years ago, the "Types of Mankind," by Messrs. Nott and Gliddon, we have an account of a cavern or fissure at Pondres, in the department of Hérault, in Southern France. Here, we are informed, M. de Cristolles "discovered human bones and pottery, mixed with the remains of the rhinoceros, bear, hyæna, and many other animals. They were imbedded in mud and fragments of the limestone rock of the neighborhood; this accumulation in some places being thirteen feet thick." It is farther stated that "these human fossils were proved, on a careful examination, to have parted with their animal matter as completely as these bones of hyænas which accompanied them." We mention this to establish farther a connection between the human and the animal bones, and then to remark that in this cave of the earliest epoch we discover fragments of pottery.

Pondres.

The "Types of Mankind" give us also an interesting piece of information, not mentioned by Lyell, or Lubbock, or Figuier, with regard to the celebrated cave of Engihoul, explored by Dr. Schmerling. Bones of man, we are told, occurred here with those of animals of extinct species, and it is added, "Near these relics, works of art were sometimes disclosed; such as fragments of *ancient urns*, and *vases of clay*, teeth of foxes and dogs pierced with holes and doubtless worn as amulets." *

Engihoul.

The same work states that "in the caverns of Bize, in France, human bones and shreds of pottery" were found in the red clay, mixed up with the remains of extinct animals.

Bize.

We find the same statements, with regard to the two caves last mentioned, in the American edition of Lyell's "Principles of Geology" for 1865. He speaks farther of "Pondres and Souvignargues," and says that in both of them "human bones and pottery (were) confusedly mixed up with remains of the rhinoceros, bear, hyæna, and other terrestrial mammifers." † It is significant that Sir Charles has

Pottery.

* See p. 348.

† See p. 738.

dropped this and other similar matter out of the recent edition of the "Principles;" he has advanced, or become more firmly fixed, in his River-Gravel and Darwinian views.

Mialet.

In this same work of Sir Charles Lyell we have an account of the cave of Mialet, in the department of Gard, which was explored by M. Tassier. Here, says Sir Charles, "the remains of the bear and other animals were mingled confusedly with human bones, coarse pottery, teeth pierced for amulets, pointed fragments of bone, bracelets of bronze, and a Roman urn."* Part of this deposit reached to the roof of the cavity, and adhered firmly to it.

The Cave-bear and Bronze bracelets.

Now, we do not believe that the cave-bear and the bronze bracelets were cotemporaneous in France; but we think it may be fairly inferred that they were not many hundreds of years apart,—that the cave-men of the bronze period were the descendants and successors of the cave-men of the flint-implement days,—keeping up the customs of their fathers, and dwelling in the same subterranean abodes.

A Recent Flood.

It is noticeable in the account of this cave that "part of the deposit reached to the roof of the cave, and adhered firmly to it." This, Sir Charles Lyell refers to a "flood" from the neighboring river, occasioned by its course being impeded and its waters turned into the cavern. We desire the reader to observe that floods of this sort are, or may be, therefore, in some instances, even *post-Roman in date.*

There is another account of this interesting cavern, by Sir H. De La Beche. The cavern, he says, is thirty yards above a valley, on a steep slope. The lowest bed is dolomitic sand, irregularly covered with thin stalagmite, and here and there by an argillo-ferruginous clay, more than a yard thick. This bed contains abundant remains of bears. Beneath the stalagmite and a bed of clayey sand, from eight to sixteen inches thick, human remains occurred in different places. At the inmost end of the cave they were decidedly mixed with those of bears, which predominated; but at the entrance the human bones were in excess. On the ossiferous clay and beneath a rocky projection, a nearly entire human skeleton was found, and close to it a lamp and a baked clay figurine, and, at a short distance, copper bracelets. In other places were the remains of coarse pottery, worked bones, and small flint tools.†

It appears from this account that the cave is "thirty yards above a valley, on a steep slope." It occurs to us that the neighboring river must have been very seriously "impeded" to have risen to this point. If the remains had been all of the palæolithic age, Sir Charles Lyell

* Principles of Geology (1865), p. 739.

† Geolog. Observ. (1850), p. 304.

would have told us that the valley had been "excavated" since the river ran at the level of the cave.

Sir H. De La Beche describes also the cave of Paviland in Glamorganshire, Wales. Dr. Buckland found here nearly "the entire left side of a female skeleton."* Also two handfuls of shells (*Nerita littoralis*) *completely decayed*, and forty or fifty fragments of small ivory rods, with fragments of ivory rings, also entirely decomposed like the shells. Also elephants' tusks, charcoal, and bones of the ox, sheep, pig, and wolf,—one of the last-named carved into a skewer. On the hill above the cave is a Roman camp.† But there seem to be no traces of the Romans in the cave.

Paviland.

The bones of the sheep in this cave were below the remains of the elephant. The ivory rods and rings appear to be cotemporary with the latter, for if they were recent they would hardly present such a condition of decomposition. We may infer, therefore, that these articles were manufactured by the cotemporaries of the mammoth.

We have spoken of the cave of Gailenreuth in Franconia. Sir Philip Egerton, in his work "On the Ossiferous Caves of the Hartz and Franconia," says that the Earl of Enniskillen and himself found in this cave, as well as in the caves of Kühloch, Scharzfeld, and Baumannis Höhle, fragments of rude pottery; in that of Rabenstein "coins and iron household implements of most ancient and uncouth forms;" and bones of pigs, dogs, birds, etc., in every cave they explored. It is in these caves, it will be remembered, that the remains of the cave-bear are so abundant. We are not sure that in this region the cave-bear did not live down to a comparatively recent period; though by this we do not design by any means to suggest that he was cotemporary with the coins and implements of iron found by Sir Philip Egerton.

In neolithic times there were manufactories of flint implements at many points, as, for example, at the lake-stations of Wangen and Moosseedorf in Switzerland. These workshops were not, however, confined to the later or second stone period. In palæolithic times extensive factories for the manufacture of the various weapons and implements of stone had already been established. We have mentioned Chaleux in Belgium and Laugerie-Basse and Laugerie-Haute in Périgord. Cotemporaneous with these was the great factory at Pressigny in Touraine (half-way between Tours and Poitiers) discovered in 1864 by Dr. Léveillé. The flints were found here "by thousands imbedded in the vegetable mould on the surface of the soil, over a superficies of twelve or fourteen acres." The Abbé Chevalier states

Palæolithic Workshops.

* Reliquiæ Diluvianæ, p. 88.

† Geol. Obs., p. 302. This skeleton is now said to be that of a male.

that they lie "on the surface," and that "there is no walking without treading on one of them." "A few of the implements," he says, "are polished,—the rest unpolished." Figuier assigns Pressigny to a period intermediate or transitional between the chipped stone and the polished stone epochs. It ran, no doubt, into the second stone period.

The Factory at Hoxne.

We can apparently trace these Factories back to the very beginning of the Palæolithic Age,—a fact showing the existence of an organized society. It appears that such a factory must have existed at Hoxne, in Suffolk. The flint implements here were exceedingly numerous, and Mr. Frere, who was the first to observe them, states that "the man who carried on the brick-work told me that before he was aware of their being objects of curiosity, he had emptied baskets full of them into the ruts of the adjoining road."* And this is the opinion of Lyell, who infers it partly from the sharpness and perfect condition of the flints,—implying that they had never been used.†

The Factory at Chaleux.

We have mentioned that at Chaleux, in Belgium, as many as thirty thousand worked flints were collected, not one of which, says Lubbock, "presents a trace of polish." M. Dupont represents, as we have stated, that they are all "foreign" to this region, and some of them, he says (in which M. de Mortillet agrees with him), came from Pressigny.

The testimony furnished by this cave is valuable in several respects. As the life of the ancient Romans has been imperishably petrified for our observation in the catastrophe that overwhelmed Herculaneum and Pompeii, so by the fall of the roof of this cavern of Chaleux an undisturbed picture of a primitive dwelling of palæolithic man has been preserved for us on the banks of the Lys. At the depth of eight feet below the compact detritus, the floor of the cavern was reached. Besides the immense number of flint implements discovered, there were others also of bone and reindeer's horn. In the middle of the cave was found the hearth, formed of flat stones, and on it lay the ashes and coals where the cave-men had prepared their rude repasts.

The fact that flints from Grand-Pressigny, in the west of France,—three or four hundred miles distant,—were obtained here, is a striking evidence of the extended journeys and the extensive traffic which characterized man in even palæolithic times. The presence of the *nephrite* from the Caucasus or the shores of the Caspian will recall to the reader what we said in a similar connection with regard to the Lake-Dwellers of Switzerland. This material indicates at once that the Cave-Dwellers of Belgium were also from the Orient; and we shall have occasion to see, when speaking of Solutré, that, on entirely independent grounds,

---

* Lyell's Antiquity of Man, Amer. ed., p. 167. † Ibid., p. 169.

M. Pruner-Bey has pronounced the primitive occupants or frequenters of that celebrated palæolithic station to have been *a Mongoloid tribe.** This nephrite proves more: it not only connects the cave-men of Belgium with the East, *but it connects them with the Lake-Dwellers of Switzerland.* Does it not bring them at once together?

Grime's Graves.

The energy and enterprise of the men of the Stone Age are well illustrated by the explorations which have been made of *Grime's Graves*, near Brandon, by Mr. Greenwell. It has been ascertained that these were not in fact graves, but excavations made in the chalk for the purpose of obtaining flint. The pits number two hundred and fifty-four, varying in diameter from twenty to sixty feet, and originally went down to a depth of some forty feet, branching out into passages, and often communicating with one another. They cover an extent of twenty acres. This locality is used at the present day for the manufacture of gun-flints. The flint is disposed in layers, which differ very much in quality. One contains flint called "wall-stone," which is much used in building. Another contains a specimen of remarkable hardness and fineness of grain, particularly suitable for gun-flints. Now, the ancient inhabitants of Britain, who resorted hither to manufacture their flint knives and axes and arrow-heads, were perfectly well acquainted with the merits of the gun-flint layer, for, disregarding the flint which was so abundant at the surface, they sunk their shafts down past the layer of "wall-stone," which occurs at a depth of nineteen and a half feet, until they reached the gun-flint layer, thirty-nine feet from the surface.

The implements employed in these excavations were the horns of the red deer, the brow tine being used as a pick. A few flint tools adapted to these operations have also been found.

Mr. Greenwell assigns these mines to the Neolithic Age, in which he is doubtless correct; but he observes that all of the implements found here "have been merely chipped into shape," and that he "did not meet with one from the immediate neighborhood of the pits which showed traces of grinding." †

It will be seen elsewhere that the palæolithic implements abound in the river-gravel at Brandon.

Evidently the men of the neolithic era had been preceded in the flint deposits of the locality of Grime's Graves by the men of the palæolithic age.

But the implements found at Grime's Graves are *unground* and rude. We see, therefore, that they are probably very ancient,—transitional between the palæolithic and the neolithic periods.

---

* Dr. Broca, however, contradicts this statement.

† Jour. Ethnolog. Soc. of London, 1870, vol. ii. p. 422.

Similar to Grime's Graves is the celebrated *atelier*, or workshop, at Spiennes, in Belgium. Great numbers of worked flints occur in the environs of this village. The flint was mined here as at Grime's Graves. Both Spiennes and Grime's Graves are referred to the Neolithic Age, although very few polished implements have been found at the former, and none at all at the latter. It is very evident, therefore, that *polishing* was not peculiar to the so-called Polished Stone Age. The presumption arises also that there was no great interval of time between Spiennes and Grime's Graves on the one hand, and Chaleux, Pressigny, and Hoxne on the other. This presumption is strengthened by the fact that at Spiennes "a magnificent dirk twenty-five centimetres in length (ten inches) has been found, which came probably from Pressigny."*

Spiennes.

We may instance also the factory at Escalles (Pas-de-Calais) discovered on Cape Blanc-Nez. Great numbers of worked flints occur here at every step, of all forms and sizes, and presenting every variety of finish, from the rudest shape to the polished hatchet. The most striking feature at this station is the multiplicity of the types. Some of the hatchets present a marked resemblance to the almond-shaped hatchets of St. Acheul. Escalles is, however, assigned to the neolithic period.†

We may mention also that a palæolithic workshop has been discovered by Captain Angelucci in the mountains of Gargano, in the province of Capitanata, on the southeastern coast of Italy, the implements of which are said to resemble those of Abbeville.‡

We have referred to the caves of the south of Europe. Some important hints are to be derived from a study of the Gibraltar, Sicilian, and Maltese caves. We shall, therefore, give a more detailed statement of the Gibraltar caves, and some account of those of Malta, which we mentioned very briefly. We have a narrative of the exploration of a fissure in the rock of Gibraltar, at Windmill Hill, by Captain Brome. The attention of this gentleman was attracted by his terrier to a hole in the plateau, which was found to lead into a rock cavity, filled almost to the roof with calcareous incrustations and soil. In a crevice close to the entrance lay the skeletons of several human beings. The skulls are described as well formed, and denoting no great antiquity. Associated with these remains were flint hatchets and knives, well polished, a metal hook, charcoal, hand-mills, and marine shells. Also the remains of living quadrupeds.

The Caves of the South of Europe.

Captain Brome, and the Gibraltar Caves.

In the Genista Cave were the bones of two species of extinct rhi-

---

* Matériaux pour l'Histoire de l'Homme, Août et Sept., 1872, p. 428.

† Ib., Oct., 1872, p. 518.

‡ Ib., p. 504.

noceros, the hare, the hog, the red and fallow deer, the aurochs (or some allied form), innumerable remains of the ibex, the African leopard, serval, brown hyæna, etc.*

In an immense fissure not far off from this cave, Captain Brome found a complete skeleton of an extinct rhinoceros.

Many recent species were found in association with the extinct species; but in general the former predominated in the upper parts near the surface, except the rabbit remains, which were abundant at all levels.

An important fact connected with these bones is that many of them are *sun-cracked,* showing that they had been exposed before they were conveyed into the fissures. It is to be added that the bones were all lying together in the greatest disorder, as if they had been washed into the chasms.

A full report up to that date of Captain Brome's explorations may be found in the volume of the "International Congress of Prehistoric Archæology" for 1868.

There are a number of fissures and caves at Gibraltar. In St. Michael's Cave he found human remains, hand-made pottery, bone needles, armlets, querns, rubstones, mouldings of pottery, stone axes, flint knives, and, near the surface, eleven Roman coins and some very large red bricks.

In the Genista Cave (already referred to) he found human remains to the depth of ten feet, in utter confusion. He found animal remains down to the lowest depths; also flint implements, an anklet, skewers or arrow-heads, and querns. Pottery to the depth of twenty feet,—hand-made.

Martin's Cave.

In Martin's Cave, excavating through the black earth, he found nine flint knives, and below, other knives and pottery. He then came upon a two-edged iron sword under six feet of earth,—partly under the stalagmite. The hilt was surmounted by a globe pommel, and the whole of this portion "appeared to be of silver" (see p. 135). The scabbard was of leather, mounted with silver or tin. The next day another sword was found, about four yards from the first,—formed of iron, mounted with copper.

Stalagmite.

A short time after this, "a copper plate" was found "under eighteen inches of hard stalagmite; close under the south side of the cave."

---

* The flints in these Gibraltar caves (if our impression is correct) all belong to the neolithic period. It may be fairly inferred that during that period (and probably in the bronze age) the leopard, the spotted hyæna, the ibex, etc., abounded in Southern Spain. We have a strong suspicion that the rhinoceros (whose remains are found also) existed in Spain either at the same time or a very short time before, and probably the African elephant.

Here we pause for a moment.

At the meeting of the British Association in 1871 there was an animated discussion on the Antiquity of Man. It was called up in the Geological section by a paper on the explorations of Kent's Cavern, already considered by us. Mr. Vivian contended that they had here a reliable chronometer of the high antiquity of the objects found in the cavern,—referring to the floors of stalagmite (there are two floors) above the remains of the extinct animals and the unpolished flints. "Flint implements," he said, "had been found below the lowest crystalline stalagmite in the cave, and if the deposition of stalagmite went on formerly as it did now, it would have required a million of years to form those two floors." *

Mr. Vivian on Stàlagmite.

Mr. Evans (p. 464), referring to the stalagmite, says, "The amount of time represented by such a coating it is, of course, impossible to calculate; but, even under the most favorable circumstances,

Mr. Evans.

* Mr. Evans and Sir John Lubbock ignore this lower floor of stalagmite, although Mr. Evans devotes many pages to the cave, and to the upper floor. Sir C. Lyell, however, in the last edition of the "Antiquity of Man," and Mr. James Geikie, in "The Great Ice Age," attach considerable importance to the fact that three flint implements and one flint chip were found beneath the second floor. This lower floor has a thickness of from three to twelve feet, and the only animal remains found in it were the bones of the cave-bear.

If the four flint specimens referred to occupied their original position, the stalagmitic covering which overlay them exceeds in thickness any other example of the same kind. There is very considerable doubt, however, whether the flints did not fall from the cave-earth in the bed above. Speaking of the remains above and below the upper stalagmitic floor, Mr. Evans remarks that "owing to previous excavations and to the presence of burrowing animals, the remains from above and below the stalagmite have become intermingled" (p. 446, Amer. edit.); and again (p. 463), speaking of the remains between the two stalagmitic floors, he states that "the mineral condition of the bones in the cave-earth varies considerably, so much so as to lead to the conclusion that some of the bones, especially of bear, are derived from an earlier deposit of the same character,"—that is, from the cave-earth below the second floor. "These more ancient remains are," he says, "according to Mr. Boyd Dawkins, much more crystalline, much heavier, and of a darker color than the ordinary teeth and bones." Again (p. 464): "In fact, among the bones themselves there are some which, as has already been pointed out, have belonged to an earlier deposit than that in which they are now found."

The teeth of the *Machairodus latidens*, or sabre-toothed tiger, were also found in the bed between the two floors of stalagmite. This animal, it is well known, belongs to an earlier fauna than that of the palæolithic age; and Mr. Dawkins is of the opinion that it came from the earth below the second floor, "which in the form of a breccia has since become partially mixed in places with the cave-earth above this floor."

Mr. Evans also refers to certain portions of the cave "in which there are variations from what may be called the typical section, these being mainly due to accidental and local causes, such as the breaking up of beds of stalagmite of earlier date than those above the cave-earth" (p. 463).

It is, therefore, very doubtful whether these four flints were originally in the position in which they were found. Admitting that they were, however, the rapid rate at which the stalagmite even now is known to accumulate in some caves, removes all occasion for calling in more than three or four centuries.

it must have been the work of hundreds, or more probably thousands of years."

Sir Charles Lyell also suggests that a long period was required for the formation of the stalagmitic floors. In enumerating the several points on which he rests the antiquity of the palæolithic remains, he specifies, "Thirdly, the changes in the course of rivers which once flowed through caves now removed from any line of drainage, *and the formation of solid floors of stalagmite.*" *

Sir C. Lyell.

Let us now proceed with Martin's Cave at Gibraltar. Capt. Brome goes on to speak of his "copper plate" "found under eighteen inches of hard stalagmite." It was, he tells us, covered with verdigris, and was an inch and a half long, with a hole through each end. On removing the earth they found a dragon enamelled on it. "The plate," continues the narrative, "is said to be of 'Limoges' work, and of the same period as the swords." "The date is probably at the end of the twelfth or the beginning of the thirteenth century." Pp. 135–6.

We have thus works of art of the twelfth or thirteenth century covered by a stalagmite floor eighteen inches thick. This stalagmite is covered by six feet of cave-earth.

As a good deal of importance has been given to these stalagmitic "floors," it is well enough to notice the matter further.

There is a rapid deposit from calcareous springs. *Tufa* and *Travertin* are formed in this way. At San Vignone, in Tuscany, there is a thermal spring issuing from the summit of a rocky hill; from whose stream the deposition of lime is so rapid, that half a foot of solid limestone is deposited every year in a conduit-pipe, inclined at an angle of thirty degrees. At the baths of San Filippo, among the Apennines, the water which supplies the baths falls into a pond, where it has been known to deposit a solid mass thirty feet thick in twenty years.

Formation of Stalagmite.

The stalactites and stalagmites of caves are formed in the same manner, by the water percolating through the limestone rock.

Mantell, in his "Fossils of the British Museum," † informs us that M. Clausen visited a cavern in Brazil, the stalagmitic floor of which was entire. On penetrating the sparry crust he found the usual ossiferous bed; but pressing engagements compelled him to leave the deposit unexplored. After an interval of some years he had an opportunity to revisit the scene of his labors, when he found that the excavation he had made was completely filled up with stalagmite, the floor being as entire as on his first entrance. On breaking through this newly-formed incrustation, it was found to be distinctly marked with lines of dark-colored sediment alternating with the crystalline stalag-

In the Brazilian caves.

* Student's Elements, p. 162.

† Page 482.

mite. He drew the conclusion that this arose from alternations of wet and dry seasons,—the dust and sediment being deposited during the summer, and the layer of spar during the winter rains.

In the Ingleborough Cave.

We have some very recent observations on the same subject. "From some measurements lately made," says the *Athenæum*,* "by Mr. Boyd Dawkins, and some other observers, on the rate at which stalagmite is being accumulated in the Ingleborough Cave, Yorkshire, it is calculated that the stalagmitic deposit, known from its shape as 'The Jockey's Cap,' is growing at the rate of 0.2946 of an inch per annum. Assuming that this rate of growth is constant, all the stalagmites and stalactites in the cave may not date further back than the time of Edward III., and hence the thickness of a layer of stalagmite can hardly be used as an argument in support of the high antiquity of any subjacent deposit."

Mr. Vivian has, therefore, fallen into the error of ante-dating the reign of Edward III. by nearly a million of years, while even Mr. Evans, so full of information on this subject, and so cautious in his statements, making an allowance for a difference of temperament, has made a chronological mistake hardly less serious. And it becomes necessary for Sir Charles Lyell to omit this from his indicia of the antiquity of the cave-fauna.

Poole's Hole.

Mr. W. Bruce Clarke writes to *Nature*, January 1, 1874, that he visited, about ten years ago, a cavern near Buxton, commonly known as "Poole's Hole," and observed some stalagmite, probably one-eighth of an inch thick, which had been deposited on the gas-pipes which were used to light the cave, and which had been laid down six months before. Granting that the deposit had been six months in acquiring a thickness of one-eighth of an inch, one inch would be deposited, at the same rate, in four years,—"a rate of deposit," observes the editor, "even more rapid than that (viz. three-fourths of an inch in fifteen years) mentioned by Mr. Curry in the number of *Nature* for Dec. 18."

Mr. Thomas K. Callard in the same January issue of *Nature* has the following observations on this point: He thinks it probable that the rate of deposit of the stalagmite in Kent's Cavern has not been uniform, "for when the thick forest (the habitat of the animals whose bones are found in the cave) left an accumulation of decayed vegetation on the soil, we had the natural laboratory where the rain would find the carbonic acid, to act as a solvent upon the calcareous earth, and as this acidulous liquid percolated through the soil and dripped into the cave, we have the origin of the stalagmite; but as, by the axe of man, the

* April 12, 1873.

forest decreased, in that proportion the chemicals lessened, and as a consequence the deposit diminished. Besides the diminution of the solvent, every year that the operation was going on the material that composed the stalagmite must have been decreasing in the superjacent soil, so that the bicarbonate of lime which now takes two centuries to cover one-eighth inch, might have been in days gone by the work of much shorter time." *

To the same purport is the statement of M. Reclus, that in 1816, in one of the caves of Adelsberg, a skeleton—probably of some bewildered visitor—was discovered, which the stone had already enveloped in a white shroud; but he adds that these bones have now for some years been firmly fixed in the thickness of the rock, added to, as it constantly is, by fresh layers. In like manner, he says, the skeletons of three hundred Cretans, who were smoked to death by the Turks in 1822 in the cave of Melidhoni, are gradually disappearing under the incrustation of stone which has enveloped them with its calcareous layers.†

Testimony of M. Reclus.

One more fact on this subject: Prof. Winchell informs us that in one of the lead-caves near Dubuque, Iowa, stalactites *three feet long* have formed *in three years.*

The other remains in Martin's Cave were bones of the ox, goat, sheep, and ibex, pottery, stone axes, flint knives, worked bones, rubstones of sandstone, sandstone querns, and charcoal. There were no traces of any previous excavations "either in the bed of dark earth, or through the stalagmitic floors." This cave is on the east side of Windmill Hill, five hundred and ninety feet above the sea.

In Figtree Cave, not far off, and two hundred feet higher up, were found animal remains, hand pottery, flint knives, charcoal, and pottery "pointing to a comparatively advanced stage of ceramic art."

In the island of Malta similar phenomena occur; *but there are no human remains* or *works of art*, and the fossils are almost exclusively of extinct species,—among them two species of pigmy elephant and the hippopotamus pentlandi. It would have been *impossible* for the animals found to have subsisted on the present islands, even if their botanical resources had been four times those of any country on the globe, irrespective of the total absence of rivers and lakes,—or even a perennial stream. Therefore, when these animals lived, Malta was

Malta.

* Our scientific men strangely ignore the fact that the supply of carbonic acid which enables spring water to dissolve limestone and deposit stalagmite is often derived in great abundance from very deep subterranean sources, and not from decaying vegetation. The quantity of this gas sent up from below in many localities is enormous, and altogether greater than that supplied by vegetation.

† The Earth, p. 253.

connected with the main-land. There are the same indications as at Gibraltar that tumultuous torrents have swept these bones into the caves. In the deposit of one rock cavity were counted the straight tusks of thirty hippopotami, representing every stage of growth,—which must have perished by some geologic convulsion. In the dry bed of a large torrent, whole skeletons of elephants and numbers of the dormouse were jammed between large water-worn blocks of sandstone, arranged in layers across the ravine.

Many of these bones also were sun-cracked, showing that they had been bleached in the sun before they were carried into those fissures and gaps. One of these, one hundred feet long by forty broad, contained the teeth of at least one hundred and fifty individual elephants, of all ages and sizes.

A *subsidence* of the land would account for this apparent destruction.

There is little doubt, we presume, that Africa and the European continent were united at no distant period. They were united between Sicily and Cape Bon, as well as at the Straits of Gibraltar. The distance between the nearest point of Sicily (Marsala) and the coast of Africa (Cape Bon) is not more than eighty miles, and Admiral Smyth, in his Memoir on the Mediterranean, informs us that there is a subaqueous plateau uniting Sicily to Africa by a succession of ridges which are not more than from forty to fifty fathoms under water.

This junction existed probably a short time before the human period.

There have been a number of caves discovered and explored within the past few years. Among the remains brought to light, a good deal of attention has been attracted to the "Fossil Man of Mentone." This cave was discovered, we believe, in 1872, by Dr. Rivière. It is near Nice, in Italy. The remains were found in the cavern of Barma, which was partially destroyed by the cutting of the railway from Mentone to Ventimiglia. From time immemorial it has served as a place of shelter to the Mentonese fishermen, from the smoke of whose fires the roof has become entirely blackened.

Mentone.

The skeleton lay in an inclined posture, and in an attitude of repose. Its legs were crossed; its arms were folded near the head; its ribs had yielded to the pressure of the earth above them. The teeth and lower jaw were in perfect preservation, also the skull, which was of a deep brick-red color, *extremely well formed, and of extraordinary size*. The thighs were of unusual length, eighteen inches, and, with the rest of the bones, indicated the subject to have belonged to a large race. A necklace of perforated teeth and shells was found, with other ornaments that may have constituted a head-dress. Around were scattered a great quantity of implements, some of the largest size ever

Fine skull.

discovered,—such as knives, punches, needles, hatchets, and bodkins of bone, of curious workmanship. Near by lay the bones and lower jaws of herbivorous animals. At the head a stone was erected, an indication of interment. All were reached at the depth of ten feet below the accumulated débris of the cavern.

The implements are all roughly worked, and belong to the oldest known stone period. A "commander's staff or baton" also occurred.

In addition to these particulars, we gather from *Les Mondes*, quoted in the *American Journal of Science* for September, 1872, p. 241, that the skull was very dolichocephalous and its facial angle good, approaching 85°. It closely resembles the skull from Cro-Magnon found in 1868.

The different species of animals occurring in the immediate vicinity were: felis spelæa, ursus spelæus, ursus arctos, canis lupus, rhinoceros, equus, sus scrofa, bos primigenius, cervus alces, cervus elephas, cervus canadensis, cervus capreolus, capra primigenia (?), antilope, rupicapra (or chamois), and a species of lepus. "Among these animals," says *Les Mondes*, "three specially, the cave felis and ursus, and the rhinoceros, indicate by their presence around the skeleton and at levels above it, the epoch to which the fossil man belonged."

Among the objects present were two flint knives, a bone pin cut from the radius of a stag, and twenty-two canines of the stag perforated.*

M. Rivière in a paper on these caverns states that among the shells obtained from them is the *Pecten maximus*, which is not found in the Mediterranean, but, as he thinks, comes from the ocean.

A similar observation has been made upon the shells occurring with the human skeleton recently found at Laugerie-Basse. Here, at the depth of twelve feet below the surface, this skeleton was discovered during the past year, and some twenty shells of the genus *Cypræa*, or cowrie, were found, pierced, and distributed in pairs all along the body, as if they had been attached to the clothing [the same arrangement was observed in the neolithic caverns of Marne, explored by M. de Baye]. The cowrie shells found belong to two species, one of which is found only in the Mediterranean, the other being found on the Atlantic coast. From this M. de Mortillet draws the inference that the occupants of the cave of Laugerie-Basse had relations with the Mediterranean. He thinks the cave-dwellers only remained in the caves during the summer, being nomadic.

M. de Mortillet also observes that the absence of the Reindeer at Mentone shows the climate of the Mediterranean at that time to have been very different from that of the Atlantic slope of France.

---

* A number of caves have since been explored here, and as many as five skeletons have been found,—two of them children.

We may add to this observation of M. de Mortillet that the reindeer was also absent from the cave of Pontil (explored by M. Gervais) in Hérault, on the Mediterranean, where the remains of the other palæolithic animals occurred; and that we are told that "the remains of the Reindeer are never found in Provence," which comprises the present departments of Basses-Alpes, Bouches-du-Rhône, Var, and a portion of Vaucluse. See Cong. d'Anthropol., 1867, p. 97.

Luchon.

In a cave near Luchon, in France, M. Piette has made some interesting discoveries. The soil of the cavern consists of several layers,—the lowermost ones being characterized by the bones of the reindeer, and by dressed flints like those of the grotto of Laugerie-Basse. These layers enclose, in addition to human bones, a large fauna, and particularly a considerable quantity of carved bones and stones. Nowhere else has so great an accumulation of pre-historic works of art been found. The figures often cannot be recognized; still on the bones are seen some designs of considerable finish; M. Piette mentions, among other carvings, some that represent flocks of wild goats, and herds of reindeer, the head of a rhinoceros, a wolf, horses, a lion's head with mane, etc. These remains are buried in a black soil, filled with ashes. Near the surface of this layer the fauna is the same as below, but the carvings are very different from those underneath, and show a marked decadence. While the lower ones reproduce Nature exactly, with extreme care and a certain minuteness of observation, the upper ones are fantastical and not after Nature, as well as ruder than the others. All the human bones, especially the bones of the skull, are reduced to small fragments, and all have notches or incisions more or less deep. This M. Piette takes as an evidence of cannibalism. The topmost layer is hard and compact.*

More Drawings.

Nuremberg, Mill-stone and Spindles.

We find in the *Galaxy* for September, 1872, and in *Nature* for May 30, 1872, an account of a cave, opened up by the construction of the railway from Nuremberg to Regensburg, in Bavaria. The lowermost layer, it is stated, afforded no traces of man, but yielded only the bones of the cave-bear, cave-hyæna, and cave-lion. Above this layer, and thence up to the top, we find the remains of human implements and the bones of the above-named extinct animals lying associated together. Flint-flakes and fragments of pottery are abundant—the latter exhibiting considerable beauty of form, and ornamented with zigzag dots. The cave-bear appears to have been most sought after for food, but the split bones of the elephant and rhinoceros are also found. Also the bones of horses, oxen, cats, wolves, pike, and carp. Also a block of granite, used probably as a mill-stone;

* Popular Science Monthly, July, 1872.

one of its sides rubbed smooth, and on the other two holes bored apparently to receive handles. There were also several *spindle-whorls* made of clay. If this cave is correctly reported, it proves that the early cave-men were *farmers* and *weavers*.

Aquitaine. Representation of Palæolithic Man.

Quite recently additional examples of pre-historic engraving on bone or horn have been found in the caverns of Aquitaine, one of the most noticeable being a sketch on a reindeer's horn, representing a male bison pursued by a naked man, the latter grasping the animal by the tail with one hand, and plunging a lance into its side with the other. The drawing of the man is said to be the best illustration of the "humanity" of the period. The absence of clothing is believed to indicate that he went habitually naked. The head is brachycephalic, with the hair standing stiffly on the cranium, and there is a short, pointed beard on the chin.*

Veyrier.

An important cave has been found near the village of Veyrier, at the foot of Mt. Salève, three miles south of Geneva, Switzerland. It has yielded an immense quantity of flint implements, and of entire and fractured bones, all of which were imbedded in a thin layer of black vegetable earth. The knives, saws, and other flint implements amount to more than a thousand, and have evidently been manufactured on the spot. In other words, we have here, as at Chaleux and Laugerie, a flint-implement manufactory. The black soil is literally paved with bones of horses, bulls, reindeers, stags,† chamois, marmots, Alpine bears, wolves, and storks; half of which are reindeer bones. We have thus the reindeer and the flint implements associated with existing animals. A sculptured bone, eight inches in length, perforated, and with twelve incisions at one end, has engraved on one side "a bold picture of some herbivorous animal with long curved horns, probably a *bouquetin*." On the side is a drawing of a long, narrow stem of a plant, probably a fern. This is the first specimen of "art" found east of the Rhone.‡ They found also in this cave a spoon-like instrument and a

* Annual Record of Science and Industry for 1871, p. 183. We by no means accept the idea that the cave-men did not wear clothing. The constant occurrence of needles in the caves implies that skins were sewed together for clothing.

† The horse and stag are "our actual horse and ordinary stag." Mat. pour l'Hist. de l'Homme.

A precisely similar collection of animal remains occurred at the grotto of Gourdan, explored in 1873 by M. Piette, near Montréjeau (Haute-Garonne). He found abundant remains of the reindeer with those of the horse, ox, wolf, fox, common bear, badger, hedgehog, hare, water-rat, wild boar, stag, goat, etc.

M. Rütimeyer seems to think that the reindeer was domesticated in Switzerland; he asks, if it was not, why it did not retire to the high Alps with the bear, the ibex, and the chamois.

‡ Since writing this, we have seen in "Matériaux pour l'Histoire de l'Homme," Livraisons 3e et 4e for 1874, the representation of a reindeer engraved on bone from the grotto of

broken needle (of bone), and seventeen perforated valves of peduncle shells.

A series of geological inquiries has determined the fact that in ancient times the waters of the neighboring lake of Geneva were twenty-five metres above the present level; but the Veyrier cave is considerably higher than this old level.

The periodical from which we obtain these statements (*Appletons' Journal*) adds that the large quantity of animal bones accumulated in this narrow cave proves that a colder temperature prevailed then at Geneva than now, "as otherwise the putrefaction of this organic matter would have made the cave uninhabitable." This idea originated with Mr. Christy, and has been caught at by Sir John Lubbock and others, who wish to prove that France had an arctic climate in the palæolithic age. We mention, therefore, next certain caves in South Africa.

Caves of South Africa.

In the *Anthropological Review* for 1869, vol. vii. p. 121, is an account of these caves, and the cannibals who inhabited them. The largest is among the mountains beyond Thaba,—its dimensions being one hundred and thirty by one hundred yards. The roof is blackened with smoke, and the floor "strewn with remains of what they had left there, consisting of heaps of human bones, piled up together or scattered at random about the cavern, and thence, down the sloping face of the rock, as far as the eye could reach. The clefts and level spots were white with bones and skulls of human beings," the marrow-bones being split, like those of the reindeer in the Dordogne caves.

The Caledon river caverns are still inhabited, though the people have abandoned cannibalism. One old savage said, with a sigh, he had formerly been at the cooking of as many as thirty people, and he seemed to think, says the writer in the *Review*, like the "Last Minstrel,"—

> "Old times were changed,
> Old manners gone."

It appears thus that we have in these South African caves—with a climate like that of Rome—the same accumulation of animal matter which the palæontologists (for example Mr. Christy and Mr. Figuier) insist could only be endured in an arctic region.

Marne.

In the department of Marne, France, M. J. de Baye has discovered some very interesting grottoes of the polished stone age. These caverns appear to have been excavated in the rock, or at least in some measure shaped by human art. The sides and arched ceilings bear

---

Thäyngen, in the canton of Schaffhausen, in Switzerland. This is the most accurate and elegant specimen of art that we have yet seen from the caves. This grotto yielded remains of the reindeer, the mammoth, the cave-bear, etc.

the marks of the stone hatchets. Some are divided by a partition into two chambers; several were receptacles for the dead, others were inhabited. The latter were more comfortably arranged, and admitted of being closed with doors, as certain grooves show. The entrances bear traces of polish from constant going in and out. On the wall of one of these grottoes is a rude bas-relief of a hatchet provided with its handle, and a sling. The sepulchral grottoes are less carefully "excavated," and their entrances closed with large stones. None of them were found empty. The bodies were disposed horizontally,* completely extended, without a remnant of covering in some cases, covered in others with carefully prepared pulverulent earth. In one of these caverns there were upwards of forty skeletons. The brachycephalous type was dominant. A few jaws of pachydermatous animals and bones of wild beasts *were found among the human remains.*† The flint implements were hatchets, knives, punches, saws, well-cut arrow-heads, etc. Some of these articles were not flint, but porphyry. There were also implements in bone. Among the ornaments were shells pierced with holes, beads of clay, and marble ear-rings. A vase was found entire, and numerous fragments of pottery.

Grottoes of the Polished Stone Age.

There was a feature (already adverted to) connected with some of these burials which was also observed at the palæolithic cave of Laugerie-Basse. Large pierced shells were deposited all along the extent of the body. It is a circumstance connecting at once the palæolithic and the neolithic caves.‡

A very important and instructive grotto has been recently explored near Blaubeuern, in Würtemberg, by M. Fraas, called the Grotto of Hohlefels. It is a few miles from the village of Schelkingen, situated on a rocky point in the valley of the Arch. M. Fraas found here more than fifty flint knives of the palæolithic type, numerous chippings of flint, many instruments in bone, and fragments of pottery. The animal remains belonged to the *Ursus spelæus; Ursus priscus*, a species larger (?) than the cave-bear; the reindeer; the horse; the rhinoceros; the mammoth, lion, fox, duck, heron, swan, etc.

Grotto of Hohlefels.

Pottery is frequently found in the German, as in the Belgian caves, in association with the remains of the mammoth and the rhinoceros. It is a fact established beyond all question—if man was cotemporary with the mammoth at all—that the European man of the mammoth epoch fabricated pottery.

* We remember Sir John Lubbock's rule that in the polished stone age the bodies were buried in a contracted or sitting posture.

† We have our doubts about this statement. The "excavation" of these grottoes is in a very soft rock.

‡ Cong. d'Anthrop., 1872, p. 401.

Dr. C. A. Jentzsch, in a paper "On the Quaternary formations in the neighborhood of Dresden," discusses the loess, the diluvial hills, etc.; the "marl of Cotta, near Dresden; and the fresh-water limestone of Robschutz, in the Trebisch Valley." In this last, he says, remains of the mammoth and rhinoceros "abound," along with human bones and pottery.*

Abundant as this testimony seems to be, Sir John Lubbock persists in discrediting the existence of pottery in the palæolithic days. As late as January, 1872, in his address before the Anthropological Institute of Great Britain, he insisted that there was no proof of pottery even in the (so-called) Reindeer Period. The case of Aurignac, and the occurrence of pottery in the Belgian caves, he regarded as "exceptional." The pottery at Solutré he doubts.† Does he doubt also the pottery in the Italian caves, and that in the German caves, and that in the Trebisch Valley? The existence of pottery among the ancient population of the Somme Valley and of the Palæolithic caves, tends strongly to discredit, of course, the theory that man began as a *mute*.

It is, of course, a highly important piece of evidence in this discussion, whether the cave-men and the river-gravel savages fabricated pottery; the archæologists and geologists will find few credulous enough to believe that pottery was manufactured in the Glacial Age, or two hundred thousand years ago. We shall, therefore, mention the following case, where the pottery must be, beyond any cavil, cotemporaneous with the other remains. Near *La Bastide de Béarn*, in France, MM. Garrigou and Duparc have discovered the traces of a very primitive lacustrine or palustrine village. M. Garrigou thought that he had found the remains of piles in the turbary, but M. Duparc states that the settlement was constructed with the trunks of trees worked by means of *fire*, the smaller end of the trunk being burned and planted in the mud. The interlaced roots above formed a sort of scaffolding. Worked flints, remains of the reindeer, and *rude pottery* were found associated together in this ancient lake-station.‡

The reader will not fail to observe farther the *transition* here indicated from the era of the caves to that of the lake-dwellings.

Painted Savages.

There are indications that the cave-men, like the ancient Britons, *painted their bodies*. M. Dupont, in a memoir to the Royal Academy of Belgium, represents that he had found, among specimens of oligist, from the banks of the Lesse, some with markings similar to those described by MM. Christy and Lartet as found in

---

* Academy, Dec. 1, 1871.

† Jour. Anthrop. Instit. of Great Britain and Ireland, 1872, p. 383.

‡ Matériaux, 2e série, tome iv., 1873, p. 457.

specimens of red hæmatite from the caverns of Périgord. He thinks the cave-men ground down these minerals to obtain paint for their bodies. Other references are made to similar discoveries,—as at La Madelaine.

A very interesting discovery has recently been made by M. Ed. Piette, at the cave of Gourdan (Haute-Garonne), from which we learn that the cave-men regaled themselves with *music*: a bone flute has been found here, having only two holes, which are perfectly round and carefully worked. The instrument is similar to those used by the natives of Tahiti when visited by Captain Cook. With such an instrument only four notes can be produced; which, however, is nearly equal to the number of musical notes among the Japanese and the Chinese, who have only five.*

The music of the Palæolithic Age.

* Academy, September 19, 1874, p. 334. See also "Matériaux" for 1874.

CHAPTER XIV.

SUMMING UP WITH REGARD TO THE CAVES.

UP to this point we have proved:

1. The cotemporaneity of the mammoth, the rhinoceros tichorinus, and the reindeer of Southern France.

2. That at the Trou des Noutons M. Dupont and M. Van Beneden found in the superficial layer money of the last century; mediæval objects; objects of the Frankish period; medals of the Roman emperors, etc.; and then in the bed below one hundred and fifty horns of the reindeer, with bones of the brown bear, fox, wolf, stag, urus, wild goat, and astragali of the goat formed into a toy for children. This second bed, and all these reindeer, cannot be very ancient. The fauna is modern. The reindeer of Belgium was the cotemporary both of the mammoth and of the recent fauna.

3. That at Veyrier, at the foot of Mt. Salève, numerous remains of the reindeer (along with flint implements) were found in association with remains of "horses, bulls, stags, Alpine bears, wolves, and storks," —again a modern fauna.

4. That these cave-men were *skillful artisans* in stone, ivory, horn, and bone.

5. That the cave-men decorated themselves with ornaments and pigments.

6. That the cave-men—as at Mentone and Aurignac—interred their dead in a spirit of reverence and decency.

7. That there are traces of certain religious rites in the caves.

8. That the palæolithic folk were sufficiently organized and settled to establish great manufactories of weapons and tools,—as at Chaleux, Laugerie, Hoxne, and Pressigny.

9. That they carried on a traffic with distant countries, and that at Chaleux we actually meet with flints from the west of France and *nephrite** from Asia.

10. That they made use of the needle.

11. That their etchings and drawings exhibit very considerable taste

* This was not traffic, but shows contact with the East.

and skill,—a sense of proportion and a faculty of execution indicating a natural capacity fully equal to that of the existing European races.

12. That they also fabricated pottery, which was not done in the present age among the Esquimaux, the New Zealanders, the Tahitians, the Australians, the Bushmen, or the Fuegians. The Hottentots, the North American Indians, and the Fijians were, we believe, the only modern savages acquainted with pottery.

13. That they were not ignorant of music, and in this art were probably equal to the semi-civilized inhabitants of the island of Tahiti, of whom Sir John Lubbock says that "on the whole they may be taken as representing the highest stage in civilization to which man has in any country raised himself before the discovery or introduction of metallic implements."

14. That at the cave near Nuremberg, along with the stone weapons and the remains of the extinct mammals, were found a mill-stone and spindle-whorls, showing a knowledge of agriculture and weaving. Along with this was pottery "exhibiting considerable beauty of form."

15. That at the Gibraltar caves we apparently find the extinct rhinoceros in association with polished stone implements; although from the disordered state of the relics it is unsafe to rely upon this fact. But the presence of the African hyæna, the African leopard, and the Barbary stag, combined with the discovery of the remains of the African elephant* near Madrid, is of great significance; showing, as it does, the cotemporaneous existence in Spain of man with these animals, and that probably at a recent period; for, if the African elephant and the other animals mentioned have lived in Spain during the human period (all but the first during the second stone age), why is it an incredible thing that man and the mammoth may have co-existed a few thousand years ago in France and England? We also found the African elephant near Palermo, in Sicily.

The absence of palæolithic implements here is significant.

16. That we find the caves still occupied in the period of polished stone implements, and even during the age of metals. It may be added that this occupation continued with succeeding generations, down to the eighth century of our era;† all this showing a probable *connection*

* In the valley of the Manzanares, associated with a flint implement like the Madras forms. Evans, 571.

† The caves were occupied long after the Christian era. We learn from Tacitus that the Germans in his day retired into caves during winter. M. Desnoyers also refers to a passage from Florus in which it is related that Cæsar ordered the caves into which the Aquitanian Gauls had retreated to be closed up. It is also on record that in the eighth century these same Aquitanians defended themselves in caverns against King Pepin. And it is notorious that the man of the Polished Stone Age and the (so-called) Bronze Age continued to occupy these caves.

between the successive occupants, which excludes the idea of the lapse of tens of thousands of years.

The sum of the matter is, that we find in the ancient cave-dwellers a race of men in almost precisely the condition of the modern Esquimaux,—and there is a considerable probability that the Arctic races of Europe and America are their descendants. It was the first race that reached Western Europe from Western Asia, and the Celts subsequently pushed them farther north.

They were, possibly, in some instances, cannibals: and so were the Irish since the Christian era: so were the Fijians, a proud, haughty, and highly intelligent race, dwelling in houses furnished with mats, and in fortified cities; eating with forks; acquainted with music; with a taste for poetry; acquainted with agriculture and navigation; worshipping in temples; with a complicated and carefully administered political system; characterized by highly finished manners and a ceremonious politeness. And yet it is true that the Fijians fattened slaves for the table, and considered human flesh such a delicacy that the women were not allowed to eat it. Ra Undre-undre, chief of Rakiraki, is said to have eaten nine hundred persons.

The Maoris of New Zealand were also cannibals—one of the finest and most advanced of all the savage races.

It must not be supposed that the rude weapons of the caves were not as deadly as the polished ones; and it must not be imagined that with such weapons man cannot contend with the most formidable animals. The caves themselves testify to this: we refer to the sketch found in one of the caves of Aquitaine, of a male bison pursued by a naked man, who holds the bison by the tail, and plunges a spear into his side. That tells the whole story. M. Figuier, in his work entitled "Mammalia," gives an account of a rhinoceros-hunt in India by the Emperor Baber, in which the rhinoceros was killed with *arrows* and *spears*.

The North American Indian, says Lubbock, "will send an arrow right through a horse, or even a buffalo." "The African savage will kill the elephant, and the Chinook fears not to attack even the whale. . . . The South Sea Islanders are even more than a match for the shark, which they attack fearlessly with a knife." *

Such is the testimony of the *Caverns*. In the succeeding chapter we shall, in addition to further evidence from some very important caves not yet mentioned, give an account of *a Palæolithic Village* or *hunting-station*, belonging, of course, to the era of the caves, and developing this whole subject in a new and generally unrecognized aspect.

So far—and resting the matter at the point reached by us—we have

* Pre-historic Times, pp. 544–45.

found no proof from the caves of any vast antiquity for the human race. The facts to be presented in addition will strengthen this conclusion.

A good deal has been said about some of the human skulls which have been found in the caves, or under circumstances which associate them with that period. The Neanderthal skull was some years ago the subject of much criticism, and much extravagant theorizing. This famous "fossil" was found in 1857 in a cave situated in that part of the valley of the Düssel, near Düsseldorf, which is called the Neanderthal. This spot is a deep ravine about seventy miles northeast of the region of the Liége caves. The fissure occurs in the precipitous southern side of the winding ravine, about sixty feet above the stream, and one hundred feet below the top of the cliff.

Skulls of Palæolithic men.

The Neanderthal skull.

This skull Prof. Huxley described to Sir C. Lyell as "the most ape-like skull he has ever beheld." And Prof. Schaaffhausen and Mr. Busk characterized it as "the most brutal of all known human skulls, resembling those of the apes not only in the prodigious development of the superciliary prominences and the forward extension of the orbits, but still more in the depressed form of the brain-case, in the straightness of the squamosal suture, and in the complete retreat of the occiput forward and upward, from the superior occipital ridges."

The discovery of this skull occasioned the greatest flutter in the anthropological world. Prof. Schaaffhausen gave an account of it in 1857 before the Lower Rhine Medical and Natural History Society at Bonn. Prof. Fuhlrott published a book on the subject. Prof. Huxley devoted a number of pages to it in "Man's Place in Nature." Prof. Schaaffhausen pronounced it "the most ancient memorial of the early inhabitants of Europe." Prof. Huxley adjudged that it possessed "a very high antiquity." Prof. Fuhlrott, in his book, determined its age to be from two hundred thousand to three hundred thousand years. Prof. William King read a paper before the British Association, in which he referred it to the Glacial Period.

All of this was without the shadow of warrant from the actual facts. The Neanderthal skull was not found in association with any of the remains of the extinct animals, nor in the glacial drift; it was simply found under five feet of mud.

The degraded type of the skull does not prove anything with regard to its age. In fact, its minimum cranial capacity is estimated by Prof. Huxley at seventy-five cubic inches. The most capacious healthy European skull yet measured (and we hope the ladies will make a note of it) was that of a female, and had a capacity of one hundred and fifteen cubic inches, and weighed one thousand eight hundred and seventy-two grammes. Next to this came the

The brain of the Neanderthal man.

brain of Cuvier, which weighed one thousand eight hundred and sixty-one grammes; then that of Byron, one thousand eight hundred and seven grammes. Huxley states that he knows of no case of a human (male adult) cranium with a less cubical capacity than sixty-two cubic inches, while on the other hand the most capacious Gorilla skull yet measured has a content of not more than thirty-four and one-half cubic inches.

The cranial capacity of the Neanderthal skull is more than double that of the most capacious Gorilla skull known. It is, assuming the average European cranial capacity at eighty or eighty-five, not very far below this average. Tiedemann states the cranial contents in the Negro at forty, thirty-eight, and thirty-five ounces of millet-seed. The capacity of the Malay skulls equalled thirty-six and thirty-three ounces. The Neanderthal specimen equalled thirty-seven ounces of millet-seed: in other words, it is nearly equal to the Negro skull, and above the Malay.

The Neanderthal skull is thus, in point of capacity, a fair average skull, and (as Prof. Huxley observes) "very far above the pithecoid maximum."

The Engis skull.

Another skull that made a great noise was the Engis skull. This was found in the Engis cavern near Liége by Dr. Schmerling. The antiquity of this skull is admitted. It was found in association with the bones of the mammoth, the cave-bear, and other extinct mammalia. But Sir John Lubbock remarks of it that "it is a perfectly well-developed skull," while Prof. Huxley observes that "there is no mark of degradation about any part of its structure. It is, in fact, a fair average human skull, which might have belonged to a philosopher, or might have contained the thoughtless brains of a savage."

The skulls from Bruniquel.

The skulls found at Bruniquel have been examined by Prof. Owen. He expresses himself with regard to them as follows (see Phil. Trans., 1870): "They exemplify," he says, "the distinct characteristics of the human genus and species as decidedly as do the corresponding parts of the present races; they show most affinity with the oldest Celtic types, the crania being oval, and rather dolicho- than brachy-cephalic in their general proportions; the cranial capacity or brain corresponding with that of the uneducated European of Celtic origin, and exceeding that of the average Australian aborigines." *

In 1856 some surprise was expressed, says Sir C. Lyell, by the assembled naturalists at Le Puy, that the skull of the "fossil man of Denise" should be "of the ordinary Caucasian or European type."

M. Broca, at a late meeting of the new French Association, in a

* Amer. Jour. Sci., vol. l. p. 423.

paper on the "Troglodytes of Les Eyzies," said the skulls found exhibited traces of ferocity, but that they also exhibited "a certain amount of superior development." Les Eyzies.

The male skull of Cro-Magnon, we are told by M. de Quatrefages, "is remarkable for its capacity,—according to Dr. Broca, gauging not less than 1590 cent. cubes, which exceeds the average European skull of the present day."

The three "Fossil Men of Mentone," belonging to the earliest stone age, have all very fine skulls. Mentone.

And to the same purport Dr. Lund tells us that with respect to the race of fossil men in Brazil, he found that their skulls differed in no respect from the acknowledged American type. Brazil.

Bearing on this point is the remarkable testimony borne by M. de Quatrefages at the meeting of the International Congress of Anthropology at Brussels in 1872. He is reported as having "summarized the results of the present Congress," and as having stated "as the principal ones that the elements of the pre-historic population—even of the age of stone—*are discernible in the present population*, and that even in the most remote ages the migrations of races took place on a much more extended scale, and with more frequency, than was believed by any one until recently." *

Farther testimony, if any is needed, is borne by the human skeletons in the cemetery at the station of Solutré (noticed in the next chapter).

The value, however, of these craniological investigations is illustrated by the following statement of M. Virchow at the Brussels Congress in 1872. The Anthropological Society of Berlin, M. Virchow remarked, had recently received two skulls, one belonging to a man, the other belonging to a woman, obtained in some excavations made at Athens, and cotemporary with the Macedonian epoch. These crania had a capacity, said M. Virchow, "which is regarded to-day as insufficient to give a normal physical development. That of the female had the capacity of the cranium of a savage of New Holland: the other, the male, was a little larger. One might regard that of the woman as Mongoloid by its anatomical characters, and if it had been found at Furfooz it would certainly have been considered as coming from a very inferior and very primitive race." Nevertheless it belonged to a woman named Glykera, and her rank was indicated by the precious relics found in her tomb, which was in the centre of the city.

---

* Nature, Sept. 5, 1872.

CHAPTER XV.

SOLUTRÉ.

Important Discoveries by MM. de Ferry and Arcelin at Solutré, in France.—The Clos du Charnier.—Belongs to the Palæolithic Age.—Probably Cotemporary with Laugerie-Haute.—Flint Implements in Great Numbers associated with Remains of the Horse and the Reindeer.—Found on the Surface and in Sub-soil.—Refuse-Heaps, at an Increased Depth, containing Bones of the Horse, Stag, Ox, Reindeer, Elephant, etc., along with Flint Implements, some of the latter highly finished.—The Horns of the Reindeer, in some instances, apparently quite fresh, yielding, when cut, the odor of Horn, and retaining a Considerable Portion of their Gelatine.—These "Amas de Débris de Cuisine" rest on Slabs which were used as Fire-Hearths.—Numerous Remains of the Horse outside of these Deposits.—The Remains represent Two Thousand Horses.—Human Graves grouped over the Space occupied by Both Deposits.—M. Pruner-Bey pronounces the Skulls to be Mongoloid.—Farther Explorations of Solutré.—Opinion of M. de Mortillet.—New Exploration by the Abbé Ducrost.—The Subject before the French Association at Lyons.—The Graves cotemporary with the Ancient Fauna.—The Superior Character of the Flint Implements.—Stemmed and Barbed Arrow-Heads.—Domestication of the Horse.—The Significance of Solutré.—Proves the Recent Existence of the Great Extinct Animals in France.—A Remarkable Cemetery of Same Age noticed by Col. Hamilton Smith in District of Figeac.—Discovery at Chagny.—The Cave of Espalungues.—Camp of Chassey.—Remains of the Cave-Bear found in association with Polished Stone Implements in Various Parts of Europe.

FARTHER and most important light is shed on the most difficult part of this whole subject—the association of human remains with those of the post-glacial mammals—by the discoveries of MM. H. de Ferry and A. Arcelin at *Solutré* in Mâconnais, France, an account of which is published in the volume of the "International Congress of Prehistoric Archæology" for 1868.* In this paper we are informed that the geological *gisement* of the Clos du Charnier exhibits in the sub-soil of an arid hillock certain heaps of débris, incontestably of the Age of the Reindeer, and cotemporary with those of Laugerie-Haute in Périgord, together with certain mysterious accumulations of the bones of the Horse, and, finally, numerous human interments.

Clos du Charnier.

The Clos (or, more properly, the Crot) du Charnier is an uncultivated eminence, naturally turfed, situated at Solutré, and presents a loose talus which is exposed towards the south. This hillock has the form of a tri-

* "L'Age du Renne en Mâconnais: Mémoire sur le Gisement Archéologique du Clos du Charnier à Solutré, Département du Saône-et-Loire," p. 319.

lobed *mamelon,* with a radius of about sixty metres at the base, and includes a superficies of about ten thousand square metres. All of the declivity north of the vale of Solutré, occupied in part by the village, is strewn with worked flints, which are sufficiently numerous to whiten the gardens and roads. In the vineyards immediately beyond the last houses of the village, at several points, are seen, besides the flints, numerous bones of *horses* mixed with some remains of the *reindeer,* dispersed by the hoe or the plough. But the focus of the dressed flints and the bones is the Crot du Charnier. Having remained uncultivated, this point has never been in any way disturbed.

Worked Flints.

Remains of the Horse and the Reindeer.

Besides the flints and the remains of the horse and the reindeer, there are also fragments of Gallo-Roman and mediæval pottery.

When we dig into this soil, we find:

1. In the sub-soil, fragments of recent pottery (probably mediæval) at the depth of from ten to fifty centimetres (four to twenty inches), and mingled with these there are flints and bones of the reindeer, the horse, and man. The flints are in some cases well worn and fretted, while others seem quite new; some of them are entire, others are broken. The bones are separated from each other, and lie in complete disorder.

2. *Amas de rebuts de cuisine.* Beneath these beds of scattered débris, we encounter deposits much richer in products of human industry, which MM. de Ferry and Arcelin denominate *refuse-heaps,* or *débris de cuisine.*

Refuse-heaps from the Kitchen.

These heaps are found concentrated on the eastern part of the hill, on each side of, and below, the road which leads to the quarry. They occupy variable levels, some being at a depth of forty or fifty centimetres, others at 1^{m}, $1^{m}.30$, $1^{m}.40$, $1^{m}.50$, and even as deep as $2^{m}.30$.

These heaps vary also in quantity and composition. At one point they are mere "threads" of ashy material, containing a few bones, burned and unburned, and a few chips of silex; elsewhere the development is more marked, but enclosing still only shivered bones, fragments of reindeers' horns, rudely incised, many flint flakes (but few specimens of any character), fragments of scrapers, and different mineral substances foreign to the region; and then, finally, at other points they assume considerable proportions, and the remains are much better preserved, and of a much more interesting character.

Foreign minerals.

These larger heaps are ordinarily remarked by the occurrence of numerous and long fragments of the horns of the reindeer, some of them fashioned into hammers, or handles for tools; of numerous shattered jaw-bones of the reindeer, broken canon bones,

Worked bones.

numerous phalanges, vertebræ, etc.; sometimes, also, of certain bones which have preserved their normal juxtaposition; and, finally, of a great quantity of worked flints, such as scrapers, arrow and lance heads, knives, punches, flakes, splinters, and nuclei. Here and there we find specimens of these last of a thorough finish.

Next come objects borrowed from the mineralogy of neighboring districts; rolled pebbles from the Saône, porphyry or granite, peroxide of manganese, bits of red chalk for coloring or polishing, etc., etc.

All of the flint weapons from Solutré are extremely thin and light,—sometimes of very large dimensions,—and very finely cut, favorably comparing with the most beautiful specimens from Denmark.

Beautiful Implements.

Nor are the Horse and the Reindeer the only animals whose remains are found here; the remains of the elephant are also found, though not in such abundance. At one spot, mention is made of finding many fragments of the horns of the reindeer, a great bone of the elephant, eighty centimetres in length, and some very fine flints, among others a superb lance-head, which lay under the bone of the elephant. At another point, we read of "vast accumulations of bones of reindeer, horse, elephant, stag, ox," etc.

Remains of the Mammoth as well as the Reindeer.

With the exception of some of the burned bones, all of the animal remains are astonishingly preserved. One can believe them to be fresh. Some of the horns of the reindeer are still extremely hard, and, when cut, yield the odor of fresh horn; while the bones have preserved a considerable proportion of their gelatine.

Freshness of the bones.

Another noticeable fact is that all of these "amas de débris de cuisine" *rest in general on rude slabs.* They are at the same time covered by other slabs, and this rule is so universally observed that whenever the picks encountered them, the explorers could always predict the existence of a "hearth" beneath. In fine, whenever a slab was raised, its lower part presented débris or ashy matter adhering to it; then the "heap" was revealed intact, with its usual composition, and sometimes flint instruments (arrow-heads, lance-heads, etc.) in such a state of preservation that they appeared to have been deposited there in order to be reclaimed on the first occasion.

Fire-places. Stone-slabs.

The Reindeer is much more abundant than the Horse.

To the Reindeer, the Horse, and the Elephant, say MM. de Ferry and Arcelin, we must add, among the remains found here, two enormous fragments of the horns of the *cervus elephas* (common stag), which are fashioned into hammers; the bones of a very large ox; the jaw-bone of a fox; three canines of the wolf; and a canine of the cave-tiger.

Cave-Tiger.

While, ordinarily, the débris are loose and uncompacted, sometimes they form *conglomerates* or solid masses—exhibiting the phenomena presented precisely as they originally existed, and precluding the possibility of any derangement since the heaps were formed.

There are but few objects of art here. The chief is the representation of a reindeer, very rudely executed, but very distinctly indicated,—carved in a soft stone. This is the only animal representation found. There are a few fragments of rude hand-made *pottery*.

3. *Amas de débris de chevaux.*

Skeletons of the Horse outside of these heaps.

Outside of, and surrounding, the deposits above described, are very numerous remains of *horses*, presenting an entirely different state of things. These remains begin where the first end, and, as it were, encircle them. They consist exclusively of the bones of the Horse. At several points they seem to sink below the kitchen-remains, and to run under them. At one point where this is the case, there was accordingly found over the "amas de débris de chevaux" a large and beautiful hearth (foyer), with the remains of the reindeer and the elephant (more than fifty fragments of the horns of the former), numerous flints (among them a large lance-head), etc., all resting on a bed, some sixty centimetres thick, of horse-bones, which enclosed within it, a little farther off, another hearth. It is only at the border of these fire-places that these intercalations occur. Beyond, the débris of the horse reign supreme and without any other remains of any sort. We have never (say the explorers) met this deposit in the interior of the *enceinte* of the kitchen-débris: so that all of their researches have resulted in bringing out this fact: *that where the fire-places cease, there the accumulations of the horse-bones commence.*

On this periphery there is *Horse*, and nothing but *Horse*. All of the bones of these horses have been subjected to the action of fire. The bones were in great numbers, representing as many, probably, as two thousand horses.

Human sepultures.

Grouped over the space occupied by the hearths on the one hand, and the horse-remains on the other, are *human sepultures*. One of these was found intact. It had the shape of a rectangular box well jointed and closed, but the stones not squared, and it rested on the *magma* of the horse. The skeleton was that of a Finnish woman,—extended on burned and powdered bones of the horse. At its side were bones of the horse and the reindeer, and three flint knives. Nearly all of the graves contained the bones of horse and reindeer, and flint knives.

Finnish skeleton and bones of reindeer.

About half of all the graves rest on the hearths, and most of the hearths support one or more human skeletons. These skeletons in general are complete, and have not been molested.

16

No metal of any kind was met with.

The bones pronounced Mongoloid.

The human bones, we are informed, were submitted to M. Pruner-Bey, who pronounces them to belong to a *Mongoloid race*.

The Crot du Charnier a Tartar camp.

The conclusion drawn from all these facts is, that the Crot du Charnier served as a *camp* for a Mongoloid tribe in the age of the Reindeer,—a "station de chasse," which was not continuously occupied, but which was constantly, and for a long period, revisited. The authors of the paper state that they were supported by MM. Lartet, Dupont, and De Mortillet, in the opinion that in every respect the station of Solutré resembled the cave of Laugerie-Haute, which was anterior to La Madelaine, Les Eyzies, and Bruniquel.

Funeral rites.

The remains of the two thousand horses are, it is believed, associated with funeral rites; the primitive Aryans, in historical times, as well as the Mongols, practising the custom of immolating their horses on their tombs.* The fact that in the "amas de débris de chevaux" no bones are found but those of the horse (if it be as stated), and the additional fact that there are no marks of the knife on these bones, would imply that the horses were buried.

The Greenlanders, we are told, bury under their huts; and this fact sheds a good deal of light on the graves at Solutré. The same custom prevails among the Indians of the Amazon, the New Zealanders, the islanders of Torres Straits, and in the great Central African kingdom of Bornou. The Tartar tribes had the same practice.

Farther information about Solutré.

So much for the paper which appears in the volume of the records of the "International Congress of Prehistoric Archæology" for 1868. The account is not very lucid, and we therefore present the substance of the notices of the same station which occur in the publication entitled "Matériaux pour l'Histoire de l'Homme," formerly edited by M. de Mortillet, and now edited by M. Cartailhac. Combining these several accounts, the reader will be enabled to get a clear idea of the phenomena presented at this important station.

In vol. iv. (1868), page 33, we have the following:

Under the rock at Solutré, in the vineyards at that point, and at the depth of about a metre, we meet with a black stratum, containing broken bones and worked flints, and varying in thickness from thirty to forty centimetres. Hearths or fire-places occur in this stratum, forming so many centres of the black deposit under consideration. These hearths

* The Indians of the Western region of the United States kill the horse of any Indian who dies, and suspend the body in the air,—which custom formerly prevailed among the Tartar tribes of Central Asia.

very regularly present coarse slabs of stone, under which occur débris of bones, burned, sometimes fractured, and worked flints. Below these slabs other slabs sometimes occur at a certain interval, and this superposition is sometimes repeated two or three times.

The bones which characterize this bed are chiefly the bones of the reindeer, those of the horse being rare. Occasionally we meet with the bones of the fox, the deer, a large ruminant (probably the aurochs), the elephant, and, finally, of man.

The worked flints which occur are beautiful pieces, finely wrought *à petits coups*, and consist of scrapers, awls, lance-heads, arrow-heads, etc. Bones and horns of the reindeer, fashioned into implements, sometimes occur. The phalanx of this animal, formed into a *whistle*, is met with. M. de Ferry found also a fragment representing some animal sculptured in soft stone.

By the side of the space covered by this kitchen-débris is another area filled exclusively with the consolidated and compact remains of the Horse, evidently cotemporary with the hearths or fire-places,—possibly even older, as M. Arcelin observed at certain points that they were *prolonged* under the hearths, which had not been disturbed. These bones are so abundant that they have given to the place the name of Cros, or Clos, du Charnier. The thickness of this deposit is about a metre. Here there are no remains but those of the *Horse*.

Finally, certain *tombs* have been discovered within the precincts of this station,—in some instances violated. One is described by M. de Ferry which had not been disturbed. The body reposed between rude slabs forming a parallelogram,—extended on a bed thick with the bones of the horse, pounded and burned. By the side of the skeleton were some bones of the horse and the reindeer.

The human crania from Solutré were presented and discussed at the Anthropological Congress which met at Paris in 1867, and it was unanimously accepted that they were Mongoloid. They have also been chemically examined, and it was ascertained that they had experienced the same degree of decomposition as those of the reindeer and the horse; and that they were covered with precisely the same incrustations. The tombs appeared to be "orientated," or turned from east to west; but the bodies did not appear to have been deposited in any particular direction.

The flint implements of Solutré.

The style of the worked flints, says M. de Mortillet, shows that they belong to the *end* of the quaternary epoch. They are no longer the rude instruments, shaped *à grands éclats*, of the first quaternary period, but beautiful pieces, finely worked *à petits coups*, which, by their form and their very careful work, appear to constitute a *transition* between the stone which was simply *chipped* and that which was *polished*.

There is a marked resemblance to the industry of Laugerie-Haute. The fauna at Laugerie-Haute is very nearly the same,—mammoth, reindeer, and hyæna.

The implements from Laugerie-Haute were so superior that this station was thought to be *an exceptional case*, and it was selected to characterize what was called the *Reindeer epoch*, and as being later than Moustier, and La Madelaine, and Les Eyzies.

But Solutré is an advance on Laugerie-Haute, and seems to belong to a period between the epoch of the Reindeer and that of Polished Stone.

M. Dupont has also discovered a third station, at Pont-à-Lesse, in Belgium, characterized by the olive-leaf-shaped flints of Laugerie-Haute and Solutré.

In the same volume of "Matériaux pour l'Histoire de l'Homme" (p. 102) there is a letter from M. de Ferry to M. de Mortillet, from which we learn that in the tomb of the Finnish female referred to, the slabs were so well joined "que l'intérieur se trouvait encore en partie vide."

At p. 108 M. Arcelin is represented as writing to say that he ought not to have been put down as assigning Solutré (along with M. de Ferry and Mr. Franks) to the period between the Reindeer epoch and that of Polished Stone. He refers it to the period of Laugerie-Haute, and regards it as a "development" of the period of Moustier. He speaks, however, of new "types" at Solutré, and of "certain fragments of hard rock which had been polished by rubbings (frottements)."

M. de Mortillet, noticing the statements with regard to the closely-jointed slabs, observes that work of that sort could not have been executed in the Palæolithic Age. Thereupon M. de Ferry (p. 154) writes that the region of Solutré furnishes naturally slabs, *parallélogrammiques*, which one can easily raise and detach with the aid only of a bit of wood of moderate strength. The slabs bear no traces of work,—except of a very rude kind.

At p. 274 M. de Mortillet has visited Solutré, and declares himself a convert to the views of M. de Ferry and M. Arcelin.

At p. 317 there is another notice of this station. The only additional statements brought out are, that in the Horse-deposit we find here and there a few flint fragments or knives; noticeable in this, that they were *new*, and had never been used. (So it was in the grave of the Finnish woman, where these flint instruments were found.)

The Sepultures.

We are told here that the sepultures occur with slabs and without slabs. The first are found over the Horse-débris, and among the kitchen-débris *on the hearths* (the hearths, in short, were used as burial-places); the second occur on the Horse-débris, on the hearths, and in the ordinary soil. These last are scattered over the area of the kitchen débris, and contain bones of the reindeer and the horse, sometimes charred, and flints.

The sepultures on the fire-places are so numerous that they frequently almost touch one another. Most of the hearths support one or more skeletons, the depth of which from the surface corresponds invariably with the depth of the hearth itself. If the hearth is found at $0^{m}.60$, the skeleton is at $0^{m}.60$; if the hearth is at $1^{m}.50$, or $1^{m}.80$, the skeleton is at the same depth. These skeletons lie extended (this reminds us of Sir John Lubbock's remarks about the peculiarity of the Iron Age) on the back, and are for the most part complete and intact,—the bones all in place and in perfect order, and having apparently been subjected to a moderate heat (the fire-places).

There are large hearths and smaller hearths. Adults lie on the former; children—often young infants—on the latter. There is (it is not stated just here, but elsewhere) a great proportion of *aged persons.* The occupants of Solutré did not destroy their aged relatives, as was the fashion in Britain and Ireland even in post-Christian times.

M. de Mortillet pronounces the Crot du Charnier simply and only a *cemetery.* In this opinion we do not concur.

The subject of Solutré is recurred to in the fifth volume of "Matériaux pour l'Histoire de l'Homme" (1869), and we are told that the lance-heads are "admirably fashioned" with an edge "the most delicate and skillful;" "comme le preuve le peu d'épaisseur des pièces, leur peu de convexité médiane, et la manière dont les éclats ont été détachés, dans bien des cas, *d'un seul coup* d'un bord à l'autre. Il faut se rapporter à l'époque des beaux instruments des pays Scandinaves pour retrouver le même savoir-faire."

This work gives representations of these implements. They are of superb execution, and (saving the polish) equal to the very best stone implements of any age. Referring to fig. No. 11, Plate XXV., M. de Mortillet speaks of it as "cette pièce magnifique," and of "la finesse de sa taille." Fig. 2, Plate XXX., he says, offers an edge which has not been surpassed in the best specimens of Denmark.

M. Pruner-Bey.

Speaking of the crania from Solutré, M. Pruner-Bey says, with enthusiasm, "Cet homme quaternaire est constitué homme dans toute la force du terme. Rien dans son physique n'indique un rapprochement avec les Simiens . . . rien de la brute dans ses us et coutumes, dans ses croyances," and much more to the same purport.

We find the next notice of this station in the second *livraison* or issue for 1873 of the publication from which the above statements are taken. It is found in a review of a paper on Solutré by MM. Ducrost and Lortet. These gentlemen have re-examined the beds of Solutré. Their conclusions agree substantially with those reached by MM. de Ferry and

Arcelin, and M. de Mortillet. There is a want of concurrence with regard to the *amas de débris de chevaux*. These the last explorers consider to be refuse bones from the kitchen, and *not* associated with any funeral rites. These authors estimate the number of horses represented in this deposit as high as ten thousand.

The station of Solutré came up, finally, before the *Association Française pour l'Avancement des Sciences* at Lyons in 1873,* where the whole ground was gone over, and certain points, hitherto doubtful, were apparently definitively settled.

The subject before the French Association at Lyons.

We learn that the fauna of this palæolithic settlement consists of the following animals: *Elephas primigenius, Cervus Canadensis, Ursus arctos, Ursus spelæus, Canis vulpes, Canis lupus, Felis spelæa, Felis lynx, Saiga, Lepus timidus, Arctomys primigenius,* the badger, the reindeer, the horse, etc.

In the *amas de chevaux*, it is believed now that we have the remains of from *thirty to forty thousand horses*. Indeed, it is stated that the number may ultimately turn out to be double or treble as many as this.

Forty thousand horses.

Another important fact now ascertained is, that this deposit does not, as was before believed, consist exclusively of the Horse: nearly all the fauna of the "fire-places"—in small quantities, it is true—has been found here, as well as knives and other fragments of flint.

Speaking of the graves, it is stated that the bodies are disposed from east to west.

The cotemporaneity of the graves and the animal bones and quaternary flints is established.

The Abbé Ducrost mentioned that he had found a fire-place or hearth, completely isolated, on which reposed a skeleton, *and which was surrounded by a circle of stones*. Is this the origin of the *cromlech?*

A valuable paper was read by M. Toussaint on "The Horse of Solutré." From this we gather that "the skeleton of the horse of Solutré, compared with that which we actually possess, exhibits very slight differences." The height varied from $1^{m}.38$ to $1^{m}.45$.

The horse domesticated.

M. Toussaint considers the question, Was the Horse of Solutré *domesticated?* and reaches an affirmative conclusion.

MM. Lartet, Christy, and Dupont, he says, ascertained that in many of the palæolithic stations one meets with *only certain parts* of the skeletons of the animals whose remains occur, such as the head, the first cervical vertebræ, etc.: the vertebræ and the sides are generally want-

* Reported in Matériaux, 7e, 8e, et 9e Livraisons for 1873.

ing. These authors conclude that the animals were hunted, slaughtered where captured, and only the more readily handled parts carried back to their caves or dwelling-places, *which shows that the animals were not domesticated.*

But at Solutré we find all the parts of the Horse in their normal number. The conclusion follows that at this place this animal was slaughtered always *at the station*, and therefore must have been domesticated.

The close resemblance of the skeleton to that of the horse of our day is alone, according to M. Steenstrup, says M. Toussaint, proof that the animal was domesticated.

The skeletons belong for the great part to horses from three to nine years of age. This points also to domestication. The young horses were not killed; but no horses were allowed to grow old.*

The non-domestication of the reindeer is explained by the absence of the dog, which is necessary to preserve the reindeer in that condition.

As regards the reindeer, only certain parts of his skeleton are found at Solutré,—a proof that he was killed at a distance from the settlement, and these portions only of the carcass brought to the village.

Dr. Gosse (of Switzerland) remarked that the observations of M. Toussaint had converted him. He spoke of the Kirghis Cossacks who practise in our day the custom, on the death of any member of the tribe, of having hecatombs proportioned to the rank of the deceased. M. de Meyendorff, who was fourteen years Governor in the Caucasus, states that he several times assisted at funeral repasts where from two hundred to three hundred horses and from three thousand to four thousand sheep were slaughtered.

The prevailing opinion at the Association seemed to be against the idea of funeral rites; but perhaps it is true that the horse contributed to the daily diet of these people, and that on special occasions there were grand funeral repasts.

The third question discussed before the Association was the Flint Implements. M. de Mortillet referred to certain specimens which had been found by M. l'Abbé Ducrost "which could not be cotemporary with the quaternary deposits: certain stemmed arrow-heads, with barbs which are characteristic of the age of polished stone."

M. l'Abbé Ducrost replied, "Here in a few words are the reasons which caused me to adopt this idea of *transition*. I find at Solutré in

---

* M. Dupont made a remark at the Stockholm meeting of the Archæological Congress last summer which gives us to understand that the palæolithic horse was, in his opinion, domesticated. In the course of a paper on the domestic animals of pre-historic times, he dwelt on the horse, and observed that it existed in enormous numbers in the quaternary period, "and probably played," he added, "the same part in domestic life *as the ox plays now*" (our italics). Academy, Aug. 29, 1874, p. 239.

the hearths of the age of the reindeer: 1. A type derived from the type *Acheuléen*; 2. A type characteristic of the station named by M. de Mortillet *Solutréen*; 3. A transition from this type proceeding towards the type of polished stone; 4. A perfection of edge entirely identical with that of the polished stone age; 5. Instruments common to these two epochs." He cited particularly two whetstones and two arrow-heads with a distinct stem between the *barbs* (barbelures). He had found these objects himself in the talus and in the hearths.

Stemmed and barbed arrow-heads.

M. Arcelin regarded these specimens as "accidental."

M. E. Cartailhac thought that M. de Mortillet went too far when he did not admit two or three of the pieces of the superb collection of M. l'Abbé Ducrost to be cotemporaneous with the quaternary *gisement*. It had not been previously ascertained, but he thought it demonstrated to-day that these hunters who worked so well the flint and rock-crystal had arrived sometimes *à un système perfectionné de pointe de flèche*. He instanced an exploration not far from Dax in which he had been concerned during the current year with Captain Pottier, at a station which M. de Mortillet and himself regarded as similar to Solutré. He found there a grand lance-head with the stem well detached at the base of the triangular arrow. He found an identical specimen, but a little less rude, at Badegol (also synchronous with Solutré). He added that it was not to be forgotten that Laugerie-Haute, Badegol, St. Martin d'Excideuil, and other stations of this epoch had yielded stemmed points of a type quite peculiar, of an admirable work, and which are no longer found in the polished stone age. M. Cartailhac proceeded then to argue that this did not prove a *transition* from the palæolithic to the neolithic period, between which, he contended, there was, on the contrary, a *gap*.

Such are the facts at Solutré. Let it be remembered that we are now living in the days of the mammoth, the cave-hyæna, the cave-lion, and the reindeer,—the locality Central France. It is the age of the River-Gravel and of Le Moustier, for all the fine distinctions and subdivisions of the archæologists, as Mr. Boyd Dawkins has stated, are practically without foundation. The mammoth still lived in France. It is by the fauna that we must discriminate the ages. The implements were ruder at Le Moustier and in the Somme Valley, but we find an abundance of unpolished implements—of the rudest forms—in the Neolithic Age. They occur by hundreds in the Danish peat. All of the implements at Cissbury and Grime's Graves are unpolished and of the very rudest forms. In different localities more or less pains was taken with these instruments. Some tribes were more skillful and more advanced than others.

The significance of these facts.

Solutré belongs by general consent to the Palæolithic Age.

And of prime significance is the fact that *the phenomena here are upon a scale that leaves no room for misconception.* The genuine life of palæolithic man is depicted here in proportions that exclude all farther speculation. Elsewhere we find a grotto or a cavern, which had been occupied by an individual or by a few families; but here we have the home or the cemetery of a tribe, and, in the words of M. Pruner-Bey, we find palæolithic man "constituted man in all the force of that term." What signify that tender regard for the dead? that touching inhumation of the little childrén on the little hearths? that preservation of the aged, so unusual among savage tribes?

The graves are closed; carefully adjusted with closely-fitting slabs; provision is made for the wanderer to that unexplored land, of which the despised artisan of the "drift" took cognizance as we do; food is deposited in his narrow dwelling-place; his trusty weapons are laid beside him; and he himself (how much of human emotion follows him there!) is placed on the warm hearth-stone that comforted him and constituted his home in life.

One of these graves we find *surrounded by a circle of stones.* Are we mistaken in recognizing here the first glimpse that the past affords of the mysterious dolmen-builders? Perhaps we should not say the first; for, as we shall see, soon we shall catch another belonging to the same palæolithic era.

The weapons and tools of the tribe who occupied this settlement bring us fairly upon the men who fabricated the polished implements of the Swiss Lake-Villages and the Danish peat. For service, and in beauty of form, they were not inferior to the implements of these rather later periods. They were not polished or rubbed. But we have the stemmed and barbed arrow-heads which are notoriously characteristic of the polished stone age, as well as the whetstones.

The cuts on the following page will give an idea of the weapons found at Solutré.

To these burials and burial-rites, to these beautifully-finished implements, let us add the remarkable state of preservation in which the animal bones were found. The horns of the reindeer, when cut, "*yield the odor of fresh horn,*" and the bones "have preserved a considerable proportion of their gelatine." What do all of these circumstances combined indicate? Is it possible that Solutré is two hundred thousand years old?

Another observation which suggests itself from the facts presented here is, that we find men in those days *living in association.* There was an Organized Society.

At a meeting of the French Association Prof. Broca and Dr. Lagneau contradicted M. Pruner-Bey with regard to the Mongoloid type of the crania at Solutré. The former seems disposed to connect them with the north of Africa. We attach very little importance to the conclusions drawn one way or the other from craniology in connection with this subject. The *savans* are too little agreed among themselves, and we have observed that up to the present time all of the talk about *dolichocephalic*, *brachycephalic*, *kumbecephalic*, etc., ends only in confusion.

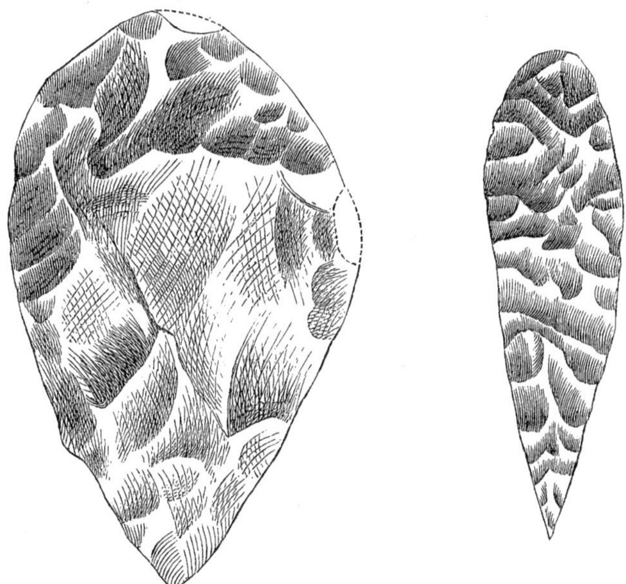

We have forty thousand—perhaps one hundred thousand horses at Solutré. We confess that this suggests to our mind the nomad tribes of Central Asia. However that be, it seems to be made out that the horse at this station was *domesticated;* and, if domesticated, this one fact alone destroys the hypothesis of a remote date for the population which lived at this time in France. The mere *number* of the horses appears to us incompatible with the belief that they were wild horses. And we see no reply to the statement of M. Toussaint that, while the reindeer is represented by only certain portions of the skeleton, all of the parts of the horse are present in their normal number.

The horse had not been domesticated in that ancient country when Abraham was in Egypt, and yet Egypt was a civilized state.

The Cave-men Esquimaux or Iberian.

The cave-men seem to be generally identified now with the Esquimaux. The similarity is so striking that it could hardly escape notice. We may add that the native term by which the Basque race designate themselves is "Escamara," which seems plainly connected with "Eskimo;" and the ancient Iberian or

Basque race, as is known, has been thought to be connected with the Finns. It was no doubt the Palæolithic race.

The reader will not fail to remark the obvious connection between the race which buried in the dolmens and barrows and the tribe which buried at Solutré. A cist was already used, and we find the same objects in the graves. We find, lastly, the circle of stones.

More than twenty years ago, Col. Hamilton Smith, in his excellent work on the "Natural History of the Human Species," described some very ancient interments, which resemble in some respects those at Solutré. In the district of Figeac, department of Lot, Southern France, are two mountains on opposite sides of the valley of the Sélé, in which occur certain caverns, at the height of three hundred feet above the level of the river. They are at a locality which seems to be connected with the ruins of certain circular and rectilinear forts, constructed with large stones. At this place, says Col. Smith, an unknown people, at a remote period, buried their dead. In 1825 one of these caverns was explored, and at the depth of three feet from the surface a human skeleton and an iron tool were found. At the depth of eighteen metres they struck a stone barrier of human work, through which having forced a passage, they came to three natural galleries. Following one of these, they came into a cavern containing many human bones, disposed around the cave, in the crevices of the rock, with evident care, some being pressed regularly into a cavity and covered with a flat slab, and surrounded by *a circle of very clean white stones.* The "barrier" to which we have referred was designed to block up the entrance to this grand vault, which Col. Smith describes as "a tribal necropolis," and which, he says, was formed with great respect for the dead.

Caves in the Valley of the Sélé.

With these remains were found the head and three teeth of a rhinoceros, the antlers of a small species of reindeer, the head of an extinct stag, the shoulder-blade of a very large bovine, and the canon bone of a horse.*

This is another example of a Palæolithic cemetery. The caves of Mentone and Aurignac testify on the same point.

We may properly mention here a very extraordinary discovery in the same department of France in which Solutré is situated (Saône-et-Loire). It is reported in the "Naturalist's Note-Book" for 1868.† The locality of this discovery was Chagny, and it was made by some workmen who were engaged in digging the foundations of a railway-station. At the depth of about nine metres, in a stratum of sandy clay and ferruginous oxides, the workmen

Remarkable discovery at Chagny.

* See Natural History of the Human Species, p. 163.

† P. 55. We cite this case, but the account is too meagre to be satisfactory.

encountered the remains of the elephant and rhinoceros, among them several back teeth and a formidable tusk in large fragments. The depth at which these remains were found was still six metres higher than the level of the highest floods of the Dheune, and in an undisturbed stratum. *Below* the remains (of "the tertiary period," as the "Naturalist's Note-Book" expresses it) was found "*an aqueduct of the most primitive kind*, and of human workmanship." This aqueduct is eighty centimetres deep by sixty broad at the bottom and forty broad at the top. M. Tremany remarks on this, that the negroes in Africa remove as little earth as possible in such works, and that this may account for the conduit being narrower at the top than at the bottom,—the small dimensions of the cavity being evidently due to the want of proper tools.

This evidence brings us in full view of the Palæolithic Age, with its fauna of the great extinct pachyderms and the cave-bear, cave-hyæna, reindeer, etc. We deem that it establishes beyond question the non-antiquity of the so-called First Stone Age.

Remains of the extinct animals occurring in the Polished Stone Age.

We now proceed, however, a step farther: we propose to show that the great animals of the Palæolithic Age (or some of them at least) were living *in the Polished Stone Age*,—in the past three thousand years. We have already mentioned Veyrier and Gourdan, which show the existence of the reindeer in France cotemporaneously with a Neolithic fauna. We will give another example of the same conditions by referring to the cave of Espalungues in the commune of Lourdes, Hautes-Pyrénées, explored by MM. Garrigou and Martin.

Cave of Espalungues.

In the upper layer of this cave the fauna was fox, horse, wild boar, stag, chamois, wild goat, reindeer, aurochs, ox, mole, field-mouse, sheep, etc. In their report MM. Garrigou and Martin say:

"Our examination of the bones collected by us from the upper bed leads to the same result that has been announced by Alph. Milne-Edwards after his investigations with M. Lartet. We conclude from the presence of the aurochs, the existence of domestic animals, the discovery of bones gnawed by dogs, the almost complete preservation of the gelatine in the bones and their deeper color, and by the discovery of a bone finely sculptured, that the upper beds belong to an age more recent than that of the lower beds. This we would call, as done by MM. Edwards and Lartet, the age of the Aurochs.

"As to the lower beds (the fauna of which corresponds with that of the upper beds) it is evident to us, from the abundant remains of the Reindeer, including large quantities of its horns; from the coarseness of its wrought objects, its worked flints, and its sculpture; from the reddish-brown color of the bones and from the absence of gelatine and their adhering to the tongue, that they pertain to an age more ancient than the preceding. It was the age of the Reindeer, parallel with that which we have distinguished in the grotto of Izeste." *

We have here together the Reindeer, the Sheep, and the Goat,—and the gelatine of their bones (in the upper bed) almost completely preserved. This fauna belongs, as we have said, to the age of Polished Stone.

The Reindeer was thus in Southern France during the Polished Stone era.

Now, if the Reindeer was in Southern France during the Neolithic Age, it is not difficult to imagine that the Mammoth was there a few centuries before.

Camp of Chassey.

We may mention another case precisely similar. We refer to the Camp of Chassey, on the Dheune (where the primitive aqueduct occurred). We learn from M. Perrault that he has examined a rock-shelter at this spot, on the summit of a steep hill between the valley of the Basses-Roches and that of the Dheune. He found here the remains of existing animals and of the reindeer, together with all kinds of polished stone implements, pottery resembling that of the Swiss lakes, earthen spoons, etc.†

We shall have occasion presently to mention the presence of the remains of the Reindeer in the Danish peat, which belongs to the Neolithic Age. They occur also in the English and Scotch peat. And we are told by M. Desor that the bones of the Great Irish Elk (which occur in the Irish peat) have been found also in the peat of the valley of the Somme, near St. Valéry.‡ We shall see farther in the progress of this work that the Irish Elk, as well as the Reindeer, lived down to a comparatively recent period.

Remains of the Cave-bear in the Neolithic Age.

We propose now to show that the cave-bear has been found with remains of the Neolithic Age,—considered by M. Figuier to be the oldest of all the palæolithic animals.

Sir John Lubbock (p. 291) informs us that the bones of this animal have been found in Italy "apparently in conjunction with a polished stone implement and even pottery." M. Regnoli has forwarded Sir John Lubbock a cast of the specimen (as we are told) on which this statement rests, and Sir John admits that it belongs to the cave-bear, "but can hardly regard it as being undoubtedly cotemporaneous with the pottery and the stone axe which were found near it." In Northern Europe, he proceeds to say, no such case has been met with.

We shall show by the following examples that the remains of the cave-

* Quoted in Amer. Jour. Sci., 1864, vol. xxxviii., S. Series, p. 277.

† American Naturalist, vol. v. p. 89.

‡ Palafittes of the Lake of Neufchâtel. Published in Smithson. Rep. for 1865, p. 400.

bear have been met with in association with polished stone implements in Northern Europe, in Southern Europe, and in Central Europe.

M. Regnoli has explored some seventy caverns in the mountains of Northern Italy. In more than one he found the bones and teeth of the cave-bear with polished stone weapons.

Grotta all' Onda.

In the Grotta all' Onda, at the foot of Mount Matanna, northwest of Camajore, near the source of the torrent Ombricese, he found instruments in bone and formed of the teeth of animals; arrow-tips, chisels, knives and scrapers of flint, obsidian, etc.; three instruments of polished stone; a polisher of serpentine; two axes, one of diorite, and the other of *jade;* fragments of rude pottery; four *barbed* arrow-heads of stone; bones and teeth of the cave-bear bearing traces of human work, and unworked bones of the cave-bear belonging to at least four individuals. The other animal remains were stag, hare, wild boar, badger, ox, sheep or goat, birds, etc.*

In noticing this case, the editor of "Matériaux pour l'Histoire de l'Homme" suggests† that there must have been some "remaniement" of the beds, and a lower bed from which the bones of the cave-bear have come. But there is no indication whatever of any disturbance of the strata; and *no lower bed,*—i.e., no bed below containing either flints or animal remains; and, in addition, some of the bones of the cave-bear are *worked,* and therefore belong, of course, to the other relics of human workmanship.

Grotto del Tamaccio.

The Grotto del Tamaccio, on the declivity east of Mount Cigoli, contained a number of human bones belonging to men, women, and children, together with bones of ox, stag, sheep, hog, etc. (the fauna of the Polished Stone Age), and the teeth of a bear which appeared to M. Regnoli to be *Ursus spelæus.* He says, "The Grotto of Tamaccio is a pre-historic sepulture probably cotemporary with the inhabitants of the Grotta all' Onda, and consequently of the epoch of the cave-bear."

Grotto of the Goths.

The Grotto of the Goths, or della Giovannina, in the mountain called Colle Maggiore, on the left of the torrent of Giannino, also explored by M. Regnoli, yielded charcoal; a human tooth; bones of the cave-bear, and bones of another species of bear; bones of stag, marmot, and ox; the worked tooth of a bear; a rude bodkin made of the cubitus of a bear; arrow-heads, pottery, etc. The objects manufactured by man belonged, we are told, to "the Neolithic period."‡

* Matériaux pour l'Histoire de l'Homme, tome iii. p. 496.

† Ib., 2e Série, tome iv., 3e Livraison, 1873, p. 142.

‡ Ib., 2e Série, tome iv., 1873, p. 144.

A similar association is mentioned by M. Lioz in a letter published in "Matériaux pour l'Histoire de l'Homme." * In the caverns of Velo, province of Verona, M. Lioz found "a complete and beautiful skull of the cave-bear," and among the numerous bones belonging to the same species he dug up a very fine (polished) axe of porphyry, and another of serpentine.

Caverns of Velo.

Here is yet another case, and this time occurring in France: we refer to the Grotto of Minerva (Aude). We find it stated that this cave "contained only bones of the Great Bear mingled with those of the horse, goat, sheep," etc.†

Also in France.

Mr. Boyd Dawkins informs us that "the presence of the sheep or goat, short-horned ox, and dog, was unknown in Europe before the Neolithic Age." ‡

We may, therefore, mention yet farther in this connection the *cavern of Nero*, in the valley of the Rhone, in the Vivarais, where were found a number of flint implements, associated with the bones of rhinoceros, elephant, horse, ibex, reindeer, stag, urus, aurochs, cave-bear, wild boar, cave-hyæna, and *dog*. The bones of the dog were found "among the flints and the other quaternary remains." "It has," says M. de Mortillet, "an appearance truly fossil, extremely ancient; it has exactly the same characters of antiquity as the other bones of the cavern of Nero: rhinoceros, bear, reindeer, hyæna." M. de Mortillet observes, however, that none of the other bones have been gnawed by dogs, and reaches, in consequence, the conclusion that the animal in question was "the domestic dog not yet domesticated." §

Cave of Nero.

We find in this cavern the same deposit of *loess* which we see in the Belgian caves and in the valley of the Somme. The waters which flooded it ran at a level seventy metres above the present level of the river.

There is, we learn, "no trace of disturbance" in the cave.||

Objects of the Neolithic Age have also been found in Austria associated with the remains of the extinct animals. In the caverns of Byciskála and of Shep, in Moravia, Dr. Wankel has discovered a great number of polished stone hatchets, worked bones, and pottery, in the same beds with the bones of the cave-bear and the cave-lion. And, so far as the existence of pottery in the Palæolithic Age is concerned, we are told that Count de Wurmbrandt found in the caverns of Peggau the same primeval carnivores and in the same earth numerous fragments of vases.¶

The extinct animals in Austria with polished stone implements.

* Tome i. p. 303.

† Ib., tome ii. p. 117.

‡ Macmillan's Mag., Dec. 1870.

§ Matériaux, Octobre, 1872, p. 432.

|| Ib., Février et Mars, 1872, p. 149.

¶ Ib., Janvier, 1872, p. 40.

Let us proceed with this testimony, which we regard as of the most important character. In the volume of the "Congrès International d'Anthropologie" for 1867,* containing the papers read at the meeting of the Congress in Paris, M. Reboux detailed before that body the discovery, in the quaternary gravel of Paris, of the remains of the reindeer, *with polished flint implements*, superimposed on the remains of the ox and rudely-worked flints, these last lying above the remains of the horse and the elephant, which were associated with flint fragments.

Same facts presented at Paris.

We have here, then, another instance of the association of the remains of the reindeer with polished stone implements; and we have below this the remains of some bovine animal; and, lastly, the remains of the elephant and horse. This brings close together again the Neolithic and Palæolithic Ages. There was no one or two hundred thousand years between the remains of the reindeer found at this place and those of the elephant; but probably a few centuries.

Once more: In the volume of the "International Congress of Prehistoric Archæology" for 1868,† we have an account of "Researches into the Caverns of Moncluses," etc., in Valencia, by Don Juan Vilanova y Piera, "belonging to the Palæolithic Age." We are informed in this paper that the author explored, among other caves in this region of Spain, that of Las Maravillas. He found here, at the depth of several metres, instruments belonging to "the first age," among them some very fine arrow-heads, "perfectly identical with those of the Swiss palafittes," mingled with the bones of the extinct mammifers. In the upper tiers of this deposit were more recent bones, mingled with fragments of Roman pottery.

Spain.

Cavern of Las Maravillas. Polished implements with bones of extinct mammalia.

So that we have here in Spain the beautiful implements of the Swiss Lake-Dwellings mingled with the remains of "the extinct mammifers" at the depth of eight or ten feet in the cave-soil. Another instance of the recent date of "the extinct mammifers" and of the nearness to each other in point of time, if not of the cotemporaneity, of the Neolithic and Palæolithic Ages.

With regard to Sir John Lubbock's remark that "in Northern Europe no such case has been met with," we have the express statement of Prof. Nilsson to the contrary. "Along the coast of the Baltic," he says, "from Ystad to Trälleborg and Falsterbo, there lies a ridge—consisting of gravel and stones—called the Jära-Wall." He then proceeds to state that under this ridge there are in several places peat-bogs, which lie beneath the surface of the sea. The Jära-Wall was

Sweden.

* Page 106–7.

† Page 398.

originated by a violent momentary motion in the waters of the Baltic, caused by a simultaneous sinking and rising of the northern part of the bottom of this sea. The stone implements, he says, are found in the peat (which was formed in fresh water) under Jära-Wall, where have also been found bones of the cave-bear in more than one place.

He farther states that in other peat-bogs (as that of Kullaberg) the bones of both the cave-bear and the reindeer have been found, and that flint flakes occur in this peat in great numbers.

He states, again, that "human productions and the bones of the cave-bear are met with together in our oldest peat-bogs, even in those that lie under Jära-Wall." *

The Holderness peat.

We have one instance mentioned of the occurrence of the remains of the cave-lion in the peat. Mr. C. Carter Blake gives an account of the finding of the bones of this animal in the peat at Holderness. The bones are in the Museum of the Hull Royal Institution. Mr. Blake states that they are from the Holderness peat, and in the museum were in juxtaposition with a series of red-deer bones from that formation.†

The caves of France still inhabited by man.

We may conclude these protracted remarks on the Bone-Caves by stating that the caves of France are inhabited even at this day. In the department of Aisne, in the north of France, as we are informed by M. Piette, the villages of the Troglodytes are yet numerous. In the canton of Craonne alone (where he resides) there are five, without counting the hamlets: Paissy, Geny, Pargnan, Comin, Neuville. Paissy has two hundred and fifty-six inhabitants; Geny, two hundred and twenty-six; Pargnan, two hundred and eleven; Comin and Neuville are now deserted. These villages consist of grottoes, formed by the hand of man, called *creutes* by the inhabitants. They are excavated in the limestone, " in beds so sandy and tender that they are disintegrated with the end of a stick. In the villages actually inhabited, houses have been constructed before the grottoes, and the rich inhabitants reside in these more elegant dwellings, leaving the *creutes* to their beasts. . . . The poor continue to live in the *creutes*, and their health is not affected by it."‡

NOTE.—We have intimated in the course of this discussion, in more than one place, that the ancient population of Western Europe probably belonged to the Iberian race. In the article on "The Antiquity of Man" in the *British Quarterly Review* for April, 1874, the opinion is expressed that this Basque or Iberian element was dominant in this region, at least, during the Neolithic Period. The writer observes that the numerous skeletons discovered in 1869 in the caves of Perthi Chwarcu, near Llandagla, in Wales, were examined

* Nilsson on the Stone Age, pp. 252, 254.

† Nature, May 11, 1871.

‡ Matériaux pour l'Histoire de l'Homme, Février et Mars, 1872, p. 124.

by Prof. Busk, and "shown to belong to a small, long-headed race, which Prof. Huxley and Dr. Thurnam believe to be represented at the present time by the modern Basques. . . . These cave-dwellers were also identified with the builders of the chambered tombs in this country." He adds that the skeletons found by Dr. Broca in the Neolithic cavern called the "Grotte de l'homme mort," in Southern France, belonged to the same race. The cave-dwellers of Gibraltar and the remains found in the caves of Andalusia by Don Gongora y Martinez, he refers likewise to the same race. "From a comparison of the skulls found in all these widely-separated spots with those obtained by Dr. Broca from the Basque cemeteries of Guipuscoa and St. Jean de Luz, and now in the collection of the Anthropological Society of Paris, it has been proved that the Basque, or Iberian, race lived, in ancient times, not merely in the Iberian Peninsula, but far to the north, away from the boundary of Cæsar's province of Aquitania, where the small, swarthy race is still ethnologically distinct from the taller, light-haired Celt, at least as far as Great Britain. In Wales it is recognized in the small, swarthy descendants of the Silures, and in Ireland in the 'dark Celts' living in the district to the west of the Shannon."

The archæologists are particularly fond of pointing out that there was a great and mysterious *lacuna* between the Palæolithic and Neolithic Ages. We shall, therefore, refer in this connection to the remarks of M. de Quatrefages before the French Academy on the occasion of the presentation of the second part of the "Crania Ethica." Describing what he calls the "Cro-Magnon race," he states that the male skull of Cro-Magnon is remarkable for its capacity,—according to M. Broca, gauging not less than 1590 cent. cubes, which is larger than the mean European skull of the present day. The characters were exemplified in the skulls found in Cro-Magnon in 1868.

With these skulls MM. de Quatrefages and Hamy class several other specimens from the palæolithic caves of Laugerie-Basse, Bruniquel, Aurignac, and Gourdan. The same race, we are told, is traced at Mentone, and beyond the Alps in the Neolithic skeletons of Cantalupo. The same skull again is found at Solutré and Grenelle, and re-appears in the celebrated Engis skull. The form is dolichocephalic. The authors remark, "Thus among these primitive savages who with their arms of stone have contended against the mammoth, we find combined almost all the craniological characters generally regarded as so many marks of a great intellectual development."

But farther: the man of Cro-Magnon, we are told, has also traversed the ages which separate us from those remote times. He is found at different pre-historic epochs: he existed down to modern times: he is still represented in a few individuals. . . . In the age of Polished Stone he left his traces in Belgium in the cavern of Hamoir, some leagues from the station of Engis; at Nieder-Ingelheim, on the Rhine (with Neolithic implements); and in the alluvions of Grenelle. We find him again at Chassemy, in a Gaulish sepulchre of the Iron Age, and in certain Basque skulls exhumed by MM. Broca and Velasco. "But it is to Africa that we must go to-day to find the representatives of the race which we are considering." The megalithic tombs of Roknia, explored by M. Bourguignot and General Faidherbe, have yielded a great many crania which resemble more or less those of Cro-Magnon. The same type occurs among the Kabyles, and especially among the Guanches of Teneriffe.*

We thus trace the Basque type through both the Neolithic and Palæolithic Ages. *The same race continued to occupy Western Europe.*

We avail ourselves of the opportunity afforded by this note to qualify what was said in the previous chapter, and in Chapter XIII., with regard to the bone flute found in the cave of Gourdan. Since those remarks were printed, we have observed that M. Piette refers this instrument of music to the Neolithic Period. It was found in the uppermost of the two principal relic-beds at Gourdan. M. Piette connects this bed with the Neolithic Age, but he remarks that no polished implements were found in it. He found one lance-head "of Neolithic form," and some knives and other flint implements very similar to those in the bed

* Comptes Rendus, No. 13, Mars, 1874, p. 861.

below, as well as fragments of rude pottery. The animal remains consisted of stag, ox, wild boar, and occasional jaw-bones of the reindeer.

This bed rested *immediately*, says M. Piette, without any intervening formation of any kind whatever, on the lower or "reindeer" bed. "On remarquera qu'entre la couche qui représente l'âge du renne et celle qui correspond aux temps néolithiques, aucun dépôt formé par le débordement des eaux ou par l'effet d'autres causes naturelles ne se trouve intercalé. Les foyers d'une époque succèdent à ceux de l'époque précédente, sans qu'on puisse saisir entre eux la trace d'une perturbation géologique. Leurs cendres n'ont été entraînées par aucun lavage; et si la présence d'une stalagmite épaisse annonce que certaines parties de la grotte ont été pendant longtemps inhabitées, dans les parties où la stalagmite n'existe pas, on dirait que les pasteurs néolithiques sont venus s'installer le lendemain du jour où les chasseurs de renne l'ont quittée pour n'y plus revenir." Matériaux, 2e Livraison, 1874.

The following animals are among those which occur in the lower bed at Gourdan: bear (*U. arctos*), beaver, wild boar, horse, wolf, fox, lynx, chamois, goat (*Capra primigenia*), ibex, stag, reindeer, rat, hare, elk, elephant, etc.

Among the drawings or etchings, there were representations of the rhinoceros, the mammoth (?), reindeer, saïga, chamois, stag, goat, lynx (?), elk, ox, horse, boar, wolf, seal, and fishes and birds.

This bed, therefore, is a genuine palæolithic bed, as proved by the presence of the mammoth and the rhinoceros. With these we find the reindeer and a modern fauna in many respects.

Among the remains of birds, M. Piette is astonished to find those of the *hen*, which, however, he says, has been signalled in several caverns, particularly at Lherm. This fowl does not seem to have been known to the Greeks in the days of Homer and Hesiod; and as late as the time of Pericles it was designated under the name of *the bird of Persia*. From Greece it passed to the table of the Romans.

Finally, in this interesting station, where we find the palæolithic and neolithic faunas apparently intermingled, and where the specimens of art are equal almost to that represented in our frontispiece from Thäyngen, the flint weapons are, perhaps, superior to those at Solutré, and among them we find in the article of M. Piette representations of *barbed arrow-heads*.

CHAPTER XVI.

THE RIVER-GRAVEL OF FRANCE AND ENGLAND.

M. Boucher de Perthes's Discoveries in the Gravel of the Somme Valley.—The "Antiquités Celtiques et Antédiluviennes."—Dr. Rigollot.—Dr. Falconer's Endorsement of the Genuineness of the Flint Implements.—The Visit of Messrs. Prestwich, Evans, Lyell, and Murchison to Abbeville.—Sir Charles Lyell's Opinion.—Works of Art in the Gravel. —Date of the Glacial Age.—Mr. John Evans on the Antiquity of these Deposits.—The Formidable Appearance of the Case.—The Implements of Human Workmanship.—Ideal Section of Valley where they are found.—Section of the Valley of the Somme.—The Theory of Sir J. Lubbock and Sir C. Lyell with regard to the Excavation of the Valley and of the Deposition of the Lower-level Gravel after this was accomplished.—The Hypothesis of a Marine Cataclysm.—M. D'Orbigny's Theory of a Fresh-Water Cataclysm.—Dr. Andrews's Paper in the American Journal of Science.—Rejects the Excavation Theory. —Believes the Volume of Water in the Somme to have reached formerly the Level of the Upper Gravel.—Ice.—Conclusions of Dr. Andrews.—His Views with regard to the Rate of Formation of the Peat.

Discoveries of M. Boucher de Perthes.

IN 1841 M. Boucher de Perthes observed in some sand containing mammalian remains, near Abbeville, on the Somme River, in France, a flint, rudely shaped into a cutting instrument. In the following years similar weapons, denominated "hatchets," were discovered in the so-called "drift" gravel in the neighborhood of Abbeville. In 1846 M. Boucher de Perthes published an account of these discoveries in a volume entitled "De l'Industrie Primitive, ou les Arts et leur Origine." He claimed to have found traces of the human race in the deposits of the drift, and in association with the remains of the great extinct pachyderms. In 1847 he published his "Antiquités Celtiques et Antédiluviennes." The scientific public, however, lent an inattentive ear to his representations, and the late "prophet of Abbeville" was, prior to 1859, regarded as merely a visionary enthusiast. Dr. Rigollot had believed, it is true, in the interim; but it was not until the year mentioned that public attention was fully aroused on the subject. The late Dr. Hugh Falconer happened at that time to be passing through Abbeville, and he took occasion to examine the collection of M. Boucher de Perthes, and was seriously impressed. On his return to England he communicated the facts to Mr. Prestwich and other geologists, and in 1860 Mr. Prestwich, Mr. Evans, Sir R. Murchison, Sir Charles Lyell, Sir John Lubbock, and other British scientists visited the valley of the Somme. These gentlemen confirmed the statements of M. Bou-

Dr. Rigollot.

Dr. Falconer.

He calls the attention of the British Geologists and Antiquarians to the subject.

cher de Perthes as to the character of the stratum in which the implements were found, as to their being the work of human hands, and as to the mammalian remains with which they were associated. Sir John Lubbock published a paper on the subject in "The Natural History Review;" Mr. Prestwich communicated the results of the visit to the Royal Society; and Mr. Evans reported to the Society of Antiquaries. Since this time a great many discoveries of similar flints have been made by MM. de Quatrefages, Lartet, etc., in France; by Messrs. Warren, Evans, Leech, Wyatt, etc., in England; by Mr. Bruce Foote in India, etc., etc.

They are all convinced.

Geologists and antiquarians in general assign an indefinite antiquity to these remains. We have already quoted from Sir Charles Lyell and Sir John Lubbock to this effect. We may add to the remarks of the former the following in the same connection: "Between the present era and that of the earliest vestiges of our race yet discovered [referring to the fluviatile drift of Amiens and Abbeville], valleys have been deepened and widened; the course of subterranean rivers which flowed through caverns has been changed; and many species of wild quadrupeds have disappeared. The bed of the sea, moreover, has in the same ages been lifted up in many places hundreds of feet above its former level, and the outlines of many a coast have been entirely altered."

Remarks of Sir C. Lyell. The antiquity of the remains.

And again: at the meeting of the British Association in 1859, Sir Charles Lyell delivered an address, in which he said, "I am fully prepared to corroborate the conclusions which have been recently laid before the Royal Society by Mr. Prestwich, in regard to the age of the flint implements associated in undisturbed gravel, in the north of France, with the bones of elephants at Abbeville and Amiens. . . . The stratified gravel resting immediately on the chalk in which these rudely-fashioned instruments are buried belongs to the post-pliocene period, all the fresh-water and land shells which accompany them being of existing species. The great number of the fossil instruments which have been likened to hatchets, spear-heads, and wedges is truly wonderful. More than a thousand of them have already been met with in the last ten years, in the valley of the Somme, in an area fifteen miles in length. I infer that a tribe of savages, to whom the use of iron was unknown, made a long sojourn in this region; and I am reminded of a large Indian mound which I saw in St. Simond's (or St. Simon's) Island, in Georgia,—a mound ten acres in area, and having an average height of five feet,—chiefly composed of castaway oyster-shells, throughout which arrow-heads, stone axes, and Indian pottery are dispersed. If the neighboring river, the Altamaha, or the sea which is at hand, should invade, sweep away, and stratify the contents of this mound, it might produce a very analogous accumulation of human implements, unmixed perhaps with human bones. Although the accompanying shells are of living species, I believe the antiquity of the Abbeville and Amiens flint instruments to be great indeed if compared to the times of history or tradition."

And once more: "The deepening and widening of valleys, indicated by the position of the river-gravels at various heights, implies an amount of change of which that which has occurred during the historical period forms a scarcely perceptible part. . . . The three or four thousand years of the historical period does not furnish us with any appreciable measure for calculating the number of centuries which would suffice for such a series of changes, which are by no means of a local character, but have operated over a considerable part of Europe."*

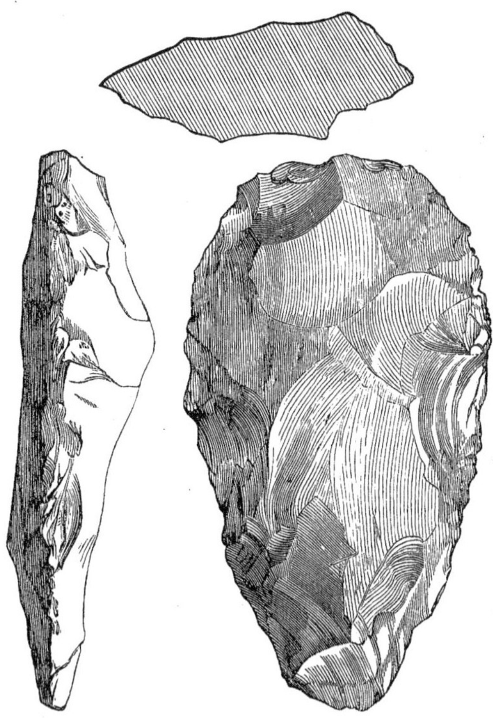

FLINT HATCHET FROM THE RIVER-GRAVEL.

M. Boucher de Perthes goes a step beyond what so far we have represented with regard to his views. He believes that he found in the "drift" other traces of human art than the rude weapons and cutting instruments which we have described. He insists that he found "sym-

* Student's Elements of Geology, p. 162.

bolical" flints shaped to represent men and animals; he affirms that he found flints carved into representations of the human head, and representing the rhinoceros, the mammoth, etc.; he even states that the human type represented belongs to the Caucasian race, and more rarely the negro race.

Carved figures alleged to have been found.

If this be true, it is a strong argument for the recent date of the remains found in the river-gravel.

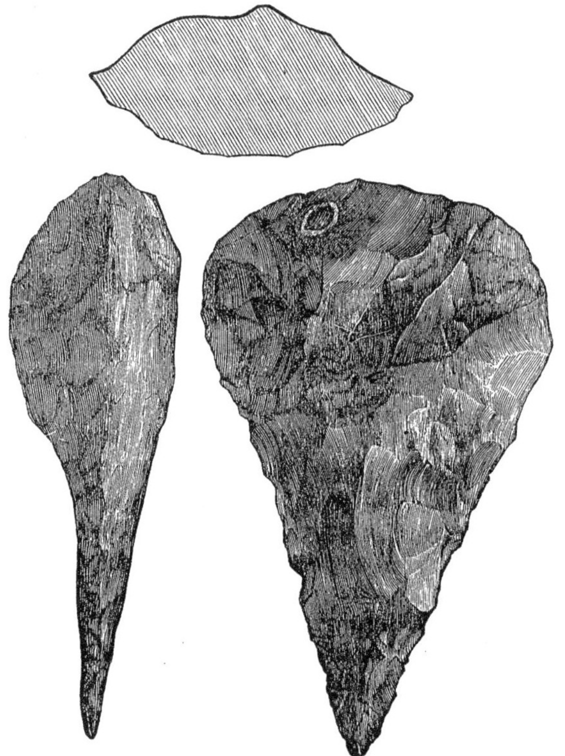

SPEAR-HEAD FROM THE RIVER-GRAVEL.

It is generally agreed that the "river-gravel" was deposited just upon the close of the Glacial Age; and Sir Charles Lyell estimates that this was about eight hundred thousand years ago.* Sir John Lubbock regards this as probably too long, and suggests in the place of it one hundred thousand to two hundred and forty thousand years.†

The Glacial Epoch.

* See Pre-historic Times, p. 412.

† Ib., p. 414. We believe that in his last edition of the "Antiquity of Man," Sir C. Lyell also fixes the date of the Glacial Age at two hundred thousand years ago; dropping abruptly from eight hundred thousand to two hundred thousand.

Mr. Evans, in his learned and elaborate work, "The Ancient Stone Implements of Great Britain," expresses himself as follows with regard to the antiquity of the implements found in the river-gravel:

Mr. John Evans on the river-gravel.

"But when we remember that the traditions of the mighty and historic city [London] now extending across the valley [of the Thames] do not carry us back even to the close of that period of many centuries when a bronze-using people occupied this island; when we bear in mind that beyond that period lies another of probably far longer duration, when our barbaric predecessors sometimes polished their stone implements, but were still unacquainted with the use of metallic tools; when to the Historic, Bronze, and Neolithic Ages we mentally add that long series of years which must have been required for the old fauna, with the mammoth and the rhinoceros, and other to us strange and unaccustomed forms, to be supplanted by a group of animals more closely resembling those of the present day; and when, remembering all this, we realize the fact that all these vast periods of years have intervened since the completion of the excavation of the valley, and the close of the Palæolithic Period, the mind is almost lost in amazement at the vista of antiquity displayed." P. 622.

It must in candor be admitted that such statements present a formidable front. In the first place we have to explain the association of the human implements with the bones of the extinct mammifers. This does not occur once, nor in one locality. It occurs at several points in the Somme Valley, and it occurs in many other river-valleys,—in Germany and Italy as well as in France and England. In the next place we have to explain the position of the flints in this ancient gravel one hundred feet above the river-level in a valley fully a mile wide; and then (at a lower level) on this gravel the peat is superimposed with a thickness of twenty-five or thirty feet.

The facts present a formidable appearance.

The advocate of the view of the recent origin of man must not only establish the probability of the recent presence in France and England of the mammoth and the reindeer, but he must also show that the gravel is a recent deposit. This is a part of the task we have assigned ourselves in this work. We ask only the reader's attention to the facts we shall lay before him.

It is admitted that the flint implements are of human workmanship, and that they are cotemporaneous with the animal remains found associated with them.

In order to a clear understanding of the question, it is important to have before us a distinct conception of the manner in which the different beds composing these river-valleys are laid down. We therefore reproduce the following ideal section of one of

Ideal section of these valleys.

these valleys from the last edition of Lyell's "Student's Elements of Geology." It is, as stated, an ideal section, and applies to other European valleys than that of the Somme.

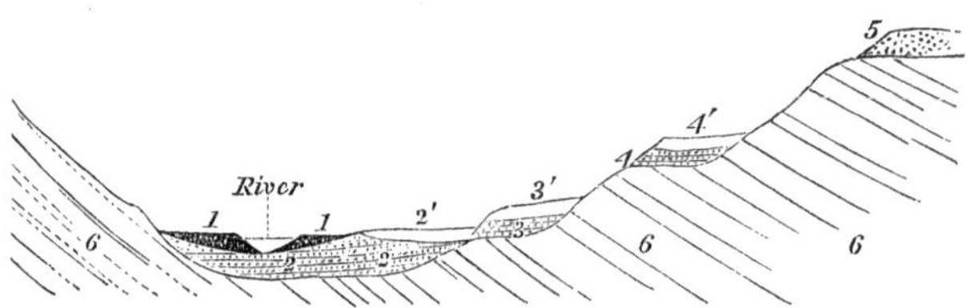

"The peat No. 1," he says, "has been formed in a low part of the modern alluvial plain, in parts of which gravel No. 2 of the recent period is seen. Over this gravel the loam or fine sediment 2' has in many places been deposited by the river during floods which covered nearly the whole alluvial plain.

"No. 3 represents an older alluvium, composed of sand and gravel, formed before the valley had been excavated to its present depth. It contains the remains of fluviatile shells of living species associated with the bones of mammalia, in part recent, and in part of extinct species. Among the latter, the mammoth (*E. primigenius*) and the Siberian rhinoceros (*R. tichorinus*) are the most common in Europe. No. 3' is a remnant of the loam or brick-earth by which No. 3 was overspread. No. 4 is a still older and more elevated terrace, similar in its composition and organic remains to No. 3, and covered in like manner with its inundation-mud, 4'. Sometimes the valley-gravels of older date are entirely missing, or there is only one, and occasionally there are more than two, marking as many successive stages in the excavation of the valley. They usually occur at heights varying from ten to one hundred feet, sometimes on the right and sometimes on the left side of the existing river-plain, but rarely in great strength on exactly opposite sides of the valley.

"Among the genera of extinct quadrupeds most frequently met with in England, France, Germany, and other parts of Europe, are the elephant, rhinoceros, hippopotamus, horse, great Irish deer, bear, tiger, and hyæna. In the peat No. 1, and in the more modern gravel and silt (No. 2), works of art of the ages of iron and bronze, and of the later or Neolithic stone period, already described, are met with. In the more ancient or Palæolithic gravels, 3 and 4, there have been found of late years in several valleys in France and England—as, for example, in those of the Seine and Somme, and of the Thames and Ouse, near Bedford—stone implements of a rude type, showing that man co-existed in those districts with the mammoth and other extinct quadrupeds of the genera above enumerated." *

Section of the Somme Valley.

Here is another diagram, from Sir Charles Lyell's "Antiquity of Man."† It represents a section of the valley of the Somme.

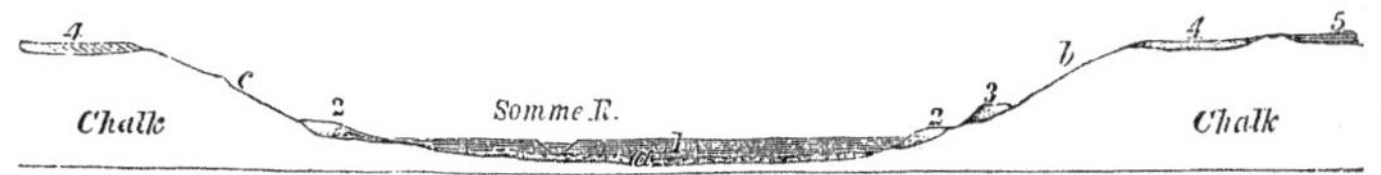

The average width of the valley of the Somme between Amiens and Abbeville is about one mile. The height, therefore, says Sir Charles, of the hills, in relation to the river-plain, could not be correctly represented in this diagram, the hills having been reduced to one-fourth of their altitude. It would have been otherwise necessary to make the space between *a* and *b* four times as great.

Lyell and Lubbock represent the flints to have been deposited before these valleys were excavated.

The theory of Sir John Lubbock and Sir Charles Lyell is that the river has excavated this valley before the formation of the peat and the deposit of the alluvium 2′ in the diagram; in which peat and alluvium we find the Roman, Gallo-Roman, and Celtic remains, and the polished stone implements of the Neolithic age. That the Somme River, for example, deposited the Palæolithic gravels during the process of excavating the valley, and with the gravel the bones of the extinct mammals, and the rude flint implements. As there are two gravel deposits,‡—the high-level and the low-level gravels,—ages are supposed to have passed between the deposit of the first and the deposit of the second; for the little stream, probably a few inches deep, as it straggled over the valley, a mile or a mile and a half wide,—and it is not supposed to have had a greater volume of water than at present,—had to excavate the valley in the mean time.

A Cataclysm.

M. Boucher de Perthes, however, attributes the formation of the gravel-beds to a cataclysm. "Cet éléphant, cette hache, ou la main qui la fabriqua, furent donc témoins du cataclysme qui donna à notre pays sa configuration présente."

The celebrated French geologist, M. D'Orbigny, connected the phenomena with "immense inundations of *fresh* water," rejecting the theory of marine action. This is based on the absence in general of marine fossils.

We are not inclined to adopt the theory of a marine inundation, but

* Lyell's Student's Elements, pp. 151–2. † P. 107.

‡ There is, as we shall urge, only one continuous deposit.

it is proper to point out that the absence of a marine fauna in the gravel does not by any means disprove that such a region was once submerged by the sea. As has been well remarked,* a marine fauna requires a marine flora to sustain it, and unless the submergence continued for a long period, there could have been no marine flora. There are extensive marine deposits of older date, in which no marine organisms are ever seen; and if the marine fossils are wanting in the river-gravel, those of the land and fresh water are usually equally wanting. There are probably hundreds of square miles of quaternary gravels in which not a single specimen has ever been discovered. In those instances in which they occur, comparatively rare, in the implement-bearing beds, they are usually lying above the gravel, and may be thus ascribed to a later date; or if of an earlier date in some instances, their occurrence would not of necessity exclude *diluvial* action, as regards the gravels.

The hypothesis of a marine cataclysm.

To the theory of a cataclysm of any sort, it is urged in reply by Sir John Lubbock, that the transport of materials has not followed any particular direction, but has in all cases followed the lines of the present valleys and the direction of the present water-courses; that the rocks of one valley are never transported into another; that the condition of the loess is irreconcilable with a great rush of water; while, finally, the perfect preservation of many of the most delicate shells is clear proof that the phenomena are not due to violent or cataclysmic action.

Lubbock's reply to the suggestion of a cataclysm.

In the *American Journal of Science and Art* for October, 1868, there is an admirable paper in reply to the views of Messrs. Prestwich, Lyell, and Lubbock, by Professor Edmund Andrews of Chicago, the substance of which is as follows:

Dr. Andrews states that the river Somme at Amiens is a small stream, apparently some fifty feet in width, meandering along the flat floor of an ancient water-course of much greater dimensions. The valley is about a mile and a half in breadth from summit to summit of the bluffs, and not far from two hundred feet in depth. In the lower part of its course it is purely a valley of erosion excavated in soft chalk; but above Amiens it expands into wide irregular basins, which are apparently the natural undulations of the surface which existed before the land rose from the sea, and which are now connected by valleys of erosion extending from one to another. Upon the floor of this valley and extending far up the slopes of the sides in many places are the famous gravel-beds, which sometimes attain a thickness of twenty feet. Upon the lowland gravels rests a bed of peat about twenty-six feet thick.

Dr. Andrews on the Valley of the Somme.

* Nature, July, 1872. Review of Mr. Evans's book.

The gravel of the Somme is not the genuine glacial drift, such as bears this name in America, but simply a river-deposit of more recent date. It is restricted exclusively to the valley, and resembles the gravel-beds flanking the river-valleys of the Western States, which also contain the bones of elephants, and are invariably found above the true drift.

Near Amiens, proceeds Dr. Andrews, whose article we are condensing, he observed evidence that at the time the deposit was formed, blocks of ice, or of mixed ice and frozen gravel, three or four feet in diameter, were laid down in the strata, and that these blocks were completely covered and had other strata laid above them, before they had time to melt. There is also proof that the river which did this work had a volume of not less than one thousand times that of the ordinary summer stream of the Somme. The facts are these: the mass of the upper gravels consists of chalk flints mixed with angular fragments, powder of crushed chalk, and rolled chalk pebbles, the whole being of a light-gray tint. Above this there is a stratum of gravelly clay of a blackish-brown color, a few inches in thickness. Over this is gravel of a lighter brown, and above that, next to the soil, there is about eighteen inches of a brown clay used for making brick. In the gray gravel there are places where the upper strata have sunk down as if into a cavity, filling it with material belonging higher up. The uppermost strata of all are undisturbed in position, as though the sinking had occurred, and the surface been washed level again, before the latter were laid down. One of the best examples was on the south side of the upper gravel-pit, above Amiens, where the perpendicular bank showed a fine section of the strata. At this place the stratum of gray gravel was missing for a horizontal distance of about four feet, the space being filled with confused materials from the dark-colored stratum above. The sides of the interrupted space were nearly perpendicular, and the dark stratum had evidently stretched across the void space,—and had settled and broken in the centre, the parts falling in against the sides of the open space, and hanging perpendicularly, the material from above then falling in. The conclusion is plain that this void space was once filled by a block of ice (containing probably gravel), which melted and left the space unoccupied for a season. On this ice the dark stratum was deposited before the ice melted, and therefore with great rapidity. An examination of the gray gravel adjacent confirms the idea of ice-action. It consists of chalk flints mixed with broken chalk of every size. Many of the fragments, which are exceedingly soft, have preserved perfectly the sharp edges which they had at the time they were broken from the cretaceous strata. It does not seem possible they could have been rolled a hundred feet in the bed of the stream without losing this sharpness. It follows that much of this material was either dropped from floating

Ice-action.

ice, or deposited by the mechanical action of ice-fields floating down the ancient river, which crushed the edges of chalk strata abutting on the valley, and pushed the débris along to be left wherever the irregularities of the channel permitted. The agency of ice is also emphatically indicated by the presence of large boulders of sandstone in the gravel, some of which weigh a ton. These must have been transported from far up the stream, as the rocks in the vicinity are exclusively chalk.

Notice of the Excavation theory.

It will be remembered that Sir John Lubbock contends that the valley of the Somme was excavated by the gentle action of the river through thousands of years, with about the present volume of water. Dr. Andrews remarks on this, that the valley is a mile and a half wide at the top,—the present river being about fifty feet in breadth. The present stream spread over the valley would have a depth of about half an inch,—making allowance for spring floods. This is entirely and obviously inadequate to the production of gravel-beds containing pebbles larger than a man's head, and boulders weighing a ton. The valley presents none of the characteristics of one widened by the fluctuations of an irregular stream, now eroding this bank and now that. "It is broad, level-floored, and parallel-banked." The stream that excavated it filled it from bluff to bluff. The marginal gravel-banks are often fifteen or twenty feet thick, and have horizontal strata. It follows that when the upper strata were laid down, the stream during its floods was a mile and a half wide and not less than twenty feet deep.

Conclusions of Dr. Andrews.

The conclusions which Dr. Andrews draws from these facts are:

1. That the ancient river, and consequently the ancient annual rainfall, were for a time, respectively, immensely larger and greater than at present.

2. The rapidity of the gravel deposit was, at least in some places, very great, and the time required for it proportionately short.*

His remarks on the peat.

Dr. Andrews next directs his attention to the *peat* (which, he says, is about twenty-six feet in thickness). M. Boucher de Perthes estimates that this was formed at the rate of about one and a half or two inches in a century, which would give an age of from fifteen thousand to twenty thousand years for the whole bed. Sir John Lubbock, we have seen, finds it at fifteen feet below the surface representative of the Neolithic period, and "of no slight antiquity." Dr. Andrews says,

* We learn from Dr. Andrews that the Somme gravels are not laid down in terraces, as Sir J. Lubbock and others affirm. They lap from the slopes like a blanket, and, though the strata are often nearly horizontal, there is no terrace-like shape.

"Mr. Boucher de Perthes has with praiseworthy care sought to determine the age of this bed; but, as he was probably unacquainted with the phenomena of forest peats in process of actual formation, he has very excusably overlooked some of the most important data." "Such an error," he says, "is not to be blamed in Europe; because where few trees are allowed to grow, and none to decay, the study of such phenomena is impossible." Boucher de Perthes states that he has found deep in the peats of the Somme numerous trunks of trees standing erect where they grew, generally birches, or alders. These trunks were sometimes a metre (39.14 inches) in height, but generally less. On this Dr. Andrews remarks that as stumps of trees do not stand long uncovered in the damp air of a swamp without decay, it follows that all which are found standing erect in the peat must have been covered to their present summits before they had time to rot away. Applying M. Boucher de Perthes's estimate of one and a half or two inches in a century for the growth of the peat, the above-mentioned stump must have stood uncovered without decay from one thousand nine hundred and fifty to two thousand six hundred years! Now, one hundred years is a long lifetime for an oak-stump under such circumstances, and every trace of almost every other tree would disappear in fifty years. Birch-stumps are especially perishable. There were prostrate trunks of oak in the peat four feet in diameter, and so sound that they were manufactured into furniture. They must have been covered by the peat in a hundred years. The rest of the calculation is easily made.

The erect stumps of trees in the peat prove its rapid formation.

Estimate of Boucher de Perthes.

Dr. Andrews remarks that the observation of Boucher de Perthes, that the growth of the peat is so slow as to be wholly imperceptible to the modern inhabitants, is doubtless true, and very easily explained. The peat-beds of the Somme belong to the class of forest peats, and not to that of moss growths. Forest peats, as may be seen in thousands of localities in the United States, are formed as follows. The annual crop of fruit, twigs, leaves, and windfall trunks, furnished by the trees and shrubbery of a dense swamp, amounts to an immense mass of vegetable matter. These, added to a thick undergrowth of grass, herbs, and moss, are all pressed against the ground by the winter snows. In the spring they are flooded and protected from decay. In the summer they are partly protected from oxygenation by the extreme wetness of the soil into which they have been pressed. Hence they are only slightly rotted when they are finally covered up by the fall of the next autumn's crop. To one who studies the actual quantity of this material, a growth of two or three feet in a century is by no means improbable. The increase of the peat *depends upon the presence of the forests.* But the forests of the Somme Valley have dis-

Forest peats.

appeared centuries ago. It is not therefore remarkable that M. Boucher de Perthes could not observe any perceptible increase of the peat at the present time. Hardly an ounce even of grass or a stick of wood ever rots at present upon the valley, every particle of vegetable matter being carefully appropriated for the use of the inhabitants. About Amiens the ground is all drained, and used for market gardens, and in other parts it is all sown for crops, mown for hay, or grazed for pasture. The peat growth, says Dr. Andrews, is therefore arrested, and no further increase will be observed though a million years should elapse. He adds that he has no means of ascertaining when the forests disappeared, but he presumes those parts occupied by Roman garrisons would be amongst the largest settlements, and the earliest cleared of timber. Probably the places where the Roman remains are found may have been destitute of timber and produced little or no peat for the past six or seven hundred years. If so, the deposit of six feet [it is often greatly more than this] over the Roman remains was accomplished in about twelve hundred years, or at the rate of about six inches in a century. This is much less than the rate required to preserve a stump three feet in height; but the latter was probably a maximum.

Most of the trunks were shorter and seem to have disappeared all together. While it is evident that the accretion in some times and places has been equal to three feet in a century, the average rate must have been lower, and very probably did not exceed six inches indicated by the depth of the Roman remains. Taking this as the probable standard, the age of the whole bed (twenty-six feet) would be not far from five thousand two hundred years down to the cessation of the peat growth, or, adding the six or seven hundred years supposed to have elapsed since the clearing of the ground, the present age of the bed would be about five thousand eight hundred years.

Dr. Andrews estimates age of peat at five thousand eight hundred years.

"It is impossible," says Dr. Andrews, "to pretend to minute accuracy, but the points made are sufficient to show that in the eyes of practical woodsmen, the enormous European estimates of time need pruning."

We shall show in the next chapter that in this calculation Dr. Andrews allows double the time really necessary for the formation of the peat. Roman remains, articles of iron, and boats (one freighted with Roman bricks) have been found in the lowest strata,—showing that two thousand or two thousand five hundred years is abundantly sufficient for the whole deposit.

Probably not half as old as this.

CHAPTER XVII.

THE PEAT,—CONTINUED.

The Peat of the Valley of the Somme.—The Subject requiring to be still further noticed.—The Erratic and Deceptive Character of M. Boucher de Perthes's Statements.—The Carelessness of Sir John Lubbock.—The "Types of Mankind."—All of the Statements on this Subject calculated to mislead and mystify the Student.—Roman Remains and Post-Roman Remains found in the Lowest Depths of the Alluvium and the Peat.—Sometimes Twenty-five Feet below the Surface.—A Ship loaded with Bricks found at the Bottom of the Peat.—Lake-Dwellings at Abbeville.—The Change in the Configuration and Character of the Valley.—The Sea formerly and recently at Abbeville.

The unreliable inferences of M. de Perthes with regard to the peat.

IN continuation of the views presented in the abstract of Dr. Andrews's paper in the preceding chapter, we shall proceed to discuss still farther the peat and the gravel of the Somme Valley; and, first, we shall have a good deal to add to Dr. Andrews's remarks on the subject of the peat. We shall show conclusively that Dr. Andrews is right in cutting down the estimates of M. de Perthes and Sir Charles Lyell for the time required for the formation of this substance; and we shall also show that the time allowed even by Dr. Andrews is probably double as great as that which really elapsed during the growth of these beds.

Lubbock and Lyell accept and countenance the remarkable views of M. de Perthes.

The "Celtic and Antediluvian Antiquities" of M. de Perthes is a work valuable for its facts, but utterly unreliable in all of its inferences. Indeed, there is hardly any correspondence between the inferences and the facts. We have been astonished at Sir John Lubbock's making use of the former and ignoring the latter. The impression made by him in his reference to the discoveries of M. de Perthes in the peat deposits of the Somme Valley is entirely unsustained by an examination of M. de Perthes's book. The same remarks are true of the use made of this work in the "Types of Mankind." And Sir Charles Lyell, although referring to the matter very briefly, has equally misrepresented the actual facts connected with the remains found in this stratum.

Sir John Lubbock is in general the most candid and fair of controversialists, and we have been more surprised at him than at even Sir Charles Lyell, who never misstates, but who sometimes omits to state, and whose *grouping* varies with his own unstable opinions.

We have seen that Sir John Lubbock tells us that at the depth of fifteen feet in the silt and peat we come to the remains of the Neolithic Period. Above it, he tells us, we find the Gallo-Roman remains at six feet in the silt or peat, and above these, at about three feet, the Roman remains. The peat, he adds, is in some places thirty feet thick. It thus appears that thirty feet of peat have been deposited since the "excavation of the valley" and the deposit of the "river-gravel," and that at three feet in this peat we find the remains of the Romans, and at six feet Gallo-Roman remains. In other words, the impression intended to be made is that it has taken about one thousand eight hundred years to deposit *about four feet of peat or silt.*

Sir Charles Lyell speaks in his usual non-committal way of the age of the peat, but leaves the impression on the mind that it is of immense age, and that M. de Perthes's observations in the valley of the Somme have reversed the judgment formerly prevailing that most of the peat of Europe was post-Roman. Sir Charles indeed had taught this doctrine himself in his earlier "editions;" but now in the "Antiquity of Man" he says, speaking of the peat of the Somme, "the antiquary finds *near the surface* Gallo-Roman remains, and still deeper Celtic weapons of the stone period. But the depth at which Roman works of art occur varies in different places, and is no sure test of age; because in some parts of the swamps, especially near the river, the peat is often so fluid that heavy substances may sink through it, carried down by their own gravity [like a boat-load of bricks, for example]. *In one case,* however, M. Boucher de Perthes observed several large flat dishes of Roman pottery lying in a horizontal position in the peat, the shape of which must have prevented them from sinking or penetrating through the underlying peat. Allowing but fourteen centuries for the growth of the superincumbent vegetable matter, he calculated that the thickness gained in a hundred years would be no more than three French centimetres. This rate of increase would demand so many *tens of thousands* of years for the formation of the entire thickness of thirty feet, *that we must hesitate before adopting it as a chronometric scale.* Yet, by multiplying observations of *this* kind, and bringing one to bear upon and check another, we may eventually succeed in obtaining data for estimating the age of the peaty deposit." * He has some remarks in the same vein in the last edition of his "Principles." We wish the reader to bear in mind these remarks about "these large flat dishes of Roman pottery," as we shall recur to them again.

An examination of the facts given in M. de Perthes's book.

We shall proceed now to show precisely what M. Boucher de Perthes does say with regard to the peat and the alluvium of the Somme: we mean his *facts,* not his theories.

---

* Antiquity of Man, pp. 110, 111. The italics are ours.

In the first place, it is necessary to point out particularly that his excavations were mainly and principally in the alluvium or silt, and not in the pure beds of peat. The peat occurs as a stratum in the alluvium, but it is in general only one of some six or seven deposits. Sir John Lubbock (p. 378) refers to M. de Perthes's explorations in the peat or silt, and says he has found "a rich harvest of interesting relics belonging to various periods." "The depth," he says, "at which these objects are found has been carefully noted by M. Boucher de Perthes." He then quotes:

"Prenant," says M. Boucher de Perthes, "pour terme moyen du sol de la vallée une hauteur de deux mètres au-dessus du niveau de la Somme, c'est à trente ou quarante centimètres de la surface que l'on rencontre le plus abondamment les traces du moyen-âge. Cinquante centimètres plus bas, on commence à trouver des débris romains, puis gallo-romains. On continue à suivre ces derniers pendant un mètre, c'est à dire jusqu'au niveau de la Somme. Après eux, viennent les vestiges gaulois purs, qui descendent sans interruption jusqu'à près de deux mètres au-dessous de ce niveau, preuve de la longue habitation de ces peuples dans la vallée. C'est à un mètre plus bas, ou à quatre mètres environ au-dessous de ce même niveau, qu'on arrive au centre du sol que nous avons nommé Celtique, celui que foulèrent les Gaulois primitives ou les peuples qui les précédèrent."

So M. de Perthes, endorsed by Sir John Lubbock; and this is the impression under which Sir John Lubbock leaves us, after telling us that the peat is in some places thirty or forty feet thick. M. Boucher de Perthes excavated at a number of points in the valley on both sides of the river, and he tells us that he found everywhere the same succession of beds, and the same antiquities occurring in the same relative positions. The several beds are as follows; and on the next page we present an ideal section from M. de Perthes's work:

I. Terrain alluvien.
II. Terre végétale.
III. Tuf calcaire poreux.
IV. Sable limoneux, bleu.
V. Tourbes renfermant des sépultures celtiques. (This is entirely gratuitous. There are no evidences ordinarily of burial in the peat.)
VI. Autre couche de sable limoneux.
VII. Terrain diluvien détritique.
VIII. Terrain secondaire, craie blanche.

What M. de Perthes really found, and where.

It will be observed that bed No. 6, below the peat, is eleven metres, or thirty-six feet, below the surface. Let us now see what M. de Perthes found in these beds.

On page 213, vol. i., he tells us that he found at Abbeville, at two or three metres, Roman objects, and many objects of the Middle Ages,—"fragments de verreries, de poteries, et d'émaux." Roman objects at three metres.

At p. 213, same volume, he says that in May, 1844, they excavated

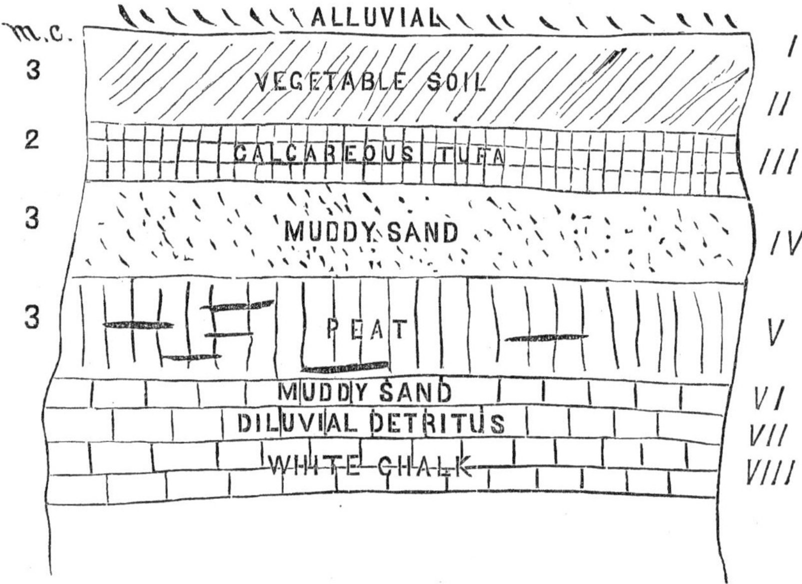

the ground between the Pont Rouge and the gate Marcadi, in order to erect a gasometer. The soil was pierced first to the depth of six metres. Here M. de Perthes found, the peat being removed, fragments of a large amphora,—of *pâte grise*, very hard,—"evidently Roman." Also on the same level, "some medals of the Lower Empire." We respectfully ask Sir Charles Lyell whether this "large amphora" *sank* to the depth of twenty feet. Roman amphora at six metres. And medals of the Lower Empire.

In vol. ii., at p. 118, we are told that at Le Marais, at Abbeville, they found flint knives one or two metres from the surface. Sir John Lubbock and M. de Perthes place the Neolithic remains at fifteen feet. Here we find them at four or five. They calculate that the Roman dishes found at the depth of one or two metres were fourteen hundred years old, and that the peat had formed at the rate of three centimetres, or nearly one and one-fifth inches, in a century. But here are the stone implements at the same depth. Flint knives near the surface.

Of course the peat forms rapidly in some places, slowly in others, not at all in others. In some places the process stops; in others it continues.

In vol. i., at p. 186, M. Boucher de Perthes finds at La Portelette, at Abbeville, at the depth of from twelve to fifteen metres, the traces of a *lake-dwelling*. At the depth of twelve or thirteen metres, he tells us, and *thirty metres from the river*, he found the "virgin earth" or the *Chalk*. Immediately above the chalk, and in a bed of peat, or oftener gravel, he found heaps of flint, pottery, and bones, which rested on a layer of carbon and decomposed plants. Between the chalk and the charcoal bed or layer the wooden platform of the lake-dwelling was discovered. Elsewhere the statement (practically the same) is that the "layers of dressed wood, or rafters," are found between the "sable limoneux" and "le terrain diluvien détritique," *i.e.*, between VI. and VII. of the diagram.

At twelve to fifteen metres finds a lake-dwelling.

At IV. of the diagram they found some beautifully polished hatchets of flint and jade, seven metres from the surface.

Immediately below the bed of tufa (III.), and near the level of these hatchets, they found morsels of dressed horn fifteen to twenty centimetres long and four or five thick.

Near the level of the hatchets, but a little higher, and six metres distant, they found a *statuette in ivory*, of fair work, representing a man holding a palm and a sort of gridiron: "*c'était probablement Saint-Laurent.*"

Statuette in ivory.

At eight metres fifty centimetres, in the peat stratum (V.), they found bone pins of delicate workmanship. At VI., in the "sable limoneux," they found a great quantity of black flints, two flint balls, and two instruments in bone; also the fragments of a little *vase en pâte noire* with two rude handles. The whole lay on a black deposit which appeared to consist of decomposed pottery, ashes, and charcoal (p. 196). They found here remains of the deer, boar, urus, ox, dog, and horse; also some hatchets of horn, and a remarkable horn dagger, which was very highly finished, and appeared to have been enamelled or dressed with paint.

Other relics.

Iron at depth of eight metres.

And now listen: "7 Septembre. Un morceau de fer, le premier qu'on eût observé dans la fouille, où peut-être *il s'était introduit accidentellement.*" Near by was a hatchet in green porphyry. This was thirty-six feet below the surface* (p. 201).

On the 11th of September, after having pierced a new bed of "sable bleu," and when at four metres below the level of the Somme, M. de Perthes struck another bed of black mud, which he recognized to be formed entirely of charcoal, ashes, and broken pottery. Under this bed was "another layer of rafters placed horizon-

Lake-dwelling.

* The reader will notice that this was just above the remains of the "lake-dwelling," and will observe also the association of the iron and the axe of porphyry.

tally." He followed this platform over a considerable area, but without coming to the limits of it. It was made of young oaks rudely squared and "with instruments which were not of iron."

Subsequently, other excavations were made at La Portelette, and there were found, at the "usual depth," the Celtic vases, the flints, the charcoal, but no polished axes. But at one metre "above the Celtic soil," that is, as we understand it, some thirty or thirty-five feet from the surface, M. de Perthes encountered "*des pièces romaines de cuivre frustes.*"

Roman copper.

A few weeks afterwards he found at V., in the peat, a "Gaulish" vase. The next day he struck a layer of wooden rafters again on a bed of gravel, at eight metres below the surface of the soil, and four metres below the level of the river.

Wooden rafters again.

We have mentioned the excavation in May, 1844, between the Pont Rouge and the gate Marcadi, where Roman amphoræ of the Lower Empire were found at the depth of six metres. We omitted to state that some very delicately-worked knives of black and blue flint and some flint axes were found at the same time and at the same depth. The same black vein of charcoal also reached here, below the peat.

And then some centimetres lower down they found an *iron chisel*, which seems to perplex M. de Perthes, as it must, according to his theory, have sunk some sixteen feet through several beds.

Iron chisel.

We mentioned finding polished stone weapons at Le Marais, at the depth of one or two metres. We may add that in the upper soil or "vegetable" stratum, in the environs of Youval, also, polished stone axes were found. (Vol. ii. p. 118.)

In 1853 M. Boucher de Perthes excavated again between the river and the Marcadi gate (Abbeville), at a point one hundred metres distant from the previous excavation (for the gasometer). He reached here the same "Celtic soil," represented by the same phenomena as at the excavation for the gasometer. It was a bed of sand, in which were vases and worked flints. He found (as usual in this bed) ashes, charcoal, funeral pottery, baked in the fire or dried in the sun, broken bones of the ox, stag, etc., and also little polished hatchets. He obtained also a fine axe of sandstone seventeen centimetres long by three and a half broad, worked with much care, and then polished, and another of *jade* of admirable polish, which seemed to be an *ex voto*. Believing that there must be others, he dug one metre deeper (two metres below the level of the river), when he reached a second "Celtic" bed. He found here a vase almost entire. "It is not," we are told, "of high antiquity,"—having been hardened in the fire and *turned on the wheel*. It was eighteen centimetres high by fourteen in diameter.

M. de Perthes's calculation.

It had a place in the side for a light of rosin, wax, or some similar substance. Near it were the head of a urus and some remains of the wild boar. There were also many carefully-wrought flints.

The fact that this vase was made on the wheel fixes its date beyond question as post-Roman. It was in bed VI.

M. de Perthes expresses the opinion that it *sank* to the position where it was found!

The stratum in which this object and the head of the urus and the worked flints were found was immediately preceded by a layer of *peat*. This stratum of peat, at a short distance, we are told, raises itself to the surface, and is no longer dominated by the *humus*. This same bed, we are also told, has been signalled at seven metres below the soil of the city. In this peat, where it shows itself at the surface, M. de Perthes found the Roman "dishes" and amphoræ on which he bases his calculation for the rate of deposit of the peat. He found them at the depth of one metre, the mean thickness of the stratum being sixty centimetres. He considers the potteries to be fourteen hundred or fifteen hundred years old, and this shows the rate of accumulation of the peat to have been four centimetres (Lyell states three) per century. The value of such a calculation is sufficiently indicated by the facts detailed in this paper. We may call attention farther to the fact that M. de Perthes seems to forget entirely that while this bed of peat is exposed on the surface of the ground at the point selected for his calculation, he has himself informed us that the same bed lies beneath the city at a depth of seven metres, or twenty-three feet; so that not only has the peat formed in the past fourteen or fifteen centuries, but the twenty-three feet of silt above it have also been deposited. It is the same bed, he also tells us, which we met with at the site of the gasometer, under which Roman amphoræ and medals of the Lower Empire were found at the depth of twenty feet from the surface.

Subterranean causeway.

In M. de Perthes's first volume, p. 54, he refers to the Marais de Boufflers, between Abbeville and Hesdin, where, he is told, at the depth of several metres, a *paved subterranean causeway* was encountered. This causeway is undoubtedly Roman.

Copper poignard at five or six metres.

At p. 147 he mentions finding *a copper poignard*, twenty-nine centimetres long, with a "little" handle. It was in the peat at three or four metres below the river-level (five or six below the surface), near the gate of Bois.

Iron at seven or eight metres.

At p. 155 he mentions finding a lump of iron, between Abbeville and Epagne, at seven or eight metres deep, in digging a well in the marl. It was *under* the marl, and "its antiquity is certainly very great." It is an oval mass, and M. de Perthes asks, "Was it a scraper or a ploughshare?" Did it "sink" through the marl?

He says another piece of iron was found in 1842, at Condé-Folie (Somme), at six metres deep. It is a kind of *spade*. And at six metres.

In 1844 another specimen was found at the gate of Hocquet, at the depth of three metres below the level of the Somme, under a stratum of gravel about a foot thick. It resembles a *hache à sapeur*. And at six metres again.

At p. 158 he mentions the finding of a canoe under the peat at Estrebœuf, near St. Valéry-sur-Somme, made of a single trunk of a tree, ten metres long.* Canoe at Estrebœuf.

Finally: in order to sum up, and state precisely the character of his explorations in the alluvium, M. de Perthes, at p. 447 of vol. i., states that he will cast a retrospective glance at the beds which he has just explored, commencing "par le sol que nous foulons, et en indiquant, lit par lit, les débris que nous avons rencontrés." He then gives the following description of the beds: M. Boucher de Perthes sums up

First Bed, or Modern Soil. Arts of civilization, scoriæ, glazed pottery of different colors, porcelain, etc.

Second Bed. Transition from modern times to the Middle Ages; iron; some copper; French, Flemish, Spanish coins; Venetian glass; etc.

Third Bed. Middle Ages. Coins of the first races and of the Lower Empire, in bronze, zinc, and gold, but little silver; less of iron than copper, etc.

Fourth Bed. Gallo-Roman Epoch. Marbles, statues, fragments of columns, stone tombs, coins of the Consular age; iron more rare; copper keys; bronze figures; etc.

Fifth Bed. Gaulish Period. Iron more and more rare; swords and lances are of copper; Gaulish coins of gold, but not of silver; some Greek pieces, etc.

Sixth Bed. First Celtic Period. We no longer find coffins or entire skeletons; there are broken bones, ashes, cinders, rude vases; no iron; a few relics of copper; stone hatchets (polished) with their sheaths, etc.

Seventh Bed. Second Celtic Period,—an undefined period:—other vases found under the first, and others under them,—these last hand-made and dried in the sun. Ashes, charcoal, broken and calcined bones. Flints roughly hewn into hatchets, knives, etc. Trees found squared and hewn without iron tools. Urns more and more rude. This is at four metres below the level of the Somme, and at eight to ten metres below soil inhabited to-day. We have traversed three or four beds of gravel or of peat intermingled with layers of sand, ashes, bones, charcoal, urns superimposed on one another and separated by these beds.

---

* This boat, in its widest part, bore some signs of having carried a mast.

Eighth Bed. The diluvium or drift; broken and rolled flints; ferruginous sand.

All this makes the matter sufficiently plain, and is full of instruction. It illustrates several points in this discussion. We find it here admitted that metallic implements are found as a general rule in the Sixth Bed, *i.e.*, at the depth of thirty-five feet.

Below this we find stone implements (as also in VI.) and the traces of the lake-dwellings.

We learn moreover: 1. That in the Middle Ages (which is the Third Bed) we find "less of iron than copper" (bronze?); 2. That in the Fourth Bed (coins of Constantine) iron is yet "more rare;" 3. That in the Gaulish period (Fifth Bed), along with Gaulish coins, the swords and lances are of *copper* (bronze). This was about B.C. 150 or 200. The Gauls had no coinage prior to B.C. 300. 4. In the Sixth Bed —just below the foregoing—there is "no iron," and "copper" is rare.

We ascertain thus from this distinguished archæologist that the date of the Bronze Age in Gaul was about B.C. 150 or 200.

From all the facts detailed by us the reader can judge how entirely inaccurate are the representations of Sir John Lubbock and Sir Charles Lyell with regard to the peat and silt of the Somme Valley; and how idle is the talk about the "thousands of years," or "the very considerable period," required for their deposition. It is quite clear that these beds are *not* very ancient; and it is highly probable that in general they hardly antedate the Christian era,—although in some cases they may go back six or eight centuries earlier.

The ship or boat freighted with Roman bricks.

Lyell's account of.

There is one other fact, referred to already, but requiring further notice: we mean the boat loaded with bricks found in the peat of the Somme Valley. It was found *at the bottom of the peat*, and before Sir Charles Lyell changed his views with regard to the rate of formation of peat, namely, prior to 1863; and in the earlier editions of his "Principles of Geology" he made the following statement:

"We are informed by Degnar that remains of ships, nautical instruments, and oars have been found in many of the Dutch mosses; and Gérard, in his History of the Valley of the Somme, mentions that in the lowest tier of that moss was found *a boat loaded with bricks, proving that these mosses were at one period* NAVIGABLE LAKES AND ARMS OF THE SEA, as were also many mosses on the coast of Picardy, Zealand, and Friesland, from which soda and salt are procured. The canoes, stone hatchets, and stone arrow-heads found in peat in different parts of Great Britain, lead to similar conclusions." *

* Principles of Geology, Am. edit., 1865, pp. 725, 726.

We know that bricks were not introduced into Gaul before the appearance of the Romans on that theatre.

We have it thus *demonstrated* that since the Christian era these peat-mosses were navigable lakes or arms of the sea. A great portion of the valley of the Somme, up to Abbeville, and beyond it, was under water.

A broad sheet of water formerly at Abbeville.

The lake-dwelling is of earlier date, but its evidence is overwhelming. It rests on the old river-gravels or the chalk. The Lake-Dwellers came right upon the heels of the Palæolithic folk. Then the waters spread in a broad sheet over the valley of the Somme at Abbeville. The Somme, at present, at Abbeville, is about fifty feet wide. The lake-dwelling was found a hundred feet from the bank. Here the water was six or eight feet deep, and a considerable distance from the margin of the ancient estuary. And this volume of water was still at Abbeville when the ancient canoe floated at La Portelette which was found in the alluvium there a few years since, and when the boat loaded with bricks, to which we have referred, came up the river from St. Valéry. It was not the body of water which once filled the valley, during heavy floods, from the upper gravels on one bank to those on the other, and when the river ran eighty or one hundred feet above its present level. But it was a broad sheet of water, and out of all proportion to the present stream. And this was the case eighteen centuries ago.

The Lake-Dwelling.

We may add that a canoe was also found near Abbeville, in the peat, at the place called Saint-Jean-des-Près, on the left bank of the canal, in 1860, at the depth of about twelve feet.*

Another canoe.

A third was found in the peat at Piquigny, between Abbeville and Amiens. In this boat were several skeletons, a bronze sword, and coins of the Roman emperor Maxentius (A.D. 306–312). We thus find the Somme at Piquigny, in the fourth century, a very different stream from what it is now.

Piquigny.

The ready suggestion of M. de Perthes that the objects known to be of recent manufacture have *sunk* in the peat, requires us to believe not only that the boats, and the Roman amphoræ and vases, the statuettes, the objects in iron and bronze, the Roman causeway, have thus made their way from ten to thirty feet beneath their first position, but we must believe also that in most cases they have pierced not only a bed of peat, but beds of gravel, sand, and marl as well,—and that, not as M. de Perthes and Sir Charles Lyell intimate, "near the river, where the peat is so fluid, etc.," but at La Portelette, for example, thirty metres distant from the river.

These boats did not sink in the peat.

* Mémoires de la Société Imp. d'Émulat. d'Abbeville, 1861, p. 625.

CHAPTER XVIII.

THE RIVER-GRAVEL FARTHER CONSIDERED.

The Views of Mr. Alfred Tylor, F.G.S., in the Quarterly Journal of the Geological Society. —Regards the Deposition of the River-Gravels as close to the Historical Period.—Rejects the Hypothesis of the Excavation of the Valley since the Deposition of the Gravel, and regards the Upper and Lower Gravels as deposited simultaneously by a Stream which formerly filled the whole Valley.—His Suggestion of a Pluvial Period following upon the Glacial Period.—Power of Floods.—Great Rain-fall in Scinde.—Amount of Rain-fall at Present.—Floods in Arctic and Tropical Regions.—Calculation of the Amount of Water given out by the Great Quaternary Glaciers.—The Anthropological Review on Mr. Tylor. —The Amount of Water called for by Dr. Andrews supplied by Mr. Tylor's Pluvial Period.—The Certainty that there was a Broad Sheet of Water at Abbeville Two Thousand Years ago.—A Well-Known Fact also that subsequent to the Glacial Age, and after the Occupation of the Bone-Caves by Man, Immense Floods or Deluges occurred.—So stated by M. Figuier and by M. Dupont.—Evidence from the Belgian Caves.—Farther Evidence on the Subject.—The Fact affirmed by Mackie, Editor of *The Geologist*.—Assumed substantially by Mr. Evans.—M. D'Orbigny and M. Boucher de Perthes.—M. Elie de Beaumont and M. de Quatrefages.—M. Belgrand.—Prof. Dawson makes the same Statement.—Consideration of the Corresponding Gravels in the South and Southeast of England.—The Hampshire Coast.—Views of Mr. Evans and Mr. Codrington.—The Old Channel of the Solent.

The Pluvial Period of Mr. Alfred Tylor. He considers the deposition of the gravel as very recent.

In the *Quarterly Journal of the Geological Society* for May, 1867 (British), Mr. Alfred Tylor, F.G.S., published a paper on this subject which has attracted much attention. In a previous paper read before the Society in 1866 (see *Quart. Jour. Geol. Soc.*, vol. xxii. p. 463) he had suggested that there was evidence of very little weathering or atmospheric action since the date of the gravels containing human remains, and that the age of the deposits was "close to the Historical period,"—also that the upper and lower valley-gravels were *continuous* and of one period.

In the present paper Mr. Tylor states that the conclusions which he has arrived at are extremely dissimilar from those of Mr. Prestwich and Sir Charles Lyell, and are as follows:

"First, that the surface of the chalk in the valley of the Somme had assumed its present form prior to the deposition of any of the gravel or loess now to be seen there, and in this respect corresponds with all other valleys in which Quaternary deposits of this character are met with.

"Second, that the whole of the Amiens-valley gravel is of one formation and of similar mineral character, and contains nearly similar organic contents, the La Neuille, Montiers, and St. Acheul gravels being of the same age, and capped with a covering of loess also of one age and mineral character, the whole deposit being of a date not much antecedent to the Historical period.

"Third, that the gravel in the valley of the Somme at Amiens is partly derived from *débris* brought down by the river Somme and by the two rivers the Celle and the Arve, and partly consists of material from the adjoining higher grounds, washed in by land-floods,—the immense quantity of chalk present in the gravel having been derived from the latter source.

"Fourth, that the Quaternary gravels of the Somme are not separated into two divisions by an escarpment of chalk parallel to the river, as has been stated. They would have formed an exception to other river-gravels if this had been the case. The St. Acheul gravels thin out gradually as they slope from the high land down to the Somme, and they pass away into the Loess formation,—and so also at Montiers. The Loess deposit, on the contrary, forms a distinct escarpment for many miles along the Somme; and this, I believe, is the bank of the ancient river whose floods produced the St. Acheul and Montiers gravels.

"Fifth, that the existence of river-floods, extending to a height of at least eighty feet above the present level of the Somme, is perfectly proved by the gradual slope and continuity of the gravels deposited by those floods upon the sloping sides of the valley towards the Somme, and also by the Loess or warp of similar mineral composition and color, extending continuously over the whole series of gravels, and finishing with a well-defined bank near the present stream.

"Sixth, that many of the Quaternary deposits in all countries, clearly posterior to the formation of the valleys in which they lie, are of such great dimensions and elevation that they must have been formed under physical conditions very different from our own. *They indicate a Pluvial period*, just as clearly as the northern drift indicates a Glacial period. This Pluvial period must have immediately preceded the true Historical period."

Glacial period almost necessitates a Pluvial period.

The existence of a Glacial period, Mr. Tylor affirms, almost necessitates that of a Pluvial period, commencing prior to the Glacial and continuing after it, occupying a region south of that occupied by the ice and snow.

Corrects Mr. Prestwich.

Mr. Tylor seems to prove that Mr. Prestwich was wrong in his measurements, and wrong in his impression that there were two gravels (a high-level and a low-level), separated by a belt of chalk all the way from Amiens to Abbeville. He has never seen a case of the kind. The gravels at Montiers are plainly continuous.

All the gravel and loess is, he believes, of one period, and has remained spread over the valley where the ground was concave enough to retain it. The absence of gravel on the steep escarpment, and near the river-channels, is a proof of great floods and rapid currents in the Quaternary period.

The gravel one continuous deposit, and all of the same age.

Sir Charles Lyell fell into the same mistake with Mr. Prestwich about the gravel at Montiers being separated by a band of chalk. Both authors represent, in several sections of the Somme, a great extent of chalk thus separating what they call the high-level and the low-level gravels; but the distinction does not exist in fact, the gravel being one and continuous.

With reference to the power of floods, Mr. Tylor mentions that in 1866 twenty inches of rain fell in Scinde in twenty-four hours, in a flat country intersected by rivers. Nine girders, weighing nearly eighty tons each, were washed off the piers by the Mulleer River from the railway bridge situated sixteen miles above Kurrachee. This bridge consisted of eighteen girders, made of wrought iron on Warren's system. The bottoms of these girders were sixty-five feet above high-water mark, spring tides, Kurrachee harbor, and seventy-four feet above low-water spring tides. They fell in six hours; and one of them, weighing eighty tons, was carried two miles down the river and buried in sand. The fall of the Mulleer River averages ten feet per mile for fifteen miles above the bridge; and, as rain rarely falls, there is generally less than a foot of water in the river-bed. This bed was nearly dry the day after, as well as the day before, this excessive rain-fall. The girders thus carried away are a measure of the rain-fall in Scinde, just as the fluviatile beds at Amiens are an index of the current of the Somme, of its flood-level, and of the force of the stream.

Power of floods.

Mr. Tylor might have cited other examples, and he might have stated that the amount of rain-fall, and the floods, of the present temperate regions, by no means represent what is experienced in the regions of either extreme cold or heat. At Paramaribo, in Dutch Guiana, rain falls annually to the amount of two hundred and twenty-nine inches, or nineteen feet per annum. At Maranham, in Brazil, the annual amount is two hundred and seventy-six inches; and at Mahableshwur, in the western Ghâts, south of Bombay, at the height of four thousand two hundred feet, it amounts to three hundred and two inches! And all this water falls in the space of a few months, and, so to speak, at once. It has been seen to fall at Cayenne twenty-one inches in a single day. This is nearly as much as falls during a whole year in the temperate regions north of the equator. Floods of forty feet rise, and even higher, are frequent at this season in the rivers of South America, the llanos of the Orinoco being changed to an inland

Rain-fall.

sea, the Amazon inundating to a vast distance its plains, and the Paraguay forming lagoons more than three hundred miles in length.*

The floods in the regions of snow and ice are on the same scale, and occur with great suddenness. The Volga, at Saratof, rises in the spring from thirty to forty feet.

Amount of water given out by the Quaternary glaciers.

A calculation has actually been made as to the quantity of water given out by the great Quaternary glaciers in a day. Thanks to the exact observations, made in 1844 and 1845, by MM. Dolfuss and Desor, in the glacier of the Aar, we know that the torrent rushing from it, carefully gauged, poured forth, between July 20 and August 4, a mean quantity of 1,278,738 cubic metres a day, the maximum being 2,100,000 and the minimum 780,000 cubic metres. The same observers studied the glaciers of Grindelwald and Rosenlaüi. Without wearying the reader with all the details, it was ascertained that a glacial surface of fifty-two square kilometres pours forth 2,100,000 cubic metres of water a day. Let this be applied to one of the great glaciers of the Alps in ancient times, west of the Rhone. It encumbered the whole upper valley of the Rhone, from Galenstock to the Lake of Geneva, a length of one hundred and fifty kilometres; from thence it extended, fan-like, over the whole surface of the lake, and its front occupied at a given time the shore between Mount Sion, near Geneva, to beyond Soleure. Its frontal moraines were deposited on the western slopes of the Jura. This glacier, with its geographical basin, its snow-fields, its peaks, occupied a surface of twelve thousand six hundred square kilometres. Adding to it the ancient glacier of Chamounix, comprising the hydrographical basin of the Arve and that of the Drome, whose waters meet those of the Rhone glacier, and which occupy fifteen thousand square kilometres, the whole ought—if they acted like the glacier of the Aar—to have poured forth six hundred and five millions of cubic metres of water per day (rather more than seven thousand cubic metres per second), on a point situated a few kilometres below Geneva.

The actual Rhone, at Geneva, gauged by General Dufour on September 24, 1840, at its flood, gave a result of 424 cubic metres; the Rhine, at Kehl, at low water, 350; in medium state, 956; and in full flood, 4635 cubic metres, per second.

---

* Guyot's "Earth and Man," p. 156.

The extreme range between low and high water of the Upper Mississippi at its mouth is thirty-five feet; that of the Missouri at its mouth, about the same; and that of the Ohio at Louisville, forty-two feet. (Prehistoric Races of the United States, by Dr. Foster, p. 173.) Coal River, West Virginia, has been known to rise forty-five feet, at its mouth, in a single night.

The Ganges at Benares and Allahabad, in September, rises from thirty to forty-five feet.

A similar calculation is made with the glacier Agelès, in the Pyrenees.

The result evolved is that the flood from these two ancient glaciers under ordinary circumstances, when there was no unusual melting of the ice, must have been fifty per cent. greater than the flood of the Rhine at Kehl (opposite Strasburg), at the present time, when the river is highest.*

We can readily understand now how in the post-glacial period, when the glaciers and snows were melting, and when the torrents were still further swelled by heavy and continued rains, the Somme and the Thames and the Solent rose high above their ordinary levels and inundated their valleys to the utmost limits of the river-gravel.

Transport of materials and erosion.

M. Collomb refers also to the mechanical effects of transport of materials and erosion of rocks by the glaciers and the river-torrents. The waters of the latter, like those of to-day, were loaded with sediment. From careful observation it is found that the waters issuing from the Aar carry on the upper surface of their currents 092.142 of fine silt per litre, while at the bottom of the torrent-bed much larger masses are transported. This 092.142 multiplied by these six hundred and five millions of cubic metres per day, of the ancient glacier of the Rhone, gives eighty-six million kilogrammes of sediment,—eighty-six thousand metric quintals a day,—and this contributed a considerable portion of the loess, the origin of which has hitherto been so problematical.

Even the *Anthropological Review*, in 1869, remarks, "The ages of the high-level and low-level gravels of the Somme Valley, since Mr. Tylor's paper, are exceedingly doubtful." †

The amount of water called for by Dr. Andrews is abundantly supplied by the "Pluvial Period" of Mr. Tylor, and the melting glaciers. Indeed, whenever these phenomena did occur—whether four thousand or four hundred thousand years ago—the valley of the Somme was undoubtedly, to the summit of the upper gravels, filled with water. *When* that was is a different question. It was certainly after the Glacial Period; and *when that was* is another question. We have seen that Sir Charles Lyell believes that it was some two hundred thousand years ago. But, whenever it was, it was followed by the presence of an immense body of water in the river-valleys. In considering the problem, we must combine with this the change of level in the land.

The fact that there was a broad sheet of water at Abbeville two

---

* The Student and Intellectual Observer, vol. ii. p. 311. "Floods from the Ancient Glaciers." By E. Collomb. Read to the French Academy.

† Page 164.

thousand years ago, prepares us to be the less surprised at this. If the Somme was two hundred yards wide at Abbeville in the days of Herodotus, it may, after great rains, and in seasons of flood, have been a mile wide in a previous age. The James River, half a mile wide at Richmond, Virginia, rose twenty-five feet in twenty-four hours in September, 1870.

But Prof. Andrews and Mr. Tylor are not alone in the opinion that immense floods occurred at this epoch. It is the general opinion among the continental *savans* of Europe, and there are plain traces of such a flood in North and South America, and in Asia, as well as in many parts of Europe.

Farther testimony to the fact of great inundations in this age.

M. Figuier, in his "Primitive Man," gives expression to the prevailing scientific opinion on the subject in France. After considering the Unpolished Stone Implements, he proceeds to discuss the Epoch of the Polished Implements, and in the opening of his chapter on this latter period he remarks, "We have now traversed the series of antediluvian ages since the era when man first made his appearance on the earth. . . . We will now leave this epoch.

Testimony of M. Figuier.

"A great catastrophe, the tradition of which is preserved in the memory of all nations, marked in Europe the end of the Quaternary Period. It is not easy to assign the exact causes of this great event in the earth's history; but, whatever may be the explanation given, it is certain that a cataclysm, caused by the violent flowing of rushing water, took place during the Quaternary geological epoch; for the traces of it are everywhere visible. Those traces consist of a reddish clayey deposit, mixed with sand and pebbles. The deposit is called in some countries *red diluvium*, and in others *gray diluvium*. In the valley of the Rhone and the Rhine it is covered with a layer of loamy deposit, which is known to geologists by the name of *loess* or *lehm*. . . . Sir Charles Lyell is of the opinion that this mud was produced by the crushing of the rocks by early Alpine glaciers, and that it was afterwards carried down by the streams of water which descended from the mountains. This mud covers a great portion of Belgium, where it is from ten to thirty feet in thickness, and supplies with materials a number of brick-fields. . . .

A great catastrophe.

"This inundation to which the *diluvium* is referred closes the series of the Quaternary ages. At this era the present geological period commences, which is characterized by the almost entire permanency of the present vertical outline of the earth, and by the formation of peat-bogs." *

Again: "The European diluvial inundation was, as we know, posterior to the glacial period." †

* Page 125. † Page 57.

The reader will remember that we pointed out the evidences of mighty currents of water in treating of the ancient bone-caves. Many of them now far above the level of all neighboring streams furnish unmistakable proof that they have been swept by water. M. Dupont insists on this as one of the most noticeable points about the Belgian caves. In the Trou des Noutons he found one hundred and fifty antlers of the reindeer broken by the violence of water, and in the Trou du Frontal, he remarks, the bones of the thirteen human skeletons were in "inexpressible disorder." "It was," he says, "unanimously admitted that they had been mingled with the stones and earth by a great inundation."*

A great inundation evidenced by the bone-caves.

M. Dupont.

Speaking of the Trou de la Rosette, he says the occupants of this cave were "overwhelmed by a deluge." And he concludes his review of the whole subject by remarking, "Do we not see traces then of that terrible phenomenon of which all races have preserved the remembrance?"

M. Le Hon, after describing the reindeer-caves of Massat, Bise, Savigné, etc., observes, "At the termination of *this* period occurred the submergence of Northern Europe, spoken of by M. Dupont, when the waters in Belgium, at the epoch of the red drift, rose two hundred and fifty metres."†

One of the most emphatic of these testimonies is contained in a paper of great ability, entitled "Man as the Cotemporary of the Mammoth and the Reindeer," translated by C. A. Alexander for the Smithsonian Institution, from "Aus der Natur: die neuesten Entdeckungen auf dem Gebiete der Naturwissenschaften." Leipzig, 1867. In this paper the evidence for the antiquity of man is reviewed, particularly in connection with the bone-caves, and the writer maintains that the First Stone Period was ages ago.

Farther testimony.

After describing the Glacial Period, he says that after this the level of the waters sank, and the submerged lands of Europe rose above the sea, the glaciers melting in part, and the valleys forming. This he denominates "The First Debacle." At this time the rounded pebbles were formed, and the caves were emptied of their clay.

Amid this grand melting of glaciers, and the floods thereby occasioned, the volcanoes of Auvergne were in full activity,—emitting flame and lava,—which activity, says our author, "was witnessed by human beings, as testified to by the human remains found in the volcanic tufa of Mt. Denise de Velais." Herds of mammoth roamed over Europe, and cotemporary with them were the cave-bear, cave-tiger, and cave-hyæna.

* This flood reached the height of four hundred and fifty feet.

† Anthropological Review, 1869, p. 167.

This first age of man, he says, "must doubtless have comprised thousands of years."

This was followed by *a recurrence of the cold*, and "the era of the Reindeer." There was "a second advance of the glaciers," and "this in consequence *of a great inundation* which was slow in attaining its ultimate limits." Europe was laid under water. In Belgium, according to M. Dupont, the flood must have reached a height of four hundred and fifty feet. "To this inundation are to be ascribed the beds of gravelly clay, or calcareous mud, which have covered a part of France and Belgium."*

This was the Second Debacle.

And this language about "floods," "inundations," "debacles," just at this juncture, is precisely what Mr. Tylor wants in corroboration of his theory of a Pluvial Period, and precisely what Dr. Andrews wants to fill the valley of the Somme with a stream running a hundred feet above its present level.

The evidence of the fact is overwhelming, and nowhere denied.

It is referred to by Mr. S. J. Mackie, F.G.S., editor of *The Geologist*: "The Glacial era was inaugurated by unequalled copious rains, and passed away as a geological age in a multitude of debacles." †

Testimony of Mr. Mackie.

Even Mr. Evans assumes that there was at the period in question "a considerably greater annual rain-fall," ‡ and, speaking of Mr. Tylor's theory of a "Pluvial Period" subsequent to the Glacial, remarks, "To some extent this opinion is probably correct." §

Mr. Evans.

We have referred to the opinions (to the same effect) of M. D'Orbigny and M. Boucher de Perthes; and we shall see hereafter that M. Elie de Beaumont and M. de Quatrefages go still farther, —considering the gravel deposit as very recent.

D'Orbigny and B. de Perthes.

We have a glimpse of a similar, but no doubt more recent, cataclysm in connection with the period of the Danish shell-mounds. Says M. Morlot, "It would seem then the age of the kjökken-möddings was ended by some catastrophe which violently agitated the waters of the sea, and the latter then rushed in at a moderate height and beyond its habitual boundary." || Prof. Steenstrup expresses the same opinion. This was doubtless due to a depression of the land.

In the *Journal of the Anthropological Institute* for January, 1873, we have an address of Mr. Busk, late President of the Anthropological Society, in which he reviews the most recent contributions to the liter-

---

* See Smiths. Rep. for 1867, p. 350.

† The Geologist, 1864, p. 118.

‡ Ancient Stone Implements, p. 579.

§ Ib., p. 613.

|| Smiths. Rep. for 1860, p. 295.

ature of this subject. He notices at some length, and speaks in favorable terms of, the work of M. Belgrand, Inspecteur-Général des Ponts et Chaussées, etc., on "Le Bassin Parisien aux âges anté-historiques." Mr. Busk says that this author has enjoyed unusual opportunities for studying this subject. M. Belgrand is an extreme advocate of the antiquity of man, remanding him, indeed, to the beginning of the Miocene Age, or the very verge of the Eocene. The following testimony is, therefore, unprejudiced.

The continent, he says, was less elevated during the Palæolithic period than at present, and the rivers much larger. The diminution in the size of the rivers, he thinks, "must have taken place rapidly." This he conceives to be proved by the fact that the river-valleys of the Seine and of Picardy are in their lower parts occupied by *beds of peat.* Now, peat does not grow in turbid, muddy water. Thus, there is no peat in the valley of the Marne, because, owing to the impermeable nature of a part of its course, it is subject to violent floods of muddy water.

The Seine Valley contains much peat down to Montereau, where it is joined by the Yonne, which receives its waters from an impermeable district of country, and below this point no peat occurs in the valley of the Seine for some distance. The floods in Palæolithic times, continues M. Belgrand, were so violent that the water became muddy in all cases. Hence no peat was then formed. The growth of peat characterizes the present régime. But if the change from the large rivers of the Palæolithic times to the small rivers of the present had been gradual, argues M. Belgrand, the valleys would have been filled, not with peat, but with gravel, sand, and alluvium.*

Again: "Dans l'âge de la pierre, les pluies étaient tellement abondantes que leurs eaux ruisselaient à la surface des terrains les plus perméables. Il résultait de là que la première partie de la crue de Paris, celle qui est due aux terrains imperméables, était considérablement augmentée, et que la deuxième partie, due aux eaux de sources, était aussi beaucoup plus grande, puisque les eaux ruisselant à la surface du sol, les sources étaient alimentées autant qu'elles pouvaient l'être, l'absorption des eaux pluviales dans les terrains perméables étant alors au maximum." . . . "When once, therefore, the latter were rendered impermeable" (Mr. Busk then proceeds to remark), "as he [M. Belgrand] supposes to have been the case in Palæolithic times, whether by saturation or any other cause, the total impermeable area, that which mainly supplies flood water, . . . would be four times as large as at present."

There is more to this effect, which it is not necessary to reproduce,—all going to show the great volume of the Palæolithic flood.

---

* Jour. Anthrop. Inst., Jan. 1873, p. 433.

The testimony is directly at war with the theory of Sir Charles Lyell and Sir John Lubbock and their little shallow stream.

We would call special attention too to the opinion of M. Belgrand with regard to the *suddenness* or *rapidity* of the change "from the large rivers of the Palæolithic times to the small rivers of the present." Precisely our theory. And so the Palæolithic age did not shade off through tens of thousands of years into the Neolithic age; the Palæolithic age rapidly passed away, followed by the age of Peat.

We must cite yet another witness: we quote from Prof. Dawson's able work, entitled "The Story of the Earth and Man." After describing the glacial period, he proceeds:

Prof. Dawson.

"Further, as the land rose, its surface was greatly and rapidly modified by rains and streams. There is the amplest evidence, both in Europe and America, that at this time the erosion by these means was enormous in comparison with anything we now experience. The rain-fall must have been excessive, the volume of water in the streams very great; and the facilities for cutting channels in the old Pliocene valleys, filled to the brim with mud and boulder-clay, were unprecedented. . . . It was the spring-time of the Glacial Era, a spring eminent for its melting snows, its rains, and its river-floods. . . . It will be readily understood how puzzling these deposits have been to geologists, especially to those who fail to present to their minds the true conditions of the period; and how difficult it is to separate the river-alluvia of the age from the deposits in the seas and estuaries, and these again from the older Glacial beds. Further, in not a few instances the animals of a cold climate must have lived in close proximity to those which belonged to ameliorated conditions, and the fossils of the older post-pliocene must often, in the process of sorting by water, have been mixed with those of the newer.

*   *   *   *   *   *   *   *   *   *

"But if man really appeared in Europe in the post-glacial era, he was destined to be exposed to one great natural vicissitude before his permanent establishment in the world. The land had reached its maximum elevation, but its foundations 'standing in the water and out of the water' were not yet securely settled, and it had to take one more plunge-bath before attaining its modern fixity. This seems to have been a comparatively rapid subsidence and re-elevation, leaving but slender traces of its occurrence, but changing to some extent the levels of the continents, and failing to restore them fully to their former elevation, so that large areas of the lower grounds still remained under the sea." *

---

* Pp. 287–290.

But it is not only in the valley of the Somme that we find the so-called River Drift containing the traces of the Palæolithic Age. In France the bones of the extinct mammals and the flint implements are also found in the valleys of the Seine and the Oise. In England they have been found in the valleys of the Thames, the Ouse, etc., and in the south of Hampshire in what Sir Charles Lyell calls "a tabular mass of drift which caps the Tertiary strata, and which is intersected both by the Solent and by the valleys of all the rivers which flow into that channel of the sea." He thinks this locality affords stronger evidence of the antiquity of pre-historic man "than any other monument of the earlier Stone age yet discovered." * Mr. Evans appears to share this opinion.

The River-Gravel of England.

The gravel is found thus all around the south coast of England (and as far in the interior as Salisbury) and along the east coast up to the mouth of the Ouse. It is found at Bournemouth, in the valley of the Avon, at Fisherton, on the Isle of Wight, near Southampton, near Folkestone, at Reculver and thence up the valley of the Thames to Hackney Down and Ealing, in the valley of the Waveney, at Shrub Hill in the valley of the Little Ouse, in the valley of the Lark, at Bedford in the valley of the Ouse, etc.

Coast of Hampshire. Lyell.

Sir C. Lyell considers that the gravel on the Hampshire coast has been deposited before that region attained its present configuration. It is a plateau or table-land along the coast, intersected by the river-valleys of the small streams near Gosport, of the Southampton, the Avon, the Stone, etc., all of which "have been excavated since Palæolithic man inhabited the region;" "for not only at various points east of the Southampton estuary, but west of it also on both sides of the opening at Bournemouth, flint tools of the ancient type have been met with in the gravel capping the cliffs."†

Reply furnished by Mr. Evans.

Sir Charles is answered by Mr. Evans (who, however, agrees with him on the chronological issue). Mr. Evans's theory is that all of these gravels were deposited by rivers, and the gravel along the south coast of England, he says, was deposited by *a* river which ran in ancient times *from west to east* and drained an extensive tract of country along this coast; and "that of this river a portion still survives in an altered and enlarged condition as the Solent, which now separates the Isle of Wight from the mainland." Mr. T. Codrington, F.G.S., in a paper published in the *Quarterly Journal of the Geological Society* in 1870, arrived on independent grounds, says Mr. Evans, at the same conclusion. And before that,—in 1862,—before any implements had been found in this

The ancient Solent.

Mr. Codrington.

* Principles of Geology, vol. ii. p. 567. † Ibid., p. 568.

region,—the Rev. W. Fox published nearly similar views as to the origin of the Solent. Mr. Fox wrote, "The severance of this island [the Isle of Wight] from the mainland, it appears to me, was effected under very unusual circumstances, and at a very distant period. The present channel of the Solent, being pretty nearly equally deep and equally broad throughout its entire length of twelve or fourteen miles, proves at once that it was not formed in the usual way of island-severing channels, that is, by gradual encroachments of the sea on the two opposite sides of a narrow neck of land:" "it is to be accounted for, therefore, not by the excavations of a gradually approaching sea, but, as I shall hereafter have to attempt to show, by its being originally the trunk or outlet of a very considerable river." "Whoever, as a geologist, examines the vertical strata of the Chalk of the Needles, nay, and throughout the whole length of the Isle of Wight, and the strata of the same rock in exactly the same unusual position on the bold white cliff on the Dorsetshire coast some twenty miles westward of the Needles, will not doubt but that the two promontories were once united, forming a rocky neck of land from Dorset to the Needles. This chain of chalk might, or might not, be so cleft in twain as to allow the rivers of Dorset and Wilts to find a passage through them to the main ocean. My opinion, however, is that they had no such outlet, but that at that far-distant period the entire drainage of more than two counties, embracing the rivers that join the sea at Poole and Christchurch, flowed through what is now Christchurch Bay, down the Solent, and joined the sea at Spithead."

"According to this theory, the Solent was at that time an estuary somewhat like the Southampton Water, having but one opening to the British Channel, but of so much more importance than the latter as it was fed by a vastly greater flow of fresh water." "Of course, according to this view, the sea would lose its original condition as an estuary at the time when the British Channel had so far made a breach through the chain of rocks connecting the Isle of Wight and Dorsetshire as to give an opening into itself for the Dorsetshire rivers, somewhere opposite to the town of Christchurch." *

The gravel occurs on the east and the west coast of the Isle of Wight, a flint implement having been found in the first by Mr. Codrington on the top of the Foreland Cliff at the height of eighty feet above the sea, and elephant-remains in the latter (on the southwest coast) at the same elevation.

At Bournemouth the gravel occurs at one hundred and thirty feet above the sea; farther east, near Boscombe, at one hundred and twenty feet; midway between that spot and Hengistbury Head, at ninety feet;

* Quoted in "Ancient Stone Implements of Great Britain," pp. 605, 606.

at High Cliff, at eighty-four feet; at Hordwell, a short distance inland, at sixty feet; and about midway along the north shore of the Solent, at fifty feet.

The only difference between us and Mr. Evans is the *time* at which all this occurred.

CHAPTER XIX.

FARTHER OBSERVATIONS ON THE RIVER-GRAVEL.

The Changes in the Physical Geography of the South Coast of England.—The Valley of the Ouse.—Activity of Geological Forces after the Glacial Period.—The Peat of the Somme Valley.—The Sea formerly at Abbeville.—The High-Level Gravels on the French Coast at an Elevation of One Hundred Feet.—Unequal Elevation of the Banks of the Somme.—The Gravel deposited at Piquigny Fifty Feet higher than at Amiens and Abbeville.—Mr. Prestwich's Testimony as to the Greater Rain-fall at this Period, and the Rapidity and Energy of the Geological Movements of that Day.—Thinks the Evidence as much requires bringing forward the Great Extinct Mammalia towards our Own Time as the carrying back of Man in Geological Time.—The South Coast of England.—Mr. Prestwich thinks the Table-Land and Overlying Gravel were formed by Marine Action, implying Elevation of the Coast.—Raised Beach on the Isle of Wight.—Valley of the Ouse. —Marine Remains far Inland.—Near Cambridge.—Submerged Forests.—Valley of the Thames.—Submerged Forests here.—Animal Remains found near Salisbury in the Gravel.—Sir Roderick Murchison on the Gravel-Beds of the South Coast of England. —Violent Geological Action.—The Celebrated Moulin-Quignon Jaw.—Is it Genuine ?— The French and English Savans.

The improbable aspects of the "Excavation" theory.

THE idea that the Somme River—a small sluggish stream fifteen or twenty yards wide, with a fall of sixty feet in forty-one miles from Amiens to St. Valéry—should have *excavated* the valley of the Somme, a mile broad and one hundred feet deep, since the appearance of man upon earth, is an opinion which seems to us to reflect on the good sense of those who entertain it. The enormous mass of chalk which filled the valley all removed, and its angular flints rolled into sand and gravel, by a river whose natural flow, says the author of "Man's Age in the World," can never have been rapid except in flood-times, owing to the absence of high grounds towards its sources. These gravels thus formed, it is to deposit in succession at its edges, *i.e.*, its higher levels, thirty feet thick,—all accompanied by heavy blocks of sandstone eight feet by three,—the scooping out of the valley progressing meantime—across a breadth, as we have said, of a mile, and more than a mile. This is the theory of Sir Charles Lyell and Sir John Lubbock.

Perhaps it will turn out that they are as unskillful in calculating the age of gravel as they are in estimating the lapse of time required for the formation of peat.

The great changes presented in the configuration of the soil on the south coast of England—and, as we have seen, in connection with the palæolithic caves—remain to be still farther spoken of. Nor has the physical geography of the south coast of England alone been greatly modified since the deposition of the River-Gravels: in the valley of the Thames and in the valley of the Ouse the changes seem to have been equally great. In the latter it is quite as difficult to connect the position of the gravel-beds with the existing drainage of the country as in the neighborhood of Southampton.

Valley of the Ouse.

The fact is, the present tranquil aspect of matters in these regions by no means reflects the geological status at the close of the glacial and the beginning of the human period. The whole tendency of the evidence now is, that the human period was ushered in by great activity in the physical world. Man came upon the scene, in all probability, right upon the close of the glacial epoch. The great pachyderms still lingered. The lion, and the tiger, and the hyæna, and the bear, and the reindeer, roamed over Western Europe. Vast floods followed upon the breaking up of the Ice. Great perturbations prevailed in the domain of physical geography.

Great activity in the Post-Glacial epoch.

Take the peat in the valley of the Somme,—a comparatively recent deposit. "If thirty feet of peat were now removed, the sea would flow up and fill the valley for miles above Abbeville." So declares Sir Charles Lyell.* There has been a change in the sea-level, or the valley has sunk. We know indeed from M. Boucher de Perthes that the peat in the Somme Valley is many feet below the level of the river,—sometimes twenty or twenty-five feet. This has occurred in the past two thousand or two thousand five hundred years.

The Peat of the Somme.

It will be recollected that at La Portelette, thirty metres from the river, M. Boucher de Perthes found traces of a lake-dwelling at the depth of fully *thirty feet* below the present level of the Somme. When that platform was laid down, the bottom of the river at that point was higher (of course), perhaps considerably higher, than the bed of the main channel. Now the spot is thirty feet lower than the river-bed.

But there were fluctuations of level before this.

The high gravels in the environs of Abbeville, as at Moulin-Quignon for example (where they are one hundred feet above the river), con-

* Antiquity of Man, Amer. ed., p. 111. He also tells us (p. 109) that "large masses of compact peat, enclosing trunks of flattened trees, have been thrown up on the coast at the mouth of the Somme; seeming to indicate that there has been a subsidence of the land and a consequent submergence of what was a westward continuation of the valley of the Somme into what is now a part of the British Channel, or La Manche."

tain only land and fresh-water shells. But the low-level gravels in the suburbs, as at Menchecourt, which are forty feet above the level of the river, contain also marine shells. In other words, the sea was at that time at Abbeville, at least twenty-five feet above its present level at high tide; and these shells were probably deposited at low tide. Sir John Lubbock refers to this fact, but very briefly. "Marine shells," he tells us, "also occur at Abbeville, about twenty-five feet above the sea-level; *and no doubt this change of level had an important bearing on the excavation of the valley*" (our italics).*

Marine shells found at Abbeville.

Referred to by Lubbock.

In a note he adds, "The higher-level gravels in some places fringe the coast at an elevation of as much as one hundred feet: this phenomenon, however, I should be disposed to refer principally to an encroachment of the sea on the land, and the consequent intersection of the sea at a higher level." †

High-level gravels along the French coast.

It thus appears that the river-gravels fringe the sea-coast at an elevation of one hundred feet! The wearing away of the coast by erosion would hardly explain this. The river entered the sea on a level with it. The sea has hardly eaten into the land sufficiently to separate those levels by one hundred feet, and the only explanation is an elevation of the land,—unless there was a cataract at St. Valéry.

We have just seen that the gravel at Menchecourt has risen some forty feet: why not account then for the elevation of the gravel at St. Valéry by a rise of the coast? ‡

The fresh-water shells found at Menchecourt, as we learn from Sir C. Lyell, consisted of "the genera Planorbis, Limnea, Paludina, Valvata, Cyclas, Cyrena, Helix, and others, *all now natives of the same part of France,* except *Cyrena fluminalis,* which no longer lives in Europe, but inhabits the Nile, and many parts of Asia." § The marine shells occurring here, mixed with these fresh-water shells, were Buccinum undatum, Littorina littorea, Nassa reticulata, Purpura lapillus, Tellina solidula, Cardium edule, and a few others,—"all littoral species now proper to the contiguous coast of France."

The *Excavation-theory* has a difficulty to encounter which we have not yet adverted to. The higher gravel at Abbeville and Amiens is one hundred feet above the river; but at Piquigny, *between* Abbeville and Amiens, it is one hundred and fifty feet above the river; thus:

Irregular upheaving of land in the Somme Valley, Piquigny.

* Pre-historic Times, p. 382.

† Ib.

‡ At p. 382 Sir John Lubbock states that "raised beaches have been observed at an elevation of from five to ten feet at various points along the coast of Sussex and the Pas de Calais," which, he says, is "recent."

§ Antiquity of Man, p. 123.

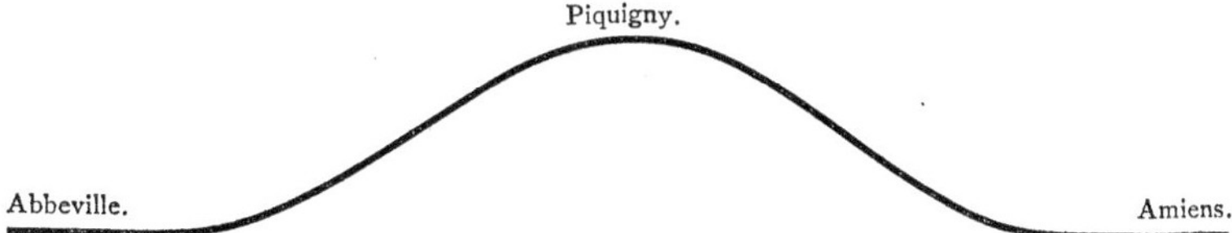

If the river then, says the author of "Man's Age in the World," cut out its channel without elevation of the land, it must have flowed up-hill. It is clear that the land rose fifty feet at Piquigny after the gravel was deposited; and this elevation of fifty feet was local and peculiar to Piquigny. This develops at once not only disturbances of the land, but demonstrates that the action was "paroxysmal" and irregular in its operation, as we know it to have been on the island of Möen and the shores of the Great American Lakes,—a most important fact in connection with what Sir Charles Lyell so frequently adverts to as "a change in the physical features of the country" and in the old "lines of drainage" since the Palæolithic Age.

Strong testimony from Mr. Prestwich.

Mr. Prestwich, whose views seem to be treated with especial deference by all scientific men in England, bears important testimony to the greater amount of rain-fall at the period of the gravel deposits, to the greater volume of water in the valley of the Somme River, to the rapid geological changes which probably characterized that epoch, and to the probable recent existence of the mammoth and the other great mammals cotemporary with him. He believes, however, in the great antiquity of the Abbeville flints, for he does not seem to be able to get rid of the idea of the *excavation* of the valley by the river since the deposit of the high-level gravels, which he considers would, after all abatements, still require a very long time. Speaking of a section at Moulin-Quignon, he is reported as saying,—

The Somme raised fifty feet by the floods of that day.

"In all probability we have in both these places part of the bed of the old river, when it flowed in a channel higher by nearly one hundred feet than the present river-bed. In the diagram of the section, fig. 3, I have given what I consider may have been the section of the valley at that period, showing a shallow and broad river with numerous, generally dry, shoals and shingle-banks, *but during floods* (our italics), *arising from the melting of the winter snows and a greater rain-fall than at the present day, rising to a height of forty or fifty feet above its ordinary level, flooding the adjacent country, and depositing, out of the course of the main current, the fine silt now forming the Loess.*" *

* Journal of the Geological Society, 1863, pp. 502, 503.

The rise of forty or fifty feet above referred to would lead to the deposit of the "high-level" gravel, some eighty or ninety feet above the present river. Therefore the bed of the river at this time (according to Mr. Prestwich) was some forty feet above the present level of the stream. He describes it as "a shallow and broad river." The rain-fall and the melting snows were so great that they raised this "shallow" river "forty or fifty feet," the valley being a mile wide.

This concedes the whole question.

What more does Mr. Tylor or Dr. Andrews ask for?

Now, we have shown that at the epoch of the lake-dwelling found in the peat or silt, and also at the date of the boats found in the peat, the Somme at Abbeville was a broad arm of the sea, and we have also stated that marine shells are found at Menchecourt at the height of forty feet above the present river-level. It is, therefore, certain that at these periods there was a great volume of water at Abbeville, *filling the valley* to a point ranging as high as forty feet. The valley was *already excavated.* There was no broad, shallow stream running, as Mr. Prestwich supposes, forty feet higher than the present valley-bottom; but there was an arm of the sea met by the waters of the Somme, and these commingled waters ranged at the time of the deposit of the sea-shells *at least* as high as forty feet above the present river. And, as Mr. Prestwich allows the floods of that day to raise his broad, shallow stream some forty or fifty feet higher, where is the occasion to hesitate about the ability of these same floods to fill the valley to the same height in the manner supposed by Dr. Andrews and Mr. Tylor?

In the proceedings of the Royal Institute for the next year we find Mr. Prestwich referring to this subject again:

Mr. Prestwich again.

"One reason" (he says) "for believing the accumulation of the silty alluvium of our valleys to have been more rapid at one time than now, is that these valleys, left rude and rugged at the end of the Quaternary period, would be subject to more frequent floods until their inequalities were filled up and levelled." Mr. Prestwich concluded by observing that "For these and various other reasons I am confirmed in the opinion I expressed in 1859, that the evidence, as it stood, *seemed to me* [our italics] *as much to necessitate the bringing forward of the great extinct animals towards our own time, as the carrying back of man in geological time.* . . . If, on the contrary, they [the modern valley-alluvia and the latest Quaternary beds] followed in immediate succession, and I think we have evidence that such was the case, for there seems reason to believe that some of the larger pachyderms still existed at the commencement of the alluvial period, whilst we know that many of the ruminants lived on uninterruptedly from one period to the other, *I do not, for my part, see any geological reasons why the extinct mammalia should* *not have lived down to comparatively recent times, possibly not further back than eight thousand or ten thousand years.*" "But this only brings us to the threshold of that dim and mysterious antiquity in which first appear those rudely-wrought flints." . . . (He then reiterates the views about the excavation of the valleys by the streams.) "But," he continues, "if the views here proposed be correct, it would follow that *with rivers so large in proportion to those now occupying the same valleys, with floods of a force now unknown in the same districts, with cold so severe as to shatter rocks and to hasten the removal of their débris, we should have, I contend, agencies in operation so far exceeding in power any now acting, that it is impossible to apply the same rules to the two periods. The change described must have progressed with a rapidity of which we at the present day can in these latitudes hardly form an adequate conception.*" *

No reason why the extinct mammalia may not have lived down to eight or ten thousand years ago.

Large rivers, mighty floods, severe cold, in that day.

Here is the judgment of probably the first geologist in England; and it proves the whole case.

The South of England.

So much in a general way. Let us now turn our attention particularly to the deposits in England. And here we must make use again of the testimony of Mr. Prestwich, quoted and accepted by Mr. Evans; who is speaking of the south coast of Hampshire, and the region between Poole and Southampton. He remarks that the formation of this table-land and the overlying deposit of gravel appear to be due to marine action, though as yet no marine remains have been discovered in it. He then proceeds:

Raised sea-beaches.

"Sea-shells have, however, been found by Mr. Prestwich in an old sea-beach at Waterbeach, near Goodwood, and similar beds at Avisford Bridge occupy a height of eighty or one hundred feet above the sea. *We seem, then, here to have evidence of a considerable elevation of the land from beneath the sea; and, as the gravel in places overlies late Tertiary beds, this must have taken place at a comparatively late geological epoch.*"†

All of this "tabular mass of drift," of which Sir Charles Lyell speaks, was then at a recent geological period under the waters of the British Channel, and the beach along the south coasts of Hampshire and Sussex has been raised "eighty or one hundred feet."

Isle of Wight.

We have spoken of the "oval flint implement" found in gravel in 1868 "at the top of the Foreland cliff on the most eastern point of the Isle of Wight, five miles southeast of Ryde." It "is of the true Palæolithic type," says Sir Charles Lyell, and was "eighty feet above the level of the sea." Now we learn that Mr.

* Proc. Roy. Inst., 1864, p. 221. † Ancient Stone Implements, p. 608.

Codrington considers that there is a raised beach here, and that "a rise of land to the extent of seventy or eighty feet must have taken place since the deposition of the brick-earth in which the flint implement was imbedded." *

Valley of the Ouse.

Altered relations between the land and the sea.

If we turn to the valley of the Ouse and its affluents, the evidences of altered relations between the land and the sea are of an extraordinary character. A little north of the Ouse, on the Nene, at Peterborough, some twenty miles, perhaps, from the sea, we find the oyster and other marine shells. In the gravel in March, on the old Nene, about twelve miles from the sea, we find *Buccinum*, *Trophon*, *Littorina*, *Cardium*, etc. In Whittlesea Mere, about fifteen miles from the sea, we find remains of the walrus and the seal, and sea-shells. At Waterbeach, ten miles from Cambridge (some forty-five from the sea), the remains of the whale have been discovered. At Icklingham, on the Lark, forty miles from the coast, "the whole surface of the country, and its drainage, have been so much modified by the invasion of the sea, which produced the wide level of the Fens, that we should expect," says Mr. Evans, "to find any deposits of an ancient river, which existed before that great planing-down of the adjacent country, in somewhat anomalous positions."†

The whale near Cambridge.

Submerged forests.

Torquay.

Apart from the more ancient and violent elevations and depressions of the land in England, there are at various points on the southern coast more recent examples of submerged forests. Sir Charles Lyell gives us an account of a submerged forest at Torquay (mentioned by us elsewhere), and much peaty matter resting on bluish clay, which may be traced from the neighborhood of Tor Abbey, at a height of about eighty-four feet above the sea, for three-quarters of a mile to the shore. This bed extends to an unknown distance seaward, many stumps and roots of trees being observed firmly fixed in the clay, and bones of the deer, wild hog, horse, and the *Bos longifrons* occurring in the peat, and with these the antler of a red deer, fashioned into a tool for piercing. The molar tooth of a mammoth, stained with the black color of the peat, and retaining much of its animal matter, was (as referred to elsewhere) found here.‡

Porlock Bay.

On the Bristol Channel, at Porlock Bay, on the coast of Somersetshire, Mr. Godwen-Austen called attention in 1866 to a submerged forest, which extends far from the land; and Sir C. Lyell believes that there was formerly a woodland tract uniting Somersetshire and Wales, through the middle of which the ancient Severn

* Ancient Stone Implements, p. 608. † Ib., p. 596.

‡ Principles of Geology, vol. i. p. 539.

flowed. And this throws some light on the Glamorganshire caves, which are fissures in the precipitous cliffs high above the sea.*

West of this some twenty-five or thirty miles, on the coast of Devonshire, we find evidences of a raised beach at Barnstaple Bay. After the elevation of this beach, a forest grew upon it, and since then the land has subsided, and we have here at present a submerged forest. This occurs at "Westward Ho," in the parish of Northam. There are also submerged peat-beds here, which may be seen at low water, and the stumps of some seventy or eighty large trees, projecting above this peat, were observed by Mr. Townshend M. Hall, F.G.S., in the winter of 1864 (after a heavy westerly gale). Mr. Hall published a paper on the subject in "The Student and Intellectual Observer," vol. iv. p. 338. He represents that the subsidence of the coast here amounts to some seventy feet. The bones and horns of the red deer are found in the submerged forest, lying among the roots of the trees, and, associated with them, flint flakes and chippings, oyster-shells, calcined flints, flint cores, pointed stakes of wood, etc.,—traces, evidently, of the Neolithic Age.

Barnstaple Bay.

But this is but half of the story. The raised beach is forty feet above the sea. This was once under the waves. It too, as we learn from the alluvial soil, lying above the "drift," must be assigned to the Neolithic Age. The level of the sea was originally one hundred and ten feet lower at this point. Then the forest flourished, and the flint-folk of the Neolithic Age left their implements in the soil and in the alluvium now marked by the traces of the sea. The land subsided until the beach was formed,—one hundred and ten feet. It then rose again until the beach became elevated forty feet above the waves. And all this has occurred since the so-called Neolithic Age.

Mr. Evans mentions also a submerged forest, occasionally visible at low water, at the foot of the cliffs at Bournemouth. The trees appear to be those of the Scotch fir, and local tradition speaks of the existence of an impassable morass so late as the commencement of the present century between the cliffs and the sea. The trees grow on the surface of a thick bed of hard peat.†

At Bournemouth.

The valley of the Thames seems also to have been disturbed. We find subterranean forests at Purfleet, Grays, Dogenham Marsh, and Tilbury Fort. In the Isle of Dogs a forest of this description was found at eight feet from the grass, consisting of elm, oak, and fir trees, some of the first of which were three feet four inches in diameter, accompanied by human bones and recent shells, but no traces of human implements.

The Thames.

* Principles of Geology, vol. i. p. 548.

† Ancient Stone Implements, p. 610.

The Thames too, like the Somme, in ancient times met the sea much higher up. Dion Cassius describes London as situated at "the *estuary* of a river," and Ptolemy describes Kent as all maritime, and not as bounded on one side by a river. Such would have been the case if the sea had flowed up to London and submerged the marshes on both sides of the river. Cæsar seems also to speak of the Thames as being higher up than the present London, locating it in the territory of King Cassivelaunus. The Romans (as the legend runs) in the beginning of the fourth century confined the river in artificial banks, such as exist at the present day. We mention elsewhere an account by Col. H. Lane Fox of the discovery of Roman remains and *piles* in layers of peat during some excavations at London Wall. Col. Fox speaks of these piles as the remains of ancient *kitchen-middens*. But they were not kitchen-middens: they indicate that there was formerly a "lake-dwelling" at London Wall. The Thames or the sea covered that spot, now far removed from the river. Piles have also been found north of the Bank, near the Mansion House, and in the line of old Wall Brook.

The sea formerly at London.

Remains of a lake-dwelling.

It is very plain, therefore, that the Thames at London formerly presented a much broader sheet of water than it does at present,—and this even after the occupation of the country by the Romans. Prior to that the river-level was, as in the case of the Somme, no doubt yet higher.

It is interesting to recognize that the great British metropolis in the time of Agricola was a *pile-village*.

In the south of England, in the county of Sussex, there is another river which bears the name of the Ouse. At Lewes, situated on this stream, about seven miles from the sea, an anchor was dug up in the last century. Another was found still higher up the Ouse, at Landport.*

There is an extraordinary example of a raised beach on the coast of Ireland, near Dublin. Dr. Mantell mentions that there is an ancient beach at this point, which has been elevated two hundred feet above the level of the sea, and which contained the bones of the Great Irish Elk.† This single example is sufficient to explain all the changes in physical geography alluded to by Sir Charles Lyell. It corresponds, in point of time, with the deposition of the river-gravels of the Somme Valley.

Coast of Ireland.

The flints in the English river-gravels "exactly resemble" those found in the valleys of the Somme and the Seine. There is also the same evidence of ice-action,—

The Palæolithic flints of England exactly like those of France.

* Archæologia, 1869, vol. xlii. p. 28.

† Wonders of Geology, vol. i. p. 133.

great blocks of sandstone occurring, some more than twenty feet in circumference and from one to two and a half feet thick. At Fisherton, near Salisbury, the remains of no less than twenty-one species of mammals were found in the gravel:—*Canis lupus, Canis vulpes, Hyæna spelæa, Felis spelæa, Bison minor, Bos primigenius, Ovibos moschatus, Cervus tarandus, Cervus* (*Guettardi ?*), *Cervus elephas, Equus* (four varieties), *Rhinoceros tichorinus, Elephas primigenius, Spermophilus* (*Superliosus ?*), *Lemmus torquatus, Lemmus* (*Norvegicus ?*), *Arvicola, Lepus timidus*, etc.

Fauna of the gravel.

Of birds there were found the bones and portions of the shells of the eggs of the wild goose and of the wild duck.

There were thirty-one species of land and fresh-water shells,—all still living in England.

Sir Roderick Murchison long ago (in 1851) pointed out the similarity between these formations, in his memoir on "The Drift of the South-East of England." He remarked that in the valleys of Kent, Sussex, Surrey, and Hampshire we find the same denudations of the chalk, the same angular flint terrace accumulations, accompanied by the remains of the same extinct species of animals, which have been observed in the valley of the Somme, and he inferred that we should (as has turned out to be the case) find the same implements of flint. He perceived that in this district the flint drift was not the lingering deposit of ages of comparative repose, but bore witness to short, though turbulent, agencies, performing, we may imagine, in a few years the work for which the uniformitarian demands his hundreds or thousands of centuries. In the first place, he points out that the denudation of the vast area of the Weald of Sussex and the neighboring counties must have been the result of upheavals, fractures, and accompanying denudations to the intensity of which existing nature offers little or no analogy. He shows that the configuration of the steep slopes of the North and South Downs facing the Wealdon Valley cannot possibly have been formed, as some theorists suppose, by ordinary diurnal action prolonged through countless ages. He next recognizes the results of an agency of vast intensity, and clear proofs of a great force that drifted the flint materials to the flanks of the denuded country in this district. He speaks of ancient mounds of drift arranged irregularly and at different altitudes upon their banks from twenty to one hundred feet above the present rivers,—the counterpart, therefore, of the Menchecourt and Moulin-Quignon beds at Abbeville. And he adds, "a glance at any of these materials at once bespeaks the tumultuous nature of their origin, for none of them contained water-worn or rounded pebbles. At Peppering, about eighty

Sir R. Murchison on the evidences of similarity between these French and English valleys.

Short, turbulent agencies.

Upheavals, fractures, and denudations.

feet above the Arun, bones of an elephant were found." (Jour. Geolog. Soc., vol. vii. p. 360.) And again:

"By no imaginable process of the longest-continued diurnal action could any portion of this detritus have been gradually derived during ages from the low chalk-hills." (Ib., p. 368.)

Again: "To my mind the circumstances of the same drift being placed in such different levels at Folkestone, and of its sloping up from the sea-board to a height of two hundred and twenty-two feet inland, are good evidences that these creatures were destroyed by violent oscillations of the land, and were swept by currents of water from their feeding-grounds into the hollows where we now find them, and where the argillaceous materials which covered them have favored their conservation."

The River-Gravel in Italy.

The worked flints, in association with the bones of extinct animals, have also been found in Italy,—at Ponte Molle, two miles from Rome; at Ponte Mammolo; at Monte Sacro; at Torre di Quinto; at Acquatraversa; and at other points.

At Ponte Molle, the ancient *Pons Milvius*, near the gates of Rome, at the depth of fifty feet is a layer of gravel, pebbles, etc. Above this are heavy layers of marl and sand; then another bed of gravel and pebbles; then sandy clays again; and, finally, the vegetable soil of Rome. The flint implements are found in both the lower and upper gravels, and with them the remains of *Elephas antiquus* and *Elephas meridionalis*, three species of Rhinoceros, three species of Hippopotamus, etc. These strata were examined by Signor Ceselli. There is an account of them in *Macmillan's Magazine* for 1867. Signor Ceselli, we are told, thinks he discovered traces of progressive handicraft between the lower and upper flints. In the upper stratum the workman was no longer content to get his edge or point by the mere chipping process. "*He begins to rub.*" In other words, the implements are partially polished. "Yet many of the flints of the lower stratum," as we are told, "show the hand of a master."

We have some farther information on this subject in the volume of the "Congrès International d'Anthropologie et d'Archéologie" for 1867.* M. de Rossi is reported as stating to the Congress that M. Indes had discovered at Ponte Molle some additional "archeolithic arms of a more highly finished character (plus perfectionnées) than those previously found:" they mark, says M. de Rossi, "the commencement of the transition to the neolithic or polished stone age."

The surface-soil of Rome yields "flint weapons of exquisite shape."†

* Pp. 109, 110.

† Macmillan's Mag., 1867, vol. xvi. pp. 357, 358.

There were found in these gravel deposits certain flint ornaments of a triangular shape, with a notch in them, and it is conjectured that they were strung originally on a thread.

It is in view of the indications here that the men of the Stone age had begun to "rub" or polish their flints, we presume, that Mr. Stevens, in his "Flint-Chips," remarks that "it is doubtful whether the Italian drift implements should be regarded as of equal age with the implements of the Somme Valley and those of Wiltshire, Hampshire, and Norfolk." *

We must not close the discussion of this branch of the subject without adding an account of the famous *Moulin-Quignon jaw*, the history of which is almost the counterpart of the "Bill Stumps, his mark," in the memorable chapter in the Pickwick memoirs.

The famous Moulin-Quignon jaw.

In 1863 a quarryman at Moulin-Quignon brought to M. Boucher de Perthes a shaped flint and a fragment of a human molar found in the gravel. Afterwards another workman informed M. Boucher de Perthes of the discovery of another bone (which proved to be a human jaw). The workman had not removed the bone, nor disturbed the earth around it. M. Boucher de Perthes with a number of friends at once visited the spot and carefully exhumed the precious relic. A flint hatchet was found near it. The spectators all remarked on the identity of the *patina* or colored crust on the jaw, the flint, and the adjacent pebbles. These remains were found in the "upper-level" gravel,—the oldest stratum of the Somme gravels. The tidings were at once sent to England, and forthwith Messrs. Prestwich, Evans, and Tylor repaired to Abbeville, where the jaw was duly submitted to their consideration. Messrs. Evans and Tylor suspected some foul play,—Mr. Evans suggesting that the axe had been artificially stained with the irony deposit which discolored it. M. Boucher de Perthes insisted that he had himself removed the articles from the earth in which they were imbedded in the presence of a number of gentlemen,—that the earth had not been previously disturbed,—and that the two workmen were men of irreproachable character.

It is true that a reward had been offered by M. Boucher de Perthes for fossils, and that a number of attempts had been made to deceive him.

Subsequently Dr. Falconer wrote an article in the London *Times* of April 25 on the subject, which led to an animated discussion as to whether the jaw was authentic. Unable to reach any satisfactory conclusion, a scientific conference was finally called to meet at Paris in May. It was attended by the following eminent *savans:* MM. de Qua-

* Page 176.

trefages, Lartet, Delesse, Desnoyers, Milne-Edwards, Gaudry, and Bourgeois, and by Messrs. Falconer, Busk, Prestwich, and W. B. Carpenter. The conference remained in session three days. The jaw was sawn across and washed,—the black coating or matrix being readily removed by the sponge. There was no appearance of *dendrites* on the surface or within the bone; nor any infiltration through it of mineral matter. The substance of the bone was dry and friable, but tolerably firm under the saw. The section was fresh-looking, *and emitted distinctly the odor of sawn bone.* The molar too which had been cut by the saw had the same appearance of freshness. The dental canal was lined with fine gray sand, indicating previous lodgment in a non-ferruginous sandy bed. Mr. Busk thought the jaw resembled many cemetery-bones, but that it was unlike the fossil bones of the Somme Valley, all of which had been covered with *dendrites.* Besides, it was found that the material of the gangue or matrix, applied soft to any solid, would adhere with great tenacity,—indicating that the deposit on the bone might be artificial. Most, if not all, of the members of the English commission pronounced the flint hatchets said to have been discovered unauthentic, until finally the French *savans* were shaken.

The conference thereupon broke up, and adjourned to Abbeville.

Fresh excavations were undertaken under the inspection of the commission. These resulted in the discovery of several hatchets which were believed to be genuine, though not possessing the characteristic *patina,* or other proofs of antiquity relied on. After a due consideration of all the facts in the case, the investigation terminated in a conviction on the part of every member of the commission that no fraud had been practised.

But all did not agree as to the *age* of the fossil bone. Dr. Falconer and Mr. Busk reaffirmed their original doubts with regard to its absolute age, considering the appearance of freshness inconsistent with the idea of its being coeval with the remains of the extinct quadrupeds.

M. Milne-Edwards, President of the Academy of Sciences, and M. de Quatrefages, the eminent physiologist, expressly held themselves uncommitted as to the age of the beds; and the distinguished geologist, M. Elie de Beaumont, created a decided sensation by announcing that the Moulin-Quignon strata were not "diluvial,"—not even alluvium deposited by the encroachment of rivers on their banks,—but were simply composed of washed soil deposited on the flanks of the valley by excessive falls of rain, such as may occur exceptionally once or twice in a thousand years. A week later, before the same learned body, M. Elie de Beaumont reiterated these views, and stated that in his opinion these formations belonged to the "stone period," and were

Elie de Beaumont.

analogous to those of the peat-mosses of Denmark and the lake-dwellings of Switzerland.

We have thus a human jaw-bone from this famous deposit, which, according to Sir Charles Lyell, Sir John Lubbock, Mr. Evans, etc., must be several hundred thousand years old—which, however, when cut with a saw, emitted distinctly the odor of fresh bone!

CHAPTER XX.

THE MAMMOTH.

The Date of the Palæolithic Age to be fixed by the Time of the Disappearance of the Mammoth, Reindeer, etc.—Popular Misconception with regard to the Disappearance of Wild Animals.—Disappearance of the Buffalo in America.—The Bear, the Wolf, the Elk, the Antelope, the Moose, etc.—The Thessalian Lion.—The Moa.—The Dodo.—The Bear, Wolf, Beaver, and Bustard in Europe.—The Hippopotamus in Southern Africa.—The Elephant and the Rhinoceros in Northern India.—Extinction of the Urus and Aurochs.—Reindeer in the Hercynian Forest in the Days of Sallust and Cæsar.—In Scotland in the Twelfth Century.—Remains found near London.—Gaston de Foix.—Prof. Nilsson's Opinion that the Reindeer of Lapland is of a Different Species from that of the Palæolithic Age.—The Great Irish Elk.—Remains found in the Peat-beds and Crannoges of Ireland.—Found in Association with Iron Sword, and with Jet Rings.—Found beneath Altar-stone on the Rhine.—Irish Lyre made of Bones of.—Freshness of some of the Bones, and Large Percentage of Animal Matter.—Remains of the Elephant.—Former Marvellous Stories with regard to.—The Knee-bone of Ajax.—The Skeleton of Orion.—Skeleton of the Cyclops.—The Remains of Orestes.—The Giant of Lucerne.—The Tooth of St. Christopher.—The Fossil Unicorn of Leibnitz.—Teutobocchus Rex.—Remains of the Mastodon and Mammoth in America.—Mr. Peale's Discoveries.—Rev. E. Fontaine's Account of the associated Bones of the Mammoth, Flint Implements, and Pottery on the Island of Petite Anse, Louisiana.—Similar Discovery by Prof. Holmes on the Ashley River, near Charleston.—The Discoveries of Dr. Koch in Missouri.—Sir C. Lyell on the Discovery of the Mastodon's Remains in Shallow Ponds.—Two Remarkable Cases from Sir C. Lyell.—Remains of the Mammoth in the Peat Deposits of Wales and England —In America, the Remains of the Mammoth and Mastodon found on the Surface and in the most Superficial and Recent Deposits.—Prof. Hall's Account of such Discoveries in New York.—Prof. Mather on Same Subject.—Sir C. Lyell.—Col. Hamilton Smith on the Remains of the Megatherium found on the Surface of the Soil in South America.—The Bones of this Animal used there by Natives for Fire-places.—Original Account of the Famous Mammoth found by Dr. Koch in Gasconade County, Missouri. —Col. Whittlesey.—Prof. Winchell.—Other Examples,—Prof. Shaler in the *American Naturalist* on the Recent Existence of the Mammoth and Mastodon.—Dr. Warren's Newburg Mastodon.—Freshness of its Bones.—Sir C. Lyell on the Remarkable Preservation of the Bones of these Animals in America.—The Siberian Mammoth.—Found imbedded in the Ice, or Frozen Soil.—Vivid Account of the Finding of the Carcass of a Mammoth.—Remains of the Mammoth in Alaska.—Mr. Boyd Dawkins pronounces the Cave-Lion identical with the Existing Lion.—The Cave-Hyæna the same with the Spotted Hyæna of Southern Africa.—The Cave-Bear pronounced by Mr. Busk to be the Grizzly Bear.—The So-called Cave-Horse.—Result of the Foregoing Evidence.

When did these things occur?

IF we inquire, And when did all this take place? the reply to the question depends mainly on the answer to another question, When was it that the reindeer was living in Southern France and on the slopes of the Pyrenees? and when did the Mammoth and the Great Irish Elk and the Tichorine Rhinoceros—and the cave-bear and the cave-lion and the cave-hyæna—disappear from Europe?

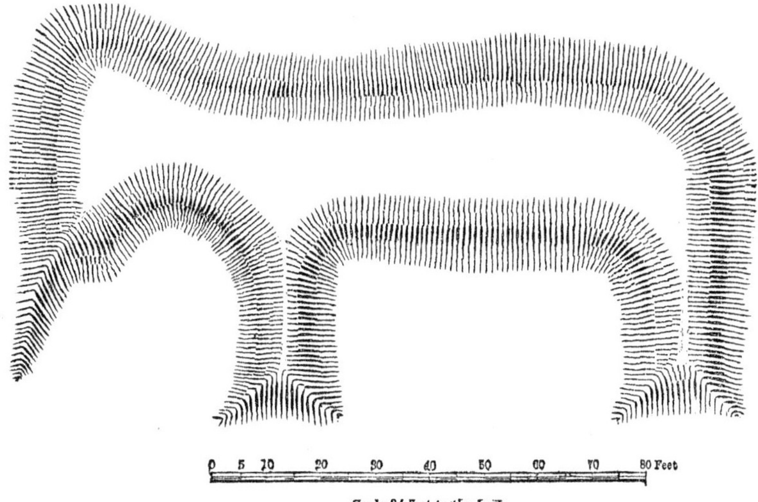

THE BIG ELEPHANT MOUND IN GRANT COUNTY, WISCONSIN.

It is the popular impression, and it is asserted by those who believe in the antiquity of man, that the Urus, the Aurochs, the Reindeer of Western and Central Europe, the Megaceros, the Mammoth, the Woolly Rhinoceros, etc., disappeared, all or most of them, long ages ago. We shall proceed to show that this opinion is erroneous, and that some of these extinct animals have lived in historic times, and that even the great pachyderms vanished from Europe, from Siberia, and from America, at a comparatively recent period. This point established, the argument for the antiquity of man is practically demolished.

The disappearance of wild animals.

The Buffalo, etc.

Great misconception exists with regard to the lapse of time naturally involved in the disappearance of wild animals. The rapid disappearance of the buffalo in America is a case in point. This animal is now driven to the western part of the United States, and will soon, no doubt, be entirely extinct. The same is true of the bear and the wolf in America, which, a few centuries ago, abounded on the Atlantic coast. Dr. Hoy, in a paper read two or three years since, before the Wisconsin Academy of Sciences, states that the elk, which existed in that State as late as 1863, is probably now extinct. The last buffalo was killed in 1832. The antelope, which was found there in the time of Father Hennepin, has also disappeared. The last wild turkey [?] was killed in 1846. The otter, the beaver, and the moose still linger.

Two centuries ago the moose ranged as far south as Pennsylvania and the Ohio River, and herds of bison grazed in the valley of the Connecticut.

The Moose.

We know from Aristotle and Herodotus that the lion was formerly common in Macedonia, Thrace, and Thessaly. It formerly abounded also in Arabia, Syria, and Babylonia. M. Figuier, in his "Mammalia," remarks that this animal is rapidly diminishing even in Africa, and observes that "our grandchildren will probably know the Lion only from our descriptions."

The Lion.

Formerly five hundred to a thousand of the stag and the fallow-deer were slain in England at a hunting-match; now they are only preserved by the greatest care. The otter, the marten, the polecat, formerly abundant, have been almost entirely destroyed.

Stag.

The moa has become extinct in New Zealand within a very recent period. Dr. Hector, in a communication to *Nature*, announces the discovery of a part of the skeleton of one of these gigantic birds, upon the posterior portion of which the skin, partially covered with feathers, is still attached by the shrivelled muscles and ligaments. Numerous localities have been discovered in New Zealand where the bones of the moa remain in immense profusion, and *usually accompanied by native implements of stone, some of which are of great perfection of finish.* Here we have in the nineteenth century of the Christian era the union and juxtaposition of extinct animals and the flint implements.

Moa.

The grotesque and gigantic dodo was found by navigators in the island of Mauritius in the sixteenth century. It too is now extinct.

The brown bear, according to M. Dupont, lingered in Belgium until the Middle Ages. It continued in Scotland, according to Mr. Boyd Dawkins, down to the middle of the eleventh century. The wolf was found in Scotland as late as 1306, and in Ireland till 1710. Giraldus Cambrensis met with the beaver in 1188, in the river Teivy, in Cardiganshire. The bustard was formerly seen on the heaths and downs of Britain in flocks of forty and fifty.

Bustard.

Figuier also informs us that the hippopotamus inhabits Southern and Eastern Africa, but that they are fast disappearing. In the time of Levaillant, that is to say, in the eighteenth century, they abounded in the colony of the Cape of Good Hope; but in 1838 there were only two left, on the property of a rich horse-breeder, who very carefully protected them. We find it represented in the ancient tombs of Egypt, but it has now retreated above the first cataract,—indeed, is rarely seen below the second.

Hippopotamus.

The disappearance of the elephant and rhinoceros in India is full of instruction on this subject. Three centuries ago, the famous Mogul emperor Báber (the great-grandson of Timour Lang,

Asiatic Elephant.

or Tamerlane), in his public memoirs, mentions the occurrence of the rhinoceros, wild buffalo, and lion in the neighborhood of Benares, and that of the elephant near Chunar. "In the jungles around Chunar," he remarks, "there are many elephants;" and he elsewhere states that they are found in the district of Kalpe (or Kulpe), and "as you advance east they increase."* The translator of this work, in a note on this passage, written fifty or sixty years ago, observes, "The improvement in Hindustan must be prodigious. The wild elephant is now confined to the forests of Himâla and to the ghâts of Malabar. A wild elephant near Karrah, Manikapore, or Kalpe, at the present day, is totally unknown."

Soon forgotten.

At this time the rhinoceros has long been extirpated, with not so much as a *tradition*, says Figuier, of it remaining, in all the parts where Báber mentions its former existence; but in the desert region northwest of Delhi the lion was numerous within the memory of living man, "and there we learn that already *hardly a tradition remains of this formidable animal.*"†

Benares and Chunar are some two hundred and fifty miles south of the Himalaya range, while Kalpe, farther west, is equally distant. And yet these great animals have entirely disappeared from the intervening region, leaving scarcely a recollection of their existence behind. Why, then, may not the American Mastodon and the Siberian Mammoth have disappeared three or four thousand years ago, and man have lost almost totally the memory of their former presence?

Recent existence of the Urus.

The Urus, or *Bos primigenius*, which is one of the extinct animals whose remains are found in the bone-caverns and river-gravels, is mentioned by Cæsar as existing in the Hercynian Forest; is alluded to in the Niebelungen Lied in the twelfth century; and, according to Herberstein, was found in Germany in the sixteenth century. In the Museum at Lund there is a skeleton of this animal (found, we presume, in the Swedish peat), in which one of the vertebræ still shows traces of a wound, made, in the opinion of Prof. Nilsson, by a flint arrow. Bones of this species have also been found in the tumuli, as well as in the lake-habitations and the shell mounds.

Recent existence of the Aurochs.

The Aurochs, or European Bison, whose remains are found also in the river-gravel and the older bone-caves, is not mentioned by Cæsar, but both Pliny and Seneca speak of it as existing in their time; and it is also named in the Niebelungen Lied. It existed in Prussia as late as 1775, and is still found wild in the Caucasus. The present Emperor of Russia, also, has twelve herds, which he carefully

* See Mammalia, by Louis Figuier, pp. 148, 150.

† Ib., p. 143.

protects in the forests of Lithuania. The stuffed skins of this animal may be seen in the British Museum.

There is now no doubt of the fact that the *Bos primigenius* and the *Bos longifrons* were found in the neighborhood of London during the period of the Roman occupation of Britain. Excavations made a few years since in the vicinity of London Wall to the depth of from seventeen to twenty-two feet reached a gravel similar to the Thames ballast. On this rests a bed of peat from seven to nine feet thick, and above this were the remains of London earth, composed of the accumulated rubbish of the city. In excavating the peat it was found to be interspersed with wooden piles of oak and elm. The peat was full of Roman relics,—planks containing Roman nails, red Samian pottery, bronze and copper pins, iron knives, tweezers, iron shears, a piece of polished metal mirror, the leathern soles of shoes and sandals, some thickly studded with hob-nails, the *caliga* of the Roman legions, etc. Mingled with these works of art were the bones of the horse, ass, red deer, wild boar, wild goat, dog, *Bos primigenius*, *Bos longifrons*, *Bos frontosus*, etc. The peat had grown some eight feet in four hundred years.

London Wall.

Prof. Steenstrup remarks that the *Veson cornipotens* of the Chronicle of St. Gall (tenth century) is nothing else than the Urus of Cæsar.*

It is of more importance to our present inquiry to ascertain when the reindeer disappeared from France and England. We have it on the authority of Cæsar that it was found in his day in the Hercynian Forest.†

Reindeer. Alluded to by Cæsar.

We know, moreover, on the authority of Torfæus, and from other evidence, that the Norwegian jarls in the twelfth century used to cross the sea to Scotland to hunt the reindeer.‡ Its bones also are found in the ruined towers (previously mentioned by us) which occur in North Scotland, called "Brochs" or "Burghs," some of which were in use in the twelfth century.

In Scotland in the twelfth century.

---

* "Man as the Cotemporary of the Mammoth and the Reindeer." See Smiths. Rep. for 1867, p. 362.

† "Est bos cervi figurâ cujus a mediâ fronte inter aures unum cornu existit, excelsius magisque directum his quæ nobis nota sunt cornibus. Ab ejus summo, sicut palmæ, rami quam lati diffunduntur." (De Bel. Gal., vi. 26.) This is the passage usually cited, and some persons refuse to believe that the reindeer is referred to. But Cæsar states elsewhere, speaking of the Germans, "et pellibus aut parvis rhenonum tegumentis utuntur." (De Bel. Gal., vi. 21.) And Sallust, to the same purpose, "Germani infectum rhenonibus corpus tegunt." Fragm. incertæ sedis. 18. Dietsch.

Isidore (A.D. 600) has a passage implying that the reindeer was hunted in his time at no remote distance from the Rhine. It is as follows: "Renones sunt velamina humerorum et pectoris usque ad umbilicum atque intortis villis adeo hispida ut imbres respuant. Dicti autem renones a Rheno Germaniæ flumine ubi iis frequenter utuntur." Isid., Orig., xix. c. 23.

‡ International Congress of Pre-hist. Lit., vol. for 1868. Paper on Pre-historic Mammalia, by Mr. W. Boyd Dawkins, p. 287.

There is a curious passage cited by Buffon from a work entitled "Le Miroir de Phébus des déduits de la Chasse," written by Gaston de Foix in the fourteenth century. This Gaston was third count of Foix and Lord of Béarn, who at an early age joined a crusade in behalf of the distressed Teutonic Knights against the Paynims of Lithuania. He was passionately fond of hunting, and usually entertained sixteen hundred dogs. According to Cuvier, after his crusade in Lithuania he crossed over into Norway and Sweden to hunt reindeer; and in the work in question, referring to that journey, he writes of the reindeer, "J'en ai veu en Nourvegue et Xuedene et en ha oultre mer, mes en Romain pays en ay je peu vus." Which plainly appears to assert that he had sometimes seen them south of those regions; but Sir John Lubbock does not think the passage should be so construed. What other construction it can bear we do not perceive. By the "Roman country" we understand Prussia, which at that time was the possession of the Teutonic order, but which, as well as Denmark, owned allegiance to the Holy Roman Empire.

Gaston de Foix.

There is other evidence of the most positive character that the reindeer was found in Southern Sweden about the tenth century. During the session of the International Archæological Congress at Stockholm last year the members of the body made an excursion to the isle of Björkö, in Lake Mälar, near Stockholm, where there is an ancient cemetery of two thousand tumuli. Within a few hundred yards from this is the site of the ancient town. Several trenches were run through this locality, and many relics obtained by the members of the Congress. On the occasion, Dr. Stolpe, who was familiar with the previous discoveries at this point, delivered a lecture on the island and its remains. They all, he stated, belong to the Second Age of Iron in Sweden, and consisted of implements of iron, ornaments of bronze, and animal bones. Kufic coins have also been found, along with cowrie-shells (*Cypræa moneta*) and silver bracelets. The number of animal bones met with is immense, more than fifty species being represented, and, what is especially noteworthy, *the marrow-bones were all crushed or split;* just as in the palæolithic times. The principal wild beasts were the lynx, the wolf, the fox, the beaver, the elk, the *reindeer*, etc.

Dr. Stolpe refers the foundation of this pre-historic city to "about the middle of the eighth century after Christ," and says it was probably destroyed "about the middle of the eleventh century." *

During this period the reindeer existed in this part of Sweden, that is, only one degree above the northern limits of Denmark.

A discovery made a year or two since would seem to settle the ques-

* Academy, August 29, 1874.

tion of the recent presence of the reindeer in England. In 1870 Mr. Henry Wood mentioned at the meeting of the British Association that certain excavations made by the East London Water-Works Company had revealed the presence of shell marl in the Walthamstow marshes, the shells being all recent. He added that in this bed they had discovered *bronze spear-heads, arrow-heads, knives*, etc., accompanied by the bones of man, the wolf, the fox, the beaver, the wild deer, the red deer, the roebuck, the fallow-deer, and the *reindeer.* Mr. Wood remarked that the discovery of the beaver, red deer, and reindeer within seven miles of London was astonishing.

Found near London with bronze weapons.

The article on "The Antiquity of Man" in the *British Quarterly Review* for April, 1874, refers to this discovery, and mentions also that this animal has been found in the layer of peat underneath the alluvium of the Thames at Crossness, in the peat of Yorkshire, and "in several places in Scotland and Ireland." The reviewer is, in consequence, compelled to admit that the reindeer lived in the British Islands during the Neolithic Period.* The writer proceeds to comment on the severity of the climate which must have prevailed in England at this time. It "must have been similar," he says, "to that of the regions in which he [the reindeer] now lives." So that it does not require ages, as the geologists say, to effect a change of climate.

Prof. Nilsson, at the meeting of the International Congress of Archaic Anthropology, at Paris, in 1867, is reported as taking the ground that "the reindeer which was found in the bogs of Sweden is not the same species of animal as that now inhabiting the North, and that the fossil reindeer might, then, enjoy and thrive in a much warmer climate." M. de Quatrefages cited Pallas

The ancient reindeer perhaps a different species.

---

* Brit. Quart. Rev., April, 1874, p. 189, Amer. Reprint.

In "Matériaux pour l'Histoire de l'Homme," 1re Livraison, 1874, we have an account of a station referred to the bronze age, in the valley of the Tardoire, in the department of Charente, in France, by M. A. Fermond. The relics discovered were found in a "rock-shelter." They consisted of worked flints, fragments of pottery, an earthen dish like those found in the Swiss lake-dwellings, three small fragments of bronze, a hair-pin of bronze, a beautiful bronze hatchet, etc. With these were found the bones and the teeth of the ox, the stag, the wild boar, and the reindeer, and also human bones. The objects occurred at the depth of one metre. See p. 14 of the work referred to.

Although there is no hint here of the "remaniement" which the French archæologists are so fond of suggesting in these cases, and apparently no trace whatever of any disturbance, we think it by no means improbable that these remains are not strictly cotemporary. They may be, but we are rather inclined to the opinion that the flints and the bones of the reindeer precede by a short interval the relics of bronze. The fauna belongs (excluding the reindeer) to the neolithic or the bronze age. We have, therefore, in any view, the bones of the reindeer in the polished stone age, a fact which, as we have seen, is often observed in other cases.

to show that even in the last century the reindeer, "assisted by great forests, found its way almost to the shores of the Caspian." He thought that the difference between the fossil and the present reindeer may be only a slight difference of breed. M. Vogt said "Yes," and cited the difference between the domestic and the wild breeds.*

The reference to the presence of this animal on the Caspian recalls the fact that Pliny† makes mention of the *Tarandus* of the Scythians.

In the well-known work of Prof. Nilsson on the Stone Age we find the same views expressed. "The reindeer," he says, "whose skeletons are found in the peat-bogs of Scania belong to quite a different race from those of Lapland. They had no doubt immigrated to Scania from some more southerly part, and may possibly belong to the same race as the reindeer which during Cæsar's time lived in the Hercynian Forest."

Prof. Nilsson then makes the statement that the reindeer had not proceeded "from Scania up towards Lapland:" this, he remarks, "*is proved by there never having been found a skeleton nor even a bone of a reindeer in any of the provinces that are situated between Scania and Lapland.*"‡

We learn from Mr. Worsaae that the reindeer is found not only in the Danish peat, but in the more recent layers of that formation. We shall see that the archæologists speak of several layers of this peat, the oldest containing remains of the primeval pine forests of Denmark, and corresponding to the Stone Age; while above this is a layer containing the remains of the oak forests which are said to have succeeded the pine forests, and which coincided in point of time with the Bronze Age. We learn from the "Primeval Antiquities of Denmark" that "at a period when the country was covered with forests of oak, in all probability, there lived animals that are now extinct, such as the reindeer, the elk, and the aurochs, the horns and bones of all which are frequently found" (he is speaking of the peat-bogs). We thus have the reindeer in Denmark in the "Bronze Age," the recent date of which in that country will elsewhere appear.

If farther evidence is necessary on this point, we may cite the high authority of Mr. Boyd Dawkins. He states in his paper on "The Classification of the Palæolithic Age by Means of the Mammalia," that the reindeer was probably living "in the bronze and iron ages." [In the same paper he speaks of the classification of the caves by M. Lartet,

---

* Anthropological Review, 1868, pp. 209, 210.

† Vol. ii. p. 304, Bohn's edit.

In America the caribou is seen even at the present day in living herds upon the northern shore of Lake Superior; while De Kay has met with their *disjecta membra* in Northern New York. Prehistoric Races of the United States, p. 88.

‡ Nilsson on the Stone Age, p. 249.

namely, the division into the Cave-bear, the Mammoth, the Reindeer, and the Aurochs periods, as "of no value." The animals, he says, are distributed in the river-gravel and the caves fairly, and generally together.]

It has been supposed that the *Megaceros*, or Great Irish Elk, is more ancient even than the *Elephas primigenius*. This magnificent animal was more than ten feet high, and measured from eight to eleven feet between the tips of its horns.

Recent existence of the Great Irish Elk.

It has been long known that its remains were found in the Irish bogs and in the Irish crannoges or lake-dwellings, but no entirely decisive evidence of its recent existence in Ireland was obtained until some few years since. The fact was suspected, but not ascertained. It is now, however, settled by several discoveries.

At the meeting of the Geological Society of Dublin in December, 1861, Dr. Petrie stated that he had in his possession *an iron sword* which had been found with the bones of the megaceros in the county of Meath; and we may add that Mr. Bailly referred to the discovery of the remains of the same animal, in association with spear-heads and pottery, in a lake in the canton of Berne, in Switzerland.

Remains found in a bog with iron sword.

The leg of a megaceros, with a portion of the tendons, skin, and hair on it, was found about 1864 in the county of Wexford, on the estate of H. Grogan Morgan, Esq., a specimen of which was sent to the Royal Dublin Society, and exhibited by Mr. Peale, Professor of Veterinary Surgery, to his class. See *Dublin Quarterly Journal of Science* for January, 1865; paper by Rob. H. Scott, Esq.

Found with the tendons, skin, etc., preserved.

It is stated also in this paper that Archdeacon Mansell mentions the discovery of a megaceros at Rathcannon, Limerick County, and with it a number of *jet rings*, and the bones of a dog or bear.

With jet rings.

There are allusions also in the "Book of Lismore," and in the "History of Ireland," published in the seventeenth century, and said to be by Peppard, to the chase of a great black deer, supposed to be the great elk.

Mentioned in the "Book of Lismore."

In an article published nearly forty years ago in the *Penny Magazine*, on the Great Irish Elk, it is stated that the head of one of these animals, some stone hatchets, and several bones of the urus, were found together in Germany in the same drain.* There is very little doubt that the "stone hatchets" referred to belonged to the age of polished stone, for at that time the palæolithic implements were not recognized, and would not have been spoken of.

---

* Ib., p. 300.

Col. Hamilton Smith mentions the discovery near Xanthen, on the Rhine, *beneath an altar of stone*, of the head of an Irish elk, and a quantity of ashes.*

Beneath an altar-stone.

The crannoges of Ireland, we have mentioned, are of recent date. In a paper on the Crannoges of Lough Crea, read before the Royal Irish Academy in Nov. 1863, it is stated that the animal remains dug up included those of the ox, sheep, goat, deer, pig, dog, wolf, and the head of a *Cervus megaceros* thirteen feet between the horns. With these were found a number of iron implements, a crozier of brass (with pieces of silver), a battle-axe, a cast for a coin, bone and stone implements, etc.† We may add that the writer concludes that iron was in use in the early age of the crannoges; and that when this crannoge on Lough Crea was built, the surface of the lake was seven feet higher than at present.

In the Irish Crannoges.

Mr. Steele, in his treatise on "Peat-Moss," tells us that "in Ireland, the horns and other remains of a gigantic species of deer, now extinct in the British Isles, have been found at the bottom of peat-bogs, many feet deep (Phil. Trans., vol. xxvii.). A nearly perfect and magnificent specimen of this fossil deer, named by some the Irish Elk, is preserved in the Royal Museum of the University of Edinburgh." ‡

Other examples.

Professor Jamieson and Dr. Mantell note the discovery in the county of Cork, Ireland, of a human body found in a peat-bog, at the depth of eleven feet. The soft parts were converted into adipocere, and the body, thus preserved, was enveloped in a deer-skin of such large dimensions as to lead them to the opinion that it belonged to the extinct elk.§ Professor Wilson, who is our authority for this case, then mentions one that indicates in an unmistakable manner a very recent period. At a meeting of the Archæological Institute, June 3, 1864, the Earl of Dunraven exhibited an imperfect *Irish lyre*, found in the moat of Desmond Castle, Adare, the material of which was pronounced by Professor Owen to be bone of the Irish elk.‖

Irish lyre made from bones of.

In the first edition of "Prehistoric Man" (we do not think the statement is contained in the second edition), Dr. Wilson affirms that "skeletons of the Irish elk have been found at Curragh, Ireland, in marshes, some of the bones of which were in such fresh condition that the marrow is described as having the appearance of fresh suet, and burning with a clear flame."¶

Fresh condition of the bones.

* Nat. Hist. Hum. Spec., p. 154.

† Dublin Quart. Jour. Sci. for 1864, p. 125.

‡ Steele on Peat-Moss, p. 11.

§ Wilson's "Prehistoric Man," 2d edit., p. 37.

‖ Ib., p. 37.

¶ Vol. i. p. 98.

The statements with reference to the freshness of some of the bones of the megaceros are corroborated by the *Dublin Quarterly Journal of Science.** According to this high authority, a centesimal analysis of a skeleton by Prof. W. Stokes yielded 43.45 of phosphates, with fluates, and 42.87 of animal matter; and Prof. Apjohn states that "the cartilage and gelatine had not been even perceptibly altered by time."

Even Prof. Agassiz admits the continuance of this great deer down to the fourteenth century to be "probable." At the meeting of the Boston Society of Natural History in 1868, he said that Brandt had proved from an examination of ancient documents in the Sclavonic tongue that the *Bos primigenius* was living in the forests of Lithuania and Poland up to the eleventh and thirteenth centuries, and added that "the presence of *Cervus megaceros* in the marshes of Europe up to the fourteenth century is also made probable."

To the same effect we read in "Matériaux pour l'Histoire de l'Homme:" "Le *Bos cervi figura* de César n'était ni un Élan, comme le suppose Lenz, ni un Cervus euryceros [megaceros], comme le croit Eichwold, mais bien un Renne, et M. Brandt croit l'avoir prouvé. Suivant lui, le *Machlis* ou l'*Achlis* que Pline distingue positivement de l'Elan, et le *Schelch* du poëme des *Niebelungen,* ne sont autre que le *Cervus euryceros.* En effet, cette grande espèce vivait en Allemagne au Xe siècle; et n'y devint complètement inconnue qu'à partir du XIIe siècle, époque à laquelle on la trouvait encore en Irlande." †

We have thus shown that the *Bos primigenius* was living in England during the occupation of the Romans, and in Germany in the twelfth century; that the aurochs existed in Prussia a century ago; that the reindeer lingered in Scotland until the twelfth century, and that it was found in Germany about the beginning of the Christian era; and that the great Irish elk continued in Ireland down to the Age of Iron, and in Germany, probably, until the twelfth century. These animals were the companions of the Mammoth and the Woolly Rhinoceros. Would it be strange if they too lingered down to a more recent period than we have been taught to believe? We have already found the remains of the existing African elephant in a cave in Central Spain.

If the elephant lived in Belgium (as he seems to have done) when the little urn figured on p. 210 was baked in the sun, and when the group of reindeer figured on p. 202 were sketched by some primeval artist, that does not *seem* very long ago. There is something exceedingly *human,* and a certain aroma of *proximity,* about that handiwork.

---

* For January, 1866, p. 22: Hart on "Fossil Deer of Ireland."

† Décembre, 1872, p. 534. It is added in a note, "D'après Hibbert, selon Ranking (Wars and Sports, London, 1826, p. 491), il aurait été détruit par les Romains."

The remains of the Elephant in Europe.

The bones of the elephant are found all over Europe at comparatively shallow depths, and it is amusing to remark now the wonder and astonishment which they excited in the minds of the ancients and even down to very recent times. The patella of a fossil elephant was believed by the Greeks to be *the knee-bone of Ajax*, and some great bones, no doubt those of an elephant, found in the island of Crete, are described by the naturalist Pliny, who states that they were "supposed to be *the skeleton of Orion.*" St. Augustine found on the sea-shore "a fossil human tooth" "which was a hundred times the size of the tooth of any person living." Much later Kircher tells us of a skeleton dug up near Rome, which, by an inscription attached to it, was known to be that of *Pallas* (slain by Turnus), and was higher than the walls of the city. The same author tells us that another skeleton was found near Palermo, that must have belonged to a man four hundred feet high, and who, therefore, could be no other than the *Cyclops*,—" most probably *Polyphemus.*" * Massigli, in his History of the Danube, describes the bones of an elephant found in Transylvania, which were conjectured to have belonged to one of the elephants which the Emperor Trajan carried with him in his expedition against the Dacians.

The body of Orestes, thirteen feet in length, discovered at Tegea by the Spartans, no doubt belonged to the same respectable animal.

In 1577 some immense bones were exposed to view by the uprooting of an oak near the cloisters of Reyden, in the canton of Lucerne, in Switzerland, which the celebrated physician Pläten declared to be those of a giant, whom he pronounced to be nineteen feet high. He proceeded to put the skeleton together, and sent it with an explanatory drawing to the Council of Lucerne. In 1706 the anatomist Blumenbach recognized the bones as those of an elephant. The good people of Lucerne in the mean time had adopted the image of the pretended giant as the supporter of the city arms.

The tooth of St. Christopher, shown at the church dedicated to that saint in the city of Valence, was the molar tooth of the *Elephas primigenius;* and M. Figuier informs us that in 1789 the canons of St. Vincent carried through the streets in public procession the arm of a saint to procure rain, which was nothing more than the femur of an elephant.

Leibnitz got hold of the bones and enormous tusks of an elephant, and constructed the skeleton of a fantastic animal which he denominated *The Fossil Unicorn.*

The best story on this subject, however, is that about Teutobocchus

* Edinburgh Review, May, 1811.

Rex, the barbarian king who invaded Gaul at the head of the Cimbri, and who was vanquished near *Aquæ Sextiæ* (Aix in Provence) by Marius, who carried him to Rome in triumphal procession. Teutobocchus Rex.

In January, 1613, the workmen in a sand-pit near the castle of Chaumont, in Dauphiny, between Montrecourt and Saint-Antoine, on the left bank of the Rhone, found a number of great bones. These were purchased by a country surgeon named Mazuyer, who gave out that he himself had made the discovery in a tomb thirty feet long by fifteen broad, *built of bricks*, upon which he found the inscription, TEUTOBOCCHUS REX. He added that in the same tomb he found a hundred medals with the effigy of Marius. In the bulletin which he issued, announcing his discovery, he reminded the public that, according to the testimony of Roman authors, the head of Teutobocchus exceeded in dimensions all the trophies borne upon the lances in the triumph. The skeleton of this Teutonic chief, as exhibited by Dr. Mazuyer, was twenty-five feet long by ten broad. It was carried through all the cities of France and Germany, and formally exhibited before Louis XIII., who contemplated it with the profoundest interest. It gave rise to an embittered controversy between the anatomist Riolan, who insisted that the bones were those of an elephant, and a physician by the name of Habicot, who defended the genuineness of the skeleton.

These bones are still in the Museum of Natural History in Paris. They remained at Bordeaux until 1832, when they were sent to Paris, where they were identified by M. de Blainville as belonging to a mastodon [mammoth?].

Bones of the mastodon were discovered near Albany, New York, in 1705, but attracted little attention. In 1759, M. de Longueil, a French officer, discovered, in what is now known as Big Bone Lick, in Kentucky, a number of these remains, which, on his return to France, he presented to Daubenton and Buffon. Daubenton referred them to the hippopotamus and the elephant, but Buffon convinced him and other French *savans* that they all belonged to the elephant, which he erroneously believed to be six or eight times the size of the existing elephant.

Bones of the American Mastodon and Mammoth.

In 1801, Peale discovered two complete skeletons in a marsh near Newburg, on the banks of the Hudson. Subsequently, Prof. Barton, of the University of Pennsylvania, discovered the bones of another skeleton at a depth of six feet in the soil. In the middle of the bones, and in a sac which was probably the stomach of the animal, he found a mass of vegetable matter, partly bruised, and composed of leaves and branches, among which was a rush belonging to a species yet common in Virginia.

Since that time remains of the mastodon and the mammoth have been found in great numbers throughout the United States.

The skeleton of a mammoth or mastodon was found on the roadside trench of the old Tezcuco road, in Mexico. In California their bones have been found in numerous instances. They occur, on the other hand, as far north as Canada.

Dr. Leidy regards the *Elephas Americanus* as a slightly different species from the mammoth of Europe. The American mastodon seems to have had no representative in Europe in the post-pliocene epoch.

Island of Petite Anse.

Remains found with pottery.

The Rev. Edward Fontaine, in his volume entitled "How the World was Peopled," gives an account of certain remains of the mammoth found on the island of Petite Anse, St. Mary's Parish, Louisiana. This island rests on an immense deposit of crystallized salt. At the depth of twelve feet, incredible quantities of pottery were thrown out of the pit by the miners, mingled with fragments of the bones of the elephant and other huge extinct quadrupeds. Mr. Fontaine, who is a geologist, examined this locality in 1867, in conjunction with Prof. Hilgard. Cane baskets, stone hatchets, a large stone anvil, and pottery of six different patterns, were thrown out in heaps with the fossil bones of the mammalia in question. The animals appear to have been bogged, and to have perished in the miry clay above the salt, which they frequented. The aborigines used the rock-salt, and the animals no doubt repaired to the spot for the same purpose. The whole island, some two thousand acres, resting upon the solid rock-salt, is, says Mr. Fontaine, of comparatively recent origin. All the formations are *Quaternary*, belonging to the "Bluff formation" of Mississippi,—a sort of loess, the remnant of the ancient valley of the great river, and overlying the "Orange Sand." The Orange Sand is newer than the Tertiary; and the valley in which the bones and the works of art are found is alluvium, washed from the surrounding hills, and the whole not more than sixteen feet thick. "In this recent deposit they are so mingled that we can only infer that the men and animals were probably coeval, and that they lived and died in an age not far removed from our own." It seems impossible to resist the conclusion that these remains are comparatively recent. The wooden coffins, the traces of which were found seven feet below the surface on the site of the gravel-pits at St.-Acheul, and assigned by Sir John Lubbock (p. 365) to the fourth century, were entirely destroyed; but here we have the cane baskets well preserved in association with the bones of the mammoth and great quantities of pottery, and an anvil for the manufacture of the pottery.

The attention of the Philadelphia Academy of Natural Sciences was called to the subject by Dr. Leidy in 1866. Dr. Leidy said that Mr. J. F. Clew, one of the proprietors of the salt-mines on the island of Petite Anse, had that day called on him, announcing a donation to the

Academy of a mass of pure rock-salt; and that Mr. Clew had mentioned in connection with the mines the discovery, at the depth of ten or fifteen feet, of the bones of the elephant, *well preserved*, and *beneath these*, near the stratum of rock-salt (which is at the depth of fifteen feet), an abundance of matting, portions of which were exhibited to Dr. Leidy. It was composed of a tough, flexible, split cane, and was plaited diagonally. The pieces were well preserved. Mr. Clew, on being asked, was under the impression that stone implements had been found. He added that at the sides of one of the pits the bones of the elephant, and pieces of matting, could *still be seen*,—as they had been allowed to remain undisturbed.*

Very similar is the testimony of Prof. Holmes, of Charleston, S.C. In 1859 he exhibited before the Philadelphia Academy of Natural Sciences a collection of fossils from the post-pliocene of Charleston, and made the following statement to the Academy: "Dr. Klipstein," he said, "who resided near Charleston, in digging a ditch for the purpose of reclaiming a large swamp, discovered and sent to me the tooth of a mastodon, with a request that I should go down and visit the place, as there were indications of the bones and teeth of the animal still remaining in the sands which underlie the peat-bed. Accordingly, with a small party of gentlemen, we visited the doctor, and succeeded not only in obtaining several other teeth and bones of this animal, but nearly one entire tusk, and immediately alongside of the tusk discovered the fragment of pottery which I hold in my hand, and which is similar to that manufactured at the present time by the American Indians." † These remains were found on the banks of the Ashley River, in a deposit of peat and sand, in an undisturbed bed. Underneath lie marine shells, corresponding to species now living on the coast of Carolina, but including also two species no longer found there, though common in the Gulf of Mexico and the West Indian seas.

Same juxtaposition near Charleston.

In 1867, Prof. Holmes is again reported as exhibiting before the Academy "specimens of extinct and recent animals, accompanied by the bones of men, together with pottery, stone arrow-heads, and hatchets" from the post-pliocene of Charleston.‡ The animal bones belonged to the hog, the horse, the mastodon, and an extinct gigantic lizard.

Dr. Koch insisted long ago, says Prof. Winchell, that he had found in Missouri such an association of mastodon and Indian remains as to prove that the two had lived cotemporaneously. And Prof. Winchell

* Proceedings Acad. Nat. Sci. of Phil., 1866, p. 109.

† Ib., July, 1859, pp. 178, 186.

‡ Ib., 1867, p. 125.

adds that he himself has seen the bones of the mastodon and elephant imbedded in peat at depths so shallow that he could readily believe the animals to have occupied the country during its possession by the Indians.*

Similar testimony is given by Sir Charles Lyell. He states that entire skeletons of the mastodon are met with in bogs and lacustrine deposits occupying hollows in "the glacial drift." "They sometimes occur in the bottom even of small ponds recently drained by the agriculturist for the sake of the shell-marl. In 1845 no less than six skeletons were found in Warren County, New Jersey, six feet below the surface, by a farmer who was digging out the rich mud from a small pond which he had drained."†

Remains of Mammoth in peat in Wales and England.

This author recites a case which affords a strong indication of the recent presence of the mammoth in Wales. A bed of peat was observed in the harbor of Holyhead by the Hon. W. Stanley, containing the stumps and roots of trees. The peat was three feet thick. It was exposed at low water, and stretched upwards to a slight elevation above the sea, where the excavations made for the railway in 1849 brought to light two perfect heads of the mammoth. The tusks and molars lay two feet below the surface in the peat.

Sir Charles naïvely remarks, "It is not improbable that this mammoth survived most of the lost species which were its contemporaries in what has been called the Cavern period." He thinks that it probably belonged to "a date intervening between the era of the lake-dwellings and that of the oldest epoch to which man has yet been traced back." ‡

This is a most important admission.

It is perfectly evident that these two mammoths belong to the period *succeeding* the deposition of the river-gravel. They are cotemporary with the *peat* of the Somme Valley. There has been a submergence of this coast. There are traces, says Sir Charles, of submerged forests "at St. Bride's Bay, in Pembrokeshire, and, proceeding farther to the north, in Cardiganshire, and again in North Wales (as in Anglesea and Denbighshire)." § The present locality is in Anglesea. At some time within the human period, the coasts have sunk. On the marshy shore, during this subsidence, the peat was formed. It is three feet thick. At the depth of two feet we find the remains of the mammoth. It is extorted from Sir Charles Lyell that "this mammoth [probably] sur-

* Sketches of Creation, p. 356.

† Elements of Geology, p. 183.

‡ Principles of Geology, vol. i. p. 550, Amer. edit.

§ Ib.

vived most of the lost species which were its contemporaries in what has been called the Cavern period." But if we can find *one single clearly-established case* of the existence of the mammoth a few centuries before the date of the Swiss Lake-Dwellings,—or, if Sir Charles Lyell chooses, a thousand or two thousand years before those settlements,—we prove that the antiquity of the great pachyderms does not exceed some 1500 or 2500 years B.C.

Another example.

We have spoken in the previous chapter, and in another connection, of the submerged forest, "and much peaty matter resting on bluish clay," at Torquay, mentioned by Sir Charles Lyell. We will recapitulate the facts, without troubling the reader to refer back. This forest is traceable for nearly a mile from the neighborhood of Tor Abbey to the sea-shore, and then running out into the sea. Many stumps and roots of trees are observable in the clay, while bones of the deer, wild hog, horse, and *Bos longifrons* occur in the peat: with these the antler of a red deer was observed by Mr. Pengelly, having several cuts on it made by a sharp instrument, and the whole fashioned into a tool for piercing. From this forest-bed, in thirty feet of water, the fishermen drew up in their trawl, a few years before 1851, the molar tooth of the mammoth, stained with the black color of the peat, and retaining much of its animal matter, its fresh condition perhaps due to the antiseptic quality of the peat.*

Here we have precisely the same state of things with that in Anglesea on the same coast. The tooth of the mammoth retained "much of its animal matter." Sir Charles thinks this was due to the preservative properties of the peat; and no doubt he is right. But the fact that the tooth was found in this peat-bed containing the bones of the *Bos longifrons* (characteristic of the neolithic and the historic period), the red deer, the deer, the hog, the horse, proves that it too belongs to a period *subsequent* to the deposition of the river-gravel, and cotemporaneous with the French peat.

There are other examples of the occurrence of the bones of the mammoth in the English peat. The Rev. D. Fisher found the remains of one which had been overwhelmed in a bog, near Colchester, the small bones of the feet being in their natural position. In an address before the (British) Geological Society (reported in *The Geologist* for 1864, p. 64) Mr. G. S. Poole stated that the remains of the mammoth and the tichorine rhinoceros had been found in a peat-moss above those of man and fragments of pottery.

As we shall see hereafter, it is the rarest occurrence to find the remains of these pachyderms in Scotland or Ireland.

---

* Principles of Geology, vol. i. p. 549.

In America the remains of the Mammoth and Mastodon found in the most superficial deposits.

The bones of the mammoth and mastodon, in America, are generally found in the most superficial deposits,—those of the mastodon ordinarily in peat-bogs, swamps, and the shell-marl of small lakes and ponds. This shell-marl is of the same age as the peat,—a parallel formation,—both of them containing, at the same time, along with the extinct animals, the remains of existing animals.

The shell-marl, like the peat, is a very recent formation, and is often deposited with great rapidity. Water holding carbonic acid in solution has the property of dissolving carbonate of lime, which is deposited in the form of a fine powder wherever carbonic acid gas escapes. Rain-water, and the water from springs, holding this gas in solution, and percolating through limestone rocks, or passing over their surfaces, will dissolve a portion of the lime, and carry it into ponds, lakes, and marshes, where it is deposited in the form of a white calcareous powder. It is there absorbed and secreted by testaceous animals, whose outer covering or shell is thus formed. In these places, where large quantities of calcareous matter are held in solution, these small testaceous animals grow in great abundance, and live but a short time, their places being taken by other generations, which in time die, and thus large deposits are formed, called *shell-marl.* Shallow ponds or lakes, where the deposit of shells and lime is rapidly carried on, finally become *filled up to the water-line.**

Skeletons of quadrupeds, says Lyell, are met with abundantly in recent shell-marls in Scotland. The remains of several hundred skeletons have been procured from five or six small lakes in Forfarshire, including the stag, ox, boar, horse, sheep, dog, hare, fox, wolf, and cat.†

Appleton's New American Cyclopædia says the mastodon is "generally found at the depth of from five to ten feet in lacustrine deposits, bogs, and beds of infusorial earth."

In the eighth volume of the "Smithsonian Contributions to Knowledge," we are told that "the remains of the mammoth and the megatherium (mastodon?) are found near the surface in the United States, and do not exhibit signs of having been rolled by floods, or seriously disturbed." An account is given of a megatherium exhumed while digging the Brunswick Canal, so near the surface that the roots of a pine penetrated its bones.

In the superb volumes of the "Natural History of New York," pub-

---

* Geology of New Jersey, by George H. Cook, State Geologist. Extract from Dr. Kirchell's Report for 1854, p. 47.

† Principles of Geology, Amer. edit., vol. ii. p. 543.

lished by the State (Part IV., Geology), we have an account by Mr. James Hall of the remains of a number of mastodons found in the Fourth Geological District of that State. Prof. Hall's testimony.

1. In the town of Perrinton, in the bank of a small stream, in gravel and sand, a tusk and several teeth.

2. In 1817, some remains in a hollow or water-course, at Rochester.

3. In 1838, while excavating the Genesee Valley Canal, at its junction with Sophia Street, Rochester, a tusk, nine feet long, and the pelvis of a mastodon, were found, intermingled with gravel and covered by clay and loam, and under these a deposit of shell-marl.

4. During the digging of the Erie Canal, at Holley, in Orleans County, a large molar tooth was found in a swamp near the village.

5. In a small muck swamp in Stafford, Genesee County, a molar tooth was found, a few years since, below the muck, and upon a deposit of clay and sand.

6. At Geneseo, in Livingston County, several years since, many bones and three teeth were found in a swamp, beneath a deposit of muck, intermingled with sandy calcareous marl.

7. At Jamestown, Chautauqua County, a tooth was found several feet below the surface in gravel.

Mr. Hall observes:

"In all situations where these remains appear to have been left undisturbed, they are associated with the most recent deposits, proving that the animal has existed upon the surface since the present condition of things prevailed.

"In speaking of this subject" (he proceeds), "Dr. Kage remarks, 'Rejecting as fabulous the accounts by Barton about twigs* in the stomach, it has certainly been discovered in positions indicating that the animal perished and left its bones on or near the surface where now found. Cuvier states that the mastodons discovered near the Great Osage River were almost all found in a vertical position, as if the animals had merely sunk in the mud. (Oss. Foss., éd. alt., vol. i. pp. 219, 222.) Since that time many others have been found in swamps, a short distance beneath the surface (frequently some of the bones appearing above the soil), in an erect position, conveying the perfect impression that the animal (probably in search of its food) had wandered into a swamp, and, unable to extricate himself, had died on the spot. Such an incident doubtless occurred to the animal whose remains we assisted to disinter, some years ago, at Long Branch, N.J. He was in a natural vertical position, his body supported by turf soil or black earth, and his feet resting on a gravelly bottom. The occurrence of bones of other ani-

* They are not fabulous, however.

mals, not yet extinct, with those of the mastodon, is not a conclusive evidence of their cotemporaneous existence; but we cannot deny that it furnishes strong reasons for believing them to have been of very recent date. We think it highly probable that the mastodon was alive in this country at a period when its surface was not materially different from its actual state, and that he may have existed cotemporaneously with man.'

No doubt of the very recent existence of the Mastodon.

"Of the very recent existence of this animal" (Prof. Hall continues) "there seems to be no doubt; the marl-beds and muck swamps where these remains occur are the most recent of all superficial accumulations (indeed, they are now forming), and the surface had arrived at its present condition generally before these began to be formed. Any great change, such as the submergence of the land, would obliterate these deposits, and mingle their contents with the surrounding drift. . . .

"The situation of the bones in the Fourth District offers no exception to the general rule, but rather confirms it in several instances."

Mr. Hall further states that Mr. Williams informed him that at the summit level of the Genesee Valley Canal, near New Hudson, four miles from Cuba, several deer-horns, and the horns of an elk, were found twelve feet below the surface, in a muck deposit. Also a piece of wood gnawed by beavers.

This is just such a deposit as we constantly find the remains of the mastodon in.

The foregoing survey of Mr. Hall, with the Report, was made in 1843.

Testimony of Prof. Mather.

In the "Geology of the First District of New York," in the same series of volumes, by Wm. W. Mather, we are told that "the bones of the Mastodon and the Fossil Elephant are frequently found in the peat bogs of Orange County. Multitudes of them are doubtless entombed in these and other marshes." They are supposed to have been mired. An account is given of one found near Hudson, Albany County, on the Helderberg Mountain, in a bed of shell or lake marl, where it appeared to have been mired, on the bank of a small pond-hole or marsh.

These remains, says Prof. Mather, "are found only in alluvial deposits, and most frequently in peat, lake or shell marl, in banks of streams, or in the vicinity of salt-licks, or where saline substances exude or effloresce from the earth" (p. 47).

In Albany and Greene Counties, New York, as we learn from the *American Journal of Science* for 1844, Mr. Lyell found remains in two swamps west of the Hudson River, at the depth of four or five feet, with the remains of the existing animals of Scotland. "Cattle have recently been mired in these same swamps." In the same work it is mentioned that Mr. Nuttall found a large collection of the bones of the mastodon below Newbern, N.C., on the Neuse, resting on a deposit containing recent shells. In South Carolina, while they were digging the Santee Canal, they found similar remains in a spot where large quadrupeds might now sink into the soft boggy ground. In Georgia the bones of the mastodon and megatherium occur in swamps formed on a marine sand containing shells now inhabiting the neighboring sea.

Testimony of Sir C. Lyell.

Sir Charles Lyell points out that these remains are found lying on strata containing fresh-water and land shells of existing species,—which proves not only the recent existence of the animals, but the prevalence of *the same climate.* Sir Charles Lyell has another remark pertinent to the point under consideration, as follows: "That they [the mastodons and mammoths] were exterminated by arrows of the Indian hunters, is the first idea presented to the mind of almost every naturalist."*

Col. Hamilton Smith on the remains of the Megatherium.

Col. Hamilton Smith, in his "Natural History of the Human Species," says the bones of the megatherium in Brazil are on or near the surface, in a recent state. "How could they," he asks, "have resisted disintegration four or five thousand years, subjected to a tropical sun and periodical rains? Yet they often occur on the surface, and the bones of the pelvis have been used for temporary fire-places by the aborigines, wandering on the pampas, beyond the memory of man."†

The Mammoth found in Gasconade County, Mo.

The following is a cotemporary account of the famous mastodon found in Gasconade County, Missouri, by the late Dr. Koch, of St. Louis. We take it from the *American Journal of Science* for 1839, vol. xxxvi. p. 199. The *Journal of Science* republishes it from the Philadelphia *Presbyterian* of January 12, 1839. It is a communication to that paper from a correspondent.

"It is with the greatest pleasure the writer of this article can state, from personal knowledge, that one of the largest of these animals has actually been stoned and burned by the Indians. The circumstances are as follows:

"A farmer in Gasconade County, Mo., wished to improve his spring, and in doing so discovered, about five feet beneath the surface of the ground, a part of the back and hip bone. Of this I was informed by Mr. Wash, and, not doubting but the whole might be found, went there,

---

* "A Second Visit to the United States," vol. ii. pp. 270–271; i. pp. 234, 298.

† Page 104.

and found, as has been stated, also a knife made of stone. I then commenced a larger opening; the first layer of earth was vegetable mould, then a blue clay, then sand and blue clay. I found a large quantity of pieces of rocks, weighing from two to twenty-five pounds, evidently thrown at some object. There is no sign of rocks or gravel nearer than four hundred or five hundred yards; and these pieces were broken from larger rocks and carried to the spot. After passing through these rocks, I came to a layer of vegetable mould; on surface of this found the first blue bone, with this a spear and axe. The spear corresponds precisely with our common Indian spear, the axe is different from any I have seen. Also in this earth was ashes, nearly six inches to twelve deep, burned wood, burned bones, broken spears, knives, axes, etc. The fire appeared to have been largest on the head and neck of the animal. The animal had sunk, it appeared, with its head fast in the mud and water, and, unable to extricate itself, had fallen on its right side; and so was found and killed by the Indians." The writer goes on to say that the hind and the fore foot were well preserved,—also large pieces of the skin, which looked like "fresh-tanned leather." Twenty witnesses, it is stated, were present when the examination was made.*

It was about a year after the foregoing excavation, Dr. Koch says, that he found another skeleton, in Benton County, on the Pomme-de-Terre River, about ten miles above its junction with the Osage River. This skeleton received the name of the *Missourium*. With it were found several stone arrow-heads,—one of which lay under the thigh-bone. The whole were found in a vegetable mould, under layers, twenty feet thick, of sand, clay, and gravel.

Dr. Koch's statements have, for some reason, been received with distrust. Dr. P. R. Hoy pronounces them to be unreliable, and that, in particular, in the case last mentioned, the animal was found much nearer the surface than Dr. Koch states,—the scapula occurring at the depth of *two feet.*†

It will be observed that the "spear" mentioned in the first example is not a "palæolithic" spear, but is stated to correspond precisely "with the common Indian spear."

Col. Whittlesey, in the fifteenth volume of the "Smithsonian Contributions," mentions an elephant found near Sandusky, Ohio, in a recent bog; also that he had seen similar remains in Ross County, Ohio, in alluvial muck. A mastodon, he also states, was found at Aurora, Illinois, in a recent swamp.

---

* See also Dr. Koch's account in the Trans. St. Louis Acad. Sciences, vol. i. p. 62, 1857.

† American Naturalist, vol. v. p. 148. Dr. Foster and Prof. Rau, however, think that there is no reason to doubt the substantial correctness of Dr. K.'s statements.

Prof. Winchell, in a paper read before the Troy meeting of the American Association for the Advancement of Science, on the Post-Tertiary Phenomena of Michigan, said that his first remark was with regard to the relics recently found in the peat-beds of Michigan. "These beds are the sites of ancient lakelets slowly filled up by the accumulation of sediment. They enclose numerous remains of the mastodon and mammoth. These are sometimes found so near the surface that one could believe they have been buried within five hundred or a thousand years. For the first time, too, the remains of the gigantic American beaver have been recently found in Michigan. What is, perhaps, most interesting of all is the discovery of flint implements in a similar situation. The arrow-head was found seven feet beneath the surface, in a ditch excavated in the southern part of Washtenaw County. The mastodon remains found near Tecumseh, but a few miles distant, lay but two and a half feet beneath the surface. The Adrian mastodon was buried about three feet." *

Testimony of Prof. Winchell.

The remains of three mastodons were found by Dr. Meyer, of Fort Wayne, Indiana, and Dr. Stimpson, of Chicago, in 1867, in the peat in Noble County, Indiana. The skeletons of a calf and one of the adults were nearly complete. They lay at the depth of four or five feet in a stratum of peat overlying blue clay, containing lacustrine shells. In the peat, among the bones, they found fragments of boughs and branches of trees, well preserved, some of them gnawed by the beaver.†

Other examples.

An entire skeleton of the mastodon was also found "in the mud" of a stream in Kansas, by Mr. J. D. Parker, of Topeka.‡

Mr. Charles Frederick Heath, in a communication to the *American Naturalist*, dated May 25, 1871, narrates the discovery of the teeth and bones of a mastodon at Mott's Corner, near Ithaca, N.Y., in a layer of clay and pebbles "a few inches thick," under peat from "a few inches to two feet" in thickness,—the whole resting on a bed of blue arenaceous clay.§

In a paper read before the American Association in 1871, Prof. A. H. Worthen detailed the circumstances of the discovery of the bones of a mastodon in Macon County, Illinois, between Illiopolis and Niantic, in September, 1870. A farmer, digging a shallow well in a low peaty bog, at the depth of four feet came upon an entire tusk, nine feet long, and upon a fragment of the other tusk, the lower jaw, the teeth of the upper jaw, and fragments of the other bones. With these he found the antlers of a large elk, the bones of an elk, and the bones of the buffalo and the

* Annual Scient. Discov., 1871, p. 239.

† Amer. Naturalist for 1869, vol. ii. p. 56.

‡ Ib., p. 52.

§ Vol. v. p. 314.

deer. They were all imbedded in quicksand containing *Physa*, *Planorbis*, and *Cyclas*, of existing species, and beneath four feet of black, peaty soil.*

Testimony of Prof. Shaler.

We have similar testimony in the *American Naturalist*† from Prof. Shaler, who, we may remark, is also, like Sir Charles Lyell, a believer in the modern theory of the Three Ages. "There can now be no doubt," says Prof. Shaler, "that a few thousand years ago these companion giants [the mammoth and the mastodon] roamed through the forests and along the streams of the Mississippi Valley." He states that they "fed upon a vegetation not materially different from that now existing in that region," and that "the fragments of wood which one finds beneath their bones seem to be of the common species of existing trees; *even the reeds and other swamp plants* which are imbedded with their remains are apparently the same as those which now spring in the soil." "Almost any swampy bit of ground in Ohio or Kentucky contains traces of the Mammoth and Mastodon;" and at Big Bone Lick "the remains are so well preserved as to seem not much more ancient than the buffalo bones which are found above them."

Dr. J. C. Warren.

Dr. J. C. Warren, of Boston, by whom the Newburg mastodon was set up in that city, publishes a monograph on the "Mastodon Giganteus." In this volume it is stated that the bones of the mastodon have been found recently in considerable numbers in North Britain, on the west side of the Connecticut River, in a marsh or muck, at the depth of three feet, lying on a bed of clay. The Newburg specimen was found on the Hudson River, about seventy miles from New York City, by Mr. Peale. It was found in a small valley, some four hundred feet in length, now free of woods and shrubs, in a pool of water, some thirty or forty feet in diameter. "Under this watery collection lay the bones of the mastodon, scarcely covered by the soil and a few feet of water; and there, almost on the surface of the earth, they had remained," says Dr. Warren, "undisturbed for unknown ages."

Dr. Warren states that twigs were found in the stomach of the Newburg mastodon, and mentions farther that the same fact presented itself in connection with the mastodon found in Wythe County, Virginia, noticed by Bishop Madison, who, in a letter to Dr. Barton, speaks of "half-masticated reeds, twigs, and grass or leaves." He also mentions that Prof. Mitchell, in the Appendix to "Cuvier's Theory," at p. 376, referring to another skeleton of the mastodon, found in Goshen County, New York, makes the statement that "beneath the bones, and immediately around them, was a stratum of coarse vegetable stems and films resembling chopped straw, or rather drift-stuff of the sea."‡

---

* American Naturalist, vol. v. pp. 606, 607.

† Vol. iv. (1871) p. 162, "Time of the Mammoths."

‡ See pp. 168, 169.

The bones of the Newburg mastodon, we learn from Dr. Warren, "are lighter than recent bones, being divested of a portion of their gelatine, but still retaining not an inconsiderable part, as appears by the following analysis: Freshness of the bones.

"A portion of the epiphysis of a vertebral bone yielded, when dried at 300° F.,—

Animal matter (bone cartilage)	27.73
Bone earth (phosphate and carbonate of lime) and phosphate of iron	72.27
	100.00

"A portion of the bone with cancelli yielded, by drying a little above 212° F.,—

Water	6
Bone earth (phosphate and carbonate of lime) and phosphate of iron	64
Bone cartilage	30
	100

"On burning the bone, the ash which remains," says Dr. W., "is of a beautiful blue color, owing to the presence of phosphate of iron, which appears to have been infiltrated into the bone from the marl surrounding the skeleton." *

Dr. Warren remarks that the bones of the *Mastodon giganteus* have been found in the post-pliocene or alluvial formations, at the depth of from five to ten feet, in lacustrine deposits, in bogs, and in beds of shell-marl. At the salt-licks, he says, they occur on the surface, and mixed with the common soil.†

We have mentioned (what is well known) that very ancient bones lose their animal matter. "Apart from the geological formation," says the "Types of Mankind,"‡ "they are found in, the only method of judging of the age of bones is by the proportion of animal and mineral matters which they contain. Where animal matter is present, the bone is hard without being brittle, and does not adhere to the tongue; when nothing but earthy matter remains, the bone is both brittle and adhesive."

Sir Charles Lyell, in his Travels in the United States, makes the following observations on the bones of the mastodon and other extinct animals found in this country: "Nothing," he says, "is more remarkable than the large proportion of animal matter in the tusks, teeth, and bones of many of these extinct mammalia, amounting in some cases, as Dr. C. T. Jackson has ascertained by analysis, to twenty-seven per cent., so that when all the earthy ingredients are removed by acids, the form of the bone remains as perfect, and the Sir C. Lyell on this point.

---

* See page 172. † Page 182. ‡ Page 345.

mass of animal matter is almost as firm, as in a recent bone subjected to similar treatment." *

Now let us go forth and find the remains of man and these extinct animals together, and what should be our inference?—that man is very old—or that the mammoth *is not* very old?

Formerly, it was stated that the "diluvium" was very old, because no remains of man, but the remains of various extinct animals, were found in it: now that man's remains are found, it is inferred, not that the mammoth is recent, but that man is ancient. And yet the tusks of the mammoth and mastodon are so sound that they are used in some instances in the arts, and their bones so fresh that they retain twenty-seven per cent. of animal matter; while in other instances the animals are found with the flesh still on their bones, and their last meal still in their stomachs. These remains, moreover, are frequently—in the case of the mastodon generally—found in shallow peat bogs and on the surface.

The remains of the Mammoth in Siberia.

This brings us to speak of Siberia. In this country the bones and tusks of the mammoth occur in extraordinary numbers, and in a number of instances entire carcasses, still undecayed, of both the mammoth and the tichorine rhinoceros have been found. Sir Charles Lyell remarks that the bones are met with "in a very fresh state" throughout all the lowland of this country,—from the borders of Europe to the extreme point nearest America, and from south to north, from lat. 60° to the shores of the Arctic Sea. Fossil ivory has been collected within this space on the banks of the Irtish, Obi, Yenisei, Lena, and other rivers. The remains do not occur (Sir Charles Lyell remarks) in the marshes, but where the banks of the rivers present lofty precipices of sand and clay. Sometimes they are imbedded with marine remains; in other cases they occur with fossil wood or lignite.

"So fresh is the ivory throughout Northern Russia," says Lyell (Principles, vol. i. p. 183), "that, according to Tilesius, thousands of fossil tusks have been collected and used in turning."

The skeletons or carcasses are found on the Lena and Indigirka,—far to the east, where the cold is intense,—imbedded in the ice or the frozen soil, in the most wonderful state of preservation. Here the soil is frozen to the depth of five hundred feet.

We shall mention some of these cases directly. In the mean time, the reader must bear in mind that these well-preserved carcasses have been

---

* Second Visit to the United States, vol. ii. p. 271.

To the same purpose Dr. Foster remarks, "Mastodon bones, however, of a much older date, recovered from peat swamps, have so much of the gelatinous matter yet remaining in them, that a nourishing soup might be extracted." Dr. Foster, Prehist. Races of the United States, p. 370.

frequently found, while the bones and tusks occur *in vast numbers*, in a high state of preservation—as a rule.

We may well ask whether *all* of them, as Lyell contends, are one or two hundred thousand years old. *That* is the position of Science.

Sir Charles Lyell conjectured that the mammoths found near the northern coast of Siberia had been drifted there by the rivers from a warmer latitude; but Mr. Boyd Dawkins, a very high authority in these matters, shows that he is mistaken by the following thrilling narrative of the discovery of one of these monsters in 1846 by a young Russian engineer, named Benkendorf, near the mouth of the Indigirka. Mr. Benkendorf *witnessed the disentombment* of a mammoth during the great thaw of the summer of that year, and ascertained positively by what he saw with his own eyes that the animal had perished on the spot in a bog, in which its remains were subsequently frozen. There were "young shoots of the fir and pine, and a quantity of young fir cones, all in a chewed state, in the stomach."

Disentombment of a Mammoth.

The account of the finding of this mammoth is so vivid, and throws so much light on the history of the remains found in Siberia, that we reproduce it:

"In 1846 there was unusually warm weather in the north of Siberia. Already in May unusual rains poured over the moors and bogs, storms shook the earth, and the streams carried not only ice to the sea, but also large tracts of land thawed by the masses of warm water fed by the southern rains.

"We steamed on the first day up the Indigirka; but there were no thoughts of land; we saw around us only a sea of dirty brown water, and knew the river only by the rushing and roaring of the stream. The river rolled against us trees, moss, and large masses of peat, so that it was only with great trouble and danger that we could proceed. At the end of the second day we were only about forty wersts up the stream; some one had to stand with the sounding-rod in hand continually, and the boat received so many shocks that it shuddered to the keel. A wooden vessel would have been smashed. Around us we saw nothing but the flooded land. . . . The Indigirka, here about three wersts wide, had torn up the land and worn itself a fresh channel, and when the waters sank, we saw, to our astonishment, that the old river-bed had become merely that of an insignificant stream. . . . The stream rolled over, and tore up the soft, wet ground like chaff, so that it was dangerous to go near the brink. While we were all quiet, we suddenly heard under our feet a sudden gurgling and stirring, which betrayed the working of the disturbed water. Suddenly our jäger, ever on the look-out, called loudly, and pointed to a singular and unshapely object, which rose and sank through the disturbed waters.

"I had already remarked it, but not given it any attention, considering it only drift-wood. Now we all hastened to the spot on shore, had the boat drawn near, and waited until the mysterious thing should again show itself. Our patience was tried, but at last a black, horrible, giant-like mass was thrust out of the water, and we beheld a colossal elephant's head, armed with mighty tusks, with its long trunk moving in the water, in an unearthly manner, as though seeking for something lost therein. Breathless with astonishment, I beheld the monster hardly twelve feet from me, with his half-open eyes yet showing the whites. It was still in good preservation.

* * * * * * * * *

"Picture to yourself an elephant with a body covered with thick fur, about thirteen feet in height, and fifteen in length, with tusks eight feet long, thick, and curving outward at their ends, a stout trunk of six feet in length, colossal limbs of one and a half feet in thickness, and a tail, naked up to the end, which was covered with thick tufty hair. The animal was fat, and well grown; death had overtaken him in the fulness of his powers. His parchment-like, large, naked ears lay turned up over the head; about the shoulders and the back he had stiff hair, about a foot in length, like a mane. The long outer hair was deep brown, and coarsely rooted. The top of the head looked so wild, and so penetrated with pitch, that it resembled the rind of an old oak-tree. On the sides it was cleaner, and under the outer hair there appeared everywhere a wool, very soft, warm, and thick, and of a fallow-brown color. The giant was well protected against the cold. The whole appearance of the animal was fearfully strange and wild. It had not the shape of our present elephants. As compared with our Indian elephants, its head was rough, the brain-case low and narrow, but the trunk and mouth were much larger. The teeth were very powerful. Our elephant is an awkward animal; but, compared with this mammoth, it is an Arabian steed to a coarse, ugly dray-horse. I could not divest myself of a feeling of fear, as I approached the head; the broken, widely-open eyes gave the animal an appearance of life, as though it might move in a moment, and destroy us with a roar. . . . The bad smell of the body warned us that it was time to save what we could, and the swelling flood, too, bade us hasten. . . . But I had the stomach separated, and brought on one side. It was well filled, and the contents instructive, and well preserved. The principal were young shoots of the fir and pine; a quantity of young fir cones, also in a chewed state, were mixed with the moss." . . .

The bones of the mammoth are found in almost incredible numbers in the islands off the northern coast of Siberia. New Siberia and the Lächow Islands are, for the most part, an agglomeration of sand, ice, and elephants' teeth; and the inhabitants of this region also carry on a profitable commerce in fossil ivory. The remains of the rhinoceros are also found. Pallas, in 1772, obtained from Wiljuiskoi, in lat. 64°, from the banks of the Wiljui, a tributary of the Lena, the carcass of a rhinoceros (*tichorinus*), taken from the sand in which it had been frozen. This carcass emitted an odor like putrid flesh, part of the skin being covered with short crisp wool and with black and gray hairs. Prof. Brandt in 1846 extracted from the cavities in the molar teeth of this skeleton a small quantity of half-chewed pine-leaves and coniferous wood. And the blood-vessels in the interior of the head appeared filled, even to the capillary vessels, with coagulated blood, which in many places still retained its original red color.

Thirty years after this discovery, that is, in 1803, Mr. Adams obtained the entire carcass of a mammoth much farther to the north, on the banks of the Lena, in lat. 70°, and "so perfectly had the carcass been preserved that the flesh, as it lay, was devoured by wolves and bears." This skeleton is in the Museum of St. Petersburg, the head retaining its integuments and many of the ligaments entire. This animal was nine feet high and sixteen feet long, without reckoning the large curved tusks; a size rarely surpassed by the largest living male elephants.

Another mammoth was discovered on the Tas, between the Obi and the Yenisei, with some parts of the flesh in so perfect a state that the ball of the eye is now preserved in the Museum of Moscow.

The remains of the mammoth are also found in great abundance in Alaska, and it was stated not long since in the San Francisco papers that parties were entering on the business of collecting fossil ivory from this region on a large scale. The condition of these bones is farther shown by the tooth of an elephant brought back in 1872 from Alaska by M. Pinart, which was reported on by Mr. A. Gandry. It was pronounced to be the sixth upper molar of the *Elephas primigenius*, and to be "in a state of preservation which will scarcely permit it to be called a fossil."

Alaska.

We must close this chapter, calling attention, first, to the fact that Mr. Boyd Dawkins and Mr. Sanford consider the cave-lion as only a large variety of the existing lion,—identical in species, in which opinion Sir John Lubbock seems to concur. And we should recall in this connection the statement of Herodotus that the camels in the army of Xerxes, near the mountains of Thessaly, were *attacked by lions*.

The identity of some so-called extinct animals with existing species.

The cave-lion.

The *Cave-hyæna*, says Sir John Lubbock (see his "Pre-historic Times," p. 293), "is now regarded as scarcely distinguishable specifically from the *Hyæna crocuta*, or spotted hyæna of Southern Africa," while Mr. Busk and M. Gervais identify the *Cave-*

The cave-hyæna.

bear with the *Ursus ferox*, or grizzly bear of North America. Highly important facts in their bearing on the question of the antiquity of the remains found in the bone-caverns.

Mr. Dawkins remarks, that "while it is undoubtedly true that the *Felis spelæa* was on the whole larger and stronger than the existing Lion, *some individuals were even smaller than the average Lion of the present day. There is not one solitary character by which the animal can be distinguished from the living Lion.*" "And thus," he adds, "we are compelled to hold that the Cave-Lion which preyed upon the Mammoth, the Woolly Rhinoceros, and Musk-Sheep in Great Britain, is a mere geographical variety of the great carnivore that is found alike in the tropical parts of Asia and throughout the whole of Africa." *

It has been the fashion to refer to all of these animals as "the great *extinct* mammalia," and to represent them all as greatly larger than the existing animals of the same kind. So Figuier in his "Primitive Man." It appears, however, from the foregoing, that three, at least, of the most important are *still living*, and that as to one of them (the cave-lion), some of the specimens were smaller than the average lion of the present day. Indeed, we now learn from Sir John Lubbock's last edition of "Prehistoric Times" that of the seventeen principal "Palæolithic" mammalia, ten until recently were regarded as "extinct;" but that it is now believed that the "Irish Elk, the elephants, and the three species of rhinoceros are perhaps the only ones which are absolutely extinct" (p. 290).

The cave-horse.

So of the Horse: we read in works on anthropology a great deal about the *Equus spelæus*. Our account of Solutré shows that during the so-called Palæolithic Age in France the horse had been probably domesticated and was used as he is now. Ekkehard mentions wild horses as existing in Switzerland in the eleventh century; and Lucas David refers to them as existing in Russia in 1240. Even as late as the seventeenth century, Herberstein mentions them as existing at that time in Lithuania. At the meeting of the Philadelphia Academy of Natural Sciences, in 1865, Dr. Leidy exhibited the bones and teeth of the so-called "Fossil Horse" of America from California and Oregon. He stated that similar bones had been found all over North America, and added that "many of these remains are undistinguishable in anatomical character from the corresponding bones and teeth of the domestic horse. . . . Most of the remains from California, among them an entire skull, are unchanged in appearance, and are undistinguishable from the corresponding parts of the Mustang, or recent Indian Horse of the West,

* Popular Science Review for 1869, p. 153: Mr. Dawkins on "The British Lion." M. Gervais, it would be more accurate to say, identifies the cave-bear with the brown bear of Europe, which, however, is so close to the grizzly bear as to be in all probability only a variety.

though taken from auriferous gravel a considerable depth from the surface." To the same effect the author of "Man as the Cotemporary of the Mammoth and the Reindeer" says that the palæolithic horse "has been improperly regarded as differing from that of the present day." *

The significance of all this is very great. It leaves none of the ancient cave and river-gravel animals to account for except the Mammoth, the Rhinoceros, the Irish Elk, the Reindeer, the Hippopotamus, and the Musk-Ox. Some of these are not extinct, but they are extinct in France and Britain. We have attempted to render the account in question in the preceding pages. But what has been said is strengthened by the fact that the great carnivores found associated in the gravel and in the caves with the animals just mentioned *are now found to be living*, though previously believed to be extinct; and we may, therefore, readily imagine that we are not very far off from the age of the Mammoth.

We have mentioned that in the fifth century the camels in the army of Xerxes were attacked, near the mountains of Thessaly, by lions. The author of the paper (already quoted) on "Man as the Cotemporary of the Mammoth and the Reindeer" adds to this that the Thessalian lion was also figured on the coins of Greece, and also observes that as this animal "endured a climate like our own, he could not, therefore, be the present African species." We learn, however, from Mr. Boyd Dawkins that *it was* of "the present African species."

Ancient animals larger than existing ones.

One observation more as to the size of the palæolithic animals. Ordinarily, it is probable that animals of that day, identical with existing species, were larger than their present representatives; and this has bewildered the palæontologists into classifying them as the *cave*-bear, the *cave*-hyæna, the *cave*-lion, etc.

A remark of the Rev. W. Greenwell, in the Journal of the Ethnological Society of London for 1870, throws much light on this point. The article is on the Neolithic Flint Mines known as Grime's Graves. He is speaking of the picks of stag's horn which the Neolithic men used to excavate these galleries. They were made of the horns of the red deer. The bones of this animal, he says, found at Grime's Graves, belonged to specimens much larger than the present Scotch red deer. This, he observes, might have been expected, because the red deer of Scotland is now confined to a small area in Britain, and that of a high elevation and almost entirely devoid of vegetation, except ling and very coarse grasses, whereas in pre-historic times, and much later, it occupied a country abounding in wood, and possessing a much more varied and nutritious flora than is now possessed by the Highlands of Scotland."†

* Smiths. Rep. for 1867, p. 352.

† Journ. Ethnol. Soc. of London, vol. ii. p. 428.

It is, therefore, easy to comprehend that other animals of a period anterior to the Neolithic Age may have been larger in size than those of the same species driven to the mountains and deserts of Asia and Africa.

The cut at the beginning of this chapter is taken from the "Report" of the Smithsonian Institution for 1872, and represents a very large animal mound in Grant County, Wisconsin, which bears the name of the "Big Elephant Mound." It is well known that many of the ancient mounds in this State are constructed to represent certain animals,—the bear, the deer, the fox, birds, reptiles, etc. The reader can judge whether the mound in question was probably intended to represent an elephant. If it is an elephant (it differs entirely in form from the Bear Mounds), it establishes the presence of this animal in this region in the time of the Mound-Builders; that is to say, within the past fifteen hundred or two thousand years.

NOTE.—While these sheets are passing through the press, we have met with a very interesting passage in the *Journal of the Anthropological Institute of Great Britain and Ireland*, which may throw much light on the vexed question of the climate of the Palæolithic Age, and on the existence of the reindeer in former times in Great Britain and France. It is contained in a paper by H. H. Howorth, Esq., entitled "Strictures on Darwinism." Mr. Howorth says:

"The conditions under which animals thrive have never been treated in a scientific manner. Such a problem as the existence of the mammoth in Siberia has been treated in an extremely empirical manner. One school of writers will have it that the mammoths must have lived in the subtropical parts of Asia, and been floated by the northern rivers to where their carcasses are now found. Another set of inquirers point to the researches of Middendorf and others to prove that the mammoth lived where his bones are now found; but the inquiry into the question of the conditions under which a mammoth, a hyæna, and a reindeer could live together has, if I am not mistaken, never been adequately made, and before it has, it is absurd to deal with the smaller question. Let us begin with the reindeer. Why will not the reindeer now live in Scotland? The attempt to introduce it has been made more than once; the experiment has been described in considerable detail in Mr. Arthur de Capell Brooke's 'Travels in Lapland,' 76, *et seq.* *Inter alia*, he says, 'The reindeer moss, contrary to expectation, was not only found abundantly in Scotland, but in most parts of England, particularly on Bagshot Heath, while the climate and even latitude of Scotland did not materially differ from the part of Norway whence they came. Notwithstanding these favorable circumstances, they died one by one, till I believe none remained in Scotland.' It cannot be that the moss is not of the same quality, for, as Mr. Brooke says, the reindeer is by no means particular; it eats the leaves of the birch, sallow, and aspen, particularly the former, and browses also upon the young herbage and the tender shoots of the mountain shrubs. He gives a long list of the plants upon which it habitually feeds in summer (*op. cit.*, 88 and 89). He also tells us that it is sometimes fed on hay in the winter. In this he is supported by Mr. Laing, who says that it eats grass and hay as well as moss. It lives on moss because there is nothing else to live on in the Fjeld ('Residence in Norway,' 264). There is, therefore, no reason in regard to its food why the reindeer should not now live in Scotland. On turning to Iceland we have a different tale to tell. Twenty-four does were embarked from Hammerfest, in Finmark, for that island. They succeeded very well, and were soon so abundant that Sir George Mackenzie, in his work on Iceland, says they are not unfrequently seen there on the mountains in herds of sixty or one hundred together.

It is more pertinent and remarkable that in Scotland the reindeer existed in comparatively recent times. One of the Norse Sagas mentions the hunting of the reindeer in Caithness; and this allusion, which alone might be suspected, has been amply confirmed, as I have the authority of my friend Mr. Boyd Dawkins for saying, by the discovery of the broken bones of reindeer in the refuse-heaps of the Pictish burghs.

" It is clear, therefore, that some change has occurred recently in Scotland adverse to the mode of life of the reindeer. The obvious cause of this, at first sight, would be said to be that the reindeer thrives best in the coldest and most exposed situations,—that Scotland and Southern Norway are too warm for it, while Spitzbergen, Greenland, and Siberia are its more natural habitats; and this proves in some measure to be confirmed by the fact that reindeer formerly in not remote times lived in Scotland, at a time when we have many reasons for believing the climate there was much more severe than it is now. This view would be partially, but only partially, correct. Mr. Capell Brooke tells us that at the same time when the imported reindeer were dying in Scotland, others kept in confinement, and experiencing the very opposite reverse to their former mode of life, not merely survived, but remained healthy and vigorous; withstood the effects of a London season and an atmosphere most unusual to them,—that of a room frequently crowded to suffocation (*op. cit.*, 79). Reindeer thrive in the mountains north and east of Mandchuria, a comparatively temperate region, and lived until quite recently, if not now, in the southern Urals. On turning to Mr. Laing's most admirable narrative of a residence in Norway, I find the following passage, which I believe solves the difficulty. Speaking of the hair and skin of the reindeer, he says, the former does not throw off wet well, and even parts from the skin after any continuance of moisture. With our damp climate and wet ground the animal would be drenched through the hair to the skin for weeks together, and would die of cold or rot, as our sheep often do in wet seasons. In Norway the heavy rains occur in spring or autumn, at which seasons what is rain below is dry snow higher up in the Fjeldes. Our highest hills do not afford in summer this kind of refuge from rain and damp to an animal whose coat keeps any degree of cold, but will not stand continued moisture. (Laing's 'Residence in Norway,' 264). It is the damp of our latitudes now-a-days that the reindeer cannot endure. It is strange that no use has been made of this fact hitherto in zoological reasoning; for it is a very potent reason why so many foreign animals die here. In our menageries the beasts do not suffer so much from cold and other assigned causes as from damp. Diseases of the lungs are the scourges of such establishments, and these induced not by cold but damp. The camel, the tiger, etc., can endure the exceedingly bitter cold of the Thibetan plateau with impunity, because the cold is a dry parching cold. The lion, which lived in historical times in the rugged mountains of Thrace, need not fear the cold of our winters, but may well dread our damp seasons, which make such havoc even among our acclimatized people. That our climate has grown damper is probable from the contemporaneous extinction of the spruce fir with the reindeer, the former of which, as well as the other linear-leaved trees, according to Ermann, especially likes a dry air. Such climatic changes would probably be first felt by the vegetation, and what affects it would naturally affect the animals feeding on it; and here we get to another cause of the extinction of certain types. With the disappearance of the forest the forest animals disappear too,—notably, the elk, the sable, etc." Jour. Anthrop. Instit., July and October, 1873, pp. 221–224.

CHAPTER XXI.

RESULT OF THE FOREGOING EVIDENCE.

Effect of combining all of the Foregoing Facts with regard to the Circumstances under which the Remains of these Palæolithic Animals are found, and with regard to the Fresh Condition of their Bones in Europe, Siberia, and North and South America.—Early Forgetfulness of the Former Presence of Extinct Animals in Unlettered Countries.—Traditions of the Mammoth and Mastodon in America.—Of the former amongst the Tartars of Southern Siberia.—The Gigantic Fossil Tortoise of the Sewalik Hills.—Associated by Dr. Falconer with the Hindoo Cosmogony.—The Tortoise and the Elephant.—The Indian Hippopotamus recognized in Ancient Indian Words.—Traditions of the Aula or Elephant-Horse.—The Elephant formerly in Ethiopia.

Effect of the foregoing evidence.

WHEN all of the foregoing evidence is *combined*, the effect of it is almost irresistible.

We might imagine that there was some mistake with regard to Cæsar's *bos cervi figurâ* if it stood alone; but he mentions the reindeer in connection with the Germans expressly elsewhere as supplying them with a covering for their bodies, while Sallust distinctly affirms the same fact. We have then the testimony of Torfæus and Gaston de Foix. We then find the remains of the animal in association with bronze implements near London. We then find them in the Scottish "burghs." We find them also in the peat of England, Scotland, and Denmark. Nor is this all; we have mentioned a number of cases in one of our chapters on the Bone-Caves, in which the remains of the reindeer occurred in association with the implements or the fauna of the Neolithic Age.

We find the remains of the great Irish elk in the Irish crannoges in association with implements of iron. The mere fact of finding them in a crannoge is sufficient; for it is not pretended that any of these go back to the Palæolithic Age; indeed, there was no palæolithic age in Ireland. We find the bones of the megaceros also in the Irish peat, the tendons still undecayed, and the bones themselves yielding forty per cent. of animal matter. We find them associated with iron in the peat, as well as with jet beads. We find in the same peat an Irish lyre made of these bones. We find references to the animal in the "Book of Lismore." We are told by Agassiz and Brandt and in "Matériaux pour l'Histoire de l'Homme," that the animal lived in Central Europe down to the tenth and even the fourteenth century of our era.

We find the remains of the Cave-bear in the Neolithic Age: indeed, we ascertain that there is no distinction between the cave-bear and the common brown bear.

We are reminded that the lion existed in Europe in the fifth century (we might say the third) before the Christian era, and that it also is identical with the Asiatic lion, while the cave-hyæna and the cave-horse are identified with the existing species of the same animals.

We find the remains of the mammoth in Siberia with the flesh still on the bones, and thousands of the teeth and tusks nearly as fresh as the ivory imported from Africa and India. We find the tusks in Scotland and England in such a state of preservation that they also have been used in the arts. We find the remains of the mammoth and the mastodon in America everywhere in the surface deposits, with their last meal still preserved in the stomach, and the bones retaining, like those of the European mammoth in some instances, and of the megaceros in Ireland, a large proportion of their animal matter. In America we do not find one, or two, or three in the surface mud or peat, but we find *great numbers*, and in all parts of the country.

Now, it may be that the Siberian mammoth is two hundred thousand years old, though it is highly improbable,—perhaps incredible. But it is out of the question that *all* of these fresh bones in different parts of the world are one hundred or two hundred thousand years old. All the facts we have stated have to be considered and met, together. If we go to South America, we find again bones of the megatherium undecayed on the surface of the soil. And so again in Mexico.

There is, indeed, every mark of *recency* in connection with these remains all over the world.

But if the mammoth lived in Western Europe or in Siberia or in America within a few thousand years, why have we no account of them?

Tradition.

There were no books in those days. If there were no books, who would know now that two hundred years ago the great Arctic moose grazed in the valleys of the Ohio and the Susquehanna? If there were no books, and no readers, how many of us would know that two centuries ago the buffalo ranged in the Atlantic States? We have seen that, according to M. Figuier, three centuries ago the Emperor Báber hunted the rhinoceros in regions in India whence it has now disappeared, and where there is now *no tradition* of its former presence; and so of the lion, which formerly abounded northwest of Delhi "within the memory of living men," and now there is *hardly a tradition of its existence.* If one or two centuries can obliterate to such a degree, is it strange that, after three thousand or four thousand years, men should have forgotten the denizens of the Palæolithic caves and valleys?

But there *are* traditions of the mammoth,—and, as we have seen, of the Irish elk. Mr. Jefferson, in his "Notes on Virginia," speaking of the animals of the country, says:

"Of these the mammoth, or big buffaloe, as called by the Indians, must certainly have been the largest. The tradition is, that he was carnivorous, and still exists in the northern parts of America. A delegation of warriors of the Delaware tribe having visited the Governor of Virginia, during the Revolution, on matters of business, after these had been discussed and settled in council, the Governor asked them some questions relative to their country, and, among others, what they knew or had heard of the animal whose bones were found at the Salt Lick on the Ohio. The chief speaker immediately put himself in an attitude of victory, and, with a dignity suited to what he conceived the elevation of his subject, informed him that it was a tradition handed down from their fathers, 'That in ancient times a herd of these tremendous animals came to the Big Bone licks, and began an universal destruction of the bear, deer, elks, buffaloes, and other animals which had been created for the use of the Indians; that the Great Man above, looking down and seeing this, was so enraged that he seized his lightning, descended on the earth, and seated himself on a neighboring mountain, on a rock, on which his seat and the prints of his feet are still to be seen, and hurled his bolts among them till the whole were slaughtered, except the big bull, who presenting his forehead to the shafts, shook them off as they fell; but missing one at length, it wounded him in the side; whereupon, springing round, he bounded over the Ohio, over the Wabash, the Illinois, and finally over the great lakes; where he is living at this day.' It is well known that on the Ohio and in many parts in America farther north, tusks, grinders, skeletons of unparalleled magnitude, are found in great numbers lying on the surface of the earth, and some a little below it. A Mr. Stanley, taken prisoner by the Indians near the mouth of the Tenassee, relates that after being transferred through several tribes, from one to another, he was at length carried over the mountains west of the Missouri to a river which runs westwardly; that these bones abounded there; and that the natives described to him the animal to which the bones belonged as still existing in the northern parts of the country, from which description he judged it to be an elephant."

Indian tradition of the Mammoth.

In the fourth volume of the "Natural History of New York" we have in a note the following interesting statement on the subject of the Indian traditions from Prof. Mather. He says that Mr. Stickney, for many years the Indian Agent of the United States for the tribes northwest of the Ohio, informed him that "particular persons in every nation were selected as the repositories of their history and traditions; that these persons had others who were younger, selected for this purpose continually, and repeatedly instructed in those things which were handed down from generation to generation; and that there was a tradition among the Indians of the existence of these animals (the mastodon); that they were often seen; that they fed on the boughs of a species of lime-tree; and that they did not lie down, but leaned against a tree to sleep."*

We hear of the same tradition from other sources. In the "Smithsonian Contributions to Knowledge," vol. iii. pp. 142, 143, we are told that in North America there are native legends which indicate a traditional knowledge of more than one species of these extinct animals; as that of the Great Elk or Buffalo, which, besides its enormous horns, had an arm protruding from the shoulder, with a hand at the extremity (proboscis). Another, the *Tagesho*, or *Yagesho*, was a giant bear, long-bodied, broad down the shoulders, thin and narrow about the hind-quarters, with large head, powerful teeth, short and thick legs, paws with very long claws, body almost destitute of hair, except about the hind-legs, and therefore called "*The Naked Bear.*" It was probably the *Megalonyx Jeffersonii.*

The Colossal Elk, which was probably the mastodon or mammoth, was referred to, says a French officer of the last century, as the *Père aux Bœufs*.

This officer, named Fabri, writing to Buffon in 1748, mentions one of the songs which he heard from the Indians in Canada: "When the great Manitou descended to the earth in order to satisfy himself that the creatures which he had made were happy, he interrogated all the animals. The bison replied that he would be quite contented with his fate in the grassy meadows, where the grass reached his belly, if he were not also compelled to keep his eyes constantly turned towards the mountains to catch the first sight of the *Père aux Bœufs*, as he descended with fury to devour him and his companions."

Among the Chavanais Indians there is a tradition that these great animals lived in former times, conjointly with a race of men of proportionate size.

According to Prof. Brandt, there is a tradition among the Tartars of Southern Siberia in regard to "giant animals" with which their ancestors contended.†

Tradition among the Tartars of Siberia.

In Scotland there are traditions of deer in the days of Fionn, and of birds far larger than any now existing. Ossian, according to the tradition, spoke of "deer as big as horses," and "birds as big as oxen."

Scotch traditions of great deer.

* Natural History of New York, Part IV., Geology. By W. W. Mather, p. 44, 1843.

† Mélange Biolog., vii. 434.

The elephant is delineated on the monuments of Central America; and Dr. Foster believed that we have in such delineations the memorial of either the mastodon or the mammoth; but we are of the opinion that these figures have reference rather to the Asiatic elephant,—though it may be otherwise.

India.

A strange voice comes to us on this question from India. Dr. Falconer (with Mr. Cantley) discovered on the Sewalik Hills the remains of a gigantic *tortoise*, in 1835. This huge chelonian had a shell twelve feet long, eight feet in diameter, and six feet high,—a fit object of comparison with the elephant. It was named the *Colossochelis Atlas*. With these remains were found those of existing species of chelonians. Dr. Falconer happily connects this extinct monster with "the traditions connected with those cosmogonic speculations of all the Eastern nations, having reference to a tortoise of such gigantic size as to be associated in these fabulous accounts with the elephant." "Was this tortoise," he asks, "a mere creature of the imagination, or was the idea of it drawn from a reality like the *Colossochelis?*"

The Colossochelis Atlas.

Traditions of the Tortoise.

The tortoise figures in the Pythagorean cosmogony, where the infant world is placed on the back of a tortoise. So in the Second Avatar of Vishnu, the god is made to assume the form of a tortoise,—and carries the world on his back. And again, in the exploits of the bird demi-god *Garuda*, we find him in one of them directed by his father to appease his hunger at a certain lake *where an elephant and a tortoise were fighting*. In *Garuda* Dr. Falconer thinks we may detect the gigantic crane of India.

Ancient Hippopotamus of India.

Dr. Falconer proceeds to state that he was informed by Raja Radhakanta Derva, the eminent Indian scholar and author of the Sanscrit Encyclopædia, that the *Hippopotamus* of India is referred to under different names of great antiquity, significant of "*Jala-Hasti*," "Water-Elephant," or "Living in the Water." This inference, he says, is confirmed by the opinion of Henry Colebrooke and H. H. Wilson.*

It is, therefore, extremely probable that the *Hippopotamus major* was an inhabitant of India in the early stages of Indian civilization.

We may add that the Iroquois Indians also have a tradition about the tortoise apparently of Oriental origin.

Col. Hamilton Smith has a statement bearing on this point, as follows: "The traditions in the East Indies," he says, "mention the *Aula*, or *Auloc*, *Elephant-horse*, a solidungulated proboscidian, supposed to be represented in Kindersley's "Specimens of Hindoo Literature," where

* Falconer, Palæontological Memoirs, vol. ii. pp. 573–580.

the *Macaira*, represented in Buddhist zodiacs, is again seen beneath the monster horse, and, still more singularly, bears the same form in a Peruvian bas-relief, always resembling the presumed figure of the *Dinotherium giganteum*, with the character of an aquatic proboscidian." *

It may be mentioned that the elephant appears to have existed in ancient times in Ethiopia. M. Lartet infers this from the circumstance that certain nations in that country were called *Elephantophagi.* He also refers to the fact that the Phœnicians brought ivory from Ethiopia.†

---

* Natural History of the Human Species, p. 162.

† It is ascertained that the ostrich formerly existed in Central Asia.

CHAPTER XXII.

RECENT CHANGES IN THE PHYSICAL GEOGRAPHY OF THE EARTH.

Geologists require Vast Periods of Time.—The Uniformitarians.—The Anthropologists rest the Antiquity of Man partly on the Physical Changes which have occurred since his Appearance.—Sir C. Lyell on Raised Beaches.—The Beach at Leith raised Twenty-Five Feet since the Roman Occupation of that Region.—The Change observed in the Physical Features of the Localities of some of the Bone-Caverns, considered by Sir C. Lyell a Strong Evidence of the Antiquity of Man.—But we find in the Geologic Records Traces of Force as well as of Time.—Many Evidences of Violent and Sudden Changes.—The Earthquake at Lisbon.—The Mountain of Jorullo in Mexico.—The Ice-Sheet.—The Fluctuations of the Sea-Level in the Glacial and Post-Glacial Ages.—The Violence exerted on the Crust of the Earth in the Post-Glacial Epoch illustrated in the Contorted Strata of the Island of Möen.—The Change of Climate since the Palæolithic Age.—The Ancient Beaches of the Great North American Lakes.—The Cagliari Pottery.—Volcanic Forces.—The Volcanic Mountain of Toinmoura.—Fusi-Yama in Japan.—Santorin.—The Earthquake of Cutch.—Volcanic Action in New Zealand.—The Earthquake of Calabria in 1783.—An Example from the Island of Java.—The Earthquake of Lisbon.—Peru.—The Observatory of Santa Lucia in Chili.—Observatory of Armagh.—The Peat in Constant Motion.—The Coast of Sweden.—Celsius.—Carl Vogt on the Elevation of these Coasts.—M. Reclus on the Same Subject.—Scania an Island in Recent Times.—The Oyster, which formerly lived in the Waters of the Baltic, no longer found there.—Due to the Loss of its Saltness by the Water.—The Oysters of the Kjökken-Möddings.—The Raised Beaches of Spitzbergen.—Siberia and Russia.—The Raised Beaches of Scotland.—Northern Africa.—The Ports of Carthage, Utica, etc., filled up.—Southern France.—The North of France.—Monastery of Mont St.-Michel.—Valley of the Somme upheaved.—The Elevation of the Shores of Asia Minor.—The Ægean Isles.—The Caspian Sea.—The Ancient Hyrcanian Ocean.—Goldsmith and Buffon on the Coasts of France, Holland, England, Germany, Prussia, etc.—The City of Tongres.—Psalmodi.—The Goodwin Sands.—Irruption of the Sea in the Territory of Dort in 1546.—The Encroachments of the Baltic Sea.—The City of Modena in Italy.—Cases cited by M. Malte-Brun.—The Pontine Marshes.—The Villas of Baiæ.—The Walls of Damietta.—The Mouth of the Pyramus.—The Cities of Miletus and Ephesus.—Ravenna.—Aquileia.—Tacitus's Description of Germany.—Col. Hamilton Smith on the City of Adria.—The Delta of the Rhine.—The Sea formerly at the Pyramids of Memphis.—The Mouths of the Nile.—Western Coast of Schleswig.—Submerged Forest and Tomb of the Age of Stone.—The Coasts of Chili.—Concepcion.—Arica.—The Bolivian Lake.—The Coasts of Texas.—The Straits of Hell Gate in New York.—The Aleutian Isles.—The Mountains of New Zealand.—The Lateritic Formation of Madras.—Mr. Darwin on Coast of South America.—The Coasts of Florida and New Jersey.—Louisburg.—The Delta of the Ganges.—Calcutta.—Sir C. Lyell on the Basin of the Mississippi and the Deltas of the Po and the Ganges.—On the Plains of Northern Italy.—The Yellow River in China.—Its Wonderful Wanderings.—Other Remarkable Changes in China.—Island of Formosa.—Tombs at Alexandria, in Egypt.—Subsidence of Land in the Valley of Cashmere, in India.—Ships found in Deserted River-beds, and along the Sea-coasts.—Buried City in India.—Inundations and Floods.—Streams dried up by the Destruction of Forests.—Lakes of Morat and Neufchâtel.—The Scamander.—The Euphrates.—Lakes in New Granada.—The Oder and the Elbe.—The Kalahari Desert.—The Hauran.—The Mississippi.—The Volga.—Streams in the South of France.—British Columbia, and the Destruction of the Beaver.—Change of Climate in the Colorado Plateau.—The Change of Climate in Greenland and Iceland.—In Norway.—In Scotland. —In Northern Russia.—In Siberia. —In France.—Marine Remains and Works of Art found far from the Sea in England and Scotland.—The Sea in Recent Times at Cambridge and Bury St. Edmund's, and at Glasgow and Falkirk.—The Wall of Antoninus.—Blair Drummond Moss.—Iron Anchor found in the Carse near Stirling.—Implements of Iron found in the Carse of Gowrie, on the Tay.—Seventeen Ancient Canoes found on the Banks of the Clyde, and far from the River, at Glasgow.—A Cork Plug in one of them.—Remarks of Sir C. Lyell and Prof. Wilson on these Facts.—Other Relics.

GEOLOGISTS have, since the development of their science, continually insisted on vast periods of time to accomplish the successive stages which seem to mark the creative work. The evidences of the lapse of incalculable ages since that "beginning" spoken of in the introductory sentence of Divine Revelation are so overwhelming that no intelligent theologian presumes any longer to call them in question. A modern school of geology has, however, become so enamored of the element of Time as necessary to the explication of all geological processes, that we are in danger of overlooking other considerations in forming our judgments with regard to the changes which have occurred on the surface of our planet. The fashionable geological philosophy in England now not only requires immense periods for all the modifications to which the earth has been subjected, but, making the operations of the present the gauge by which to measure all the occurrences of the past, seeks to expound all the appearances in the strata of the earth by the same tranquil operations which are carried on by Nature in the present era of comparative repose. It is assumed that the causes which are at work to-day are the causes which have been at work in the past, and that it is unphilosophical to admit of any more violent energies than those which a survey of existing operations presents to the geologist. It is assumed that the Glacial Epoch is removed from our days by a vast cycle of time; it is assumed that the physical geography of the earth has not been substantially modified for tens or hundreds of thousands of years; it is assumed that it requires long ages to effect the extinction of an existing fauna; it is assumed that elevations and subsidences of the land which are indicated by the presence of marine shells on lofty beaches and by submerged coasts, have occurred at the rate of two and a half feet per century; it is assumed that the rivers of to-day are the same streams, with the same volume of water, which existed at the close of the Glacial Period; it is assumed that it requires the sequence of innumerable centuries to effect a transition from a harsh to a temperate climate; it is assumed that because no great river-horses or huge proboscidians or powerful carnivores roam in our age through civilized Europe, a long and protracted period must have intervened since the hippopotamus wallowed in the marshes of the Thames and the cave-lion roared on the Mendip Hills. Lyell derives his principal arguments for the antiquity of man from the great physical changes which have taken place during the human period, assuming that such changes could not have been effected in a few thousand years, and that the conditions were precisely the same formerly that they are in 1874. In such an argument the *presumption* is with those who maintain the brief sojourn of man upon the earth, because we cannot discover or hear of any human history back of some six or eight thousand years ago. It therefore devolves upon the geologists to prove positively that there was something behind the beginnings of Egyptian and Babylonian and Arabian history. It is *possible* that physical changes may have occurred more energetically and more rapidly six or eight thousand years ago than they do now. It is *possible* it was a *transitional* period about the time that man was introduced upon the earth. The fitting up of the planet for his reception *may* have involved some rapid shiftings of the scenes,—glacial movements,—increased rain-fall,—melting snows,—upheavals and depressions of continents or sea-bottoms,—changes of temperature,—migrations of animals and plants,—the formation of lakes and river-beds.

The beginnings of the human race possibly an epoch of great geological activity.

A writer in the *Princeton Review*, to whose article we have already made reference, says that in 1853 Lyell reasoned that if human remains should be found in the raised beaches of the drift or glacial era, it would compel us to ascribe a much higher antiquity to our species than even the boldest speculations of the ethnologist required,—viz., from sixty to one hundred thousand years. He instanced especially the beaches of Great Britain. The remains have since been found. "In a raised beach at Leith, fragments of Roman pottery, along with bones apparently of deer, and littoral shells, have been discovered at a height of twenty-five feet above the sea. This is an important fact; for it shows that since the time when the Roman legions marched along the shores of the Frith of Forth, and their galleys sailed into its harbors, the land has actually been upheaved, slowly and imperceptibly, to a height of twenty-five feet. So great a change within so recent a period tempts us to pause before we give assent to the enormous intervals of time which some geologists demand for the accomplishment of other changes that have occurred since the advent of man. It may be that man appeared on earth at a much earlier period than is generally supposed, but such a discovery as that of the raised beach at Leith seems to teach us that we cannot be too cautious

Lyell on Raised Beaches.

in sifting the evidence on which his antiquity is sought to be established." *

In referring to the caves in which human remains have been found in association with those of the extinct mammifers, Sir Charles lays great stress on the alterations in the physical geography of the localities of these caves which have occurred since the fossils were deposited. He refers to the alterations which have taken place in the shape of the valley of the Meuse, where the mouths of the fossiliferous caverns often open abruptly in the face of perpendicular precipices two hundred feet or more in height above the present streams. These caves have all been swept by water since the human period.

Sir C. Lyell on the alterations in the physical geography of the localities of the caves.

So at Kent's Hole, at Torquay, the cave—also manifestly at one time invaded by torrents since the existence of man—is nearly one hundred feet above the streams of the neighboring valleys. There is a similar state of things at Brixham Cave, and at King Arthur's Cave, in Glamorganshire.

Sir Charles and his school demand for all such geological operations *Time;* and Time is no doubt the chief element in geological changes. It must have required Time for the formation of the coal measures: the growth and mineralization of their contents conclude this at once. But, as a writer in the *North British Review* remarks of the geologic record, the gigantic revolutions indicated by the faults, elevations, submergences, marvellous plications and contortions, complete inversions of strata, etc., betoken *forces* quite unexampled in the historical period. These displacements appear also to have been consummated with rapidity. Even Lyell admits that in the case of the denudation of rivers, with their subsequent deposition of alluvia, such rivers as the Thames could never (according to the present rate of change), not even in a million of years, have excavated the valleys through which they flow.

Force an element of geological change, as well as Time.

If a shock may be felt in the course of a few minutes from the Great Lakes of the United States to the coasts of Sweden and the Mediterranean,—over an area four times greater than the extent of Europe,—and the sea may rise in a moment fifty feet above its ordinary level, and sweep over the adjacent coasts,—and the larger portion of a capital like Lisbon, at the same time, may be shaken down almost in a breath, and sixty thousand of its inhabitants overwhelmed in the ruins,—one of the quays of the harbor, on which a great concourse of people had assembled, also suddenly sinking down into the sea so deep that not one of the dead bodies ever floated to the surface,—if all this may happen in-

---

* North British Review, No. lxix. p. 77, quoted in Princeton Review, Oct., 1868.

stantly and abruptly, it is idle to insist upon absolute uniformity in geology. If, as Humboldt affirms, the mountain of Jorullo was seen to rise from a level plain, on the 14th of September, 1759, to a height of one thousand six hundred and eighty-one feet, it is obvious that *Force* as well as *Time* is an element in the transformations exhibited by the surface of the earth.

The phenomenon of the Glacial Age itself is in the nature of a "paroxysm."

Contortions of strata in the Island of Möen.

The violent character of the forces in operation in the Post-Glacial Age have been vividly represented by Sir Charles Lyell himself. In his "Antiquity of Man" he describes the contortions of the strata of this date in the Danish island of Möen. The accompanying figures will illustrate what we mean.

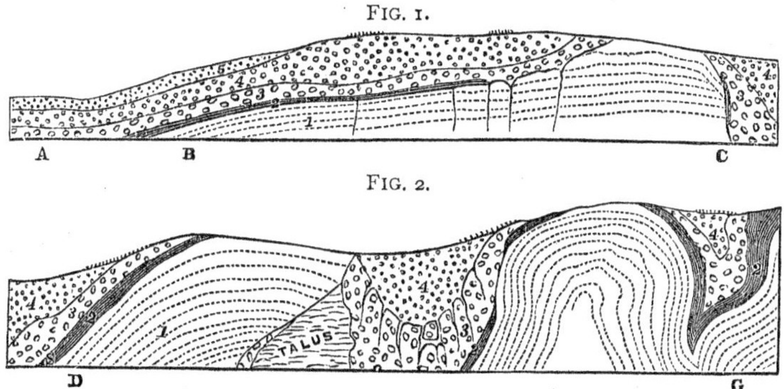

FIG. 1.

FIG. 2.

These figures (from the "Antiquity of Man") represent the cliffs on the northeast coast of Möen. In the low part of the island, at A, fig. 1, the drift is horizontal. At B it changes. At C, where the cliff is one hundred and eighty feet high, there is a sharp flexure. Passing to fig. 2, between D and G we observe a great fracture in the rocks, with synclinal and anticlinal folds exhibited in cliffs nearly three hundred feet high.

But the most wonderful shiftings and faultings of the beds occur in the Dronningestol, part of the same cliff, where the drift becomes thoroughly entangled and mixed up with the dislocated chalks.

Change of climate, and sudden elevations and subsidences of land.

The ice-covering which succeeded (in the north of Europe) the palms of the Pliocene era implies some great reversal of the geological processes. In the Palæolithic Age, as we are told, the temperature in England was 20° lower than it was in the Neolithic Age; and this is connected (if it be true) with some abrupt change in the influences operating upon the earth. We know that during the Glacial Period the land rose and fell from one thousand to fifteen hundred feet in Scotland and

Wales; and that these alternations were repeated more than once. Dr. Andrews has shown that the waters of the Great American Lakes rose and fell several times at the close of this period, and that these changes occurred *abruptly and suddenly*.

Sir Charles Lyell refers also to certain pieces of pottery found at Cagliari, in the south of Sardinia, three hundred feet (as he states it, but two hundred and forty-two feet as given in Reclus's "The Earth") above the existing sea-level. He calculates that this pottery must be twelve thousand years old, assuming the rate of elevation to be that now observed in Sweden,—to wit, two and a half feet per century.

Cagliari.

It is not at all improbable—indeed, it is highly probable—that volcanic action has had something to do with the raising of this beach, though that is not absolutely necessary to account for the elevation in a period of a few thousand years. We know that this locality is a focus of volcanic activity. According to the Chinese and Japanese accounts, several volcanoes have risen from the bed of the sea on the coasts of Japan and Corea during the historical period. In the year 1007 a roar of thunder announced the appearance of the volcano of Toinmoura on the south of Corea, and after seven days a mountain four leagues in circumference appeared, towering up to the height of one thousand feet. The Japanese affirm that the celebrated Fusi-Yama, the highest mountain in Japan, was upheaved in a single night from the sea, twenty-one centuries and a half ago. M. Reclus instances also Stromboli, St. Paul in the Indian Ocean, Momotombo in the Lake of Nicaragua, and the Santorin group in the Ægean Sea. In the centre of this last-named group an island of lava emerged about 196 B.C. It was named Hiera, and a temple to Neptune was erected on its summit. This island was added to in the years 46, 713, 726, and 1427, and is now called Palæo-Kaïmeni. Not far off, a smaller one, Mikro-Kaïmeni, rose in 1570 or 1573. At the beginning of the eighteenth century, Neo-Kaïmeni was formed. At a point near Mikro-Kaïmeni, a bank of rocks, situated in 1794 at a depth of eighty or one hundred feet, was in 1835 only thirteen feet from the surface.

Volcanic action.

There has been another eruption of this volcano since M. Reclus recorded the foregoing, viz., in February, 1867. An island three hundred and fifty feet by one hundred feet was raised up.

The changes which may be wrought by an earthquake are vividly illustrated in the instance of the earthquake at Cutch, in the delta of the Indus, in 1819. The principal town, Bhooj, was converted into a heap of ruins, and the movement was felt over an area having a radius of one thousand miles from this point,—extending to Khatmandoo, Calcutta, and Pondicherry. The vibra-

Earthquake of Cutch.

23

tions were felt in Northwest India, at a distance of eight hundred miles, after an interval of about fifteen minutes after the shock at Bhooj. The eastern channel of the Indus (which had been almost deserted) had before the earthquake been fordable at Luckput, being only one foot deep when the tide was at ebb, and at flood-tide never more than six feet; after the convulsion this channel was found to be more than eighteen feet deep at low water. The fort and village of Sindree, on the eastern arm of the Indus, were submerged, the sea flowing in by the eastern mouth of the Indus, and in a few hours a tract of land two thousand square miles in area was converted into an inland sea, or lagoon. A tract of country, about five miles from Sindree, about fifty miles in length from east to west, and sixteen miles in breadth in some parts, was elevated to the height of ten feet above the original level of the delta. To this tract the natives gave the name of *Ullah Bund*, or the *Mound of God*.

More recent geographical changes, of great magnitude, have occurred in the district of Cutch, near the mouth of the Koree, or eastern branch of the Indus, by which a large area appears to have subsided, and the Sindree lake has been converted into a salt marsh.*

The Valley of the Mississippi.

In the year 1812 a great convulsion occurred in the neighborhood of the village of New Madrid, in the valley of the Mississippi. A tract of many miles in extent, near the Little Prairie, became covered with water some four feet deep, and large lakes, twenty miles in extent, were formed in the course of an hour. The grave-yard at New Madrid was precipitated into the bed of the Mississippi, and the river-bank sank eight feet. This region west of New Madrid is now called *The Sunk Country*, and extends along the course of the White River a distance of seventy-five miles north and south and thirty miles east and west.

New Zealand.

In the year 1823 there was a small cove called the Jail, about eighty miles north of Dusky Bay, in New Zealand, which was much visited by sealers, and where the deep water ran up close to the shore. "After a succession of earthquakes," says Sir Charles Lyell, "in 1826 and 1827, so complete was the transformation of this coast that its former features could no longer be recognized." In 1847 the hull of a vessel—supposed to be the "Active," which was lost in 1814—was found on the west coast, two hundred yards from the shore, with a small tree growing through its bottom.

There was another earthquake in New Zealand in 1855. The shocks were felt at sea to the distance of one hundred and fifty miles from the coast, and embraced an area of three hundred and sixty thousand square

* Lyell's Principles, vol. ii. p. 98.

miles. Near Wellington, in the North Island, a tract of land comprising four thousand square miles is believed to have been permanently elevated from one to nine feet.

Vivenzio states that by the earthquake of Calabria, in 1783, some fifty lakes were formed. In Sicily and the two Calabrias the loss of life amounted to about forty thousand.

In the year 1772, Papandayang, a volcanic mountain in the island of Java, nine thousand feet high, experienced an eruption which reduced its height to five thousand feet.

Earthquake of Lisbon.

Sixty thousand persons perished in the course of about six minutes by the earthquake of Lisbon in 1755. The sea rose fifty feet. The mountains of Arrabida, Estrella, Julio, Marvan, and Cintra were "impetuously shaken, as it were, from their very foundations; and some of them opened at their summits, which were split and rent in a wonderful manner, huge masses of them being thrown down into the subjacent valleys." Flames are reported to have issued from these mountains which are supposed to have been electric. The shock of this earthquake was felt in the Alps, on the coast of Sweden, in Thuringia, in Northern Germany, and in Great Britain. In the islands of Antigua, Barbadoes, and Martinique, the tide (which usually rises in this region about two feet) suddenly rose twenty feet, the water assuming an inky blackness. The movement was also felt in the great lakes between the United States and Canada. The water in Loch Lomond, Scotland, rose two feet four inches. At Cadiz the sea rose sixty feet.

Peru.

Peru was visited in 1746 by a tremendous earthquake. Two hundred shocks were experienced in twenty-four hours. The ocean twice retired and returned upon the land; Lima was destroyed, and part of the coast of Callao converted into a bay. Fifty-nine years before, a similar convulsion had occurred. The sea at that time retired and advanced again, overwhelming Callao, and drowning man and beast for fifty leagues along the shore.

Great Earthquake of August, 1868.

The coast of Peru was visited again by these convulsions on the 13th of August, 1868, the shocks being felt on the coast of Bolivia as well. The sea retired and returned at the rate of ten miles an hour, with a wave fifty feet high, that covered many towns and left many ships upon the land. Arequipa, a city of fifty thousand inhabitants, about forty miles from the coast, was almost entirely destroyed. Iquique, another city, in the southern part of Peru, was also almost totally destroyed. Arica, after being destroyed by the earthquake, was obliterated by the sea. The town of Tambo was entirely washed away. The towns of Tiabaga Vitor, Molliendo, and Mahia, and all the villages within one hundred and fifty miles, were destroyed. At Islay the earthquake-wave rose to the height of sixty feet.

In the Chincha Islands the shocks were very severe. In Ecuador repeated shocks were felt between the 13th and the 16th, and at the termination of these shocks the cities of Ibarra, San Pablo, Atuntaqui, Imantad, Otovala, and many other places had been laid in ruins. In Ibarra, Otovala, and Cotacachi, almost the entire population perished. The site of Cotacachi was covered by a lake. Severe shocks were felt at Talcahuano, in Chili, and the sea was greatly agitated.

This convulsion of the earth was not confined to the coasts of South America. It was observed at the Sandwich Islands on the 14th, and at Yokohama, Japan, on the 15th. The sea rose and fell on the coasts of the Sandwich Islands from six to twelve feet.

On the morning of the 17th (the 16th as compared with time at the Sandwich Islands) earthquake-shocks were felt in New Zealand at several points. In Eastern Australia there were unusual waves and tidal disturbances.

Sicily.

In Sicily, in 1693, the city of Catania and forty-nine other places were destroyed by an earthquake, and about one hundred thousand people perished.

Jamaica.

In 1692 a violent earthquake in the island of Jamaica caused the town of Port Royal to *sink down* into the water, only about one-fourth of the houses escaping. The large store-houses on the harbor sank down,—some of them forty-eight feet under the sea. The mountains of the island were fearfully shaken, and many of them were stripped of their verdure. The rivers on these mountains ceased to flow for about twenty-four hours, and then brought down immense quantities of timber into the sea.

This is volcanic action; and we do not insist that the beach at Cagliari was raised in this manner. It may have been, without resorting to any improbable hypothesis.* We take occasion here to enter a protest

* Strabo expressly affirms that Sicily was broken from the continent by earthquakes. Æschylus, in a missing work, refers to the same convulsion; and Rhegium is said to have gotten its name from this event. (Strab., i. 386. See also Virgil, Æneid, iii. 414.) Col. Hamilton Smith observes that "no author states at what period, and to what extent, volcanic convulsions changed the surface of Eastern Italy and separated Calabria from Sicily by a disruption now denominated the Straits of Messina. The event can only be surmised by approximation, for, although it confessedly took place before within the historical record, it was not so remote as to have obliterated the terror impressed upon the memories of subsequent generations living in the vicinity, or to have worn away the dangerous impediment of Scylla and Charybdis, . . . and may synchronize with the close of the transition-era of convulsive phenomena which includes the bursting of the Thracian Bosphorus at the volcanic Cyanean islands; the Greek deluge; the separation of the Eubœa from Attica; and the passage of a large diluvian wave across the Isthmus of Corinth, which has left indelible

against the dogmatism of scientific men. It is certainly rash to reverse all of our conclusions with regard to human chronology by examples of this sort, in which the energetic forces of volcanic action are first unceremoniously discarded, and then a chronometric scale of two and a half feet per century arbitrarily assumed from some observations of what is now in progress on the coasts of the Baltic, as the general rate of the secular elevations of the land in all parts of the world,—when it is *known* that the rate varies in every part of the world and in different ages.

We propose in this chapter to show that the crust of the earth is in a state of perpetual movement, and that the coasts of Europe, Asia, Africa, America, Australia, and the islands of the sea have within the present era experienced important upheavals or depressions, thereby effecting serious modifications in the geography and physical conformation of the earth.

Movements of Peat formations, etc.

The Chilian astronomer Moesta has ascertained that the National Observatory of Chili, on the hill of Santa Lucia, near Santiago, rises and descends alternately in the space of twenty-four hours. Similar observations have been made with reference to the Observatory of Armagh, in Ireland. In the first case the particles of the rock dilate during the day under the solar rays, and contract in consequence of the radiation during the night. At Armagh, after heavy rains the hill swells or rises perceptibly; and after the evaporation of the extra water it contracts. These movements are, however, due to local or temporary influences, and are not occasioned by the steady and slow pressure or the quick and violent energy of subterranean forces.

The coast of Sweden.

More than a hundred and forty years ago, Celsius, the Swedish astronomer, had his attention called to the fact that the Gulf of Bothnia was steadily diminishing in depth and extent. Old men pointed out to him various places on the coast over which the sea used to flow. He observed also the sites of former sea-ports removed inland from the sea, the remains of boats found at a distance from the coast, and edifices built originally upon the shore abandoned by the sea. In 1730 he propounded the hypothesis that the Baltic sank about three feet four inches every century. Then in the course of the following year, in conjunction with Linnæus, having made a mark at the base of a rock in the island of Loeffgrund, he was enabled to verify thirteen years afterwards that the retreat of the Baltic was taking place quite as rapidly as he supposed. It did not occur to Celsius that the solid earth,

---

marks on all the coasts in the vicinity, and was particularly recorded at Dodona." Natural History of the Human Species, p. 138.

This Samothracian Deluge is mentioned by Diodorus Siculus, with the circumstance of the bursting of the Black Sea through the Thracian Bosphorus.

as he regarded it, was in motion: he considered that the phenomenon was due to the gradual depression of the level of the sea. But even in this modified form his views shocked the orthodox divines of Stockholm and Upsal. He was accused of impiety. In the parliament the representatives of the clergy, followed by the burgesses, condemned the new opinion as an abominable heresy. But the fact remained, and more recent observations have confirmed the correctness of the philosopher's averments; save that it has been ascertained that it is the land and not the sea that is in motion. At the northern extremity of the Gulf of Bothnia, at the mouth of the Tornea, the continent is emerging at the rate of five feet three inches in a century; by the side of the Aland Isles it rises only three and a quarter feet in a century; south of this archipelago it rises still more slowly, and farther down the movement seems to cease. The terminal point of Scania is gradually being buried under the waters of the Baltic, as is proved by the submerged forests. Several streets of the towns of Trälleborg, Ystad, and Malmoe have disappeared, the latter having sunk five feet two inches since observations made by Linnæus.*

The west coasts of the Scandinavian peninsula have also been elevated within recent times. The terminal point of Jutland, bounded by an ideal line trending obliquely from Fredericia towards the northwest, rises at the rate of 11.70 inches in a century. In the island of Munkholm, farther to the north, the ground has risen about twenty feet in a thousand years. The portion of the coast nearest the pole is rising most rapidly. Elevated beaches, which can be traced by the eye like the steps of an amphitheatre, are observed at various heights on the slopes of the mountains. Heaps of modern shells are found at heights of five hundred to six hundred and fifty feet above the level of the sea, and the great branches of pink coral formed by the *Lophohelia prolifera*, which lives in the sea at a depth ranging from one thousand to two thousand feet, are now raised up to the base of the cliff.†

Remarks of M. Reclus.

Reclus adds that if the elevation of the beds of the Gulfs of Bothnia and Finland continues with the same regularity as during the historic ages, in three or four thousand years the archipelago of Qvarken, between Umea and Vasa, will be changed into an isthmus, and the Gulf of Tornea will be converted into a lake similar to that of Ladoga. Later still, the Aland Islands will become connected with the continent, and will serve as a bridge between Stockholm and the empire of Russia. It is, besides, very probable that the great lakes and numberless sheets of water which fill all the granite basins of Finland have taken the place of an arm of the sea which once united

* The Earth, p. 532.

† Carl Vogt: quoted by Reclus, pp. 532, 533.

the Baltic to the great Polar Ocean. The shells belonging to polar waters, which are found as far as the basin of the Volga, demonstrate the existence of a former arm of the sea. The name of Scandinavia itself signifies the "Isle of Scand," and the name of Bothnia (Botten) suggests that these coast provinces were formerly a marine bed.* M. Reclus proceeds:

Scandinavia recently an island.

"This is not all. The Baltic Mediterranean communicated with the North Sea by a wide channel, the deepest depressions of which are now occupied by the lakes Mälar, Hjelmar, and Wenern. Considerable heaps of oyster-shells are found in several places on the heights which command these great lakes of Southern Sweden. On the rocks now laid dry, which surround the Gulf of Bothnia, banks of these molluscs have also been discovered exactly similar to those of Norway and the western coasts of Denmark. With regard to the celebrated *kjökken-möddings* of the Danish islands, they are in great part composed of oyster-shells, which the inhabitants, in the Age of Stone, evidently used to collect in the bottoms of the neighboring bays. It has been proved by the investigations of M. de Baer that the oyster cannot live and grow in water holding more than thirty-seven parts in one thousand of salt, or less than sixteen or seventeen parts in one thousand. Now, the Baltic Sea, into which its numerous tributaries bring a large quantity of fresh water, does not contain, on the average, more than five parts in one thousand of salt; and indeed in some of the gulfs the water, now devoid of all its former inhabitants, has become entirely fresh. And yet—the heaps of oyster-shells prove it—the Baltic Sea and the inland lakes were once as salt as the North Sea is at the present day. Whence, then, could this saltness proceed, except from some former strait which occupied the depressions in which the Swedish engineers have dug out the Trolhätta Canal? Besides, when the sluices were being constructed, there were found, not far from the cataracts, and at a height of forty feet above the Cattegat, various marine remains, mingled with relics of human industry,—boats, anchors, and piles. According to M. de Baer, it is not, at the most, more than five thousand years before our century that we must date the closing up of the straits which used to exist between Southern Sweden and the great mass of the northern plateaux."

The oyster no longer found in the Baltic.

We have given the statement of M. Reclus. Sir C. Lyell's ("Principles," vol. ii. p. 193) is different. He affirms that the oyster is not found on the raised beaches near Lake Mälar and the east coast of Sweden, but only the dwarfed mussels, cockles, and periwinkle of the brackish waters of the Baltic. To this we may recur in a future chapter.

* The Earth, p. 533.

We shall also show that the five thousand years suggested by M. de Baer is much too great.

Sir C. Lyell considers that the Swedish coast has been raised by a uniform secular movement of about two and a half feet per century. But the "uniformitarian" hypothesis is a pure assumption, and is directly contradicted by ascertained facts. It has been shown by recent investigators that the upheaval of Northern Scandinavia "does not take place in a mode that is perfectly uniform." The movement has sometimes been accelerated and sometimes slackened. It has also been shown by M. Bravais that the lines of erosion of Altenfjord are not parallel, and that the rocky masses situated at the ends of the gulfs have been displaced much more than the layers nearer the sea. Thus the upper bank of Altenfjord has risen at the eastern end two hundred and nineteen feet above the level of the sea, while at the entrance of the bay it has risen only ninety-one feet.

The movement a paroxysmal movement.

Touching the rise of land in Sweden, we find the following statement in *The Academy* of March 1, 1872: "Not far from Morup, on the Holland shore, is a large block (of stone), ten feet high and fifteen broad, which served as a beacon as far back as the eleventh century. In September, 1816, this stone was, according to the measurements of Bexell, four feet above high-water mark, and it still bears an inscription to that effect. This block of stone in the summer of 1871 was one hundred and twenty feet from the shore, indicating a comparatively recent and rapid upheaval along this coast. In no historic records of this stone is it stated to have been in, but invariably at, the water; from which it appears that the upheaval commenced with the present century, and is now rapidly progressing."

The beaches of the islands of Spitzbergen exhibit, up to the height of one hundred and forty-seven feet above the sea, heaps of bones of whales and shells of the present period.

Spitzbergen.

The northern coasts of Russia and Siberia are likewise rising, as is attested by popular tradition and the observations of travellers. M. de Keyserling and Sir Roderick Murchison found (says Reclus) at points two hundred and fifty miles to the south of the White Sea, on the banks of the Dwina and the Vaga, beds of sand and mud containing several kinds of shells similar to those which inhabit the neighboring seas, and *so well preserved that they have not lost their colors*. In like manner M. de Middendorf states that the ground of the Siberian *tundras* is in great part covered with a thin coating of sand and fine clay, exactly similar to that which is now deposited on the shores of the Frozen Ocean: in this clay, too, which contains in such large quantities the buried remains of mammoths, there are also found heaps of shells perfectly identical with those of the adjacent ocean. Far

Russia.

Siberia.

inland, besides, traces of drift-wood are seen, the trees forming what once grew in the forests of Southern Siberia: these trees, having been first carried into the sea by the current of the rivers, have been thrown up by the waves on the former coasts, which are now deserted by the sea.* How recent this upheaval of Siberia is, is shown by the further statement that "the island of Diomida, which Chalaourof noticed in 1760 to the east of Cape Sviatoj, was found to be joined to the continent at the date of Wrangell's voyage, sixty years later." †

Again: "Quite recently Russian travellers have discovered, on the coast of the great island Saghalien, heaps of modern shells, lying not far from the shore, on beds of marine clay, and also former bays, which are now converted into lakes or salt marshes." ‡

To the same purport Ermann mentions, speaking of the Kirgis Steppe, and the eastern border of the Oural, in the Government of Orenburg, that "a depression of the level of several of the existing lakes is also suspected to be continually taking place; but it can be fully demonstrated in the instance of one situate near Turdoysk, between Slatousk and Miask, which was once capable of driving a mill. Between the years 1795 and 1812, it has been proved, by observation, to have sunk two hundred and ninety-one feet." §

Raised beaches of Scotland.

The cliffs of Scotland present phenomena similar to those observed in the foregoing countries. We have referred to the raised beach of the Frith of Forth. The upheaval has been from twenty-four to twenty-six and a half feet, or some (since the time of the Romans) 0.195 inch a year. But since 1810 this rate has increased to 0.546 inch in a year. On the coast of Wales Mr. Darbishire has found, at a height of thirteen hundred and fifty-seven feet, shells similar to those at present existing in the seas of Northern Europe.

Former African Sea.

Within a recent period there was a sea, or at least a strait, several hundred miles in width, which commenced at the Gulf of Syrtes, and, filling up the depressions of the Berber Sahara, joined the Atlantic in front of the archipelago of the Canaries. The sands of these regions are entirely identical with those of the nearest Mediterranean shores, and contain the same shells. The common cockle is found not only on the surface, but also at some depth, and likewise at a height of nine hundred feet on the sides of the hills. The Algerian Sahara has therefore risen to this extent during a recent geological period.||

To the existence of this African Mediterranean, Lyell and Escher

---

* See p. 536, Translation by Mr. Woodward, Am. edit.

† Ib., pp. 536, 537.

‡ Ib., p. 563.

§ Travels in Siberia, i. 213, Trans., Amer. edit.

|| The Earth, p. 538.

von der Linth in a great measure attribute the enormous extent of the former glaciers of Europe.

At a recent, and perhaps historical, epoch, Lake Tritonis of the ancients, now the Sebkha Faraoun, into which flowed the Igharghar, has ceased to be a prolongation of the Gulf of Gabes, and has become a mere marsh.

Ports of Carthage, Utica, etc.

On the southern coasts of the Mediterranean also the ancient ports of Carthage, Utica, Mahedia, Porto Farina, Bizerta, etc., are now filled up.

The shores of this sea afford many instances of raised beaches. In the island of Sicily there are caves (which we have already considered) so recently elevated that *serpulæ* are still found clinging to their walls. Of these the cave of San Ciro, near Palermo, is a good example. It is one hundred and eighty feet above the sea. Within it is found an ancient beach of pebbles of various rocks, many of which must have come from places far remote. Broken pieces of coral and shell, especially of oysters and pectens, are mingled with the pebbles; and immediately above the level of this beach, *serpulæ* are still found adhering to the rock, while the walls of the cave are perforated by *lithodomi*. Dr. Philippi found forty-five different species of shells in this cave,—all, with two or three exceptions, still inhabiting the adjoining sea; while overlying this shell-gravel is a deposit of bone breccia, containing remains of the elephant, hippopotamus, and several species of deer.

Raised beaches of Sicily.

At Puzzuoli, on the Bay of Baiæ, it is well known, the Temple of Serapis and other Roman remains give evidence of marked changes in the level of the coast. Lyell discusses the subject at considerable length. He reaches the conclusion that "since the beginning of the Christian era the relative level of land and sea has changed twice," and that "each movement, both of elevation and subsidence, has exceeded twenty feet." At one point on the coast the elevation was "more than thirty feet." Other writers state in general terms that the temple has been raised twenty-five feet. Including both movements, there is here an example of changes in the level of the coast amounting to some fifty feet since the beginning of the Christian era.

Puzzuoli.

The following striking examples are from Spain. M. de Botella, in a letter to M. Elie de Beaumont, writes, "From Villar don Diego, in the province of Zamora, it is now possible to see half of the bell-tower of the Benifarzes, a village in the province of Valladolid, while twenty-three years ago (1847) it was scarcely possible to see the top of the same tower.

Spain.

"A similar fact has been noticed in the province of Alava, it now being possible to perceive from the village of Salvatierra the whole village of Salduente, while in 1847 it was difficult to distinguish the vane of the bell-tower." The four points are on a line passing through Burgos,—W. 28° S. The extremities of this line are three hundred kilometres apart.*

In Southern France it has been proved that in the times of the Romans, and as late as the Middle Ages, the marshes extended much further inland. Astruc points out the remarkable fact that the Romans, who highly appreciated thermal springs, were not aware of the abundant wells of Balaruc, although the eddies of steam could not have failed to point them out if they had not been covered by the waters of Lake Thau. In the north of France, on the other hand, the coasts appear to be sinking. On the coast of Brittany and Normandy, numerous forests have been submerged. In 709 the monastery of Mont St.-Michel was built in the midst of a forest ten leagues (?) from the sea: it now stands, like an island, in the midst of sand-banks. Reclus also affirms that at some remote epoch, but cotemporary with man, the valley of the Somme was upheaved, but for thousands of years it has been slowly subsiding, as submarine forests are found along the coast, and the peat bogs of Abbeville, the bottom of which is situated below the Bay of Somme, afford no other *débris* than the remains of animals and vegetables which lived on the earth or in fresh water.† M. Beauvais believes that the whole of France is being slowly upheaved on the southern side, and turns on a base-line passing through the peninsula of Brittany. At all events, the coasts of Poitou, Aunis, and Saintonge appear to have risen since the commencement of the historical epoch. The former Gulf of Poitou, the entrance to which two thousand years ago was some eighteen to twenty-five miles in width, is now nothing but a small bay, known as the Creek of Aiguillon. Brouage is now some distance from the sea. In the Middle Ages it was a port of some importance.

France.

The shores of Asia Minor have risen with a rapid movement during the historical period. The ruins of Troy, Smyrna, Ephesus, and Miletus have gradually become more distant from the sea. Many of the Ægean Isles have become united, or have been connected with the mainland. The mountain of Lade in the time of Herodotus was an island, near which the Ionian galleys and the Persian fleet fought a battle. At the present day it stands in the midst of the plain of the Meander. The town of Priene, which in the time of Strabo was four and a half miles from the shore, had been originally built on the coast. The village Ayasoulouk, the site of the city of Ephesus, is now two

Asia Minor.

* Comptes-Rendus, May, 1870, quoted in An. Sci. Dis., 1871, p. 250.

† The Earth, p. 546.

leagues from the coast, and the former estuary which was commanded by the town is a marshy plain.

Banks of modern shells have been left by the sea at considerable heights on the hills of Thrace and Anatolia; round the Crimea, salt lakes and stagnant marshes now exist far inland in the place of the former gulfs.

Caspian Sea.

The Caspian Sea, the Sea of Aral, and the sheets of water scattered over the steppes of that region were separated from the Euxine and the Gulf of Obi by a gradual upheaval of the continent. The plains are still covered with salt and marine remains. The inland seas and the scattered lakes are still inhabited by seals, and thus present an altogether oceanic character. Herodotus, Strabo, Ptolemæus, and all the writers of antiquity attribute to the ancient Hyrcanian Ocean an extent far larger than that of the Caspian of our day, most of them, indeed, considering it as a prolongation of the Frozen Ocean.* We may venture to assume that during some portion of the present period a vast strait, like that which once ran along the base of the Atlas, extended from the Black Sea to the Gulf of Obi and the Frozen Ocean.†

Venice.

In the sixteenth century, Angiolo Eremitano suggested that the isles of Venice were sinking at the rate of about a foot in a century. This hypothesis, derived from a comparison of the buildings and the pavements of the streets with the water, has been since fully confirmed. The town of Conca, once situated near the mouth of the Crustummio, has been entirely under the sea for some centuries, and the remains of two of its towers may still be seen beneath the waves. At Trieste, pavements may be seen below the level of the sea.

Submerged forests.

The coasts of the south of England, of Cornwall, and of Yorkshire, as well as those of Hanover and Schleswig, present submerged forests and submarine peat mosses. The western coast of Schleswig has subsided thirteen feet during the present period. "In this locality, at the bottom of the port of Husum, there was discovered, in the midst of a submerged forest of birches, *a tomb of the Age of Stone* [our italics], necessarily dating from a period anterior to the subsidence of the ground on which it stood."‡ On the eastern coast, near the mouth of the Schlei, the stumps of the trees of an ancient deer-forest of the Middle Ages may be seen under the water about half a mile from the shore. According to John Paton, Denmark and Schleswig-Holstein have lost since the year 1240 an area of about one thousand two hundred and twenty-five square miles,—*i.e.*, one-eighteenth of their territory.

* The Earth, pp. 543, 544. † Ib., p. 534. ‡ Ib., p. 548.

Further to the east, round the southern basin of the Baltic, we find Rügen broken up into islets and peninsulas, and Bornholm surrounded by submarine forests, one of which is twenty-six feet below the line of the shore. Other submerged forests fringe the coasts of Pomerania and Eastern Prussia. On the point of Samland the church of St. Adalbert, built, at the close of the fifteenth century, some four and a half miles from the sea, is now only one hundred paces from the beach.

The Baltic coasts.

The encroachments of the sea on the one hand, and the formation of new land on the other, is not a matter of simply recent observation. A hundred years ago, Goldsmith, in his "History of the Earth," recorded many instances of this kind. Buffon, he tells us, mentions that on many parts of the coasts of France, Holland, England, Germany, and Prussia, the sea had been sensibly known to retire. Hubert Thomas, he also says, asserts, in his Description of the Country of Liège, that the sea formerly encompassed the city of Tongres, which, however, was in his day *thirty-five leagues* distant from it: this assertion he supports by many strong reasons, and, among others, by the iron rings affixed in the walls of the town, for fastening the ships which came into that port. In Italy, he remarks, there is a considerable piece of ground gained at the mouth of the river Arno; and Ravenna, that once stood by the seaside, is now considerably removed from it. But, he adds, we need scarce mention these, when we find that the whole republic of Holland seems to be a conquest from the sea. The surface of the earth in this country is below the level of the bed of the sea; and he remembers, on approaching its coast, to have looked down upon it from the sea, as into a valley. . . . In France, the town of Aigues-Mortes was a port in the time of St. Louis, which is now removed more than four miles from the sea. Psalmodi, in the same kingdom, was an island in the year 815, but is now more than six miles from the shore. All along the coasts of Norfolk, as he was informed, in the memory of man the sea had gained fifty yards in some places, and lost as much in others.*

Similar facts chronicled by Goldsmith, Buffon, and Malte-Brun.

He proceeds to mention the inundation which happened in the reign of Henry I., when the sea overflowed the estates of Earl Godwin and formed what is now known as the Goodwin Sands; also the irruption of the sea in the territory of Dort in 1546, by which one hundred thousand persons were destroyed, and a yet greater number around the Dollart. In Friesland and Zealand more than three hundred villages were overwhelmed; "and their ruins still continue visible at the bottom of the water, in a

The Goodwin Sands.

Irruption of the sea in 1546.

* History of the Earth, vol. i. p. 112, Philadelphia, 1852.

clear day." The Baltic Sea has, by slow degrees, covered a large part of Pomerania, and, among others, destroyed and overwhelmed the famous port of Vineta. The German Sea has advanced upon the shores of Holland, near Catt; so that the ruins of an ancient citadel of the Romans are now under water.

Submergence of Pomerania.

At the mouth of the river Ness, near Bruges, in Flanders, at the depth of fifty feet, are found great quantities of trees lying close to each other, —the trunks, the branches, and the leaves in such preservation that each kind of tree is immediately distinguished.

At the city of Modena, in Italy, and about four miles round it, wherever the ground is dug, at the depth of fourteen feet are found the ruins of an ancient city, paved streets, houses, floors, and pieces of mosaic-work. Beneath this is a solid earth; and under this, at twenty-six feet, are large trees, such as walnuts, with the walnuts still sticking on the stems. In many of the layers are found pieces of charcoal, bones, and bits of iron.

The city of Modena.

To the same purport M. Malte-Brun in his "Universal Geography." The Pontine Marshes, he says, now cover part of the Appian Way, while the renowned villas of Baiæ are now found buried beneath the water. In Egypt, the town of Damietta, whose walls in the time of Louis IX. were washed by the sea, is now (that is, when M. Malte-Brun wrote) at a considerable distance from it. The island of Tyre is joined to the continent by a more powerful hand than that of Alexander. At the mouth of the Pyramus, in Cilicia, a deposit of sand has extended the modern coast six miles beyond the ancient boundary. The Meander has, by little and little, filled up the valley into which it flows, and which was formerly a gulf. The inhabitants of Miletus and Ephesus have several times been compelled to change the situation of their towns, in order to follow the sea, which retired from their walls. The environs of Ravenna, Aquileia, and Venice present similar phenomena. Although the ground near Ravenna has sunk to such a degree that the pavement of the cathedral is only six inches above the level of high water, yet the land is extended in such a manner that this town, formerly situated in the midst of the marshes and canals and furnished with an excellent port, is now three Italian miles from the sea, and surrounded by meadows and fields.*

The Appian Way and the Villas of Baiæ.

Miletus and Ephesus.

Ravenna.

Tacitus, says M. Malte-Brun, describes Germany as full of inaccessible marshes, "which are now in great measure dried up." Rudbeck admits (he says) that, according to the tradition of the country, the low parts of Scandinavia presented the same aspect.†

* Universal Geography, vol. i. p. 207.

† Ib., vol. i. p. 231.

Col. Hamilton Smith mentions also that the town of Adria, said to have been built on the *sea-shore* by Tarchon, leader of the ancient Etruscan people, about the time of the Trojan war, is now fifteen and a half miles from the mouth of the river Tartarus, which is still six miles within the furthest point of land projecting in the sea. Excavations at the depth of several feet reveal a former level of the town, with Etruscan and Roman pottery, and at a still greater depth another settlement was reached, where all the earthenware was Etruscan, and there were vestiges of a theatre.

Adria.

The delta of the Rhone, where this river enters Lake Geneva, illustrates the immense amount of earthy matter transported by some streams. An ancient town, Port Vellais, once situated at the water's edge at the point where the river entered the lake, is now more than a mile and a half inland; this intervening tract having been acquired in about eight centuries. The remainder of the delta consists of a flat alluvial plain, about five or six miles in length, composed of sand and mud, a little raised above the level of the river, and full of marshes. The alluvial deposits continue for two miles into the lake. If we could obtain a section of the accumulation formed in the last eight hundred years, we should see a series of strata from six hundred to nine hundred feet thick, along this whole extent, at a very slight angle.

Delta of the Rhone.

On the coasts of Chili the evidences of upheaval are very manifest. Here the coast was not raised by any uniform movement. There seem to have been intervals of comparative repose. On the hills of Chiloe, Darwin found heaps of modern shells at a height of three hundred and forty-seven feet. On the north of Concepcion, traces of the waves during the present period are found at an elevation of six hundred to one thousand feet.

Upheaval of the coast o Chili.

At Valparaiso these levels are as high as twelve hundred and ninety-five feet above the sea.

In front of Arica, on the coast of Peru, the sea has receded one hundred and sixty-five yards in the space of forty years. In front of Callao, on one of the cliffs of the island of San Lorenzo, at a height of eighty-five feet above the sea, Darwin discovered, in a bed of modern shells deposited on a terrace, roots of sea-weed, bones of birds, ears of maize, plaited reeds, and some cotton thread almost entirely decomposed. These relics of human industry almost exactly resemble those which are found in the *huacas* or burial-places of the ancient Peruvians.*

Arica.

Callao.

Mr. Darwin, in the "Naturalist's Voyage around the World," narrates the following remarkable example of the change in the physical

* The Earth, p. 552.

geography of a locality near Lima. When at this city, he says, he met with a civil engineer, Mr. Gill, who informed him that while travelling from Casme to Huarez (not far from Lima) he found a plain covered with the ruins and marks of civilization, which was quite deserted and barren. Near it was the dry bed of a considerable river, from which the water had formerly been conducted for the purposes of irrigation. There was nothing to indicate that the river had not flowed there a few years before; in some parts sand and gravel were spread out, in others the solid rock had been worn into a deep channel. Walking up the bed of the stream, he was astonished to find that he was going *down hill.* The downward slope was about forty feet. "We have here," says Mr. Darwin, "unequivocal evidence that a ridge had been uplifted right across the bed of the stream." The water, he observes, was then, of course, thrown back and a new channel formed, and the neighboring plain became a desert.

The Bolivian Lake.

Travellers assert, says M. Reclus, that the area of the immense Bolivian lake has always been diminishing since the commencement of the historical period. Its water once bathed the walls of Tia-Huanacu, one of the principal cities of the Incas; but this locality is now situated twelve and a half miles from the lake, and more than one hundred and thirty feet above the level of its water.* This change, however, is not due to the elevation of land, but to a different cause, to be noticed presently; namely, the diminution in the amount of the rain-fall. We mention it now simply as one of the changes in this region of the world.

Coast of Texas.

On the coast of Texas, the shores of the Bay of Matagorda have risen from eleven to twenty-two inches from 1845 to 1863. In consequence of the gradual increase in the land, which is also proved by the heaps of shells left far from the shore, it has been necessary to transfer the port of Indianola to Powderhorn, a place four and a half miles nearer the entry. The coasts of Labrador and Newfoundland are also rising. The straits of Hell Gate, which form the entry to the port of New York, are, according to tradition, of recent origin. Two centuries ago, the natives related to the Dutch colonists established in the island of Manhattan that at the time of the fathers of their grandfathers it was possible to cross dry-shod from one bank to the other, and that the sea entered the straits only at the time of the great equinoctial floods. This portion of the coast seems to be subsiding at the rate of twenty-three and a half inches in a century.

Hell Gate.

The bridge of islands which extends diagonally across the Pacific from

* The Earth, p. 384.

the coasts of California to the Malay Peninsula is now sinking, and constitutes the remnants of a former continent which has gradually been sinking in the waves. Several of these islands have disappeared since the first Europeans visited these seas.

Pacific Islands.

There is corresponding to this area of depression a wave of upheaval which coincides with the semicircle of volcanoes running round the western side of the basin of the South Sea. At the commencement of the present geological period the mountains of New Zealand were nineteen hundred feet lower than they are at present. These mountains, as is proved by the series of terraces, have since risen ten successive times. This process of elevation is still going on. In ten years the shores at Lyttelton have risen three feet.

The "lateritic" formation of Madras and North Arcot may be an example of a raised beach on a large scale. Mr. Bruce Foote has found here stone implements similar to those found in the river-gravels of Europe. Other works of human skill show that the bed of the sea has been raised up into dry land [?] since the appearance of man.

Madras.

Mr. Darwin, in his "Voyage of the Beagle," traced a raised beach from the Rio Colorado southward a distance of six or seven hundred miles, spreading itself over the plains of Patagonia two hundred miles inland from the coast. He believes that the land from the Rio de la Plata to Tierra del Fuego—twelve hundred nautical miles—has been raised in mass, in some parts to a height of four hundred feet, within the period of existing sea-shells, which are found on the surface retaining their colors.

Raised Beach twelve hundred miles in length.

Prof. Winchell, of the University of Michigan, in his work entitled "Sketches of Creation," informs us that at St. Augustine, in Florida, the stumps of cedar-trees stand beneath the hard beach shell-rock, immersed in the water at the lowest tides. Some of the sounds of North Carolina which have been navigable within the memory of living sea-captains are now impassable bars or emerging sand-flats. Along the coast of New Jersey the sea has encroached, within sixty years, upon the sites of former habitations, and entire forests have been prostrated by the inundation. In the harbor of Nantucket the upright stumps of trees are found eight feet below the lowest tide, with their roots still buried in the native soil. Similar remains of ancient submarine forests occur on Martha's Vineyard, and on the north side of Cape Cod, and again at Portland. In the region of the St. Croix River, separating Maine from New Brunswick, the coast has been raised, carrying deposits of recent shells and sea-weeds in one instance to the height of twenty-eight feet above the present level of the sea. The island of Grand Menan, off the mouth of the St. Croix River, is slowly rotating on an axis, the south side

St. Augustine, Florida.

Coast of New Jersey.

gradually dipping beneath the waves, while the north is lifted into high bluffs. The north side of Nova Scotia is sinking, while the south is rising. The ancient city of Louisburg, on the island of Cape Breton, was in the eighteenth century the stronghold of France in America. It was well fortified, and had a population of twenty thousand souls. It was destroyed during the French and Indian wars, and the inhabitants dispersed. But Nature had decreed its abandonment. The rock on which the brave General Wolfe landed has nearly disappeared. The sea now flows within the walls of the city.

City of Louisburg.

The entire chain of the Aleutian Islands, between Alaska and Kamschatka, constitutes the vestiges of an ancient ridge, originally raised by volcanic fires.

Aleutian Isles.

A depression in the Valley of the Lower Mississippi of only three hundred feet would admit the waters of the Gulf of Mexico up to the mouth of the Ohio River. A trifling depression in Northern Illinois would furnish an outlet to the Gulf for the Lakes Michigan, Superior, and Huron.*

There is no doubt that the sea once washed the base of the rocks on which the Pyramids of Memphis stand; the *present* base of which is washed by the inundation of the Nile, at an elevation of seventy or eighty feet above the Mediterranean. The Nile once entered the sea by seven principal mouths, two of which have now entirely disappeared. The city of Foah, which stood in the fifteenth century on one of these branches, is now more than a mile inland, and Pharos, anciently an island, which Homer describes as *one day's voyage* by sea from Egypt, is now joined to the continent.†

The Pyramids.

Pharos.

The head of the delta of the Ganges commences two hundred and twenty miles in a direct line from the sea. The sediment transported by the river colors the sea for a distance of sixty miles from the shore.

Delta of the Ganges.

Mr. James Fergusson, in some remarks on this delta before the Geological Society, pointed out that in historical times the Brahmapootra and Ganges (which now run parallel to each other), on entering the plains of Bengal,—passing Goalparah and Rajmahal respectively,—ran originally to the sea in a nearly due north-and-south course, parallel to each other. This symmetry was first disturbed by an *upheaval* of the Midnapore jungle, north of Dacca, by which the Brahmapootra was diverted in a southeast direction into the depression known as the Sylhet Jheels, which were the result of the upheaval in question. The river then filled these Jheels, and returned to its former bed within the limits

* Sketches of Creation, pp. 24, 25.

† Odys., Book iv., v. 355.

of the present century. Mr. Fergusson stated that we have sufficient reason to believe that in the past five thousand years the plain of Bengal has been nearly in the same condition that the valley of Assam now is, —a jungly swamp.*

Sir Charles Lyell informs us that, in the process of boring a well at Calcutta in 1835–40, at the depth of about seventy feet they came to a stratum of black peat, about two feet in thickness, and he therefore concludes that "*there has been a sinking down of what was originally land in this region, to the amount of seventy feet or more.*" Continuing the boring, at the depth of three hundred and fifty feet they encountered the bony shell of a tortoise resembling the living species of Bengal, and also a portion of the humerus of a ruminant, of the size and shape of the common hog-deer of India. At the depth of three hundred and eighty feet they reached a stratum of decayed wood, implying a period of repose, and the existence of a forest, "which must have subsided three hundred feet, to admit of the subsequent superposition of the overlying deposits." †

Calcutta.

In the same connection Sir Charles Lyell says that "in the basin of the Mississippi, proofs both of the descending and ascending movements to a vertical amount of several hundred feet can be shown to have taken place since the existing species of land and fresh-water shells lived in that region."

Basin of the Mississippi.

"The deltas of the Po and Ganges," he also remarks, "when probed by the Artesian auger, have borne testimony to a gradual subsidence of land to the extent of several hundred feet,—old terrestrial surfaces or dirt-beds, turf, peat, forest-land, having been pierced at various depths." ‡

Sir Charles Lyell states also § that the changes gradually effected in the plains of Northern Italy since the time of the Roman republic have been considerable. Extensive lakes and marshes have been gradually filled up, as those near Placentia, Parma, and Cremona, and many have been drained naturally by the deepening of the beds of the rivers. Deserted river-courses are not unfrequent, as that of the Serio Morto, which formerly fell into the Adda, in Lombardy. The Po itself has often deviated from its course, having, after 1390, deserted part of the territory of Cremona and entered that of Parma; its old channel being still recognizable, and bearing the name of *Po Morto*. There is another old channel of the Po in Parma, called Po Vecchio, which was abandoned in the twelfth century, when a great number of towns were destroyed.

Lyell on changes in Northern Italy.

---

* Intellectual Observer, vol. iii. p. 384.

† Lyell, Principles, vol. i. p. 476.

‡ Ib., vol. i. p. 483.

§ Ib., p. 419.

"In the Adriatic," he says, "from the northern part of the Gulf of Trieste, where the Isonzo enters, down to the south of Ravenna, *there is an uninterrupted series of recent accessions of land, more than one hundred miles in length, which within the last two thousand years has increased from two to twenty miles in breadth.*"* And all this notwithstanding the fact that, according to the observations of M. Morlot, the coast between the points indicated has since the time of the Romans subsided five feet.

The wanderings of the Yellow River.

No river has shifted its bed more than the Yellow River in Northern China. It changed its course in the year 602 B.C. It changed again about 350 B.C.; again in 132 B.C.; in 11 B.C.; A.D. 70; A.D. 1034; A.D. 1048, etc. Within the last twenty years one of these great changes has taken place. Instead of emptying into the Yellow Sea, the Hwang-Ho now has its mouth in the Gulf of Pecheli. This course is nearly at a right angle with the old one to Hwaingan; and the distance from its present mouth to where it emptied before into the Yellow Sea *is more than three hundred and eighty miles in a straight line, and more than twice that distance along the sea-shore.*†

Cities that were built on the delta-plain of the Hwang-Ho many centuries ago are now far removed from the sea. Putai, which is said to have been, in the year 220 B.C., one li (about one-third of a mile) west of the sea-shore, in A.D. 1740 was *one hundred and forty li inland,*—nearly *fifty miles.* Hienshuikan, on the Pei-Ho, is said to have been on the sea-shore in A.D. 500, and is at present about *eighteen miles inland.*

We hear of this river in 1725, in the description of China compiled by Du Halde from the diaries of the Jesuit missionaries who between 1708 and 1717 travelled over and mapped out the Chinese empire. We learn from this work that at that time the Yellow River emptied into the sea near Hwaingan, about lat. 34°; whereas formerly it had entered the sea in lat. 40°,—*i.e.*, in the Gulf of Pecheli, as it does to-day.

The mountain of Ki-she-shan.

We learn from the same work that "the mountain Ki-she-shan, which formerly was united to the territory of Yungping-fu, is now *five hundred li* (*about one hundred and sixty miles*) distant in the sea from this city." Du Halde argues, and adduces facts to prove, that Corea and the ancient Chantsien were formerly contiguous,—that the whole Gulf of Pecheli was *dry land,* and indeed that there was, when the Chinese abridgment of chorography entitled Kwang-in-ki was prepared, *a continuous plain* from Peking to Corea. If the land in this region were raised two hundred and forty feet, this would now be the case, and if it were raised only one hundred and twenty feet, the Gulf of Pecheli would disappear.

---

* Lyell's Principles, vol. i. p. 420.

† Amer. Jour. Sci., vol. xlv. (Second Series) pp. 213, 221.

It appears that the land around the Gulf of Pecheli has risen about fourteen feet in the last two hundred and fifty years. If, instead of rising fourteen feet, the land had *subsided* fourteen feet, "*probably one-third of the low, thickly-populated parts of China would then be beneath the sea.*" *

Gulf of Pecheli.

At Takao, in the island of Formosa, recent crabs and recent shells are found at a height of one thousand one hundred and eleven feet above the sea.

Formosa.

Sir Charles Lyell mentions that the land in Egypt has sunk within the historical period. This is proved by the position of certain tombs near Alexandria, and their present level relatively to the Mediterranean, and also by the ruins in the lake Menzaleh.†

Egypt.

Proving how universal are these disturbances, we learn from the Transactions of the Philosophical Institute of Victoria, Australia, that in twelve months the bottom of Hobson's Bay rose four inches; that the beach at Williamstown, which five years before was covered by the tide, was at the date of the statement covered with a green vegetation and was occupied by tents and houses. Flinders's soundings are no longer trustworthy, for where he found ten fathoms of water there were then but seven. The railway between Adelaide City and the port rose four inches in the year after it was opened. The conclusion drawn from these facts is, that for some time a rise of four inches per annum has been going on.‡

Victoria.

A very recently observed example of raised land is reported in *Notice No.* 89, published in the year 1874 by the Hydrographic Office at Washington, giving an account of the results of the explorations in the Northern seas, about Nova Zembla, during 1872. One of these results is the discovery of the Gulf Stream islands in the exact place where the examinations of the Dutch expeditions in 1594 to 1597 located a sand-bank with eighteen fathoms of water over it, the depth of water between it and the coast being fifty to sixty fathoms. This would indicate that the sea-bottom in that region has risen more than one hundred and ten feet in three hundred years. According to Sir Charles Lyell, a period of four thousand four hundred years ought to have passed.

The Sea-bottom raised one hundred and ten feet in three centuries.

The effects of the subsidence of the land are strikingly exemplified in the celebrated valley of Cashmere in India, at the southern foot of the Himalaya range. In the cliffs of the river Jelam, which traverses this valley, strata of fine

Subsidence of land in the valley of Cashmere.

* See Amer. Jour. Sci., vol. xlv., S. S.

† Principles, vol. i. p. 434.

‡ Chambers's Journal, 1860, art. on "Progress of Science."

clay, sand, etc., are exposed to view, containing fresh-water shells and land shells of recent species, and precisely such as would be formed if the whole valley were now converted into a great lake and the numerous mountain-torrents should have time to fill up the lake-basin with sediment and gravel. *Fragments of pottery* are met with at the depth of forty or fifty feet in this lacustrine formation, showing that the upper part, at least, has accumulated in the human period. On a low table-land in this valley, near the ruins of Avantipura, portions of two buried temples are to be seen, which were explored by Major Cunningham in 1847. In one of these structures he found a magnificent colonnade of seventy pillars beneath the soil. This edifice is supposed to have been erected about A.D. 850, and was certainly submerged before 1450, when the Mohammedan king Sikandar, called Butshikan, or the Idol-breaker, destroyed all the images of the Hindoo temples in Cashmere; as the human-headed birds and other images in this buried edifice are unharmed.*

Buried ships.

Ships (to proceed with our illustrations) have been found in deserted river-beds, and inland away from the shores of the sea. In an old channel of the river Rother, in Sussex, a Dutch vessel was found. Another vessel was found in a deserted bed of the Mersey; and another in the alluvial plain of the Thames, in excavating the St. Katherine Docks. Many ships have been found preserved entire along the southern shores of the Baltic, especially in Pomerania. Between Bromberg and Nakel, for example, a vessel and two anchors, in a very perfect state, were dug up far from the sea.†

Several vessels have been discovered in the delta of the Indus, in the numerous deserted branches of that river, far from the present bed of the stream. Near Vikkar, in Scinde, a vessel of four hundred tons, pierced for fourteen guns, was found, and in a region where it has been questioned whether the Indus had ever been navigable for large vessels.

Subterranean town.

In 1833 a very ancient subterranean town, apparently of Hindoo origin, was discovered in digging the Doab Canal, in the vicinity of Behat, north of Saharunpore. It was buried seventeen feet below the present surface of the country. More than one hundred and seventy coins of silver and copper were found, and many articles in copper and earthenware. In the neighborhood are several rivers and torrents.

M. Bobhaye states that in the Morea the formation termed céramique, consisting of pottery, tiles, and bricks, intermixed with various works of art, enters so largely into the alluvium that it constitutes an important stratum.‡

---

* See Lyell, Prin. Geol., vol. ii. p. 560. † Ib., p. 554. ‡ Ib., p. 519.

In this connection we may appropriately mention the destruction occasioned by *floods*, and that not only in their effects on the configuration of the country and the removal of buildings and other human constructions, but also in the loss of animal life. Humboldt tells us that in South America great numbers of animals are annually drowned. Thousands of wild horses are said to perish every year when the river Apure (a tributary of the Orinoco) is swollen, before they have time to reach the more elevated ground of the Llanos. The mares, during the season of high water, may be seen, with their colts, swimming about and feeding on the grass, of which the top alone waves above the waters. Sir W. Parish states that the Paraná, flowing from the mountains of Brazil to the estuary of the Plata, is liable to great floods, and during one of these, in the year 1812, vast numbers of cattle were carried away, "and when the waters began to subside, and the islands which they had covered again became visible, the whole atmosphere for a time was poisoned by the effluvia from the innumerable carcasses of skunks, capybaras, tigers, and other wild beasts which had been drowned."

Floods.

"On the coast of Orissa," says Heynes ("Tracts on India"), "I have seen tigers and whole herds of black cattle carried along by what are called freshes."

Sir Charles Lyell speaks of "hundreds of carcasses of rhinoceroses and buffaloes swept away by the Tandoi in Java during a flood which accompanied a volcanic eruption."

A dreadful inundation of the sea was caused in 1787, at Coringa, Ingeram, and other places, on the coast of Coromandel, by a hurricane blowing from the northeast, which raised the waters so that they rolled inland to the distance of twenty miles. Many villages were swept away, more than ten thousand people were drowned, and one hundred thousand carcasses of cattle were left strewed over the inundated region. An old tradition of the natives of a similar flood about a century before had, up to this time, been discredited by the Europeans. Another catastrophe of the same kind occurred in 1832.

In speaking of the Swiss lakes, we called attention to the fall of the level of the water in some of them. M. de Saussure long ago spoke of this, particularly of the fact as noticed in the lakes of Bienne, Morat, and Neufchâtel, and referred it to *the clearing away of the forests*. The drying up of the river Scamander is, in a similar manner, attributed to the destruction of the cedars which covered its source. Strabo informs us that in his day great precautions had to be taken against the floods of the Euphrates. M. Oppert now informs us that the volume of water in the river is greatly diminished,—

The Swiss Lakes. Change of level.

Attributed to the clearing away of the forests.

The Euphrates.

that the inundations no longer occur,—that the canals are dry,—the marshes exhausted by the heats of summer; and he attributes this great change to the clearing away of the forests on the mountains of Armenia.

The mouth of the Euphrates is now in 30° north latitude. In the earliest historic age it is thought to have been as high as 31°, so that at that time the Euphrates and the Tigris flowed separately into the Persian Gulf. Its immense alluvial deposits are said to advance its exit into the gulf at the rate of a mile in from thirty to seventy years.

At the village of Dubaté, on the table-lands of New Granada, situated near two lakes which sixty years ago were united, we have another example of the change effected by the destruction of the forests. The waters here have, in thirty years, subsided to such an extent that lands then under water are now cultivated. M. Boussingault was satisfied that this was attributable to the disappearance of the forests. Where the woods have been undisturbed, as on the lake of Tota, at a short distance from the above, the level of the water has not changed.*

The Oder and the Elbe.

It is not due to the same cause, but it has been observed that the water in the Oder diminished from 1778 to 1835, and that in the Elbe from 1823 to 1835. In this instance the cause assigned is "change of climate, due to the process of civilization."

Kalahari Desert.

To the indiscriminate felling of the timber by the natives and colonists, however, the steady expansion of the Kalahari Desert in Southern Africa, and the drying up of its rivers, are attributed by Mr. James F. Wilson.

Hauran. Mississippi River. Volga. France. India.

So Mr. Cyril Graham has shown that the once populous region of Hauran, east of Damascus, full of the ruins of great cities, became the uninhabited desert it now is from the same cause. And so Generals Humphreys and Abbott have demonstrated that the volume of water in the Mississippi has been diminished in consequence of the clearing of the upper country. Sir Roderick Murchison makes similar remarks with reference to the amount of water in the Volga. In like manner, the wooded regions in the Pyrenees were greatly devastated during the French Revolution, and the south of France was beginning to be converted into a desert, when Napoleon interposed and restored the law to protect the forests. And so, finally, Col. Balfour has shown that the replanting of trees in India has reopened its lost springs.†

---

* Smithsonian Report for 1869, p. 412: paper by M. Becquerel, of the French Institute.

† Lesley, "Man's Origin and Destiny," p. 142.

In a paper read before the British Association, in 1864, on the country west of the Rocky Mountains, in British Columbia, along the line of the Thompson River, by Dr. Cheadle and Viscount Milton, it is stated that a great portion of the country to the east of the mountains has completely changed in character through the agency of the *beaver*, which formerly existed here in great numbers. The rivers and chains of lakes, being dammed up, became a series of marshes; and now there is hardly a stream for two hundred miles, excepting the large rivers.

Work of the Beaver in British Columbia.

We are informed that there has been a great change of climate in the Pacific regions of the United States. In an address before the American Association, in 1870, Dr. J. W. Foster stated that "there are evidences in the Great Basin and on the Colorado Plateau that at no remote day there was a much more genial climate and a soil more productive than now prevail. This is seen in the dead forests that line the mountain-side; in the water-lines of the lakes and streams high above the greatest floods; in the deep cañons through which now course trickling streams, but which must have formed the channels of voluminous rivers; and in the alluvial bottoms, now bare and desolate, in which is imbedded a robust vegetation." *

Change in climate of the Colorado Plateau.

Nowhere are the changes which have occurred more striking than in Greenland and Iceland, and nowhere have a few centuries produced such a complete revolution. "A thousand years ago," says Mr. Evan Hopkins, "Greenland, according to Icelandic histories, was a fertile land in the south, and supported a large population. Iceland at that period was covered with forests of birch and fir, and the inhabitants cultivated barley and other grains."†

Change of climate in Greenland and Iceland.

There is much testimony to the same purport. "There is no doubt on my mind," says Dr. Kane, "that at a time within historical and even recent limits, the climate of this region was milder than it is now. I might base this opinion on the fact, abundantly developed by our expedition, of a secular elevation of the coast-line. But independent of the ancient beaches and terraces and other geological marks which show that the shore has risen, the stone huts of the natives are found scattered along the line of the bay in spots now so fenced in by ice as to preclude all possibility of the hunt, and, of course, of habitation by men who rely on it for subsistence.

"Tradition points to these as once favorite hunting-grounds near

* American Naturalist for 1871, p. 462.

† Quoted in "World before the Deluge," p. 21.

open water. At Rensselaer Harbor, called by the natives *Aunatok*, or the Thawing Place, we met with huts in quite good preservation, with the stone pedestals still standing which used to sustain the carcasses of the captured seals and walrus. Sunny Gorge, and a large indentation in Dallas Bay which bears the Esquimaux name of the Inhabited Place, showed us the remains of a village, surrounded by the bones of seals, walrus, and whales,—all now cased in ice. In impressive connection with the same facts, showing not only the former extension of the Esquimaux race to higher north, but the climatic changes which may perhaps be still in progress there, is the sledge-runner which Mr. Morton saw on the shores of Morris Bay, in lat. 81°. It was made of the bone of a whale, and worked out with skilful labor." *

Dr. Hayes expresses a similar opinion:

Dr. Hayes.

"The fiord on the banks of which stands this modern town of Julianashaab extends some forty miles; but, while the modern town stands alone, in ancient days hamlets were dotted beside it everywhere; thousands of cattle once browsed where there are now but a few cows; and peace and plenty reigned here once among a Christian people."†

Julianashaab is in lat. 60° 44′. When Eric the Red landed at Cape Farewell from Iceland in the year 983, and proceeded thence to this place, we are told that "upon the meadow-land beside the fiord immense herds of reindeer were browsing on the luxurious grass; sparrows chirruped among the branches of the little trees." He called it *Greenland.*

Afterwards the Icelanders or Northmen explored as far north as 75°, a point where the stoutest ships run great risk in venturing now. At Upernavik, lat. 72° 50′, a stone was found in 1824 by Sir Edward Parry, bearing an inscription in Runic characters, as follows:

"'Erling Sigvatson and Biorn Thordarson and Eindred Oddson on Saturday before Ascension week raised these marks and cleared ground. 1135.'

"Think," says Dr. Hayes, "of clearing ground up in lat. 72° 50′! What kind of ground would now be found to clear? Naked wastes alone; and the desert sands are not more unproductive. But, as intimated already, the climate has certainly changed during the seven hundred years since this event happened; in evidence of which it is not unimportant to observe that in old chronicles of the voyages of these ancient Northmen there is very little mention made of ice as a disturbing element in navigation."‡

---

* Arctic Explorations, vol. i. p. 308.

† Land of Desolation, p. 37. ‡ Ib., p. 43.

The changes in Iceland are similarly attested. Von Troil, writing in 1773, states that no wood grows in this country,—scarcely a tree being found in the whole island, "though there are certain proofs," he says, "of wood having formerly grown there in great abundance. They have low shrubs and bushes. Von Troil.

"That wood has formerly grown in Iceland can be proved from the Sagas, or tradition stories, of Landnama, Kialnesinga, Soarfdala, and Egil Skallagrimsonare. It is likewise proved by pieces which are frequently dug up in marshes and fens, where not a single bush is to be seen at present. The substance called by the natives *suturbrand* is likewise a clear proof of it. This suturbrand is evidently wood, not quite petrified, which drops asunder as soon as it comes into air, but keeps well in water, and never rots." *

"As to what relates to agriculture, it may be discovered, by many passages of the ancient Icelandic accounts, that corn formerly grew in Iceland. In later times several trials have been made with it, but they have been attended with little success." †

"Are Frode, in Scheda de Icelandia, Oxon., 1716, cap. 2, p. 10, says that at the first landing of the Norwegian colonists, Iceland was covered with woods and forests in the space between the shores and mountains." ‡

Von Troil speaks also of Greenland: "The eastern shores," he says, "were formerly inhabited by a colony of Norwegians, and they had there a bishop's see, called Gardar, to which belonged farms, woods, pastures for cattle, granges, and tillage-lands. See Crantz's History of Greenland, vol. i. p. 245, which evidently proves the mildness of these now inhospitable regions. Ships sailed formerly to the eastern coast, whereas for a great number of years past it has been inaccessible on account of the immense masses of ice found there." §

In *Nature*, May 9, 1872, Mr. H. H. Howorth quotes from Henderson's Journal in Iceland, pp. 6 and 7, that "it is evident from ancient Icelandic documents that on the arrival of the Norwegians, and for centuries afterwards, pretty extensive forests grew on different parts of the island, and furnished the inhabitants with wood, both for domestic and nautical purposes. Owing, however, to the improvident treatment of them, and the increased severity of the climate, they have almost entirely disappeared." . . . Howorth.

"That grain," he says, "was produced in Iceland in former times appears from the names of many places, such as *akrar*, *akrances*, *akraheron*, etc., the word *akr* signifying a cornfield, and from certain laws

---

* Von Troil's Letters on Iceland, in Pinkerton's Voyages, vol. i. pp. 636–639.

† Ib., p. 641. ‡ Ib., p. 642. § Ib., p. 642.

in the ancient code, in which express mention is made of such fields, and a number of regulations are prescribed relative to their division and cultivation." Grain is no longer raised there.

Mr. Howorth proceeds to say that the same is true of Norway, in the most northern parts of which we find many names compounded with the Norse word for barley, proving that, as is agreed, barley grew there where it grows no longer. In Scotland many places show signs of the plough, and of having been sown with cereals, where arable farming is now unproductive. It is notorious that not only in Scotland, but in England as far south as Lancashire, large districts that were once covered with forests are now entirely bare of trees, *and trees cannot be made to grow there.* The Romans planted vineyards and made wine in parts of England where the hop will now hardly grow.

Scotland.

In Northern Russia, he remarks, beyond the Dwina, is a vast area, formerly known as Biarmia, studded with graves and other remains of a prosperous people, whose wealth and civilization are much descanted on by the Saga-writers. Othere, the navigator, whose story is translated by Alfred, tells us that on arriving in this country he met with tilled fields and an agricultural race. This area is now *deserted* except by hunters and fishermen. The old inhabitants have moved west and south into Finland. The climate has increased in severity so that agriculture is almost unendurable there. The Norse traders used to visit Cholmogorod, the port of Biarmia, in great numbers, for traffic and fishing. This navigation continued till the early part of the thirteenth century. But the ice increased so in the White Sea that it was put an end to; and when the English found their way to Archangel in the sixteenth century, so forgotten was this trade that the journey was treated as one of discovery.

Great change in Northern Russia.

Von Wrangel in his Voyage writes that

Von Wrangel on Siberia.

"In 1810, Hendenstrom went across the tundra direct to Utsjouk. He says, 'On the tundra, *equally remote from the present line of trees* among the steep banks of the lakes and rivers, are found large birch-trees complete with bark, branches, and roots. At first sight they appear well preserved, but on digging them up they are found to be in a thorough state of decay. *The first living birch-trees are not now found nearer than* 3° *to the south, and then only as shrubs.*' . . . 'Another cliff, thirty or thirty-five feet high, beyond the Maluya Kurspataschnaja River, consists of ice, clay, and black earth. On drawing out some interspersed roots, we found them to be birch, and as fresh as if only just severed from the trees. *The nearest woods are one hundred versts off!*'"

These facts show how much more severe the Siberian climate has become,—a fact perhaps connected with the persistent southwesterly drifting of the Ugrian tribes from this area in historic times.

Similar testimony is derived from Mr. Draper's "Year Book of Nature and Popular Science." We find it stated here that the increasing cold of the Arctic regions is driving the Esquimaux slowly southward, while the forests and grain-growing districts of Norway, Iceland, and Greenland are steadily diminishing in size.

The cause of these changes is believed to be the elevation of the lands in the northern regions. Near Spitzbergen and in the Polar Sea of Siberia, in the memory of the seal-fishers and others, the waters have shallowed so fast as to have excluded the right whale.

The mean temperature of Iceland is now 41° F., and is steadily decreasing.

Change of climate in France.

The Romans, we are told, introduced the vine into the southern parts of Gaul, "and though in the time of Strabo the cold of the northern provinces was so intense that it was considered the grape would not ripen, yet this was not long considered an obstacle."*

Aristotle speaks of the climate of the Kelts as "too cold for the ass."†

The climate of Gaul has experienced great changes (as we are told by M. Fuster) since the days of Julius Cæsar. In Cæsar's time Gaul had a very rigorous climate. The winters were very severe and of very long duration, and the frost so hard that the navigable rivers, including even the Rhone, were frozen hard. The winters sometimes lasted from October to April, when heavy rains accompanied by tempests came on. In the time of Julian the climate had undergone an extraordinary change; and when the Franks became masters of Gaul, in the fifth century of our era, the climate was still milder, and the vine, which was unknown under Julius Cæsar, was flourishing in even the most northern parts of the country. The ninth century marked the limits of the change, but the climate remained unaltered to the twelfth century. At that time the winters consisted chiefly of rainy weather and storms, and vines grew and flourished in all the northern parts of the territory. The harvest in the north commenced at the end of July, and the vintage at the end of September.‡

Change of climate in Italy.

Dr. Arnold, in his History of Rome, remarks that the woods and marshes of Cisalpine Gaul, and the perpetual snows of the Alps, far more extensive than at present, owing to

---

* Article on the Roman remains at Lillebonne, in Penny Magazine for 1840, p. 117.

† De Mirab. Auscult., 1157; De Gent. An., lib. ii. c. 8.

‡ Athenæum, quoted in Eclectic Magazine for April, 1844, p. 570.

the uncultivated and uncleared state of Switzerland and Germany, could not but have been felt even in the neighborhood of Rome in ancient times. Even on the Apennines, he says, and in Etruria and Latium, the forests occupied a far greater space than at present; which would increase the quantity of rain, and consequently the volume of water in the rivers; the floods would be greater and more frequent [?], and before man's dominion had completely subdued the whole country, there would be large accumulations of water in the low grounds, which would still further increase the coldness of the atmosphere. The language of ancient writers confirms the conclusion that the Roman winter was, in their days, more severe than in modern times. The elder Pliny (xvii. 2) speaks of long snows being useful to the corn, which shows that he is not speaking of the mountains; and a long snow lying in the valleys of Central or Southern Italy would surely be an unheard-of phenomenon now. Virgil and Horace, too, speak of the freezing of the rivers, an image of winter which would hardly be employed by an Italian poet of the present day at any point to the south of the Apennines. It agrees with this that the olive, which cannot bear a continuance of severe cold, was not introduced into Italy till long after the vine; Fenestella asserted that its cultivation was unknown as late as the reign of Tarquinius Priscus; and such was the notion entertained of the cold of all inland countries, even in the latitude of Greece, that Theophrastus held it impossible to cultivate the olive at the distance of more than four hundred stadia from the sea.* The winter of 355 A.U.C., which, however, was one of unusual severity, caused the Tiber to be choked with ice, and the snow lay seven feet deep, where it was not drifted.

We have spoken elsewhere of the former presence of the sea on lofty beaches in the south of England, and far in the interior along the coasts of Cambridge and Lincoln and Norfolk,—the remains of the whale, the walrus, and shells of marine origin testifying that the waves once extended almost to Cambridge and Bury St. Edmund's and Huntingdon. On the west, in Gloucestershire, near Cheltenham, there is an old sea-shore gravel-bed stretching to the base of the Cotswold Hills, and forming a level terrace, at an elevation of about forty feet.

We have spoken also of the raised beaches of Scotland. There have been alterations of level on these coasts both since and shortly prior to the Roman period. The foundations of the old Roman docks are several miles up a small stream near Falkirk, considerably beyond the reach of the tides. We called attention to the raised beach (twenty-five feet) at Leith. There is a similar presentation at Inveresk, a few miles below Edinburgh. At Cramond, at the mouth of the Almond,

---

* History of Rome, Appletons' edit., p. 191.

above Edinburgh, was Alaterva, the chief Roman harbor on the southern coast of the Forth. The old quays have been lifted up some twenty feet, or more, and thrown far back from the shore.

At a period prior to this, but still quite recent, the sea extended *beyond* Falkirk. In Blair Drummond Moss, seven miles above Stirling, that is, nearly twenty miles above Falkirk, were found, not many years since, the remains of a whale, and beside them a rude harpoon (of horn) with a wooden handle, an oaken quern, a wooden wheel, and flint arrowheads. Not quite so far inland, at the base of Dunmyat, one of the Ochil Hills, near Stirling, twenty feet above the highest tide of the Forth, the skeleton of another whale had been previously found (in 1819). Beside it was a perforated harpoon of deer's horn. In the neighborhood of Falkirk, in 1821, at the depth of thirty feet below the surface of the carse or alluvium, an ancient canoe was found. One had been found previously—in the beginning of the century—at the depth of fifteen feet. In the same carse land, in 1843, a human skull was disinterred. So far we appear to be in the Stone Age; but in the carse below Stirling an *iron anchor*, as we are informed by Sir Charles Lyell, has been found. This anchor is older than the Roman period, because the sea had retired from the carse near Stirling in the Roman period, as is proved by the facts that a Roman road crossed the carse near Stirling, and the river at a ford called the "Drip," west of the town; and that another Roman road passed below Stirling (crossing the river probably by ferry). The carse of Stirling is about twenty-five feet above high-water mark. The sea must have been thirty-five feet higher than it is at present when the whales spoken of, and the iron anchor, were left on this spot.

Iron anchor in the Carse of Stirling.

Farther north, in the carse of Gowrie, on the Tay, implements of iron have been found. In the same vicinity we find a number of hillocks designated by the Celtic name of *Inch*, showing that they were once surrounded by water or marshy ground.

Traces of upheaval are found also at Elie, on the south coast of Fife, and on the borders of the Solway Frith.

Let us now pass to the western coast. No less than seventeen* canoes have been dug out of the flat lands along the banks of the Clyde within the past century. Five of them lay buried under the streets of Glasgow, one of which contained marine shells. Twelve others were found about a hundred (one of them one hundred and thirty) yards back from the river, at the average depth of about nineteen feet from the surface of the soil, or seven feet above high-water mark; but a few of them were only four or five feet deep, and

Canoes found at Glasgow.

---

* Indeed, the number is greater: several additional ones have been recently found.

consequently more than twenty feet above the sea-level. Most of them appeared to have sunk in smooth water.* Sir Charles Lyell goes on to tell us that nearly all of these canoes were formed out of a single trunk of oak, "hollowed out by blunt tools, *probably stone axes.*" "A few," he says, "were cut beautifully smooth, evidently with metallic tools." Two of them were built of planks, one of which, dug up on the property of Bankton, was eighteen feet in length, and "very elaborately constructed." Its prow was "not unlike the beak of an antique galley; its stern formed of a triangular-shaped piece of oak, fitted in exactly like those of our day. The planks were fastened to the ribs, partly by singularly-shaped oaken pins, and partly by what must have been *square nails of some kind of metal;* these had entirely disappeared,† but some of the oaken pins remained." In one of the canoes a beautifully polished celt or axe of greenstone was found; "in the bottom of another, a plug of cork," which he says "could only have come from the latitudes of Spain, Southern France, or Italy."

The comments of Sir Charles on these facts are curious. "There can be no doubt," he says, "that some of these buried vessels are more ancient than the others. Those most roughly hewn may be relics of the stone period; those more smoothly cut, of the bronze age; and the regularly built boat of Bankton may perhaps come within the age of iron."

It is rather a crushing retort to all this that the *cork* plug, referred to above, stopped up a round hole in that one of all the above canoes which was considered *the most ancient.* Professor W. King, in the *Christian Observer* of May, 1863, makes this statement, and adds that this boat was "a large rude one hollowed out of the trunk of an oak, which, when found, was quite black, as hard as marble, and very heavy." He also states that "canoes formed of the solid stem of the oak were in use in Ireland about two hundred years ago."

There is reason to believe that these canoes are of the same period with the iron anchor and the harpoons found in the carse of Stirling,—all pre-Roman, but of a date when the natives living on the bays and estuaries procured materials (such as metal and cork) from vessels visiting their coasts to build their rude and primitive canoes. The Roman roads to which we have referred across the alluvial plain of Stirling date probably from the latter part of the second century. The canoes under consideration may be five or six hundred years older, although it is much more probable they are little older than the beginning of our era. Iron does not appear at the Swiss Lake-Dwellings until a century or so before the advent of the Romans. It was in use in Britain (that is, on the

* Antiquity of Man, Amer. ed., p. 48.

† Which shows that they were probably iron.

coasts) in the time of Julius Cæsar. It is evident that in the case before us the natives were using stone; and there are marks of metallic tools on some of the boats. On this coast metallic weapons may have been in use. But our researches have shown us that in Switzerland metal tools were sometimes employed in the construction of the pile-dwellings prior to what is called the bronze or the iron age. Doubtless such tools were exceedingly precious. The bulk of the population continued to use stone.

Reflections of Dr. Wilson.

The comments of Prof. Wilson on these canoes in his "Prehistoric Man" are also interesting, as showing the sanguine spirit of archæology. "It is difficult," he says, "to apply any satisfactory chronological test whereby to gauge the lapse of centuries since this primitive fleet plied in the far-inland estuary that then occupied the modern area through which the Clyde has wrought its later channel; but that the changes in geological no less than in technological aspects indicate a greatly prolonged interval, cannot admit of doubt; and primitive man, alike in Africa and in the New World, is still practising the rude ingenuity of the builder's art, which the allophylian of the Clyde pursued thousands of years ago."*

Another canoe was found in 1791, four or five feet in the peat, in Lochar Moss, Dumfriesshire, which extends to Solway Firth. It was four miles from the reach of the highest tide.

In the same region, twelve miles from present flood-mark, a bronze vessel, and anchors, oars, and other naval implements, were found.†

* Second edit., p. 104.

† Wilson's "Prehistoric Annals of Scotland," vol. i. p. 45.

CHAPTER XXIII.

STONE, BRONZE, AND IRON.

The Precise Sense in which the Distinction of the Three Ages is recognized in this Volume. —The Prevalence of Stone Implements testifies rather to a Stage of Civilization than to an Epoch in Chronology.—Confusion of the Three Ages.—Early Appearance of the Metals in Egypt and Babylonia.—Use of Stone Implements among the Ethiopians down to the Fifth Century B.C.—Use of among the Egyptians, Hebrews, Phœnicians, Romans, etc., in Religious Rites.—The Tumulus opened in the Tauric Chersonese near the Ancient Panticapæum.—Recent Use of Stone in Japan and China.—Sir Gardiner Wilkinson on the Use of Flint Weapons in Egypt.—Stone Implements found in the Ruins of Troy, and their Continued Use in this Locality down to the Seventh or Sixth Century B.C.—Stone Implements in Italy down to the Fourth or Third Century B.C. —The Hewn Stones in the Megalithic Monuments of Western and Northern Europe, and the Perforated Stone Axes, fashioned with Metal Tools.—Mr. Worsaae and Sir John Lubbock at Fault on this Point.—The Inhabitants of Polynesia and their Architecture. -The Vast Period demanded by the Archæologists for the Duration of the Palæolithic Age and the Transition to the Neolithic Age.—Facts in Contravention of this Theory.—Discovery of Stone and Bronze Implements at the Ford of Pas de Grigny, in France.—Col. A. Lane Fox on the Excavations and Discoveries at Cissbury and Highdown, in Sussex.—Flint Implements found at Baggy Point, in Devonshire.—Stone Implements from the Cape of Good Hope.—The Rude and the Polished Stone Implements found also together in the Surface-Soil of North America.—Dr. Abbot in the American Naturalist on the Implements of Stone found in New Jersey.—Objects found on the Coast of Cheshire, between the Dee and the Mersey, showing the Recent Date of the Paleolithic Age.—The Shadowy Nature of the So-called Bronze Age.—No Evidences of it in the Gravel, or the Caves, or the Lake-Dwellings, or the Kjökken-Möddings, or the Dolmens and Tombs.—In the Opinion of Mr. Thomas Wright, the Bronze Weapons found in the West and North of Europe are of Roman Origin.—Sir W. R. Wilde on the Use of Stone Weapons down to a Late Date in Ireland.—Other Facts bearing on this Point.—Mr. Evans on the Occurrence of Stone Implements with Roman Remains, and in Saxon and Merovingian Graves.—Examples of the Occurrence of Bronze and Iron Weapons together at Kingston on the Thames, in the Trenches at Alise, near Annan in Dumfriesshire, in the Forest of Bretonne in France, at the Cueva de los Merculagos in Spain, etc., etc.—Stone Implements found on Shores of Lough Neagh.—Forty Skeletons buried with Stone and Bronze Weapons at Cumarola, in Italy.—Numerous other Examples.

The Three Ages.

It would not be correct in this discussion to say that the division by the archæologists of the human period into the three ages of Stone; Bronze, and Iron is wholly unfounded. That is not our position. Any race which uses exclusively stone implements is in its Stone Age; and, therefore, the inhabitants of certain regions in

America, Australia,* and Polynesia, are to-day in their Stone Age. So the rude populations of France and England were in their Stone Age

---

* The Australians, for the most part, use unpolished stone implements, and may, therefore, be said to be still in their palæolithic age. See Matériaux pour l'Histoire de l'Homme, Livraisons 5e et 6e, 1873, p. 279.

One hundred years ago the Finns, the Woguls on the Obi River, and the Tchouktchis inhabiting the extreme eastern promontory of Siberia, were living precisely as the ancient occupants of the caverns of the valley of the Isère lived in the days of the mammoth and the great cave-bear. We have an account of them in a work which appeared at St. Petersburg in 1770, entitled " Déscription de toutes les Nations de l'Empire de Russie." The Finns lived on the reindeer, on fish, and by hunting. The pagan Woguls ate even the beasts of prey, and in times of scarcity they nourished themselves with a soup which they made of pounded bones, the grease and marrow of which furnished them with a kind of broth.

The Tchouktchis lived in subterranean dens and caves, the opening to which they closed by suspending the skins of the reindeer before the entrance. They had no instrument of iron or any other metal; their knives were of stone; their piercers or punches, of bone; their vessels, of wood or hide; their arms consisted of the bow, the pike, and the sling. The pikes were armed with pointed bone. The women tanned the skins of animals killed in the chase, scraping them to take off the hair, after which they rubbed them with grease and the roe of fish. They used the sinews of animals to sew with, their needles being of pointed bones and the bones of fish.

Our author informs us that not far from the Tchouktchis and the other tribes of Kamschatka, on the petty islands, there lived tribes yet more savage. One cannot imagine an existence more rude, and at the same time more perfectly identical with that of the palæolithic caves, than that portrayed in the following extract:

" Ils ne connaissent ni lettres, ni écriture, ni hiéroglyphes, ni chronologie, et ne savent rien de leur histoire nationale.

" Leurs occupations et leurs ouvrages n'ont d'autre but que les besoins les plus naturels et les plus indispensables de la vie.

" Ils n'ont aucune espèce de bestiaux domestiques, pas même le chien, et ils font la chasse à ceux que les Russes y amènent comme si c'était quelque autre gibier.

" Leurs armes, leurs meubles sont une image de l'enfance du monde, l'arc et la flèche, le dard et la lance, le tout sans armure de fer. C'est avec des os et des pierres pointues qu'ils tâchent de les rendre meurtrières.

" Leurs habitations (*oullaa*), qui sont des tanières souterraines, ressemblent à celles des Kamtchadales et aussi à celles des Groënlandais (Ilgous). Un *oullaa* a une longueur de 10 à 50 brasses, une largeur de 3 à 5, et une profondeur d'environ une brasse et demie. Il est divisé en compartiments au moyen de perches. Il y a un ou plusieurs foyers.

" Quelques-uns de ces caveaux contiennent cinquante, cent, deux cents, et même trois cents personnes.

" Plusieurs passent leur vie dans des antres de rochers ou dans des cavernes qu'ils tâchent d'arranger aussi bien qu'ils peuvent avec du bois flotté, des peaux et des nattes."

This is the Palæolithic Age photographed in the eighteenth century.

We need not be in any degree surprised at this picture, for, as we have already seen, the occupants of the pre-historic city of Björkö, in Lake Mälar, in the south of Sweden, in the eleventh century, continued to feast on the lynx and the wolf and to split their long bones to get at the marrow; and, more extraordinary still, the inhabitants of Scandinavia, north of the province of Nordland, in Norway, we are told by Prof. Rygh, of Christiania (at the Stockholm meeting of the International Congress of Pre-historic Archæology), "although they lived for many centuries in communication with people who used iron, *remained themselves in the practice of the Stone Age till the beginning of the eighteenth century.*" Academy Aug. 29, 1874, p. 238.

in the River-Gravel and Bone-Cave period. We find traces of a Stone Age in Greece, which, however, must have been brief. It was succeeded by a Stone-and-Bronze Age, in which the stone and bronze implements were used together. So the Mexicans and Peruvians, in the days of Cortez and Pizarro, used stone and bronze, and had no iron.

The error of the archæologists.

The error which the archæologists have fallen into consists in the prominence which they have given to these periods, and the sharpness of the lines by which they have divided them off the one from the other; in applying them universally to all the races of mankind; in assigning to them, respectively, a *duration* which they never possessed; and in associating, as a general rule, the idea of an immense antiquity with the use of stone, and even of bronze. The fact that the inhabitants of Mexico and Central America, as well as the Peruvians, used weapons of obsidian and implements of bronze at the time of the Spanish Conquest, proves that the Bronze or the Stone Age is not necessarily associated with *antiquity*. It is a stage of civilization, not a measure of time.

A question of the *duration* of these ages.

Nor did these ages have the protracted existence which is assigned to them, nor were they, even in Western and Northern Europe, marked off from each other, in most instances, in the manner represented by the archæologists.* The Bronze Age especially, in Western and Central Europe, as well as in Britain, rests on a very equivocal foundation. We have a glimpse sometimes of a preponderance of bronze weapons over those of stone and iron, but this is extremely rare, and only for a moment. On the contrary, the presence of bronze appears merely to mark in general the rapid transition from stone to iron; that is to say, the moment we find the use of stone *discontinued*, almost *at once* we observe the introduction of iron. The bronze does not exhibit any solid and independent existence. It is first used with stone, and afterwards with iron. And then, again, when the iron becomes plainly visible in one part of Britain, we still find stone weapons and tools in another,—and continuing in some regions down to recent periods. And in fact the question between us and the more intelligent archæologists reduces itself to the *duration* of these ages, rather than to the mere technicality of one of these materials being more primitive than another. In Egypt only very faint traces of the use of stone are observable. Implements of the neolithic type have been found in some instances, and, as we have already stated, a stone celt is figured in the Third Dynasty. We,

* We shall see that in Eastern Europe and Asia Minor the ages of bronze and of stone existed together: they are not marked off from each other at all, saving the faint traces of the palæolithic age in Greece.

moreover, do not doubt that in certain districts and among the poorer classes flint arrow-heads continued to be long used. But we assert that, strictly speaking, there cannot be said to have been *a Stone Age* in Egypt. It is a mere speck, and, if it ever had any independent existence (which we do not believe), it did not endure beyond a period of one or two centuries. And so of bronze: Egypt seems to have had a Bronze Age,* but it lasted only a few hundred years.

No Stone Age in Egypt.

The Stone Age in Western and Northern and Central Europe lasted much longer, owing to the rude social state which continued to prevail until the imposition of the Roman yoke. By a very imperfect system of communication—overland and by water—a certain traffic had long before been maintained even with the tribes on the North Sea and the Baltic; but this did not civilize the Northern nations, or materially influence their mode of life. The same merchant who carried to the Swiss mountains the coral of the Mediterranean, or the glass beads of Etruria or Phœnicia, could have carried there bronze celts and bronze swords and bronze knives; but the Swiss lake-dwellers on Constance and at Meilen and at Robenhausen continued to manufacture their stone weapons, and to rely upon them in their wars. Nay, more, this Mediterranean peddler could have carried them *iron*: why he did not do it may be answered when we learn why the civilized American races used stone knives and swords when they possessed metal tools capable of shaping the immense blocks of stone in their temples and palaces; or why the Portuguese continue to use a farm-cart furnished with solid wooden wheels, the axle of which revolves with the wheels; or why the inhabitants of Syria and Palestine, at this day, continue to plough their fields with a sharpened stake.†

The Stone Age in Europe.

One would naturally expect that the establishment of a Greek colony like that of Massilia on the coast of Gaul would speedily lead to the general and exclusive use of iron weapons and utensils in that country; but it was not until the people were *conquered* that any real impression was made upon their methods of life.

After a careful study of this subject, while recognizing, then, as we have said, a succession in a general sense of the Stone, the Bronze, and the Iron Ages, that which particularly impresses us, in view of the positions taken by modern archæology, is

The Confusion of the Three Ages.

* M. Chabas believes that there was no age of stone, no age of bronze, and no pre-historic age in Egypt,—nor, indeed, in Europe.

† We cannot tell why "the modern improvements" frequently do not penetrate into certain regions. Some races are constitutionally tenacious of the ideas which they have inherited. Herodotus describes the *Argippæans*. Erman, during his travels, ascertained that the existing Baschkirs of the Ural Mountains are the descendants of this tribe, and that their present mode of life is exactly like that described by Herodotus more than twenty-three hundred years ago.

the confusion of these periods. They cross each other at every point, and run into each other to an extent which constitutes an entirely different state of things from that represented by the archæologists. Rapidly the palæolithic implements of the gravel and of the type of Moustier pass into those of Laugerie-Haute, Gourdan, and Solutré; and from Laugerie and Solutré rapidly we pass into the polished forms at Concise and Wangen; rapidly the bronze makes its appearance in the Swiss lakes, and flourishes side by side with the weapons of nephrite and serpentine and diorite; suddenly the bronze and the iron are intermingled, and we find in the North the bronze weapons continuing in use even down to the ninth and tenth centuries of our era. And, as if to confound still farther any attempt at a systematic classification, we find the Stone Age in progress at one point on the map, while in the neighboring district of the same country the population are extensively employing metal. All of this has been abundantly illustrated in our previous discussions, and particularly in our chapters on the Megalithic Monuments and the Swiss Lake-Dwellings.

Early use of metal in Egypt and Mesopotamia.

At the very first glimpse that we catch of the human race in the region of their primeval home, we find them erecting great structures which could have been prepared only with metal tools. In one of the oldest of the pyramids there has been found a bronze "celt." It is equally certain that the builders of Erech and Calneh and Babel were acquainted with the use of metal. "The objects found in the ruins prove a knowledge of the art of working metals for ornament as well as use."*

We find the flints, on the other hand, in tumuli and dolmens that we know to be as late as the fifth century.

The Ethiopians.

We know that the Ethiopians of the Upper Nile had attained a high degree of civilization centuries before the invasion of Greece by Xerxes, and yet we find the contingent of soldiers furnished by this nation towards that expedition pointing their arrows with sharpened stones instead of iron, and using antelope's horn for the heads of their javelins, while the nations around them used iron and bronze. Here we have a vivid example of the stone, the bronze, and the iron ages all existing side by side. We have already mentioned that the Egyptians used a black flint, known as Ethiopian stone, to cut open the body in the process of embalming. The same knife was used by the Phœnicians and Arabians for the performance of certain religious rites. Flint knives were also used by the Jews in performing the rite of circumcision. They were also used for sacrificial purposes by the Romans.

The Jews and Romans.

* The Ancient History of the East, by Philip Smith, p. 234.

In the magnificent tomb discovered near the ancient Panticapæum in the Tauric Chersonese the flint implements again appear. The tomb found under a burial-mound one hundred and sixty-five feet in diameter belonged to one of the early kings. It contained a shield of gold, a gilded quiver, a sword with a curiously-embossed hilt, metal knives with carved ivory handles, statuettes, bronze cauldrons, and "a hundred and twenty pounds weight of gold jewelry."

Kertch.

It is a highly interesting and important fact in this discussion that it now appears that stone implements were used in Japan at a very recent period, and that the metals do not appear to have been used to any great extent until about the seventh or eighth century of our era. Mr. Franks, in a paper published some few years since on "Stone Implements in Japan," quotes from Dr. O. Mohnike, formerly a physician in the Dutch East Indian army, who presented a report on this subject to the Society of Northern Antiquaries in 1853.*

Recent use of stone in Japan.

Dr. Mohnike states that "though the useful metals may have been known in Japan before the commencement of our era, I believe they were first imported from China, and employed but rarely in Japan before the seventh or eighth century after Christ, when copper-mines were discovered." Before that, stone was used, and perhaps till the ninth or tenth century. Prior to this date, however, we find far earlier traces of copper swords.

In the well-known Japanese historical work, Niponki, written in 720 A.D., it is stated that "in the spring of the year 27 before Christ, a ship went to Japan from Sinra in Corea, with a son of the king of Sinra on board, who brought to Japan presents for the Mikado, including spears of stone." (Siebold, French edit., l. v. p. 138.) This also shows that these stone weapons were then used in Corea.

Stone weapons *are still used* by the inhabitants of the Kurile Islands.†

It appears from the statement of Mr. E. B. Tylor, that the stone weapons *are also still used in some parts of China.* He quotes from Grossier in 1818.

And in China.

In the annals of the Song dynasty (A.D. 964–1279), in the life of Tchang-sun, soldiers are mentioned armed with arrows having stone points. They were probably Tartars.

In the annals of Northern China, composed under the Thang dynasty (A.D. 619–907), it is said that in the country east of Fo-ni all the arrows had stone points. In these same annals mention is made of stone

* Volume of the "Internat. Cong. Prehist. Archæol." for 1868, pp. 261, 262.

† Ib., p. 262.

axes (*chi-fon*). In various other passages are mentioned a stone knife (*chi-t'ao*), a stone sword (*chi-kien*), and an agricultural instrument in stone (*chi-jin*).

The archæologists (Lepsius, for example) tell us that the date of the fourth Egyptian dynasty was more than 3000 years B.C. Sir Gardiner Wilkinson informs us that "the Egyptians continued occasionally to use stone-tipped arrows after the eighteenth dynasty." Those who wanted better weapons, he says, used bronze at that time for arrows.* The date of this eighteenth dynasty was about 1500 B.C., and it was the Augustan era of the great Theban monarchy,—when Egypt under Thothmes III. and Amen-hotop III. was at the very summit of her power.

Egypt.

Knives of flint have been repeatedly found placed in the Egyptian tombs by the side of the mummies. This fact was mentioned long ago by Rosellini, the companion of Champollion. Prism-shaped implements of flint have been obtained also from the tombs by Passalacqua and Lepsius. At the meeting of the Institut Égyptien, May 19, 1870, M. Mariette-Bey expressed himself as follows: "The fact that there are found [in Egypt] flints worked by the hand of man cannot be contested. . . . The flints in question do not go back to the age of stone. They belong to the historic age of Egypt, and their great number on the plateau of Biban-el-Molouk simply shows that, in all historic antiquity, even to the time of the Ptolemies, flints were worked on this plateau, on account of its proximity to Thebes, in order to supply the demand for instruments of this material which have been always used. There are found in the tombs of Gournah, which date back to the eleventh dynasty, arrows in great numbers, made of reeds and armed either with a point of wood hardened in the fire, or with the bone of a fish, or with a point of flint. Sometimes also the point is formed from the reed itself; but what is particularly remarkable is that in all antiquity *pharaonique*, and even in the tombs of the Greek epoch, there are no arrow-heads of metal; the Greek tombs alone yield points of bronze.

"With the flints they made knife-blades, which they fixed in handles of wood. One finds them even among the Greeks. These knives are also sometimes *toothed* in the form of a saw.

"In the third place, they made lance-heads.

* * * * * * * * * *

"In a geological point of view it remains to be observed that the worked flints up to this time have always been found at the surface of the soil. This is their position on the plateau of Biban-el-Molouk, in another *gisement* situated at the entrance of the same valley, in another

---

* See this part of the statement contradicted below by M. Mariette.

which is found at the entrance to the turquoise-mines of Mount Sinai, and in a fourth at Monfalont. It is the same with those which are found in the quarries. But, on the contrary, if the flints were truly pre-historic, it would happen that we would encounter them in certain beds in the interior of the soil, which has never yet occurred.

"The flints of Egypt have no patina, no change of tint."*

Stone implements in Babylonia.

We find also stone implements in the first age of Babylonia, but, as we learn from the historian of this region, they were used by a people who had made very considerable progress in the arts of agriculture and commerce, and, as we know, *along with implements of metal.*†

This discovery of stone and metal together in the Chaldæan plain is a striking example of the utter worthlessness of the archæological system of the Three Ages. In the ancient tombs, and elsewhere among the ruins, of this region, we are informed that "knives, hatchets, arrow-heads, and other implements both of *flint* and *bronze*, . . . chains, nails, fish-hooks, etc., of the same metal, . . . leaden pipes and jars, . . . armlets, bracelets, and finger-rings of *iron*" were found,‡—showing the cotemporaneous employment at this early date of stone, bronze, and iron.

We shall learn also, in the progress of this investigation, that stone weapons were used by the Trojan soldiers in the Trojan war, and that they continued to be used by the race or races which occupied the site of Troy, down to 700 or 600 B.C.

Khorsabad.

Stone implements continued to be used in the valleys of the Euphrates and the Tigris to a much later date than that referred to above in connection with Babylonia. The magnificent palace at Khorsabad, near Nineveh, was built by Sargon about B.C. 715. The ruins of this royal city and residence were discovered by M. Botta in 1842. In 1852 they were farther explored by M. Place. In raising the great stone bulls, which weighed fifteen thousand kilogrammes, and which had never been disturbed, M. Place found beneath them a number of bracelets and necklaces of carnelian, emerald, amethyst, and other hard stones, polished and fashioned in the shape of beads and the heads of animals. Among these objects (products of an advanced civilization),—some of them *scarabæi* with Phœnician inscriptions,—M. Place found two knives of black flint similar to those of Mexico and, more especially, those of Bethlehem.§

---

* Reported in Matériaux, 1re Livraison, 1874, p. 17.

† Five Great Monarchies, vol. i. pp. 119, 120.

‡ Smith's Ancient History of the East, p. 375.

§ Congrès d'Anthropologie et d'Archéologie, 1867, p. 118.

The Abbé Richard has examined the so-called tomb of Joshua, at Gilgal, on the banks of the Jordan. He found here a great number of knives, saws, and fragments of flint.*

Flint implements in Palestine.

This was (say) about 1500 B.C. The Israelites had come up from the civilization of Egypt. If this be in fact the tomb of Joshua (which we very much doubt), we thus ascertain that during the grand culmination of Egyptian development, seven or eight centuries after they had been using metal, flint *knives* and *saws* were still fabricated.

The Abbé Richard also found *on the surface*, on a plateau between Mount Tabor and the Sea of Tiberias, a flint implement of the palæolithic type.

At the village of Bethsaour, near Bethlehem in Judæa, the Abbé Moretain has found a number of worked flints and articles of worked bone which M. Louis Lartet regards as similar to those found in the caves of Périgord of the "Reindeer" epoch. They were found, it was stated by those who picked them up, on the surface of the ground. With them were found stone balls and mealing-stones. Similar flints were also found in certain grottoes in the neighborhood. The Duke de Luynes found a specimen of pottery made on the wheel mingled with these flints in one of these grottoes. M. Arcelin, also, found in these grottoes pottery of a ruder character in association with the flints. This evidence is similar to that afforded by the Babylonian and Egyptian tombs.

There is another interesting fact connected with the implements which occur on the surface near Bethsaour. M. Lartet mentions that he saw at the house of M. le Comte de Vogüé an instrument of flint, of discoidal shape, which nearly approached certain of the palæolithic types of Europe, and "could well have served the same purposes as the hatchets of the drift."† The occurrence of this palæolithic type of the flint implements in the East, and that in connection with objects pertaining to a state of civilization, is of course destructive of the presumption that such types are probably associated with any antiquity in the West. We shall see that similar instances occur in Babylonia.

It is not a remarkable thing that the ancient Egyptians should have made use of stone implements. After the lapse of three thousand years, stone and metal are *still in use* in Northern Abyssinia. M. Arthur Issel, who made an excursion into this country in 1870, in company with the Marquis Butinori, learned from a very intelligent young Abyssinian, named Said, who was in the service of the Marquis Butinori, that the Bogos, who dwell in this region, are in the

The Bogos of Abyssinia.

---

* Comptes-Rendus, Juil.–Déc., 1871, p. 541.

† Matériaux, 4e Livraison, 1873, p. 179.

habit of manufacturing and using stone hatchets and flint knives at the present day. These people use at the same time hatchets and poignards of iron.*

It is probable that the Bogos, or their predecessors, have been thus using metal and stone together for three or four thousand years. If an archæologist had found in some cave or pile-village in Northern Abyssinia iron hatchets and flint knives in association, he would have explained that there had been a "remaniement" of the bed in which they were found, or he would have remarked, "This cave belongs to the end of the neolithic, and the beginning of the metal age;" when in fact these two "ages" began about the same time and have existed side by side from the Pharaohs down to King Theodore.

Bronze and Stone in India.

We have the means, perhaps, of fixing the date of the so-called Bronze Age in Ceylon. At the International Congress of Brussels (1872), M. Leemans remarked that in Ceylon several ancient Buddhist monuments had been opened, which had been closed after their construction, and which were designed never to be afterwards seen. There were found in these, he tells us, objects of bronze, but none of iron. Iron, it thus appears, was probably not known at this time in Ceylon. Buddhism, as is well known, originated about the sixth century B.C.

In the same Congress, M. Leemans called attention to an ancient Buddhist temple in the island of Java, the walls of which are covered with a great number of bas-reliefs forming a complete illustration of the life of Buddha. This temple was erected by architects from the continent in the seventh century of our era. On the reliefs are figured perforated flint tools furnished with handles of wood. There are also delineations of pile-dwellings. These sculptures illustrate the life of India, rather than of Java, in the seventh century.

The Massagetæ.

We know positively also the date of the "Bronze Age" among the Massagetæ, a Scythian tribe occupying the vast region east of the Caspian Sea, known as Turkestan or Tartary. It was with this people that Cyrus the Great, according to Herodotus, fought his last battle. His army was defeated, and he himself was killed. Now, Herodotus, as is his custom, gives us a brief sketch of these Massagetæ or *Massa Goths* (according to Dr. Donaldson), and, among other things, he tells us that "they fight on horseback and on foot, and are both ways formidable. They have spears, arrows, and battle-axes. They make much use both of gold and brass. Their spears, the points of their arrows, and their battle-axes are made of brass; their helmets, their belts, and their breast-plates are decorated with gold. They use

* Matériaux pour l'Histoire de l'Homme, Juin et Juillet, 1872, p. 290.

neither iron nor silver, which indeed their country does not produce, though it abounds with gold and brass." *

This was written 450 years B.C., so that these Parthians, Scythians, or Tartars, armed with breast-plates and helmets, and mounted on horseback,—with decorations of gold,—and coping successfully with the conqueror of Babylon,—were at this time ignorant of iron.

We hear of the same people again at a yet later date. Strabo (who wrote about the beginning of our era) says of them that they have no silver, little iron, but abundance of gold and bronze. They touched India, China, and Persia. Would it be strange if the barbarians of Northern Europe were no farther advanced at that time in their knowledge of the metals? And is it not preposterous when the anthropologists inform us that the Iron Age in this last-named region commenced 2000 B.C.?

The Ichthyophagi.

Beloochistan has Southern Arabia (of whose ancient civilization we hear so much) on the west, Persia on the north, India on the east, and yet Strabo tells us of a people—the Ichthyophagi—belonging to this country, and inhabiting the coast of the Arabian Sea, who were in his day in their "Stone Age." They lived on fish, which, for the most part, they ate raw, and on bread,—for, although without the metals, they raised a little wheat.

Italy.

A writer in the *Popular Science Monthly*, criticising a statement of Mommsen in his History of Rome to the effect that there are no traces of a Stone Age in Italy, expresses his surprise that the historian should have fallen into such an error, and cites a number of localities in that country—such as Ponte Molle, Torre di Quinto, Imola, Alatri, etc.—where flint implements have been found. He adds that "Prof. Issel believes the evidence quite sufficient to show that the Ligurians remained stone-using savages, without knowledge of the metals, up to the time of their subjugation by the Celts and the Romans." The Ligurians were in immediate contact with the Northern Etruscans, and they were conquered by the Gauls about 400 or 500 B.C., the Romans following a century or so later. Now, if these people were "stone-using savages, without knowledge of the metals," as late as this, right in contact with the civilization of the Etruscans, what was probably the condition of the Helvetii and the Britons about the same time? and what was probably the date of the Swiss Stone Age lake-villages? †

* Herodotus, Clio, ccxv.

† Diodorus Siculus wrote a century before the Christian era: he gives us a portrait of the Ligurians. "Many of them," he says, "drink only water, and live on the flesh of domestic and wild animals, and, sometimes, herbs which grow naturally on their soil. . . . These men sleep in the fields, and rarely take refuge in miserable cottages, or rather huts, and oftenest the hollows of the rocks and the caverns offer them a shelter."

There is one point connected with the subject of the Stone Implements with regard to which some remarks are necessary. We have touched upon it in our chapter on the Megalithic Monuments. Archæologists speak of monuments like those at Locmariaker, where the stones are hewn, as belonging to the Stone Age. Now, we lay it down as a fact that a hewn stone monument is an infallible evidence of the use of a metal tool. Mr. Worsaae, speaking of the "cromlechs and giants' chambers" of Denmark, observes that "It is still more remarkable if, being destitute of tools of metal, they were in a situation so to split the large roofing and supporting masses of stone that they are completely flat on the side which is turned towards the chamber." He then suggests that the early population were acquainted with the method of splitting large blocks of granite by boring holes in a certain direction along the veins,* which are filled with water. Wedges are then introduced into these holes, and struck with heavy mallets till the rock is split into two flat pieces. "It must be supposed," he adds, "that in this case the aborigines knew how, by means of other stones, to form these holes or perforations in the granite; but this supposition is by no means incredible." Many of these monuments, we may remark, referred to the Stone Age, have the stones not only split, but they have been smoothed and hewn after they were split.

Hewn stone monuments imply metal tools.

Worsaae's opinion.

We have been astonished to find that even the good hard sense of Sir John Lubbock has not sufficed to make him reject the idea that the stones of the great morai of Oberea in Tahiti, the material of which he does not intimate to be very soft or easily worked, were shaped and prepared by the present inhabitants with stone tools; and he also represents that the celebrated statues of Easter Island were executed in the same way.†

Sir J. Lubbock's opinion.

The morai of Oberea is a pile of stonework, raised pyramidically, upon an oblong base, or square, two hundred and sixty-seven feet long by eighty-seven wide. The top is reached by a succession of steps, of which there were eleven, each four feet high, so that the height of the pile was forty-four feet. Each step was formed of white coral stone, *which was neatly squared and polished.*

The morai of Oberea.

This, says Sir John, "is perhaps the most important monument which is positively known to have been constructed with stone tools only, and renders it the less unlikely that some of the large tumuli and other ancient monuments of Europe may belong to the Stone Age."

* The first difficulty is to bore the holes. We have considered this in our discussion of the Megalithic Monuments. (See Prim. Antiq., p. 92.) The holes would have to be often several feet in depth.

† See Pre-historic Times, pp. 483, 549.

Captain Cook is the authority quoted for this remarkable statement. We have been unable to find any such statement in his works, but, as Mr. Huxley also refers such a statement to him (namely, that this morai was erected by the natives of Tahiti, when Captain Cook was at that island), we must have failed to search his "Voyages" with sufficient diligence. But we do not believe that the Tahitians hewed and shaped great hard stones with stone tools: that is simply incredible. Captain Cook may have seen them erect the morai, but he never saw them *hew the stones*,—as we believe; *that is, provided the "white coral" is a hard rock.*

The Polynesians.

It has been generally represented that, when those islands were discovered by Europeans, the inhabitants of Polynesia were not equal to the construction of any buildings of hewn stone; although they had the most beautiful stone implements. Their dwellings were all of wood. With the exception of the morai referred to, "they do not," says Mr. J. H. Lamprey, "seem to have built anything in stone since the time of their earliest discovery by Europeans." *

With regard to the Easter Island statues, Captain Cook remarks that "the present inhabitants *have most certainly* had no hand in them, as they do not even repair the foundations of those which are going to decay."

Traces of a primitive population.

The traces of a primitive population, in the shape of numerous and extensive ruins, are found all through the islands of the Pacific, and it is from these ruins that the modern inhabitants procure the hewn stones sometimes observed in the foundations of their buildings.

Melville, writing of Nukaheva, in the Marquesas Islands, describes "the curious massive stone foundations called by the natives *pi-pis*." He says that some of these are so extensive, and such a vast amount of labor must have been involved in constructing them, that he cannot believe that they were built by the ancestors of the *present* inhabitants. He asks, "How could they, with their rude implements, have chiselled them into shape?"

These foundations, he tells us, are selected by the natives to erect their bamboo dwellings on.†

T. H. Hood, says the author of the paper from which we quote, in his notes of a cruise in H. M. S. "Fawn," in the West Pacific, in 1862, speaks of the burial-ground at Moa, where he saw large slabs of red porphyry, which is brought from an island in the lagoon. This is the rock, Mr. Hood tells us, of which large blocks were conveyed in former times to Tongataboo in the great war-canoes.

---

* Internat. Cong. Prehist. Archæol., 1868, p. 56.

† Ib., p. 63: paper by M. J. H. Lamprey.

"This circumstance," says the article in the volume from which we quote, "renders more accountable the existence of the ruins of ancient buildings and circles of stone, composed of materials not obtained except from distant localities, as those at Strong's or Kunaie Island, at Paadsen, Easter Island, Waiahu, etc. *Now* all tradition of their origin is lost."

In Walpole's "Four Years in the Pacific," p. 101, he relates that in Tahiti "we came upon vast squares of stones similar to the pieces on which the houses are built." The whole island, he says, "bears evidence, in the numerous dwellings found in the bush, of a former and much more numerous population."

And so of Hawaii. In Ellis's "Missionary Tour," in 1826, p. 141, he says, "We passed over the ruins of deserted heathen temples and demolished altars in the Sandwich Islands;" and he mentions that he himself had frequently visited similar ruins in other groups. He states that the burying-place at Keanhou was a space surrounded by high stone walls, appearing like a *heian* or temple. At p. 65 he speaks of the Temple of Bukohola, two hundred and twenty-four feet by one hundred and ten feet in size, with large stones six feet wide forming a wall, and on the top of the wall, twenty feet high in places, were pillars to support the altar. "The pavement," he adds, "was perfect." He states that this edifice was constructed of smooth stones brought from a distance, and that it had been erected thirty years before; but Mr. Lamprey remarks that "it can be proved that it stood there in the earliest times of the discovery of the Sandwich Islands."

Ruins.

Mr. Baldwin informs us, in his work on the archæology of America, that the ruins of a great temple of stone, connected with canals and earthworks, exist on the island of Ascension or Fanife, constructed by an older race than the present inhabitants. He mentions similar ruins on Strong's Island; and at Lale, he says, is a "conical mountain surrounded by a wall twenty feet high, and of enormous thickness;" and the whole island appears to present "a series of cyclopean enclosures and lines of great walls everywhere overgrown with forest." There are also the remains of great stone structures on some of the Navigators' Islands, of which the natives can give no account. Similar ruins, he states, are found in the Sandwich Islands. At Hawaii, some thirty miles from Hilo, is the hill of Kukü, resembling in form the pyramid of Cholula. Near the summit are found great hewn blocks of stone overgrown by shrubbery, while the summit itself is paved, and levelled and squared to correspond with the cardinal points. The upper portion of the hill had been terraced and faced with hewn stones, which are in perfect squares not less than three feet in diameter. The material is a dark, vitreous basalt. Each slab was faced and polished on every side, so that they fit together like sheets of paper. Many blocks were, when observed, lying detached,—"probably some had been removed." The natives could give no account of these remains.*

As to Easter Island, also relied on by Sir John Lubbock, Mr. Baldwin (who contends strongly for the "Antiquity of Man") says that all who have examined the remains refer them to some former race. He alludes also to the remarkable ruins on some of the Marquesas Islands.

It is very evident from these facts that any hewn stones in any of the modern structures of these Pacific islands may have been readily derived from the materials belonging to the ruins abundantly found in nearly all of them. This is a much more credible theory of the origin of the morai at Oberea than Sir John Lubbock's opinion that the great blocks were hewn with stone implements. If the Tahitians are capable of such work, and in view of their great energy and activity as artisans, why do we not hear of *some other* structure of stone erected by them?

The coral of Tahiti frequently a very soft rock.

But there is yet another explanation (if the facts be correctly stated) of these hewn white coral blocks. Prof. Huxley, commenting on the foregoing paper by Mr. Lamprey, remarked "that there were evidences in Captain Cook's Voyages, and elsewhere, that the inhabitants of Tahiti were then building with large blocks of stone;" and (he added) they may well do this with stone implements, because the coral rock which they used was "a soft rock" "which could be had *of every description of hardness*."† Sir John Lubbock, however, wrote in ignorance of this fact.

This disposes of the only example yet brought forward to prove that the flint or stone implements are equal to the task of hewing and shaping the blocks in edifices of stone. Common sense ought to have decided the question on *a priori* grounds. It might be possible to work a single block, or two, or three; but it would require untold years to erect a structure of any dimensions in this way. It is *possible* that a small funeral monument of hewn stones should be prepared with stone tools; it is not *probable* that it has been prepared with such instruments.

From the Palæolithic to the Neolithic Age.

We have seen that the Neolithic or Polished Stone Age shades off into the Bronze Age, or exists in conjunction with it, and that in like manner the Bronze Age passes into the Iron Age, or exists in conjunction with it: in neither case is an extreme (independent) duration of more than a few thousand years claimed on any hand. But the Palæolithic Age, as is represented, has peculiar characteristics of its own; its duration is represented to have been "immense," and the archæologists most generally represent that there is *a lacuna or gap* between the two stone ages, which implies the

* Ancient America, note C at the end of the volume, p. 288.

† Internat. Cong. Prehist. Archæol., 1868, p. 67.

operation of geological agencies. Sir Charles Lyell estimates, if we remember correctly, a period of one hundred and fifty thousand years between the upper- and lower-level gravels of the Somme Valley; and then thousands of years roll away from the date of the deposit of the lower-level gravels and the bones of the accompanying fauna of great extinct mammals to the opening of the Neolithic Age at Wangen and Moosseedorf.

The implements of the drift and the older caves, we are told, are entirely different from the implements of the Danish peat and the Swiss lakes, being excessively rude, and without a trace of grinding or polish. The very shapes are uncouth; and everything savors of the Primal Age.

They are not widely apart.

There are facts, however, which the archæologists themselves cannot deny, going to show that there is no great gulf between even the Palæolithic and the Neolithic Age. Let us give an illustration:

Pas de Grigny.

It is stated in the volume of the "Congrès International" for 1869 that M. de Mortillet presented to the Congress, whose proceedings are here reported, a number of implements found by M. Campagne, Inspector of Navigation at Corbeil. These implements were discovered at Pas de Grigny, in the department of Seine-et-Oise, in a ford which was in use in the bronze and stone ages. They consisted of instruments of flint "which came certainly from Grand-Pressigny," perforated stone hammers, polished flint hatchets, bronze hatchets, a bronze fish-hook, bronze sickles, bronze blades of swords or poignards, bronze lance-heads, and a number of bronze pins. There were also bones of the *Bos primigenius* and the stag.

The flint-implement manufactory of Grand-Pressigny dates in the transition-period from the Palæolithic to the Neolithic Age. Flints manufactured here were found at the palæolithic cave of Chaleux, in Belgium; while, on the other hand, a few of the flints are polished. The perforated stone hammers at Pas de Grigny, and the polished flint hatchets, show that the Pressigny flints found in the ford must be assigned to the later period of that manufactory. The bones of the *Bos primigenius* indicate a period as old as the Stone Age of the Swiss Lake-Dwellings. This ford, therefore, connects the Bronze Age with the perforated stone hammers and the polished flint hatchets, and we are carried back to the age of Robenhausen and Concise; and Grand-Pressigny must at this date have been a flint-implement factory; and thus the Neolithic Age is linked to Chaleux, where we find the Pressigny flints of an earlier period. The Palæolithic, the Neolithic, and the Bronze Age are thus all linked together—separated evidently by not more than a few centuries—at Pas de Grigny. We are told that the

Bronze Age lasted a couple of thousand years; the Neolithic, some five (?) thousand years; the Palæolithic, fifty, a hundred, five hundred thousand years. And we should therefore have to believe that the ford at Pas de Grigny was in use (prior to our era) five or ten thousand years, and that the factory at Grand-Pressigny, which lasted from Chaleux to Pas de Grigny, was in operation thousands, perhaps tens of thousands, of years in addition.

The honey-colored flints of Pressigny have also been found in the dolmens of Central France,* as well as in a "sarcophagus" of rude stones at Agen, on the Garonne.

Let us give another example:

Cissbury.

Certain remains of the "palæolithic" type are described by the distinguished archæologist (President at the time, we believe, of the Anthropological Society) Col. A. Lane Fox, in the *Archæologia* for 1869, in an account entitled "Excavations at Cissbury and Highdown," in which he discusses the hill-forts in the county of Sussex. Here are a series of extensive "pre-historic" fortifications, erected by the earliest flint-folk. Colonel Fox examined some twenty-five pits on the Sussex hills, and obtained a large number of unpolished implements; those obtained by him, with the specimens secured by others, numbered between five and six hundred, exclusive of flakes. The fortifications consist of a rampart and a ditch, and are found on some half-dozen contiguous hills in the neighborhood of Cissbury. These flints, he says, are "of nearly every type known to have been found amongst the flint implements from the drift, and caves, and up to the surface period." † All of the specimens were "*chipped*, and without the slightest trace of *grinding* or *polish*, nor was any vestige of metal found in the place." Some of the forms, he says, "exactly resemble" some found in the ancient cave of Le Moustier, which belongs to the very earliest period. He also states that the Cissbury flints resemble those from the manufactory of Spiennes in Belgium. There are no arrow-heads at all. Most of the implements are "of large size." Nor is there any trace of sandstone for grinding-purposes.

The animal remains were *Cervus elephas*, *Bos longifrons*, *Capra hircus*, *Equus* (*sp. ?*), *Sus scrofa*. No trace of the fallow-deer. This fauna corresponds with the "surface period."

The intrenchment he affirms to be cotemporary with the flints, which are found in the space enclosed by it, and not beyond, with trivial exceptions.

Colonel Fox considers, as already stated, that these remains are

* Flint Chips, by Stevens, p. 105.

† See Archæologia, 1869, vol. xlii. p. 69.

palæolithic. One of two things is certain: either they belong to the age of the Moustier Cave, *or* the pretended distinction between the Palæolithic and the Neolithic Age, as founded on the character of the flints, is *without foundation*. If they are palæolithic, then the palæolithic people *went to war* and *erected elaborate defences*. If they are not palæolithic, then these rude implements are no longer evidences of a great antiquity: there is no distinction between the Palæolithic Age and the Polished Stone Age. The anthropologist can select between the alternatives.

Our own confident opinion* is that they are not as old as Le Moustier or the River-Gravels, but that only a few centuries intervened between them; and that rude and unpolished flints remained in use by the side of the finer specimens, according to the locality, the opportunities, and the capacity of the population.

Here is another illustration of the rapid sequence of these ages. Mr. Townsend M. Hall, F.G.S. (reported in the *Intellectual Observer* for 1865, vol. viii. p. 350), found at Baggy Point, in North Devon,—a bold promontory bounding Barnstaple Bay,—great numbers of rude unpolished flint implements, precisely like those from the Somme Valley, except that they are smaller. They were associated with pottery, and were found in the alluvial soil, at the depth of four feet, *immediately above* the drift. (It is a raised beach,—forty feet above the sea.)

Baggy Point.

Now, this is the age of the fauna of Cissbury; the mammoth has disappeared. We are, indeed, in the Neolithic Age; nevertheless, the flints are just like those from the Somme Valley.

So again, at a meeting of the International Congress of Pre-historic Archæology, reported in the volume for 1868, Mr. George Busk, F.R.S., presented some stone implements found at the Cape of Good Hope, some of which were "highly polished," while others were "very rude;" but all were of the same age.

Cape of Good Hope. Polished and unpolished stone implements found together.

In North America we frequently find the rude unpolished implements lying on the surface, or a few feet beneath the surface, promiscuously mingled with the most highly-wrought specimens. Dr. Charles C. Abbot, in the *American Naturalist* for March, 1872, and April, 1872, describes a number of stone implements found in the State of New Jersey, which abundantly illustrate this remark. Stone weapons and implements, he says, are found scattered all over the State, from the mountains of Sussex to the sea-

North American Indians. Another example.

* Based on the fauna, which is the only criterion; although the French archæologists (M. de Mortillet especially) fix the chronology of the caves by the type of the flints.

beach at Cape May. Axes, arrow-heads, lance-heads, javelins, harpoons, spears, knives, scrapers, hammers, adzes, mortars and pestles, pipes, etc., are yearly turned up by the plough. Sometimes a "deposit" is found deep in the soil. These relics occur chiefly on the banks of the larger rivers and creeks. Many of them are picked up on the surface of the soil. The difference in the workmanship of these implements is so great that Dr. Abbot is sorely perplexed by it, and he remarks that "when a hundred or more are gathered together, and carefully compared, we must come to one of two conclusions; either that there were many execrable workmen among their tool-makers, or that the age of the crude specimens far exceeds that of the finely-wrought relics." Here are two specimens, both found on the surface; one of them unground and unpolished, the other carefully shaped and polished.

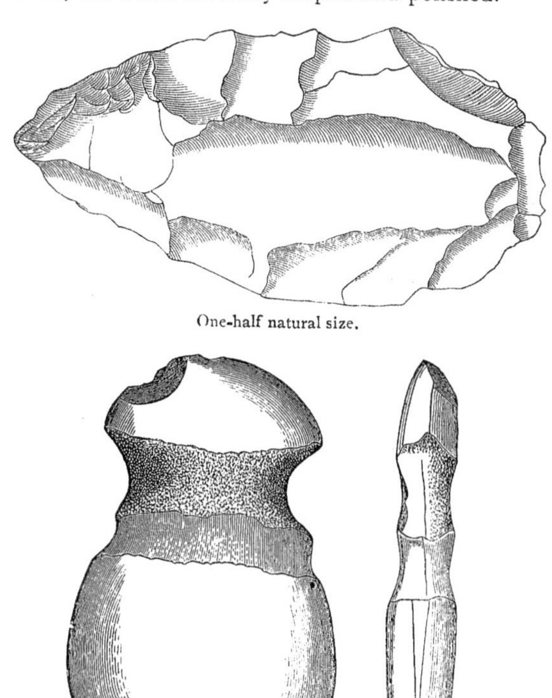

One-half natural size.

One-half natural size (side view). One-half natural size (end view).

The first of these specimens Dr. Abbot refers to the Palæolithic Age; the second, to the Neolithic Age.

The following is another example of the "palæolithic" type:

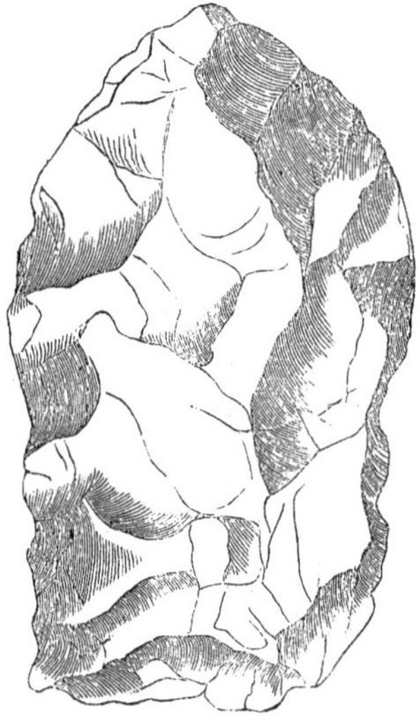

Natural size.

The cuts on page 406 are examples of the "neolithic" age.

The resemblance of these forms (rude and polished) to the European forms will at once arrest the attention of any one familiar with the subject. But our immediate object is to place side by side the so-called palæolithic and neolithic types. Dr. Abbot does not hesitate to assign these to the Indians who lived on the Delaware River a few centuries ago, and those to the "autochthones" who inhabited America ages ago. When the anthropologist finds human remains with the remains of the cave-bear and the mammoth, he argues that man must have been cotemporary with the great extinct mammalia; when he finds the rude flint implements with the polished implements, he assigns to one a date of A.D. 1600 and to the other an antiquity of one hundred thousand years; and this when all occur *on the surface.*

The Erie Indians.

We may cite a precisely similar example from Canada. In the *Anthropological Review* for 1864* there is an account of a lot of flint implements from Lake Erie shore, procured by F. R. Fairbank, M.D. They were found lying in mould a few inches from the surface. Similar implements, it is stated, are found scattered over most of the neighboring valleys. It is believed that they belonged to the tribe of the Eries, exterminated about the year 1650. In some respects they are superior to the implements obtained from the

* Page 64.

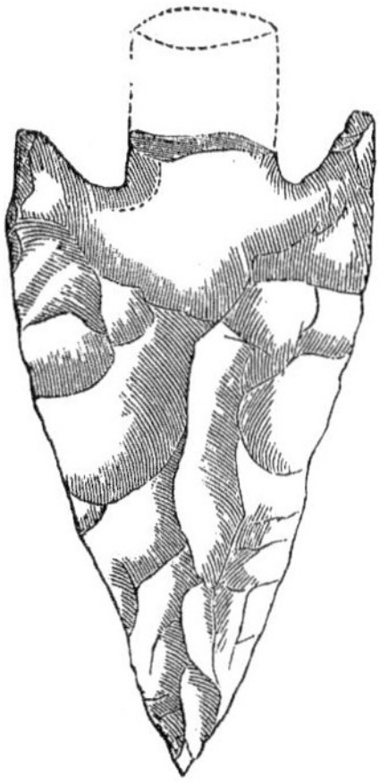

Natural size.

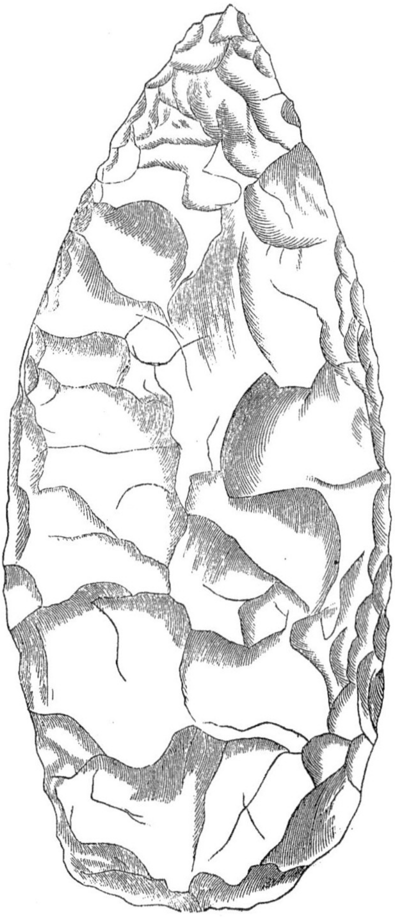

Natural size.

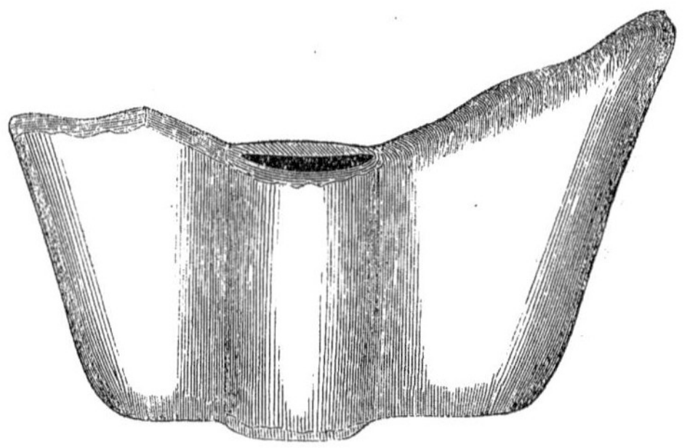

Natural size.

drift of France and England, says the writer; but "their general character is the same." They are "rough-hewn, and exhibited no signs of friction."

Then there is the factory of Spiennes in Belgium. This is assigned to the Neolithic Age; but the implements are rude and unpolished, and of all shapes.

Then, again, there are the great Flint Mines of the Neolithic Age at Grime's Graves. We are informed by the Rev. W. Greenwell that "all the implements here have been merely *chipped into shape*," and that he has "not met with one from the immediate neighborhood of the pits which shows traces of grinding."

Prof. Charles Rau informs us, in the last Smithsonian Report, that "flint implements of the European 'drift type' are by no means scarce in North America, although they cannot (thus far) be referred to any particular period, but must be classed with the other chipped and ground implements in use among the North American aborigines during historical times." He then proceeds to mention certain leaf-shaped flint implements of the palæolithic type which have been found in the mounds and on the surface. The most important deposit of this character, he states, is that discovered by Messrs. Squier and Davies in one of the "sacrificial" mounds of Clark's Work, on the North Fork of Paint Creek, Ross County, Ohio. More than six hundred flint discs were found in this mound. They are roundish, oval, or heart-shaped, and of various sizes, but on an average six inches long by four inches wide,—are clumsy and very roughly chipped. They bear, says Prof. Rau, "a striking resemblance to the flint 'hatchets' discovered by Boucher de Perthes and Dr. Rigollet in the diluvial gravels of the valley of the Somme."

Mr. Stevens, in his "Flint Chips," remarks that it is to be concluded "that implements resembling in form some of the European palæolithic types were made by the aborigines of America at a comparatively late period, and that the people usually termed the 'mound-builders' were probably the makers of these implements." Prof. Rau observes on this that, as he thinks, "there is no sufficient evidence for referring these implements exclusively to the mound-builders, considering that they occur on the surface, and in deposits below it, in regions where the people designated as mound-builders are not supposed to have left their traces." *

The argument in hand is farther corroborated by the *Grotta dei Colombi*, on the island of Palmaria, which was examined by Signor Capellini. The flints here were so extremely rude that

Grotta dei Colombi.

* Smithsonian Report, 1872, pp. 398–403.

Signor Capellini assigns them to the close of the palæolithic period. The fauna, however, belongs to the polished stone age,—*Bos taurus*, *Capra hircus*, *Sus scrofa*, *Lepus caniculus*, *Canis lupus*, *Felis cattus*, *Macacus inus*, etc.

Vicarello. In the basin of the thermal springs of Vicarello, near Lake Sabatino, there have been found in successive layers: 1. Coins and vases of the imperial epoch; 2. Coins of the Republic; 3. We then pass from the *æs signatum* to the early and rude *æs*. The metal here ceases, and we encounter *immediately* flint knives, scrapers, etc., "of the archæolithic epoch." There are no intermediate flints of the polished stone age.* It is probable that the true interpretation of such a series as this is, first, that the archæolithic or palæolithic age, in this region, came down to a very recent period; secondly, that the stone age, at this point, continued down to the dawn of a coinage among the inhabitants of this district.

One of the most interesting and instructive of the "transition" caves or grottoes is in the southwest of France, near Peyrehorade, in the southern part of the department of Landes. We find here, situated in a promontory formed between the Pau and the Oléron where they unite to form the Adour, the "Grottoes of Sorde," in one of which, *La grotte Duruthy*, MM. Louis Lartet and Chaplain Duparc have discovered a great number of worked flints, worked bones, a human skull, perforated teeth of the lion and the bear, and unworked bones of the reindeer, the horse, the ox, and the stag. The canine teeth are nearly all pierced with a hole, and a number of them contain etchings or drawings, among which are arrow-heads and delineations of fishes and *a seal*. We learn from the last that these troglodytes visited the sea, some twenty-five miles distant. A human cranium, examined by M. Hamy, is pronounced to belong to the race of Cro-Magnon. The worked flints are similar to the types of Cro-Magnon, La Madelaine, Les Eyzies, and Laugerie. Immediately above the bed containing the foregoing remains were found some thirty human skeletons, ascertained by MM. de Quatrefages and Hamy also to belong to the race of Cro-Magnon. Apparently, the reindeer had disappeared when this second occupation of the grotto was in progress. The worked flints and nuclei are similar in part to the preceding, but several of the implements are retouched and of very superior workmanship, while there is one very beautiful lance-head which on one side is carefully polished.

---

* Congrès d'Anthropologie, 1867, p. 110. It is conjectured that the relics found here were offerings thrown into the springs in accordance with a well-known custom of the ancients. M. de Rossi refers the ruder coins to the Bronze Age. The bed containing the flints, we are told, was "directly" beneath those containing these coins. See Matériaux, 1873, tome iv. p. 447.

We appear, therefore, to have here a direct *sequence* of the palæolithic and neolithic ages, *the same race* continuing to inhabit the same rock-shelter.

MM. Lartet and Duparc are forcibly struck with this fact, and conclude their lengthened examination of these remains with the following remarks:

"Voici la race humaine que nous trouvons à Cro-Magnon, vivant avec le mammouth, le grand lion des cavernes, le renne, l'aurochs, le spermophile, se servant de flèches, d'os triangulaires, et ne sachant décorer ses outils que d'ornements grossiers.

"Nous la voyons, à l'époque suivante, à La Madelaine et à Laugerie, employer des flèches barbelées et des aiguilles d'os, graver avec un véritable sentiment artistique, les images du mammouth, du renne, de l'aurochs, et du glutton, ses contemporains.

"Dans la grotte Duruthy, que nous venons d'étudier, après l'avoir rencontrée à la base, dans sa période artistique, en compagnie d'un ours, d'un lion et du renne, nous la retrouvons encore représentée dans une sépulture superposée aux foyers de cette dernière époque, avec des armes qui paraissent inaugurer l'ère de la pierre poli, pendant laquelle n'existaient plus, sur notre sol, les animaux dont nous venons de parler."

There is no *gap* here between the First Age and the Second Age. We take the man of the palæolithic age in the very act of inaugurating the polished stone age.

There is one other mark that connects this grotto with a transitional period. In the lower bed there are no remains of the great pachyderms, while we are told that the lion and the bear represented are not the *Felis spelæa* and the *Ursus spelæus*, but the modern lion and the *Ursus priscus*, the latter an intermediate form in point of size between the *Ursus spelæus* and the *Ursus arctos.**

We shall add only one more example in this connection, to show the proximity of the different ages to each other, and how quickly we pass from one to another.

The Coast of Cheshire.

The coast of Cheshire, from the mouth of the Dee to that of the Mersey, especially near the village of Hoylake, has long yielded objects to the antiquary. The coast is formed by great hills of loose, shifting sand, which rests on a layer of marshy deposit of little depth and of no very remote date. In or under this have been found human bones, estimated to be about three hundred years old.

Then, beneath this, comes a much thicker bed of fine drift sand, containing mediæval objects.

---

* See Matériaux, 3e et 4e Livraisons, 1874, p. 101.

Then, below this, a still deeper bed of artificial arable soil, composed of bog and sand with a little marl. This contains also mediæval articles, bones of domestic animals and of *Bos longifrons*,—dating about the twelfth or thirteenth century.

Then, under this, is another thinner stratum of blue marl or silt; and here we find Norman and Anglo-Saxon coins.

Then, under this, is a thicker bed of forest bog soil, filled with trees and shrubs and many stumps of large trees. Here we find remains of the deer, ox, horse, boar, etc., with shells; and Roman objects, and a few Saxon objects, including a Saxon coin; and, finally, in lower portions of the bed, a few arrow-heads of flint, stone, and shell.

Then, under this, we have a bed of some thickness of blue marl, containing the remains of *Bos primigenius*, the great Irish elk, and cetacea, and a few "primeval flints." *

During the Roman period, we are informed, this district, now buried in sand, was covered by forests, and ran out far into the present sea.

The "primeval flints" with the remains of the urus and the megaceros take us back to the "palæolithic" age,—so that we have here, in rapid succession apparently, a complete series of all the epochs from the River-Gravel to the age of Queen Elizabeth. It appears to us that no one can inspect this record without receiving from it the impression that as the modern stratum followed on the mediæval, and the mediæval on the Saxon and Roman and neolithic, so these followed quickly on the palæolithic stratum.

We have spoken elsewhere of the similarity of the stone implements all over the world. This similarity exists also between the types of different ages. "A comparison of different types," says Mr. E. B. Tylor, "with what is found elsewhere, breaks down any imaginary line of severance between the men of the Drift and the rest of the human species. The flake knives are very rude, but they are like what are found elsewhere, and there is no break in the series which ends in the beautiful specimens from Mexico and Scandinavia. The Tasmanians sometimes used for cutting or notching wood a very rude instrument. Eye-witnesses describe how they would pick up a suitable flat stone, knock off chips from one side, partly or all around the edge, and use it without more ado; and there is a specimen corresponding to this description exactly in the Taunton Museum. An implement found in the Drift near Clermont would seem to be much like this. . . . The leaf-shaped instruments of the Drift differ principally from those of the Scandinavian shell-heaps, and of America, in being made less neatly and by chipping off larger flakes. . . . Even the most special type of the

* Intellectual Observer, vol. vii. p. 390.

Drift, namely, the pointed tapering implement like a great spear-head, differs from some American implements only in being much rougher and heavier."

"There have been found in Asia," says Mr. Tylor, "stone implements resembling most closely the best marked of the Drift types. Mr. I. E. Taylor, British Consul at Basrah, obtained some years ago from the sun-dried brick mound of Abu Shahrein, in Southern Babylonia, two taper-pointed instruments of chipped flint, which, to judge from a cast of one of them, would be passed without hesitation as Drift implements. . . . A stone implement, found in a cave at Bethlehem, does not differ specifically from the Drift type." *We trace thus the palæolithic age to its primeval home, and fix its date by the chronology of Babylonia and Palestine.* We have already referred to the finding of an implement of this type among the flints which occur at the village of Bethsaour.

Another instance of the finding of an implement of the palæolithic type in Babylonia is mentioned by M. Louis Lartet in his work on the Geology of Palestine. It was a flint hatchet "in every respect similar to the finest types from our quaternary beds of the Somme and those of England." It is in the British Museum.

The Bronze Age, no distinct traces of.

With regard to the BRONZE AGE, while, as we have admitted, there are traces of such a period, its existence in Western and Northern Europe is, nevertheless, a very shadowy and faintly-defined reality. Except, possibly, in Denmark, one is almost tempted to reject it altogether. Where do we find it? Not in the Caves.* Not in the Danish Kjökken-möddings. It must, then, be either in the Tumuli and Dolmens, in the Peat, or in the Swiss Lakes. Let us keep in mind the definition of the Bronze Age. Bronze ornaments occur abundantly in the Iron, as in the Bronze Age. The Bronze Age, as we have stated elsewhere, is defined by Sir John Lubbock to be "that in which bronze was used *for weapons and cutting instruments* of all kinds."

No evidence of a Bronze Age from the Tumuli.

This is all clear enough. Weapons and cutting instruments are battle-axes, swords, spear-heads, knives, razors, arrow-heads, daggers. Sir John Lubbock gives us in his volume the contents of some two hundred and fifty tumuli, barrows, and dolmens, which have been examined in Great Britain and France; and he constantly speaks of a large proportion of these tombs as belonging to the "Bronze Age," *i.e.*, to the era of bronze weapons. Now,

* "Up to the present time," says Mr. Boyd Dawkins, "all the pre-historic caves discovered in Britain belong either to the age of stone or of iron." (Macmillan's Magazine, December, 1870.) And yet the archæologists tell us that the Bronze Age lasted some two thousand years.

in all of these two hundred and fifty interments all of the bronze weapons found consist of fifteen bronze daggers, two bronze battle-axes, and one bronze spear-head. That is the Bronze Age. Fifteen dirks, two celts, and one lance-head. Astonishing as it may appear, this is the foundation on which this great and careful archæologist erects the Bronze Era of the Rude Stone Monuments. Fifteen dirks, two celts, and one lance-head. The dirks are partly in the category of "ornaments," and do not really belong to the class of genuine weapons. They continued in use down to the Middle Ages. There is not a solitary sword, not a knife, not an arrow-head.

There *is* an account in Sir John Lubbock's work of the finding of some bronze swords—three in number—in certain tumuli in Jutland, two of which we have already noticed, from an account by Prof. Worsaae. They were met with near Ribe, where there are four tumuli, known as Great Kongehoi, Little Kongehoi, Guldhoi, and Treenhoi. In these were found seven wooden coffins, and in the coffins some woollen caps, two woollen shawls, a woollen cloak, traces of leather (perhaps the remains of shoes), an ox-hide, a pair of woollen leggings, a small comb, a small bronze razor-knife, three bronze swords, a bronze brooch, a bronze knife, a bronze awl, a pair of bronze tweezers, a bronze stud, an amber bead (baby's coffin), a small bronze bracelet, two bronze daggers, a wooden bowl ornamented with tin nails, a vase of wood, a box of bark, and a javelin-head of flint.

Here we have apparently the Bronze Age pure and simple,—not a trace of iron, and only one flint. And what do we see? A "prehistoric" man? In these comfortable woollen garments, caps, shoes, and wooden coffins with movable lids. And a baby's bracelet. Besides all which, the condition of one of the bodies indicated anything but an ancient burial. The brain had undergone little decay, and was found lying at one end of the coffin, covered by a thick hemispherical woollen cap. Sir John Lubbock attributes this to the action of water impregnated with iron. But will water impregnated with iron keep a dead man's brain three or four or five thousand years?

The cuts given of the "woollen" articles represent as neat and substantial garments as can now be found in our clothing establishments. When were woollen garments introduced into Denmark? Probably after the Christian era; and this "bronze" find is probably not fifteen hundred years old.

It appears, therefore, that it would hardly be appropriate to speak of a "bronze age" as derived from the character of the relics found in the barrows and dolmens, and if (we argue further) there be a "bronze age" at all, it must be found in connection with the relics obtained from either the ancient lake-villages or the Irish and Danish peat.

Nor from the Lake-Dwellings.

Sir John Lubbock makes an ingenious effort to demonstrate the existence of a Bronze Age among the lake-dwellers. He selects four of the oldest Stone-Age villages,—Wangen, Moosseedorf, Nussdorf, and Wauwyl,—and five of the so-called Bronze-Age villages, namely, Nidau, Cortaillod, Estavayer, Corcelettes, and Morges; and these he contrasts, proposing to show that the four yield vast numbers of stone implements, and no bronze, and the five bronze stations vast numbers of bronze implements and very few stone implements. This he does by the following table, which includes also the iron station of Marin:

	Stone.					Bronze.								Iron.							
	Axes.	Arrows.	Flakes.	Other objects.	Total.	Axes.	Knives.	Lances.	Sickles.	Fish-hooks.	Ornaments.	Sundries.	Total.	Swords.	Axes.	Knives.	Lances.	Ornaments.	Sundries.	Total.	Coins.
Switzerland																					
Wangen	1500	...	2500	450	4450	...	...	...	...	...	...	...	...	...	...	...	...	...	...	...	o
Moosseedorf	100	25	2300	277	2702	...	...	...	...	...	...	...	...	...	...	...	...	...	...	...	o
Nussdorf	1000	100	100	30	1230	...	...	...	...	..	...	...	...	...	...	...	...	...	...	...	o
Wauwyl	43	36	200	147	426	...	...	...	...	...	...	...	...	...	...	...	...	...	...	...	o
Nidau	33	?	?	335 Corn-crushers.	368	23	102	27	18	109	1420	305	2004	...	...	...	...	...	...	...	o
Cortaillod	?	?	?	?	...	13	22	4	2	71	515	208	835	...	...	...	...	...	...	...	o
Estavayer	?	?	?	?	...	6	14	...	1	43	403	150	617	...	...	...	...	...	...	...	o
Corcelettes	?	?	?	?	...	1	19	2	7	...	465	16	510	...	...	...	...	...	...	...	o
Morges	o	?	?	Many corn-crushers.	...	50	20	11	11	10	108	?	210	...	...	...	...	...	1	1	o
Marin	...	...	Some	12 Balls.	...	1	...	...	...	...	1	13	15	50	5	4	23	More than 100	61	250	9

It is perfectly true that no metal occurred at Wangen, Moosseedorf, Nussdorf, or Wauwyl. Perforated stone celts and nephrite celts (fifty of these at Nussdorf), however, did occur. This may fairly be called the Stone Age,—although even here we get upon the trail of the presence of metal, and recognize the plain evidence of some sort of contact with the East.

It will be observed that the stone implements at the bronze stations of the table are not reported. The blank is merely filled with a mark of interrogation. It is difficult to draw inferences from a table constructed in this manner: the very point in question has reference to the number of stone implements found at the bronze stations, and a mark of interrogation throws no light on the subject. We derive an important hint, however, from a remark of Sir John Lubbock on page 13; this is, that "the manner in which the collections were made accounts, probably, for the absence of whetstones, and perhaps, to a great extent, for that of the flint flakes, etc." But he is impressed with the absence of stone axes at Morges, and "their rarity at Nidau and Estavayer."

On p. 43 Sir John Lubbock has another table furnished him by Dr. Keller, showing the number and character of the bronze objects obtained from the Swiss lakes. This table is given below. It includes all of the bronze stations mentioned in the above table, except Morges, and adds Möringen, Auvernier, and "other places."

	Nidau.	Möringen.	Estavayer.	Cortaillod.	Corcelettes.	Auvernier.	Other Places.	Total.
Celts and fragments	23	7	6	13	1	6	11	67
Swords	....	...	...	...	...	...	4	4
Hammers	4	...	1	...	...	...	...	5
Knives and fragments	102	19	14	22	19	8	9	193
Hair-pins	611	53	239	183	237	22	22	1367
Small rings	496	28	115	195	202	14	3	1053
Ear-rings	238	42	36	116	...	3	5	440
Bracelets and fragments	55	14	16	21	26	11	2	145
Fish-hooks	189	12	43	71	9	2	1	248
Awls	95	3	49	98	17	...	...	262
Spiral wires	...	...	46	50	5	...	...	101
Lance-heads	27	7	...	4	2	5	2	47
Arrow-heads	...	...	5	1	...	...	...	6
Buttons	...	1	28	10	10	...	...	49
Needles	20	2	3	4	1	...	...	30
Various ornaments	15	5	7	18	3	1	...	49
Saws	...	...	3	...	...	...	...	3
Daggers	...	...	...	...	...	...	2	2
Sickles	18	12	1	2	7	1	4	45
Double-pointed pins	75	...	...	...	...	...	...	75
Small bracelets	20	...	...	11	...	...	...	31
Sundries	96	3	5	16	...	...	4	124
Total	2004	208	618	835	539	73	69	4346

An examination of this table shows that if *bronze weapons* are the characteristic of the Bronze Age, that age could never have existed at any one of these six stations selected as the special representatives of the Bronze Age by Sir John Lubbock. Take Corcelettes. According to Sir John Lubbock, not a solitary iron implement or object was found here; and he *reports* (in his tables) none of stone. But five hundred and thirty-nine bronze objects are reported; of which three are weapons. This is the Bronze Age at Corcelettes. There is not one sword, not one dagger, not one arrow-point. There are one celt and two lance-heads,—and, if they are to be counted, nineteen knives. All of the rest (with a few exceptions) are *ornaments;* and we naturally ask, Did these people never go to war? Take Estavayer: six hundred and eighteen bronze objects were found here. According to Sir John Lubbock's tables, not a solitary object of iron was found, and no stone is reported.* How many bronze weapons were found here? how did the people of Estavayer defend themselves and pursue the wild beasts of the forest? According to our table, six celts and five arrow-heads represent the armory of Estavayer, and constitute at this point *the Bronze Age.* There is not a sword, nor a lance-head, nor a dagger. Take Cortaillod: the bronze relics number eight hundred and thirty-five; the weapons number eighteen.†

Now, at the iron station of Marin (see the first table), where the whole find consisted of fifteen objects of bronze and two hundred and fifty of iron, the iron weapons amounted to seventy-eight,—nearly one-third. And this, we say, is *the Bronze Age* in the Swiss lakes.

The entire number of bronze objects contained in the second table is four thousand three hundred and forty-six. The entire number of weapons is four swords, six arrow-heads, sixty-seven celts, one hundred and ninety-three knives, forty-seven lance-heads, and two daggers. It does not seem reasonable to rear a Bronze Age on four swords and sixty-seven battle-axes and forty-seven spear-heads,—occurring at six of the principal bronze stations in the Swiss lakes, where more than four thousand three hundred objects of bronze were obtained in all. This is entirely out of proportion to the number of weapons at the iron station of Marin. It is equally out of proportion to the number of weapons at the Stone Age stations. Thus, at Wangen there were fifteen hundred stone axes; at Nussdorf there were one thousand; at Moosseedorf there were one hundred axes and twenty-five arrow-points out of some four hundred objects of stone (exclusive of twenty-three hundred flakes).

At one of the bronze stations (Nidau) in the table, the number of stone axes is, fortunately, reported; and at this, the greatest of all the bronze stations, where the objects in bronze amounted to two thousand and four, *the stone axes outnumber the bronze celts.*

But this is but a partial view. Sir John Lubbock does not mention the bronze station of Unter Uhldingen, where three hundred stone celts were found, besides "arrow-heads, chisels, stone hammers, etc.;" nor Greng, where we have "a mixture of stone and bronze;" nor Montellier, where Col. Schwab found a "number of stone implements, along with bronze knobs, dishes, screws, a bronze knife, etc.;" nor Chevroux, where we have "stone celts, bronze sickles, knives, etc.;" nor Ebersburg (land station), where were found stone celts, bronze knives, etc.; nor other similar places.

---

* Dr. Keller, however, informs us that stone celts, grinding-stones, etc., were found.

† Dr. Keller says that objects of stone and iron were found here.

It therefore appears that neither in the Swiss lakes nor in the ancient tombs is there any evidence of a Bronze Age.*

We have intimated that possibly there might be clearer traces of such an age in Denmark, and perhaps we might have added Ireland. We shall say enough elsewhere about the Irish peat to show that if any Bronze Age is represented there, it was a very recent thing. We have also referred to Denmark. But we shall in a future chapter speak more particularly with regard to the very great number of bronze weapons which have been found in these countries.

At present, we shall proceed to speak of the miscellaneous "finds" of bronze and stone implements (frequently associated with iron), which occur under varying circumstances,—in old river-beds, among ancient ruins, on battle-fields, in the lakes, in peat, etc., etc. We shall in this connection devote a brief chapter to the Ruins of Troy; and in another chapter we shall take occasion to speak of the use of stone and bronze in America.

The Bronze weapons pronounced to be Roman.

Sir John Lubbock not only insists on a Bronze Age in Western and Northern Europe, but he affirms that in the north "the use of bronze weapons had been discontinued before, and probably long before, the commencement of our era." (P. 12.) Many persons think, however, that the bronze swords and daggers and celts are even *Roman*. This is the opinion of that eminent archæologist Mr. Thos. Wright, who affirms that "instead of our not finding the bronze swords in juxtaposition with Roman remains, in every case where they have been found in Britain or Gaul, where the details of the discovery have been carefully observed, it has occurred under circumstances which lead to the strong presumption of their being Roman." He mentions the discovery of a bronze sword, with the skeletons of a man and horse, in 1801, in a peat moss at Heilly, in France, and with these four coins of the emperor Caracalla. Another bronze sword, he says, was found in a turbary at Piquigny (already noticed), near Abbeville, in a large boat, which appeared to have been sunk, and in which were several skeletons, with some coins of the Roman emperor Maxentius, who reigned from 306 to 312 A.D. There was also a bronze helmet on the head of the skeleton

* M. Bertrand gave expression to similar views at the Congress of Anthropologists held in August last at Stockholm. He attacked the divisions of the Bronze Age, "because" (to use his own language) "not only did the Bronze and the Iron Ages overlap one another, but they had positively been cotemporaneous. . . . In Germany the Bronze Age prevailed in the fourth century after Christ." Mr. Evans "agreed with M. Bertrand that it was unadvisable to insist on the divisions of the Bronze Age." M. Desor stated that "as far as the First Iron Age was concerned, it belonged in Scandinavia to the fourth and sixth centuries" (of our era). Academy, August 29, 1874.

to which the sword belonged. Outside of the boat a similar sword was found.*

Mr. Wright admits the truth of the objection that the bronze swords are not ordinarily met with in connection with Roman remains, but he says that this is explained by the fact that the Romans did not bury their weapons with the dead, but, on the contrary, preserved them with great care. He says it is equally true that "a Roman sword of iron is one of the rarest objects of antiquarian discovery," and that he remembers, in his own observations, hardly a case where one was discovered in Roman Britain. At Wroxeter, the relics from which filled a whole museum, not one Roman sword was met with, "nor do I remember," he says, "one on any site of a Roman town or villa." He mentions that a few years since a Roman sword in a bronze scabbard, the blade appearing from the rust to be iron, was dredged out of the Thames along with a very fine specimen of the well-known leaf-shaped bronze swords and a large stone celt, all of which are now in the museum of Lord Londesborough, at Grimston Park, Yorkshire. And also that a similar iron sword in a bronze scabbard was found with a bronze one in the river below Lincoln, at a spot where a circular bronze shield had been previously found.

Whether they were Roman or not, we learn from these cases that bronze swords were in use in Gaul and Britain in the Roman period, and that certainly as late as the fourth century. We recognize also the cotemporaneous use of bronze and iron.

The swords found in the Thames at London, says Mr. Wright, are *nearly all bronze*, and in the city limits, as he believes, no relic of any kind has been found earlier than the Romans. Mr. Roach Smith, he proceeds to remark, who has examined the subject of these Roman antiquities in London more extensively and deeply than any one else, and who is the first authority on the antiquities of the Romans in England or even in Europe, "is equally convinced with me that the bronze swords are of Roman manufacture or origin."

The bronze axes, chisels, etc., he remarks, are still more clearly of Roman origin.

He then cites the authority of M. de Caumont, who states in his *Cours d'Antiquités Monumentales*, tom. i. p. 232, that "we find also very frequently these bronze axes in places covered with Roman ruins, and I have acquired the certainty of this by my (his) own observations and by the information I have collected in my (his) travels." M. de Caumont, Mr. Wright says, is the highest authority among archæologists.

* Trans. Ethnolog. Soc., N. S., vol. iv. p. 176: paper on Bronze Weapons, by Thomas Wright, M.A., F.S.A., etc.

Some light is thrown on the date of the Bronze Age by an account, in the Proceedings of the Anthropological Congress of 1867, of a "pre-historic workshop of the Age of Bronze."* We learn from this account that an *atelier* of bronze was found in a turbary in the commune of Amiens, near St.-Acheul, the objects obtained consisting of bronze hatchets, lance-heads, bracelets, razors, swords, pruning-bills, and an "*éperon préhistorique!*" We thus ascertain that in the Bronze Age the inhabitants of the Somme Valley rode on horseback wearing *brass spurs.* Is it possible that these things occurred in the region known as Gaul three thousand years before the Christian era? Did it occur before the conquest of Gaul by Julius Cæsar? Is it not probable that this "pre-historic" spur belongs to the "Lower Empire"?

In the diary of the late Matthew Lee, Esq., as we are told, there is the following entry: "July, 1763. The laborers on Lovepayne farm, Colyton, near Southleigh, destroyed a stone barrow in order to procure a supply of stones for the new turnpike road. Upon one side of the barrow they found about a hundred Roman chisels for cutting stones, of a metal between a copper and brass color, rough and unhardened." Of course Mr. Lee's statement does not prove the chisels to be Roman, but they are more recent than the barrow, and the fact that similar "finds" of bronze implements are very common in England in the vicinity, as Mr. Wright affirms, almost always of Roman roads, creates a strong probability that these from the Lovepayne farm are of Roman date. They probably belonged to an itinerant manufacturer, who moved from place to place, disposing of his wares. At the time of the meeting of the British Archæological Association at Ludlow, in 1867, a discovery of a similar character was made in the neighborhood, at Broadward, which is close upon the line of a Roman road. In draining a piece of swampy land, the laborers came upon a very large deposit of spear-heads, swords, axes or chisels (commonly called celts), knives, and other implements, made of bronze, amounting (so far as they had proceeded) to a hundred-weight. With them some pottery was found, regarded by the writer from whom we take this account as probably Roman.†

Another collection of bronze implements, believed to be Roman, and consisting of swords, celts, and two fragments of *ferrules*, was found in 1862, in a field near Guilsfield, in Montgomeryshire, known as "The Camp."‡

We shall not undertake to decide this question; the decision of it does not fall within the object of this volume; but the fact that leading

---

* See Congrès d'Anthropologie, 1867, p. 223.

† The Student and Intellectual Observer, vol. i. p. 70.

‡ Ib.

archæologists refer these bronze weapons to the Romans—archæologists far better informed than Sir John Lubbock on such a point—is relevant to our discussion. If the relics of bronze found were not in some measure recent, no such views would have been advanced; and it makes little difference whether they are Roman or British. We shall only add that Mr. Llewellyn Jewett, F.S.A., in his recent work on "Grave Mounds and their Contents," advances precisely the same opinion with Mr. Wright, stating that the swords of bronze which have been generally attributed to the British period are now "considered Roman." *

We do not know a more striking evidence of the recent date of the employment of bronze in Britain for cutting instruments than one casually mentioned in a late number of the *London Quarterly Review* in an article on "The Isle of Wight." Speaking of the Anglo-Saxon occupancy of this island, and of the sepulchral barrows of that period, we are told that in one of these barrows belonging to the cemetery on Chessell Down, near Freshwater, was found "the skeleton of a female, with the bodkin which had confined her hair still lying at the back of her head, and *her bronze needle and scissors* by her side." In others were found the bronze rattle of an infant, a silver spoon, balls of crystal with silver mountings, etc.† The Saxon, or rather Jutish, occupation of the island dates from A.D. 530, when Cerdic of Wessex, and his son Cynric, subsequently to their conquests on the mainland, crossed the Solent, and, after a bloody battle, stormed the *burgh* or stronghold of Carisbrooke and made themselves masters of Wight. And yet we are told that the Bronze Age in the north had terminated before, "and probably long before," the commencement of our era.

Bronze scissors of the sixth century.

Sir W. R. Wilde mentions, in his Catalogue of Bronze Implements, etc., a very fine sword of bronze (No. 5) found at Kildrinagh ford, on the river Nore, in Queen's County, with three other bronze swords (Nos. 48, 49, 50), and two iron swords, two iron spear-heads, and three skulls.‡

Bronze and iron found together.

On the other hand, he mentions the finding at Toome Bar, in the river Bann, at the depth of three feet, of a stone celt and a bronze celt together.

Sir W. R. Wilde mentions also the discovery at the depth of five feet in a bog, in a side-cutting of the river Deel, of five hundred bronze spear-heads, near a crannoge which contained iron spear-heads. This was in the parish of Killucan, Westmeath.

The same authority also shows us that stones were used as missiles in battle, in Ireland, as late as the tenth century. He quotes from the

* Page 190. † Lond. Quar. Rev., July, 1874, p. 5, Amer. reprint. ‡ Page 444.

Book of Lismore that in the battle fought near Limerick by Callachen Cashel against the Danes, about A.D. 920, "their youths, and their champions, and their proud, haughty veterans, came to the front of the battle *to cast their stones*, and their small arrows, and their smooth spears on all sides." He also cites a number of examples of *naked celts* without handles, used in this way, about the same date.

Recent use of bronze weapons in Ireland.

The recent use of bronze in Ireland, and its employment cotemporaneously with iron, is also further illustrated by the following statement of Sir W. R. Wilde: he remarks that the swords figured on the sculptured crosses of Ireland are always of the iron pattern, long, straight, round, or angle-pointed, and cross-hilted. On these same crosses celts are also figured, and therefore, he says, bronze celts must have continued in use after the introduction of iron swords,—and, he might have added, after the date of the sculptured crosses, which are hardly earlier than the seventh century.*

Bronze was unquestionably used in Ireland (and, as we shall see, by the Danes) as late as twelve hundred years ago, and, what is still more noticeable in this connection, stone hammers and stone anvils were used "until a very recent period."†

Recent use of stone implements.

Stones seem also to have been used in battle as missiles in England as late as the eleventh century. Speaking of the Saxons at the battle of Hastings, William of Poitiers says, "Jactant cuspides ac diversorum generum tela, sævissimas quasque secures ac lignis imposita saxa."‡

Mealing-stones, similar to those found in the Swiss lakes, "not improbably," says Mr. Evans, "remained in use [in Ireland] until a comparatively late period."

The large thin blades of stone found in the Shetland and Orkney Islands, and called "Picts' knives," have also been used at no distant period. Mr. Evans informs us that "there are traditions extant of their having been in use *in the present century*."

In our chapter on the Megalithic Monuments and Tumuli we had occasion to mention a number of cases where stone implements were found with Roman, Saxon, and Frankish remains. We departed a little from the subject immediately under consideration to quote the statement of Mr. Evans, that the stone axes are said to have been found "in many cases" in Germany in association with objects of iron,—that they had been found in Denmark with the same metal,—that flint arrow-heads are also frequently found with objects of iron and objects of the Roman and Saxon periods.

---

* Page 440. † Evans's Stone Implements, on authority of Sir W. R. Wilde, p. 11.

‡ "Celt, Roman, and Saxon," p. 72.

We cited also from Mr. Evans the finding of flint battle-axes in a Merovingian cemetery at Labruyère; of a fibrolite hatchet at Mont Beuvray with Gaulish coins of the time of Augustus; of flint or stone implements with Roman remains at Ash, in Kent; at Leicester; at Great Whitcombe, Gloucestershire; at Ickleton, Essex; at Alchester, Oxfordshire; and at Eastbourne.

We may add here the case mentioned by him of the discovery of five polished stone celts with Roman remains at Kastrich, near Gonsenheim, one of which was nine and one-quarter inches long. The smallest of these was of greenstone, the others of chloritic albite. They are said to have been found in a sort of leather case.

In Saxon graves.

Flakes and rudely-chipped pieces of flint, we also learn from Mr. Evans's work, are found in both the Saxon and Merovingian graves, and are also "a very common occurrence on the sites of Roman occupation," as at Hardham, Sussex, where Roman pottery was found; at Moel Fenlli, in the vale of Clwyd, where Roman pottery was also found; and at Reculver (Regulbium), St. Alban's (Verulamium), etc.*

Mr. Evans mentions that he has in his own collection a stone celt said to have been found in Ireland with a hoard of Anglo-Saxon coins of the tenth century.

Runic inscriptions.

He also mentions a perforated stone axe found in the last century, and now in the Museum of Upsala, having on it a Runic inscription,—"Owns Oltha this Axe." Another, with four Runic characters, was found in Denmark. The Runes *may* have been used as early as the third or fourth century of the Christian era; but they were certainly used about A.D. 900 and for some centuries afterwards; and, therefore, while this axe may be as old as A.D. 300, it is *probably* not older than A.D. 600 or 700.

Tacitus distinctly tells us (Germ., ii. 19) "Literarum secreta viri pariter ac feminæ ignorant." This was written about A.D. 100.

Bronze and iron weapons found together.

In one of the early volumes of the *Archæological Journal* (perhaps the fifth) is an account of the finding of a number of bronze and iron weapons together, at Kingston, on the Thames, in the bed of the river. It is surmised that it was the scene of a battle between Julius Cæsar and the Britons. The bronzes were celts, a sword, and a fibula. Within a few yards, at the same depth, lay iron spear-heads and an iron hatchet imbedded in blue clay, under the gravel. The hatchet is a weapon of war, and resembles closely a hatchet found in the bed of the Witham, near Horsley Deep, where many Roman remains have been found.

* Evans, p. 255.

But, curious to relate, with these was found a thumb-ring (bronze) of probably *the fifteenth century*,—certainly not older than the Middle Ages.

Sepulchral interments found near by yielded bronze weapons and large masses of unwrought metal, indicating an armorer's establishment.

With the bronze weapons in the bed of the river there was found also an elegant object of bronze, which appeared to support a standard or Roman eagle.

Stone implements with Roman remains.

An extensive discovery of Roman remains was made in 1869 at Stonham, in Suffolk. Great quantities of iron, lead, pottery, glass, querns, flue-tiles, coins, and other objects were found, and with them "many flint implements, such as celts, arrow-heads, spear-heads, scrapers," etc. The coins were chiefly third brass of the *Lower Empire*, mostly in a bad state of preservation, but those which could be read were of Claudius Gothicus, Diocletian, Carausius, Constantine I., Constantine II., Magnentius, and Valens; and also one of the late coins called by numismatists *minimi*.*

The following example not only illustrates the use of stone in Roman times, but also gives us an important piece of information on another point.

Col. A. Lane Fox's testimony.

In an article in the "Journal of the Ethnological Society of London"† for 1869, Col. A. Lane Fox, at that time Hon. Secretary of the Society, gives an account of the finding of flint implements in association with Roman remains by himself in Oxfordshire and the Isle of Thanet. Colonel Fox stated that his object was to lay before the Society some evidence that he had stumbled on, going to show that there must have existed during the Roman period in Britain "a class of people who employed flint tools such as we are in the habit of associating with a very early condition of human culture." "There is now good reason for supposing," he says, "that flint implements continued in use among the Britons during the Roman and perhaps even during the earlier part of the Saxon period." He proceeds to give an account of his observations on which these conclusions are based,—of his finding Roman pottery mixed with very rude worked flints in Oxfordshire and in the Isle of Thanet; and in his judgment the relics were all cotemporary, though this was by no means absolutely *certain*. It is important to remark—if these remains really are of the same date—that the flint implements are described as being *very rude*.

---

* The Student and Intellectual Observer, vol. ii. p. 152.

† Vol. i., N. S., p. 1.

In accordance with this, we have in the "Sussex Archæological Collections"* an account of the early British races formerly settled on the low hills overlooking the water-courses of North Hampshire. On both sides of the Test Valley occur spots, which were evidently places of temporary occupation, at which are found rudely-worked stone celts, scrapers, spear-heads, arrow-heads, hammers, mullers, etc.; while on the east side of the valley there is a cluster of *hut-circles*. These were the dwellings of the fabricators of the flints. In them were found wrought flints similar to those just described, and, along with them, the split bones of *Bos longifrons*, *Cervus elephas*, *Capra hircus*, *Sus*, and *Canis*. There was coarse hand-made pottery, but no metal, except one specimen, which was an early British *coin*, found in clearing away the mould from around the circles.

Stone implements with British coin.

This coin could not have been a century older than the Roman invasion; it is probably cotemporary with the Roman period.

Mr. Boyd Dawkins gives similar testimony, stating in the "Journal of the Ethnological Society of London" that he had found flint flakes in the cinder-heaps of the Wealdon Iron-Works, and in a Romano-British cemetery at Hardham, in Sussex. "A club or axe armed with stone," he says, "was used even at the battle of Senlac," and "a cargo of stones for missile purposes formed an important part of a Viking's equipment."†

Mr. Boyd Dawkins.

Prof. Wilson, in his "Prehistoric Annals of Scotland," mentions the finding of vast quantities of iron arms in 1834 in a field near the burgh of Annan, in Dumfriesshire, and with them a brass battle-axe. (Vol. ii. p. 123.) At the same place, and associated with these articles, they found a number of iron horse-shoes, which are said to have been first introduced into England by William the Conqueror (A.D. 1066). This bronze axe is, therefore, probably as late as the eleventh century.

Stone and bronze.

In 1843 a bath was discovered in the forest of Bretonne, in France. It was reached by a staircase of hewn stones. A bronze hatchet, fragments of mosaic, cups and rings in bronze, broken household vessels, oyster-shells, bones of human beings and animals, were found.‡ This, of course, is Roman.

Bronze celts were also found with Roman antiquities at Ladbrook, in the town of Old Flint.§

They were also found in Herculaneum.

Great numbers of stone implements were found, according to Mr.

* Vol. xxiv. p. 164. † Vol. ii. p. 145.

‡ Eclectic Magazine for January, 1844, p. 139.

§ Gentleman's Magazine, part i. vol. xciv. p. 162.

Evans, on the shores of Lough Neagh, and on the banks of the river Bann, which flows out of the lake. Some of these implements were also found in the old bed of the river, at the depth of six feet.

Lough Neagh.

Stone hatchets were obtained to the number of three or four hundred, and the worked flints occurred by "thousands." Some piles were also found in the lake, evidently shaped with metal tools. The main locality is at Toome's Bridge, where the river flows out of the lake. Several iron or steel axes also were found on the lake-shore at Toome, which appeared, from the form, to be of considerable antiquity. Some of the stone implements were found on the surface of the peat.

In the cave of Longberry Bank, we are told, near Penally, in Pembrokeshire, flint flakes occurred in association with red, fine-grained pottery, *turned in the lathe* (and, therefore, of Roman age), and the remains of *Bos longifrons*, badger, sheep, and wolf or dog.

At a meeting of the Royal Archæological Society in 1869, Mr. Richard Meeson presented a celt of grayish flint and a perforated stone disc, found in deepening the bed of the Mardyke, at Stifford, near Gray's Thurrock, with which was found a bronze dagger.*

Mr. Meeson also presented a bronze sword found on the surface of the peat in the Mardyke.

The foregoing examples are chiefly from Great Britain and Ireland. The French archæologists afford us similar information with regard to France.

The Three Ages in France.

It would seem that the city of Bordeaux, in France, was at one time a kjökken-mödding, and, apparently, in Roman times. In "Matériaux pour l'Histoire de l'Homme," † we are told that in 1867 some laborers, constructing sewers in the streets, at a considerable depth below Roman remains, struck a bed of peat containing ashes, charcoal, numerous broken and worked bones, still more numerous marine shells, and worked flints. "It must have been," says M. de Mortillet, "a deposit analogous to the kjökken-möddings of Denmark." He adds, however, that the designs which he had seen represent some bones "evidently sawed with *steel,* and not with silex, certainly of Roman origin." He thinks the beds have not been "properly studied."

Bordeaux.

On the following page of the sàme anthropological journal we are told that at the hamlet of Ladroix, commune of Serrigny, Côte-d'Or, there is a magnificent spring, which from time immemorial has attracted the population of the neighborhood. Here, under some Gallo-Roman remains, were discovered, says the work in question, two coins in bronze of the type *Éduen.* Also there was found an

Ladroix.

---

* Arch. Jour., No. 102, p. 190, 1869.

† Tome iv. p. 4.

axe of jadeite, well preserved, associated with splinters of flint and a nucleus.

The same work* mentions also that in a Gaulish tumulus in the forest of Brumath, near Strasbourg, a bronze celt, cotemporary with the Roman conquest, was found in a wooden box.

The next case deserves special attention. Our account is taken from the volume of the "Congrès International d'Anthropologie et d'Archéologie Préhistoriques" for 1871 (the Congress at Bologna).† M. Anatole Ronjon details the examination of the "station of Champsperlard," in the environs of Choisy-le-Roi, department of the Seine. This he describes to have been a genuine *terramare*, like those in the north of Italy. Remains of dwellings are found, as well as implements and utensils. The locality is elevated about five feet above the level of the plain. The surface of the *tertre* or hillock, we are told, was formerly covered with fragments of pottery, débris of bones, and *worked flints*. Ten years of research have, however, caused these to disappear.

Station of Champsperlard.

Excavating, M. Ronjon found at thirty or forty centimetres (twelve or sixteen inches) not only objects "préhistoriques," but also some rare bits of pottery and Roman tiles. Lower down, this mélange disappears, and the relics consist of fragments of millstones; calcined sandstone; cinders; charcoal; fragments of baked earthen vessels; remains of the mud or plastering of the huts, which still exhibit the impressions of the boughs which sustained it; pottery; worked flints; bits of *bronze*, broken animal bones, etc. Among the flint implements are arrow-heads, knives, scrapers, awls, nuclei, polished axes of flint and sometimes of crystalline rock, etc. The pottery is sometimes fine, sometimes coarse,—all made by hand. Among the bronzes were a bracelet, formed of a thin bronze wire bent in the form of a rude spiral, and a fragment of a javelin.

Almost at the surface was found a small bronze coin "belonging to the second age of iron, or the époque gauloise."

There were also worked bones. The fauna was ox, sheep, goat, stag, horse, etc.

We learn from these facts that on the surface, and *above* the Roman tiles (which were twelve or sixteen inches below), the flint implements occurred; that in the bed below that containing the fine pottery and the Roman tiles they found stone implements associated with bronze implements and ornaments; and, finally, that near the surface occurred a Gaulish coin,—either in or above the Roman stratum.

The iron that was doubtless once here has perished, and probably much of the bronze.

* Tome v. p. 73.

† Pages 374–378.

We have here the Stone and Bronze Ages and the Roman (or Iron) Age all confounded. Obviously, the stone and bronze were, during the period represented by the lower bed, used cotemporaneously; and then the stone continued to be used through (according to the archæologists) the two thousand years of the Bronze Age and the fifteen hundred of the Iron Age down to the advent of the Romans.

Grotto of Saint-Jean-d'Alcas.

At Saint-Jean-d'Alcas,* in Aveyron, we have an example of the association of numerous stone implements with bronze in a sepulchral grotto. The entrance was closed by two large slabs, and M. Cartailhac naturally inferred that the remains within had not been disturbed. The contents were great numbers of human bones (men, women, and children); a number of flint arrow-heads and lance-heads (these of large size); some small axes in serpentine, and one of green jade; and rings, beads, and pendants in stone, jade, *copper*, *glass*, etc.

(The dolmens in Aveyron number some two hundred; those in the neighborhood of Saint-Jean-d'Alcas are identical in the remains found with this grotto.)

Corberon.

M. Beauvais informs us of the occurrence of a stone axe in a deposit of Roman date. During some excavations on the site of a Roman villa at Corberon, Côte-d'Or, a polished stone axe was found, together with Samian pottery, and a sword, key, fragments of knives, etc. (all of iron). They belonged to the second or third century of our era.†

Isle de la Cité.

M. Figuier mentions the discovery of an ancient canoe in the bed of the Seine, at the extremity of the Cité, in Paris, which was presented to the late Emperor. Close by it were found a worked flint and various objects of bronze, among them a helmet and several swords.‡

Not far from the hamlet of Cernois, in a region called *Le Bâtardeau*, M. Morlot discovered, immediately beneath the soil, five slabs, which, he thinks, originally constituted a box designed to cover a sepulture. He found below these slabs the fragment of a polished hatchet in diorite, two knives, one of them of a beautiful red flint, fragments of pottery, and finally, "chose embarrassante," *a very small Gaulish medal.*

Some days afterwards, "perplexed by this strange fact," he resumed his explorations over a wider surface, and, "more and more astonished," he found—1, a beautiful flint lance-head; 2, an arrow-head; 3, two other flints; 4, a fragment of a bronze hatchet. Various objects of stone and bronze occurred in the neighborhood or environs of the

---

* Matériaux pour l'Histoire de l'Homme, tome iii. p. 487.

† Ib.

‡ Prim. Man, p. 178.

hamlet,—apparently of the same age. The fragment of an iron fibula has also been found at Cernois.*

If the archæologists were open to conviction, the facts at Alise would alone impress them with the unstable foundation on which their theory of the Three Ages rests. Alesia was the scene of the last battle between Cæsar and the Gauls. In B.C. 52, Cæsar, with six legions, laid siege to Gergovia. He was compelled by the revolt of the Ædui to raise the siege and march southward into the country of the Sequani, where he was followed by swarms of Gauls, who attacked him on his road. Vercingetorix, a noble Arvernian, who commanded the forces of the Ædui, was by far the ablest general whom Cæsar had yet encountered in Gaul. It was into Alesia, the capital of Burgundy, that Vercingetorix retreated, pursued by Cæsar. The town was regularly invested and besieged. An immense army of Gauls, however, soon approached for the relief of the place. These Cæsar defeated, and ultimately compelled Vercingetorix to surrender at discretion.

The trenches at Alise.

Now, in the trenches before Alise *the arms of the three eras have been found*,—stone, bronze, and iron,—all of the same date. The Gauls were decidedly in advance of the Germans and Britons, and, nevertheless, in the days of Julius Cæsar we find them armed with arrow-heads of flint and bronze swords, showing how utterly idle is the endeavor to throw back the Stone Age of the Swiss lakes five or six thousand years before the Christian era. The evidence from these trenches entirely corresponds with the express testimony of Tacitus with regard to the Germans, and with the evidence of the commingled bronze and iron arms found at Kingston on the Thames.†

In "Matériaux pour l'Histoire de l'Homme" a number of other places in France are specified where the stone implements have been found, belonging to the Gallo-Roman, the Merovingian, and even the Carlovingian epochs.

Thus, in Brittany, in the funeral vault of Plouvenez-Lochrist there were found twenty-two arrow-heads of flint and a poignard of bronze; in a Gallo-Roman sepulture at La Souterraine (Creuse), an arrow-head of flint; in the Gallo-Roman necropolis of Varennes-sur-Allier, flint arrow-heads; in the Merovingian sepultures of Puxieux (Moselle), an arrow-head and a lance-head of flint; in the funeral pits of Beaugency, stone axes; in the Gallo-Roman sepultures of Luneray (Seine-Inférieure), stone axes; in the grave of a Gallo-Roman oculist of the third century, stone axes, at St.-Privat-d'Allier; in the ruins of the Gallo-Roman villa of La Touratte (Cher), stone axes; in a Roman *sacellum*,

---

* Matériaux, 2e série, tome iv., 1873, p. 465.

† See Napoleon's Life of Cæsar, Eng. trans., vol. ii.

near Conches (Eure), the same; in another *sacellum*, near the Château des Roches (Sarthe), the same; in the Frankish cemetery of Labruyère (Côte-d'Or), the same; in the sarcophagi of Bray (Oise), the same; in a tumulus of the tower St.-Austrille (Creuse), certainly not earlier than the sixth and most probably as late as the eighth century, the same; and, finally, there is mention of these axes in the Life of St. Eloi by St.-Ouen.*

In an ancient iron-mine near Guéret (Creuse) M. Bouchardon obtained flint flakes and fragments of tiles.

At the oppidum of the Puy-de-Gaudy, assigned to the Bronze Age, a great number of polished stone axes were found.

In the grotto of La Magdeleine, described by M. Munier, in a paper entitled "Découvertes préhistoriques faites dans la chaine des Montagnes de la Gardéole," we are informed that he found many remains of the ox, horse, hog, deer, goat, rabbit, etc., along with bone awls, worked flints, two beautiful axes of jade, a beautiful bronze bracelet, a bronze pin, two bronze rings, passed the one through the other, a bronze rod, etc.†

The *Grotte des Morts*, near Durfort (Gard), is pronounced to be a sepulchral grotto of the age of polished stone. Some sixty implements of flint were found here,—lance-heads, arrow-heads, etc.,—along with worked bones. There were also found some twenty-five or thirty beads of copper, and a small copper punch or awl.‡

Here is an example from Lot-et-Garonne. In "Matériaux," M. L. Combes narrates the finding of a polished flint hatchet side by side with three instruments of iron, in the commune of Monsempron, fifty metres from the Lot, at the depth of more than a metre, under a kind of stone vessel. This vessel was broken, and contained ashes; and there were traces of fire on the hatchet. The iron implements were a pruning-knife; a gimlet; and a bit of squared iron, use unknown. This is called a "sepulture," but it appears to be a matter of doubt whether such was the fact.§

Dolmen of Caranda.

We find in the *Galaxy* for December, 1873, under the title of "Ancient Dolmen," a short account of the discovery of a dolmen in the vicinity of Caranda, department of Aisne, France, in which were found a skeleton, some lance- and arrow-tips, and a flint knife. From the description of the dolmen, it appears to us to have little antiquity; but the information given is too meagre to

* Matériaux, Août et Septembre, 1872, pp. 339–341.

† Ib., p. 383. Stone and metal and Roman coins were found together in the dolmen of Beaumont-sur-Oise. We are not acquainted with the details of the discovery, and can only make this general statement.

‡ Mat. pour l'Hist. de l'Homme, tome v. p. 249.

§ Tome iii. p. 63.

permit us to form any decided opinion. We only infer that the monument is not a "rude" one from the employment of such expressions as "pilasters" and "slabs" in describing it. But we are told that "around the dolmen, and on the same eminence," are some "ancient graves, in which occurred a number of flint implements." We are further told that with these flint implements occurred also "iron weapons." It is very likely the dolmen and the graves are of the same date; but this is unimportant. The point of interest is that "a number of flint implements" are found associated with the "iron weapons,"—showing beyond controversy that the flint implements continued in use after the introduction of iron.

The following examples occur in Italy: Italy.

In Dr. Keller's "Lake-Dwellings of Switzerland," mention is made of the discovery of forty skeletons in the year 1856, at Cumarola, near Modena, in Italy, simply buried in the earth three feet deep. Each had on its right side a socketed lance-head of copper, and on the left side a flint arrow-head. In addition, some of the skeletons had beside them, on the right side, a lance-head of very hard serpentine, while others had at the head a perforated stone celt.* It is a remarkable example of the cotemporaneous employment of bronze and stone weapons, on account of the number of the skeletons.

Cumarola.

Objects of flint were found in the *Caverna del Re Tiberio*, in the Apennines, near Imola, in the north of Italy, in association with pottery made on the wheel. M. Scarabelli found in this cave fragments of zinc, bronze, and iron, and at one metre below this upper bed, seventy-two little vases (black and red) made with the hand, fragments of wheel-made pottery, Roman and Etruscan vases, worked bones, and three flint knives.†

Caverna del Re Tiberio.

Objects of stone and bronze were found also at the sepulchral grotto of *Porco-Spino*, in Sicily. Polished stone hatchets and bronze hatchets occurred here together, along with very beautiful and entire vases, made with the hand.‡

Grotto of Porco-Spino.

The work quoted ("Matériaux pour l'Histoire de l'Homme") mentions also the occurrence of bronze and stone together in the cavern of *La Grande Barme*, near the city of Aix-les-Bains, in Savoy. A number of instruments in serpentine, diorite, flint, and bone were obtained here at the depth of several metres, and mingled with them were the remains of *bronze rings*.§

La Grande Barme.

---

* Keller, p. 237.

† Matériaux pour l'Histoire de l'Homme, Avril et Mai, 1872, p. 192.

‡ Ib., 3e Livraison, 1873, p. 117.

§ Ib., 4e Livraison, 1873, p. 159.

The Abbé Cherieci found stone implements mingled with bronze objects in an undisturbed stratum in a cave in the province of Reggio, at the foot of the Apennines. The account is contained in the Proceedings of the International Congress of Anthropology and Archæology, held in 1872, at Brussels. There were two beds or layers in the cave, the lower one of which contained no human traces except charcoal. The upper bed contained a hearth, from which three distinct floors of charcoal departed,—separated the one from the other by a thin layer of mud (two or three inches thick). About the fire-place, and in the two upper floors of this charcoal, were found several objects of bronze, and various stone implements, such as axes, awls, knife, saw, etc., together with fragments of hand-made pottery.

Cave of Reggio.

The objects seem to have been all found strictly together, and we are told by M. l'Abbé Cherieci that "since its deposition the soil had remained intact," excepting a single excavation, of little importance, undertaken by an amateur of natural history, who found seven stone axes, a bone awl, and some pottery.*

In the province of Terra di Bari, in Apulia, if we apprehend correctly the statement in "Matériaux pour l'Histoire de l'Homme,"† M. Bonucci found a great number of stone weapons and implements,—of flint, chalcedony, jasper, obsidian, etc.,—some of them very highly finished. With them he found a number of *sharks' teeth*, mounted with *silver*, so as to permit them to be suspended as ornaments.

Flint and silver.

An extremely interesting discovery has been made in Spain. The *Cueva de los Murciélagos*, or the Cave of the Bats, is in Andalusia, and has been described by Señor Don Manuel de Gongora y Martinez.‡ This cave has several chambers. In one of these, three human skeletons were found, around the skull of one of which was a diadem of pure gold of twenty-four carats, valued at twelve pounds. At another point—perhaps in a different chamber—were three other skeletons, and a cap of *esparto* (Spanish broom), with marks, apparently, of blood upon it. In another chamber twelve skeletons were found, surrounding a female skeleton, which last was "admirably preserved," and which was clothed in a garment of skins, open at the side. About the neck was a necklace of *esparto,* from the rings of which hung marine shells, and (from the centre) a carved boar's tusk. Ear-rings of black stone were also by the skeleton.

Spain.

Cave of the Bats.

The skeleton with the gold diadem was clothed in a fine short tunic of *esparto*,—the other male skeletons being clothed similarly, but in

* Congrès d'Anthropologie et d'Archéologie Préhistoriques, 1872, p. 363.

† See 2e série, tome iv., 1873, p. 434.

‡ See Archæological Journal, No. 108, 1870: paper by Lord Talbot de Malahide, F.S.A., p. 235.

coarser material. Some of them wore sandals of *esparto*, several of which were elaborately worked. Close to the skeletons were found flint knives; hatchets; arrows with flint points fixed to rough sticks with bitumen; rude, but sharp, arms of silex, some of them kept in purses of *esparto;* vessels of clay; a large piece of skin; very thick knives and pickaxes of bone; and spoons of wood, with large low bowls.

At E (another point in a diagram given of the cave) lay fifty bodies, all with sandals and dresses of *esparto*, arms of stone, etc. There occurred here also a number of small baskets. The bodies were reduced to the condition of mummies, and "were covered with flesh." The dresses and the baskets still retained their original colors. The vases were very rude, but had spouts and handles. Some of them were sun-dried, others were baked.

We have here the Stone Age in all its purity; and this is in Spain, which had its Phœnician cities 1200 B.C., and which was conquered in great part by the Carthaginians. It is obvious that the remains have little claim to antiquity. They are almost certainly of a date later than the Christian era.

Example from Portugal.

The following example is from Portugal. It is mentioned by M. Ribeiro, well known as the discoverer of certain alleged traces of man in the Miocene strata of the vicinity of Lisbon. During a discussion in the International Congress of Anthropology, at Brussels, in 1872, with regard to the antiquity of iron, M. Ribeiro made the statement that he had found in the soil of a cavern near the town of Otta, some twenty-five miles from Lisbon, a fragment of iron (apparently part of a nail) consolidated in a breccia with worked flints and broken animal bones. M. Ribeiro regards these remains as, of course, post-quaternary, but is entirely unable to indicate any age for the deposit. "Voilà," he exclaims, "une question que de nouvelles explorations seules peuvent élucider." *

Mr. Boyd Dawkins gives us an account of the caves of this country. The *Casada-Moura*, he tells us, presents two strata. The lower contained flint weapons, and remains of the fox, lynx, brown bear, etc. The upper had implements of stone and bone, and *bronze arrow-heads*, with the remains of horse, bat, rabbit, dormouse, sheep, goat, etc.

The other caverns of Portugal examined by him, he informs us, present "the same features." †

Germany.

M. Pruner-Bey gives an account of the discovery of iron arms and flint arms in a tumulus in Germany (farther illustrating our previous statement from Mr. Evans with regard to that country), at the village of Minsleben (county of Wernigerode). They found

* Congrès Internat. d'Anthrop. et d'Archéolog. Préhist., 1872, p. 504.

† Internat. Cong. Prehist. Archæol., 1868, p. 82.

here forty-six skeletons lying side by side in contiguous graves, along with urns filled with ornaments and ashes. By the side of the fragments of pottery were a great number of flint knives and arrow-heads. With these were two knives of iron, one by the skeleton of a child, the other by that of an adult. The only animal bones occurring were those of the head of a horse.* It is as clear as the noonday sun that the warriors who used these flint weapons were living (in point of time) in the (so-called) Iron Age.

Other examples from this country were mentioned by M. Schaaffhausen at the Brussels International Congress in 1872. "The Museum of Bonn," he said, "has one of these axes of jade, which is in appearance *new*. . . . It was found among Roman remains. . . . There are other similar axes in the Museum of Mayence; these have been discovered in the midst of Roman fortifications. It is therefore that I consider them [the axes of jade] as having belonged to the last period of the age of stone."†

---

* Matériaux pour l'Histoire de l'Homme, tome i. p. 400.

† Cong. d'Anthrop. et d'Archéol., 1872, p. 356.

CHAPTER XXIV.

THE STONE AGE AND THE BRONZE AGE AMONG THE MEXICANS AND PERUVIANS.

These Nations found by the Spaniards using simultaneously both Stone and Bronze.—Their Great Hewn Stone Edifices erected with the Use of Bronze Tools.—Obsidian used also in the Arts.—Bronze and Obsidian Weapons in their Armies.

WHEN the Spaniards appeared in Mexico and Peru a few centuries ago, they found in both of those countries, the civilization of one being entirely independent of that of the other, and no communication existing between them, a state of things which entirely subverts the Three Ages of the archæologists. They found there the Stone Age and the Metal Age both in existence at one and the same time,—stone weapons and stone tools side by side with bronze weapons and bronze tools. The subjects of the Incas and the Aztecs were both highly-enlightened and skilful nations, the remains of whose cities and edifices and public works astonish us like the Pyramids and Theban temples, and the aqueducts of Rome. They seem to have had copper in the greatest abundance; they understood how to convert it into a bronze capable of shaping and cutting the most massive and the hardest stones; and yet we find them freely using obsidian for swords, spear-heads, knives, scissors, chisels, and other implements.

Co-existence of the Stone and the Bronze Age.

We have mentioned particularly the Aztecs of Mexico and the Inca race of Peru, but our remarks apply equally to the yet more advanced people of Central America.

Prescott informs us that the Peruvians had neither the iron ploughshare nor draught-animals. They used as a plough "a strong, sharp-pointed stake, traversed by a horizontal piece, ten or twelve inches from the point, on which the ploughman might set his foot and force it into the ground." Six or eight strong men dragged it along. This rude implement, Mr. Prescott remarks, "was perhaps not much inferior to the wooden instrument introduced into its stead by the European conquerors."*

Testimony of Prescott.

Similar ploughs are used at this day in the East. A writer in the

* See Prescott's Conquest of Peru, vol. i. pp. 136, 137.

"Biblical Treasury"* makes the following statement: "The ploughs consist of a great block of wood, somewhat resembling a shoe with a pointed toe, and are without coulter or share, with one handle and long curved tongue. . . . I saw several yoke of bullocks dragging a cart with massive stone wheels, whose weight, I should think, was greater than the whole burden of the cart."

Eastern agricultural implements.

The Palestine plough, he remarks, consists of two poles, which cross each other at the ends near the ground. The pole turned to the oxen is fastened to the yoke, and draws the implement; the one towards the driver serves at one extremity as a ploughshare, and at the other as a handle.

All this is in the midst of the abounding stores of metal found in this age all over the world. Is it astonishing that the rude Britons of Yorkshire, or the rude dwellers on Constance, should have used polished stone weapons, when the Peruvians of the sixteenth century, as well as the Spaniards of the sixteenth century, used sharpened poles to plough their fields, surrounded in the one instance by the splendid monuments of the Augustan era of Spain, and in the other by the wonderful structures and arts of the dynasty of the Incas? when on the eastern shores of the Mediterranean to-day the same plough is used, and stone is employed instead of wood and iron for the wheels of their farm-carts? This single fact lights up at once this whole question of the Stone Age so much talked about in the works on archæology. It illustrates perfectly how the metals may have abounded in Southern Europe when the Northern races continued, notwithstanding a certain measure of intercourse with the South, to persist in the use of flint, and porphyry, and serpentine.

"The tools of the Peruvians," says Mr. Prescott, "were of stone, or more frequently of copper. But the material on which they relied for the execution of their most difficult tasks was formed by combining a very small portion of tin with copper. This composition gave a hardness to the metal which seems to have been little inferior to that of steel." M. de Humboldt brought back to Europe one of these tools, a chisel, found in a silver-mine near Cuzco. It contained 0.94 of copper and 0.06 of tin.†

Farther evidence from Prescott.

With these tools the Peruvian not only hewed into shape porphyry and granite, "but by his patient industry accomplished works which the European would not have ventured to undertake."

The Mexicans had the same bronze tool, an alloy of tin and copper, and with this they cut not only metals, but, with the aid of a siliceous dust, such substances as basalt, porphyry, amethysts, and emeralds.‡

* Vol. i. pp. 1, 2.

† Conquest of Peru, vol. i. p. 152.

‡ Conquest of Mexico, vol. i. p. 139.

The Peruvian edifices were usually built of porphyry or granite, sometimes of brick.

Besides their bronze tools, the Mexicans, we are informed, used others "of *itztli*, or obsidian, a dark, transparent mineral, exceedingly hard, found in abundance in their hills. They made it into knives, razors, and their serrated swords. It took a keen edge, though soon blunted." *

At the battle in the region of Tlascala which took place between the Mexicans and Cortez, the Indians are described as having "their naked bodies gaudily painted," and carrying "spears and darts tipped with points of transparent *itztli* or fiery copper."

Their "various weapons," the historian states elsewhere, "were pointed with bone, or the mineral *itztli* (obsidian)." Again: "Their spears and arrows were also frequently headed with copper. Instead of a sword, they bore a two-handed staff, about three feet and a half long, in which, at regular distances, were inserted, transversely, sharp blades of *itztli*." †

---

* Conquest of Mexico, vol. i. p. 140. † Ib., pp. 441, 442.

CHAPTER XXV.

A GREEK HERCULANEUM.

THIS is the title of an article in the *Dublin University Magazine* for 1870, referring to the discovery of a buried Greek city in one of the volcanic islands of Santorin. It appears that the cliffs here consist of horizontal beds of black lava, alternating with layers of reddish scoriæ and violet-gray ashes, and, capping all, a stratum of *pumice-stone* of a brilliant white color.

This pumice has been long quarried for, and, mixed with lime, used as a cement. During the excavations a few years since, the workmen, digging deeper than had been done before, came upon regular courses of stones. Further investigation brought to light several rooms built of irregular blocks of lava, uncemented, but having the interstices filled with red volcanic earth, intermingled with tortuous branches of olive in a charred condition. The roof was supported by wooden posts. Outside of one of the walls of one of these rooms there was found a curious set of *hewn stone blocks* of large size, laid regularly over each other, in the top of which occurred a cylindrical cavity an inch in depth. Great quantities of pottery were also found, among which were terra-cotta jars,—some with a capacity of several gallons,—and which were the counterpart of those in which the modern islanders store their corn. These jars contained barley, chick-pease, and coriander-seed. There were found also smaller specimens of much finer work, one form of which was a bright-yellow vase with beautiful arabesques. There were, besides, broad basins with little handles, cups, platters, etc. Some of the basins were found "in the stables" (which are mentioned), containing chopped straw. The mangers and horse-troughs were large blocks of lava, with shallow rectangular cavities cut in them. A number of skeletons of sheep, both old and young, were also found. Other articles were a lava oil-press, hand-mills, weavers' stone discs, a stone knife or lance-head, and a flint saw with very regular teeth. Obsidian arrow-heads (chipped) and knives of obsidian were also found. But not a morsel of iron or bronze was met with. The only metal obtained was two gold rings, which were the links of a chain.

These relics were either procured or examined by M. Fouquet,* who

* Or Fouqué.

seems to be an archæologist, and who has published an account of them in the *Revue des Deux Mondes* for October, 1869. He believes that we have here the traces of a very ancient civilization. He tells us that Greece was at one time united to Africa and Asia, from which it was separated by a great convulsion, speaks of the period of the great pachyderms, and refers Santorin and Therasia to the Stone Age.

The Reviewer reaches the conclusion that the remains must be older than 1500 years B.C., and regards them as perhaps dating at least 2000 years before our era. He informs us that the Phœnicians invaded Greece 1500 years B.C., and remarks that all of their remains are *above* the pumice, as are also remains similar to those below the pumice. M. Fouquet considers the old Therasians even more ancient than this, and calls attention to the fact that the pottery (there being no clay in the island) proves the existence of a foreign trade, as do the flint and the obsidian. But there is no trace of Egyptian art among the remains, and therefore these people must have lived before the Egyptians of the third and fourth dynasties!

It is astonishing that people can gravely write such nonsense as this. The pottery and the gold ought to be sufficient to shut out the idea that these islanders were barbarians in their "Stone Age." It appears, farther, that they had *horses*, which they fed out of hewn stone troughs. The horse does not appear to have been known in Egypt before the time of Joseph; he is not represented on the monuments earlier than the eighteenth dynasty. The hewn stone steps, and the lava troughs, prove also, positively, the use of metal tools. That stone implements were in use along with metal, was no doubt the fact in the case.

The author of the article in the *British Quarterly Review* for October, 1872, entitled "The Present Phase of Prehistoric Archæology," to which we have already referred, gives us what may be taken to be an authoritative judgment with regard to the remains found in Therasia. "The absence of metal," he tells us, "implies that they were living in the Neolithic Age." In the very next line he says that "the dressed blocks of stone used in some parts of the walls implies that they were good stone-masons, while their pottery proves them to have been possessed of a taste almost Eastern in its delicacy." For our part, we consider it very certain that these "good stone-masons," and the fabricators or importers of this beautiful yellow pottery "almost Eastern in its delicacy," were in the possession of metal. But it serves our argument better to admit the Reviewer to be correct: we have then the Stone Age in Greece in association with the most elegant vases and vessels, gold, the horse, and walls of masonry,—a civilization like that of Peru and Mexico, *without* the Peruvian and the Mexican bronze. We may grant that it was 1500 or 2000 years B.C.; and from this it would result that the people of the Stone Age were neither very ancient nor very savage; that M. Morlot, Sir Charles Lyell, and Sir John Lubbock are unwarranted in assigning to the Neolithic Age an antiquity of seven thousand years; and that it may be fairly inferred that the Neolithic Age in Britain was about B.C. 700 or 1000, as the races there were certainly eight hundred or one thousand years behind the Greeks of the Ægean Sea.

Testimony of Homer.

We shall be the better prepared, however, to form an opinion about the chronology of this "Greek Herculaneum" when we have explored a Dardanian "Pompeii" which has just been exhumed in the vicinity of the same Grecian Archipelago.

Before narrating these wonderful revelations, we may premise that Dr. Smith, in his "Dictionary of Greek and Roman Antiquities," makes the statement that the Greeks used commonly arrow-heads of bronze, as is expressed by the epithet χαλκῆρης, "fitted with bronze," which Homer applies to an arrow. (Il., xiii. 650, 662.)* Another Homeric epithet (τριγλώχιν) is illustrated by the forms of the arrow-heads, all of bronze, represented (says Dr. Smith) in the wood-cuts (which he gives). Two of these, he says, are from the plains of Marathon. The fourth specimen was also found in Attica. With regard to the spear, Homer defines it as δορυ χαλκοβαρές, "a pole heavy with bronze." (Od., xi. 532.)†

The Roman *pugio*, or dagger, says the same authority, was "commonly of bronze." It was worn by the Romans and Gauls, and the custom continued in England and the adjacent nations to the Middle Ages.‡

Mr. Evans.

Mr. Evans speaks to the same effect. We learn from Pausanias, he says (see Laconica, cap. 3), that all the weapons of the Homeric heroes were of *bronze*. He quotes Homer's description of the axe of Pisander and the arrow of Meriones; and cites also the spear of Achilles in the temple of Minerva at Phaselis, the point and ferrule of which were of bronze; and he mentions also the sword of Memnon in the temple of Æsculapius, at Nicomedia, which was of bronze. "There is," says Mr. Evans, "in Homer, constant mention of arms, axes, and adzes of bronze, and though iron is also named, it is of far less frequent occurrence. According to the Arundelian marbles (Wilk. Anc. Egyp., iii. 241), it was discovered only one hundred and eighty-eight years before the Trojan war, though of course such a date must be purely conjectural."§ In the time of Pausanias (A.D. 174) the Sarmatians are mentioned as unacquainted with iron.

---

* See Smith, art. *Sagitta*, p. 1001.

† Smith, art. *Hasta*, p. 587.

‡ See p. 975.

§ Anc. Stone Imp., p. 4.

With regard to the date of bronze implements among the Romans, we may remark that eight guilds of craftsmen were numbered among the institutions of king Numa: to wit, the flute-blowers, the goldsmiths, the coppersmiths, the carpenters, the fullers, the dyers, the potters, and the shoemakers. "It is remarkable," says the historian who makes this statement, "that there appears no special guild of workers in iron. This affords fresh confirmation of the fact that the manufacture of iron was of comparatively late introduction in Latium." *

Bronze among the Romans.

* Mommsen's History of Rome, vol. i. p. 258.

CHAPTER XXVI.

THE RUINS OF TROY.

The Complete Subversion of the Theory of the Archæologists by the Discoveries of Dr. Schliemann on the Site of Ancient Troy.—The Trojans of Homer a Stone-using People.—No Traces of Iron.—The Five Beds of Relics, indicating as many Settlements.—The Bronze found *under* the Stone.—Fine Pottery.—Recent Use of Stone.—A Link between the Successors of the Homeric Trojans and the Lake-Dwellers of Northern Italy.—Discovery of an Earlier Occupation than that of the Trojans.—Consideration of the Question whether this is actually the Site of Troy.

A WHOLE page of the New York *Herald* for December 21, 1872, is taken up with a letter from Dr. Henry Schliemann, accompanied by a map, giving an account of his researches at Troy. Dr. Schliemann was engaged during 1871 and 1872 in conducting these explorations, and has, it appears, succeeded at last in discovering the site of this famous city.

The ruins of the "historic" times, he tells us, extend to the depth of one and a half metres, and never more than two metres. From two to four metres there were no stones. It was evident that during this period the houses were of wood, as was shown by the calcined ruins of wood. At four to seven metres there was an entire absence of metal, but great quantities of stone implements of all sorts were found, along with fine pottery. The houses in this stratum were built of small stones, cemented with earth. At seven to ten metres all the houses were built of unburned brick, and a great many copper weapons and tools occurred, though "for the most part the implements were of black stone (diorite)." At ten metres he came upon an immense mass of large stones, and at once "concluded that he had reached the veritable ruins." This progress had been made by the end of November, 1871.

In April, 1872, he began operations again with a force of one hundred or one hundred and twenty men. He opened a cutting or platform seventy metres broad by fourteen metres deep, but did not find the virgin soil even at this depth. He thereupon cleared out a well discovered in the previous October, and found the natural rock at the depth of sixteen metres.

Subsequently he continued his investigations, which his letter goes on to describe.

1. *Remains of the Ancient City.* At the depth of from ten to sixteen metres he found thousands of round objects of terra-cotta. On the virgin soil he found a number of copper nails, but there was no trace of metal weapons or implements. On the other hand, he found hammers and axes of diorite, weights of granite, beautifully polished wedges of a splendid transparent greenstone, a number of small flint saws, hand millstones of lava,* pieces of alabaster and punches of bone, terra-cotta discs, a lamp in the form of a bowl, boars' teeth, small shells, sharks' bones, and great quantities of fine pottery. There were black urns with Assyrian ornamentation, shining black bowls with a tube on each side, small black pots representing the human face, etc., etc., bespeaking "the opulence and fine taste" of the primitive Trojans, and evidently made by a very different people from those represented in the relic-bed at the depth of seven to ten metres. Many of these vessels were ornamented on the inner surface, as well as without.

Stone and bronze in the first relic-bed.

The Trojan palaces, says Dr. Schliemann, were of great size, as is evidenced by the quantity or number of the immense hewn and unhewn stones which cover the fragments of pottery in layers of from four to six metres thick.

After the Trojans came another race.

2. On the ruins of the old city the successors of the first population erected buildings whose foundations consisted of small stones held together with clay; the walls being constructed of unburnt brick. This is at the depth of seven to ten metres. In this stratum the weapons and implements, as we have stated, were chiefly of stone and bone, but a number of copper weapons and instruments were found. The stone implements were hammers, millstones, wedges, pestles, weights, mortars, discs, saws, etc. Many and various specimens of pottery were found: drinking-cups, "with a handle below in the shape of a crown;" fantastic red goblets in the form of a gigantic champagne-glass, with a large handle on each side; drinking-cups ten to twelve centimetres high, ornamented with a female face in high relief, and without handles; a great profusion of finely-burned but uncolored pottery, from a metre to one and a half metres in diameter; curious vessels in the form of an animal with a long tail and long projecting neck and mouth; terra-cottas representing the priapus, etc., etc.

Stone and bronze in the second relic-bed.

The Sun invariably appears on *all* the terra-cottas in all of the beds,

---

* Probably from Santorin.

showing that it was a symbol common to all of the races which occupied the site of Troy. And the same remark is true of the symbol of the Cross.

Stone alone in the third age of Troy.

3. At from four to seven metres there are the relics of a third occupation, the remains being still characteristic of an Aryan race, by whom Troy was again destroyed. There is here *no trace at all of metal.* The implements are stone, and not so finely finished as those in the layer just described. The architecture has also changed. For the walls of the buildings here were constructed of small stones and clay. The terra-cottas are also of inferior quality to those in the stratum below, though the forms are graceful. Some of them are after the pattern of hour-glasses, and probably were such; others resemble teacups. We find also goblets with the human face as in the specimens above mentioned, but the work is very rudely done.

Stone and bronze in the fourth age of Troy.

4. There was yet another epoch at Troy prior to the so-called "historic" period. This is represented by the relic-bed at the depth of two to four metres. The city was destroyed for the third time, and a yet ruder and poorer race succeeded the people represented by the four to seven metres bed. They are still Aryans. The pottery is scarcer and coarser still. The weapons and implements were of copper. Many lances, knives, and nails of this metal were found. There were no stone implements, excepting weights and handmills, and saws and knives of volcanic glass and silex. A saw, twelve centimetres long by four wide, beautifully made, was among these implements.

The Hellenic city.

5. Above these remains, that is, at the depth of one and two metres, are the remains of the "historic" or Greek period. Here there is Hellenic masonry of very large stones.

The excavations of Dr. Schliemann were continued in 1873. He has published a volume in Leipsic, narrating his discoveries, which we have not seen. We have, however, in the New York *Tribune* of March 2, 1874, a long letter (illustrated with cuts) from Mr. Bayard Taylor (who saw the proof-sheets of Dr. Schliemann's work in Germany), giving a synopsis of the volume. We have also seen in European periodicals reviews of the work. From these sources we gather the following additional facts:

The Homeric Troy represented by bed No. 2.

Dr. Schliemann now believes that bed No. 2 represents the ruins of the Homeric Troy, and bed No. 1 he refers to an occupation of this site antedating the Homeric Troy. He naturally refers in this connection to the tradition of an earlier destruction of Troy by Hercules.* In bed No. 2 he dis-

* Iliad, v. 642.

covered a tower forty feet in diameter, the foundations (as he believes) of the Temple of Minerva; a house with eight rooms, adjoining the tower; and many human bones, among them two entire skeletons, wearing copper helmets. He found also a number of copper lance-heads, fourteen copper weapons which he considers to be battle-axes, seven double-edged copper daggers, a copper knife, and also the fragment of a sword, and many beautiful vases with the owl-faced Minerva upon them. Also a large copper dish, forty-nine centimetres in diameter, surrounded by a rim four centimetres high,—probably a shield; a copper kettle; a silver vase; a copper vase; a round bottle of pure gold; a heavy gold goblet, and a drinking-vessel of gold in the form of a ship; five silver vases, a silver goblet, and a silver bowl; in one of the silver vases, two magnificent golden head-bands, one frontlet, and four splendid golden ear-pendants; fifty-six golden ear-rings, and thousands of very small rings, pendants, dice, buttons, etc., all of gold; six golden bracelets, etc., etc. Also many stone weapons.

Farther discoveries.

At thirty feet below the surface he discovered a street, near the tower. It was sixteen feet wide, and paved with stone blocks about four feet square. Believing that he was near the Scæan Gate, he followed this street with his excavations until he came to a large massive double gate, the copper bolts of which were found among the rubbish. Between this gate and the tower he discovered the foundations of a large Trojan (using his own language) house, whose dimensions with the treasures found in it lead Dr. Schliemann to the belief that it may properly be called the House of Priam. It was in the immediate neighborhood of this house that the treasures referred to above were found. They were closely packed in a quadrangular space, surrounded with wood ashes, and near them lay a copper key, four inches in length. The fashion of the Trojan jewelry is entirely original, and offers no resemblance to that of Assyria or Egypt.

Among other evidences of the destruction of Troy by a fierce conflagration, Dr. Schliemann found "a layer of slags of melted lead and copper, in some places an inch thick, extending over the whole site of the city." With the exception of the stately edifice of massive stone near the "Scæan Gate," nearly all the houses of Troy were built of unburned brick, with sills of hewn stone.

We are now told that in stratum No. 3 "a few copper implements have been found," though the stone implements occur by "thousands." The fragments of two lyres of stone and one of ivory show that this stone-age race possessed a knowledge of music.

Wheel-made pottery occurs first in bed No. 2.

Some of the hand-made pottery in the several beds bears a close resemblance to that of Cyprus and Santorin.

From Mr. Bayard Taylor's account we derive the very interesting statement that in bed 3 several of the terra-cotta discs "prove to be precisely identical, in shape, size, and emblematic decoration, *with those found in the Lake-Dwellings of Northern Italy.*" Both refer directly to India, "to the Sanskrit myths of *Pramantha*, the far earlier origin of the Greek Prometheus."

A link with the Lake-Dwellers.

We get thus an approximate date for the lacustrine habitations of North Italy: they are more recent than the Trojan war.

Many of the patterns on these discs, and also on certain terra-cotta *bells*, are well-known Vedic symbols,—such as the hare (a symbol of the moon), the tree of life, the caterpillar, the peculiar cross called in Sanskrit *swastika*, etc.

Vedic symbols.

A few fragments of inscriptions have been found, belonging apparently to the Trojan era. Prof. Max Müller thinks he has recognized one containing Semitic letters, and another, appearing on a bone or a piece of red slate, discovered in the Palace of Priam, contains, he remarks, "some decidedly Phœnician letters in their earliest form."

Inscriptions.

Other inscriptions appear to have been read by Professor Gomperz, of Vienna, by the application of the Cyprian alphabet. One he reads as ἴλαι or ἴλα, "Be gracious;" another as ἐγώ ταπατόρῳ, which he translates, "I dedicate this to the goddess Apaturos," a name of Athene or Aphrodite; a third, by being read from right to left, yielded the words ταγῷ δίῳ, "to the divine leader or prince." Prof. Max Müller remarks on these readings that "if I speak still with some diffidence, it is chiefly because I only know the Cyprian letters from the types cast by the Berlin Academy, not from the original Cyprian inscriptions. . . . The reading of the last inscription in particular inspires confidence."

The most important variation from the early papers of Dr. Schliemann which appears in his book, as the reader will have observed, is the identification of the Homeric Ilium with bed No. 2, and the recognition of an earlier race than the Homeric Trojans in bed No. 1.

The positions taken in our present work are strikingly corroborated by the evidence of these facts.

Our views confirmed by these discoveries.

The first occupiers of this locality—an early Aryan race —used bronze* and stone cotemporaneously. They seem

* Dr. Schliemann constantly speaks of *copper;* but he ought to have known that blocks of stone are not hewn with copper or stone tools. He has now satisfied himself that some of the implements, at least, which he described as copper, are *bronze.* Up to the last moment Dr. Schliemann insisted that all of the metallic implements found, except in the Hellenic stratum, were of *pure copper.* He had them analyzed by Prof. Landerer, Professor of Chemistry at Athens. A more recent analysis of some other specimens, made by M. Damour of Lyons, and mentioned at the close of Dr. Schliemann's book, shows that

to have been, in civilization, superior to any race which followed them, until we come to the Greek settlement. We have in this stratum, taken alone, and leaving what follows out of the account, a complete refutation of the Stone, Bronze, and Iron Ages.

Like the Mexicans and the Peruvians, the first settlers on the hill of Hissarlik, along with their weapons and tools of bronze and copper, used weapons and tools of diorite, granite, greenstone, flint, and lava. There is no room for equivocation here. The case is conclusive. The example is on an extended scale,—like Solutré.

Like the Mexicans and Peruvians, this pre-Trojan population were surrounded by objects of luxury and refinement, and enjoyed doubtless a civilization similar, if inferior, to that prevailing at the same time on the Euphrates and the Tigris and in Phœnicia.

The Trojans of the Iliad follow this race. *They continue the cotemporaneous use of bronze and stone:* so that we actually have at Troy in beds Nos. 1 and 2—that is, at the depth of seven metres and down to the native rock at the depth of sixteen metres—*the continued cotemporaneous use of bronze and stone throughout the entire period or periods represented by these two relic-beds.* The archæologists are willing to admit, as we have stated, that one age sometimes runs into that which follows, but it is only, as they allege, for a brief period, and does not affect the substantial, independent, and separate existence of the Three Ages, which, as they further allege, were each for a protracted period, and, during each of those protracted periods, plainly distinguishable the one from the other. But at Troy the occupiers of stratum "ten to sixteen" have used during their occupation both metal and stone; and then the race which succeeded them—from seven to ten metres—kept up the conjoint employment of these materials until their city was destroyed.

Then follows settlement No. 3; and here *there is hardly any trace of metal at all.* The Stone Age, confounding the entire system of the Archæologists and Anthropologists, follows the Bronze Age! When was this?

The Trojans were originally called *Dardanians.* Homer places Hector and Paris in the seventh generation from Dardanos; thus: 1. Dardanos; 2. Erichthonios; 3. Tros; 4. Ilos; 5. Laomedon; 6. Priam; 7. Hector. We may suppose, therefore, that the interval between Dardanos and Hector was about two hundred years.

In the Egyptian records it is mentioned that in the fourth year of Rameses II. (the Sesostris of the Greeks) the Khita (that is, the Hit-

these, at least, are bronze,—one containing four per cent. of tin, and the other nine per cent. If this last analysis had not been made, Sir John Lubbock would doubtless have believed firmly that the hewn stones of the first settlement were cut with stone tools.

tites) organized a confederacy against him, which included, besides other Asiatic nations, the peoples of Asia Minor. Among the latter the following are enumerated: the Mysians, the Lycians, the Pisidians, and the Dardanians. According to the French Egyptologists, this was in the year B.C. 1406. We have thus (approximately fixed) a date when the inhabitants of Troas were called Dardanians. They were called Trojans two hundred years later; *i.e.*, B.C. 1206. The fall of Troy may have been as recent as this; it may have been one hundred and fifty years earlier. It ought to date between B.C. 1356 and B.C. 1206.

Herodotus adopts the date 1270 B.C.

The date (1184 B.C.) which has been transmitted to us from antiquity is after Eratosthenes.

We may fairly conclude that the date assigned by Herodotus is near the mark; and as the thickness of bed No. 3 (some ten feet) may presumably represent an occupation of a couple of centuries, we have the Stone Age in full flower on the Hellespont as late as about 1070 B.C., amid the blaze of the Phrygian, the Lydian, the Carian, the Phœnician —not to add, the Assyrian—civilization.

Probable connection with the invasions of the Cimmerians.

As there is little doubt that the tribes on the north coasts of the Black Sea frequently invaded Asia Minor, it is highly probable that this third relic-bed belongs to some such irruption. We know from Herodotus that the Cimmerians, in the reign of Ardys, the son of Gyges, "driven from their homes by the nomads of Scythia, entered Asia, and captured Sardis, all but the citadel." * This was in the seventh century B.C. They carried their devastations over all the fairest regions of Lower Asia. In Ionia they ravaged the valley of the Caÿster, besieged Ephesus, and, according to some accounts, burned the temple of Artemis in its vicinity; after which they proceeded southward into the plain of the Mæander, and (as is said) sacked the city of Magnesia.†

The Cimmerians.

Strabo tells us, however, that "the Cimmerians, who are also named Trerones, or some tribe of them, *frequently* overran the right-hand shores of the Pontus, and the parts adjacent,—invading sometimes the Paphlagonians, sometimes the Phrygians." ‡ Elsewhere § he speaks of their invasions of Æolis and Ionia about the time of Homer by the way of the Bosporus; while Eusebius places an incursion of the Cimmerians into Asia in the reign of Cadmus, King of Attica, three hundred years before the first Olympiad,—about 1076 B.C.

Even the fourth relic-bed (two to four metres) at Troy, which termi-

* Herod., p. 15.

† See Rawlinson.

‡ Strabo, i. p. 61. The Cimmerians, from this statement, were no doubt mingled with Thracian tribes.

§ Strabo, i. p. 6, iii. p. 149.

nates about 650 B.C., is strewn with flint implements. We have even flint *saws*. There is no iron in any of the beds below the uppermost one: it is possible that it may have perished; but the probability is that it was never used (unless in rare instances) until the foundation of the later Greek city.

It may be profitable to compare with what we have thus discovered by actually *digging* on the plains of Troy, the declaration of Sir John Lubbock as to what *ought* to have been found on the principles of archæology. On page 5 of "Pre-historic Times" this able writer remarks, "We may, therefore, consider that the Trojan war took place during the period of transition from the Bronze* to the Iron Age." We can imagine Sir John's bewilderment when he hears from Dr. Schliemann.

Is this really the site of Troy?

Of course we are aware that a question has been raised as to whether it is really *Troy* which is represented by these remains: indeed, some of our modern philosophers (reminding us of Bishop Berkeley's metaphysical system) doubt whether there ever was such a place at all! The decision of this question one way or the other does not affect the main value of Dr. Schliemann's discoveries. Whatever the name of the people or of the city formerly occupying this site, we find that implements of bronze and stone were used at the same time during the periods represented by the first and second settlements; and that a stone age, represented by bed No. 3, succeeded the bronze of Nos. 2 and 1,—a yet ruder people, using bronze and stone, next succeeding, and who are represented by bed No. 4. We have also an approximate date for this bronze-and-stone people of the fourth bed: they immediately preceded the Greek city of historic times, which had its beginning about 650 or 600 B.C. We know, therefore, that stone implements, along with bronze implements, were used in this region of the world down to the time of Tyrtæus and the birth of Solon.

This question does not affect the main results.

We learn also that races may use flint knives and saws without being savages; for we find in the first three beds, along with stone implements, beautiful objects in gold and silver, finely-wrought pottery, objects in ivory and ebony, and, we may add, evidences that these ancient people were acquainted with the alphabet.

We think, however, that there is no reason to doubt that we have here the veritable Troy of Homer. It is very well known that in modern times there has been much controversy about the site of Troy. There was none in ancient times until a certain Demetrius of Skepsis, about B.C. 250, raised a question on the subject, suggesting that the

* The Bronze Age is represented to have lasted about two thousand years.

Greek city which bore the name of Troy, and which Alexander and Xerxes had visited as the traditional site of the Homeric Ilium, was too near the sea for the battles described in the Iliad. To allow more space for the theatre of these conflicts, he located old Troy at a place called the village of the Ilians (the modern *Akshi-kuhi*). Strabo, two hundred and fifty years afterwards, adopted this opinion, which, however, met with little acceptance among the ancients. Up to this time the concurrent voice of antiquity had located Ilium where Dr. Schliemann has found it. When Xerxes was about to cross the Hellespont, we learn from Herodotus that he went up to the "Pergamus of Priam" (on the site of Hissarlik) and sacrificed a thousand oxen to the Ilian Athena. A similar visit was paid to the sacred spot by Alexander the Great when he marched to the conquest of Asia. He dedicated there his armor, and took away some preserved in the temple which was traditionally connected with some of the Homeric heroes. Dr. Schliemann has effectually disposed of the theory of Demetrius and Strabo by digging into the site of the "Village of the Ilians." He found nothing but the virgin rock.

In modern times (towards the close of the last century) a French traveller, named Chevalier, found, as he conceived, the sources of the Scamander in two springs, one hot and the other cold (in conformity with Homer's statement), near the Turkish village of *Bunarbashi*, some eight or nine miles from the sea; and he accordingly fixed upon Bunarbashi as the site of Troy. This suggestion met with acceptance, and many scholars have been inclined to adopt it; although the traditional site has still had able advocates. The claims of Bunarbashi have been urged by Major Rennell, Colonel Leake, and Professors Welcker and Forchhammer: on the other hand, Mr. Grote has a long argument in favor of *Hissarlik* (the traditional site), and Dr. Smith in his "Dictionary of Greek and Roman Antiquities" advocates the same side of the question. Mr. Maclaren, Dr. Eckenbrecher, and other learned men also maintained that *Hissarlik* was the true site.

We cannot, of course, go into the numerous petty points involved in the discussion: the leading objection against Hissarlik was the fact that it is only some three miles from the sea, Bunarbashi, as we have stated, being eight or nine. It was conceived that the Greeks and the Trojans must have had armies like those of modern Europe, and that they could not have been manœuvred between Hissarlik and the Grecian camp. Dr. Schliemann had indulged a similar idea about the size of Troy, and he has been very much astonished to find that the city which he has reached could not have accommodated more than a population of five thousand souls. He could discover no traces of a city beyond the limits of the acropolis: the Pergamus of Priam was Troy. But this is in fact an argument in favor of Hissarlik: the ancient cities were often mere citadels,—fortified hills,—resembling in this respect the feudal castles. The court and the better class lived within the walls; the common people lived on the plain outside of and around the fortress. It was thus with the hill-fortress of Zion, with the Byrsa of Carthage, with the citadel of Mycenæ, which was an inconsiderable village in the time of Thucydides, who expressly refers to the fact, and guards his readers not on that account to doubt the magnitude of its armament in the Trojan war. So the space covered by the city of Tiryns, as indicated by the walls, was only about two hundred and fifty by one hundred yards.

The claims of Bunarbashi have, however, been settled in the same conclusive way that Dr. Schliemann tested the pretensions of Strabo's Troy. Excavations made here in 1864 by Hahn, followed by the researches of Sir John Lubbock in 1872, revealed only the fortifications of a small town, with nothing to connect them in any way with the Homeric Troy or the heroic age.

It appears also that instead of the two springs observed by Chevalier at Bunarbashi—one hot and one cold—there are *forty* of them, and none of them hot.

The theory that Bunarbashi is the site of Troy also requires us to identify the river *Mendere* (whose etymology points to the Scamander) with the Simois, and to identify the Scamander with a much more insignificant stream. It is well known that Homer represents the Scamander as the principal stream.

We have mentioned that the great difficulty in the minds of those who rejected the Hissarlik site was the fact that it is too near the sea,—now about three miles distant,—in the time of Strabo not two miles. As we have stated, the idea has prevailed that the operations of the contending parties in the war of the Iliad were on a very extended scale; and we have suggested that this idea was very erroneous. But, as the question was raised, we wonder that it did not occur to Chevalier and his followers that the element of distance presented a formidable difficulty against accepting the site of Bunarbashi. This place is eight or nine miles from the sea-shore, and we are told in the Iliad that on one occasion the Greeks twice pursued the Trojans from their camp to the walls of the city, and were twice driven back to their ships,—which would involve their fighting over a space of thirty miles in a day.

CHAPTER XXVII.

THE BRONZE WEAPONS OF DENMARK AND IRELAND.

We promised to speak farther of the Bronze Age in these countries. This seemed called for by the *number* of bronze weapons found in the peat and in the graves of Denmark, and in the peat of Ireland. Elsewhere, as we have seen, the bronze weapons are rare. Here they are quite numerous, and of very fine workmanship. In the great Museum at Dublin are seven hundred and twenty-five celts and chisels, two hundred and eighty-two swords and daggers,* and two hundred and seventy-six lances, javelins, and arrow-heads. Of course we do not mean to say that all of them were found in the peat-beds; they are also sometimes found in the river-beds, in the graves, and elsewhere. More than two thousand bronze celts are known to exist in the different Irish collections.

Of bronze swords alone, the Museum at Copenhagen contains three hundred and fifty specimens. Many of these were found in the barrows.

There is a marked parallelism in the archæology of Ireland and Denmark. Neither had a Palæolithic Age; in neither (one or two exceptional cases excluded) do we find the remains of the great pachyderms. Man entered Ireland, Scotland, Denmark, and Scandinavia at a period subsequent to the River-Gravel and Bone-Caverns of England and France and Germany. The stone weapons, though often rude, belong, in point of time, to the Neolithic Age. The great abundance of bronze, and the comparative scarcity of iron, is another point of resemblance between them. And, finally, it does not appear that the Romans ever entered either country.

No Palæolithic Age in these countries.

We shall take occasion in a succeeding chapter to speak of the Irish peat, as well as of the peat mosses of Denmark. We shall learn that the bronze objects found in both of these are not very ancient: that bronze weapons, indeed, continued to be used in Ireland down to the sixth, seventh, and eighth centuries of our era, and that cotemporaneously with stone, has already appeared from previous statements.

* There are many of these specimens intermediate in form between the sword and the dagger.

We have also had occasion to speak of the bronze weapons found in the Danish barrows. We found these also very recent. In Denmark the bronze swords found in the barrows are associated with tree and plank coffins and fine woollen garments.

We learn from Mr. Worsaae that the Bronze Age in Denmark extended to the seventh century of our era. About the second century of our era, he says, at the time of the Roman invasions of the countries of the Black Sea, new tribes probably entered Sweden and Norway. These, on their arrival, either completely subdued the nomadic Finnic tribes, or drove them to the most northern part of Europe, where remnants of them still exist. It was thus that the civilization of the iron period was developed so suddenly in Sweden and Norway, which is evidently built on the Roman civilization. This is confirmed by the many Byzantine coins of the fifth and sixth centuries found in the North, the gold bracteates found there, and the constant intercourse which, from that time, existed between the North and Byzantium, where the Northmen so frequently served as the life-guards of the emperors.

Worsaae on the Bronze Age.

On the Iron Age.

Denmark received its iron civilization from this quarter. "In Götaland [that is, Southern Sweden] the use of iron had probably completely superseded the use of bronze, for weapons and implements, as early as the sixth century, as there were then frequent attacks both from Norway and Sweden, and as Götaland, not long after, became connected with Sweden. In Denmark it took, of course, more time; but from the fifth or sixth century, the civilization of the iron period had been completely introduced into Mecklenburg, by the Slavonic tribes; into England, by the Anglo-Saxons; into Norway and Sweden, by the Norwegians and the Svear. It is probable that bronze and iron were in use together in Denmark during one or two centuries, until about the year 700, when the use of iron completely superseded that of bronze, for implements and weapons." *

This does not require comment.

In Norway and Sweden "it is well known that, comparatively speaking," says Mr. Worsaae, "bronze objects belong to the rarest finds." †

"At length," he remarks in another connection, "and as appears about the eighth century, the third age, or the iron period, was com-

---

* Worsaae's "Primeval Antiquities of Denmark," p. 147.

† Ib., p. 124. M. Oscar Montelius, in his beautiful work entitled "Antiquités Suédoises," remarks, "L'âge du bronze a probablement fini en Suède peu de temps après le commencement de l'ère chrétienne."

On the other hand, Prof. Leemans remarked at the Stockholm Congress of Archæologists, held in August last, that "three or four thousand years is the highest age which can be attributed to the Stone Age in Sweden." See The Academy, Aug. 29, 1874, p. 240.

pletely established. With it came into use in Denmark two metals hitherto unknown and unused,—iron and silver."*

We thus have the Iron Age in Denmark somewhere about 600 or 700 A.D.

Now, M. Morlot remarks that, in the Iron Age, we find in Switzerland and Denmark "the same iron sword, without guard or crosier, the same iron hatchet, shaped like the bronze hatchet, the same bridle-bit, and even the same coat of mail."† "Iron arms of this epoch," he says, "show in the North a forge-workmanship of rare perfection, and which probably has never since been surpassed."

We must believe, then, that there was no great interval between the Iron Age in Switzerland and the Iron Age in Denmark.

The Bronze Period, according to Mr. Worsaae, "must have prevailed in Denmark five or six hundred years before the birth of Christ."‡

There is no evidence whatever, that we are aware of, to warrant the statement that the bronze implements in Denmark date, some of them, from the sixth century before Christ. The probabilities are that they do not go back so far. The barrows of the early Bronze Age, described by Mr. Worsaae in the paper published in the *Archæological Journal* for 1866, and to which we have referred, contained magnificent bronze swords and "well-woven woollen cloths, with thicker mantles, and caps of a peculiar kind of felt; a spiral bracelet of gold; wooden cups turned in the lathe; horn combs," etc. The bodies were in hollow and split oak trunks. These barrows Mr. Worsaae assigns, as heretofore stated, to the *Early* Bronze Age; *i.e.*, to B.C. 600, when it is notorious that there are no traces of the turning-lathe before the Christian era in Northern and Western Europe, and when it is obvious that the woollen garments and oaken coffins also, in all probability, are later than the empire.

In the same paper he says that in the barrows at Kongehoi and Treenhoi the woollen clothes "are so well preserved that they are now fit for use."

The Stone Age in Denmark.

We have shown also in our chapter on the tumuli and dolmens that the Danish barrows and dolmens, assigned to the Stone Age, are no older than the same monuments in England, if so old. These contained stone implements, and we thus ascertain that the Stone Age in Denmark came down to our era, and probably to a much later period. The tomb of Harold Hildetand, at Lethra, in Zeeland, contained "stone wedges," and was of the eighth century. This tomb is one of the grand "cromlechs" described by Mr. Worsaae, and which he refers to the Stone Age. The Giants' Chambers, he

* Worsaae's Primeval Antiquities, p. 123.

† Paper republished in Smithsonian Reports for 1860, p. 329.

‡ Primeval Antiquities, p. 135.

says, are also of equal antiquity, and contain, like the long "cromlechs," "implements and weapons of flint or bone, pieces of amber, and urns of clay." Yet he tells us that the large stones of which these are composed are "smooth on the surface which is turned inwards," —showing the probable employment of metal tools. One example has on two of these stones markings "which are regarded by some as Runic inscriptions." And at Herrestrup, in Zeeland, there are figures of ships, showing the era of the Vikings. All of which proves, what might have been surmised from the other facts of the case, that the Stone Age of Denmark *continued* to co-exist with the Bronze Age.

We have also mentioned elsewhere that Mr. Rose, in his account of the stone implements collected by him in Denmark, stated that the arrow-heads were all found at the depth of three or four feet in the peat.

Mr. Worsaae himself, indeed, states that, owing to the fact that "neither copper nor tin occurs, so that these metals, being introduced from other countries, were necessarily expensive, the poorer classes continued for a long series of years to make use of stone as their material;" and that it further appears "that the richer, at all events in the earlier periods, in addition to their bronze implements, still used others of stone, particularly such as would have required a large quantity of metal for their formation." * He tells us, moreover, that "the aborigines had stone implements, which were bored with regular holes for handles,—that is, mauls or hammers,—among which those which have perforations close to the neck are commonly called axes." † These were undoubtedly bored with metallic tubes, as in Switzerland.

The reader can judge from the evidence whether the Bronze Age, even in Denmark, was a distinct and independent era. Even if it be true that the use of bronze in this country (which we do not believe) constituted such a distinctly-defined epoch, it is at the same time true that Sir John Lubbock is wide of the mark in the declaration that "it appears evident that the use of bronze weapons had been discontinued in the North before, probably long before, the commencement of our era;" ‡ it is true that the Bronze Age in Denmark, while it may have been "pre-historic" in the sense that it prevailed before the development of letters and monumental records in that country, does not possess any great *antiquity*, and even comes down almost to mediæval times. History does not commence in Denmark until the establishment of Christianity, which was about the reign of Gorm the Old,—that is, about the middle of the tenth century. And when archæologists speak of "pre-historic" times, if this is all they mean, the system is free from objection.

---

* Primeval Antiquities, p. 24. † Ib., p. 15. ‡ Pre-hist. Times, p. 12.

CHAPTER XXVIII.

HALLSTADT.

It would not be proper to omit in this discussion some account of the great cemetery of Hallstadt, near Salzburg, in Austria, discovered by M. Ramsaneur, who opened here as many as nine hundred and eighty graves. These belong to the ancient people who centuries ago worked the yet unexhausted salt-mines at this place. In them was found immense wealth of bronze and iron. The table on the next page, taken from Sir John Lubbock's work, will instruct and interest the reader.

It will be observed that we have here, on an extensive scale, all together, iron, bronze, and stone.

There are some three thousand six hundred objects of bronze; of which one hundred and nine are weapons.

There are some six hundred objects of iron; of which five hundred and ten are weapons.

The "stone" is not described; but it is probable that the stone weapons were about as numerous as those of bronze.

There are nearly two hundred "vessels" of bronze, some of them three feet high, and some of which, delineated in M. Figuier's work, are evidently of superb workmanship.

There are nearly twelve hundred and fifty specimens of pottery, some of which, as we learn from M. Figuier, was made with the wheel.

There are seventy-three objects of glass,—a sure sign of a very recent date.

There is also African ivory.

It will be remembered that Sir John Lubbock distinguishes the burials of the Bronze Age by the circumstance that the corpse was burned. The second half of our table belongs, therefore, to the Bronze Age. But, while there are nearly two thousand bronze objects, there are only ninety-one bronze weapons, but three hundred and forty-nine iron ones.

Mr. Evans, in his work on Stone Implements, speaks of this place as "the ancient cemetery of Hallstadt," and Sir John Lubbock evidently regards it as older than the Roman occupation of that country. Others place it four centuries before the Christian era.

TABLE.

HALLSTADT.		GRAVES WITH BODIES BURIED IN THE ORDINARY MANNER.											
		ANTIQUITIES.											
	Number of Graves.	Gold Orna-ments.	Bronze.				Iron.		Amber.	Glass.	Pottery.	Stone.	
			Orna-ments.	Vessels.	Sundries.	Weapons.	Weapons.	Other Objects.	Ornaments.				
	527	6	1471	3	35	18	161	33	165	38	334	57	
		GRAVES WITH BURNT CORPSES.											
		ANTIQUITIES.											
	Number of Graves.	Gold Orna-ments.	Bronze.				Iron.		Amber.	Glass.	Pottery.	Different Objects.	
			Orna-ments.	Vessels.	Sundries.	Weapons.	Weapons.	Other Objects.	Ornaments.				
	453	58	1744	179	54	91	349	41	105	35	908	100	
Totals . . .	980	64	3215	182	89	109	510	74	270	73	1242		5985

Hallstadt is in Central Europe, some seventy miles southeast of Munich. It was in the ancient kingdom of Noricum, and in the territory of the Boii, the most important tribe of that country. The region was occupied by the Romans about the close of the first century; and no rational person can believe that these graves, with such contents as we have described, were dug before that time. The wheel-made pottery and the glass are decisive. How much later it may have been is a more difficult question; for the arts of Rome followed rapidly in the wake of her arms.

M. Desor, speaking of La Tène, remarks that "we have not yet discovered in the palafittes of La Tène those armlets covered with fine engravings, nor those discs with concentric circles, still less those cinctures of bronze, presenting casts of small human figures and quadrupeds, which exist at Hallstadt and in certain cairns of Switzerland; *nothing, in a word, which approaches those overloaded ornaments frequent in Helveto-Burgundian and Merovingian tombs.*"

M. Desor believes in all the ages. We know also the date of La Tène. It appears that Hallstadt is later, by the admission of one of the first archæologists of Europe.

CHAPTER XXIX.

FARTHER CONSIDERATION OF THE PEAT MOSSES.

Peat.—Farther consideration of.—The Danish Peat, and the Successive Remains of the Pine, the Oak, and the Beech therein.—Sir Charles Lyell and Dr. McCausland.—The Implements of Stone alleged to be found in the Pine Stratum, the Implements of Bronze in the Oak Stratum, and the Implements of Iron in the Beech Stratum.—The Pine alleged to have been extinct in Denmark in Historical Times.—Proves nothing, if true. —That the Pine, the Oak, and the Beech all grew together, proved by Example of Bog on Earl of Arran's Estate.—M. Morlot.—Mr. Pattison, F.G.S.—His Reply to Sir Charles Lyell, and Statement that the Forests are all cotemporaneous.—Woollen Clothes found in the Pine Stratum.—Peat growing at the rate of Two Inches in a Year.—Dr. Rennie on the Formation of Peat.—Recent Date assigned by him to many of these Mosses.—Mar Forest.—Hatfield Moss.—Roman Remains.—Kincardine or Blair Drummond Moss in Perthshire.—Roman Roadways under the Peat.—De Luc's Statement that many of the Continental Mosses are Post-Roman.—Coin of Emperor Gordian.—Sir W. R. Wilde.—Account of Objects found in the Irish Peat.—Bog Butter.—Shoe found in Tipperary.—Human Body found in the Peat in Parish of Killery.—Steele on Peat Moss.—Human Bodies found in Derbyshire.—Other Remains in the Peat.—Coins of Edward IV. at Depth of Eighteen Feet.—Steele on the Growth of Peat Mosses.—Earl of Cromarty.—His Account of the Formation of a Peat Moss in Loch Broom Parish in less than Fifty Years.—Barton Park.—Excavations near London Wall.—Rapid Formation of Peat.

We have spoken in a previous chapter of the Peat of the Somme Valley. We have mentioned the "thousands of years" which Sir C. Lyell requires for its deposition, and that Sir J. Lubbock believes it to date back to the Polished Stone Age, to which he assigns an antiquity of some seven thousand years. We mentioned also that the calculation of M. Boucher de Perthes would demand a period of thirty thousand years. Mr. Hudson Tuttle, of Boston, on data furnished by M. Boucher de Perthes, believes that it took one hundred and twenty thousand years for that peat to form.* The stone implements at the bottom of the Danish peat he believes to have been dropped there about 22000 B.C.†

Age of the peat according to the Anthropologists.

We have mentioned the various articles of iron and bronze, and the various specimens of pottery of the Roman and Gallo-Roman eras, found in the very lowest strata of the French peat. Also the boats—one of them freighted with Roman bricks—found in the same deposits.

* "The Origin and Antiquity of Man Scientifically Considered," p. 55. † Ibid., p. 52.

We propose in the present chapter to discuss this subject farther, and to consider the peat-deposits of other countries, particularly Ireland, England, and Denmark. A very large (and the most important) part of the antiquities collected in the Danish Museums has been obtained from the peat-beds of that country. A special argument for the antiquity of the human race has been derived from the discovery of the polished stone implements found in these mosses. It is alleged that there are two periods distinctly traceable in the peat: 1, the period of the pine forests of Denmark, the remains of which are found in the lowest stratum of the beds; 2, the period of the oak forests, the remains of which occur in the layers above the pine layer. A yet later, and third period, it is alleged, is marked by the existing beech forests, which have in turn superseded the oak forests. We are told that stone implements occur in the pine stratum of the peat, and that bronze implements occur in, and correspond to, the oak stratum. Lastly, we are told, the beech forests are representative of the Iron Age. Thus Sir C. Lyell: "The Age of Stone coincides with the period of the first vegetation, or that of the Scotch fir, and in part, at least, with the second vegetation, or that of the oak. But a considerable portion of the oak epoch coincided with the Age of Bronze, for swords and shields of that metal have been taken out of the peat in which oaks abound. The Age of Iron coincided more nearly with that of the beech-tree."

The Danish peat.

The peat-deposits of Denmark, as we learn from the "Antiquity of Man," vary in depth from ten to thirty feet. "Around the borders of the bogs," says Lyell, "and at various depths in them, lie trunks of trees, especially of the Scotch fir (*Pinus sylvestris*), often three feet in diameter, which must have grown on the margin of the peat mosses, and have frequently fallen into them."

"What," says Dr. McCausland,* "was the extent of the epoch of the oak forests coeval with the bronze age, which had preceded and died out before the commencement of the iron age? And what, again, was the duration of the second stone epoch, and its population that had passed away before the commencement of the bronze age?" "The minimum of time required for the formation of the peat which was grown above the pines of Denmark must, according to the Danish geologist Steenstrup and other competent authorities, have amounted to at least four thousand years; and Sir Charles Lyell remarks that there is nothing in the observed rate of the growth of the peat opposed to the conclusion that the number of centuries may not have been four times as great."

Lyell on the age of the peat.

* Adam and the Adamite.

Let us admit all of the facts as stated: they do not prove any great antiquity.

Dr. McCausland tells us that "Steenstrup and other competent authorities" believe that the formation of this peat requires a minimum time of "four thousand years." That would only take us to about 2100 B.C.

But Prof. Worsaae is even more moderate than this: his remark is, that "it is therefore no exaggeration if we attribute to the stone period an antiquity of at least *three thousand years.*"* That would fix the settlement of Denmark about 1100 B.C.,—which is very near the truth.

Any one who knows the rapidity with which the chestnuts of the forests of the United States are succeeded by pines, will deem three thousand years abundantly sufficient to admit of the succession of forests in Denmark claimed by Sir Charles Lyell.

The pine, we are told, has not been a native of the Danish islands "in historical times;" and the oak is now almost superseded by the beech.

However this be, the pine and the oak both flourished in Denmark in former times, as we know; and the fact that they may not flourish there now, does not prove anything. Such changes are common.

But the point, it will be urged, is, that we have exhibited a regular *succession* of these forests, corresponding to the three archæological ages. As we have said, even this may be so, and yet three thousand years will cover all the requirements of the case.

But it is denied [by us] that these forests were not formerly *cotemporary*—all growing at one and the same time—in Denmark.

"There is," says a writer in the *Princeton Review,* "a piece of primeval bog and forest on the Earl of Arran's estate in Scotland which makes it apparent that the pine, oak, and beech *were not successive,* but cotemporaneous at different levels; the bog growing as well as the trees. Holes from which peat has been cut have been observed to fill up at the rate of a foot in four years. And, finally, the frequent discovery of similar Danish remains in the Danish forts of Ireland determines the stone and bronze ages to the era of the Danish invasion, A.D. 827.†

"From the pine stratum of the bogs of Ireland, skeletons of warriors with gold epaulets and clasps, bronze battle-axes, and stone arrow-heads have been frequently raised in the process of cutting out peat for fuel."‡

It will be observed that Sir C. Lyell speaks of bronze *swords* and *shields* as found in the so-called oak stratum of the peat. Sir Charles ought to know that bronze swords and shields in Denmark cannot be much earlier than the Christian era. We are told also by Dr. McCaus-

* Primeval Antiquities, p. 135.

† Princeton Review for October, 1868.

‡ Ib.

land that the oak layer is "several feet" below the beech layer. If there is only "several feet," it might have been formed in a century.

Morlot and Lyell on the Scotch fir.

M. Morlot has also a good deal to say about the succession of forests in the Danish peat. He affirms, as does also Sir C. Lyell, that the Scotch fir (*Pinus sylvestris*) has not grown in Denmark in the historic period.

We do not see the pertinence of this, even if it be true. The historic period of Denmark does not go back farther than the tenth century of our era. We may add also that it is well known that trunks of this tree have been found in English mosses, which are known to have been accumulated since the presence of the Romans in that country. Cæsar, in his Commentaries, it is true, affirms that the tree did not grow in Britain; but in this he was only mistaken. It is found abundantly with Roman remains,—as, for example, in Hatfield Chase, where the Romans after Cæsar's time cut down forests of pine, oak, birch, and beech, and where trunks of the pine ninety feet long have been found in the peat. This—the destruction of this forest—was some eighteen centuries ago; and there is every probability that the tree grew at the same date in Denmark on the opposite shores of the North Sea.

More than this: we learn from Prof. James Geikie's work on "The Great Ice Age,"* that the Scotch fir *does not now grow in England;* its range is confined to lat. 56°–59°,—from Perthshire to Sutherland. From the fact just stated above,—namely, that during the Roman domination it grew in Yorkshire (at Hatfield Chase),—we ascertain that its disappearance in England does not date farther back than eighteen hundred years ago. Why should it have disappeared at an earlier date from Denmark?

Mr. Pattison, in his reply to Sir C. Lyell, on the question of the antiquity of man, observes on the point under consideration,—

"The superposition of the oak timber in the bogs is easily accounted for without calling in the aid of thousands of years. The process and its progress are matters of ordinary observation. A clump of pine-trees grows with here and there an oak; the firs are the first to become old and feeble; some of them fall and begin to decay; the tiny streamlet meandering through the wood is dammed up; mosses grow; the firs all fall; the bog increases; the more hardy oak yields next; the birch and the alder survive on the driest spots; but these, too, are ultimately engulfed."

Statement of Mr. Worsaae.

An incidental remark of Mr. Worsaae throws considerable light on the age of these peats. In his section on the "Antiquities of the Stone Age," in his "Primeval Antiquities," he mentions

* Page 296, Amer. edit.

that the apparel of the aborigines of Denmark consisted chiefly of skins, and that bodies clad in such skins have from time to time been dug up from the peat bogs, and with some of them primitive leather shoes or sandals, made of a single piece of hide sewn together behind. He then remarks that *with these* there have been found also *remains of woollen cloth.** So that the Stone Folk of Denmark sometimes clad themselves in woollen garments,—and this in the time of the pine stratum of the peat.

Peat may all have grown in two thousand years.

The Earl of Cromarty (to whom we have referred, and shall refer again) makes the statement that "the frequent discoveries of mediæval objects low down in fen-deposits, and the experience of all those who have had to do with the management of peat lands, lead to the conclusion that two thousand years constitute ample allowance for the growth of all the peat on the present surface of the globe."

M. Morlot assigns the beech forests of Denmark to the Iron Age, and he tells us that the oak forests are now being replaced by beech, the oak corresponding with the Bronze Age. He is quite sure that the oaks belong to the Bronze Age, because in this layer, in a kjaermose or bog-meadow, were found "the magnificent bronze bucklers of the Museum of Copenhagen." These statements by no means suggest to our mind the idea of great antiquity for either the oaks or the bronzes. The oaks are in existence now, and "magnificent bronze bucklers" had hardly found their way to Denmark before the Christian era. The cuts on the next page represent some of the ancient bronzes found in Denmark. Do they look "pre-historic"?

"The climate," he also tells us, "has scarcely changed since the appearance of man," for the terrestrial molluscs found in the shell-mounds, and the fluviatile molluscs found in the marly peat bogs, "are, without exception, *identical*" with those of the present day, and "we know what good climatometers snails are." Only the vineyard snail is missing, and this was introduced, as we know, by the monks in the Middle Ages.†

It may have been *sixteen thousand years*, says Sir Charles Lyell (who erred so greatly about the age of the Delta of the Mississippi, and indicated Dr. Dowler's Red Indian to be about fifty-seven thousand years old), since the Danish peat-beds commenced to form. That is a long time, if (as we shall learn) the peat moss near Loch Broom, in Rossshire, formed at such a rate that the inhabitants dug the peat in less than half

---

* Primeval Antiquities of Denmark, p. 19.

† Smithsonian Reports for 1860, p. 309: General Views on Archæology, by A. Morlot. Translated.

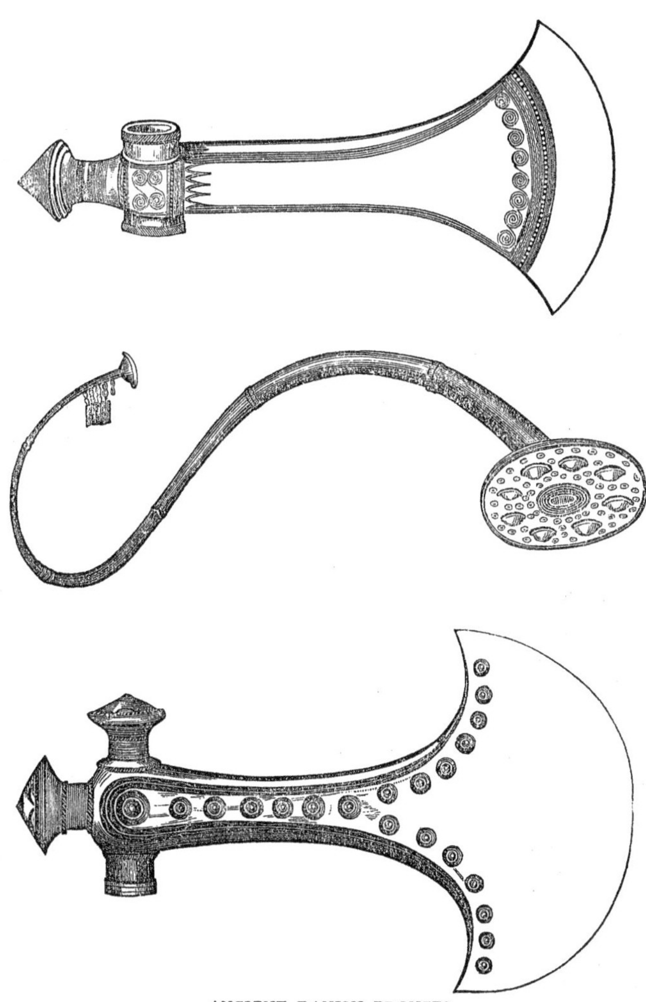

ANCIENT DANISH BRONZES.

a century. It is a long time, if it be true, as alleged by the author of the article on Peat in Appleton's New American Cyclopædia, that "an increase in the Irish bogs of *two inches a year has been observed.*" This—two inches a year—would give us in sixteen thousand years a depth of two thousand six hundred and sixty-six feet and eight inches,—considerably more than the thickness of all the deposits of the Tertiary Period!

Peat forming at the rate of two inches a year.

Testimony of Rennie.

Mr. Rennie, in his "Essays on Peat," quoted by Sir Charles Lyell, informs us that "many of these mosses of the north of Europe occupy the place of forests of pine and oak, which have, many of them, *disappeared within the historical era.*" In Mar Forest, in Aberdeenshire, large trunks of Scotch fir, which had fallen from age and decay, are said to have been soon immured in peat, formed partly out of their perishing leaves and branches, and partly from the growth of other plants. In Hatfield Moss, in Yorkshire, referred to a short space back, where the original forest was cut down by the Roman general Ostorius, in the reign of Vespasian, the peat has formed since that period. This moss covered an area of ninety thousand acres, and was one of the largest in England. Here, "many feet deep at the bottom of the moss or fen mould," when the bog was drained, old Roman axes, somewhat in shape resembling the axes used for sacrificial purposes, and other axes and knives, were found. Trees of Scotch fir, oak, birch, beech, yew, thorn, willow, ash, etc., the roots standing in the hard soil at the bottom of the moss, were also found in vast numbers. The Scotch firs were, some of them, ninety feet long, and were so firm and strong as to be sold for masts and keels of ships; while some of the oaks were one hundred and one hundred and twenty feet long, and were sold for from ten to twenty pounds, and were so hard and durable as to be fit for any purpose. Some of these trees had been burnt,—some quite through, and some on one side. In other places some trees were found chopped and squared, some bored through, others riven with great wooden wedges and stones. Near a great root were found eight or nine coins of some of the Roman emperors. Afterwards, on cutting the great new drain of Hatfield, four or five miles long, and three hundred feet wide, there were found at the bottom of the moss-ground many great trees, some of them squared and cut; rails, bars, old links of chains, horses' heads, an old axe, something like a battle-axe, two or three coins of Vespasian, etc.*

Mar Forest.

Hatfield Moss.

Roman relics.

Roman coins.

We have here, it will be observed, the fir, oak, and beech *all growing together* in Yorkshire in the time of Vespasian.

In this peat, as also in that of Kincardine, Perthshire, Scotland, Roman roads are said to have been discovered at the depth of eight feet, and it has been stated that all the coins, axes, arms, and other objects found in the British and French mosses are *Roman.*†

The Roman way over Kincardine Moss is twelve feet wide, and regularly formed by trees or logs of wood laid across each other. The character of this road seems to imply that the bog had already begun to form when the road was constructed.

Kincardine Moss.

---

* Steele, pp. 282–285. See also Phil. Trans., vol. xxii., No. 275.

† See Lyell's "Principles of Geology," vol. ii. p. 506, who, however, does not *now* accept this, fortifying himself with the assertions of M. Boucher de Perthes.

The average depth of the peat here is seven feet, but there are parts of it fourteen feet deep.

The Moss of Kincardine, including the adjoining moss of Blair Drummond, covers some ten thousand acres betwixt the Forth and the Teith, beginning a mile above the confluence of the rivers, and extending thence up the Forth. It lies upon a field of clay which is a continuation of those rich, extensive flats in the neighborhood of Falkirk and Stirling which we have mentioned as distinguished by the name of *Carses*. In this peat, as at Hatfield, we find the oak and the birch, but, apparently, not the fir or the beech.

Mr. Steele thinks it probable the Roman roadway was constructed in the expedition of Severus, A.D. 207, whilst Donald I. reigned in Caledonia. The road, we presume, was used and kept open for a certain period, we cannot tell how long. Finally the peat gathered over it. It is highly probable that the growth of the peat has been arrested for many centuries.

Isle of Axholm.

Adjacent to Hatfield Chase is the tract called the Isle of Axholm, in Lincolnshire. Several human bodies have been found in the deep peat-moss grounds of this quarter, and also Roman roads, pavements, and platforms, and large quantities of Roman coins, all among vast heaps of fallen trees. The body of a lady was found here, with antique sandals on her feet.

Testimony of De Luc.

According to De Luc, the very sites of the aboriginal forests of Hercynia, Semena, Ardennes, and several others, are now occupied by mosses and fens. A great part of these changes has, with much probability, been attributed to the strict orders given by Severus, and other emperors, to destroy all the wood in the conquered provinces.*

Coin of Gordian found at depth of thirty feet.

De Luc also informs us that a coin of the Emperor Gordian, A.D. 237, was found thirty feet deep in the peat at Groningen.

Degner states that the remains of ships and nautical instruments have been found in many of the Dutch mosses. The peat has formed over these remains since the retirement of the sea, and the sea has retired since it was navigated by the ships.

In the Bernese Jura we find traces of ancient iron-furnaces. At some of them coins both Roman and Gallic have been found, some of the former belonging to the time of the Constantines, or the fourth century. M. Quiquerez describes one of these furnaces which was covered by twenty feet of peat, which must have accumulated in the past two thousand years.

---

* Lyell's "Principles of Geology," vol. ii. p. 507.

Sir W. R. Wilde, in his "Catalogue of the Antiquities of Animal Materials and Bronze in the Museum of the Royal Irish Academy," mentions several cases in which vessels containing *butter* were found in the Irish peat at great depths. Number 37 of the catalogue was found at the depth of nine feet below the surface in Grallagh bog, near Abbeyleix, Queen's County.

Sir W. R. Wilde.

Bog butter.

Number 38 was found at the depth of fifteen feet in Ballyconnell bog, Donegal County. It is a hard, yellowish-white substance, like old Stilton cheese, and in taste resembles spermaceti. It was contained in a large, square, thin "mether," apparently intended originally for a butter or milk vessel. This vessel is nine inches high and five inches across, is made of willow wood, and is double-handled.

Number 41 is another and larger vessel of butter, found eighteen feet below the surface, in the county of Kilkenny.*

In the same work Sir W. R. Wilde mentions a *shoe* (Number 28 of the catalogue) found at the depth of twenty feet in a turf bog near Templemore, Tipperary. It is "a right, thong-sewn, turned shoe," of thick, well-tanned leather, with a double sole.†

Shoe found in the peat.

According to Sir C. Lyell, this bog-butter and this shoe are perhaps sixteen thousand years old; and if M. Boucher de Perthes is right, the Irish were making butter and wearing double-soled shoes some fifteen thousand years ago. But, as butter and shoes were little used even in Rome, this statement is highly improbable.

Probable age.

When was butter introduced into Ireland? We do not know; but we cannot believe that the specimens referred to can be as much as a thousand years old. Nor do we know when they commenced to wear shoes of the pattern described. The Irish princes probably used them as early as the fifth or sixth century. With regard to the people generally, Giraldus Cambrensis, in the twelfth century, informs us that they "went naked and unarmed to battle;" and Dincley, in his account of his visit to Ireland in the reign of Charles II., states that "the common people of both sexes weare no shoes, after the English fashion, but a sort of pumps called brogues."

Sir W. R. Wilde mentions also that in 1824 a male body, completely clad in woollen garments, was found in a bog in the parish of Killery, at the depth of six feet. He assumes that it belonged to the fifteenth or sixteenth century. A silver coin was also found, which was illegible.

Coin of fifteenth century.

In his "Catalogue of Antiquities of Stone, Earthen, and Vegetable Remains," he mentions that Number 97 of the catalogue is an ancient wooden candlestick of fir, eight and a half inches high, found at the

* See pp. 267, 268.

† Page 292.

depth of sixteen feet in the bog of Lower Lyrane, near Blackstones, Kerry.*

Similar examples, illustrating the rapid formation of peat, are mentioned by Mr. Andrew Steele in his work on "Peat Moss or Turf Bog," published in Edinburgh in 1826.

Steele on Peat.

A man and a woman, he says, were found in a peat moss in Derbyshire in 1703, at the depth of three feet. The man's name was Barber. He was a grazier, who, being reduced in his circumstances, was going off with his servant-maid for Ireland, and was lost in this bog during a great fall of snow on the 14th of January, 1674. When found, they had lain in the peat moss twenty-eight or twenty-nine years. Their appearance was in no way altered, and the flesh was soft as that of persons newly dead.†

Human bodies found.

A butter-kit, Mr. Steele informs us, was found, filled with butter, *in the bottom* of Cormaskae Moss, in Perthshire. "It was evident it had lain in the moss very long, from this, that the kit was made of bark of trees, which has not been the fashion for such articles in the Highlands of Scotland for a century past at least."‡

Butter-kit.

Mr. Arthur Young, he states, in his Irish Tour, mentions a peat moss in which, at the depth of fourteen feet, "evident marks of the plough in the soil at the bottom, also remains of cabins, cribs for cattle, moose's horns, oaks, yews, and fir, being good red deal," were found.

Traces of the plough below the peat.

Here is a very remarkable case. Dr. Plott, in his "Natural History of Stafford," "mentions that a parcel of coins of Edward IV. were discovered in a peat moss eighteen feet deep, which, supposing them to have been dropt on the surface in that reign, led him, by the latest date of the coins, to the arithmetical conclusion that the moss must have risen or grown upwards of an inch every year."§ Sir John Lubbock, however, would refer these coins to the Neolithic Age.

Coins of Edward IV. eighteen feet in the peat.

"The growth of mosses," says Mr. Steele, "is occasioned by the continual accession of fresh vegetables growing over those that have decayed.

Remarks of Mr. Steele.

"By some the growth of peat has been thought to be the operation of ages; but those who are intimately acquainted with botanic researches know well that the tribe of cryptogamous plants grow in general with extraordinary rapidity. . . . I have myself observed the *Sphagnum* grow four feet in a year, springing from the bottom and covering the surface of stagnated water of that depth. The *Hypnum fluitans*, which also grows in water and floats on its surface, has been known to grow two

* See p. 218. † Page 9. ‡ Page 11. § Steele on Peat Moss, p. 13.

or three feet in length in a season, and to form a stratum of peat in twenty years. Mr. Lightfoot, in his Flora Scotica, says that the *Polytrichum commune* grows sometimes annually a yard in length, which, with the other musci that flourish in bogs or marshes, he adds, by continual increase and decay, soon fill up and convert them into peat bogs. . . . Now, it may be further remarked that, although the musci do often very quickly fill up wet valleys in this climate, and convert them into peat bogs, yet it must be obvious that a wood, decaying all at once, from the stagnation of water, or other causes, may, with the assistance of the musci, and the gramineous and other plants that are natives of wet soils, *form a very considerable depth of peat in a very few years.* The roots of the *Eriophorum vaginatum*, mixed with *Scirpus cæspitosus*, *Schænus albus*, *Carex pulicans*, and *limosa*, form very quickly entire strata of peat. By replacing the surface turf of a moss cut for fuel, I am informed, a peat moss near Cupar-Angus grew again, so as to admit of being cut for fuel *twice in fifty years.*

"I have also observed the *Conferva bullosa*, and others of the algæ tribe, cover the surface of deep stagnated water an inch or two in thickness, in appearance like a green scum, in the course of a very few weeks in summer; while shallow pools, in the same time, having the addition of musci growing from the bottom, are entirely filled up with vegetable matter. . . . Also the *Ranunculus fluviatilis* assists to cover very rapidly the whole surface of large stagnant lakes, and to convert them into peat mosses. Boats have indeed been frequently found buried beneath the turf in extensive mosses." *

"A very curious instance of the growth of an extensive moss, viz., Cree, in the north of Scotland, was reported in 1785, as follows: About nineteen years before, a gentleman who lived near one side of it could, from a certain window of his house, observe the door of a cottage which was built on the opposite side of the moss; whereas then, from the same place, he could scarcely see the top of its chimney." †

Example from Irish crannoge.

Fifteen feet of peat, according to Sir J. Lubbock, take us back to the Stone Age,—according to M. Boucher de Perthes, they represent eleven thousand years: in the "Antiquity of Man," ‡ Sir C. Lyell, while speaking of the Irish crannoges, informs us that in one of these at Lagore the relics were covered by fifteen feet of peat, among which occurred antiquities "referable to the ages of stone, bronze, and iron." It would follow, therefore, according to the "Prophet of Abbeville," that iron was introduced into Ireland eleven thousand years ago. It was almost certainly not introduced earlier than the Christian era; and, if so, this peat is not more than eighteen

---

* Steele on Peat Moss, pp. 14–16. † Ib., pp. 16, 17. ‡ Page 30.

hundred and seventy years old,—supposing that the peat commenced to form the very moment the iron relics were deposited.

Many of the peat mosses were forests in Saxon times.

Mr. Maxwell, in his Statistical Account of the parish of Kilbarchan, in Renfrewshire, describes a moss, consisting of five hundred acres, from seven to nine feet deep, where a forest formerly stood. The stumps of the trees are in general in their original position, and the trees are broken over at the height of three feet. He alleges that this moss is not very ancient, which inference he draws from the fact that there are places around the moss "still denominated by the Saxon name of *Wood*." He might have added, says Mr. Steele, that a great proportion of the mosses in the Lowlands of Scotland retain the name of Woods, though there does not now exist a growing tree in their vicinity. The fact that the trunks of the trees are standing three feet high in the peat is precisely analogous to what we observed in the peat of the Somme Valley, and proves, as in that case, that at least three feet of peat was formed in a century.

Earl of Cromarty's account of the rapid formation of a peat moss.

There is an account of the formation of a peat moss recorded in the Philosophical Transactions of the Royal Society of London, vol. xxvii., given by the Earl of Cromarty, which we will transcribe in his own words:

"In 1651 (he says) I went by a very high hill in the parish of Loch Broom, which rose in a constant steepness from the sea; only about half a mile up there is a plain of about a half-mile round, and from thence the hill rises as before more than a mile in ascent. This little plain was at that time all covered over with a firm standing wood, which was so very old that not only the trees had no green leaves, but the bark was totally thrown off, which the old countrymen told me was the universal manner in which fir woods did terminate, and that, in twenty or thirty years after, the trees would ordinarily cast themselves up by the root, and that they would lie in heaps till the people would cut them and carry them away. They likewise shewed me that the outside of those standing trees, for the space of an inch inward, was dead white timber, but what was within that was good solid timber, even to the pith, and was as full of rosin as it could stand in the wood. About fifteen years after, I came the same way, and saw not so much as a tree, or appearance of the root of any; but, in the place thereof, the whole bounds where the wood had stood was all over a plain green ground, covered with a plain green moss. I asked the country-people who were with me what became of the wood, and who carried it away. They told me that nobody was at the pains to carry it away, but that, it being all overturned at the root by the wind, the trees did lie so thick and swarving over one another, that the green moss, there called fog, had overgrown the whole timber, which they said was occasioned by the moisture that came down from the high hills which were above it, and stagnated on the plain. They said none could pass over, because the scurf of the fog would not support them. I would needs try it; and accordingly I fell in to the armpits, but was immediately pulled out by them. Before the year 1699, that whole piece of ground was turned into a common moss, where the country-people are digging turf and peat. The peats were still soft and spongy, but are always growing better and better, and I am informed it now yields good peat."

Peat formed and cut in fifty years.

We have here a bed of peat forming in less than fifty years,—evidently of considerable depth, and in condition to be cut and carried away for fuel.

In Mr. Steele's book is an extract from Mr. Vancouver's Agricultural Report of Cambridgeshire, giving an account of the draining of a peat bog in Ireland. In this it is stated that under peat some twelve or fifteen feet thick there were seen ridges and furrows, the indisputable marks of a former cultivation, and at the bottom they found "the dash and lid of a hand-churn, and a large crane-necked brass spur, with a rowel a full inch in diameter." *

Plough-marks.

There is a tract of land lying between Manchester and Warrington, in the county of Lancaster, the principal part of which lies in the township and royalty of Barton-upon-Irwell. This moss is from ten to thirty feet thick. It appears that a part of this area formerly presented a very different surface, for it is certain that it was at one time imparked by the name of *Barton Park.* The impalement and enclosure of this park are laid down in the map of the county palatine of Lancaster, by Robert Morden, in Camden's Britannia; and in cutting the drains of the moss in the beginning of the present century, the ancient oak palings were found under the ground.†

Barton Park.

In our chapter on the "Mammoth," (p. 313) we gave an account of certain excavations at London Wall, where the traces of a pile-settlement and Roman remains were met with. These refuse-heaps and Roman remains were found at the bottom and up to the top of a stratum of peat eight feet in thickness, showing that the entire peat-formation had been deposited during the Roman occupation of Britain,—that is, in a period of four hundred years. In other words, the peat had formed here at the rate of two feet in a century.

Excavations at London Wall.

* Steele, p. 136. How old is this spur?

† Ib., p. 304.

CHAPTER XXX.

THE MUD OF THE MISSISSIPPI AND THE NILE, AND THE CONE OF THE TINIÈRE.

Dr. Dowler's Red Indian.—Answered by Prof. Andrews and Rev. Mr. Fontaine.—The Excavations of Mr. Leonard Horner in the Mud of the Nile.—The Evidence adduced apparently countenanced by Sir C. Lyell and Sir J. Lubbock.—A Brick bearing the Stamp of Mohammed Ali found at a Greater Depth than Mr. Horner's Pottery at Damietta.—The Figure of the Grecian Honeysuckle also found stamped on some of Mr. Horner's Specimens.—The Improbability that the Deposit around the Statue of Rameses is older than some Fourteen Hundred Years.—The Cone of the Tinière.

THE idle and extravagant manner in which the most distinguished *savans* figure up the vast antiquity of the present mundane economy is ludicrously illustrated by Sir Charles Lyell's and Sir John Lubbock's calculations about the antiquity of Dr. Dowler's Red Indian found in the mud in the city of New Orleans, sixteen feet beneath the surface, and beneath four successive tiers of cypress forests. Dr. Dowler estimates that this relic is fifty-seven thousand years old, and Lyell quotes with apparent approval his calculation, while Lubbock remarks that, if the facts as stated can be relied on, "this skeleton must carry back the existence of man in America *to a very early period.*" Says Lubbock, "The plain on which the city of New Orleans is built, and which rises only about ten feet above the sea-level, consists of alluvial soil which has been proved by borings to have a depth of more than five hundred feet, and which contains several successive layers of cypresses. The river-banks show similar remains of ancient forests, and Messrs. Dickeson and Brown have found remains of no less than ten cypress forests, at different levels below the present surface. These trees are not unfrequently as much as ten feet in diameter, and there are from ninety-five to one hundred and twenty rings on each. The human skeleton above referred to was found at a depth of sixteen feet," etc., etc. As a commentary on this, we will quote from our friend Dr. Andrews again (in the *Chicago Advance*, May 28, 1868, cited in the *Princeton Review*, Oct. 1868):

Dr. Dowler's Red Indian.

Endorsed by Lyell and Lubbock.

"In New Orleans, while digging a pit for the gas-works, the workmen came upon the skeleton of a Red Indian sixteen feet beneath the surface, and overlaid by earth in which stood the stumps of four successive cypress forests. Dr. Dowler, who investigated the

Dr. Andrews's reply.

matter, concluded that it required fifty thousand years to accumulate the sixteen feet of material above the skeleton, and Lyell quotes and partly approves the calculation. Dr. Dowler is well known in the medical profession as an enthusiastic but unsound investigator, who is very prone to come to startling, but erroneous, conclusions; but that Lyell should be led astray by sûch enormous blunders may well excite astonishment. The accretion both of vegetable matter and of river-mud in the region of the Lower Mississippi is very rapid, and the United States Army Engineers* have calculated that the whole ground on which New Orleans stands, down to the depth of forty feet, has been deposited within the period of four thousand four hundred years. Lyell himself states that he has seen many stumps of trees standing erect in the banks of the river, a fact which should have shown him that the accretion was rapid enough to cover these stumps to their summits before they had time to decay. I have myself seen in that region young cottonwood saplings only seven years old, around whose trunks the annual overflow of the river had deposited two or three feet of earth above their original roots. It is possible that the New Orleans man may be one or two thousand years of age; but to claim fifty thousand years for him is provocative of laughter."

Both Lyell and Lubbock make reference also to the "Natchez man" found by Dr. Dickeson, which was associated with the bones of the mastodon, and Lyell argues that if he be right in calculating a hundred thousand years for the growth of the Delta of the Mississippi, and if it be admitted that the Natchez man was cotemporary with the mastodon, North America must have been peopled a hundred thousand years ago! †

The precise age claimed by Dr. Dowler for his fossil man was fifty-seven thousand six hundred years, and these figures were accepted by Messrs. Nott and Gliddon.

Observations of Rev. Mr. Fontaine.

Commenting on this, Mr. Fontaine, in his work previously referred to, remarks that similar specimens of antiquity, and probably more abundantly, may be found between the present levee and Tamaulipas Street, where the whole area, to the depth of more than one hundred feet, has certainly been deposited within the period of sixty years. He states that since the gas-works were constructed, the New Orleans Academy of Sciences was agitated by a report that in making some deep excavations at Port Jackson, at a considerable distance from the

New Orleans "Academy of Sciences."

* Messrs. Humphreys and Abbott, who estimate the age of the Mississippi delta to be four thousand four hundred and forty years. Sir C. Lyell made it one hundred thousand. The late Professor Hitchcock made it fourteen thousand two hundred and four years.

† Antiquity of Man, p. 204, Amer. edit.

Mississippi River, and at a depth of fifteen or twenty feet below the surface, a piece of wood had been exhumed which had evidently been shaped by "human art" and dressed with tools which indicated the work of a highly-civilized race of men. It was decided by the advocates of the pre-Adamite origin of the "autochthones" of America, that these aborigines, who had inhabited Louisiana fifty-seven thousand six hundred years ago, were an exceedingly cultivated and highly enlightened people. Several members of the Academy determined to examine the matter thoroughly. They found the facts to have been correctly stated. A large piece of yellow poplar had been unburied at a great depth, and a considerable distance from the river,—a distance as great as that occupied by the aboriginal mound in the graveyard of Point à la Hache above the forts. It was squared with a broad-axe, bored with an auger, cut with a hand-saw, and was unmistakably *the gunwale of a Kentucky flat-boat!* *

Discover the gunwale of a Kentucky flat-boat.

Mr. Fontaine says the Artesian auger has brought wood up unpetrified, and but little changed from common seasoned timber, from a depth of three hundred and twenty-five feet; and he mentions the finding of the skeleton of a man "fifty feet below the levee, and beneath two tiers of stumps, buried in the deposit only four years." †

This author has some remarks upon the age of *trees*, or their dead trunks, in the valley of the Mississippi. He observes that the forest-trees of all the country east of the Rocky Mountains which he has examined are very short-lived, and that he has never found one whose age will compare with that attributed to the chestnuts of Sicily, the oaks of England, the cedars of Lebanon, the cypresses of Mexico, or the *sequoias* of California. He has found that all the forests on soils growing large crops of grass were once prairies, and had covered the earth recently, or since the annual burnings practised by the Indians had ceased. He found no oaks, or other trees, more than two hundred years old, except in bottoms, etc. In Virginia, and in Mississippi, the red oak, the white oak, and many other forest-trees, attain nearly their greatest size in fifty years.‡

The trees of the Mississippi Valley.

"The age of no fossil found in the alluvium of the present delta of Louisiana can be determined. The average depth of the river is about one hundred feet for the lower one hundred and twenty-five miles of its course, and its bottom current flows as swiftly as its surface, and the average velocity is about four miles per hour. Opposite New Orleans, the soundings of Harrison's map of 1847, in the New Orleans Academy of Sciences, showed a depth of from one hundred and sixty-two to one

Impossible to determine the age of remains found in this alluvium.

* How the World was Peopled, pp. 86, 87. † Ib., p. 330. ‡ See pp. 84, 85.

hundred and eighty-seven feet. Mr. Alfred Henson, who had lived in the city sixty years in 1867, told me that he recollected when the deep channel of the river flowed where Tchoupitoulas Street is now built, in the heart of the business part of it, a quarter of a mile from the present shore. By undermining and engulfing its banks, with everything upon them, logs tangled in vines and bedded in mud, cypress stumps, Indian graves, and modern works of art, are suddenly swallowed up and buried, at all depths, by its waters, from ten to one hundred and eighty-seven feet. The deep channel then works its way from them, and leaves them beneath a deep soil of inconceivable fertility, which quickly produces above them a dense forest of rapid and short-lived growth; first of cypress remote from the shore, with willows and cottonwood next to its receding current; then of live-oak, hackberry, and elm, with a variety of other trees. But the restless and resistless giant soon returns with a sweeping curve, and invades the land of the oaks, and of the cypress also; and undoes quickly all the work of a quarter of a century, or of an age, to do it over again. In 1856, an Artesian auger penetrated a cedar log eighteen inches thick, which it had buried one hundred and fifty-seven feet beneath the pavement of Canal Street."*

Mr. Horner's explorations in the mud of the Nile.

All this throws light on Mr. Horner's "Researches in Egypt," as Sir John Lubbock denominates his observations touching the sediment from the Nile which has accumulated around the obelisk at Heliopolis and the statue of Rameses II. at Memphis, and above a certain piece of pottery which he found in this deposit at the depth of thirty-nine feet. The obelisk "is believed" to have been erected about 2300 B.C., and adding 1850, the year when the observation was made, we have four thousand one hundred and fifty years for the age of the same. Eleven feet of sediment have accumulated around it, or some 3.18 inches in a century. In the case of the colossal statue at Memphis, the present surface is ten feet six and three-quarter inches above the base of the platform on which the statue stood. Assuming that the platform was sunk fourteen and three-quarter inches below the surface of the ground at the time it was laid, we have a depth of sediment from the present surface to that level of nine feet four inches. Rameses, according to Lepsius, reigned between 1394 and 1328 B.C., which gives an antiquity of three thousand two hundred and fifteen years, and consequently a mean increase of three and a half inches in a century. With this unit of measure Mr. Horner ascertains that the piece of pottery "had been buried thirteen thousand years."†

Sir John Lubbock hesitates to accept "unreservedly" the conclusions of Mr. Horner, but regards his calculations as "of great importance."

---

* Pages 85, 86.

† See "Pre-historic Times," p. 395.

The subject is earnestly discussed in the "Antiquity of Man," and has exercised various scientific societies. The resulting estimates for the antiquity of bricks and pottery in Egypt range from twelve thousand to sixty thousand years. A writer in the *London Quarterly Review* answers all this with the remark that the late Sir Robert Stephenson found in the delta near Damietta, at a greater depth than was ever reached by Mr. Horner, a brick bearing upon it the stamp of Mohammed Ali.

The answer.

It is farther stated by the Rev. Mr. Savile, in his work entitled "The Truth of the Bible," that in the deepest boring at the foot of the statue of Rameses II. there was found the Grecian honeysuckle stamped upon some of the supposed palæolithic fragments, which belonged to the age of Alexander the Great at the earliest.

And farther: Mr. Horner, in his papers in the Philosophical Transactions for 1855–58, represents that there were some ninety-five excavations made in the mud near Memphis, besides a number near Heliopolis, and that in nearly all of these excavations fragments of *burnt brick* were brought up from greater depths than that from which the pottery was obtained. Now, the brick used in ancient times in Egypt was almost invariably sun-dried, and not burnt. The burnt brick was not commonly used till the Roman period. If, then, Mr. Horner brought up burnt brick from so many places, it was probably Roman brick.

And again: Mr. Osburn, the author of the "Monumental History of Egypt," in a letter to the *Literary Gazette*, states that Abd-al-Latif, a historian of Bagdad, visited Memphis about six centuries ago, and that he describes this statue as standing at that time. The mud of the nine feet four inches must then be dated from the thirteenth century of our era, instead of from the seventeenth century before that era.

And again: If the mud deposits of the Nile have been accumulating around this statue ever since it was set up in the city of Memphis, then the inundations of that river must have annually submerged the city. The more probable fact is that the inundation was banked out, and that the floods of the river never reached the statue till Memphis became a ruin in the fifth century of our era.

Even the *Anthropological Review* pronounces Mr. Horner's evidence "preposterous," and laments that Sir Charles Lyell "should have thought it worth while to notice *such absurdities*."

THE CONE OF THE TINIÈRE.

This is another prominent witness relied on by the archæologists to prove the "antiquity of man." Sir John Lubbock and Sir Charles Lyell consider it with the utmost gravity. At the eastern extremity of the Lake of Geneva, at the city of Villeneuve, the torrent of the Tinière descends abruptly from the mountains. It brings down annually a certain amount of gravel, which has been deposited in the form of a half-cone on the plateau on the border of the lake. The apex of the cone rests against the side of the mountain, and the base extends in a semicircle around the mouth of the gorge from which the torrent descends. A railroad cut through the cone has exposed a section nearly to the base of the cone. Four feet from the top were found Roman relics; at ten feet were found bronze implements; and at nineteen feet Morlot found stone implements. The entire depth of the cone is thirty-two feet and six inches. Some two hundred years ago the increase of the cone was stopped by confining the torrent between stone walls. This leaves about fourteen hundred or fifteen hundred years for the Roman period. In this time about four feet of gravel (as the calculation runs) were deposited, or about three and a half inches in a century. From this datum Morlot calculates that the antiquity of the bronze relics is about three thousand eight hundred years, that of the stone relics about six thousand four hundred years, and that of the whole cone about ten thousand years.*

Relied on by the anthropologists.

M. Morlot's calculation.

Dr. Andrews has also demolished this calculation. "It is with great hesitation," he says, "that I question the conclusions of a European savant, made respecting his own country; but, having twice examined these cones with great care, and followed the torrent a mile into the mountains to study its appearance and action, I cannot avoid the conclusion that there is a very singular mathematical error in estimating the age of the cones, and an omission of several important geological facts, which vitiate the whole calculation. The nature of the mathematical error will be made obvious by a few facts. The gravel cones of Switzerland are very numerous, and the principle of their formation easily understood. On the supposition that the torrent brings down about the same amount of gravel every year,† it will readily be seen that the first year's deposit will lie upon the plateau in a conical heap of no great breadth, but of considerable height. The second year's gravel, however, will be spread over the entire surface of the first, and, extending wider, it must be much thinner. The third year's accretion will be broader and thinner still; and so on to the last. It follows that the superficial annual layers are always the thinnest, because the broadest. Now, if Morlot is correctly quoted, he first derives his scale of from three and three-tenths to four inches increase per century from the superficial layers where they are thinnest, and then applies

Dr. Andrews's reply.

* Pre-historic Times, p. 393, Amer. edit.

† Which is not probable, comparing modern with ancient times.

it without modification to the interior where the annual accretions were much thicker. His unit of measure is, therefore, too small, and exaggerates the total age. It is perfectly plain that the true method is to take the cubic contents of the strata whose age is known, and compare the amount with the cubic contents of the whole cone; or, in plain language, if the annual rain-fall and gravel-wash has been uniform, then as the quantity of gravel in the layers deposited since the Roman conquest is to the quantity in the whole cone, so is the time required for the deposit of these layers to the time required for the formation of the whole cone.

"The revised data and calculation would be as follows: The lower cone is really a half-cone, the apex resting against the declivity of the upper one, and the base being a semicircle. The dimensions are nearly as follows:

"Height of apex, 38 feet.

"Radius of the base, 900 feet.

"Cubic feet in the strata deposited since the Roman conquest, 5,283,205.

"Time of deposition of the same, 1300 to 1500 years.

"Cubic feet in the whole lower cone,* 16,116,408.

"Time of deposit of same, 3965 to 4576 years.

"Adding the three hundred years which have elapsed since the deposit ceased, the present age of the lower cone would be from four thousand two hundred and sixty-five to four thousand eight hundred and seventy-six years."

The whole cone, therefore, is, at the maximum, only four thousand five hundred years old. The stone implements lie about midway between the apex and the base. It is plain, therefore, that they are not more than three thousand years old. This, of course, is merely an approximation. And the whole calculation would be still farther changed if it should be true either that the deposition of the gravel was arrested earlier than two hundred or three hundred years ago, or that the Roman coin found (which Lubbock says was very much worn) was dropped a couple of centuries later than has been assumed, or that three thousand years ago the torrent of the Tinière flowed with a bolder current than it did in the Middle Ages.

M. de Ferry and M. Arcelin have both made calculations designed to fix approximately the dates of the Iron, Bronze, and Stone Ages. The river Saône is gradually raising the plain through which it flows, and these *savans*, taking the position of the Roman remains as the basis of their calculations, have esti-

Calculations of MM. de Ferry and Arcelin.

* There is an older and much larger cone above the one under consideration.

mated the probable age of the subjacent beds. Comparing a number of observations, M. de Ferry fixes the accumulation since the Roman period at a thickness of 1.1^{mm}; of the Bronze Age layer at 1.30; of the Stone Age layer at 1.50. This would give for the Bronze Age an antiquity of three thousand years; for the Neolithic Age an antiquity of four thousand or five thousand years; and for the Palæolithic Age about nine thousand or ten thousand years. M. Arcelin adopts a somewhat different scale: assuming for the Roman layer a depth of one metre, deduced from twenty-four stations, he thus obtains for the Celtic Iron Age an antiquity of from one thousand eight hundred to two thousand seven hundred years; for the Bronze Age an antiquity of from two thousand seven hundred to three thousand six hundred years; for the Neolithic Age an antiquity of from three thousand six hundred to six thousand seven hundred, and for the Palæolithic Age an antiquity of from six thousand seven hundred to eight thousand years.

This is a considerable improvement on Sir Charles Lyell and Sir John Lubbock,—a decided abatement from two hundred thousand years for palæolithic man. If we make some allowance for the difference in the volume of the Saône at the different periods, the calculations would appear to be nearly correct.

To illustrate what widely-different conclusions are reached by the anthropologists from calculations like these, we may state that at the meeting of the British Association at Dundee, some years since, Mr. Vivian presented an estimate which he had made of the age of man from observations at Kent's Cavern. Roman remains were found under stalagmite five millimetres thick, which represented two thousand years. With this unit, Mr. Vivian fixed the duration of man's residence in England at two hundred and sixty-four thousand years.* It will be remembered that at the meeting of the Association in 1871, Mr. Vivian expands this estimate to "more than a million of years."

* Matériaux, tome iv. p. 48.

CHAPTER XXXI.

THE ABSENCE OF THE PALÆOLITHIC AGE IN EGYPT.

If the modern theory of a Palæolithic Age, dating back two or three hundred thousand years ago, is correct, of all countries in the world Egypt is the place where we ought to find some traces of it. We ought to find there, in the geological deposits which are the equivalent of the River-Gravel, the palæolithic implements, and the remains of an extinct fauna. If there is no deposit of the so-called "drift" in the Valley of the Nile, there is, of course, some geological deposit of corresponding age; and in this we should find hatchets of the St. Acheul type, and the bones of extinct animals, as we do in England, France, Spain, Italy, and India.

Nothing of the kind, however, occurs. There are no indications whatever of a Palæolithic Age. Flint implements have been found in Egypt, but they belong to the Neolithic Age, and occur on the surface, or near the surface—or in the tombs. We have little doubt that, as in Babylonia, a few stone implements of the palæolithic form will ultimately be found in Egypt; but it will be remembered that in Babylonia these have occurred in association with *metal*. No doubt some of the earliest flint implements of Egypt were very primitive, but they were, as in Babylonia, cotemporary, or nearly cotemporary, with bronze and iron. Indeed, *one* such implement is reported by M. Arcelin as found in the Valley of the Nile.

In the volume of the Congrès d'Anthropologie for 1872,* M. J. Delanoüe asks, "How is it then that, being one of the countries most anciently inhabited, it [Egypt] never offers, up to the present time, to the numerous archæologists who have explored it, any human prehistoric station, nor any rough-hewn flints *in situ* in the diluvium, as at St. Acheul, for example?" "That," he continues, "is easily explained by the fact that there is no quaternary *terrain* visible in Egypt. I know well that several geologists have affirmed the existence of *ancient terraces* all along the Nile. The fact is exact, but quite exceptional, and it is wrong to generalize it.

"The Nile, which has excavated so great a valley, had evidently formerly a much greater volume and a higher level; but there remain no traces of its *high levels*. The accidental deposits of gravel and mud

* Page 314.

which travellers have long signalled at ten, fifteen, and thirty metres above the present floods, are all situated near ancient natural barriers, now no longer existing. They are, then, purely local and accidental. It is there only that the true quaternary can be observed at the surface of the soil, and that tools of flint occur *in situ.*"

M. Delanoüe professes to have found at such a point a collection of pre-historic tools on the summit of the hillock of Fatira, situated thirty metres above the floods of the Nile, and five kilometres from Djebel Salsile (Mont de la Chaine). He gives a cut of a beautiful polished instrument in white flint found at this place, associated with shells and pebbles. There was at this point, he says, according to the opinion of M. Linant-Bey and the most competent engineers, an ancient *digue* which has been broken by the river.* This ancient barrier had created at this point a sort of lake and a cataract, until the river broke through and fell to its present level. These terraces are found at Ouadi Alfa, Assouan, Djebel Ein, etc.

M. Delanoüe then mentions the discovery of a workshop of *rude* flints at Chersonna, twelve kilometres from Esne.

This is all the evidence that M. Delanoüe can collect for the existence of a palæolithic age in Egypt. A fatal objection to the opinion that the deposits are *palæolithic* presents itself at the threshold: the beautiful specimen of polished white flint to which we have referred is *neolithic.*

Again, these flints occur *at the surface*, and have no associated remains of any extinct animals.

With regard to the antiquity of the "barriers" to which M. Delanoüe refers, we may remark that in one instance we have the data by means of which to fix the period during which it was broken. "In remote ages," says Mr. Smith, in his "Ancient History of the East," "the hills which border the valley of the Nile approached so close to one another at some points as either to form lakes, or at least to dam up the waters of the inundation in certain parts, till the river forced its way through the barrier of rocks. Such a barrier once existed at Silsilis (*Hadjar Selseleh*), some forty miles below the first cataract. The effect of this in spreading the water of the inundation over the now barren plains of Nubia is still seen in ancient alluvial deposits, which reach northward as far as Silsilis, and in water-worn rocks at a considerable distance from the river. But this is not all: we can determine the historic period within which the barrier was broken down. On the rocks at Semneh, *inscriptions of Amenemes III.* and other kings of the Twelfth Dynasty show that the inundation then reached twenty-seven feet above

* M. Linant-Bey, who, M. Delanoüe says, has studied better than any one else the hydrography of the Nile, has only seen in Egypt and in Nubia *local terraces*, occasioned by these obstructions to the course of the river.

its present height; while, on the other hand, the foundations of buildings on the old deposit, and the caves in the rocks near the Nile, prove that the lower level was permanently established by the time of the Eighteenth Dynasty. . . . But it must be observed that the name of this king [Amenemes III.] gives us only an *upward limit;* and among the inscriptions at Semneh, some are now said to bring down the period of the river's higher rise into the Thirteenth Dynasty." *

If palæolithic man lived in Egypt, there is one other quarter in which we might expect to find some traces of his existence. The remains of the "palæolithic" man of France are found not only in the river-gravel, but also in the ancient *caves.* There are no traces of palæolithic man in caves in Egypt.

If it should be alleged that, owing to the long occupation of Egypt by civilized man, all such traces would have disappeared from the caves, then we must call attention to the fact that such caves and such traces of man are found in Italy.

But, on the other hand, the question may now be asked, If the extinct animals lived a few thousand years ago, and left their remains (mingled with the flint implements) in the Somme Valley, as we contend, how do *we* explain the absence of such remains in Egypt? That the argument is as damaging to one hypothesis as to the other.

Our reply is this: 1. That after the Flood, Egypt was occupied *immediately* by civilized man, and by a considerable population; and that, under such circumstances, the wild beasts of the forest would rapidly disappear. Of the river-gravel deposit there seems to have been none; of the cave-life of palæolithic Europe there would be little. We do not find the remains of wild beasts with the Egyptian relics, for the same reason that we do not find them with Roman relics. 2. That, in all probability, Egypt was inhabited *before the Flood* for many centuries, and in that case the cave-fauna had probably disappeared from that region before it was re-occupied by the descendants of Noah.

Thus the argument with which we set out in the first chapter of this book, that in Egypt and Babylonia we find man in the beginning *civilized,* is signally corroborated, after our recognition of the "palæolithic" fauna and implements in Western Europe and elsewhere, *by the failure of this phenomenon in the Valleys of the Nile and the Euphrates.* Had such remains been found in these valleys, we should also have necessarily found the traces of the intermediate progress from the Palæolithic Age to the Temple-towers and the Pyramids. We find neither. Man appears rotund and complete in Egypt, as the sun suddenly presents itself above the horizon in the morning.

---

* Ancient History of the East, p. 88, Amer. edit.

CHAPTER XXXII.

THE ABSENCE OF PALÆOLITHIC REMAINS IN THE NORTH OF ENGLAND, AND IN SCOTLAND, IRELAND, NORWAY, SWEDEN, AND DENMARK.

A Clue to the Date of the Palæolithic Age.—No Flint Implements of this Age found in these Countries, and no Remains of a Palæolithic Fauna.—Due to the Fact that the North of Europe was still in the Glacial Age when the Gravels of the Somme Valley were deposited.—First Traces of Man in the North found in the Scotch Carses and the Danish Peat.—Date of the Glacial Age in the North.—Came down to the Era of Polished Stone.—Prof. Jamieson on the Geological Changes in Scotland.—Recent Shell-Mounds.—Recent Use of Stone Implements.—Remains of the Mammoth, Reindeer, Urus, etc., found in the Scotch Glacial Deposits.—A Mild Inter-Glacial Period.—Corresponded with the Period just preceding the Palæolithic Flood and the Deposition of the River-Gravel.—The Occurrence of both an Arctic and a Southern Fauna in the Palæolithic Gravels and Caves explained.—The Glacial and the Neolithic Ages.—Elevation and Subsidence of Land in Sweden.—Recent Erratics observed in Sweden and Scotland.

A clue to the date of the Palæolithic Age.

WE are not without a clue to the date of the Palæolithic Age; and it is most astonishing that in this connection, although the facts are well known, it has escaped the attention of all of the writers on this subject. THERE ARE NO PALÆOLITHIC IMPLEMENTS IN THE NORTH OF EUROPE,—that is to say, in Norway, Sweden, Denmark, Scotland, and Ireland. Nor do we find these implements in the river-gravel of the north of England. In this last-named country they occur in the valleys of the Ouse, the Waveney, the Thames, and their tributaries, and at various places along the southern coast; but never in the gravel north of the Ouse or west of the valley of the Axe.

All of the stone implements found in the regions indicated belong to the Neolithic Age.* In other words, Palæolithic man never penetrated into the north of Europe.

Absence of the great pachyderms.

Nor do we find, with a qualification to be presently noticed, in Scandinavia, Denmark, Scotland, or Ireland,† any traces of the mammoth, the woolly rhinoceros, the cave-lion, or

* Excepting a few bone-caves in England north of the line indicated.

† It has been recently stated that "worked flints" have been found in the river-gravel of the northeast of Ireland. It is *not* stated that they were of the palæolithic type, nor that they were associated with the remains of the Quaternary fauna. An occasional discovery of this sort may, perhaps, be naturally looked for.

the cave-hyæna. The reindeer and the Irish elk occur in the peat, having lived, as we have shown, in Neolithic times; and the same seems to be true of the cave-bear in Denmark. The absence of the great extinct animals mentioned in these northern regions finds a ready explanation: it is referred by Mr. Boyd Dawkins to the fact that the Ice had not yet retired from these higher latitudes. They were still in the Glacial Age. Neither man nor beast ventured beyond the regions of the palæolithic gravels. The gravels of Scotland and the other northern districts of Europe contain neither flints nor the bones of the extinct mammals.

The North still in the Glacial Age.

The first traces of man in Northern Europe occur in the *carses* of Scotland and in the Danish and Irish peat bogs, and the implements found are all of the Polished Stone Age.

First traces of man in the North.

"It has been estimated," says Sir Charles Lyell, "that the number of flint implements of the Palæolithic type already found in Northern France and *Southern England*, exclusive of flakes, is not less than three thousand. *No similar tools have been met with in Denmark, Sweden, or Norway*, where Nilsson, Thomsen, and other antiquaries have collected with so much care the relics of the Stone Age. Hence it is supposed that Palæolithic man never penetrated into Scandinavia, which may perhaps have been as much covered with ice and snow as the greater part of Greenland is at present." *

We have thus the means of fixing the date of the Glacial Epoch: it lasted in Ireland, Scotland, and Denmark *down to the beginning of the Neolithic Age;* down to the date of the older Swiss lake-dwellings.†

Date of the Glacial Age.

In France, the Glacial Age had just terminated at the beginning of the Palæolithic period.

The Palæolithic period covers the interval between the appearance of man in France and the appearance of man in Scotland and in the north of England. We thus ascertain the *duration* of the Palæolithic Age with absolute certainty. By as much longer as the Ice age lingered in the north of England than it lingered in the valley of the Somme, by that much is the dawn of the Palæolithic Age removed from the dawn of the Neolithic Age,—using these terms always in the sense employed by the archæologists, and as descriptive of the periods represented by the fauna of the mammoth, etc., on the one

Duration of the Palæolithic Age.

* Principles of Geology, vol. ii. p. 567, Amer. edit.

† So Sir Charles Lyell remarks: "The close of the glacial period in the Grampians may have coincided in time with the existence of man in those parts of Europe where the climate was less severe, as, for example, in the basins of the Thames, Somme, and Seine, in which the bones of many extinct mammalia are associated with flint implements of the antique type." Antiquity of Man, Amer. edit., p. 252.

hand, and the aurochs, *Ursus arctos,* beaver, common deer, ox, sheep, wolf, fox, dog, etc., on the other.

In the "Journal of the Geological Society"* Prof. Thomas F. Jamieson, F.G.S., has a paper on the "History of the Last Geological Changes in Scotland," which illustrates these positions. There are, he tells us, no remains of the mammoth or the Rhinoceros tichorinus in Scotland after the Glacial era; and the valley-gravel is singularly destitute of fossils of every kind. The first traces of man are found in the raised estuarine beds represented by the flat country of the *carses.* Prof. Jamieson then mentions that several primitive *canoes* have been found in the silt of the Clyde at Glasgow, and that with the whale found in the carse of the Forth, at Blair Drummond, there was found a fragment of stag's horn, similar to that found with the Airthrey whale, and having a similar round hole bored through it. Canoes, he says, have also been found in the carse of the Forth. The group of mollusca occurring in these beds are all still living at present both in the seas of Britain and to the south of this country, while some of them are not known to live in the Arctic regions.

Last geological changes in Scotland.

He recognizes (we by no means accept all he says) the following as the order of events during the post-tertiary period:

1. After the deposit of the crag-gravel, and the mammoth had lived in Scotland, the country was covered with a great depth of snow and ice, which extinguished the preceding fauna. The ice moved in great streams from the great water-sheds, carrying along the stony débris and boulders which constitute the boulder-clay or till.

2. This was followed by a depression of the land to the extent of several hundred feet, so that all the lower grounds were below the sea-level. It was at this time that the brick-clays containing arctic shells were formed, the boulders being drifted hither and thither by the floating ice, the ice probably still covering much of the land. The condition of the country was similar to the present state of things in Spitzbergen.

3. The country emerged from the water, but the ice still lay on much of the land.

4. The glaciers began finally to retreat in earnest, leaving behind them heaps of débris. The floods occasioned by the rapid thaws strewed the valleys with large quantities of rolled gravel.

5. By this time the land had attained a higher level than its present level, so that Britain formed a mass united to the continent. Woods of birch, alder, and hazel grew on the soil, while the Great Irish Elk, the Red Deer, the Great Wild Bull, the Wolf, the Bear, the Beaver,

* Vol. xxi. p. 180 (1865).

and probably the Reindeer, made their appearance. In the valleys the rivers were gradually cutting their way to lower levels, and in doing so spread out much gravel and alluvial soil along the banks. This period is represented by the submarine forests and peat-beds underlying the carses of the Tay and the Forth.

6. A depression now took place, cutting off the land from the continent. In the valleys of the Tay and the Forth the coast-line was twenty-five or thirty feet above the present, and on the coast of Aberdeenshire eight or ten feet higher than the present line. Now are formed the old estuarine beds, or carses, of the Forth and the Tay; and MAN APPEARS.

7. There is yet another movement of elevation, the natives using stone implements, and the peat (which is eight or twelve feet deep) in the vicinity of Blair Drummond forming. [This peat, as we have shown, is post-Roman.]

Shell-mounds examined by Prof. Jamieson. Very recent.

Prof. Jamieson gives an account in the same paper of certain *shell-mounds* examined by him on the raised beach at the mouth of the Ythan, on the northeast coast of Scotland. The examination was made in company with Mr. Robert Dawson. They found no metal, but quantities of chipped flint. "Their antiquity, however, does not seem to be very great. The base of the largest of them is not four feet above the present reach of the tides in the estuary of the river, which shows that the land *must have been as high as it is at present when they were formed.* They are therefore later than the raised beaches* and estuary beds, some of them, perhaps, a good deal later, seeing that there is much blown sand underneath them."

The chipped flints, says Prof. Jamieson, occur also abundantly in the immediate neighborhood of one of these mounds, and are also found in great numbers at certain places along the coast, both north and south of the Ythan, "*often in positions a very few feet above high-water mark.*"

Stone implements probably in use to a late period among poorer classes.

He then adds that it is "very probable that among the poorer and less civilized inhabitants the use of stone tools may have continued to a comparatively late period. No one who has seen the primeval implements *still in use* in some of the Western Isles of Scotland will think this unlikely."†

These beaches post-Roman.

As it is certain that the second of these raised beaches of Scotland (that represented at Leith) is post-Roman, we ascertain from the foregoing that the Stone Age (apparently unpolished) existed in Scotland in the past eighteen hundred years; and that

* One of these beaches, as we have shown, has been elevated since the Roman occupation of Britain.

† Page 193.

the shell-mounds of the Stone Age ("no trace of metal") are of the same recent date.

It will be remembered that in one of the "primitive" canoes from the carse at Glasgow a piece of *cork* was found, while an iron anchor was obtained from the carse of Falkirk. These represent the older beach, and possess no great antiquity, while the beach above Edinburgh has certainly been raised since the Romans used the port of Cramond as a naval station.

We have now, however, as was indicated, to qualify the foregoing remarks: while there are no traces of the mammoth in Scotland after the Glacial Epoch, such remains do occasionally occur in the glacial deposits themselves.

Mammoth in the Scotch till.

There are evidences, says Prof. James Geikie, of two periods of glaciation in Scotland,—characterized by the lower and the upper till.* Between these two beds there have been found intercalated veins or beds of peat and sand (or sand and gravel). These intercalated beds imply an *inter-glacial* mild period, and it is here that we occasionally meet with the remains of the mammoth, the reindeer, the Irish elk, the *Bos primigenius*, and the horse, sometimes with marine shells. A railway-cutting in Cowden Glen, Renfrewshire, exposed two beds of till, and interposed between them a bed of silt, clay, mud, sand, and gravel, with here and there a line of peat. This intercalated bed yielded a skull of the great ox, and bones of the Irish elk and the horse. At Woodhill Quarry, near Kilmaurs, in Ayrshire, the remains of the mammoth and reindeer, with marine shells, have been found. So at Chapelhall, at Cliftonhall, and elsewhere. At Cliftonhall, in the valley of the Almond, a tusk of the mammoth was found in very stiff glacial clay, "in so fresh a state," says Sir Charles Lyell, "that an ivory-turner purchased it, and turned part of it into chessmen before it was rescued from destruction."

A mild inter-glacial period.

Traces of a similar inter-glacial period have been noted, says Prof. Geikie, by Messrs. Törnebohm, Holmström, and Nathorst, in Sweden. The lower blue till in this country, says Mr. Holmström, is very thick, and extends almost continuously over the whole country. He has found shells and plants in fresh-water clays, resting on this lower till, and a bed of yellow till above the fresh-water clays. These shells and plants he supposes to have come in from the south

Sweden.

* We make these statements about an "inter-glacial" period entirely on the authority of others. We feel that very little is known about the glacial age. No satisfactory theory has yet been propounded. The Iceberg theory does not account for the facts; and the Ice-sheet theory does not account for the facts. We need a third theory; and any such theory must take cognizance of *all* the facts, and not of local phenomena only.

when the ice retired. Then at a subsequent period some local glaciers, he thinks, crept down from the great mass of ice still lingering in the north, covering with morainic matter the fresh-water clays.

Switzerland.

In Switzerland we find, Prof. Geikie proceeds, what are presumed to be inter-glacial beds at Dürnten and Wetzeken, in the canton of Zurich, and at Utanach and Mörschweil, in the canton of St. Gall. Certain beds of lignite, from two to five feet thick,* occur at these places, made up chiefly of peat-forming plants, but containing remains of trees. In this peat-bed are found the bones of the "Asiatic" elephant, a species of rhinoceros, the cave-bear, the stag, and the urus. At Dürnten the lignite rests on the equivalent of the Scotch till, called in Switzerland the *grund-moräne*. Above the lignite is a thick deposit of gravel and sand, on which repose several Alpine erratics.

This second glaciation in Switzerland was characterized by glaciers of much smaller dimensions than those which prevailed in the first ice-period.

There is a remarkable parallelism between the glacial phenomena of Switzerland and those of the north of Europe. We find the extinct animals occupying the same geological position. In Switzerland, as in Scotland, the close of the Glacial period corresponds with the opening of the Neolithic Age,—for Palæolithic man is not represented in the Alpine valleys. The ice excluded him also from this part of Europe.

Corresponds with pre-river-gravel period.

It is pretty evident that this so-called inter-glacial period of Switzerland, Scotland, and Scandinavia corresponds in point of time with the period immediately preceding the deposition of the river-gravel in the valley of the Somme. The glaciers withdrew partially, and a few of the Palæolithic animals wandered into Scotland and into Switzerland. At the date of the Palæolithic Flood, when the remains of the mammoth and the Palæolithic implements were buried in the gravel of the Somme and the Thames Valleys, the cold (though with mitigated severity) set in again in Scotland and amid the Alps. After an interval the ice retired again, and finally disappeared in most localities. The mammoth and the rhinoceros became extinct, and we meet with the fauna of the Scotch and Irish peat, and the Swiss lake-dwellings.

A measure of the *duration* of the "inter-glacial epoch" is afforded by the intercalated peat-beds at Dürnten.

Human remains in glacial clay.

We are now prepared to estimate correctly the human fibula recently found in the Victoria Cave, in the north of England,† "beneath a bed of stiff glacial clay,"—supposing, as may

* It reaches occasionally a thickness of twelve feet.

† In the mountains of West Yorkshire.

be the case, that the bone was found in its original position,—and which seems to have occasioned Mr. Geikie so much excitement.

There were, doubtless, centres of local glaciation even after the second retreat of the ice; and the Victoria fibula may be even as late as one of these. There is plenty of glacial clay in Switzerland that is not five hundred years old.*

In America the Glacial Age lingered in the far north, as in Scotland and Scandinavia; and we accordingly find (with trivial exceptions) no remains of the mammoth or mastodon in Canada or New England. We are also told that America had its inter-glacial period. Prof. Newbury, according to Prof. Geikie, mentions the occurrence of an intercalated forest-bed in the glacial deposits of Ohio, and states that the bones of the mammoth, the mastodon, and the great beaver have been found in the same position.

Ice age in America.

We desire to state (as intimated in a previous page) that we by no means give our assent to Mr. Geikie's theory of "The Great Ice Age." That great riddle remains to be solved yet. We cannot, for example, comprehend how, as Mr. Geikie represents to have been the process, it is *possible* for the "till" to have been deposited or formed underneath and by means of an *ice-sheet*,—sometimes (the deposit) thirty, or forty, or fifty feet thick. We have glaciers in Switzerland: has any one ever known the "till" to accumulate under one of them? The Glacier de

* From the learned work of Mr. Boyd Dawkins just published, entitled "Cave-Hunting," it appears that there is no evidence that this human fibula is either pre-glacial or inter-glacial. It was found, we are told, under "stiff glacial clay," and there are ice-scratched Silurian grit-stones at the entrance to the cave, imbedded in this "glacial" clay.

Now, we learn from Mr. Dawkins that these ice-scratched stones are probably derived from the waste of boulder-clay which has dropped from a higher level. This, he says, "appears the more likely because some of the boulders have been deprived of the clay in which they were imbedded, and are piled on each other with empty space between them, the clay being carried down to a lower level and re-deposited."

The deposits above the cave-earth, he proceeds to say, occupying the interior and the entrance to the cave, have been introduced by the rains, either through the entrance or through the crevices which penetrate the roof, and consist of a finer detritus washed out of the boulder-clay on the surface at a higher level.

"The laminated portions of the gray clay are considered by Mr. Tiddemann," Mr. Dawkins remarks, "to have been formed by the flow of water through the entrance, derived from the daily melting of the glacier which occupied the valley." To this Mr. Dawkins replies that "since similar accumulations are being formed at the present time at the bottom of pools in many caves, they cannot be taken to imply a glacial origin." Cave-Hunting, pp. 121–123.

Mr. Dawkins believes, however, that the fibula is "pre-glacial;" this conclusion he reaches from the consideration of the fact that the bones of the cave-hyæna, mammoth, reindeer, etc., were found in the Victoria Cave,—in a region north of the line which is the boundary of the implement-bearing gravels. Is it strange that in a few instances these animals wandered across the line?

Bossons, about 1817 we believe, had been continually advancing, until it not only covered part of a man's farm, but began to topple stones over the moraine down upon his house. The good Catholics there made a religious procession, and stuck a cross on the moraine; when the glacier stopped; and it has now receded some four hundred yards. If this ice-sheet had possessed the power to lay down a stratum of "till" like those described by Mr. Geikie in Scotland, one might repair to Chamounix and dig up cats and dogs, and tobacco-pipes, under a bed of true till. As it is, the ground is covered over with a desolate stone moraine at the lower border, and scattered blocks of stone above.

In regard to another point, we observe that, whatever be true of Scotland, according to Mr. Geikie's own showing, in Switzerland and America we recognize no return of the "ice-sheet,"—in other words, no upper till. Let us take the so-called "inter-glacial" bed at Dürnten. The lignite, we are told, rests upon "a layer of fine yellow sand and clay, beneath which comes an unknown thickness of grund-moräne. Overlying the lignite we find a considerable thickness of *gravel and sand*, in beds which are surmounted with several large Alpine erratics." * Now, what is this upper bed but the "river-gravel"?

"A similar succession of deposits has been detected," we are told, "by Professor Hans Höfer, as occurring in Carinthia. In the lower reaches of the valleys of that region ground-moraine is well developed, and perched blocks and erratics are found at great elevations, while the glaciated aspect of the mountains further shows that the valleys must have brimmed with ice. Overlying the ground-moraine come massive deposits of *river-gravel*, etc. (near Klagenfurt), which have yielded remains of the woolly rhinoceros, the steinbock (*Ibex cebennarum*), and *Bos taurus*. These fresh-water beds Professor Höfer correlates with *the gravel-beds* that immediately overlie the Dürnten lignites (corresponding to the *Inter-glaciale Gerollbildung* of Heer)." †

The upper till in Scotland, therefore, corresponds with this river-gravel in Switzerland.

There are a number of unwarranted assumptions in Mr. Geikie's work besides that which concerns the formation of till. He assumes that a glacier filling a main valley "dams back" the streams of side-valleys, in utter disregard of the fact that the glaciers are not quite equal to a sieve for holding water. Side-streams plunge into, through, and under them without serious obstruction, like all the other waters connected with the glacier. The same absurdity is repeated about the terminal moraine damming the valleys and making lakes, when they are not a whit better for such a purpose than a row of stakes driven across a

* The Great Ice Age, p. 375.

† Ib., p. 377. The italics are ours.

valley. Another remarkable assertion is that running water never cuts basins at any point deeper than places further down stream, because the river-bottom "cannot run up hill." The truth is, as every observer knows, that a river may scoop out a hollow a hundred feet deep, and a few miles below the water may be so shallow that a horse may ford it on a rock bottom, the top of the water not having descended five feet in that distance. The deep parts of our rivers were often cut out enormously in the rush of the Loess floods, especially in the earthy formations, and everywhere streams cut their beds according to the mechanical laws of force, velocity, and resistance, giving undulating bottoms, which in many places "run up-hill" for some distance.

Elsewhere, Mr. Geikie states that mastodon remains have been found underneath the glacial drift in America. So far from this being the fact, they *always* occur on the *top* of the boulder drift, and covered only by swamp or river deposits. In a few instances the remains have been found under the loess. Mr. Geikie also states that the remains of the Asiatic elephant were found in the Dürnten lignite-beds,*—which can hardly be true; and, again, that the remains of the mammoth and the woolly rhinoceros are found in the "post-glacial" deposits of Switzerland which are characterized by polished stone implements; † which is, at least, new to us. If this latter statement be true, it is a very conclusive evidence of the very recent existence of the mammoth and the rhinoceros in Switzerland.

The mixed fauna of the river-gravels explained.

If we be right in identifying the period of the Palæolithic Flood with the "second" cold period of the interglacialists, some light is thrown by the hypothesis on a fact which has been the source of great perplexity to the archæologists and geologists. We find, as has been shown, in the river-gravels of France and England, a strange mixture of a Southern and a Northern fauna,—the remains of the hippopotamus and the hyæna mingled with those of the musk-sheep, the reindeer, and the glutton. The bones of the hippopotamus occur in the valleys of the Somme and the Seine, at Bedford, Grays, Ilford, Peckham, Barton, etc.; and in the bone-caves of Kirkdale, Kent's Cavern, Durdham Down, and Ravenscliff. Mr. Geikie (with others) gives us a "geological" explanation of this: there were, he suggests, "great oscillations of climate" during the accumulation of the river-gravels. These deposits are of pre-glacial and inter-glacial age. "To some mild and genial inter-glacial period or periods" he would refer "the hippopotamus and the other Southern forms met with in the English caves." So Sir John Lubbock (adopting the suggestion of Mr. Croll) thinks there was during "the excavation of the river-valleys"

* See p. 375, Amer. edit.

† Page 379, Amer. edit.

a change of climate "every ten or twelve thousand years," whereby the hippopotamus and the reindeer were alternately accommodated.*

Apart from the monstrous character of this hypothesis, one fatal objection exists against it. We have been taught to infer the cotemporaneity of man and the mammoth from the fact that their remains are commingled in the river-gravel and in the cave-earth. Now, the bones of the Northern and Southern faunas are found "side by side."† It is impossible, therefore (unless we reject at the same time the argument from the juxtaposition of the remains of men and the mammoth), to admit the suggestion that "ten or twelve thousand years" intervened between the Arctic and Southern faunas of the Palæolithic gravels.

Our theory supposes the River-Gravel period in Southern England and France to synchronize with the "second glaciation" of Scotland. The climate of the former countries was of course adapted to the reindeer and the musk-ox and the great snowy owl. Preceding this the climate of France had been milder,—corresponding with the mild "inter-glacial" period of the north of England and Scotland. It was mild enough in Southern England (even as far north, indeed, as Leeds) for the hippopotamus. The remains of this animal do not occur often. Our theory of the Palæolithic period only calls for hundreds where that of the archæologists calls for thousands of years. The Palæolithic Flood might readily have brought together remains only separated by a very brief interval.

Again: Mr. Geikie and Sir John Lubbock believe that the river-valleys were slowly excavated by the rivers,—requiring a hundred or two hundred thousand years to complete the work. The Arctic fauna, therefore, ought to occur at one level, and the Southern fauna at another. But we find the Arctic fauna among the high-level gravels and equally among the low-level gravels. And so the Southern fauna is found also at both of these levels. The gravel was laid down, twenty or thirty feet thick, as the work of excavation proceeded. When the river (a very small stream sometimes, like the Somme) had cut its way down fifty feet, we may suppose the mild æon to set in, and the hippopotamus to appear. Gradually, as the river sank lower and lower in the

* The archæologists as a general rule represent that the climate of the Palæolithic period was intensely cold. At the International Congress of Pre-historic Archæology held at Stockholm last summer, Count de Saperta, however, narrated the discovery of fragments of tufa near Fontainebleau, in a Quaternary deposit, on which were impressed the outlines of fig-leaves, which apparently belong to a species now confined to Japan and the Chinese islands. M. Dupont observed on this that it was "another proof that the climate of Europe in the Quaternary period was warmer and more uniform than in late times, and that it was then the lion, the reindeer, the hippopotamus, and the hyæna existed side by side." The Academy, Aug. 29, 1874, p. 239.

† Pre-historic Times, p. 415, Amer. edit.

valley, the bones of this animal would be buried in the low-level gravel. Now, according to Mr. Geikie, how should these bones get up among those fifty feet higher? And *vice versa?* Sir John Lubbock sees the difficulty, and invokes a number—a series—of alternating periods, running from the top to the bottom of the valley.

The Glacial Age and the Neolithic Age.

The bringing down of the Glacial Period in Denmark and Scotland to the date of the Polished Stone Age is a great fact in this discussion. Singularly enough, Sir C. Lyell and Mr. Geikie admit the fact without realizing its significance. For the archæologists ordinarily fix the antiquity of the Polished Stone Age at five thousand or seven thousand years ago. But if the glaciation of Scotland and Southern Sweden terminated only some six thousand years ago, why assign a vast antiquity (two hundred thousand years) to the Glacial Age as represented in Southern England?

The raised beaches of Sweden.

The ascertainment of this date of the Glacial Age in the north of Europe throws great light also on the elevations and subsidences of the land in those regions.

M. Brongniart found at Uddevalla, on the west coast of Sweden, at the height of two hundred feet, a deposit of shells, "all of them identical with those now inhabiting the contiguous ocean."

In 1862, Mr. J. Gwyn Jeffreys visited Uddevalla and collected eighty-three species of shells from other beds, "*characteristic of the Glacial Period.*" "He also," continues Sir C. Lyell, from whom we are quoting, "obtained evidence that a littoral and shallow-water deposit underlaid the shells proper to deeper water; a fact clearly implying a depression of the bed of the sea previous to that upheaval which has since carried up the land where the marine shells are found to the height of more than two hundred feet. As to the date of this last upheaval, Mr. Torell has shown *that it by no means reaches back to the Glacial Period*, to which the shells above alluded to belong. Those shells, so characteristic of a cold climate, are specifically identical with those now living in the seas of Spitzbergen, ten degrees of latitude north of Uddevalla. Mr. Torell detected at the height of two hundred feet above the sea the remains of a marine testacea *agreeing with species now proper to the fauna of the adjacent and more temperate seas.* It appears, therefore, that the series of movements in the district under consideration consisted, first, of a depression converting the shallow water into deep sea at a time when the cold was very severe, and then of an elevation of more than two hundred feet when the waters of the sea had acquired their present milder temperature." *

* Principles of Geology, vol. ii. p. 192. The italics are ours.

We would remark, on this, first, that the *depression* spoken of seems to have been *sudden*. We pass at once from the shells of the shallow water to those of the deep sea.

Secondly, the upheaval "*by no means* reaches back to the Glacial Period." The climate had become what it is now. Since this date the land at Uddevalla has risen two hundred feet.

When was this? It was after the foundation of the Swiss lake-dwellings of the Polished Stone Age. If we place that at B.C. 1200, it will be liberal. It was about three thousand years ago; and if the movement has been uniform, it has proceeded at the rate of nearly seven feet per century,—instead of two and one-half feet per century, the unit of measure which Sir Charles Lyell has arbitrarily adopted to measure these movements all over the world,—including even a volcanic region like Sardinia.

Still farther light will be thrown on the recent date of some of these great movements by noticing another instance of a similar rise and fall of the land on the east coast of Sweden. We give this also in the words of Sir Charles Lyell:

"Some phenomena," he says, "in the neighborhood of Stockholm appear to me only explicable on the supposition of the alternate rising and sinking of the ground since the country was inhabited by man. In digging a canal, in 1819, at Södertelje, about sixteen miles to the south of Stockholm, to unite Lake Mälar with the Baltic, marine strata, containing fossil shells of Baltic species, were passed through. At a depth of about sixty feet they came down upon what seems to have been a buried fishing-hut, constructed of wood in a state of decomposition, which soon crumbled away on exposure to the air. The lowest part, however, which had stood on a level with the sea, was in a more perfect state of preservation. On the floor of this hut was a rude fire-place, consisting of a ring of stones, and within these were cinders and charred wood. On the outside lay boughs of the fir, cut as with an axe, with the leaves or needles still attached. It seems impossible to explain the position of this buried hut without imagining first a subsidence to the depth of more than sixty feet, then a re-elevation. During the period of submergence the hut must have been covered over with gravel and shelly marl, under which not only the hut but several vessels also were found, of a very antique form, and having their timbers fastened together by wooden pegs instead of nails."

We now understand the presence of the marine shells on the heights above Lakes Mälar, Hjelmar, and Wenern, and on the rocks which surround the Gulf of Bothnia. We understand also the "boats, anchors [iron, we presume], and piles" found at a height of forty feet above the Cattegat.

We do not know when it was that a deep strait connected the Baltic and the North Sea. Sir Charles Lyell attempts to prove that it was long ago. He infers this from the fact that an elevation of one hundred feet has occurred on the coast of the Baltic since these waters were separated.

But the ancient geographers represent that Southern Sweden was an island, and their positive statements are met by merely affirming that they were ignorant;* and we have just seen that at Uddevalla the coast is ascertained to have risen two hundred feet in less than three thousand years.

We cannot be accurate about such points. No one, however, we may add, can read these remarks without realizing the absurdity of drawing any inferences with regard to the antiquity of man from a change in the drainage of the locality of a cave.†

Sir Charles Lyell informs us in this connection that he observed in 1834, near Upsala, a ridge of stratified sand and gravel, containing a layer of marl evidently formed at the bottom of the Baltic by the slow growth of the mussel, cockle, and other marine species, all of dwarfish size, like those now inhabiting the brackish waters of this sea,—the bed being one hundred feet above the level of the Gulf of Bothnia. Upon the top of this ridge repose several huge erratics, which must have been brought into their present position since the neighboring gulf was already characterized by its peculiar fauna. We thus learn that the transportation of erratics continued after this region had assumed that remarkable feature of its physical geography by which the Baltic was separated from the North Sea, and which causes the Gulf of Bothnia to have only one-fourth of the saltness belonging to the ocean.‡

These erratics are probably cotemporary with the buried hut.

This agrees with the statement of Mr. James Smith, of Jordanhill, who on the lowest ancient beach of the west of Scotland found a large ancient boulder, which, in his opinion, could only have come there on floating ice. Sir Charles Lyell refers to this statement, and in the same connection refers also to the position of the whales (in association with human implements) found in the carse of Stirling, some twenty feet above high-water mark. On this he observes, "The position of these whales, and their association with human implements, imply that at the time when they were cast ashore by a tide rising twenty or thirty feet

---

* Lyell, Principles, vol. ii. p. 181.

† We gather another very important fact with regard to this buried hut from a discussion which took place at the Archæological Congress last year at Stockholm. It appears that the hut was buried under a deposit of "*glacial sand.*" How much light does this throw on the date of the retirement of the ice in the North? See Matériaux, Livraisons 5e, 6e et 7e, 1874, pp. 246, 247.

‡ Antiquity of Man, p. 239.

beyond the present high-water mark, man was already an inhabitant of Scotland; and their great size indicating that they belonged to the Greenland whale—which only frequents seas of floating ice—*would point to an arctic climate* [our italics] in these regions before the last change of level occurred."*

The estuarine silt of this carse was, therefore, deposited beneath "seas of floating ice" and during the prevalence of "an arctic climate." Did such a climate prevail in Scotland, following the Glacial Age, some two hundred thousand years ago,—or did it prevail there at a much more recent period? The answer may be gathered from the fact (already mentioned by us) that *an iron anchor* was found in this carse, and *iron implements* (the character not stated) in the carse of Gowrie. Ships carrying implements of iron sailed upon this "arctic sea."

---

* Antiquity of Man, p. 60, edit. of 1873.

CHAPTER XXXIII.

THE RECENT DATE OF THE GLACIAL AGE.

Dr. Andrews on the Great Lakes of North America.—The Oscillations of Level in the Lakes.—Lakes Michigan and Huron.—Erosion of the Bluffs by the Waves, and the Formation of Beaches with the Detached Sand.—Lakes have existed since the Drift Period.—The Close of the Drift in this Region *very sudden*.—The Orange Loam.—Sudden Retirement of the Waters.—Age of the Lower Beach.—Soundings.—The Terrace of Erosion.—A Calculation.—Annual Rate of Erosion.—The Upper Beaches.—The Amount of Sand drifted.—The Beaches probably Five Thousand Three Hundred or Seven Thousand Five Hundred Years Old.—Out of the question, therefore, to allow such a Period as One Hundred Thousand Years for the Antiquity of the Glacial Age.—Another Calculation.—Even Twenty-Five Thousand Years an Impossible Admission.—Changes of Level in this Region.—Flexures and Contortions in the Strata.—Rapidity with which the Lakes fell and rose.—Probable Identification of the Loess with the Period of the Middle Beach.—General Results reached.

WE have argued in a previous chapter that the Glacial Epoch has been erroneously assigned by the geologists to a remote antiquity. We have gathered this from the ages of the estuarine beds in Scotland, and the peat-beds in Ireland and Denmark, which followed the disappearance of the glaciers in those countries, as well as from the absence of all Palæolithic remains in those countries.

We shall now call attention to a remarkable and independent evidence of the same fact in America. These observations are due to one of the ablest and most original masters of geological science in the United States: we refer to Prof. Edmund Andrews, President of the Chicago Academy of Sciences, and Professor of Surgery in the Chicago Medical College,—whom we have already had occasion to quote in connection with the phenomena of the Somme Valley and the formation of the cone of the Tinière in Switzerland.

Prof. Andrews.

In the second volume of the Transactions of the Chicago Academy of Sciences is a paper by Prof. Andrews on "The North American Lakes considered as Chronometers of Post-Glacial Time," which appears beyond all contradiction to be a complete demonstration of the error of the prevailing opinion with regard to the extreme antiquity of the Glacial Period; but, on the contrary, to show that the true date of that period does not extend beyond a few thousand years ago. Dr. Andrews reaches the

His paper on the American Lakes.

Recent date of the Glacial Epoch.

conclusion that "the total time of all the deposits [since the Glacial Period] appears to be somewhere between five thousand three hundred and seven thousand five hundred years." This is a startling declaration,—accustomed as we are to the eight hundred thousand or the two hundred thousand years of Sir Charles Lyell.

The observations of Dr. Andrews were made on Lakes Michigan and Huron, which, he says, are hydrographically one sheet of water, with the same level, and connected by a strait several miles in width. Lake Michigan is three hundred and fifty miles in length from north to south, and about eighty-five miles in width. Its outlet is at the north, the southern extremity being a *cul-de-sac.* Its waves are continually in motion, and rapidly erode the drift-clay of the shores. This erosion, taking place upon material nearly uniform in character, varies mainly with the violence of the waves, and hence, when long periods are taken, has a very regular rate.

In Lake Michigan the material washed down by the waves is sorted by the same agency into clay and sand; the clay floating about settles whenever it reaches deep water where the wave-action is too slight to keep it longer suspended, while the sand is carried by the currents along shore southward, and deposited in beaches and dunes on the low sloping plain around the south end of the lake. The *beaches* thus formed have mapped out on the country around the head of the lake every successive level occupied by its waters, and show, by their relative size, the length of time during which each one was deposited; while the same periods further north are indicated by the ancient *bluffs* from the erosion of which the sands of the beaches were derived. It is by the combined study of the erosion and the beaches that the total post-glacial time can be deduced.

The shifting levels of the lakes.

The elements of the calculation are the following:

1. The average rate of erosion.
2. The width of the subaqueous plateau formed by the erosion since the lake stood at its present level.
3. The amount and direction of the sand movement.
4. The amount of sand in the several beaches.

It should be observed, says Dr. Andrews, that our lakes have existed ever since the close of the Drift Period, a time which is rather sharply defined, because the close of the Drift in this region *occurred with a suddenness unusual in geological phenomena.*

Suddenness of the close of the "Drift."

The last member of the Drift in Wisconsin and Michigan is the Orange Loam, which is a well-stratified layer, covering all the Drift hills and valleys like a sheet, and usually only a few inches in thickness. It shows its relation to the rest of the Drift by displaying a few boulders, some of which are three or four feet in

The Orange Loam.

diameter; but their numbers are comparatively small. Disregarding, says Dr. Andrews, the dispute whether the heavy Boulder Drift below was laid down by glaciers, or by icebergs and water, it is evident that this upper sheet is a water deposit, and that this region was under water during its formation. Again, there is never any trace of peat or vegetable mould between it and the drift, showing that no period of land-vegetation intervened between the two. In short, *the Orange Loam is the closing member of the Boulder Drift.*

The waters, proceeds Dr. Andrews, which deposited the Orange Loam *retired suddenly to the south, closing abruptly the Drift period.*

"I make this statement deliberately," says Dr. Andrews, "after several years of investigation. It is the unanimous testimony of civil engineers that no great body of water can retire gradually from a region without leaving numerous beaches and bluffs to mark the shore-lines. Beaches form with great rapidity, ridges ten feet high being thrown up sometimes in a single storm, and all the sand and gravel tossed beyond the water's edge is left as it retires, a permanent monument of the former level. Now, the waters at the close of the Drift fell with such abruptness, that outside of the basin of the lakes they have left no beach-lines between the highlands of Wisconsin and the Ohio River, a fact attested by railroad engineers and geologists alike. . . . This recession of course left the basins of the great lakes like so many cups filled with water, and the waves, being never still, must of necessity begin at once to erode their shores and cast up their beaches, as they have continued to do ever since. It follows, therefore, that the history of our lake-shores covers the whole time from now back to the close of the Drift period, meaning by that term the time of retirement of the waters that deposited the Orange Loam. From that time to the present the history of the lakes is mapped out on their shores, and may be read with more certainty than is usually possible in geological phenomena."

Three different levels.

The waters of Lake Michigan have stood at three different levels, which are marked in the north by three bluffs which they have cut at different heights on the shores; and in the region around the southern extremity of the lake, where the vast amount of sand thrown in by the currents shielded the shores from wash, the three shore-lines are accurately mapped out by sand beaches, which are on the same level as the bluffs with which they were severally cotemporaneous.

The lower beach.

Age of the Lower Beach.—The shores of Lake Michigan are nowhere stationary for long periods. The waves are continually either tearing down the clay, or else piling sand upon it, according to the location; and both these processes go on with an energy and rapidity astonishing to one not accustomed to the investigation. Dr.

Andrews's personal observations were mainly on the west shore of Lake Michigan. From Manitowoc southward to Evanston, a distance of about one hundred and eighty miles, the waves are eroding the shores into drift-clay bluffs, which are caving down under the lashing of the waves. The sand and gravel resulting from the sorting of this material is swept southward and thrown into beaches and dunes about the head of the lake, so that the lower bluff and the lower beach are cotemporaneous, and the latter is made of the sand derived from the former. Now, we have, in the contour of the lake-bottom, a ready means of determining approximately the original position of the shore, and consequently the distance which the bluffs have receded since the water occupied its present level. The waves of our great lakes cease to have

Terrace of erosion.

any erosive power upon the bottom at the depth of about sixty feet: hence when the shores are worn back there is left under water a sort of shelf or terrace, the surface of which slopes gently outward to the depth of about sixty feet, when the bottom dips down more suddenly to the deep water, below the reach of wave-action. It is obvious that this terrace is the product of wave-action, and it will be convenient to denominate it the terrace of erosion. It exists almost everywhere along the lake-shores where the circumstances admit of it. . . . The existence of this terrace has long been known to some observers, and has been noticed by some of the United States engineers engaged in lake-survey. It is shown very finely among the islands and shores of the northern part of Lake Michigan. The following figure shows the profile of the bottom from north to south across North and South Manitou Islands, and thence to the mainland near Sleeping Bear, Michigan. The terrace surrounds both islands, and skirts the mainland, and the sudden dip of the bottom from the plane of sixty feet depth is well illustrated.

FIG. 1.

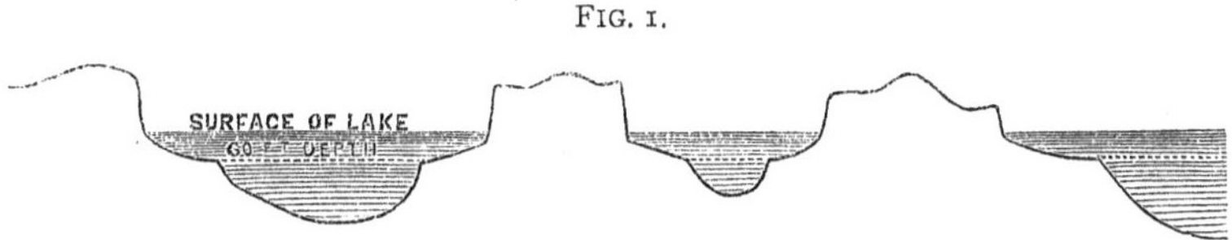

Fig. 2, also derived from the soundings on the United States charts, shows the average contour of the terrace on the east shore of Lake Huron, from Brewster's Mills to Point Clark, a distance of fifty miles.

A calculation.

Where the shores are of drift-clay, the terrace has generally a breadth of from two to six miles, and occasionally more; but where it is of rock the width is much less. On some of the hard rocks of Lake Superior the terrace is scarcely two hundred feet wide.

Softer rocks frequently show a breadth of one thousand or fifteen hundred feet. It is a curious and unexpected fact that the depth of the

FIG. 2.

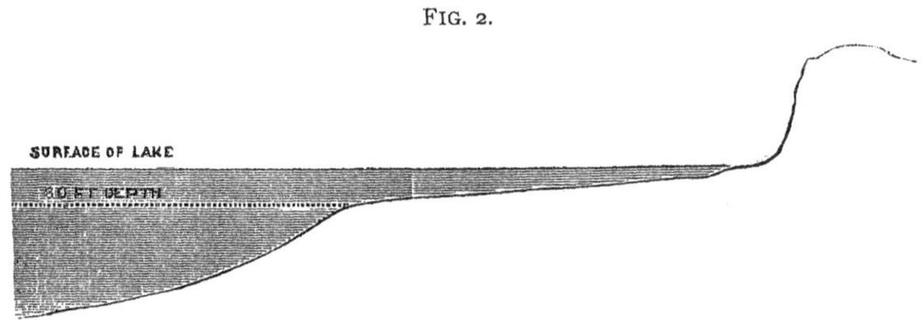

erosion is much less affected than the breadth of it by the hardness of the material. Even rock shores often show the edge of the terrace to be sixty feet down.

Seven lines of soundings to determine the breadth of the terrace on the west shore of Lake Michigan, between Chicago and Manitowoc, a distance of one hundred and eighty miles, were taken by an expedition fitted out by President Burroughs of Chicago University. Two more lines were taken by the United States engineers and others,—making nine observations of breadth between Chicago and Manitowoc. The edge of the terrace of erosion was found to average 3.98 miles from the present bluffs, and the position of the old shore about 2.72 miles. The latter figures, therefore, represent the total recession of the bluffs of the west shore of Lake Michigan during the period of the lower beach.

It is obvious, says Dr. Andrews, that the outer edge of the terrace represents the line where sixty feet of water was when the erosion commenced, and the old shore-line must be somewhere between this and the present bluffs. The clue to the position of the old shore is found by taking the steepest part of the slope, just outside the edge of the terrace, and prolonging it upward till it meets the surface of the water. This of course involves some error, but on the average must approximate the truth.

Fig. 3 is the profile of the terrace averaged from the nine lines of soundings referred to. The dotted line represents the original surface of the clay, and O. S. the position of the old shore.

Annual Rate of Erosion.—The next point is to ascertain the annual amount of destruction of the bluffs. This varies considerably in single years, but, taking long periods, it appears to be quite uniform for the same region. The rate varies according to the exposure of the coast to the prevailing winds, and according to the hardness of the material. For shores of boulder drift, exposed to the full action of the waves, it appears everywhere to amount to from three to six feet a year, and often much more. At Cleveland, Ohio, for forty years it has averaged six feet per annum. On the Canada shore opposite, it has been about the

FIG. 3.

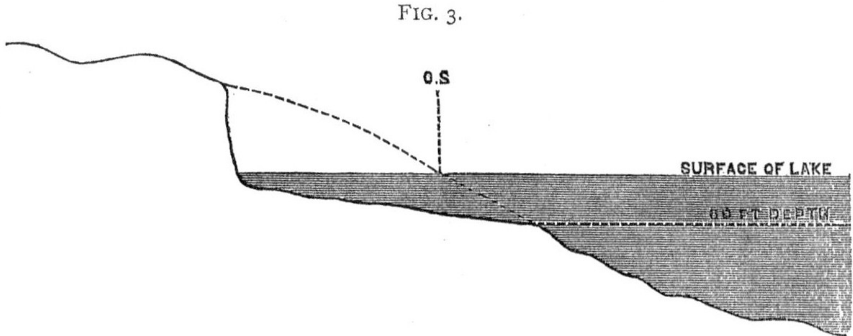

same. Rev. Thos. Hurlbut found that on Lake Huron it varied in different places from one to twelve feet,—an average of six feet per annum. A civil engineer at Goderich, on the same shore, found the erosion in front of that town to amount to eight feet per annum; but in the adjacent regions north and south about four feet per annum. The County Surveyor of Van Buren County, Michigan, judges the erosion to be about six feet a year.

Dr. Andrews, to determine the rate on the west coast of Lake Michigan, has through several years accumulated a large number of observations, of which he publishes a table, embracing twenty-three places. The greatest erosion was at Evanston, where it reached nearly seventeen feet a year. North of Milwaukee the erosion is less rapid than south of it, and the terrace of erosion is narrower. From Milwaukee to Manitowoc (about eighty miles) it averages four and one-third feet a year, while between Milwaukee and Evanston it averages six and one-quarter feet a year. The average of the two is 5.28, which is therefore the average erosion along the whole line. Numerous other less exact observations confirm this result.

We have seen that the total recession of the bluffs from the old shore-line amounted to 2.72 miles, or fourteen thousand three hundred and sixty-two feet. Dividing this by 5.28, the annual rate of erosion, we find that the total age of the lower terrace is two thousand seven hundred and twenty years. If we compare this with the same beach in Lake Huron, we find some variation, but still a confirmation of the general calculation. Taking the east shore, from Brewster's Mills to Point Clark (fifty miles), we find, from the United States charts, that the edge of the terrace is about six miles from the present bluffs, and the original shore-line about 4.02 miles. The erosions there have been less carefully ascertained, but appear to be about five and one-half feet per annum; which would give three thousand eight hundred and fifty-nine years as the age of the terrace.

We must add to this result the amount of time covered by the periods during which the water stood at the higher levels.

The antiquity of the lower beach is of necessity the same as that of the lower terrace of erosion. The time required to form this terrace is the time which elapsed during the accumulation of the sand of the lower beach. It has been calculated that the amount of this sand is 1,747,570,000 cubic yards. We must refer the reader to Dr. Andrews's paper for the details of the calculation.

The total of the upper sands, that is, the sands in the upper and the middle beaches, is stated at 1,659,881,000 cubic yards.

The upper beaches.

That is, the total lower sands are to the total of the two beaches above nearly as seventeen to sixteen. The time of accretion of the lower beach has already been stated to be two thousand seven hundred and twenty years: therefore the period required for the deposition of all the sands above must have been two thousand five hundred and seventy years,—making the combined periods for *all* of the beaches five thousand two hundred and ninety years.

If we take the results of the Lake Huron erosion as the proper estimate of the age of the lower terrace, viz., three thousand eight hundred and fifty-nine years, the total time for all the beaches would be seven thousand four hundred and ninety-one years.

It is very evident that if we could ascertain the total annual sand-drift we could make a third and independent calculation, by simply dividing the total amount of sands by the annual drift.

The body of water along the shores of Lake Michigan is in motion southward (the return waters passing northward again along the middle of the lake), and every handful of sand lifted by the waves, as they lash the shore-line, falls a few feet southward; and this process going on without cessation, the shore-sands are in constant motion southward, and the amount transported by the converging currents from the east and the west shores is enormous. Where piers are built out into the lake, they act as obstructions, which cause the sand to accumulate on the side from which the current comes. In the opinion of engineers, no pier stops more than a fraction of the sand, because the current is deflected, and, passing around the end of the pier, carries most of the loose material with it. Captain Sanders, of the United States army, in charge of the harbor works at Grand Haven, Michigan, estimates that the piers at that place (one of which, however, had a gap in it) stop only one-eleventh of the sand. There are piers at Chicago and Michigan City, and Dr. Andrews estimates the amount of sand stopped by them at one hundred and twenty-nine thousand cubic yards annually, "while probably five or six times as much passes into the head of the lake."

Now (as stated), the total amount of sand south of these two cities is 3,407,451,000 cubic yards. The annual amount of sand stopped by the piers is a very small proportion of all the drift-sand; but if we divide 3,407,451,000 cubic yards by 129,000 (the annual amount stopped by the piers), we obtain 26,000 years as a maximum and extreme limit of time for the accumulation of the 3,407,451,000 cubic yards of sand. It cannot be more than this. And, as there is every reason to believe that the stoppage by the piers only amounts to one-fourth or one-fifth of the whole drift, we obtain five thousand two hundred or six thousand five hundred years as the probable period for the accumulation of the beaches. "This maximum," says Dr. Andrews, "is useful as showing that it is impossible to allow, even on the most liberal estimates, any such post-glacial antiquity as one hundred thousand years, such as has been often claimed. The narrowness of the terraces proves the same thing; for had the erosions gone on as they do now for one hundred thousand years, the lower terrace would have been *forty-nine miles* wide, which, counting the terrace of both shores, is actually more than the whole breadth of the lake, and the places where our west shore towns now stand would have been *in sixty feet of water and forty-six miles from the nearest land.*"

A period of one hundred thousand or even twenty-five thousand years for the antiquity of the Glacial Age, therefore, impossible.

"Another calculation will illustrate the same idea. If we estimate the total annual sand-drift at only twice the amount actually stopped by the very imperfect piers built,—which, in the opinion of engineers, is setting it far too low,—and compare it with the capacity of the clay basin of Lake Michigan, we shall find that, had this process continued one hundred thousand years, the whole south end of Lake Michigan, up to the line connecting Chicago and Michigan City, would have been full, and converted into dry land, twenty-five thousand years ago, and the coast-line would now be found many miles north of Chicago. It is needless to say no such enormous quantity of sand exists in this region."

Another estimate.

It is proper to add to this that no sand in the south part of Lake Michigan (according to Dr. Andrews) is ever washed out into deep water, nor is any ever brought up from it. Beyond thirty-six feet, in the region of the beaches, the bottom is always of a smooth, impalpable clay. The waves here cease to have power to move sand at the depth of from twenty-four to thirty-six feet.* It follows that the sand in our

* This assertion may seem to conflict with the previous one, that boulder clay is eroded sixty feet deep. But we are informed by Dr. Andrews that the reason of the difference is

beach-lines around the head of the lake all came from the north, along the sand-bearing currents of the shores, there being no other possible source for it. Conversely, it follows that as the sand cannot pass out into deep water it has no avenue of escape, and must lodge in the bight at the end of the lake, being caught in the *cul-de-sac*.

The sand deposits, as we have stated, are at the southern extremity of the lake; and they have a curved length of one hundred miles, and a maximum breadth of ten miles. The subsoil is boulder drift, which has here a gently sloping surface of remarkable uniformity. On this smooth incline the sands lie for the most part in three concentric beach-lines. The uppermost beach or ridge was the first formed, and must have commenced immediately after the close of the Drift period. It is interesting, says Dr. Andrews, to remark that this upper beach, which appears all around the lakes where not worn away by subsequent erosion, and which originally must have been level, has now been thrown *into a sinuous form, showing that the country has undergone changes of level since that time.* Around the south end of Lake Michigan, and for a hundred miles north on the Wisconsin shore, it is everywhere about fifty-two feet above the present level of the water; while on the east side of the lake, south of Grand Haven, it is shown by the survey of Captain Sanders, of the United States army, to be at the elevation of only twenty-one feet. On both sides of the southern front of Lake Huron, which then was continuous both of Lake Michigan and Lake Erie, it presents an elevation, where cut by the Grand Trunk Railway, of about one hundred and forty feet. The western beach there makes a wide détour into the State of Michigan, and then sweeps around the southern shore of Lake Erie into Ohio, where, according to Prof. Newberry, it has an elevation of two hundred and fifty feet above the present water, or about two hundred and thirty-five feet above Lake Michigan. As this old shore-line must have been originally level, its present distorted grade can only be due to flexures of the strata of the continent occurring since the beach was laid down.* The fall of the waters from the line of the upper beach, which probably occurred at the

Paroxysmal action.

that in the southern section of the lake, where the beaches lie, the water is shallow and the waves act less deeply, but further north they erode to sixty feet. Dredgings, nevertheless, show that in neither region is beach-sand ever carried into deep water. The sand sometimes brought up on the greased lead from greater depths is different, and consists of gravel left in the boulder clay by the washing away of the clayey particles, at depths where the waves were unable to stir the pebbles, thus leaving them on the surface. They differ from the beach-sand by the angular form of the grains and their larger average size.

* This throws a flood of light on the positions in which the river-gravel in the east of England is found, and which sometimes seem to be dissociated altogether from the present lines of drainage.

time of this disturbance of the strata, appears to have been *very sudden.* This is shown by a peculiarity in the contour of the deposit, which is uniform in all the sand shores of this part of the coast. As you go out into the lake, the bottom gradually descends from the water-line to the depth of about five feet, when it rises again as you recede from the shore, and then descends toward deep water, forming a subaqueous ridge or "bar" parallel to the beach, and some ten or twenty rods from the shore. This is shown at the point marked B in the section, Fig. 4.

Fall and rise of the waters very sudden.

FIG. 4.

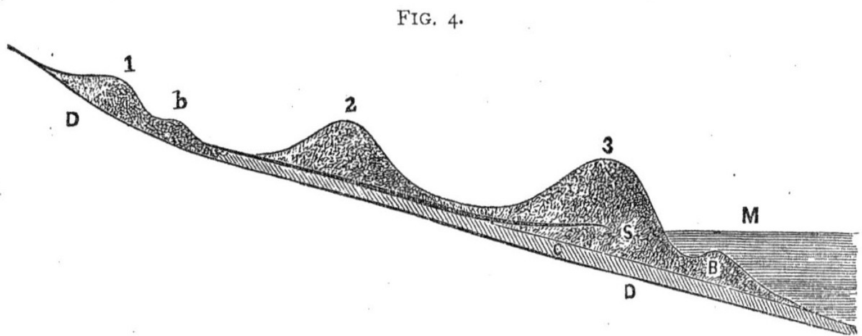

The upper beach preserves its old bar perfectly (marked *b* in the cut), as if the lake had left it but yesterday. The quickness of the change is obvious to any one accustomed to lake-shore action; for had the water occupied even two months in receding from the bar, the waves would have torn it in pieces and covered it with new sand, leaving nothing distinguishable of its form. Another proof of the suddenness of the retirement is, that there are no sand ridges between the upper and middle beaches. The ground is bare clay, just as the waters left it, and the valley between the two beaches, which is generally about two miles wide, is absolutely continuous for a hundred miles, surrounding the head of the lake. . . . The waves of Lake Michigan act upon their shores with tremendous force, and are always engaged in either piling up the sand or tearing down the clay. There is no possibility that they could effect a slow retreat down such a slope without leaving marks which no time could erase. We have on this shore examples both of slow and of rapid recession, and the comparison of the two establishes the above conclusions.

Singularly enough, says Dr. Andrews, this subsidence was at first not to the middle beach, but to the lower one. . . . The waters fell from the upper beach to about the present level so suddenly that they not only left the subaqueous "bar" almost undisturbed, but they did not throw up a single intermediate beach-line, which, at the rate of sand deposit prevailing in this region, would have been visible if there had been a pause even of six months. The waters remained here long enough for a thin stratum of peat to form, and then rose again over the soil-bed and deposited the middle beach upon it. . . . From the upper edge of the middle beach the water receded very slowly, occupying probably two thousand years or more in falling a few feet, and throwing up, where the sand-supply was most abundant, numerous parallel ridges. It then fell perhaps ten feet more, pretty rapidly, to the upper part of the present beach, leaving a continuous valley between the middle and the modern sands. This last recession, however, was not so sudden as that from the upper line, as shown by the fact that the subaqueous bar was demolished by the retiring wave action, and a considerable amount of sand was left between the middle and lower beaches.

Identification of the Loess with period of the middle beach.

One of the most important results of this investigation is *the probable identification of the high water of the middle beach with the more general submergence of the Loess.* The Loess is not a continuation of the Boulder Drift, as is often supposed (says Dr. Andrews); on the contrary, it is separated from the true Drift by a stratum of vegetable mould, marked with subaerial denudations, showing that a period of dry land and vegetation intervened between the close of the Drift and the submergence called the Loess. . . . The following sections will show the relations of the deposits on the lakes and on the Mississippi:

SECTION OF THE MISSISSIPPI.	SECTION OF THE LAKE SHORES.
Modern Soil. (Water at its lower level.)	Modern Soil. (Water at its lower level.)
Loess. (General submergence near the rivers.)	Middle Beach. (Extensive submergence about the lakes.)
Ancient Soil. (Water at its lower level.)	Ancient Soil. (Water first at upper and then at lower beach.)
Boulder Drift.	Boulder Drift.

General results reached.

It appears, therefore, that the general order of events on the lakes and on the Mississippi has been identical, and that the high water of the middle beach occupies exactly the same place in the series as the high water of the Loess near the Mississippi. There can hardly be a doubt, therefore, that the two were cotemporaneous.

Dr. Andrews sums up the history and chronology of the lakes as follows:

1. The upper beach began to form immediately after the Boulder Drift period, and continued to accrete for about nine hundred years. No animal fossils have yet been found in it.

2. The waters then fell suddenly to about their present level, where they remained till a thin bed of peat accreted on the marshy slope

vacated by the waves. He has not been able to collect data for a calculation of this first low-water period, but, from the position of the soil-bed in the eastern dunes, inclines to think it lasted five hundred or one thousand years.

3. The water rose again, submerging for a short time the upper beach, but soon fell to the line of the middle one, where it remained about one thousand six hundred or two thousand years. This period appears to be cotemporary with the Loess.

4. The water, which had already slowly fallen some feet, now retired more rapidly to near its present level, which it has maintained with only moderate fluctuations ever since.

5. The total time of all these deposits appears to be somewhere between five thousand three hundred and seven thousand five hundred years.

This result is, of course, entirely at variance with the enormous figures demanded by Sir Charles Lyell and the deriders of "the current cosmogony;" but it corresponds with the conclusions we have reached on other and independent evidence; and it is for an intelligent public to decide who is right.

NOTE.—We learn from Dr. Andrews that Dr. Lapham, of Milwaukee, suggests that the lakes may have stood for long periods at lower levels than the present one, and that he (Dr. Andrews) has not allowed anything for such lower-level periods. In support of this, Dr. Lapham calls attention to the fact that the channels of the rivers running into the lake are often much deeper than the adjacent bottom of the lake itself, indicating ancient lower channels. To this Dr. Andrews replies, that rivers, like brooks, cut deepest where the current is swiftest, and that the ancient greater size of the streams, as well as the modern spring floods, would cut out these deeper places, while at the point of entrance into the lake the motion is checked, and the channel is either cut less deeply, or, if cut, is filled again by the waves. There is a narrow, swift place in Wisconsin River which is one hundred feet deep, yet two miles lower down the stream the rock bottom rises nearly to the surface, though the descent of the surface itself is very slight.

Furthermore, numerous borings and deep-water dredgings, as well as a regular shaft sunk in the bottom of the lake two miles from shore, and a tunnel dug from the shore to the shaft, fail to find any traces of the submerged beaches which ought to exist under the lake if it ever had a much lower level than the present.

Dr. Andrews also writes us that since he wrote his article on the lake beaches he has discovered that the deluge of the middle beach went temporarily much higher, and even laid a stratum of muddy gravel over the black soil which had accumulated on the upper beach. This higher part of the inundation is probably, he remarks, the true analogue of the Loess deluge. The water remained at this upper limit for a very brief period—not long enough to lay down a definite shore-line.

On page 501 we state that "the body of water along the shores of Lake Michigan is in motion southward," etc. This is spoken of the currents which affect the sand beaches of the calculation there made. The well-known northward current on the northern portion of the east shore is too far away to influence this region.

CHAPTER XXXIV.

SIBERIA.

Preservation of the Mammoth.—The Bones found as far South as Lat. 56°.—Mr. Howorth on the Extinction of the Mammoth.—Great Changes in the Climate and Physical Geography of Siberia.—The Former Existence of a Great Asiatic Mediterranean.—The Sudden Draining of this Sea, by which the Mammoth was destroyed.—Sudden Change in the Siberian Climate.—The Tundras of Siberia.—The Ancient Hyrcanian Ocean.—Evidences that the Caspian formerly covered a much greater Area.—No Glacial Age in Siberia.—The Destruction of the Mammoth and the Preservation of his Remains in the Ice subsequent to the Date of the Glacial Age in Europe.—Tartar Traditions of the Mammoth.—M. Dupont on the Climate of the Quaternary Period.—A Pre-historic "Find" in Siberia.—Bronze Relics.—Representation possibly of the Mammoth.—Observations of M. Desor.—The Bronze-Workers of Siberia cotemporary with the Mammoth.—Are these Bronzes Etruscan?—The "Tomb-Building" Races.—Connection between the Etruscans and the Altaic Tribes.—Mr. Taylor's "Etruscan Researches."

THE preservation of the carcasses of the mammoth in Siberia is referred to the fact of their being imbedded in the ice or in the frozen soil. The bones of the mammoth, as we have stated, are found, however, in all the lowland of Siberia,—in the west as well as in the east, and between lat. 60° and the Arctic Ocean. Lyell mentions that Pallas observed them as far south as lat. 56°, below the city of Krasnojarsk, on the Yenisei, in strata of yellow and red loam, alternating with sand and gravel.* The ground has hardly remained permanently frozen in this region, as the climate of Siberia is much milder in the west than in the east, and as the summers at Krasnojarsk, though short, are very hot. The well-preserved carcasses of the mammoth are found ordinarily beyond the Arctic Circle, and in the east.†

The fresh state of these bones, or of the ivory associated with them, precludes, therefore, it appears to us, the idea that they can have any such antiquity as several hundred thousand years, even if we could be-

---

* Erman mentions that many well-preserved mammoths' skulls were seen by him at Malmish, which had been dug up from the alluvial sand and mud of the low valley of the Vyatka. (Travels in Siberia, vol. i. p. 132, Amer. edit.) Malmish is in about the same latitude as Krasnojarsk; but it is forty degrees of longitude farther to the west, where the climate is much milder.

† We are not aware that any specimen has been found south of 64°; and this was on the Wiljui, a tributary of the Lena.

lieve that the frozen earth of the more northern and eastern regions might have preserved for some vast period the carcasses of the mammoth and rhinoceros which are found there.

The ice and frozen mud have undoubtedly been the agent which has contributed to preserve the flesh of these animals in Northeastern Siberia; but is it credible that even there these carcasses have rested without decay during the enormous periods demanded by the geologists?

We have pointed out elsewhere that the climate of Northern Russia and Siberia was formerly much less severe than it is at present.* The fact that the mammoth was sustained in such large numbers is a testimony to the same effect.

Mr. Howorth on the extinction of the mammoth.

In a Report to the British Association, in 1869, on the subject of the extinction of the mammoth in Siberia, Mr. Howorth reaches the following conclusions:

1. That the mammoth lived where its remains are found.

2. That a great portion of this area is now a moss-covered *tundra*, or an ice- and boulder-heap.

3. That no herbivore of the size and development of the mammoth could find subsistence in that area now.

4. That, although covered with wool, and therefore adapted to a more rigorous climate than that of India or Africa, neither the mammoth nor the rhinoceros could survive the present winter temperature of Northern Siberia.

5. That the remains of the food eaten by the mammoth, and found and examined by Middendorff and Brandt, are remains of plants only found now in more southern latitudes.

Mr. Howorth concludes farther, therefore:

That the climate and condition of things in Siberia have *changed* very greatly since the mammoth existed there. In support of this conclusion, he calls attention to the fact that the bed of the Arctic Sea north of Siberia is rapidly rising, and exposing banks of sand containing mammoth-remains, the land rapidly gaining on the sea along the whole coast-line.

The appearance of the tundra, says Mr. Howorth, seems to point to a not very distant submergence of the whole of Siberia as far south as the highlands, which roughly mark the present northern limit of trees.

What, then, has led to the extinction of the mammoth? The hand of man, says Mr. H., is quite inadequate; and we must seek for the cause in the draining of the vast mediterranean sea which once existed from the Euxine to the Klingar Mountains. The drainage of this sea

* Chap. xxii. p. 380. See, also, "Matériaux pour l'Histoire de l'Homme," Décembre, 1872, p. 550.

must have been sudden and overwhelming; for we find the mammoth-remains aggregated in hecatombs on the pieces of high ground, and not scattered indiscriminately. This alone would account also for such an immediate change of climate (from an insular one to a continental) as should allow the bodies of the mammoth to be immediately frozen and thus preserved intact.*

This is a bold conjecture, but some attention to the facts of the case renders it in a high degree probable.

Physical geography of Siberia.

Northern Siberia is one vast lowland or plain, sloping gradually to the ocean. Between the Obi and the Yenisei, from lat. 60° to the sea, and between the Yenisei and the Lena, from the Arctic Circle to the sea, the country consists of *tundras*, or mossy deserts, which have very recently been covered by the Arctic Ocean. This is proved by the thin coating of sand and fine clay which extends over these plains, and which contains heaps of shells perfectly identical (at least in the high latitudes) with those of the adjacent seas.† (In this sand and clay the bones and tusks of the mammoth are found.) Trains of drift-wood are also seen far inland,—trees first carried out to sea by the rivers, and then thrown up on the ancient shores.

M. Reclus remarks that "after Humboldt's profound investigations on Central Asia, we shall not, at the present day, show too great temerity in assuming that during some portion of the present period a vast strait, like that which once ran along the southern base of the Atlas, *extended from the Black Sea to the Gulf of Obi and the Frozen Ocean.*"‡

And now as to the reality of that ancient *Hyrcanian Ocean* of which the ancients speak:

The ancient Hyrcanian Ocean.

"Nearly in the middle of the south border of the Great Plain," says McCulloch, in his Geographical Dictionary,§ "on both sides of the hills of Mugodsharsk, and the countries lying south of it,

---

* Rep. Brit. Assoc. at Exeter (1869), p. 90.

The very same thought had occurred to Sir Roderick Murchison. "The final destruction of the mammoth," he says, "may have resulted from aqueous debacles dependent on oscillations of the mountain chains, and the formation of much local detritus." Geology of Russia, vol. i. chap. 19.

† See Reclus's The Earth, p. 536; Lyell's Principles of Geology, vol. i. pp. 181, 183.

An idea of this region may be formed from the fact that Tobolsk, which is situated on the Irtisch, a tributary of the Obi, five hundred and twenty-five geographical miles in a direct line from the mouth of the former, is only one hundred and fifteen feet above the level of the sea. Bernaoul, on the Obi, nine hundred and twenty geographical miles from its mouth, is three hundred and eighty-three feet above the sea. The Yenisei, after leaving the mountains, traverses a similar flat region for nearly eight hundred miles to the head of its estuary.

‡ The Earth, p. 544.

§ Art. Asia, vol. i. p. 162, Amer. edit.

between 45° and 64° E. long., occurs the most remarkable depression on the surface of the earth. A tract of country extending over an area of more than three hundred thousand square miles, exclusive of the Caspian Sea, is, according to the supposition of Humboldt, lower than the surface of the ocean. The lowest part of it is occupied by the Caspian Sea, which was supposed by Humboldt to be no less than three hundred and forty-eight feet below the surface of the Black Sea; but later and, it is believed, more correct measurements make the level of the Caspian Sea only one hundred and sixteen feet below, and that of the Lake of Aral fourteen feet above, the level of the Black Sea. According to Humboldt, this depression extends between the rivers Kooma, Wolga, and Oural, up to a line drawn from Saratow to Orenburg, whence its boundary runs to the Lake of Ak-sa-kal (48° N. lat. and 63° E. long.), and then includes the countries traversed by the lower courses of the Sir-Daria (Sihoon, *Jaxartes*) and Amoo-Daria (*Oxus*). This country is so little elevated above the level of the great lakes which lie in the midst of it, that a strong northwest wind of some continuance forces their waters over many miles of the adjacent tracts. Its soil consists partly of sand, and partly of hard clay, on which neither trees nor shrubs grow, and which only in spring, after the melting of the snow, is covered with a scanty but nourishing grass and numerous flowers. . . . Along the shores of the Caspian Sea this low and desert country extends to the very edge of the table-land of Iran (Persia), where it terminates between 36° and 37° N. lat.; but from the table-land of Eastern Asia it is separated by a mountain region. . . . The Caspian Sea, which covers a surface of one hundred and twenty thousand square miles, is very deep towards its south extremity, where it is surrounded by the mountain ranges of Iran; but where it borders on the desert it is shallow. Its waters are salt. The lake or sea of Aral, lying farther east, has a surface of between forty thousand and fifty thousand square miles, and its waters are likewise salt, as is the case with all the numerous smaller lakes which occur in the above-mentioned depression."

In the article on the "Caspian Sea," in the same work, we are told that "there can be little doubt that it was formerly much more extensive on three sides,—the north, northwest, and east; and it is still most likely diminishing;" that "it has been observed that the present bed appears to descend in terraces, and on the east and northwest shores the land rises in the same manner;" that "this land presents also incontestable proofs of having formerly been covered with sea-water; being uniformly flat, except when it rises in sandy ridges to form the terraces before mentioned; being uniform in soil, which consists of sand combined with marine slime, without a trace of terrestrial vegetation (except the common desert plants), or the slightest indication of minerals; the substratum being clay, at a considerable depth from the surface; and the surface itself abounding in sea-salt, sea-weed marshes, salt-pits, and lakes, together with innumerable shells exactly resembling those of the Caspian Sea, *and which are not found in any of the rivers.* . . . These high grounds formed, therefore, in all probability, the ancient shores of the Caspian; but that to the northwest terminates abruptly on the little river Mantysh, near the 46th parallel, between which and the Caucasian mountains a low and narrow tract, exactly resembling that on the immediate borders of the Caspian, stretches without interruption to those of the Sea of Azoph, having every appearance of the deserted bed of a strait formerly uniting the two waters. Towards the east the whole country has the same appearance of a deserted sea-bed; and the conclusion, therefore, appears inevitable, that at comparatively no distant period the Sea of Aral, the Caspian, and the Black Sea, formed one body of water, *uniting the present anomalous salt lakes of Asia with the ocean.* This conclusion is further strengthened by the presence of the same species of fish, seals, etc., in the three seas; a fact which it is impossible to account for on the supposition that they were always separated." *

MM. Lenormant and Chevallier, in their "Ancient History of the East," alluding to the first appearance of man on the earth, tell us that at that time "in the north of Asia a vast mediterranean sea, which subsequent elevations of the soil have removed, occupied the whole basin of the Caspian and Sea of Aral, covered great part of the Steppes situated between the Oural Mountains and the Volga, as well as the country of the Kalmucks, and reached southward to the base of the Caucasus. Its eastern limits are uncertain; but, according to the observations of travellers, and *indications drawn from the annals of China*, it seems to have occupied all the desert of Gobi to the north of Thibet." †

Herodotus, Strabo, Ptolemy, and all the authors of antiquity who allude to the subject, attribute to the ancient Hyrcanian Ocean an extent far larger than that of the Caspian of our day; most of them, indeed, considered this inland sea as a prolongation of the Frozen Ocean. Herodotus describes it as an ocean by itself, communicating with no other, and of such size that a swift-oared boat would traverse its length in fifteen days.‡ Strabo speaks of the Caspian as *a gulf of the Northern Ocean.*§ Ptolemy gives the greatest length from east to west, and makes it (says McCulloch) "a vast deal too large."

---

* McCulloch's Geographical Dictionary, vol. i. p. 569.

† Ancient History of the East, by Lenormant and Chevallier, vol. i. p. 26, Translation.

‡ Clio, 203.

§ Geography, xi. 507.

Lyell correctly observes that the ice or congealed mud in which the bodies of the great pachyderms were enveloped "has never once been melted since the day when they perished." If, therefore, Siberia experienced, like Northern Europe and the northeastern part of the North American continent, *a glacial epoch*, it might be supposed that these animals were buried in the frozen soil at that time.

No Glacial Age in Siberia.

*It appears, however, that Siberia and Northeastern Russia exhibit no traces of glaciation.**

The same has been affirmed by some of British Columbia.

The Siberian mammoth and rhinoceros were doubtless living in Siberia and Russia when Northern Europe was covered with ice, and at the close of that period they wandered into Europe. The climate of Siberia was far milder than it is now. The ocean advanced up to the Arctic Circle, and even beyond; while further south a vast inland sea, covering five hundred thousand square miles, and communicating with the Northern Ocean, spread out like a second Mediterranean. It was *subsequent to* the disappearance of the glaciers from Europe that the climate of Siberia grew intensely cold. We now have some idea of the time when the carcasses of the mammoth and the rhinoceros were entombed in the frozen banks of the Yenisei and the Lena.

The severe cold in Siberia followed upon the elevation of the land, the destruction of the great inland ocean of Central Asia, and the retirement of the Arctic Sea; it was due, as Mr. Howorth says, not only to the elevation of the land, but to the consolidation of the continental area of Asia, which had not previously existed, in consequence of the separation of Siberia from the central regions by the expanse of the Hyrcanian Ocean.

The physical evidence of these facts is very strong; but when we find them confirmed by the express statements of the historians and geographers of antiquity, there is strong reason to confide in this interpretation of the record.

It is corroborative of the idea that the mammoth lived down to a recent period in Siberia, that the Tartars who inhabit the south of that country have a tradition of certain great extinct animals with which their ancestors contended, and that the remains of the mammoth found

---

* Geology of the Ural Mountains, by R. I. Murchison, pp. 554, 555.

Sir R. I. Murchison, after stating that Siberia is entirely free from erratic blocks, remarks, "All lands, therefore, in the Northern hemisphere, which are as void of such drift as large portions of Siberia on the one hand, and Siluria on the other, may have been, like them, for ages the habitation of the great extinct quadrupeds."

See also Congrès International d'Anthrop., 1871, p. 128. M. Vogt observes, "L'époque glaciaire n'a pas existé dans l'Asie Centrale; on n'en trouve du moins aucune trace dans l'Altaï."

in the caves of the Altai Mountains are associated with the remains of other animals, the most of which still inhabit these mountains.*

At the Anthropological Congress of 1871, at Bologna, M. Dupont made some remarks touching the Quaternary fauna of Belgium. Referring to the presence of the hippopotamus, the lion, the hyæna, on the one hand, and that of the reindeer, the musk-ox, the glutton, etc., on the other, he observed that this assemblage of diverse species was one of the most curious facts of the Quaternary epoch. He proceeded:

M. Dupont on the climate of the Quaternary period.

"It is evident that the hippopotamus proves the absence of rigorous winters, and the species of the north excludes very warm summers. It is necessary, then, to suppose at this epoch a climate more equal and temperatures less extreme than in our days. But it is the northeast wind which brings the cold in winter and the heat in summer, a double effect which seems to hold with the existence of a great plain in that direction. It is necessary, then, to seek the explanation of the climate of the Quaternary epoch in the absence of those lands, and the presence, at that epoch, *of a great sea to the northeast of Europe.*" †

That sea, as we have attempted to show, did actually exist during the days of the mammoth in Siberia. When it was suddenly drained, the mammoth was destroyed; the climate of Siberia changed; and the climate of Europe changed. The change was sudden in Siberia, for the carcasses of the great pachyderms did not have time to putrefy before they were locked in that icy embrace, which, like some process of the embalmer, has preserved them these several thousand years fresher and more life-like than the forms from Egyptian and Peruvian graves. The change may, therefore, have been sudden in Europe; and this may explain the rapid disappearance of the great animals whose remains are found in the river-gravels and caves.

The views presented by Erman, in his "Travels in Siberia," are strikingly in accordance with the theory of Mr. Howorth and the conjecture of Sir Roderick Murchison. Speaking of the mammoth-remains found in Siberia, he remarks, "The ground in Yakutsk, the internal condition of which was found in sinking M. Shergin's well, consists, to the depth of at least one hundred feet, of strata of loam, fine sand, and magnetic sand. They have been deposited from waters which at one time, and, it may be presumed, suddenly, overflowed the whole country as far as the Polar Sea. In these deepest strata are found twigs, rocks, and leaves of trees of the birch and willow kinds. . . . Everywhere throughout these immense alluvial deposits are now

* Brandt, Mélange Biologique, viii. 424.

† Matériaux pour l'Histoire de l'Homme, Janv. 1872, p. 35.

lying the bones of antediluvian quadrupeds along with vegetable remains. In the lower valley of the Lena, . . . and at both sides of the mouths of this river, are found the teeth and bones of mammoths, rhinoceroses, and other quadrupeds, and even whole carcasses.

"It cannot escape notice that, as we go nearer to the coast, the deposits of wood below the earth, and also the deposit of bones which accompanies the wood, increases in extent and frequency. Here, beneath the soil of Yakutsk, the trunks of birch-trees lie scattered only singly; but, on the other hand, they form such great and well-stored strata, under the tundras between the Lena and the Indigirka, that the Yukogirs there never think of using any other fuel than fossil wood. . . . In the same proportion the search for ivory grows continually more certain and productive, from the banks of the lakes in the interior to the hills along the coast of the Icy Sea.

"Both these kindred phenomena attain the greatest extent and importance at the furthest chain of the islands above mentioned, which are separated from the coast of the mainland by a strait about one hundred and fifty miles wide, of very moderate depth. Thus, in New Siberia lie hills two hundred and fifty or three hundred feet high, formed of drift-wood; . . . other hills on the same island, and on Kotélnoi, which lies further to the west, are heaped up to an equal height with skeletons of pachyderms, bisons, etc., which are cemented together by frozen sand as well as by strata of ice. It is only in the lower strata of the New Siberian wood-hills that the trunks have that position which they would assume in swimming or sinking undisturbed. On the summit of the hills they lie flung upon one another in the wildest disorder, forced upright in spite of gravitation, and with their tops broken off or crushed, as if they had been thrown with great violence from the south on a bank, and then heaped up. Now, a smooth sea covering the top of these hills on the islands would, even with the present form of the interjacent ground, extend to Yakutsk, which is but two hundred and seventy feet above the sea. But before the latest deposits of mud and sand had settled down, and had raised the ground more than one hundred feet, the surface of such a sea as we have supposed would have reached much further up, even to the cliffs in the valley of the Lena. So it is clear that at the time when the elephants and trunks of trees were heaped up together, one flood extended from the centre of the continent to the furthest barrier existing in the sea as it now is." *

Pre-historic bronzes from Siberia.

There is an account by M. Desor, in the 4th "livraison" of "Matériaux pour l'Histoire de l'Homme" for 1873,† of certain "pre-historic" objects found in Siberia. These consist

* Vol. ii. pp. 285, 287, Trans., Amer. edit.

† Page 197.

of a number of articles in *bronze* obtained by a Russian engineer, M. Lapatine, from the Tartars in the neighborhood of Krasnojarsk, on the southern frontier of Siberia. The objects mentioned are two poniards, two hatchets, six knives, a pair of scissors, a pike, a bridle-bit, and five buckles. Most of these articles are coated with a beautiful brown patina; others are covered with a green patina, similar to that observed on the antiquities found in the ancient European tombs. Their antiquity, we are told, is beyond question. They are far superior to, and entirely different from, the utensils or weapons in use among the Tartars; they have nothing in common with the classic forms, nor with those of the pre-historic epochs of Europe. Nor are they Chinese or Hindoo. That they are the product of an indigenous civilization seems to be confirmed by the tombs which are found in great numbers on the banks of the Yenisei, and which Pallas referred to an ancient people, no longer in existence, but whose culture is attested by a funeral *mobilier* quite complete, which is composed in part of the same objects as those under consideration. The workmanship of the articles indicates a measure of skill beyond that of the Lake-Dwellers of the Bronze Age. The objects are not only of elegant shapes and gracefully ornamented with various designs, but a good number of them have a distinct and peculiar stamp, and represent, under various and divers aspects and with divers applications, animal forms, such as the wild goat, the stag, the eagle, the wolf, etc.*

In "livraisons" 5 and 6 of "Matériaux" for 1873 (the issue succeeding the one containing the above account) we have a plate containing drawings of the objects referred to; and, wonderful to relate, we have among the animal forms (fig. 1, p. 516) executed in bronze by these ancient Siberian artists, what appears to be *a representation of the mammoth!* Some of these sketches we reproduce; for nothing half so interesting has been in many years reclaimed from the Past by modern archæology.

We do not think that there can be any reasonable question that we have in this figure a delineation of the Siberian elephant. Very certainly it cannot represent *any other* animal: it is not a lion, nor a tiger, nor a bear, nor a deer, nor an ox, nor a sheep, nor a wolf: it is *some* animal, and must be an elephant.

It is easy (if this be indeed an elephant) now to explain the traditions of the mammoth among the Tartars and in China; and, if we cannot explain in detail how their bodies have been preserved undecayed, we

* Erman, in his "Travels in Siberia," mentions a collection of ancient relics at Krasnojarsk, consisting of articles of bronze found in the so-called Kurgans, or Strangers' Graves, in the circle of Minusinsk, at the foot of the Sayan and Kusnetsk Mountains. Vol. ii. p. 112, Translation, Amer. ed.

can at least reject the extravagant suggestion that they have been thus preserved for two hundred thousand years,—or, as the French archæologists put it, from the Tertiary age.

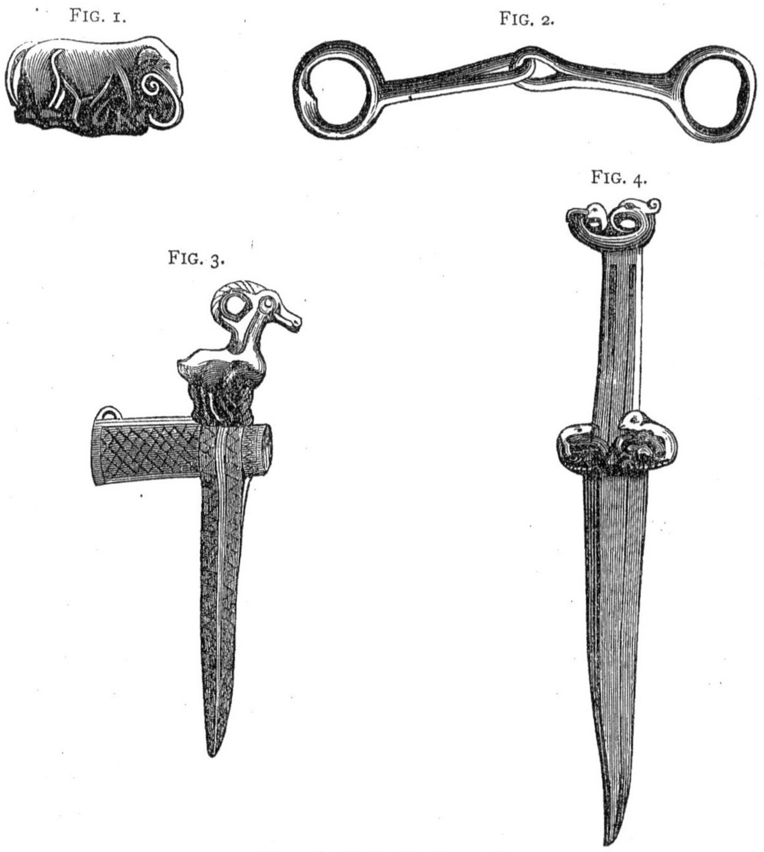

ANCIENT SIBERIAN BRONZES.

The effect of the present evidence is so utterly subversive of Modern Anthropology, that M. Desor, one of the most distinguished and eminent of all the European expounders of this science, treats it as follows (having first mentioned that various animal forms, such as the wolf, the wild goat, the eagle, etc., are represented): "Il y en a d'autres qu'il est plus difficile d'identifier; ainsi une sorte de grand chat (tigre ou lion), dont le corps est très-caractéristique, mais dont le museau est prolongé en forme de trompe, si bien que plusieurs personnes seraient tentées d'y voir une réminiscence du mammouth. Nous préférons, jusqu'à plus ample information, y voir un animal fantastique, comme l'imagination de tous les peuples s'est plu à en créer."

We leave it to the reader to determine which is the more "fantastic," —the picture which we are considering, or this archæological verdict.

The *tail* of the animal is too long; but this was treated in this way, we suppose, to finish off and balance that side of the ornament. Those who have seen the *originals* will testify that the present delineation is more distinct than the mammoths figured in the Dordogne caves. We do not perceive the resemblance to a cat.

Conclusions of M. Desor.

With regard to these people, M. Desor, in conjecturing who they might have been, remarks, "Perhaps one might evoke here the vague memories which tradition has preserved in Northern Asia of a people, the *Tschudi*, whose power must have been considerable, and whose influence seems to have extended even to the confines of Europe."

But, asks M. Desor, could a culture as advanced as that indicated by the evidences before us have been developed under the climatic conditions existing to-day at Krasnojarsk? where the mean annual temperature oscillates around zero, and the mean winter temperature is —20° C.?

He then suggests (as we know was indeed the fact) that the climate of Siberia may have formerly been *milder*. "It must be admitted," he says, "without fear of contradiction, that if, by means of a slow subsidence, the northern part of Siberia were submerged to-day, *the northern slopes of the Altai would enjoy a climate much more temperate;*" and then, in this connection, he makes this most important statement: that shells of the oyster have been found on the banks of the Ischim, one of the affluents of the Irtisch. This is in the southwestern part of Siberia, intermediate between the Sea of Aral and the Gulf of Obi,—in the direct line of the great interior sea which we have indicated. This, says M. Desor, "*proves that the sea has sojourned here since the last great revolution of the globe*" (the Glacial epoch). And the existence of this sea, or rather the presence of the sea at this point, would involve, M. Desor thinks, a milder climate.

A doubt, however, is raised in M. Desor's mind by "the relatively *modern stamp* of most of the objects which we have before us, as well as by the description which Pallas has left of several tombs in which he found similar objects in compartments separated by beams and partitions of wood."

The perplexities of the archæologists proceed from their false theory: unable to comprehend how the stone axes, and the mammoths, and the cromlechs can belong to our present horizon, they are constantly bewildered by the stubborn evidences of the recent date of these objects in different parts of the world.

The mammoth was in Siberia down to the inauguration of that cold climate now characteristic of that region; this was *after* the Glacial period in Europe, probably at the close of the Glacial period in Sweden and Scotland; when France and England were occupied by the cave-men, Siberia was enjoying, at least the middle and southern parts of that country, a comparatively temperate climate; it was inhabited at that time by a bronze-using people, who were skilful workers in that metal; the mammoth, the rhinoceros, and the megaceros ranged in its forests; by some sudden and swift geological disturbance the great inland sea, which communicated by the valley of the Obi with the Northern Ocean, was emptied of the greater part of its waters, which swept over Siberia, destroying many of these animals; the sudden elevation of the land, and the draining of this sea, occasioned a sudden change in the climate, which completed the destruction of the mammoth. The cold became so intense that the carcasses of the mammoths and the rhinoceroses were quickly frozen in the mud and sand in which they had been buried; this climate has continued to increase in severity, and that frozen mud has never since thawed. Such seems to be the story of pre-historic man and the mammoth in Siberia.

The bronze-workers of Siberia contemporary with the mammoth.

Bone-caverns have been explored in the basin of the Tscharysch, an affluent of the Obi, in Southwestern Siberia. Pallas was the first to call attention to them. He was followed by other explorers, and M. Brandt has recently published a considerable work on the fauna by which they are characterized. No human remains or works of art have been found. The remains of the animals so far described belong, we are told, for the most part to species still inhabiting the same region, or to those which lived there at a very recent period (as the *Sus scrofa* and the *Castor fiber*). Among the more ancient forms are the mammoth, the *Rhinoceros tichorhinus*, the great Irish elk, the cave-hyæna, the European bison (aurochs), and the urus or *Bos primigenius*. No remains of the reindeer have been found, nor does the musk-ox occur. This fact, and the presence of the bones of the *Hyæna spelæa* (the spotted or African species), while there are no traces of the striped hyæna, now spread over Western Asia, is another circumstance to show that the climate of this region was formerly much milder than it is to-day. The remains of the tiger are also found, but, so far, none of the *Felis spelæa*. Nor has the *Ursus spelæus* yet been met with, the bones which were referred to that animal being referred by Brandt to the *Ursus arctos*.

Caves of the Altai Mountains.

The fact that no human remains or works of art are found in the Altai caves is another concurrent fact in our argument. It is a collateral testimony that the early inhabitants of Siberia were a civilized, or a semi-civilized, race. It is negative evidence that the bronze objects found at Krasnojarsk are a true reflection of the primitive state of man in these regions.

It may be well to add that when the subject of these pre-historic Siberian bronzes was brought to the attention of the Société d'Archéologie de Paris, in May, 1873, by M. Hamy, who read a letter from M. Desor, the eminent ethnologist M. de Quatrefages observed, in some comments on that communication, that "the Samoyedes appear to have executed works which indicate their acquaintance with iron. They must have had then, in the past, a civilization superior to that which they have to-day. There were also strong reasons to believe that at a certain epoch Siberia enjoyed a much milder temperature than now."*

We have a strong suspicion that these bronzes are *Etruscan*,—we mean, intimately connected with the art of that mysterious race.

Are these bronzes Etruscan?

Now, it is significant that a very interesting and a very ingenious work has just appeared, identifying the Etruscans with the Ugric tribes of Central Asia.

We were compelled to refer the megalithic tombs and the great sepulchral mounds to the Turanian family. The monuments of Aryan and Semitic races consist mainly of temples, palaces, and theatres. But the Egyptians, the Lydians, the Lycians, the Etruscans, the Chinese, the Tartars, the Mongols, the Iberians, the Finns, were (and are) pre-eminently TOMB-BUILDERS. Their tombs were their temples, to which they repaired to worship their ancestors. Egypt reared its great sepulchral pyramids; at Sardis we find the great tumulus of Alyattes, the father of Crœsus, two hundred feet in height and eleven hundred and eighty feet in diameter; near Smyrna we find the tumuli of Tantalais; in China we find the great tumulus of Yung-lo, near Pekin,—a mile in circumference; in India we find the mausoleum of Hyder Ali, the last Tartar king who ruled in that country; near Alexandropol, between the Dnieper and the Bazaolouk, is a tumulus one thousand feet in circumference and seventy feet high; in Tuscany we find the tumulus of Cucumella, at Vulci, that called the Regulini-Galeazzi tomb at Cære, with many others. Tradition, it is well known, connects the Etruscans with the Lydians. It is a noteworthy coincidence that the great tumulus of Cucumella has two towers or steles on its summit, and that the tumulus of Alyattes is also turreted; while Rubruquis informs us that the same peculiarity characterizes many of the tumuli on the steppes of Upper Asia. Most of these tumuli have sepulchral chambers. Some of them cover concentric stone circles.

The tomb-builders.

* Matériaux pour l'Histoire de l'Homme, Livraisons 5e et 6e, 1873, p. 280.

They occur to the eastern limits of Siberia. The traveller Bell tells us that they exist in thousands near Tomsk. These, too, consist of a central chamber and a mound of earth. The vast tomb of Yung-lo, in China, contains a stone chamber enclosing a sarcophagus. A passage-way leads to this chamber, the entrance to the former being approached by a paved causeway lined with colossal figures in marble,—not unrelated, perhaps, to the avenues which we find associated with the European stone circles.

The argument of Mr. Isaac Taylor in his "Etruscan Researches" to prove a connection between the tribes of the Altai and the Etruscans is chiefly a linguistic and philological one. He refers, however, to the fact that both the Etruscan and the Turko-Finnic races belonged to the great *tomb-building* branch of the human family, and that the essence of their religion consisted in *the worship of their ancestors.*

The hut-urns at Albano.

It will be remembered that certain "hut-urns" have been mentioned as discovered under the peperino at Albano. Mr. Taylor thinks that these cinerary urns are intended to be imitations of tents or huts framed with boughs and covered over with skins. Some of them, he says, are exact reproductions of the Tartar tent as now in use on the Siberian steppes. In Greenland and Siberia, at the present day, we know that the tent is surrounded with a circle of heavy stones, designed to keep down by their weight the skins of which the tent is composed. Mr. Taylor thinks that we find here the origin of the sepulchral tumulus. When a man died, he was left, with all of his possessions, in his tent, which, to keep the body from the wolves, was covered with a mound of earth or stones. Long after the tumulus-builders had ceased to dwell in tents, this circle of stones continued to be erected around the base of the funeral mound. The stone circle is commonly found around the base of the British tumuli, and is represented, we are told, in the Etruscan tumuli by the *podium*, or low encircling wall of masonry.

M. de Rossi has recently found, on Mount Crescenzio, some additional cabin-urns in the peperino. They contained Etruscan vases, and M. de Rossi informs us that one of these was placed in a kind of little dolmen formed of six slabs of peperino about twenty inches in length. A second dolmen, but of yet smaller dimensions, was found near this.*

Bronze mirrors.

We remember in reading Erman's volumes (which are not now before us) to have been struck with an account of certain *bronze mirrors* which were found in some ancient graves in Siberia, and which Erman conjectured might be *Buddhist.* We have been startled in reading Mr. Taylor's book (he apparently not being aware

* Matériaux pour l'Histoire de l'Homme, 2e série, tome iv., 1873, p. 422.

of the discovery of these mirrors in Siberia) to find repeated references to "bronze mirrors" as found in the tombs of the Etruscans. He mentions them on pp. 105, 139, 142, 282, and 366. Some archæologist can inform us whether they have been found in the tombs of any other nations.

The dice of Toscanella.

Mr. Taylor thinks that the key to the affiliations of the Etruscan language has been at last found by the discovery of TWO DICE in a tomb near Toscanella, the supposed site of the ancient Etruscan city of Tuscania. The faces of these dice, instead of being marked in the usual manner by pips, were each inscribed with Etruscan letters, which are naturally presumed to represent the first six Etruscan numerals. These six numerals, Mr. Taylor remarks, are clearly and decisively Ugric. He institutes a comparison also of the names and functions of the Etruscan deities with those of the Kalevala, the ancient epic of the Finnic race; and compares in like manner the funeral inscriptions found in the Etruscan tombs with the languages of the Altaic, Ugric, or Finno-Turkic tribes.

The very name—TURRHENOI (or TURSENOI)—by which the Greek writers designate the Etruscans is supposed by Mr. Taylor to be equivalent to the name TURAN by which the Aryan Persians called their nearest non-Aryan neighbors, the Turkic or Turcoman tribes to the north of them. In various Siberian languages—the Kot, Koibal, Samoyede, Mongol, etc.—the word *tura* means a "tent." We see the root in TURK, TURKOMAN, TURANIAN, and, perhaps, in TURRHENOI and TURSCI (the original form, according to Lepsius, of TUSCI or ETRUSCI).

The legend of Romulus.

We cannot undertake to follow the details of Mr. Taylor's work. We have been struck, however, with an allusion he makes to the legend of Romulus and Remus and the she-wolf. Rome in its origin was an Etruscan city, and this legend of the eponymic founder of the Roman city is doubtless Etruscan. Now, according to the Chinese historians, the forefathers of the Turkic race belonged to a Hunnic horde which was wellnigh exterminated by its enemies. The sole survivor, a boy ten years of age, took refuge in a morass. There he was found by a she-wolf, who suckled him and fostered him in a cave. The boy, taking the name of his foster-mother, was called TSENA, from the Mongolic *schino* or *tschino*, a "wolf." When he had grown to manhood, he took his foster-mother to wife. She bore him ten cubs, who became mighty warriors. Having captured wives from a neighboring tribe, they became fathers of the race of the Asena, whose banner was adorned with the heads of wolves.

In the Roman myth, we have the MORASS—the SHE-WOLF—and the CAVE. After a while ACCA LARENTIA takes the place of the she-wolf as the foster-mother of Romulus, and she becomes the mother of twelve sons. Acca Larentia was called also LUPA, the "she-wolf." Moreover, the Ugric character of Acca Larentia (says Mr. Taylor) is indisputable; she is the "mother of the mighty ones;" the mythic ancestress of the twelve khans of the twelve tribes of the Rasenna. The Siberian version speaks of *ten* tribes. This seems to be preserved in the division of the tribe of Ramnes, the tribe of Romulus, into ten curiæ or sub-tribes. Another element in the Roman myth—the rape of the Sabine women—we may trace in the Siberian legend; and this itself may refer to the primitive Turanian custom of exogamy.

Various other points are made, but we cannot go farther into the subject.

As to Mr. Taylor's philological argument, we are not competent to judge of its value, and we have, therefore, no opinion about it. We see that it is even questioned whether the objects found at Toscanella are in fact DICE. However all this may be, we cannot, and do not, believe that the Etruscans were, as it is fashionable to say, *Aryan.* We believe (whatever their language may have been) that they were Turanian; and the conviction of this fact creates the belief with us that Mr. Taylor is on the right track, whatever Prof. Max Müller or the philologists may say to the contrary. We are satisfied that *the result* will sustain Mr. Taylor, while it may be that his reasoning is bad.

We shall only add that Mommsen, in his History of Rome, recognizes a Finnish substratum for the ancient population of Italy.

CHAPTER XXXV.

THE GERMANS AND BRITONS AS DESCRIBED BY TACITUS AND CÆSAR AND OTHER ANCIENT WRITERS.

Gaul in the Time of Julius Cæsar.—The Soldiers of Brennus.—The Caledonians in the Time of Agricola.—Tacitus on the Weapons of the Germans.—The Scarcity of Iron.—Spears of Wood hardened in the Fire.—No Reference to Bronze.—The Æstians.—The Fennians.—Clothing of the Germans.—Herodian's Testimony.—The Classical Writers never refer to any Rude Stone Monuments.—Tacitus on the Burial Customs of the Germans.—The Testimony of Cæsar.—His Account of the Britons and the Germans.—The Suevi.—Pomponius Mela.—Strabo.—Cannibalism in Scotland.—Testimony of Jerome.—The Ancient Irish Cannibals.—The Irish in the Twelfth Century,—and in the Sixteenth Century.—Mommsen on the Inhabitants of Spain.—Prof. Worsaae on the Introduction of Iron in Northern Europe.

It will naturally occur that we may derive some information with regard to the ancient people of Northern Europe from the Roman historians. Iron was in pretty common use in Gaul in the time of Julius Cæsar, and had been for, perhaps, a century; although it is certain that bronze and stone were both also in use. Iron begins also to appear in the southern parts of Britain, and in some parts of Germany. The maritime tribes would naturally obtain it first. After the conquest of the North by the Romans, it was rapidly introduced.

Iron.

Sir John Lubbock says the soldiers of Brennus were armed with iron swords. No doubt they were by the time they reached Rome, just as the Cimbri, B.C. 100, were armed with steel helmets. There were plenty of such arms in the Roman and Etruscan territory,* as well as among the colonies of Marseilles at the head of the Sinus Ligusticus. Sir John Lubbock also quotes Tacitus to prove that the Caledonians had swords of iron. The Romans had been in Britain a century and a quarter when Agricola encountered the Caledonians, and no doubt there were iron weapons in the army of the latter. But let us hear what else Tacitus says on this subject: he gives us in the second book of his Annals, chapter xiv., a speech of Germanicus

Soldiers of Brennus.

The Caledonians.

Tacitus on the weapons of the Germans.

* It is most important also to remember that while the chiefs and the better class might have weapons of metal (procured by traffic or on the march), it would by no means follow that the mass of the barbarian host were armed in the same way. The historians do not condescend to write of these; they would not know much about them.

to his army on the banks of the Weser, in the modern province of Hanover, where he defeated Arminius. Germanicus tells his soldiers, "The unwieldy buckler of the Germans, and that enormous length of spear, which, amid surrounding trees and interwoven thickets, was scarcely manageable, could not be compared to the Roman sword, the javelin, and their defensive armor. . . . Redouble your blows, and strike at the face of the enemy. *They have neither helmet nor breast-plates. Their shields are neither riveted with iron nor covered with hides; they are nothing but osier twigs intertwined, or slight boards, daubed over with glaring colors. In their foremost ranks a few are provided with pikes and javelins; in the rest of their army you see nothing but stakes hardened in the fire, or weapons too short for execution.*"

Armed with stakes hardened in the fire.

These words were spoken of the Chaucians, whom Tacitus characterizes as "beyond all question" "the most respectable of all the German nations."

We find in this author another reference to the use of iron among the Germans. "Iron," he says, "does not abound in Germany, if we may judge from the weapons in general use. Swords and large lances are seldom seen. The soldier grasps his javelin, or, as it is called in their language, his *fram;* an instrument tipped with a short and narrow piece of iron, sharply pointed, and so commodious that, as occasion requires, he can manage it in close engagement or in distant combat. With this, and a shield, the cavalry is completely armed. The infantry have an addition of missive weapons. Each man carries a considerable number, and, *being naked,* or, at least, not encumbered by his light mantle, he throws his weapon to a distance almost incredible. . . . Breast-plates are uncommon. In a whole army you will not see more than one or two helmets."*

Scarcity of iron.

Naked savages.

* Manners of the Germans, § 6. Murphy's translation.

In a note on this, Mr. Murphy observes:

"Abundance of iron was to be found in the bowels of the earth; but to extract it, to soften it by fire, and render it pliant and malleable, required more skill and patience than consisted with the rough genius of a savage race.

"Accordingly, swords and javelins were not much in use. A spear tipped with iron, in their language called, as Brotier informs us, *friem*, or *priem*, was their weapon in almost all the battles recorded by Tacitus. From the word friem the Roman writer easily made the term *framea*, more consonant to the idiom of the Latin language. It appears in the Annals, book 2, s. 14, that those instruments of war were of an enormous size, and unwieldy in close engagements. The number was not sufficient to arm more than the front line of their army. The rest carried short darts or clubs hardened by fire. In general, pointed stones were affixed to their weapons; and many of these, Brotier says, have been discovered in German sepulchres."

In all the pages of Tacitus, so far as we are aware, we read nothing about *bronze;* in all the battles which he describes between the Romans and the Germans, we read little or nothing about the Germans being armed with swords. We read of weapons tipped with bone or iron, we read of clubs of wood, of missile stones, of sharpened stakes hardened in the fire, but never, we think, of a bronze weapon of any kind. Had bronze been in use and departed?

No reference to Bronze.

The Suiones, he tells us,—the Swedes and Danes,—"may be said to inhabit the ocean itself," and "in addition to the strength of their armies they have a powerful naval force."* He then tells us in the next section that on the coast to the right of the Suevian (the Baltic) ocean the Æstians have fixed their habitation. This is the present kingdom of Prussia, Livonia, etc. Among these, it is remarked, "the use of iron is unknown, and their general weapon is a club."

The Æstians.

The Fennians (Finns), says Tacitus, are exceedingly ferocious; their food is the common herbage; the skins of beasts their only clothing. "For their chief support they depend on their arrows, to which, for the want of iron, they prefix a pointed bone."†

The Fennians.

The Germans do not appear to have worn much more clothing than the Fennians. Tacitus says, speaking generally, they wore "a loose mantle, made fast with a clasp, or, when that cannot be had, with a thorn." "Naked in other respects, they loiter away whole days by the fireside. . . . The skins of wild animals are also much in use."‡

The Germans went nearly naked.

The ancient Britons, we also know, wore a scanty covering of untanned skins, and covered the exposed portions of their bodies with blue paint.

From these facts the reader can form an opinion whether Sir John Lubbock's Bronze Age tumuli on the peninsula of Jutland, near Ribe, where they found the beautiful woollen cloaks and shawls and shirts and caps and leggings, with the fine bronze razor-knives and brooches, etc., date, as Sir John represents, fifteen hundred or two thousand years before the time of Tacitus.

The Germans had no cities, Tacitus informs us,—and in winter they retreated from the cold into "subterranean caves, dug by their own labor, and carefully covered over with dung."

No cities.

Herodian, who wrote some two hundred and fifty or three hundred

* Tacitus, Manners of the Germans, § 44. This was about A.D. 100–120.

† Ib., § 46.

‡ Ib., § 17.

years after the invasion of Britain by Julius Cæsar, speaks of iron as even then very precious in that country. He says that the Britons "wear iron about their bellies and necks, which they esteem as fine and rich an ornament as others do gold."*

Herodian on the Britons.

Tacitus has some remarks with regard to the funeral rites of the Germans, which imply, we think, that they buried their dead in tumuli, with their arms and horses. He makes no allusion to stone monuments in the form of either dolmens or megalithic chambers; and he represents that the dead were *burned*. This last statement was probably only partially true: they doubtless buried with and without cremation. We give the passage, and the reader can draw his own conclusions.

Funerals of the Germans.

"Their funerals," he says, "have neither pomp nor vain ambition. When the bodies of illustrious men are to be burned [Sir John Lubbock's Bronze Age], they choose a particular kind of wood for the purpose, and have no other attention. The funeral pile is neither strewn with garments nor enriched with fragrant spices. The arms of the deceased are committed to the flames, and sometimes his horse. A mound of turf is raised to his memory; and this, in their opinion, is a better sepulchre than those structures of labored grandeur which display the weakness of human vanity, and are, at best, a burden to the dead."†

The testimony of Cæsar with regard to the Germans and Britons presents us with a picture fully answering to that of Tacitus. With regard to Britain, he discriminates between the Belgæ of the coast and the population of the interior. The Cantii, or people of Kent, he says, pursued agriculture, but the tribes of the interior lived on milk and flesh, and clothed themselves with skins.‡

Testimony of Cæsar with regard to the Germans and Britons.

And speaking of the Germans, he says that they did not pursue agriculture, but that their food was milk, cheese, and flesh; nor did any one own any particular piece of land, but occupied the portion allotted him by the magistrate.§

---

* Quoted in Prehistoric Annals of Scotland, ii. 8. Prof. Wilson remarks in the same connection that Sweden (excepting a small district adjacent to Denmark) appears to have had no Bronze Age, the Stone Age in that country having been immediately succeeded by the Iron Age. There is some doubt about this.

† Manners of the Germans, § 27.

‡ De Bello Gallico, v. 14. It is exceedingly important for the student of this subject to bear this distinction constantly in mind. The inhabitants of the coasts are always found in advance of those in the interior. They would often have ships and carry on a commerce with the adjacent coasts; or, if they had no ships of their own, ships from other countries would visit them.

§ Ib., vi. 22.

For garments, he tells us, they wore skins, or pieces cut from the skin of the reindeer.*

Even the Suevi, (according to Cæsar) the most numerous and powerful of the Germans, are represented as living chiefly on milk and the meat of their flocks, and by hunting.† Their clothing, he says, consisted of nothing but skins, and even this covering was so scant that a large portion of the body was exposed; and this was the case even in the coldest regions.

The Suevi.

Pomponius Mela has also given us an account of the Britons. The country, he says, presented to the Romans a succession of forests, lakes, and great rivers, and he represents the people as in general not only uncivilized, but much behind the nations of the Continent in their social culture. Their cattle constituted their wealth.‡

Mela.

Strabo informs us that they had a community of women among eight or ten men,—fathers and brothers and sons,—like the Arreoy Society of Tahiti. Their houses, he says, were built of reeds or wood in the midst of the forest. Some of them knew nothing of agriculture.§

Strabo.

Herodian speaks of those in the northern districts, with whom Severus fought, as usually naked.‖

This was about the beginning of, and a century or two after, the Christian era.

A few centuries later,—but after the Romans had put a new face, at least, on England,—we have an account, by St. Jerome, of a Scottish tribe, the Attacotti, who were in the habit of making predatory incursions into England. St. Jerome tells us that in his youth he had seen some of these people in Gaul,—no doubt prisoners taken in Britain. He describes them as savages of the lowest character, who were so accustomed to eating human flesh that when they made raids into districts which abounded in cattle they preferred the men as diet to the animals; and he informs us particularly of the parts of either sex which they considered as the most delicate for eating,—*pastorum nates et fœminarum, et papillas solere abscindere, et has solas ciborum, delicias arbitrari.* Richard of Cirencester places the Attacotti on the banks of the Clyde.

Cannibalism in Scotland in the fourth century.

It is now a well-established fact that the ancient Irish were cannibals, and it is said to have been a matter "of religious observance with them to *eat their parents.*" ¶

The ancient Irish cannibals.

M. Spring, at the meeting of the Anthropological Congress at Brus-

---

* De Bello Gallico, vi. 21.

† Herod., iv. 1.

‡ Lib. iii. c. vi.

§ Strabo, iv. 305.

‖ Herod., iii. 83.

¶ Amer. Rec. Science for 1872, p. 160.

sels, in 1872, referred again to this fact, and quoted Strabo as his authority.

We get a glimpse of their condition in the twelfth century from Giraldus Cambrensis, who states that some sailors, driven on the coast of Connaught, met two men, who were naked, except that they were girded with loose belts of untanned hides of animals, and they stated that they used only skins, and lived on flesh, fish, and milk.

The Irish in the twelfth century.

Fynes Moryson gives us a description four centuries later,—that is, in the sixteenth century.*

In the sixteenth century.

The wild or "mere" Irish, he states, did not, as a general rule, *eat bread at all*, though they grew a few oats, which they did not thrash, but burned the straw, and so made cakes thereof. Flesh they seethed, lapped in a raw hide, over the fire. Horses dying were considered delicate morsels. They willingly ate the herb shamrock. Their milk was warmed with a stone, which was first heated. They had no tables, but ate seated on the grass. They slept in the open air, or in a poor house of clay. The men and women in many parts went naked all the winter, except a rag about the loins, and a loose mantle on the body. At night they lay naked in a circle about a fire, with their feet towards it.†

As for the "civilized" Irish, he met at Cork "young maidens stark naked grinding corn with stones to make cakes of."

If such scenes were witnessed in Ireland in the sixteenth century, what must have been the condition of things in Northern and Western Europe two thousand five hundred or three thousand years ago? Is a flint axe a matter of astonishment?

We may mention here the statement of Mommsen, in his History of Rome, that although in the south and east of Spain the natives had made great progress, yet in West and Central Spain, and in the north, the tribes were more or less barbarous, and that in Intercatia, for example, the use of gold and silver was unknown about 150 B.C.‡ We must remember that there had been Phœnician settlements in Spain for a thousand years, and that before the conquest by the Romans it had been to a great extent conquered by the Carthaginians.

Spain.

With regard to the introduction of iron among the races of Europe, we will add in conclusion on this subject the testimony of Prof. Worsaae:

Testimony of Prof. Worsaae as to introduction of iron in Northern Europe.

"Already," he says, "in the time of Homer the Greeks had iron, although it was very scarce and expensive; the Romans seem to have had, and used, iron, before the kings were ex-

* Itinerary, part iii. p. 156.

† See Archæologia, vol. xli. p. 406.

‡ Mommsen, vol. ii. p. 256.

pelled. . . . Polybius mentions, however, that the Gauls, who, about two hundred years before Christ, fought against the Romans in the north of Italy, were obliged in their battles to straighten their swords by putting their feet upon them, because they bent when exposed to a heavy blow; a fact which shows that the Gauls did not then possess steel. The invention of making the iron hard is attributed to the Celts of Noricum; in the time of Augustus, the Noric swords were famous in Rome.

"But if the people in the neighborhood of Rome, and influenced by Roman civilization, at the commencement of the Christian era, generally possessed weapons of iron, it does not follow that the people of the North had also, at so early a time, plenty of that metal. Cæsar says distinctly that in Britain iron was only to be found at the coasts, and that in such small quantities that the inhabitants used imported bronze (*ære utuntur importato*). It must also be remembered that he speaks of their using iron rings as money. A century after Christ, the Britons seem to have got a great deal more iron, but the Germans had so little of it that they very rarely had swords, or large lance-heads, of that metal. It was when the Romans got colonies in Hungary, Germany, Gaul, and Britain, or about from the third century of the Christian era, that their civilization first got some influence in the northern part of Germany, and in Scandinavia, where, however, it had a hard struggle with the old civilization.

"This view is strongly supported by the antiquities and tombs in the different countries. . . . But it is particularly important that *all the antiquities* which hitherto have been found in the large burying-places *of the iron-period* in Switzerland, Bavaria, Baden, France, England, and the North, exhibit traces, more or less, of Roman influence. . . . In some of the large burying-places, as near Basle, in Switzerland, the tombs were built of broken Roman tomb-stones; and in other tombs of the same period, both in Germany and England, there have frequently been found Roman coins, belonging to the first centuries after Christ, but none older.

* * * * * * * * * *

"The remains of the iron-period in Denmark are scarcely sufficient to fill up a couple of centuries, before the first commencement of Christianity (826); and we cannot therefore carry the complete introduction of the civilization of the iron-period into Denmark farther back than to the sixth and seventh centuries.

"About the year 500, it seems to have been introduced into Mecklenburg, as the Slavonic people took possession of the land, which was left by the Saxon people, who went over to England." *

* Primeval Antiquities of Denmark, pp. 139–142. Eng. trans.

CHAPTER XXXVI.

THE ANTIQUITY OF MAN IN AMERICA.

Writers on American Archæology.—Captain Dupaix on the Antiquity of the Cities of Central America.—Sir J. Lubbock on the Antiquity of the Mound-Builders.—The Aztecs, and their Recent Origin.—The Toltecs.—The Age of the Central American Ruins.—Age of the Mound-Builders.—Opinion of Mr. Schoolcraft.—Opinion of Mr. Squier.—Identity of the Iroquois and the Mound-Builders.—Wide Prevalence of the Communal System among the North American Races.—Unity of the American Races.—The Natchez.—Mounds supposed to have been erected by them.—Earth-works and Mounds in Dakota.—They represent at once the Works of the Mound-Builders and the Adobe Structures of the Aztecs.—Adobe Structures in Arkansas.—The Red Indians have greatly depreciated since the Advent of the Europeans.—Former Industry and Arts of the Indians.—Character of the Objects found in the Mounds.—Extended Intercourse of the American Nations.—Mr. Baldwin's Identification of the Mound-Builders with the Ancient Inhabitants of Mexico and Central America.—Judgment of Mr. Charles C. Jones.—Other Evidences of the Antiquity of Man in America.—Dr. Foster's Table of the Antiquity of Man on this Continent and in Europe.—The Shell-Mounds of North America.—No Great Age.—Ancient Hearths in the Alluvium of the Ohio Valley.—The Human Skeleton found by Dr. Dowler.—No Great Age.—The Mastodon-Remains found by Dr. Koch.—The Human Relics in the Loess at Natchez.—Establish Nothing.—Stone Hatchet from the Modified Drift of Illinois.—Polished Plummet from the San Joaquin Valley.—The Calaveras Skull.—Pre-historic Remains in Wyoming and Colorado.—Another Case.

WE have said nothing so far, except incidentally, of the antiquity of man in America.

The archæology of America has been treated by Mr. Atwater, in the "Archæologia Americana;" by Messrs. Squier and Davis, in the "Ancient Monuments of the Mississippi Valley;" by Mr. Squier, in the "Aboriginal Monuments of the State of New York;" by Dr. Lapham, in the "Antiquities of Wisconsin;" by Mr. Haven, in the "Archæology of the United States;" by Mr. Schoolcraft, in his History of the Indian Tribes of the United States; by Mr. Baldwin, in his "Ancient America;" by Dr. Wilson, in his "Prehistoric Man;" by Waldeck, in his "Voyage en Yucatan;" by Dupaix, in his "Antiquités Mexicaines;" by Stephens, in his "Travels in Central America;" by Prescott, in his "Conquest of Peru" and "Conquest of Mexico;" by Jones, in his "Antiquities of the Southern Indians;" by the Abbé Brasseur de Bourbourg, in his "Sources de l'Histoire du Mexique," his "Quatre Lettres," etc.; by the late Dr. Foster, in his "Prehistoric Races of the United States;" and by others.

The last work named is one of the most recent, and has reference more particularly to the antiquity of man in America.

Central America.

No antiquity is claimed, we believe, for the Red Indians. Captain Dupaix, in his "Antiquités Mexicaines," attributed to the ruined cities of Central America an *antediluvian* origin.

The Mound-Builders.

Sir John Lubbock thinks that the Mound-Builders *need* not be assigned a greater antiquity than three thousand years,—although he does not "deny" that it *may be* much greater.

Mexico. The Aztecs.

It is admitted on all hands that the Aztecs moved into the Valley of Anahuac or Mexico about three hundred years before the Spanish conquest.* Up to the advent of the Spaniards they had failed to consolidate their empire, and it was through an alliance with the Tlascalans and other malcontent tribes that Cortez was enabled to overthrow it. They founded Tenochtitlan, as their new capital was at first named, in A.D. 1326. The Indians of New Mexico claim that Montezuma was born in their country and signalized his early career by founding pueblos as he moved southward into Mexico, where he finally attained supreme power.

These Mexicans or Aztecs came, as is represented, from the northwest.

The Toltecs.

They succeeded the Toltecs, who, according to Prescott, advancing from a northerly direction, entered the territory of Anahuac "probably before the close of the seventh century" of our era. According to Dr. Wilson, following Mr. Gallatin, the oldest dates bring the Toltec wanderers to Huehuetlapalan, A.D. 387.

Dr. Foster considers them (and not improbably) as identical with the Mound-Builders of the Ohio and Mississippi Valleys. The ancient Mexican records make repeated mention of an empire situated to the northeast, and known as Huehue Tlapalan, from which the Toltecs came to Mexico, broken up either by foreign invasion or by internal disturbances. The journey is described as a long one. The simple name of the country was Tlapalan, but it was called Huehue (Old) Tlapalan to distinguish it from three other places which they settled in the new region, and to which they gave the same name. Torquemada discovered an old record which describes them as skilled in the working of stones and metals.

It is represented also that the forced emigration of the Toltecs was occasioned by their being assailed by the barbarous tribes (the Chichemecs) of the continent, who were united under one great leader; that there was a terrible conflict, when, after thirteen years, the Toltecs abandoned their country, and at length reached a region near the sea,

* See Foster, p. 340; Prescott, Conquest of Mexico, vol. i. p. 15.

called Tlapalan Conco, where they remained several years, when they undertook another migration, and reached Mexico, where they built a town called Tollantzinco, and subsequently the city of Tollan,—their future capital.*

It is further stated that the Toltecs dispossessed a race called the Colhuas, who came in ships, it is suggested probably from South America.

Age of the Ruins in Central America.

With regard to the ruins in Central America, which Captain Dupaix regarded as antediluvian, and of which Catlin affirms that the ocean rolled over them for thousands of years, it is sufficient to remark that Mr. Stephens observed at Uxmal that the lintels of the doorways were formed of *wood*, and that many of them were in a perfect state of preservation ;† and that in three hundred and fifty years, since the period of the Spanish conquest, structures described as existing at that time have crumbled into dust. The climate of Central America is particularly unfavorable to the preservation of ruins of any sort,—very different in this particular from the dry atmosphere of Egypt. The old Tezcucan chronicler, Ixtlilxochitl, "the best authority," says Prescott, "for the traditions of his country," reports that the Toltecs, on the breaking up of their empire,—which he places, earlier than most authorities, in the middle of the tenth century of our era,—migrating from Anahuac, spread themselves over Guatemala, Tehuantepec, Campeachy, and the coasts of the Isthmus; a statement confirmed by the fact that the nations in that quarter adopted systems of astronomy and chronology, as well as sacerdotal institutions, very similar to the Aztec, which are believed to have been derived from the Toltecs.‡

Age of the Mound-Builders.

With regard to the antiquity of the Mound-Builders, "the character of the arborescent vegetation," says Dr. Foster, "found covering their works, may be taken to some extent, but not absolutely, as a chronometric scale in estimating the time which has elapsed since their abandonment." §

---

* Foster, p. 342.

† Mr. Stephens states that "all the lintels had been of wood, and throughout the entire ruins most of them were still in their places over the doors." At Palenque he found also a specimen of wood.' (See vol. ii. p. 430.) There were wooden lintels also at Orosingo. Vol. ii. p. 313.

Copan is regarded as very ancient by Mr. Baldwin,—as more ancient than Palenque. We are told, however, in the "Transactions of the American Antiquarian Society," that the Spaniards found Copan inhabited and in the summit of its perfection. Vol. ii. p. 549: Letter to Hon. Thos. L. Winthrop, Pres. Am. Antiq. Soc., dated June 9, 1835, from Col. Juan Galindo, member Roy. Geolog. Soc. of London, etc.

‡ Prescott, Conquest of Mexico, vol. iii. p. 413.

§ Prehistoric Races of the United States, p. 371.

Five or six centuries, he tells us, would, in his opinion, mark the extreme age of the trees ordinarily found growing on the mounds and on the rubbish-heaps thrown up in the mining operations.*

Schoolcraft, accordingly, fixes the date of the Mound-Builders, or "the active period of tumult among the tribes of the Mississippi Valley," in the twelfth or thirteenth century.

Dr. Foster urges, however, that this is unreliable, because there may have been several generations of trees of the same, or even different species, succeeding each other on the mounds.

This, of course, is possible. But, on the other hand, there is no evidence that there *have been* several generations; and, moreover, the *average* life of these forest-trees in these regions is much less than five or six centuries. "In Wisconsin," according to Dr. Lapham, quoted by Dr. Foster, "it requires a lapse of from fifty-four to one hundred and thirty years for a tree to increase its diameter one foot; three or four feet is a large tree; few exceed that size; and hence we may infer that few of the trees now growing in Wisconsin can antedate the discovery of this continent by Columbus."

Three hundred years would be a fair average. Thus, even if two generations of trees have grown on the mounds, we should only be carried back to the thirteenth century.

"Further south," says Dr. Lapham, "where trees attain a larger size, they have had at the same time, owing to the genial climate and more fertile soil, a much more rapid growth, so that they probably do not exceed the trees of Wisconsin in age."

Adjacent to Lake Erie, in Western New York and Northern Ohio, the works of the Mound-Builders occur, as well as in the valleys of the Ohio and the Mississippi, in Wisconsin, etc.

Connection between the Iroquois and the Mound-Builders.

Mr. Squier has written a book on the Mounds of New York; and he comes to the conclusion, "little anticipated," he says, "when I started on my trip of exploration, *that they were erected by the Iroquois, or their western neighbors, and do not possess any very great antiquity.*"

The famous Iroquois League, or Confederation of the Five Nations, is a matter of familiar history. They not only maintained a kind of confederated government, but they were partially civilized,—as indeed that would imply. Agriculture was practised systematically, and to a considerable extent. Settled between the Hudson and Genesee Rivers, they maintained their position from the beginning of the seventeenth century for nearly two hundred years against the Dutch and the French. Their power was felt, says Dr. Wilson, from the St. Lawrence to the

* Prehistoric Races of the United States, p. 372.

Tennessee, and from the Atlantic to the Mississippi. Captain John Smith encountered their canoes on the upper part of the Chesapeake Bay. It is interesting to remark that Mr. Lewis H. Morgan mentions that in their mounds rows of arrow-heads or flint blades have been found lying side by side, like teeth, the row being about two feet long; which has suggested the idea "that they were set in a frame and fastened with thongs, thus making a species of sword." This is evidently the serrated sword, or *mahquahwitl*, of the Mexicans and of Yucatan.*

Mr. Greenhalgh, who visited Tiotshatton, one of the Seneca villages (the Senecas belonged to the Iroquois Confederation), in 1677, describes it as consisting of one hundred and twenty houses, averaging fifty to sixty feet in length, and with from twelve to fifteen fires in a house.†

And between the Iroquois and the Indians of New Mexico and South America.

Mr. Swann, who visited the Creeks in 1870, says, "Their houses stand in clusters of four, five, six, seven, and eight together. . . . Each cluster containing a clan or family of relatives, who eat and live in common."‡ Lewis and Clarke, speaking of a village of the Chopunnish, in the valley of the Columbia River, say, "The village of Tumachemootool is in fact only a single house one hundred and fifty feet long. . . . It contains twenty-four fires, and about double that number of families." So the Dirt Lodge of the Mandans and Minitares is a communal house forty feet in diameter, polygonal in form, and accommodating seven or eight families. And so again in New Mexico, Chiapas, and Yucatan, the houses were great communal edifices, built of adobe brick, or of rubble-stone and mud mortar, or of slate-stone, or of stone fractured or cut, and laid with mortar. The pueblo of Taos, New Mexico, consists of two such houses, one of which is two hundred and sixty feet long, one hundred feet deep, and five stories high,—the stories retreating in terrace form. This is built of adobe brick, and accommodates about four hundred persons. The second house is one hundred and forty feet long by two hundred

* Stephens mentions this sword in connection with a battle fought near Copan in 1530, between the Spaniards under Hernando de Cháres and the Indians, under the Cacique of Copan, Copan Cabel by name. The camp of the latter consisted of thirty thousand men, "well disciplined, and veterans in war, armed with wooden swords having stone edges, arrows, and slings. . . . The infantry wore coats stuffed with cotton, . . . had swords and shields, . . . the horsemen wore breastplates and helmets, and their horses were covered." Vol. i. p. 100. (This corroborates our statement that Copan at this time was still inhabited.)

On the same subject, Prescott says, "Instead of a sword, they bore a two-handed staff, about three feet and a half long, in which, at regular distances, were inserted, transversely, sharp blades of *itztli*." Conquest of Mexico, vol. i. p. 442.

The same sword (sharks' teeth being substituted for stone) was used in the South Sea Islands.

† Documentary History of New York, vol. i. p. 13.

‡ Schoolcraft, vol. v. p. 262. See also Smiths. Contrib., vol. xvii. pp. 488, 489.

and twenty feet deep. They are now occupied by three hundred and sixty-one Taos Indians. In the cañon of Rio de Chaco, one hundred and forty miles northwest of Santa Fé, is a remarkable group of seven pueblos, in ruins, built of stone. That of Hungo Pavie is three hundred feet long by one hundred and thirty feet deep, three stories high, and had one hundred and forty-four chambers, each fifteen by eighteen feet. It accommodated seven or eight hundred people. This too is terraced. These structures in Mexico were mistaken for *palaces*. The so-called palaces of Palenque, Uxmal, and Chichen-Itza fade away thus into *communal houses*, crowded with Indians through all their apartments.*

---

* Smiths. Contrib., vol. xvii. p. 488.

Bryan Edwards, in his History of the West Indies, speaking of the Caribs, refers to this communal feature among that race (many tribes of which existed in South America). They resided, he says, in villages, and in the centre of each village there was "a public hall or state house, wherein we are assured that the men (excluding the women) had their meals in common." Vol. i. p. 45.

In Purchas's "Pilgrimage" (London, 1617), speaking of the Indians of Brazil, that writer says, "The Petiuares have houses two hundred yards long, without partition" (p. 839); that "some houses have fiftie, threescore, or threescore and tenne roomes, and some are without partition: ordinarily in one house they are of a kindred, and one is principall" (p. 847); that "*Stadius* saith, there are few villages of above seuen houses, but those houses are a hundred and fiftie foote long, and two fathoms high, without diuision into pluralitie of roomes; and therein liue many families, all of one kinred" (p. 849).

Samuel Champlain, in his account of his voyage to Canada in 1603, speaking of the natives, says, "their cabins are low, like tents, . . . ten households sometimes together." Purchas, p. 750.

"The Iroquois," says Purchas, "have no Townes: their dwellings and Forts are *three or foure stories high, as in New Mexico*." Page 751.

The same communal houses were found near three hundred years ago in Guiana among the Jayos, the Arwakos, and the Saspayes. Purchas tells us, speaking of these, that "their houses are like Barnes, but longer; some hundred and fiftie paces long, and twentie broad, an hundred of them keep together in one." Page 831.

It is simply impossible that these people are not all related.

There were many other practices widely diffused over both North and South America which we cannot pause to consider: as, for example, the use of feathers and shells as ornaments; the painting of the body; the employment of the bow and arrow; the marrying of men to men; the use of the pipe; the use of wampum by the North American Indians and of quipu cords in Peru; the use of the drum or of *rattles* in the dance; the elaborate and methodized torturing of captives; the burial of the dead in a sitting posture; the use of stimulants; the plucking out of the beard, etc. The traditions of the Mexicans and Central Americans constantly speak of the advent among those people of "bearded white men,"—showing that, like the Red Indians and the Caribs, the Mexicans and Central Americans were not bearded. So the Natchez spoke of the invasion of Mexico by "bearded white men,"—referring, in this instance, to the Spaniards.

There was one custom which prevailed among the Indians of Brazil, and among the Caribs of the West Indies, which is too strange to have originated independently in different families of mankind. On the birth of the first son, in Brazil and among the Caribs, the father took to his bed, the women assiduously attending him. The same custom prevailed among the Tybareni of Asia Minor, and prevailed in modern times among the

These facts point directly to a connection between the Red Indians of North America and the Mound-Builders, on the one hand, and between these and the Pueblo Indians of New Mexico and the Southern Mexicans on the other; they further indicate the essential unity of the Indians of North and South America. There are other facts that lead to the same conclusion.

The Red Indians, the Mound-Builders, the South American Indians, and the Pueblo Indians, all connected.

Dr. Foster seems to entertain the opinion that the mounds some thirty miles west-southwest of Natchez, at or below the junction of the Ouachita, the Tensas, and the Ocatahoola Rivers, in the parish of Catahoula, Louisiana, were erected by the Natchez Indians after the massacre of the French at Natchez in 1729. In this group "the great temple" has a base of more than two acres,—about three hundred feet square. The trees on these mounds were none of them older than a century when the latter were examined by Prof. Forshey, who first suggested that they had probably been constructed by the Natchez Indians, who took refuge at this spot after the massacre referred to.

The Natchez.

The Natchez are represented to have been superior in intelligence to most of the Indian tribes. They were first visited by La Salle in 1681, and his companion, Tonty, speaks of "their large square dwellings, built of sun-baked mud, mixed with straw [adobe ?], arched over with a dome-shaped roof of canes, and placed in regular order around an open area. . . . Over the temple were rude wooden figures, representing three eagles turned towards the east. A strong mud wall surrounded it, flanked with stakes, on which were stuck the skulls of enemies sacrificed to the sun."

While the trees growing on the mounds referred to were only about a century old, those adjacent to the mounds seemed to indicate a growth of four or five centuries.*

There is an account of some ancient works on the Upper Missouri, by Mr. A. Barrandt, in the "Smithsonian Report" for 1870, which

---

Iberians of Spain, and in Japan. See Purchas, p. 323, and Edwards's History of the West Indies, vol. i. p. 49.

To all this we may add that from the St. Lawrence to Cape Horn the Indians of America were strikingly similar "in color, features, and every circumstance of external appearance." Pedro de Cieca de Leon, who was one of the conquerors of Peru, and had travelled through many provinces of America, gives this account of the inhabitants: "The people, men and women, although there is such a multitude of tribes and nations as to be almost innumerable, and such diversity of climates, appear nevertheless like the children of one father and mother." Ulloa, an able philosopher and an accurate observer, visited and observed many of the Indian tribes and nations of South America. He observed also the Indians at Cape Breton in North America. He says of the latter that they were the same people with the Indians of Peru, resembling them in complexion, in manners, and in customs. "If we have seen one American," he says, "we may be said to have seen them all, their color and make are so nearly the same." See Williams's History of Vermont, vol. i. p. 226.

* Prehistoric Races of the United States, pp. 116–118.

seems to point out an unmistakable connection between the Mound-Builders and the Pueblo Indians of New Mexico, who claim to be descended from the Aztecs. These remains are found from the mouth of the Yellowstone River as far down as Bonhomme Island, below Fort Randall. One of the works is about nine miles southeast of the Missouri and within half a mile of Clark's Creek, Dakota. The main construction is a parallelogram, three hundred and forty feet long, one hundred and ninety feet wide, and twenty-five feet high. The walls are on an average seven feet thick at the summit. Several large blocks of sandstone, roughly hewn, were found, but the walls were of *calcined clay, changed by burning into a brick color.* Following the banks of the creek for half a mile, they came to the remains of a wall some five feet thick, and in some places from three to five feet high, which they traced for four hundred yards.

Mounds in Dakota.

About two hundred and fifty miles up the Bighorn River they found another large mass of ruins, all crumbled away; and from a large oak-tree which they felled, "I found," says Mr. Barrandt, "that they must have occupied this spot at least six hundred years ago, as the tree grew on the remains of what had been probably the largest mound." "We found that these mounds had, for the most part, been constructed of turf and *adobe* or *sun-dried bricks* of inferior manufacture, which accounts for their decay."

Sun-dried Bricks.

Near Grand River he visited a spot called by the Indians *Matontipre* (Bear-House),—a large mound constructed of "*calcinated clay*" which by burning was changed into a brick color. It is encircled by the remains of gigantic walls, which enclose also a number of smaller mounds, some ten or fifteen feet high, and some twenty or forty feet in circumference.

Further up the Yellowstone he found "the remains of an ancient city of mounds,"—with streets regularly laid out, and the mounds equidistant from each other. One of these mounds was sixty-three feet in diameter at the summit, and twenty-seven feet high. There were one hundred and fifty in all. They contained pottery, arrow-heads of stone, fragments of flint, etc. This is one hundred and forty miles above the mouth of the Yellowstone River.

Again, on the Moreau River, near its mouth, they found another mound-city, containing two hundred mounds. There is another group on the banks of the Great Cheyenne. And there are remains of fortifications on Bonhomme Island.

We have thus, near the frontier of British America and a few hundred miles east of the Rocky Mountains,—a thousand miles west of Wisconsin,—a union of the mounds of the Valley of the Ohio with the adobe structures of New Mexico, Chiapas, and Central America. The Aztec and the Mound-Builder have met.

The sites of ancient towns and cities are found very often in Eastern Arkansas and Southeastern Missouri. Mr. J. Dille, in the "Smithsonian Report" for 1866, remarks that "the sites of those ancient towns and cities are indicated by a series of little, square-shaped mounds, raised above the general surface of the land but one or two feet, all ranged in straight lines in two directions, indicating that the streets crossed each other at right angles, and that every dwelling stood upon a street." These mounds, he states, are "the remains of mud [adobe] dwellings," and contain broken pottery similar to that found on the shores of Lake Erie and throughout the Mississippi Valley. "In a country of so much rain," he says, "as Missouri and Arkansas, adobe houses would soon moulder down to a heap, unless well protected by a roof-covering."

Adobe structures in Arkansas.

So Prof. Cox remarks that, "In Phillips County, there are many remains of old fortifications or aboriginal towns to be seen. . . . One of these ancient works of art, four miles west of Helena, at the terminus of Crowley's Ridge, was visited. The embankments, now nearly destroyed by the washing of the rains and the cultivation of a part of the lands, were built of sun-dried bricks, mixed with stems and leaves of the cane." *

We have seen that the Natchez Indians also constructed their houses of sun-baked mud mixed with straw.

We have a particular statement of the fauna of a mound opened in 1865, near Newark, Ohio, by Messrs. O. C. Marsh and G. P. Russell. It was ten feet high and eighty feet in diameter, and was situated "in the midst of a stately forest." Oak-trees with a diameter of two and a half or three feet were growing on it, and near them were stumps evidently older. A number of human skeletons occurred, with stone, bone, and copper implements. The animal remains belonged to elk, deer, black bear, prairie wolf, hare, woodchuck, mussel,—all existing species in Ohio, with one or two exceptions. The bones were very brittle, but, on application of hydrochloric acid, were shown to retain a considerable portion of the cartilage.†

Fauna of the mounds.

Well-preserved specimens of wood are found also in the mounds. At the great stone mound about eight miles south of Newark, Ohio, in one of the small mounds adjacent was found a wooden trough, overlaid by small logs of wood, serving as a cover. In this were the skeleton of a man, and fifteen copper rings and a breastplate of the same metal. The trough and the logs were "in a good state of preservation." The logs were so well preserved that they showed

Objects found in the mounds.

* Quoted in "Prehistoric Races of the United States," p. 113.

† Amer. Jour. Sci., 1866, p. 1.

the axe-marks, "and the steepness of the kerf seemed to indicate that some instrument sharper than the stone axe had been employed."* These remains were immediately beneath a layer of hard, white clay, which was "impervious to the air, as well as to water." This, of course, tended to preserve them. The occurrence of wood is, however, not uncommon.

Specimens of regularly woven *cloth* have been found in a mound in Madison Township, Butler County, Ohio, on the Great Miami River, and elsewhere.

Ornaments of silver, copper, stone, and bone; beads of silver, copper, and shell; spear- and arrow-heads of flint, quartz, garnet, and obsidian; fossil teeth of the shark; sculptured pipes, representing the human head and various animal forms; pottery, mica, etc., are among the objects which constantly occur.

Lead is also found, and in one or two instances, we think, bronze, but no iron. The copper is wrought solely by the hammer, without the melting-pot or the aid of fire.

Extended intercourse among the American nations.

A singular evidence at once of the kinship and the enterprise of the American races is the presence in the mounds of Ohio of the pearls and shells of the Gulf; of the obsidian of Mexico; of the mica of North Carolina; of the jade of Chili; of the lead of Wisconsin; of the copper, and probably the silver, of Ontonagon and the Keweenaw peninsula; and of carvings representing the *Manatee* of South America or the Antilles, and the jaguar, the cougar, the toucan, and the paroquet. These sculptures are very similar to those of Peru, and are not inferior as works of art.

Dr. Wilson asks whether this remarkable fact indicates the intercourse of a common race throughout America, or a *migration* from the South to the North. He decides that it indicates a migration. We cannot agree with him. If the Mound-Builders migrated from the South, the first generation might recall the fauna of the tropics which they had left behind them, and carve from memory representations of animals which were specially characteristic of those latitudes. This is not probable, but it is possible. In the second generation, however, the Mound-Builders in the Scioto Valley would be as unable to make a drawing of the paroquet or the toucan as the generation born in the Wilderness of Sinai would have been to delineate the Sphinx or the Temple of Luxor. True, their fathers might have brought with them images of the animals or birds of South America or Florida, and those images might have remained as heir-looms in the family. But this would not have exerted an influence after a few generations. This hypothesis is, therefore,

* Smithsonian Report, 1866, p. 360.

untenable, and we are compelled to believe that the relations and intercourse (of course there may have been migrations also) of the Mound-Builders were of the most extensive character,—reaching certainly into Mexico, to the mica-mines of North Carolina, to the copper-mines of Wisconsin, and to the peninsula of Florida; possibly to the West India Islands and South America; and we must believe also that the same blood coursed through the veins of these widely-separated nations,—modified, no doubt, by varying admixtures, but characterized in all cases by a predominating, primeval race-mark.*

The mounds of the Southern States.

The southern region of the United States (like the northern) abounds in tumuli, earth-works, fortified hills, and other remains of an ancient population. The mounds in the neighborhood of New Madrid, on the Mississippi, are particularly rich in pottery and stone ornaments. There are many mounds also in the neighborhood of Memphis. Numerous traces of the same race occur again in the valleys of the upper tributaries of the Tombigbee and all the affluents of the Yazoo and Big Black. Ancient works appear, says Mr. Fontaine, in all the lower valley of the Mississippi, from Cairo to the mound of Pointe à la Hache, on the bank of the river, fifty miles below New Orleans. They are found again in Texas, in Alabama, and in Georgia. The Yazoo River, in the Choctaw language, is called *Yazoo-ok-hinnah*, The River of Ancient Ruins. Tumuli, which Mr. Fontaine describes as being constructed with geometrical precision, of the truncated pyramidal form,—their sides corresponding with the cardinal points,—occur near Florence, Alabama, in the valley of the Tennessee River, one of which is seventy feet high and covers an acre of ground.† The great mound

* The lead from Wisconsin, the North Carolina mica, etc., were of course procured by traffic; and why not the obsidian of Mexico or shells from Florida?

† Dr. Foster (as well as Messrs. Squier and Davis) distinguish this class of mounds as *Temple-Mounds*. They are characterized by great regularity of form and their large dimensions, and consist chiefly of pyramidal structures, truncated, and ordinarily with graded avenues to the top. In some instances they are terraced, or have successive stages. They have invariably flat or level tops. It is supposed that the summits were crowned with temples. We find traces of this form at Aztalan, in Wisconsin; at Cahokia, in Illinois; at several points in Ohio; frequently in Kentucky; at Florence and Claiborne, in Alabama; at Seltzertown, in Mississippi; and, indeed, most of the mounds of the Gulf States are of this type, which culminates in the teocallis of Mexico and Central America. We have thus conclusive evidence that the mounds of the South and those of the North belong to the same race.

Mr. Baldwin (like Dr. Foster) refers the Mound-Builders and the ancient inhabitants of Central America and Mexico to the same race. He mentions, in proof of this, that we find among the works of the Mound-Builders the same (orientated) pyramidal platforms (truncated pyramids) ascended by terraces which are represented by the teocallis of Mexico and Yucatan. In a mound in the Ohio Valley two chambers were found in which the timber of which the walls were formed was still partially preserved, and in which were arched ceilings, "precisely like those in Central America."

of Seltzertown, Mississippi, is a truncated pyramid, six hundred by four hundred feet at the base, and covering nearly six acres of ground. The north side of the mound is supported by a wall of sun-dried brick, two feet thick (reminding us of New Mexico), filled with grass and leaves. In Georgia these works are found in the valley of every considerable stream. At Silver Bluff, on the Savannah River (the village of the Cacique of Cutifachiqui, according to tradition), Mr. Bartram saw "various monuments and vestiges of the residence of the ancients: as Indian conical mounds, terraces, areas, etc., as well as remains or traces of fortresses of regular formation." He observed the same works near the confluence of the Broad and Savannah Rivers, and on the east bank of the Ocmulgee River, near Macon. The council-house of the Cherokee town of Cowe, he tells us, was a large rotunda capable of accommodating several hundred persons. It stood on the top of one of the ancient mounds. Numbers of these tumuli occur in the valley of the Etowah River,—the most remarkable of which are on the plantation of Colonel Tumlin, near Cartersville, in Bartow County. Idol-pipes, stone plates, implements of copper, terra-cotta vases, stone axes, perforated shells, mica mirrors, in one instance beads of gold, etc., are found in these mounds.

Stupendous remains occur also on the Chattahoochee, the Nacoochee, and the Oostenaula.

The mounds are found again in Florida, and in South Carolina.

The Mound-Builders, in a word, have been traced from Dakota and Wisconsin to the Gulf, and from Texas and Arkansas to the Atlantic.

Mr. Jones on the connection between the Indians and the Mound-Builders.

Mr. Charles C. Jones ("Antiquities of the Southern Indians") is disposed to connect the Mound-Builders with the Red Indians of the South. "In the light of the Spanish narratives," says this author, "after a careful consideration of the relics themselves, and in view of all the facts which have thus far been disclosed, . . . we see no good reason for supposing that these more prominent tumuli and enclosures may not have been constructed in the olden times by peoples akin to and in the main by no means farther advanced in semi-civilization than the red men native at the dawn of the historic period. In a word, we do not concur in the opinion, so often expressed, that the mound-builders were a race distinct from and superior in art, government, and religion to the Southern Indians of the fifteenth and sixteenth centuries." *

The Indians, we are informed by this careful investigator, were in the habit of erecting mounds when the southern parts of the United States were first occupied by the Europeans; afterwards the custom was

* Antiquities of the Southern Indians, p. 135.

discontinued. Mr. Jones opened a mound, twenty feet in diameter and seven feet high, below Savannah, and found in it, along with arrow-heads and celts of stone, the fragment of an old-fashioned sword. These relics lay beside a skeleton, and all were at the bottom of the mound, on a level with the surface of the surrounding plain. The oak handle of the sword was in a good state of preservation, but of the blade only about seven inches remained.

Mr. Jefferson, in his "Notes on Virginia," describes an Indian mound on the Rivanna River, in Albemarle County, Virginia.*

Bartram commemorates the fact that in his day the Choctaws covered the pyramid of coffins, taken from the bone-house, with earth, thus raising a conical hill or mount; and To-mo-chi-chi pointed out to General Oglethorpe a large conical mound near Savannah, in which, he said, the Yamacraw chief was interred who had, many years before, entertained a great white man with a red beard, who entered the Savannah River in a large vessel.†

Mr. Jones also describes an ancient fortification on Brown's Mount, situated on the line between Bibb and Twiggs Counties, not far from Macon, in Georgia. The entire top of this mount was fortified by a stone and earth wall, which enclosed about sixty acres. This wall was accompanied by both an inside and an outside ditch, the former being originally three feet wide and between two and three feet deep, and the latter ten feet wide and four feet deep. Within the recollection of persons still living, this wall was four feet high and four or five feet thick. Along the wall, at intervals of about thirty yards, were elevated platforms and lunettes. "This," we are told, "was, without doubt, the work of the red men, and in ancient times constituted a fortified retreat." "Similar structures exist within the limits of Georgia, and in many portions of the United States."‡

Within the enclosure of Brown's Mount are the traces of two small earth mounds, and near the northeastern side is an elliptical pond or basin, the bottom of which, it is said, had been plastered with clay at some remote period, for the purpose of retaining the rain-water which fell in it.

Former condition of the Indians.

That the condition of the Indians of the United States was not so degraded as is generally assumed, when the country was first occupied by Europeans, has appeared from what we have stated about the Iroquois and the Natchez. The same fact appears from Strachey's "Historie of Travaile into Virginia Britannia," in the beginning of the seventeenth century. He found the Virginia

* Notes on Virginia, p. 133.

† Antiquities of the Southern Indians, p. 131.

‡ Ib., p. 164.

Indians inhabiting wooden houses in the midst of gardens, cultivating maize, tobacco, peas, beans, and fruits, and the women and children "continually keeping the ground with weeding,"—some of them breeding tame turkeys about their houses. He describes their "great emperor," Powhatan, "with his divers seats of houses, . . . and at every house provision for his entertainment;" attended constantly by a guard of forty or fifty "of the tallest men his country does afford;" sentinels posted every night about his house; his country divided into provinces, each with a "weroanc" or commander; receiving tithes of corn, tobacco, and garden-fruit, or a tax on fowls, fish, hides, copper, etc.

In 1528, Ferdinand de Soto encountered in Florida a settled and somewhat advanced people, occupying towns, engaged in agriculture, fabricating very pretty pottery, breeding fowls, and clothing themselves with garments made out of the inner bark of trees and grass. He was informed, we are told, of a "foundry of gold and copper;" and the Fidalgo de Elvas mentions some chopping-knives at Cutifachiqui in the hands of the natives. The province of Cutifachiqui (on the Savannah River) was governed by a Cacica, who extended to him a ceremonious and formal welcome. The stern of her canoe was covered with awning, and she sat upon cushions. The natives displayed garments and shawls and richly-colored feathers of white, gray, vermilion, and yellow; well-dressed deer-skins with various designs depicted on them; and many pearls. The Knight of Elvas informs us that the inhabitants not only wore clothing for the body, but also "shoes." At Talomeco was a mausoleum one hundred paces long by forty broad, guarded by gigantic wooden statues carved with considerable skill.

Elsewhere the same chronicler informs us, giving an account of the discovery of Florida, that "on Wednesday, the 19th of June, the Governor entered Pacaha and took quarters in the town where the Cacique was accustomed to reside. It was enclosed and very large. In the towers and palisades were many loop-holes. There was much dry maize, and the new was in great quantity throughout the fields. At the distance of half a league to a league off were large towns, all of them surrounded with stockades. Where the Governor stayed was a great lake near to the enclosure; and the water entered a ditch that wellnigh went round the town. From the River Grande to the lake was a canal, through which the fish came into it, and where the Chief kept them for his eating and pastime. With nets that were found in the place, as many were taken as need required. The Cacique of Casqui many times sent large presents of fish, shawls, and skins." *

This was in Florida (and the present State of Georgia) in the six-

* Quoted in "Antiquities of the Southern Indians," p. 143.

teenth century. Why should we suppose that the Mound-Builders were of much greater antiquity? Were their arts superior?

The manufacture of pottery prevailed among many of the Indian tribes,—as the Iroquois, the Natchez, the Delawares, the natives of Florida and Louisiana, the Mandans, etc. The Knight of Elvas, speaking of that fabricated in the province of Naguatex, says that "clay vessels were made which differed little from those of Estremez and Montemor,"—two towns in Portugal noted for their earthenware. Du Pratz mentions that the women of Louisiana made pots or jugs for preserving bear-oil, holding forty pints; jars with a small opening; bowls; two-pint bottles with long necks; plates and dishes in the French fashion, etc. They also painted this pottery with ochre.

Pottery of the Cahokia Indians.

Mr. Charles Rau discovered some years ago on the left bank of Cahokia Creek, opposite St. Louis,—a locality formerly occupied by the Cahokia Indians,—the site of an Indian pottery-manufactory. It is described in the "Smithsonian Report" for 1866. He remarks, "Having seen the best specimens of 'mound' pottery obtained during the survey of Messrs. Squier and Davis, I do not hesitate to assert that the clay vessels fabricated at the Cahokia Creek were in every respect equal to those exhumed from the mounds of the Mississippi Valley; and Dr. Davis himself, who examined my specimens from the first-named locality, expressed the same opinion."

Mr. Bartram, in his "Travels through North and South Carolina, Georgia," etc. (1792), speaking of the large and handsome canoes formed out of the trunks of cypress-trees, which were in use among the Indians of Southern Florida, states that in these canoes they "sometimes cross the Gulph, extending their navigations to the Bahama Islands, and even to Cuba;" "a crew of these adventurers," he proceeds, "had just arrived, having returned from Cuba but a few days before our arrival, with a cargo of spirituous liquors, coffee, sugar, and tobacco." *

Similar testimony is borne by Dr. Bell with regard to the roving and the civilized Indians of New Mexico, in his work entitled "New Tracks in North America." We are told by him that the Navajos of the present day "for love of plunder and rapine . . . have no equals." Formerly, as we learn from the same writer, "they had fixed abodes in their country, around which they raised crops almost rivalling those of the Pimas [civilized Indians] of the Gila; they carried one art—the weaving of blankets—to a state of perfection which, in closeness of texture and arrangement of color, is scarcely equalled even by the labored and costly seraphes [*serapes*] of Mexico and South America." These were, however, uncivilized and marauding Indians. Relentless war has been

* Quoted in "Antiquities of the Southern Indians," p. 58.

made on them ever since General Kearney occupied that region. The Spaniards had made relentless war on them before. They are nearly exterminated.

It is of equal importance that the Navajos claim to be of the same stock as the town-building tribes.

The Pimas were "civilized" Indians. They were powerful and rich, and lived in great communal houses four or five stories high. The Spaniards almost destroyed them, but they rallied and became moderately prosperous again until they came in contact with the "Americans" of the United States; not having rebuilt the stately mansions of their ancestors, but living in lowly huts,—yet "a healthy race, the men brave and honest, the women chaste." But, says a paper in the Smithsonian Report for 1871, "since Butterfield's mail-coaches first passed through their land" there has been another change, and "to-day foul diseases prevail to an alarming extent, many of the women are public prostitutes, and all will pilfer whenever opportunity offers." These facts greatly diminish, if they do not entirely remove, the wide gap which has been supposed to exist between the arts of the Mound-Builders and those of the red men. A general paralysis seems to have smitten the Indian races (civilized and uncivilized) of both North and South America after the intrusion of the Europeans. The Aztecs and the Inca race of Peru are represented to-day by miserable, torpid, half-naked Indians (some of them roving Indians) but little in advance of the Indians of the United States.

If we examine into the arts and burial-customs of the modern Indians, we are astonished at the similarity or identity between them and those of the Mound-Builders.

Resemblance between the arts of the two races.

We find in a modern Indian grave the same stone implements, the same unsmelted copper, the same delicately-sculptured pipes, the same perforated shells, the same plates of mica, the same pottery, agricultural implements, ornaments, etc., that we have found in those of the Mound-Builders. The weapons have the same forms. The materials are the same. In some Indian graves near Nashville, Tennessee, Dr. Joseph Jones (see p. 222, "Antiquities of the Southern Indians") found "stone and clay images, marine shells, stone implements, arrow- and spear-heads, *a stone sword*, agricultural implements, various ornaments of stone, clay, and shell, pots, vases of curious devices, and copper crosses." We only give this as an example. It reads like an exploration of one of the great mounds of Ohio or Missouri. "A stone sword" is mentioned,—evidently the serrated sword of the Mound-Builders, the Mexicans, and the Caribs.

The commercial intercourse carried on among the Indians, as described by the author of the "Antiquities of the Southern Indians," reads like another chapter from Messrs. Squier and Davis. "The TRADE RELATIONS," says Mr. Jones, "existing among these primitive peoples were extensive. The principal articles of barter were copper, flint, and stone implements, pipes, shell ornaments, pearls, and skins. Galena, obsidian, mica, and small masses of native gold and silver, also formed subjects of merchandise. Between the coast and the interior a constant interchange of commodities was maintained. The beautiful jasper and flint arrow- and spear-points, stone pipes, discoidal stones, and various articles manufactured by the dwellers among the mountains were readily sold to the coast tribes, who gave in exchange for them shells, pearls, and commodities native to the region, and held in esteem by those at a distance. . . . From the same stone grave in Nacoochee Valley were taken an ornamental copper axe from the shores of Lake Superior, a large cassis from the Gulf of Mexico, and stone weapons made of materials entirely foreign to the locality." *

Mr. Schoolcraft mentions the discovery in one of the mounds of the Elizabethtown group, West Virginia, of "an antique telescopic tube of steatite, skilfully cut and polished, and similar to one found in Peru." † Messrs. Squier and Davis mention similar stone tubes in their "Ancient Monuments of the Mississippi Valley." Now we learn from the "Antiquities of the Southern Indians" that these tubes were in use among the Southern Indians, and also among the Indians of California, and it is suggested that they were cupping-tubes, or, in some instances, ornaments.

The game of Chungke.

Once more: Mr. Jones devotes a chapter to the game of *Chungke*, which prevailed among the Southern Indians throughout Tennessee, Alabama, Mississippi, Louisiana, Kentucky, Virginia, and elsewhere. Carefully-prepared areas were dedicated to this game, which was played with certain discoidal stones. The Indians of Georgia and Florida, says Captain Bernard Romans, play at this game "from morning till night," and "bet high," staking on it "all of their skins, then their pipes, their beads, trinkets, and ornaments, and, lastly, their blankets and other garments, and even all their arms." Messrs. Squier and Davis, we are told, found these discs in the mounds of the West, which, they say, "are related to a very numerous class of relics scattered over the surface from the valley of the Ohio to Peru." Mr. Schoolcraft tells us that "numerous discoidal stones that are found in the tumuli and at the sites of ancient occupancy in the Mississippi Valley serve to denote that this game was practised among the earlier tribes of that valley at the Mound period. These antique quoits are made with great labor and skill from very hard and heavy pieces of stone. They are generally exact discs, of a concave surface, with an orifice in the

* Pages 63, 64.

† See Baldwin's Ancient America, pp. 40–42, 70–74.

centre, and a broad rim." * They are found also in the ancient mounds of the Southern States. This game of *chungke* was a national game among all of the Southern Indians. Its prevalence among the Mound-Builders necessarily suggests some bond of connection between them and the red men.

Manufacture of cloth.

Dr. Foster gives a good deal of prominence to the recent discovery of *cloth* in the mounds of Ohio. "This fact," he says, "was so novel in itself, and so at variance with the prevailing ideas as to the degree of civilization and knowledge of the arts among the mound-builders, that I hesitated about making it public." A discovery subsequent to that of Dr. Foster assured him that there was no doubt of the knowledge of the art of weaving among this race. They clothed themselves, he says, in part at least, not in skins like the Indian; not, like the Sandwich Islander, in cloth made of the macerated bark of certain trees; nor, like the dwellers of the Swiss lakes, in matted sheets of vegetable fibre; but in a cloth regularly spun with a uniform thread, and woven with a warp and woof." † The fabric, we are told, appears to be composed "of some material allied to *hemp*," and the original texture corresponded with that of "coarse sail-cloth." ‡

"There is no evidence," says Dr. Foster, "that the Indians possessed this art when first known to the white man." "These facts," it is farther stated, "go far to dissever the present race of Indians from the mound-builders, and to link the latter to the civilized races of Central America." §

It appears, however, from Mr. Jones's work, that the Southern Indians did manufacture cloth, and, so far as we can judge, just as good cloth as that described from the Ohio mounds.

"Formerly," says Adair, "the Indians made very handsome carpets. They have a wild hemp that grows about six feet high in open, rich, level lands, and which usually ripens in July; it is plenty on our frontier settlements. When it is fit for use, they pull, steep, peel, and beat it; and the old women spin it off the distaffs with wooden machines, having some clay on the middle of them to hasten the motion. When the coarse thread is prepared, they put it into a frame about six feet square, and, instead of a shuttle, they thrust through the thread with a long cane, having a large string through the web, which they shift at every second course of the thread. When they have thus finished their arduous labor, they paint each side of the carpet with such figures of various colors as their fruitful imaginations devise; particularly the images of birds and beasts they are acquainted with; and likewise of themselves,

---

* Quoted in "Antiquities of the Southern Indians," p. 353.

† Prehistoric Races of the United States, p. 223. ‡ Ib., p. 225. § Ib., p. 226.

acting in their social and martial relations." He was informed that the Muscogees, time out of mind, passed the woof with a shuttle, "having a couple of threddles which they move with the hand so as to enable them to make good dispatch, something after our manner of weaving."

Buffalo's wool, we are also told by Mr. Jones, "was extensively used for spinning and weaving." The Choctaws made turkey-feather blankets. The inner bark of the mulberry was also used for making shawls and cloaks. It was first dried in the sun, and then beaten so as to cause all the woody parts to fall off. The remaining threads were then beaten a second time, and bleached by exposure to the dew. When well whitened, they were spun and twisted into thread.

We are informed by the Knight of Elvas that the companions of De Soto observed blankets or shawls among the natives while passing through the region now constituting Middle Georgia. "Some of these were made from the inner bark of trees, and others of a grass resembling the nettle, which, when beaten, becomes like flax." *

We have thus spinning and weaving among the Southern Indians, the material (like that of the Mound-Builders) *hemp;* or, in other cases, a species of grass, or the bark of the mulberry, or the wool of the buffalo.

We are told, moreover, that certain tribes in the Rocky Mountains spun and wove the wool of the sheep.†

Shell-mounds.

The southern coasts of the United States, we have mentioned elsewhere, present great numbers of shell-mounds. We are told that many of them are very ancient, and it is supposed that they were cotemporary with the Mound-Builders. Mr. Jones mentions a group of more than forty tumuli on Colonel's Island, in Liberty County, Georgia. Besides these sepulchral tumuli, the adjacent fields are "hoary," we are told, with shell-mounds.

It appears to us that we ascertain thus an important characteristic of the Mound-Builders' civilization. Some of them lived on the coast, and after the manner of the ancient fishermen of the Danish kjökken-möddings.

The modern Indians often lived in the same way. Many of the Southern shell-mounds (and, we believe, all on the northeast coasts of the United States) belonged to them.

The circumstance illustrates at once another practice common to these two races, and the rude and primitive condition of their society.

Other alleged evidences of the antiquity of the American races.

There are other evidences adduced of the antiquity of man in America. Dr. Foster mentions them in order. The Mound-Builders he assigns to the Historic Epoch. His scheme is as follows:

* See Antiquities of the Southern Indians, pp. 73, 78, 86, 87.

† American Cyclopædia, 1873, vol. i. p. 402.

MIOCENE (?).

EUROPE.	NORTH AMERICA.
Flints in Calcaire de Beauce, Pontleroy, with Acerotherium, Mastodon, Dinotherium, Rhinoceros. Flint flake in beds of Aurillac, with remains of *Dinotherium* and *Machairodus latidens.* Hacked bones at Pouancé, Maine-et-Loire, with *Halitherium fossile.* All these instances require, he says, further authentication.	Flint flakes, etc., in the gravel-beds of Colorado and Wyoming, with shells belonging to the genera *Corbicula* and *Rangia.* Further authentication required.

PLIOCENE (?)

Hacked bones in the beds of St. Prest associated with *Elephas meridionalis, Rhinoceros leptorhinus, Hippopotamus major.* Evidence not conclusive.	Human skull found in Calaveras County, California.

DRIFT (*closing period*).

Epoch of Extinct Animals. — Terrace gravels of the Somme, Seine, in France; Surrey, Kent, and Middlesex, in England, with flint implements, etc. The caves in France, Belgium, England, and Wales (in part) with flint implements. *Epoch of the Migrated Existing Animals* (Reindeer Period).—Dordogne caves, France, Belgian caves (in part), loess of the Rhine, skeletons, improved flint implements, etc., with remains of living and extinct animals.	Plummet from San Joaquin Valley. Stone hatchet (?) found in Jersey County, Illinois. Loess of Mississippi Valley, Natchez, enclosing *os innominatum* of man, with bones of extinct animals. Flint implements found in the lacustrine deposit in the Osage Valley, and Bourbeuse Valley, of Missouri, with bones of mastodon.

RECENT.

Epoch of the Domesticated Existing Animals. Shell-mounds of Denmark. Stone implements in Danish (Scotch fir) peat. Lake-dwellings of Switzerland of the Stone Age. Clyde marine strata with canoes. Peat of the Somme Valley. Works of art in the Nile mud.	Human skeleton in the Delta of the Mississippi. Ancient hearths in alluvium of Ohio Valley. Shells of the Busycon in the alluvium. Shell-accumulations on the Gulf coast (in part).

MORE RECENT.

Bronze Epoch.—Bronze implements of Switzerland, Denmark, Ireland, and England.	Mound-Builders of the Ohio and Mississippi Valleys. Shell-accumulations, marine and fresh-water, on the Gulf coast and in the interior (in part).

Having commenced with the Mound-Builders, we shall proceed backwards in noticing these periods.

1. *The Shell-Mounds.*—No antiquity is claimed for the shell-mounds of the northeast. They evidently belonged to the modern Indians, and relics of European origin are found in them.

On the Gulf coast they are older, apparently. At Grand Lake, on the Tèche, the accumulations are from six to ten feet high, forty feet broad, and three-fourths of a mile in length. Large live-oak trees are growing upon them. This region is now fifteen miles inland, "thus showing that marked changes in the sea-level have occurred in comparatively recent times."

It is sufficient to say that *glazed pottery* was found in these mounds. We have here, therefore, not an evidence for the antiquity of man, but an evidence that a great physical alteration in the character of this coast has occurred within a very recent period.

The fact that this pottery is *glazed* connects it at once with Chiriqui, or some nation far advanced in the ceramic art.

On the Pacific coast, near San Francisco, three miles from San Pablo, there is a shell-mound almost a mile long and half a mile wide. Two years ago, at a depth of twenty feet, numerous human skeletons were found, and "some bones of dogs and birds, and many implements of stone." "One baby had been rolled in a long piece of red silk, like the mummies, which had been covered with a coating of a sort of asphaltum." From the skulls, the skeletons were referred to an extinct tribe of Indians. These skeletons were in a sitting posture.

Dr. Foster considers the corpse in "the long piece of red silk" an "intrusive burial." This might be the case if "intrusive burials" were usual as deep down as twenty feet.*

The fresh-water shell-heaps of Florida are also on a scale that almost surpasses belief. With reference to their age, Prof. Wyman mentions one covering twenty acres, at Silver Spring, on which grows a grove of live-oaks. Six of these, at five feet from the ground, measured as follows: one, thirteen feet; three, fifteen feet; one, nineteen feet; and one between twenty-six and twenty-seven feet, in circumference. The two last he calculates to be six hundred years old. On the same basis of calculation, the least age of the mounds near Blue Spring, and at Old Town, would be about four hundred years.

With this we may dismiss the shell-mounds. It will be noticed that Dr. Foster assigns the most ancient of these to the era of the Stone Age Lake-Dwellings of Switzerland. What evidence is there?

* This piece of red silk proves communication with Asia. See also the remarkable idol represented in Harper's Magazine for February, 1875, found in a mound in Tennessee,—apparently Japanese.

2. *Ancient Hearths in the Alluvium of the Ohio Valley.*—At Portsmouth, Ohio, Col. Whittlesey, in examining the fluviatile deposits on the Ohio River, observed two ancient hearths. They were from eighteen to twenty feet above low water, and about fifteen feet below the surface. They are in or near the bottom of the usual loamy yellow clay of the valley, which is fifteen to thirty feet thick, and on which are extensive works of the Mound-Builders.

The substance of this statement is that in the river-mud, on the banks of the Ohio, fifteen feet below the mounds, two ancient hearths have been found. A solitary example of this sort, in the first place, proves nothing; because it may be the result of accidental circumstances of which we of course know nothing. In the second place, it is a mere question of the action of the Ohio River in depositing this mud on its banks. We have already seen the freaks of the Mississippi in this respect; the present deposit may all have been the work of a single freshet. The Ohio River rises sixty feet at Cincinnati.

3. *The Human Skeleton found by Dr. Dowler at New Orleans.*—We have already considered this. Dr. Foster himself rejects the antiquity of the skeleton. After reviewing the evidence, he says,—

"Thus, then, with these carefully-observed computations before us [of the U. S. Engineers, Humphreys and Abbot], we are not prepared to accept the antiquity assigned by Dr. Dowler to the human remains found beneath the surface at New Orleans. What he regards as four buried forests, which once flourished on the spot, may be nothing more than drift-wood brought down by the river in former times, which became imbedded in the silts and sediments which were deposited on what was then the floor of the Gulf." *

4. *The Mastodon-remains found by Dr. Koch with flint arrow-heads.*—We have detailed one of these two cases. We have no disposition to discredit them. Dr. Foster seems in doubt about them. He desires to show that the association of the remains of man and the mastodon proves the great antiquity of man. We, on the other hand, use the same facts to prove the very recent existence of the mastodon in America,—a fact abundantly illustrated by the finding of the mastodon-remains constantly, all over the country, in the surface peat and mud, at the depth of a few feet,—often *on* the surface.

5. *The Human Pelvis in the Loess at Natchez.*—In the bottom of a ravine cut through this fluviatile deposit at Natchez, Dr. Dickeson, many

* Dr. Foster adds the following in a note at the bottom of the page: "Since the above was written, I have seen the remarks of Prof. C. G. Forshey, made before the New Orleans Academy of Sciences, in which he discredits the observations of Humphreys and Abbot, as to the nature of the river-bed, the meagre thickness of the alluvium, and the insufficient age of the delta." See p. 76.

years ago, found the pelvic bone of a man, mingled with those of the mastodon and megalonyx.

Dr. Leidy, of Philadelphia, in his "Extinct Mammalia of North America," remarks on this, "The specimen may have been cotemporary with the remains of extinct animals, with which it is said to have been found, though it appears to me to be equally if not more probable that it may have fallen into the formation from an Indian grave above, at a comparatively recent date, and become stained, like the true fossils, from ferruginous infiltration."

Professor C. G. Forshey (quoted by Dr. Foster as a highly competent observer) speaks of these remains as follows: "I examined the spot where the bone was found,—in Bernard's Bayou, just above the bridge, on the Pine-ridge road, two and one-half miles from Natchez. The material from which it was taken was a dark loam in the bottom of the thirty-feet bayou. It was probably not *in situ*, but this loam, and the bone too, probably, had caved in from some point above, and had been drifted thither from fields of several miles square, above the road. A dozen plantation burial-places, and Indian mounds and camps, had been exposed above for centuries; and in recent years, since inhabited by the whites (for a hundred years), the drains had cut through the surface to the depth of twenty and even forty feet in the bluff loam-beds. The probabilities are a hundred to one that this bone was not of the Bluff (mastodon) formation, but of the present era."

Dr. Foster accepts, apparently, these views.*

6. *Stone hatchet from the modified drift of Jersey County, Illinois.*—We are told by Dr. Foster that this object was found in the river-

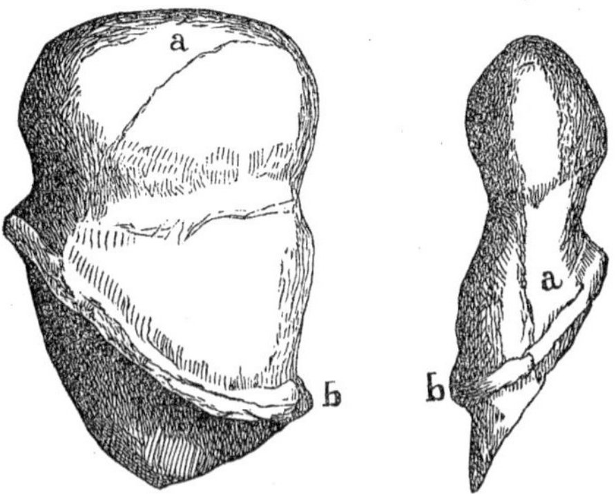

gravel, which, with the loess, fills the lateral valleys of this region of Illinois to the depth of from sixty to one hundred feet. A section of

* See Prehistoric Races of the United States, p. 59.

this formation is exhibited at the spot where this stone relic was found, being exposed by the cutting of Otter Creek through the beds. The exposure here exhibited twenty feet of yellowish-brown clay at the top, overlying twenty to thirty feet of sand and gravel with boulders; and beneath this last, about fifteen feet of blue clay, extending below the bed of the creek. From a mass of cemented pebbles and sand, which had become detached and had fallen to the margin of the stream, the hatchet was procured which is represented in the preceding figure (given by Dr. Foster).

The material is sienite. We will quote from Dr. Foster: "The portion which projected from the matrix has been so long exposed to atmospheric agents as to present a nearly uniform surface, except along the line *a*, which appears to be a thin leaf of more durable material, standing slightly out from the general ground; and the bold ridge *b*, which differs in no respect from the mass in chemical composition, and extends obliquely around the whole specimen. I can conceive that if the lower part had been imbedded in a conglomerate rock for a time, the upper part might have weathered so as to leave a projection; but this projection is equally prominent on the lower side. If this had been a finished hatchet, the workman would not have left the ridge which we have described [we imagine not], as it would have interfered with its cutting properties. On the other hand, it may be claimed that after having worked out the head he undertook to flake off a portion from the edge, but the fracture extended too deep, and the work was spoiled; and the conchoidal nature of the fracture on one side lends plausibility to this view." P. 68.

It is admitted that this rude fragment is disqualified for serving as a cutting instrument in consequence of "the bold ridge *b*," which extends entirely around the whole specimen, just above the sharp edge. It would be most natural, therefore, as the object bears no special resemblance to anything, to conclude that it is a natural form with which man has had nothing to do. But Dr. Foster first sets aside the improbability of finding a cotemporary human implement in the river-gravel of Illinois, and then reasons himself into the possibility that the object found is a stone hatchet, when it is entirely unfitted to perform the functions of a cutting implement of any sort.

Furthermore, this "object," having been found not *in situ*, but in a fallen mass of "cemented" gravel, need not possess any great antiquity. This cementation of gravel is often a modern process, and may have occurred at any iron or lime spring whose waters may have reached the gravel in question.

7. *Plummet from the San Joaquin Valley.*—The next testimony to the antiquity of man in America is from the gravel-deposits of California.

The material here is also of sienite, and there is no question of its having been shaped by human hands. Below we give a representation of this highly-finished specimen.

This plummet, as Dr. Foster calls it, is ground and polished so as to display in marked contrast the pure white of the feldspar and the dark green or black of the hornblende. It is in the form of a double cone, one end terminating in a point. The other end is perforated. Dr. Foster says "it affords an exhibition of the lapidary's skill superior to anything yet furnished by either continent."

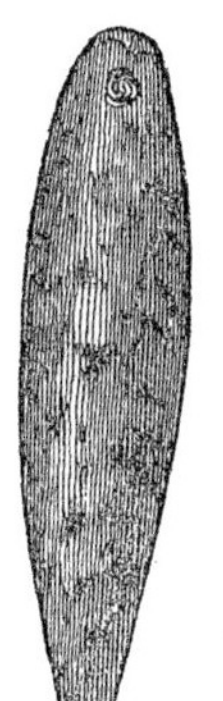

It was discovered by some workmen who were digging a well on the lands of Mr. Lafayette Nealy, in the valley of the San Joaquin. It was (*as alleged*) imbedded in the gravel thirty feet below the surface.

In connection with this case, we may mention that the bones of the mastodon and elephant occur throughout California *at the surface* and to the depth of a hundred feet in the "Post-pliocene." Such is the statement of Prof. Whitney.

What, then, is the age of this beautiful specimen of the "lapidary's skill"? Dr. Foster assigns it to the era of the "Drift," by which he evidently means the "River-Gravel."

The age of the river-gravel we have already discussed. But we do not believe that man appeared in America even as early as this. Dr. Foster himself informs us that "no remains of the mastodon [p. 84] have been found in deposits older than the Loess; . . . that the peat swamps are the great sepulchres of this animal" (as, ordinarily, according to the same authority, the river-gravels are of the elephant).

(Leaving California out), in every case in America, as at Petit-Anse, on the Ashley River, in Missouri, at Natchez, where human remains or works of art have been asserted to have been found with elephantine remains, the animal was the *mastodon*, and not the *mammoth*. (It is true, however, at the same time, that even the mammoth-remains occur on the surface, and in later formations than the river-gravel.)

Prof. Whitney states, farther, that artificial implements have been frequently found in California in connection with the bones of the "elephant and mastodon." (This is probably much too strongly stated: we should like to have the specifications.)

From all of these facts it is probable that this sienite "net-sinker,"* or whatever it is, may be as old as the flint implements found in the

* It is very probable, Dr. Andrews suggests, that the implement was part of the outfit of a "medicine-man." Before the great fire, there were in the Chicago Academy of Sciences three quite similar stone implements, which had been taken from the pouch of an Apache "medicine-man" killed in battle. They are said to have been used for plugging wounds.

Bourbeuse and Pomme-de-Terre Valleys (Missouri), at Petit-Anse, and on the Ashley River. These (if we accept the cotemporaneity of the remains found) were of the age of the Mastodon, or of the American Peat and Shell-marl.

The workmanship of this stone negatives the idea of any extreme antiquity. It belonged, obviously, to such a race as those which have left their memorials in Mexico and in Central America. As to the *depth* at which it was found, it is an isolated case, and a thousand accidents may account for that,—might, indeed, remand it to a very modern date; and, besides all this, the facts are not properly authenticated.

We might also ask how the polished stone axe referred to by Sir John Lubbock (p. 609) as found at Malton, below a band of undisturbed clay, in the river-gravel, got into this palæolithic bed. We might ask Dr. Foster how the copper knife figured on p. 256 of his work, and found in the valley of Rock River, Illinois, got into the "river-drift," where it is represented by the Assistant State Geologist of Illinois to have been found.

8. *Human Skull found in Calaveras County, California.*—This skull is alleged to have been found in a shaft, near Angelos, one hundred and fifty feet deep, in the "gold-drift," or gold-bearing gravel. This bed of auriferous gravel was covered by five beds of lava and other volcanic matter, one hundred and fifty feet thick.

The authenticity of this account has been seriously questioned, and Prof. Whitney, who secured the skull for the museum of the State Geological Survey, was thought in California to have been made the victim of a hoax.

But there are other stories of the same kind. In 1857, Dr. C. F. Winslow sent to the Boston Natural History Society the fragment of a human cranium, which he represented to have been found in the "pay-dirt" (gold-gravel), in connection with the bones of the mastodon and elephant, one hundred and eighty feet below the surface of Table Mountain, California. And again, in 1868, Prof. Blake read before the American Association at Chicago an account of the finding of "the teeth of extinct mammalia as well as the relics of human art" in this same Table Mountain, at the depth of from one to two hundred feet.

The auriferous gravel of California is referred by Prof. Whitney to the Pliocene strata, and therefore the Calaveras skull is allotted to the Pliocene Age. But this gold-gravel is a surface-deposit, "covering the face of the country" in some regions, and therefore an ancient inhabitant of California might leave his bones in it without belonging to the Pliocene Period.

What shall we say to the one hundred and fifty feet of lava and volcanic matter superimposed? That at Santorin there is a buried city under one hundred feet of lava and volcanic matter, in which beautiful pottery and gold and copper implements have been found. And we might add that near Rome the relics of the Iron Age—some 700 B.C., perhaps—are found under similar consolidated volcanic matter.

Herculaneum is buried from seventy-six to one hundred and twelve feet under the lava and ashes of Vesuvius.

When Humboldt visited the volcano of Jorullo, in Mexico, in the beginning of this century, he found the lava (from the eruption of 1759) five hundred feet thick around the base of the cones, and spreading from them over an area of four square miles.

In 1783 the volcano of Skaptár Jokul in Iceland threw out, at intervals, two branches of lava, flowing in opposite directions, the greater of which was fifty and the lesser forty-five miles in length. The channel of the river Skaptâ, in many places from four hundred to six hundred feet in depth, and two hundred broad, was filled, and the river dried up. This column, issuing from this rocky gorge, then discharged itself into a deep lake, which it also completely filled up. Issuing thence, it overflowed the level country, in a stream from ten to fifteen miles wide. The other branch of the lava discharged itself into the bed of the river Hverfisfliot, and spread over the plains, attaining a breadth of seven miles. The ordinary depth of both currents was one hundred feet, but in narrow defiles it sometimes amounted to six hundred. Professor Bischoff calculated the entire volume of this lava to exceed in magnitude the bulk of Mont Blanc.*

There are at the present day active volcanoes in Oregon and in Washington Territory to the north of California, in Mexico to the south of it, as well as in the peninsula of California; while within the past few years the shocks of earthquakes have been serious and frequent in the city of San Francisco.

But why descend into these particulars? The Geological Survey of the Territories by Prof. Hayden (published by the Government) represents the great Snake River Basin, from seventy-five to one hundred miles wide by one hundred and seventy-five miles long,—shut in by mountains,—as "entirely covered by a bed of basalt of modern date." Prof. Hayden gives the same account of the Yellowstone Valley, in Montana. This basaltic cap was traced again in Colorado. The whole region has been the theatre apparently of volcanic action on the most tremendous scale and of the most violent character. We are repeatedly told, moreover, by Prof. Hayden, that all of this is very "recent." "The lake-deposits," he says, "are certainly of very moderate date, at least as late, and perhaps later than the Pliocene. Upon this rests

* Lyell, Principles of Geology, vol. ii. pp. 49-51.

a huge bed of drift, which was deposited still later, and then comes the outflow of basalt."

"As I have frequently stated," he says, "the effusion of the basalt is a modern event, probably occurring, for the most part, near the commencement of our present period, after the entire surface reached nearly, or quite, the present elevation."

This whole region, we learn also, is marked by hot springs and geysers: the evidence seems clear, says Prof. Hayden, that "all over the West during this great period of volcanic activity the hot springs and perhaps even geysers were numerous. The hot springs which are now slowly dying out are, of course, the last of this series of events,"—so that we are not out of this Volcanic Epoch yet. All this bears not only upon the point under immediate discussion; it has a most emphatic bearing upon the Uniformitarian Theory of Geology. When Sir Charles Lyell supposes the beach at Cagliari, or the coast of Scandinavia, to have been rising at the rate of two and a half feet per century, the Pacific region of this continent from Montana and Idaho to Utah, and at the same time probably California and Mexico, were in the throes of a convulsion—or a series of convulsions—that have altered the whole face of the country.*

We know that a considerable portion of the State of California is similarly covered by an outflow of lava, and that geysers and hot springs occur there also.

But there are some data to fix the age of this relic. If it belongs to the Pliocene Age, it ought to be associated with Pliocene animals. The mastodon and the mammoth (or *Elephas Americanus*) neither date back of the river-gravel. They belong to the days of the floods of the loess and the peat and shell-marl deposits.

And again: the implements found in connection with the case mentioned by Prof. Blake were "two stone objects which were supposed to be shovels used in cooking; a mortar or dish, some instruments resembling plummets, and several spear-heads." The spear-heads, if our memory serves us, were polished and thoroughly finished implements,—which is conclusive against any great antiquity.

The skull of the Calaveras man is described as being "highly developed."

These facts render it absurd to refer these remains to the "Pliocene." They are as old, probably, as the sienite "plummet" of the neighboring San Joaquin Valley.†

---

* See U. S. Geological Survey of the Territories, 1871, pp. 30, 42, 48; and the volume for 1872, pp. 35, 36, 43, 44, 50, 51, etc.

† Since the above was written, we have obtained from Prof. Andrews and Prof. Blake

9. *Pre-historic Remains in Wyoming and Colorado.*—There is yet another example; and in this instance our American man is carried back to the Miocene Period.

The account of these remains is so incoherent and obscure that we shall not undertake to interpret it, but shall quote from Mr. E. L. Berthoud, who has made the discovery. This account was laid before the Academy of Natural Sciences of Philadelphia in 1872. The observations were made on Crow Creek, lat. 40° N., long. 104° W. While investigating the bluffs, he found many beautiful moss-agates, and numerous flakes of stone implements, mixed in Tertiary gravel and seemingly (in his judgment) coeval with it. On leaving Crow Creek, he proceeds to say,—

"I obtained a complete suite of stone implements and rude fragments which occur in a gravel and sand deposit that composes the summit and sides of the low bluff on the east bank. I found them in the gravel, in the soil, in every kind of position, and sometimes weather-beaten or stained by weather and rain. The accompanying gravel is composed of pebbles of quartzite, jasper, agate, granite, mica-slate, basalt, with a few shells, fossil wood, and wood-opal; while in the low grounds at the foot

---

additional information with regard to the Calaveras skull and the stone implements from Table Mountain.

1. Dr. Andrews informs us that the Rev. Dr. R. W. Patterson, of Chicago (who is well known), tells him that he (Dr. Patterson) was informed by the Rev. W. W. Brier, a reliable minister of Alvarado, Cal., that his (Brier's) brother, a miner, was one of two men who took the so-called Calaveras skull from a cave in the sides of the valley and placed it in the shaft where it was found, and that the whole object was a practical joke to deceive Prof. Whitney, the geologist. This, says Dr. Andrews, explains the stalagmite found adherent to the skull. The skull, we may add, was not found by Prof. Whitney himself, but was received by him from others after the lapse of a considerable period from the time when it was represented to have been found.

The plummet referred to above, which Dr. Foster treats of, was also received without any positive scientific proof that its position was thirty feet below the surface. It was forwarded with that statement, but unaccompanied by that clear evidence which is known to be necessary in such cases by those who know the readiness with which workmen or their overseers adopt as specimens from the bottom of a pit objects which have fallen by accident or design from above.

2. The stone implements described by Prof. Blake as found under the lava of Table Mountain at the depth of one hundred or two hundred feet were not found by him. They were obtained from an old man in the neighborhood, who gave this account of them. Prof. Blake entertains very great doubts as to their antiquity. He deems it by no means impossible that they may have been washed into their position through lateral fissures or crevices in the mountain.

Among the objects alleged to have been obtained from this mountain were arrow-heads, lance-heads, utensils, formed of steatite, in the shape of large spoons with rude handles, *mortars* and pestles (of *trachyte*), etc. Prof. B. informs us that some (possibly all) of the spear-heads were *polished*, and superior to anything produced by the present aborigines of the country.

According to Prof. Whitney, these objects belong to the Pliocene Age!

of the bluffs, ancient fire-places, burnt fragments of bone and wood, with flint and agate chips and implements, almost distinct from those on the summit of the low hills bordering Crow Creek, are observed. So much is this the case that the two seem to point to a distinct era, the latter presenting some progress and refinement even in stone implements.

"The evidences of the oldest and rudest do not even show traces of fire or fire-places; rough implements, irregular piles of pebbles, are all that are left us to show and identify to the observer the obscure seat of a still more obscure barbarism.

"Another fact puzzles me: that wherever on Cache la Poudre, Big Thompson River, Clear Creek, Crow Creek, and Platte River we find evidences of pre-aboriginal occupation, it is invariably on the low bluffs bordering these valleys, and in a Tertiary gravel deposit; but if we go back into the higher region of the prairies, they almost disappear, or present a difference in form or material.

"The shape, the material, the rude barbarism, of these first attempts of art, irresistibly lead us to compare them to the rude tools of Abbeville, in France, etc.

"We are fast nearing the high table-land between South Platte River, Crow Creek, and Pole Creek. This is a dividing ridge capped by conglomerate in many places, and under this, on Low Wet, Little Crow Creek, etc., Miocene beds with Oreodon, Titanotherium, and fresh-water turtles. The gravel-beds of Crow Creek may be Quaternary (?), but they seem made up from the decomposed capping north of us, and at Golden City apparently underlie the Newer Tertiary beds capped with basalt (?)."

Following up Crow Creek, he noticed "in two places in the steep bluff bordering the stream the burnt stones and black carbonaceous remains of old fire-places, from four to eight feet below the present surface."

On a small dry affluent of Crow Creek, he continues, "I found at the foot of the first ridge the evidences of the deserted site of an ancient village, the stone-heaps and circles, the projecting and polished boulders, the stray flint tools and weapons, the multitudes of broken flakes or fragments left in the primeval workshop; while all around, dispersed in rude circles, the boulders of quartzite, of jaspery rocks, yellow, red, or gray, nowhere else *in situ*, speak of some method or manner of industry totally unlike our modern Indian or mound-builders' vestiges." (We should expect something a little different in the Miocene.)

The shells above referred to, we are told by Dr. Foster, are *Corbicula* and *Rangia*, so far as recognized, and are estuary shells "certainly not later than the older Pliocene, probably Miocene, but there is no trace of *Eocene*."

It appears that these flint implements, stone circles, hearths,* etc., all occur on the surface of the ground. Apart, then, from the rudeness of the implements, what evidence there is of antiquity we are at a loss to discover. The finding of flint implements and "stone circles" in a Miocene gravel, exposed at the surface of the earth, does not prove the objects in question to be of the Miocene Age, any more than the finding of a pocket-knife in the coal that crops out from the surface near Clarksburg, West Virginia, would prove that the manufacture of cutlery had been practised in West Virginia in the Palæozoic Age.

10. Mr. Baldwin, in his "Ancient America," cites yet another evidence of the antiquity of man in this part of the world. The facts are these: In 1860, Mr. James S. Wilson found along the coast of Peru ancient pottery, vessels, images, etc., all finely wrought, some of gold, in a stratum of ancient surface-earth, covered with marine remains six feet thick. "The geological formation where these remains were found is," he says, "reported to be as old as the Drift strata of Europe, and identical with that of Guayaquil in which bones of the mastodon are met with." He traced six terraces in going up from the sea through the province of Esmeraldas towards Quito, and in all cases these relics were found below high-tide mark, which proves that this region, after human occupancy, must have been submerged and again elevated to its present position.†

This case makes a different impression on us from what it does on Messrs. Baldwin and Foster. If the facts are correctly stated, it proves that the land on this coast has subsided and risen since "finely-wrought" vessels and images, "and some" even "of gold," were in use among the ancient Peruvians; and that the mastodon was living in the region of Guayaquil at that time; all of which must be of comparatively recent date. No one in his senses can believe that finely-wrought vessels of gold were fabricated tens of thousands of years ago anywhere.

NOTE.—Before closing this chapter on the antiquity of man in America, we may remark that Sir John Lubbock (p. 326) lays great stress on the absence of the domesticated animals in the Palæolithic bone-caves: what, then, shall we say to the fact that in America, when discovered by the Europeans, no animals had been domesticated except the dog and the llama of Peru? The Mexicans had no domesticated animals.

---

* There were two hearths (as stated) at one point on Crow Creek "from four to eight feet" beneath the surface. Such dwellings were common and are common among savages.

† Ancient America, p. 274; Foster's Prehistoric Races of the United States, p. 96.

CHAPTER XXXVII.

THE UNITY OF THE AMERICAN RACES FARTHER CONSIDERED, AND THEIR CONNECTION WITH THE OLD WORLD.

Mr. Morgan's Systems of Consanguinity and Affinity of the Human Family.—Divided into the Descriptive and Classificatory Methods.—The first includes the Aryan, Semitic, and Uralian Families.—Illustrated by the Roman Method of Computation.—Characteristics of the Descriptive System.—Its Value as indicating a Common Origin for Races employing it.—The Classificatory System.—The Ganowánian Family.—Programme of the System.—It extends to all the North and South American Indians, to the Turanians, and the Malays.—Unity of the Village Indians of New Mexico, Central America, and South America with the Red Indians of North America shown by other Facts.—Nevertheless, there are Traces of more than one Race in America.—Intercourse between the Old World and the New.—China.—Japan.—The Malays.—Polynesian Canoes.—Navigation among the Polynesians.—Vessels driven from Asia to the Coasts of America.—From Europe to America.—Discovery of Brazil.—Remarkable Passage from Diodorus Siculus.

MR. LEWIS H. MORGAN argues from a new stand-point that all the Indian nations of North and South America belong to the same stock. He has developed this in a highly interesting and valuable disquisition in the seventeenth volume of the Smithsonian Contributions, entitled "Systems of Consanguinity and Affinity of the Human Family."

Systems of Consanguinity.

He exhibits the systems of six of the great families of mankind, viz., the Aryan, the Semitic, the Uralian, the Ganowánian (American Indians), the Turanian, and the Malayan. These include about four-fifths of the human race. His investigations have not as yet been extended to the Mongolian, Tungusian, Australian, and Negroid races. Among the six families above specified, he shows that there are only two systems of consanguinity: the *Descriptive* and the *Classificatory*. The first, which is that of the Aryan, Semitic, and Uralian families, rejecting classification of kindred, except so far as it is in accordance with the numerical system, describes collateral consanguinei, for the most part, by an augmentation or combination of the primary terms of relationship. These terms, which are those of husband and wife, brother and sister, and son and daughter, to which must be added, in such languages as possess them, grandfather and grandmother, and grandson and granddaughter, are thus restricted to the primary sense in which they are thus employed. All other terms are secondary. Each relationship is thus made inde-

Either descriptive or classificatory.

36

pendent and distinct from every other. But the second system, which is that of the Turanian, American Indian, and Malayan families, rejecting descriptive phrases in every instance, and reducing consanguinei to great classes by a series of apparently arbitrary generalizations, applies the same terms to all the members of the same class. It thus confounds relationships which, under the descriptive system, are distinct, and enlarges the signification both of the primary and of the secondary terms beyond their seemingly appropriate sense.

The Roman method, example of first.

The Roman method is the completest and fairest type of the Descriptive System. Mr. Morgan gives the accompanying table of consanguinity according to the scheme of the Romans.

This table represents the method of computing relationships among the Aryan, Semitic, and Uralian families. It supposes marriage between *single pairs*.

This system common to the Aryan, Semitic, and Uralian families.

Another diagram, with an entire change of terms, except in the first collateral line, is necessary to exhibit the right lineal line, female, and the collateral lines, male and female, beyond the first. The necessity for independent terms for uncle and aunt on the mother's side, to complete the Roman method, is, therefore, apparent. These terms are found in *avunculus*, maternal uncle, *matertera*, maternal aunt, etc.

The Greek, Italian, French, Spanish, English, German, Swedish, Icelandic, and cognate methods are then reviewed. As are, then, those of the Sanskrit, Slavonic, Celtic (Erse, Gaelic, Manx, Welsh), Persian, and Armenian nations.

He finds them all "descriptive," which he characterizes as "a natural system, following the streams of the blood, and maintaining the several collateral lines distinct from each other, and divergent from the lineal line."

He then passes in review the methods of the Semitic nations, and finds that "their radical characteristics are identical with the Aryan."

"It is rendered manifest by the comparison that the system of the two families was originally purely descriptive, the description being effected by the primary terms; and that the further development of each respectively, by the same generalizations, limited to the same relationships, was, in each case, the work of civilians and scholars to provide for a new want incident to changes of condition."

The question arises whether the system in its present form is of natural and necessary origin, or whether it started at some epoch in a common family stock and was transmitted to such races as now possess it by the streams of the blood.

"The descriptive system is simple rather than complex, and has a

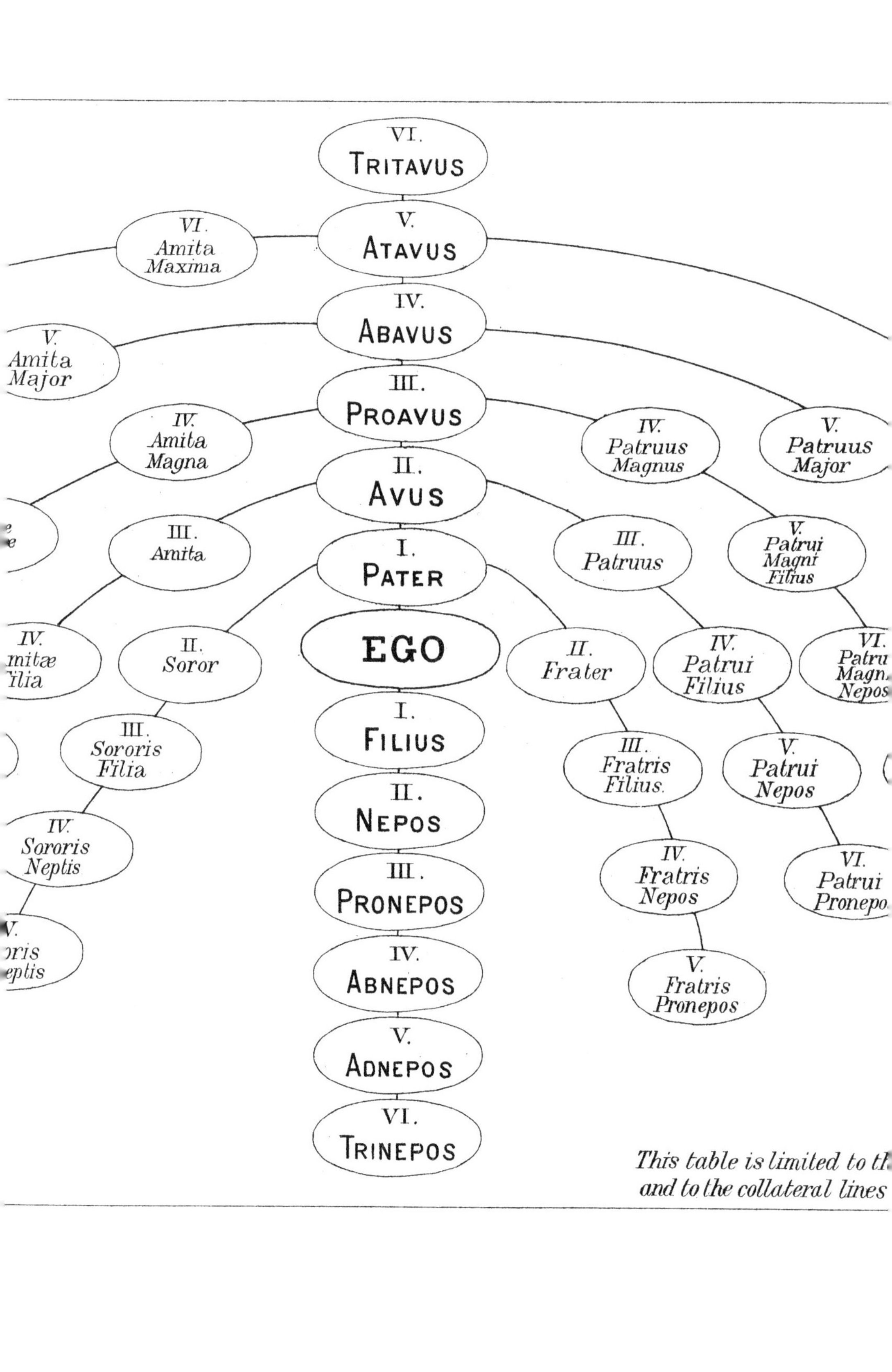
VI. Tritavus
V. Atavus
VI. Amita Maxima
IV. Abavus
V. Amita Major
III. Proavus
IV. Amita Magna
IV. Patruus Magnus
V. Patruus Major
II. Avus
III. Amita
III. Patruus
V. Patrui Magni Filius
I. Pater
EGO
II. Soror
II. Frater
IV. Patrui Filius
I. Filius
III. Sororis Filia
III. Fratris Filius.
V. Patrui Nepos
II. Nepos
IV. Sororis Neptis
III. Pronepos
IV. Fratris Nepos
VI. Patrui
IV. Abnepos
V. Fratris Pronepos
V. Adnepos
VI. Trinepos
This table is limited to
and to the collateral lines

natural basis in the nature of descents, where marriage subsists between single pairs. For these reasons it might have been framed by different families, starting with an antecedent system either differing or agreeing; and its perpetuation in such a case might be in virtue of its foundation upon the nature of descents. And yet these conclusions are not free from doubt. With the fact established that the plan of consanguinity of the two families is identical in whatever is radical, and with the further fact extremely probable that it had become established in each at a time long anterior to their civilization, the final inference is encouraged that it prevailed in the two original nations from which these families were respectively derived. Standing alone, without any contrasting form, the descriptive system of the two families mentioned would scarcely attract attention. But it so happens that in other portions of the human family a system of relationship now exists radically different in its structure and elaborate and complicated in its forms, which is spread out over large areas of human speech, and which has perpetuated itself through equal periods of time as well as changes of condition. The conditions of society, then, may have some influence in determining the system of relationship. In other words, the descriptive form is not inevitable; neither is it fortuitous. Some form of consanguinity was an indispensable necessity of each family. Its formation involved an arrangement of kindred into lines of descent, with the adoption of a method for distinguishing one kinsman from another. Whatever plan was finally adopted would acquire the stability of a domestic institution as soon as it came into general use and had proved its sufficiency. . . . The choice of a descriptive method for the purpose of specializing each relationship, by the Semitic family, and the adoption of the classificatory by the Turanian, for the purpose of arranging consanguinei into groups and placing the members of each group in the same relationship to *Ego*, were generally acts of intelligence and knowledge. . . . The descriptive system is simple in its elements, and embraces but a few fundamental conceptions. It is therefore incapable of affording such a body of evidence upon these questions as the classificatory; but it does not follow that it is entirely without significance. It is something that the Aryan and Semitic families have a system which can be definitely traced to the same original form, and to a period of time when each family, in all probability, existed in a single nation. It is something more that this system has positive elements as a product of human intelligence; and that it has perpetuated itself through so many centuries of time, in so many independent channels, and under such eventful changes of condition. To these may be added the further fact that the several systems of the Aryan nations, taken in connection with the terms of relationship as vocables, demonstrate the unity of origin

Significance of this system.

of these nations, and their descent from the same stem of the human family. In like manner the systems of the several Semitic nations, considered in connection with the terms as vocables, demonstrate the unity of origin of the latter nations, and perform this work in the most simple and natural way. Upon the present showing it will not be claimed, against the testimony of the vocables, and in the face of the radical differences in the grammatical structure of the Aryan and Semitic languages, that it affords any positive evidence of the unity of origin of the two families. It will be sufficient to say that the descriptive system separates these families and the Uralian from all the other families of mankind by a clearly-defined line."

Mr. Morgan then proceeds to show the system of consanguinity of the Ganowánian family.

The Classificatory System. The Ganowánian family.

The American Indians always speak to each other (when related) by the employment of the term expressing the relationship, and never by calling the *name* of the party. Addressing a relative, they say, *my father*, *my elder brother*, *my grandson*, etc. Where the parties are not related, they say, *my friend*. It is thus that these rude people have kept up their complicated system of relationship. It is a *tribal* affair, and every member of the tribe is addressed by another member through the employment of a term which expresses their kinship.

Includes the Ganowánian, Turanian, and Malay families.

The Classificatory System, as has been said, includes the Ganowánians, the Turanians, and the Malays. Among these, consanguinei are never described "by a combination of the primary terms;" but they are arranged into great classes. All the individuals of one class are admitted into one and the same relationship, and the same special term is applied indiscriminately to each and all of them. For example, my father's brother's son is my *brother*, and I apply to him the same term I apply to my real brother. The son of this collateral brother and the son of my own brother are both my *sons*, and I apply to them the same term I would use to designate my own son. . . .

It is impossible to explain the origin of this system on the assumption of the existence of marriage between single pairs: it probably originated from a series of customs and institutions, improving on each other, and commencing with promiscuous intercourse, and ending with a family resting on marriage between single pairs.

The following is a concise statement of the system:

Principles of the System.

I. Consanguinei are not described by a combination of primary terms, but are classified into categories, under some one of the recognized relationships, each of which is expressed by a particular term.

II. The several collateral lines are alternately merged in the lineal line.

III. Consanguinei address each other by the term of kinship.

IV. From *Ego*, a male, to the children of his brother, a male, and from *Ego*, a female, to the children of her sister, a female, the relationship of these children to *Ego* approaches in the degree of its nearness; but from *Ego* a male to the children of a female, or from *Ego* a female to the children of a male, it recedes.

V. Ascending one degree above *Ego* in the lineal line, and crossing over to the first members of the four branches of the second collateral line, it follows again that from male line to male line and from female to female the relationship to *Ego* approaches in the degree of its nearness, while from the male line to the female line, and vice versa, it recedes, and that irrespective of the sex of *Ego*.

VI. There are original terms for grandfather and grandmother, father and mother, son and daughter, and grandson and granddaughter, in all the languages of these races.

VII. All my ancestors above grandfather and grandmother are my grandfathers and grandmothers.

VIII. All the brothers and sisters of my grandfather and grandmother, and all the brothers and sisters of my several ancestors above these, are my grandfathers and grandmothers.

IX. All my descendants below my grandson and granddaughter are my grandsons and granddaughters.

X. There is one term for an elder brother and another for a younger brother,—and so for sisters,—and no term for brother or sister in the abstract except in the plural.

XI. All the children of my several own brothers, and of my several collateral brothers, myself a male, are my sons and daughters, and all the children of these are my grandsons and granddaughters.

XII. All the children of my own sisters, and of my several collateral sisters, myself a male, are my nephews and nieces.

XIII. So the children of my own brothers and of my collateral brothers, myself a female, are my nephews and nieces.

XIV. The children of my own sisters and of my collateral sisters, myself a female, are my sons and daughters.

XV. The brothers of my father are my fathers,—and so of all the brothers of such other persons as stand to me in the relation of father; and all the sisters of my mother are my mothers, etc.

XVI. The brothers of my mother are my uncles,—and so of all the brothers of other persons who stand to me in the relation of mother.

XVII. All the children of several brothers are brothers and sisters to each other.

XVIII. All sons of sons of several brothers are brothers to each other, elder or younger; all the sons of these are again brothers to each other; and the same relationship in the male line continues downwards indefinitely, so long as each of these persons stands at the same degree of remove from the original brother.

XIX. The children of sisters are brothers and sisters.

XX. The daughters of the daughters of several sisters are sisters, and the daughters of these are sisters again, etc. (as above).

XXI. All the children of several brothers, on the one hand, and of their several sisters, on the other, are *cousins*, among some of these nations.

XXII. The children of cousins are cousins again.

XXIII. It follows, as a general result, that the descendants of brothers and sisters, or of an original pair, can never pass in theory beyond the degree of cousin or grandchild,—nor, ascending, beyond grandfather.

XXIV. All the wives of my nephews and collateral sons are my daughters-in-law; and all the husbands of my nieces and collateral daughters are my sons-in-law.

XXV. The wives of my collateral brothers and of my male cousins are my sisters-in-law, etc.

XXVI. In all of the preceding relationships the correlative terms are strictly applied: thus, the one I call son calls me father, etc.

Such, according to Mr. Morgan, are the laws of the Classificatory System of Consanguinity and Affinity.

Extends to all the American Indians.

He then shows that in substance the system prevails among all the North and South American Indians: among the Iroquois, the Hurons, the Dakotas, the Missouri nations, the Winnebagoes, the Mandans, the Minitares, the Crows, the Algonquins of the Great Lake Region, the Mississippi nations, the Atlantic tribes, the Rocky Mountain tribes, the Athabascan nations, the Apaches, the Sanoptin stock, the Shoshonee nations, etc.

He shows that it prevails equally among the Village Indians of New Mexico and Arizona, and of Central America and South America.

To the Turanians and Malays.

A similar examination is then made of the methods of computing relationship among the Turanian and Malayan nations, and all of them are shown to correspond with those of the American Indians.

The Chinese method, which seems to be classificatory, at the same time distinguishes relations in a manner similar to that of the Descriptive System; probably for the better regulation of the law of descents.

An ethnic connection is thus established between all these races.

Mr. Morgan remarks that in his treatise he has shown the prevalence of the Classificatory System in more than a hundred Indian (American) nations,—thus proving them to be of one family, and the system to be coeval with the first appearance of the Ganowánian race on the North American continent; that he has found the Turanian method identical, on a comparison, with the Ganowánian in their radical characteristics; that the methods of the Turanian races and the Malayan race are one and the same,—the Malayan being the older and original form,—the East Indian element, left on the continent, having modified the system after the departure of the Malayan branch. The Ganowánians, he says, are descended from the inhabitants of India, and not from the Malays. "The Tamilian Indian and the Seneca Indian alike address their kinsmen, not by their names, but by the degree of relationship."

Unity of American Indians indicated by other facts.

The unity of the Village Indians of New Mexico, Arizona, Mexico, Central America, and South America with the Red Indians of North America is inferred by Mr. Morgan from other considerations.

The Village Indians, he says, are surrounded by Roving Indians,—a fact very well known, and of great significance. Intermediate between these he places the Iroquois and some other semi-civilized tribes.

The present Village Indians of New Mexico are, he remarks, the lineal descendants of those of the time of the Conquest.

He submits the following evidences of the identity of the Village Indians with the Roving Indians:

1. The Unity of Physical Type. There is a marked resemblance between them.

2. The Unity of the Grammatical Structure of their Languages.

3. Similarity of Usages, Arts, and Inventions,—in those relating to social life, to warfare, to marriage, burial, and especially in mechanic arts, such as pottery, weaving (whether with filaments of bark or threads of cotton), the tanning of skins, the manufacture of similar weapons, and, above all, their *architecture*, which is founded on the communal system of living, a principle which prevailed among all Indian nations, from near the confines of the Arctic Sea to the Isthmus of Panama.

4. The Dance. Among all of these nations the Dance is a domestic institution. No other people on earth have raised it to such a degree of studied development as the American Indian nations. Each has a large number, ranging from ten to thirty, which have been handed down from generation to generation. These dances, which have special names, as the Buffalo Dance, the War Dance, the Feather Dance, the Fish Dance, are sometimes the recognized property of a particular society or brotherhood; but usually belong to the nation at large. Each has its own peculiar plan, steps, and method, its songs and choruses and musical instruments, and each is adapted to some particular occasion. The Dance is among these tribes universally recognized as

a mode of worship. Among the Village Indians of New Mexico their dances are the same to-day that they were centuries ago; and they are not distinguishable in their steps, order, and method, or in their songs, choruses, and musical instruments, from the dances of the Iroquois, the Dakotas, the Ojibwas, or the Blackfoot Indians.*

5. The Structure of Indian Society,—the tribal organization, and, more especially, their form of government, by chiefs and councils,—the same social structure and the same forms prevailing as well among the Village Indians as among the Roving Tribes.

6. The Resemblance in Cranial Characteristics.

The Esquimaux, we may add, are considered by Mr. Morgan to be a recent people on the American continent. Their system of consanguinity is classificatory, but differs radically from that described above.

More than one race in America.

It would be a great mistake to conclude, however, that there were no diversities among the nations of America. The differences between the Peruvians of the time of Pizarro and the Mexicans who were subjugated by Cortez were very marked. One race may have spread over both continents, but it does not follow that there were no other intrusive races. These elements may have been more or less mixed in different regions. It is highly probable, also, that, after the aborigines of America had occupied both continents, *civilization* was introduced at certain points among them by settlers from Eastern Asia,—as from China, Japan, or India. The Peruvians present the characteristics of a race who were civilized in this way, and many analogies are pointed out between the customs of that country and those of China:—as the artificial frame of society in both countries, and that minute and elaborate system of regulation, inspection, and control, which interferes with the most trifling actions of ordinary life; the ostentatious patronage to agriculture which characterized the Incas, and which is practised by the Emperors of China, an annual festival being celebrated in China, as it was in Peru, in which the emperor proceeds to the field with great pomp and takes a part in the labor of cultivating the ground with his own hands; the use of manures and a laborious system of irrigation in the agriculture of Peru, precisely like what is observed in China, while in both countries, in other respects, agriculture was in a very rude state; the payment of internal taxes in kind; the maintenance of public roads, even in those districts where neither carriages nor beasts of burden were used, and of course for the use of pedestrians, with storehouses or places of

American civilization.

* For the dances of the ancient Mexicans and Nicaraguans, see Purchas's "Pilgrimage," London, 1617, pp. 809, 816. See also Prescott's "Conquest of Mexico." See also Purchas concerning the dances of the natives of Hispaniola (Hayti), p. 907.

refreshment for them at proper distances; the uniformity of the architecture, and the power shown of cutting and moving immense masses of stone; the existence of the drama and dramatic spectacles; the remarkable use in both countries of suspension-bridges made of ropes; the use of rafts with sails; the striking fact that, like the Peruvians, the Chinese in ancient times made use of quipus or knotted cords for the purposes of calculation; the division of the year into twelve months, and beginning it in January (while the Mexicans and other Northern nations had a year of eighteen months), etc. Manco Capac and his sister Mama Oello, according to the Peruvian annals, appeared as strangers on the banks of Lake Titicaca in the year 1100 of our era. They are represented as persons of majestic appearance, who announced themselves as "children of the sun," sent by their beneficent parent to reclaim the tribes living there from the miseries of savage life. The Peruvians represent this to be the origin of their civilization. If a colony of Chinese did in fact in such a manner inaugurate the dynasty of the Incas, and the forms of civilization, in this country, it does not follow that they must have introduced *all* the arts of China; for such settlers would not themselves be acquainted with all the arts practised in China, or competent to introduce them in a strange country.*

Dr. Pickering, we believe, on the other hand, connects the Peruvians with the Malays.

The contact of the Polynesian race with Peru is suggested by this fact: In New Zealand the natives had a well-known weapon, the *mére*, or *pátu-pátu*, an edged club of bone or stone, which has been compared to a beaver's tail, or, as Mr. Tylor expresses it, "is still more like a soda-water bottle with the bulb flattened," and which is exceedingly sharp. Through the neck it has a hole for a wrist-cord.

The *mére* is made of the bone of the whale, or of stone,—the finest of green jade, worked with immense labor, being among the most precious heir-looms of the Maori chiefs. The Peruvians had a precisely similar weapon.

The civilization of Mexico may have been long subsequent to the first occupation of the country, and may have come through the Malays, or may have been derived, as has been suggested, from a few emigrants from China, Japan, or Chinese Tartary, bringing with them picture-writing, the arts of building and weaving, and the calendar which was common to the Mexicans, along with the Chinese, Japanese, Hindoos, Thibetans, and Tartars. Such, possibly, was the origin of the Toltec civilization.

It may be, on the other hand, true that the northwestern coasts of North America were settled at a very early period by that ancient race

* Encyclopædia Britannica, art. Peru.

which, as we have seen, occupied Siberia in the days of the mammoth, and who, if their relics may be trusted, were already, at that remote epoch, in a state of considerable advancement.*

The difficulty is not how the races of the Old World got to the New, but to determine which, and how many of them, actually did so. The two continents of Asia and North America are almost in contact at the Arctic Circle,† while in latitude 55° N. the Aleutian Isles, as if by design, stretch like the piers of a bridge from Kamschatka to Alaska.

Between the tropics the myriad isles of the mid-Pacific stretch again two-thirds of the way across this vast but peaceful ocean.

The southern points of Greenland and the coasts of New England, we know, had been reached from Iceland and Norway in the tenth century, and probably by other European nations.

We do not suppose there is any doubt of the fact that America was known to the nations of Southeastern Asia. "In possession of the magnet," says a writer in the *Edinburgh Review*, "the most ancient of the Eastern nations boldly navigated the wide ocean in vessels of great burden." Some of the natives of India were enterprising mariners, says the same authority, "from the remotest antiquity," as were, doubtless, the people of the Eastern Archipelago. The oldest Javanese maps extend their voyages to Behring's Straits and to the coast of America. The Abbé Brasseur de Bourbourg, in his introduction to the Popol-Vuh, remarks that the Chinese were acquainted with the American continent in the fifth century of our era. They called it *Fu-Sang*, and represented it to be twenty thousand *li* (some seven thousand miles) distant from Ta-Han. M. Leon de Rosny, he adds, has ascertained that

China.

* We mentioned in Chapter II. the close resemblance which has been observed between the religious practices of the Aztecs and the Etruscans, and the close correspondence between their calendars. We have seen also that the Etruscans may probably be traced to the great Altaic race: may we not catch a glimpse here of the link which may exist between the ancient Rasenna and the bronze-using people whom Cortez found around the Lake of Tezcuco?

And just here let us remark that the observance of resemblances between the Mexicans and the Etruscans, on the one hand, and between the Mexicans and the Hindoos or the Egyptians, on the other, does not result in showing that the correspondences in all the cases are fanciful or accidental. When we go back to primeval times, one Turanian race might carry its customs into Siberia, into China, into India, at the same time; and so a fourth nation, descended from, or deriving its civilization from, one of them, might offer points of resemblance with all.

† "Many of the Chúckchi, at the fair of Nijnei Koluimsk, relate," says Erman, in his "Travels in Siberia," "that they, with others of their tribe, have crossed from East Cape to America by the Gvòsdev rocks in Behring's Straits, and have brought back furs with them from thence. They tell the names of many places on the shores of the other continent, and their intercourse with the Americans is the more credible, as the language of the Chúckchi at East Cape is found to be connected with that of the Aleutes at Kadjak." Vol. ii. p. 283, American edition.

Fu-Sang is the subject of a curious notice in the "Wa-kan-san-taï-dzon-yé," or the great Japanese Encyclopædia. In that work *Fu-Sang* is stated to be twenty thousand *li* distant from *Ta-nan-kouëk*. Japan.

According to the Arabian writer El-Mas'údí (tenth century), the Malays were a very important people, and controlled a vast empire, at that time,—the number of the troops under the Maharajh, or Lord of the Sixth Sea, being almost countless, and the islands under his sceptre "so numerous that the fastest-sailing vessel is not able to go round them in two years." There seem to have been two races inhabiting this archipelago, one of which was a black race. The Polynesians are evidently the descendants of these races. Some of these Pacific islands are inhabited by *negritos*, to which category the Fijians belong, although their language is of Malay origin. These negritos were also found originally in some parts of America, as, for example, along the coast of the Gulf of Darien. The Malays.

The inhabitants of the Pacific islands use a double canoe, made of the trunks of trees lashed together, and furnished with "outriggers," formed of light and buoyant logs of *bamboo* attached to their gunwales and projected some distance beyond their sides, thus making it almost impossible for them to be capsized. The freedom of these seas from storms, the strong and regular winds which prevail over them, and the copious showers which fall during the prevalence of the monsoons, are all strongly favorable to the accomplishment of long journeys by these frail barks. Polynesian canoes.

We might, therefore, naturally expect to find traces of the Malay family in America; and Dr. Pickering is no doubt correct in assigning a Malay origin to the natives of Peru and Chili, and to the Nootka Indians. All of the other aborigines of America are, in his opinion (excepting the Esquimaux), of Mongolian descent.

It has been pointed out that at the remote epoch of the earliest Vedas the Aryan Asiatics were already a maritime and mercantile people.

"A glance at a hydrographic chart of the Pacific," says Dr. Daniel Wilson, "will show that a boat driven a few degrees to the south of Pitcairn, Easter, or the Austral Islands would come within the range of the Antarctic drift current, which sets directly towards the Chili and Peruvian coasts."

It is not merely a matter of theory that long voyages may be made on the Pacific in Polynesian canoes, or that vessels might have reached America from the coast of Asia.

The map obtained by Forster and Cook from a native of the Society Islands contained not only the Marquesas, and the islands south and east of Tahiti, but the Samoan, Fiji, and even more distant groups. From the Society Islands to the Marquesas is Navigation among the Polynesians.

some thousand miles; and to the Fiji Islands, some twelve hundred miles. One of the Hawaiian headlands has been found to bear the name of *The Starting-place for Tahiti*,—nearly three thousand miles distant.

Dr. Pickering tells us that before the times of Columbus, the Polynesians were accustomed to take voyages nearly as long as his, and exposed to equal dangers, and in vessels of far inferior construction. The Tonga people are known, he says, to hold intercourse with Vavao, Samoa, the Fiji Islands, Rotuma, and the New Hebrides.

Madagascar is more than three thousand miles distant from the Indian Islands, an open sea intervening, and yet Malay and Polynesian words are met with in the vocabulary of this distant land.

Vessels driven to the coast of America.

In the year 1833, a Japanese junk was wrecked on the coast of Oregon (lat. 46° N.). A Japanese junk was stranded on the Aleutian Isles in 1871. It was dismasted in a typhoon off Jesso, and, driven by winds and currents for nine months, finally went ashore on the island of Adahk, where the crew was rescued by a hunting-party of natives and subsequently sent down in the schooner Johnson to San Francisco. These instances are taken from a number of like character.

A Chinese colony found in Peru.

We have intimated that the Peruvians may have derived their civilization from the Chinese. Whether this be so or not, we have, it would seem, positive evidence of the presence of this race in Peru. In a lecture entitled "Vestiges of Antiquity," delivered before the New York Geographical Society in January, 1873, by Dr. A. Le Plongeon, we find the following statement: "That some of the inhabitants of these countries landed in South America is certain; but it is certain also that they did not influence the civilization or religion of the population among which they commingled; nay, more, they even retained their own habits and language. To-day, on the northern coast of Peru, exists a small village called Eten, the dwellers of which speak a language that their neighbors are unable to understand, but they find no difficulty in holding communion with the Chinese coolies who of late years have been imported thither. Besides, in searching among the ruins in the Grand Chimu's City, situated between Trujillo and the pool of Huanchaco, some silver idols have been found, inscribed with very ancient Chinese characters. Some have likewise been dug up from the mounds in the valley of Chinca Alta, four hundred miles to the southward. I have examined these idols carefully. They bore marks of being very ancient. Two that were in my possession represented a man sitting cross-legged on the back of a tortoise. The head was shaved, except the top, from which depended, hanging on the back, a lock of long hair, braided Chinese fashion. . . . The arms of the figure were extended; the hands rested on short pillars; . . . and notwithstanding this relic was very much eaten by the rust and the salts contained in the earth, where for centuries it had lain undisturbed, some signs were plainly visible on the pillars. They somewhat resembled the Chinese writing, but seemed somewhat different from those in use to-day.

"The finding of these relics was quite important, in my estimation. I set forth in search of a person who could interpret them for me and dispel my doubts. I knew a very intelligent Chinaman, acknowledged to be by his countrymen a gentleman of great literary attainments. He examined the queer object for a long time; looked at it on every side; then, without speaking a word, looked at me,—looked at my relic again, his features betraying astonishment, nay, veneration, not altogether free from awe. He was evidently overcome by a strange feeling. 'Very old,' said he at last. 'These are very ancient characters, used in China thousands of years ago, before the invention of those now employed. They mean Fo-hi.' This was sufficient. In remote times the Chinese had visited this country, and, no doubt, the present dwellers of Eten are their descendants."

There is evidence that vessels have been driven across the Atlantic as well as across the Pacific. Humboldt, in his "Views of Nature," refers to well-authenticated cases of natives of America (supposed to have been from Labrador or Greenland) having been carried by currents from the Western to the Eastern Continent. There is a canoe in the museum of Marischal College, Aberdeen, which was picked up by a ship on the Aberdeen coast, with an Esquimaux in it, still alive, and surrounded by his fishing-gear.

Vessels driven across the Atlantic.

In his "History of the Canary Islands," Captain Glass relates that a small bark bound from Lancerota to Teneriffe was forced out of her course, and obliged to run before the wind, until she came within two days' sail of the coast of Caraccas; where she fortunately met with an English cruiser which relieved her distresses and directed her to the port of Laguayra on that coast.

Another instance is mentioned by Gumilla, as follows: In December, 1731, while he was in the town of St. Joseph, Trinidad, a small vessel belonging to Teneriffe, with six seamen, was driven into that island by stress of weather. The vessel was laden with wine, on which the crew, reduced to the last extremity, were compelled to live until they discovered Trinidad and came to anchor on that island.*

Columbus himself, says Edwards, in his second expedition to the West Indies, found the stern-post of a vessel lying on the shore at Guadaloupe, a circumstance which affords a strong presumption that a ship had been in the New World before him.

* Edwards's History of the West Indies, vol. i. p. 117.

We owe the European discovery of Japan to three Portuguese exiles who were shipwrecked there in 1542.

In 1626, when Sir Dodmore Cotton was sent on an embassy to the Persian court, the fleet in which he sailed was forced within a few leagues of the island of Trinidad, near the coast of Venezuela.

Accidental discovery of Brazil.

It was by a similar accident that Brazil was discovered, in 1500, by the Portuguese. A fleet under the command of Pedro Alvarez Cabral was bound to the East Indies. In order to avoid the coast of Africa, where he was certain to meet with variable breezes or frequent calms, he stood out to sea, and kept so far to the west that, to his surprise, he found himself upon the shore of an unknown country, in the tenth degree beyond the line. He was upon the coast of Brazil, where he landed, and took possession of the country in the name of the king of Portugal.*

Remarkable passage from Diodorus Siculus.

It is impossible to ignore in this connection the testimony of Diodorus Siculus. It is so explicit and so striking that, although it has been frequently recited by modern writers, we shall quote it again.

"To the west of Africa," he says, "lies a very large island, distant many days' sail from that part of our continent. Its fertile soil is partly plain and partly mountainous. The plain country is most sweet and pleasant, being watered everywhere with rivulets and navigable rivers; it is beautified with many gardens, which are planted with all kinds of trees, and the orchards particularly are watered with pleasant streams. The villages are adorned with houses built in a magnificent taste, having parterres ornamented with arbors covered with flowers. Hither the inhabitants retire during the summer to enjoy the fruits which the country furnishes them with in the greatest abundance. The mountainous part is covered with large woods, and all manner of fruit-trees, and in the valleys, which are watered with rivulets, the inhabitants meet with everything that can render life agreeable. In a word, the whole island, by its fertility and abundance of springs, furnishes the inhabitants not only with everything that may flatter their wishes, but with what may also contribute to their health and strength of body. Hunting furnishes them with such an infinite number of animals, that in their feasts they have nothing to wish for in regard either to plenty or delicacy. Besides, the sea which surrounds the island supplies them plentifully with all kinds of fish, and indeed the sea in general is very abundant. The air of this island is so temperate that the trees bear leaves and fruit almost the whole year round.

"In a word, this island is so delicious that it seems rather the abode

* Robertson's History of America, quoted by Edwards.

of God than of men. Anciently, on account of its remote situation, it was altogether unknown; but afterwards it was discovered by accident. It is well known that from the earliest ages the Phœnicians undertook long voyages in order to extend their commerce, and in consequence of those voyages established several colonies in Africa and the western part of Europe. Everything succeeding to their wish, and being become very powerful, they attempted to pass the pillars of Hercules and enter the ocean. They accordingly passed those pillars, and in their neighborhood built a city upon a peninsula of Spain, which they named Gades. There, amongst the other buildings proper for the place, they built a temple to Hercules, to whom they instituted splendid sacrifices, after the manner of their country. This temple is in great veneration at this day, and several Romans who have rendered themselves illustrious by their exploits have performed their vows to Hercules for the success of their enterprises.

"The Phœnicians, accordingly, have passed the straits of Spain, sailed along Africa, when by the violence of the winds they were driven far out to sea, and, the storm continuing several days, they were at length thrown on this island. Being the first who were acquainted with its beauty and fertility, they published them to other nations. The Tuscans, when they were masters at sea, designed to send a colony thither, but the Carthaginians found means to prevent them, on the two following accounts: first, they were afraid lest their citizens, tempted by the charms of that island, should pass over thither in too great numbers and desert their own country; next, they looked upon it as a secure asylum for themselves if ever any terrible disaster should befall their republic."

We may observe upon this account that it bears the aspect of truth,—of resting apparently on observed facts. There was a land "to the west of Africa,"—"distant many days' sail,"—with "a fertile soil," "partly plain and partly mountainous." There were "villages" "adorned with houses built in a magnificent taste." The land abounded in fruits and flowers. "The air of this island," says the historian, "is so temperate that the trees bear leaves and fruits almost the whole year round." Another very accurate observation. The Phœnicians, he says, sailing along Africa, were "driven far out to sea,"—and "at length thrown on this island." This is precisely what happened to Pedro Alvarez Cabral in the year 1500.

Other ancient writers—as Plutarch, Claudius Ælianus, etc.—confirm the declarations of Diodorus Siculus.

ADDITIONS AND CORRECTIONS.

Page 17, line 15, after "Young" insert "and Grotefend."

Page 22, line 7, for "2700" read "2300."

Page 23, line 12, for "Abyssinia" read "Nubia."

Page 25, line 5, the photograph of Prince *Ra-Hotep*, at p. 224 of "The Journal of the Anthropological Institute" for April and July, 1874, is a decidedly negroid face with close-cut crisp or woolly hair. It is taken from the statue of this prince discovered by M. Mariette near the pyramid of Meydoum. From a hieroglyphic inscription we learn that Prince Ra-Hotep lived in the reign of Phra *Snefrou*, the last king of the third dynasty. This statue proves beyond controversy that the Egyptians were first cousins to the negroes.

Page 26, line 5 from bottom, for "Joktan" read "Bedouin."

Page 56. With regard to the time required for the cooling of the earth's crust, Mr. Darwin estimates that the denudation of the weald alone occupied 306,662,400 years.

Page 56, line 11, for "and" read "or."

Page 59, line 6 from bottom, omit "THAT."

Page 60, line 14, for "eighty" read "twenty."

Page 67, paragraph 4, line 2, for "scepticism" read "skepticism."

Page 102, line 4, see pp. 146, 149. There are many dolmens in the extreme southwest of England (Cornwall).

Page 129, line 10. Worsaae states in his "Primeval Antiquities" that the Iron Age in Denmark commenced about A.D. 600.

Page 129. M. Lorange, at the Stockholm Congress in 1874, called attention to the tumuli of Norway. There are, he stated, from Christiansand to North Cape a vast number of tumuli of the Iron Age. He divides them into three classes: 1. Those without a chamber, and containing iron, but no trace of Roman influence; 2. Those with small chambers composed of slabs, containing objects of Roman origin; 3. Those with grand chambers, formed of slabs, and containing objects of Roman origin dating from the third to the seventh century. Matériaux, 8e, 9e, et 10e Livraisons, 1874, p. 329.

Page 182. The statement that M. Przezdziecki has discovered a pile-village on the Vistula, is incorrect.

Page 183. The lake-dwellings of the sixth and ninth centuries in Switzerland and France are not the most recent. At the late Stockholm Congress M. Virchow stated that there had existed in the North (as at Björkö, in Sweden, and Julin, in Pomerania) a series of lacustrine settlements down to the tenth or eleventh century. (Matériaux, 8e, 9e, et 10e Livraisons, 1874, p. 320.) Julin is the modern Wollin, in the island of Wollin, surrounded partly by the waters of the lagoon at the mouth of the Oder called *The Haff.*

Page 192, paragraph 4, for "Külhock" read "Kühloch."

Page 209, at the bottom of the page, for "fluvine" read "fluorine," and for "Fernay" read "Fumay."

Page 241, first marginal note, for "skeletons" read "remains."

Page 258, line 18, and p. 286, *note*, for "Academy" read "Academy of Sciences."

Page 285, *note*. The Ohio River, as we state on p. 551, rises sixty feet at Cincinnati. In the winter of (we believe it was) 1869 it rose sixty-three feet. The Tennessee River, on the 2d day of March, 1875, according to the newspapers, rose fifty-one and a half feet at Chattanooga. It was still higher, we believe, in 1867.

Page 299. At line 3, for "Therefore" read "And"; at line 4, for "some forty" read "a hundred"; and at line 18, for "forty" read "one hundred."

Page 311. The brown bear is still found in the Vosges, the Pyrenees, and in various other parts of Europe. The wolf, during the late war between France and Germany, after some of the battles in France, preyed upon the slain. The beaver still lives in the waters of the Rhone.

Page 315, line 22. The *Edinburgh Review* for October, 1870 (p. 234, Amer. reprint), is yet more explicit with regard to the recent existence of the reindeer. The writer, like the writer in the *British Quarterly*, is arguing for the antiquity of man; but he makes the following admissions: the reindeer, he says, has been found in the peat of the valley of the Thames at the Abbey Mills pumping station in Kent; a fine pair of antlers also was figured, in 1846, from the Norfolk Fens by Professor Owen; and more recently the remains of the animal have been found in the West Riding of Yorkshire. He proceeds to state that in the peat-bogs of Scotland the animal is "by no means rare in Ross-shire, Perthshire, and Dumfries-shire." Its remains, we are also told, have been found in the ruins of a burgh near Broca, and in another burgh, at Keiss, with the bones of the red-deer, short-horned ox, horse, goat, etc.

Page 325. Another instance recorded of the discovery of the bones of the mammoth in the peat is mentioned in the "Quarterly Review," vol. cxiv. p. 378. The locality was Sprottau, in Silesia. The remains were associated with cones of the *Pinus sylvestris*. See Meyer, Palæol., 540.

Page 329, marginal note, for "Mammoth" read "Mastodon."

Page 340. This mound seemed to us so important that we wrote to make inquiries with regard to it, and, through a friend, have received a letter written by Dr. P. R. Hoy, of Racine, Wisconsin. Dr. Hoy wrote to a friend living near Boscobel, in Grant County, on the subject, and after some delay received a letter in reply from this gentleman, stating that he had never heard of the Elephant Mound, and could not learn anything with regard to it. A few days after the receipt of this letter Dr. Hoy received, however, another letter from the same gentleman, stating that he had procured precise information on the subject; that the mound is situated in an unfrequented spot, and that it accurately represents a great elephant. "It is certainly interesting," Dr. Hoy remarks, "and goes far to prove that the Mound-Builders 'had seen the elephant.' Perhaps it is a mastodon, and this a record of man's being cotemporaneous with the mastodon, or, more likely, perhaps it represents the Fossil Elephant." Dr. Hoy in the same letter proceeds to give an account of a discovery (in which he participated) just made of the remains of a mastodon in a small bog in Racine County. They excavated through fifteen inches of peat and six inches of sand, and six inches below this they found the first bone. The bones were imbedded in a miry clay, the bottom of which could not be reached with an iron rod ten feet long. The tusks were four feet eight inches long, one of them being in perfect preservation, not a fragment missing. The remains were scattered about, and Dr. Hoy asks what is the cause of this dispersion of the bones of the mastodon, which are nearly always found in this condition? The marsh where the present remains occurred was, he says, once a little lake, and he suggests that the freezing of the pond may, through the breaking up of the ice, have had something to do with the separation and distribution of the bones.

The account of the Big Elephant Mound in the Smithsonian Report is by Mr. Jared Warner, of Patch Grove, Wisconsin. It is situated, Mr. Warner tells us, on the high, sandy bottom lands of the Mississippi, about eight miles below the mouth of the Wisconsin River, and is only about eight feet above high water,—showing "a very small change, if any, in the present bed of the Mississippi River." The total length of the mound is one hundred and thirty-five feet, the general height above the surrounding ground being five feet. "The head is large, and the proportions of the whole so symmetrical that the mound well deserves the name of the 'Big Elephant Mound.'"

Page 346. On farther reflection we think the elephant delineated on the monuments of Central America must be the mammoth or mastodon, and not the Asiatic elephant: the visitors to Central America from Southern Asia must have been few and far between, and even if such persons participated in erecting the edifices or monuments of Central America, it is highly improbable that they should have represented the animals of Hindostan or Burmah; and if they had represented one they would probably have represented others.

Page 347. The elephant is found in the southern parts of Meroë (formerly embraced in Ethiopia) at the present day. The name of the island of Elephantiné signifies in hieroglyphics, as in Greek, "Elephant-land," and indicates unmistakably that the elephant formerly ranged in Southern Egypt.

Page 367. The following remarkable instance of the subsidence of the land is mentioned in "Appletons' Journal" of February 20, 1875, p. 252: Lacondamine, in 1745, found the elevation of the city of Quito above the sea to be 9596 feet; in 1803 Humboldt ascertained it to be 9570; in 1831 Boussingault found it to be 9567; in 1867 Mr. Orton found it to be only 9520; and in 1870 Reiss and Stübel found it to be only 9356 feet. This is a subsidence of two hundred and forty feet in one hundred and twenty-five years; and the movement amounted to one hundred and sixty-four feet from 1867 to 1870, if the facts be as stated.

Page 407. For "Rigollet" read "Rigollot."

Page 429. Aix-les-Bains and Savoy belong to France.

Page 433, line 9, for "skilful" read "skillful."

Page 448, second paragraph, line 12, for "Antiquities" read "Geography."

Page 449. We learn from a report recently made by Professor Joly to the Academy of Sciences of Toulouse "On the Pottery of the Troad," discovered by Dr. Schliemann, that various *animals* are delineated on the vases which have been recovered: "de ce nombre," says Dr. Joly, "sont le bœuf, l'hippopotame, le porc, la tortue, le serpent cornu." The owl, the antelope, and the hare are also represented,—and on the handle of a sceptre (in crystal) the head of a lion. Matériaux, 8e, 9e, et 10e Livraisons, 1874, p. 370.

It will be remarked that we find, therefore, decisive proof that the hippopotamus formerly lived on the shores of the Hellespont,—for the pottery was manufactured on the spot; there is certainly no trace of Egyptian influence. The vases containing these representations of animals were found at the depth of six or seven metres; that is to say, in the relic-bed above the Trojan bed (the sculptured lion's head was found at eight metres). The hippopotamus existed in this region then (and, as we may presume, in Thrace) since the Trojan war. If the hippopotamus existed in the Troad and in Thrace about 1200 B.C., it is probable that it existed at that date as well in Spain and Italy, and then it would not be remarkable if five hundred or a thousand years earlier it had existed in France, or even Britain, where its remains are occasionally found.

We can better comprehend now the description of the hippopotamus in the fortieth chapter of the Book of Job. Heretofore it was difficult to believe that the writer of this book was describing the hippopotamus, as it was necessary to assume that he had visited Egypt, and as the animal dwelt on was presumably familiar to those whom he addressed.

We are confirmed in this view by the description in the forty-first chapter of Job of the crocodile. This animal, too, it has been supposed, was the Egyptian crocodile; but we learn from the recent book of the Rev. J. G. Wood, entitled "Bible Animals," p. 519, that several of the older writers have stated that the crocodile yet inhabits the Nhar Zurka, a river of Samaria which flows through the valley of Sharon and empties into the Mediterranean Sea. This statement, he says, has now been corroborated by the recent capture of a crocodile eight feet long in the Nhar Zurka.

It is not improbable that the Asiatic crocodile is also the subject of the reference in Psalm civ. 26, and Isaiah xxvii. 1. Pliny speaks of the crocodile "at the mouth of the Nile." N. H., viii. 25.

The language in Job is quite explicit, we think, in verse 23 of chapter xl. with regard to the hippopotamus: "Behold, he drinketh up a river, and hasteth not: he trusteth that he can draw up *Jordan* into his mouth." Hitherto the critics have explained away the word "Jordan."

The bones of the hippopotamus, we are told by Mr. Tristram, are found in the débris of the rivers of Algiers flowing into the Mediterranean.

The remains of the rhinoceros, it will be remembered, were found in the neolithic caves at Gibraltar, along with the bones of the African hyæna, leopard, stag, lynx, ibex, etc.

The remains of the African elephant, as we have seen, occur in Spain and Sicily.

There is a curious memorial of the elephant on the famous Black Obelisk from Nimrud, which stands in the British Museum. The inscriptions on this obelisk have reference to the campaigns of Shalmaneser II. (B.C. 858–823); the upper half being occupied by twenty bas-reliefs, five on each face, which represent the king receiving the tribute of five nations. The gifts brought are, in part, gold, silver, copper, elephants' tusks, etc., and, in part, "animals, such as horses, camels, monkeys, and baboons of different kinds, stags, lions, wild bulls, antelopes, and—strangest of all—the rhinoceros and the elephant." "The first of these nations is ISRAEL; the second are the people of *Kirzan*, on the borders of Armenia, which still retains the name; the central row represents the *Muzri*, in Northern *Kurdistan;* the fourth, the *Tsukhi*, or *Shuhites*, from the Euphrates; and the last, the *Patena*, from the Orontes." (Smith's Ancient History of the East, 290.) "The *Muzri*," says Mr. Smith, "are the people who bring the Bactrian camel, the *Indian* rhinoceros, and elephant (which is depicted so as to be clearly distinguished from the African), and other animals, almost certainly Indian, among them a sacred ox,—all pointing to a traffic with India."

We deem it incredible that the *Muzri*, inhabiting the valley of the Upper Tigris (south of Armenia), should have brought to the King of Assyria the elephant and rhinoceros of India,—more than fifteen hundred miles distant; and we suspect that the elephant and rhinoceros were neither confined at that time to the South of Asia. Where did they get them? And again: where did the "elephants' tusks," also mentioned, come from?

Page 454, line 3, for "M. Ramsaneur" read "M. Ramsauer."

Page 490, *note*, for "Count de Saperta" read "Count de Saporta."

Page 511. In addition to what is said here and elsewhere with regard to the former extent of the Asiatic Mediterranean, and the greater extension southwards of the Arctic Ocean, we may add that Colonel Hamilton Smith has the statement that Chinese documents of great antiquity report the land towards the north to have terminated at no great distance beyond the mountain chain of Northern Tartary. Colonel Smith adds in a note that the shadow of a gnomon set up in A.D. 1260, by order of Kobi-lay, Emperor of China, proves that the northern coast of Northeastern Asia then ranged between 63° and 64° north latitude, it being now above 70°. (Memoir read at Geographical Society, 8th February, 1841; see also Biblioth. Orientale d'Herbelot, t. iv. p. 171.) The skeletons of whales, we are farther told, have been found eight hundred miles up the Lena. Nat. Hist. Hum. Spec., p. 119.

Page 559. It was announced a very few years since that M. Delaunay had found certain human cuttings or markings on a rib belonging to the *Halitherium fossile*, a well-known miocene species.

It was also announced that M. Desnoyers had discovered in the pliocene beds of Saint-Prest certain bones belonging to the *Elephas meridionalis*, *Rhinoceros leptorhinus*, etc., which contained incisions or hackings "tout à fait analogues à celles que produiraient les outils de silex tranchants à point plus ou moins aiguë, à bords plus ou moins dentelés."

Similarly notched bones from the pliocene beds of the Val d'Arno, "said to bear marks of knives," were exhibited by Prof. Ramorino to the Italian Society of Natural Sciences.

It is now conceded on all hands that these announcements were premature;

precisely similar striæ and cuts are made on bones which have been gnawed by the porcupine, and in the beds at Saint-Prest the remains of an extinct rodent of the beaver family (*Trogontherium*) were found with the bones of the *Elephas meridionalis*.

In 1873, Mr. Frank Calvert announced in one of the English journals that he had had the good fortune to discover manifest proofs of the existence of man in the miocene age; that he had himself extracted from a formation of this period at the depth of eight hundred feet below the surface, in the face of a cliff near the Dardanelles, the bone of a dinotherium or mastodon on which was graven "the unmistakable figure of an animal with horns," etc. He had also found near this engraved bone a flint implement and the bones of animals, "evidently broken by man, according to the custom of the primitive races."

Sir John Lubbock endorsed Mr. Calvert as a conscientious geologist.

This matter was investigated by Prof. George Washburn, of Roberts College, Constantinople, who sent a paper on the subject to the American Association, which met at Portland in 1873. He declares that there is not the slightest trace of human workmanship on the specimens; that the scratches on the bones do not appear to be artificial, and represent nothing; that the flints (Mr. Calvert found a number of these at another point) are mere natural fragments; and that the bones alleged to be split by the hands of man are a delusion—Prof. Washburn having himself found at the locality old bones, which, on being dropped, split open of themselves in the same way.

INDEX.

A.

B.

D.

E.

H.

I.

J.

K.

L.

M.

N.

O.

Q.

R.

S.

T.

U.

V.

THE END.

www.ingramcontent.com/pod-product-compliance
Lightning Source LLC
LaVergne TN
LVHW021218110826
845150LV00002B/196

* 9 7 8 1 4 2 5 5 6 4 5 9 9 *